WOMEN AND SOCIAL PROTEST

EDITED BY
Guida West
Rhoda Lois Blumberg

New York   Oxford
OXFORD UNIVERSITY PRESS
1990

For H. B., Laurie, and Paul
Guida West

For Aunt Bess
Rhoda Lois Blumberg

Oxford University Press

Oxford New York Toronto
Delhi Bombay Calcutta Madras Karachi
Petaling Jaya Singapore Hong Kong Tokyo
Nairobi Dar es Salaam Cape Town
Melbourne Auckland

and associated companies in
Berlin Ibadan

Library of Congress Cataloging-in-Publication Data
Women and social protest / edited by Guida West, Rhoda Lois Blumberg.
p. cm. Includes bibliographical references.
ISBN 0-19-506118-7. — ISBN 0-19-506517-4 (pbk.)
1. Women in politics. 2. Women's rights.
3. Social movements. 4. Feminism.
I. West, Guida. II. Blumberg, Rhoda Lois.
HQ1236.W6365 1990 305.42—dc20
89-78129

9 8 7 6 5 4 3 2 1

Printed in the United States of America
on acid-free paper

Women and Social Protest

Preface

The idea for this book had its origin in our experiences as activists, teachers, researchers, and writers about protest who were confronted with a dearth of material on women and politics. The contradiction of our lives as political women and the information available in the sociological literature sparked our desire to examine why such data were so scarce. It became clear that women's participation in social protest was an arena that begged for analysis, especially from a feminist perspective.

A workshop on women and political action at the National Women's Studies Association Conference in 1984 provided the catalyst for us to commit ourselves to this project as co-editors. At first we hoped to conduct a review of the literature and write a book that synthesized existing research. It soon became apparent that the material was so scattered that there was no way to adequately review it. Consequently, we decided to put out a "call for papers" as a means of bringing together a selection of articles on women and social protest. Establishing this as our broad core concept, we tapped the sociological and political science disciplines and networks for relevant research. The intended literature review was incorporated, selectively, into an introductory theoretical chapter.

We purposely did *not* specify a common theoretical or methodological framework in our call for papers. We hoped for diversity and we got it. Clearly, a common framework might have made for a more integrated volume. However, we both felt that setting hard-and-fast boundaries on a research topic that was in the early stages of development would be less than useful, and might even be detrimental to our better understanding of women's involvement in social protest.

Among the articles submitted, several authors focused on women's struggles for their own rights and those of other women. Other authors dealt with women's participation in a variety of movements throughout the world and in different eras. We then sought a few specific articles to strengthen and balance the manuscript, while recognizing the impossibility of being holistic or all-inclusive. Although we have referred to (in Chapter 1) such diverse protests as those of Las Madres de Plaza de Mayo, of black and white women in the South African anti-apartheid movement, and of Indian women in the Chipko tree movement, we have not dealt with women activists and revolutionaries in other places, such as the Philippines, Northern Ireland, the *favelas* in Brazil, Australia, the Soviet Union, or Eastern Europe.

Nor have we included articles on every important movement, such as that of abortion rights. The boundaries of our topic are still unclear, and data still need to be synthesized, as we and other feminists redefine what we mean by social protest. This volume is offered as the beginning of such an effort, in the hope that it will stimulate and challenge others. Most of the articles were written for this collection.

The book represents diversity in a number of respects. First, it includes women's participation in various types of protest at the grass-roots, national, and international levels. Second, the women involved in these protests come from various classes, races, and cultures. Third, the types of movements vary with respect to gender structure. Some include women working with men (gender integrated); some, women working independently; and some, women working in parallel with men—in separate auxiliaries or caucuses linked to groups controlled by men. Fourth, the articles span various centuries and cover different regions of the world. Finally, the authors themselves represent a spectrum of race, class, culture, gender, and sex orientation, as well as academic disciplines.

While the diversity adds to the "sampler" effect of a volume on women and social protest, common themes integrate the various articles and link them to the theoretical discussion in Chapter 1. From Blumberg's research on women in the civil rights movement and West's on women in the welfare rights movements, as well as our review of the literature, similar concerns that attracted women into the protest arena became salient. The articles could be, and were, categorized in terms of the type of protest in which the women were involved. Thus the book is organized into four parts, reflecting four types of issues that draw women into protest.

We have many people to thank who helped to make our idea a reality. First and foremost, we thank all our contributors for their cooperation, responsiveness, and loyalty. Second, we acknowledge the love and support throughout the years of our families and friends who made it possible for us to stay with it. For Rhoda Blumberg, they include, in particular, her daughters, Leah and Helena Jo; her Aunt Bess; and three very supportive friends: Miriam Goldberg, Lynda Glennon, and Annie Gandon. Blumberg thanks the Rutgers University Research Council and Douglass Fellows Opportunity Fund for financial support, and Stanford University for an appointment as visiting scholar at the Institute for Research on Women and Gender. Guida West thanks Alison Jaggar and her other colleagues in the Laurie New Jersey Women's Studies Seminar at Rutgers University for their ideas and encouragement. West especially acknowledges the invaluable support of her partner and friend of thirty-nine years, John or H. B.; her children, Laura Lea and Paul; her sister, Landa; and her special friend, Mitzi Law.

Both of us are grateful to our editor, Valerie Aubry, who gave us direction and support throughout the publishing process. We appreciatively acknowledge the artwork for the cover contributed by Ann S. Walker, director of the International Women's Tribune Center. We would also like to thank our anonymous reviewers for their helpful suggestions and comments, some of which have been incorporated. Of course, we assume full responsibility for the volume as a whole, asking that our readers view it as one additional contribution to the growing feminist literature on women's lives within the political realm.

Montclair, N. J.   G.W.
New York   R.L.B.
February 1990

Contents

Part III   Women in Social-Nurturing/Humanistic Protests, 205

Part IV   Women in Women's Rights Protests, 257

Women and Social Protest

INTRODUCTION

CHAPTER 1

Reconstructing Social Protest from a Feminist Perspective

GUIDA WEST AND
RHODA LOIS BLUMBERG

SOCIAL PROTEST AND GENDER BIAS

Television, newspapers, magazines, books, and journal articles have tended to portray politics in general and social protest in particular as an almost exclusively male domain. Women are visible mainly through their participation in feminist causes. We join other contemporary critics in questioning the accuracy of this imagery. Either women have only recently become activists, just as some have now gained elective office, or their participation in social protest has been ignored by the media as well as by scholars. If the extent of their activism in the protest arena (independently or in coalition with men) has been lost in history, as many scholars now contend, views—and stereotypes—about women in the political world must be reexamined. Concepts of what constitutes political action must be reconsidered, for inaccurate presentation of women in this or any other area is poor and misleading social science. Furthermore, how we see and describe our lives—including the arena of political protest—has consequences for these very lives. This interdisciplinary collection of historical and contemporary research has been brought together to answer the need for expansion of scientific knowledge about women and social protest.

This chapter first explores the meaning of social protest and some of the newer critical conceptualizations of what are sometimes called social movements and sometimes called collective behavior. Second, the chapter examines the feminist critique of social science, particularly as it deals with politics and social protest. We then discuss some general propositions that emerge out of the evidence in this volume, the existing literature on women and social protest, and our own research in this area. Four types of social protests in which women have been involved are identified and illustrated; these provide the framework for the four parts of the book. A key question that underlies this first chapter is: How must the study of social protest be reconstructed if it is to include women's lives, experiences, feelings, and visions? That is, what do we learn when the analysis of social protest is women-centered?

We proceed with the following assumptions:

1. Throughout the ages and cross-culturally, women of different classes and races have acted on their felt concerns whenever and however they were able (that is, they have been actors—not passive bystanders—in social protest).
2. Women's participation in collective actions to bring about or resist change throughout history has been expressed in rational attempts to achieve desired ends.
3. Social protest is a form of politics which occurs more commonly than conventional wisdom suggests.
4. Social protest cuts across gender lines as well as race, class, age, and other stratification determinants.

However, resources and opportunities available to women (and men) vary over time and place, reflecting shifts in the political conditions under which they organize and resist. Established gender-related legal codes, religious doctrines, and cultural ideologies have greatly affected women's ability to enter and stay in the protest arena. These factors tend to establish the accepted definitions of what constitutes politics, who is political, and what the rewards and punishments are for being political, based on gender as well as race and class. They determine "appropriate" boundaries of political behavior for women and for men. Whereas men in most cultures have been taught to be aggressive and openly political in social interactions, including the protest arena, women have not. Historically, when men revolt, their behavior still falls within, rather than violates, masculine cultural norms—whether the action succeeds or fails. In contrast, women across cultures and throughout the ages have generally been socialized to be "apolitical" and have often been punished for ignoring gender boundaries when they have dared to venture into this masculine "political" sphere. We assume also (and it is becoming increasingly evident today) that the history of women and social protest has been largely ignored, misrepresented, or repressed.

In sum, politics, including protest politics, has been socially constructed, or, more accurately, male-constructed. While the contributors to this volume vary in their approaches, collectively they contribute to the multidisciplinary feminist literature that is examining and reconstructing theories about women and their lives. In varying ways they ask what happens to theory, interpretation, and narrative when woman is integrated into the analysis (see J. Martin 1986; Schuster and Van Dyne 1985, 1988). A major aim of this chapter, then, is to contribute to the emerging women-centered analysis of social protest within political discourse and debate.

The Definition of Social Protest

The definition of "social protest"—what it includes or excludes—will vary, depending on the place, the time, and who is observing and recording the "facts." As political conditions change, so do established concepts and bodies of knowledge. Similarly, what is defined as "politics" or "political behavior" is historically linked to power conflicts and, at times, specifically to gender power struggles. Thus the degree of political gender-blindness varies over history (K. Jones 1988:20).

Until recently, politics was viewed in the Western free world as comprising primarily such formal activities as registering to vote, voting, running for office and being involved in the mainstream electoral process. This approach resulted in studies revealing that women participate less than men in "politics." These findings were then interpreted by male scholars as evidence to support the image and the theories of the "apolitical" woman (K. Jones 1988:21). With the rise of feminist research, as we discuss later, new theories emerged, such as those about socially embedded obstacles to women's political participation.

In the nineteenth century, conservative political philosophers viewed collective actions as threats to the established ruling order. Consequently, they defined such actions as crowdlike, emotional, or deviant rather than as rational behavior by people organizing to make known their grievances (Le Bon 1969). Today, most political scholars reject this narrow interpretation of group behavior (H. Becker 1963:7; Cloward and Piven 1979; Horowitz 1972:350; Piven 1976, 1980:1) and argue for theories that use availability of resources and opportunity structures to explain why, when, and how people protest and make claims (McCarthy and Zald 1977; Tilly 1978; Wilson 1973; Zald and Ash 1966).[1]

Political scholars also tend to agree that social protest and social movements are political, and also that they overlap, despite differences in degree of organization, numbers of people involved, duration, degree of spontaneous actions by individuals as well as groups, and other dimensions (Gamson 1975; Lipsky 1970; Lofland 1985; Piven 1980, 1981; Piven and Cloward 1977; Useem 1975). Most now view social movements as collective organized actions to bring about or resist change by means of various historically conditioned strategies. Charles Tilly (1981:17) argues in favor of the use of the term "collective action" rather than "protest," "rebellion," or similar terms because the use of such words "prejudges the intentions and political position of actors, usually from the perspectives of the authorities." But, along with others, Tilly agrees that social movements or social protests should be seen as "an established way of doing political business." In sum, political theorists have moved from defining social protest as irrational, deviant behavior to affirming collective mobilization by groups and individuals as a rational and political means of challenging the status quo in society.

As the definition of "political behavior" has become more inclusive and more ordinary, women and their life experiences, previously ignored, have come to be included in reconstructed theories. Thus changing political conditions both mirror and model what we understand as social protest today.

As Piven and Cloward (1977:36–37) insightfully conclude from their studies of poor people's protests in the United States, *mass* social protest is rare. One's ability to participate and one's choice of strategies and tactics are limited by the political climate, one's cultural and class location, and available resources (see Gamson 1975). Historically, for women, for the poor, and for blacks and other people of color, opportunities for asserting rights under the law have been greatly restricted by those in power.

While academics have now begun to recognize the rational and political elements in protest, many authorities and the public still tend to characterize much protest behavior as irrational, thereby legitimating greater social control of the so-called deviants. For example, when massive civil disturbances occurred in cities throughout the United States in the late 1960s, and African-Americans, students, women, and gay people organized and protested in the streets, their behavior was viewed by many as threatening, irrational, senseless, and malign (Skolnick 1969:330). Even today, public-opinion data continue to reflect the belief that women are simply not designed for the rough-and-tumble world of male politics.[2]

Nonetheless, people find ways to protest wherever they are. Throughout history, those trapped in their own neighborhoods by poverty have taken action where they live. For example, poor women, mostly black, relegated to urban ghettos in the United States, marched to demand food, clothing, and shelter and took over welfare offices in the late 1960s. The "powerless" have always tried to resist their oppressors, creatively using whatever resources they possess—their bodies, time, talents, energy, children. As one welfare rights woman observed, "We protested where we were 'planted' " (West n.d.).

Similarly, we know that African-Americans, Native Americans, and Chicana(o)s have fought in many different ways for their rights in the United States; women around the globe have fought for basic survival needs, as well as to stop violence against themselves and their children and to gain the right to be heard within the political arena (Jayawardena 1986). Indeed, protest politics is an everyday experience in the lives of people around the world, whether reflected in open confrontations—peaceful or violent—with authorities or in less evident but no less conflictual events within the polity *and* other institutions in society. However, many local protest activities are crushed or lose support before they reach the level of mass movements, while others are never recorded as part of political history. Women's protest activities in particular have often suffered this fate.

The Feminist Critique of Gender Bias in Social and Political Thought

The absence of gender analysis (except, of course, in research on the women's movement) stands out starkly in almost all academic works on social protest. Interested readers are hard-pressed to find the *mention* of women, let alone comparative analysis of men and women's roles, attitudes, and feelings as social protestors. Some researchers mention the importance of gender analysis but then justify not doing it because of its alleged complexity (Fendrich and Krauss 1978:236). Others simply do not consider gender a heuristic tool in the analysis of social protest, an assumption now challenged by new feminist research. Gender-neutral terms (such as "challengers," "dissidents," "beneficiaries," "adherents," "demonstrators," "rebels," "terrorists," and so on) mask information about who is involved—men, women or both. Similarly, use of the terms "leaders" and "organizers" in the analysis of social protest without gender specification implicitly reinforces dominant notions that men are playing these roles. Within a patriarchal context, men are assumed to be leaders and organizers in the public sphere, while women who enter it are viewed as their supporters. Furthermore, sexist language that uses generic terms such as "he," "him," "men," "chairmen," and so forth continues to reinforce the impression that men, not women, are the political activists. Thus language, along with other patriarchal institutions, shapes as well as reflects reality about women and social protest.

Several feminist scholars highlight the gender bias in political science. Bourque and Grossholtz (1974) point out how political science has tended to look at female participation as an "unnatural practice." Boals (1975) notes the scarcity of information about women in this field and the male bias inherent in its basic concepts and definitions. Jones and Jonasdottir (1988:8) highlight the "peculiar irony of modern political theory"—that as the ideals of freedom and equality are becoming universally promoted, "the specific presence of women and men in the political field is denied." Thus they find that in current discourse, "the sexless and genderless member of an organized interest group" is portrayed as the political norm. Nelson (1989:1) also documents "the gendered nature of the assumptions and traditions of political science." A feminist perspective on politics requires a definition and a theory that are women-centered, that include women's actions, desires, needs, and feelings in any and all arenas, and that explicitly identify and analyze them as an integral part of political life.

While class and race as analytic categories in protest theory may have also been neglected, they are receiving increased attention, especially with the rise of Marxist revolutions, the growing revolt by blacks in South Africa, and racial minority group protests in the United States.

Jonasdottir (1988:42) points out that recent political studies have revealed "unequivocally that the background variable of gender is one of the most, sometimes *the* most, differentiating factor in studies of political behavior." The evidence, she adds, shows that "women, to a greater *degree* than men, and in different *ways*, initiate, pursue and support issues concerning bio-social production and reproduction, that is, those questions having to do with control over, responsibility for, and care of people and other natural resources" (Jonasdottir's italics). She notes that in Western capitalistic societies, the possibility that women and men are competing interest groups is usually not acknowledged in mainstream political science or even by many women's organizations. Paradoxically, Jonasdottir observes, as more women are organizing to protect themselves from patriarchal power and its consequences, and in reaction "men seem to be moving towards a new phase of organizing vis-a-vis women" (1988:44). Gender in social protest is emerging in theoretical debates, despite resistance, as the reality of women's historical place in protest becomes more widely recognized. In a similar vein, Hernes (1988:203) finds in her study of Sweden that gender is a critical element in the study of sources and modes of citizenship. Finally, Siim (1988:160–86) argues that as long as politics is conceptualized narrowly as participation in formal "power from above," we will continue to ignore women's involvement in social movements and protests, or what she terms "power from below."

Other general themes that emerge in the basic feminist critique of supposedly scientific literature are now familiar: women's contributions have been ignored, misrepresented, or erased from history in a patriarchal world. Men (especially those in authority) have had the power to define what knowledge is and what part of it gets transmitted from generation to generation. This fact has crucial practical and policy implications. Knowledge of women's past struggles and achievements is a political resource needed in raising consciousness and mobilizing others to dismantle patriarchal institutions.

Spender (1983c:9–12), following Dorothy Smith (1978), brilliantly shows how circles of powerful men who control the world are able to describe and order it. In the process, women are excluded from these circles in which society's meanings are constructed. By making political women "invisible," men reinforce the dualistic world-view of themselves as political and women as apolitical. Women who construct their own meanings and traditions threaten patriarchal values; they cease to be invisible and unreal, as they challenge the records that men have created.

Inclusion of women changes the assumptions and categories that men have set up. Consequently, feminists argue that any analysis of politics and social protest (like the analysis of the sciences, arts, humanities, religion, and so on) must include the actions, attitudes and subjective meanings of diverse groups of women as they organize to gain power to change (or resist change in) their lives. The actions and attitudes of men cannot be generalized to cover the entire population (see also Wittner 1984). Spender (1985:200–202) maintains that the inclusion of the experiences of other than white races requires a similar transformation.[3]

In addition, feminists assert that the personal is political and that the political is personal. From this perspective, all persons are political beings from the time they are born, and, as members of a group, are involved episodically in varying forms of protest (limited only by their resources, opportunities, and sociopolitical conditions). With this feminist reconceptualization, we can identify myriad collective events and ways in which groups generally defined as powerless, passive victims, gain power as they mobilize and act to control their lives.

The need to transform knowledge has led feminists to *"rethink the basic conceptual and theoretical frameworks of their respective fields"* (Stacey and Thorne 1985:302).[4] The solution is not simply to graft women onto male-created models, but, as sociologists Stacey and Thorne (1985) and others (Jones and Jonasdottir 1988) suggest, to examine traditional concepts and methods of analysis that continue to focus on gender (or race or ethnicity) as only an attribute of an *individual* or a group of individuals rather than as a hierarchical system of organizing power within society. By reexamining such traditional notions and methods of analysis, feminists are making visible the impact of gender power differentials in various settings (see for example, Jaquette and Staudt's [1988] feminist analysis of U.S. population policy in the Third World).

Not only have theories of politics and protest come under increasing scrutiny, but so too have methodologies. Women from diverse groups are now urged to tell their stories and express their feelings and visions, most of which have been previously suppressed. For example, the crucial role of African-American women in starting the Montgomery bus boycott, which triggered the civil rights movement, has emerged more than thirty years after it occurred. How black women experienced this event and how they developed their strategies is only now being integrated into the protest literature (Robinson 1987). Similarly, the role of African-American women in the Marcus Garvey movement in the early twentieth century signals the growing feminist concern with racial and class inclusiveness in studying the political behavior of women (Bair n.d.).

Virginia Sapiro (1984:245–46), while focusing on electoral politics, also examines women's alleged absence from other kinds of political involvement. Scholars are now beginning to acknowledge that women participate politically in ways that are rarely recognized or documented as political behavior or social protest—for example, by engaging in action through churches, clubs, and other organizations—a theme to which we return later in the chapter. In addition to the women's suffrage and liberation movements, large numbers of women were involved in most of the social movements in America such as abolition, temperance, health reform, peace, progressivism and municipal reform, and civil rights. Traditionally oriented women defined these activities as an extension of their nurturing and caring in the home. An interesting case is that of the "Club Movement" of the late nineteenth century, which, according to Sapiro, was "instrumental in establishing the early framework for public social welfare programs through their work in health, education, poverty relief, and municipal reform" (1984:246). White women's clubs lobbied extensively, pushing local and state governments to accept public responsibility for social welfare. Similarly, the national club movement of black women that emerged in the late nineteenth century created new resources and opportunities for a variety of collective actions to improve the lives of black people in the United States (Giddings 1984; Griffin 1988; J. Jones 1985) .

Women have also emerged as political protestors out of their historic ties with religious institutions and beliefs. Religious convictions have propelled

and undergirded protest activities for both black and white women throughout history (Blumberg 1980, 1988; Giddings 1984; Sapiro 1984; West 1981).
Many white Victorian women in social reform movements were convinced
that God had commanded them to move into the public sphere to assert their
public voices on behalf of racial, class, and other injustices. Similarly, black
women in the abolitionist, antilynching, civil rights, and welfare rights movements, among others, were sustained by their religious convictions and justified their political roles as the command of their God. Smith-Rosenberg
(1986:22) also uncovers this "lost world of female militancy" in women's religiously grounded activities and destroys the male-constructed myths of
"women as passive victims without resources isolated in a world of powerful
men" (1986:25). Protest for many women was a creative mode of resistance to
what they perceived as the evil consequences of men's rules.

     In labor struggles, men's domination helps to account for the lower re-
ported rate of female protest. Although working women and spouses of working men have always participated in labor actions, their contributions have
only recently been noted (Bookman and Morgen 1988; Foner 1979, 1980; Milkman 1985; Siltanen and Stanworth 1984; Tax 1980; Thomis and Grimmett
1982).

     Thus the structure of "voluntarism" emerges as a central means by which
women mobilized and exerted political pressures within various institutions
(the churches, the schools, the social welfare agencies, and even men's fraternal organizations), as well as within the polity. In the traditional literature,
women's actions and views within "volunteer" networks have often been
defined and dismissed as "moral" rather than "political" behavior. Later in
this chapter, we suggest that women's participation in voluntary organizations should be integrated into theories and analyses of social protest.

     The role of the male-dominated state also has to be included in the analysis
of social protest. By the state, we mean the executive, legislative, and juridical
branches of government at all levels (see also Siim 1988). Feminist scholars of
contrasting perspectives agree that it is important to examine empirically how,
when, and why the state has intervened to support or obstruct women's organized goals and protests in different historical periods. They challenge the
assumption that the state is neutral in gender-based conflicts. Some support
the view that the state (especially the welfare state in the twentieth century) has
more often than not been a "friend" in the fight for women's claims in society
(Piven 1985:265); others choose to see the state as the "foe" and oppressor of
women and a major source of patriarchal power (Barrett 1983; Eisenstein 1983;
Elshtain 1983; Pearce 1984); a few view the role of the state as potentially both
friend and foe, depending on specific issues and historical contexts (Siim
1988:175). In developing a feminist sociology, Dorothy Smith (1988:3) suggests
replacing the concepts of "state" and "class" with the term "relations of ruling."
Smith argues that this new concept "grasps" the dimensions of power, organization, direction, and regulation much more sharply than the traditional ones.
Obviously, in any feminist analysis the roles of *all* actors in the social protest
arena must be carefully analyzed and past assumptions (such as the

benevolent-father state, the autocratic-father state, or the neutral state) examined empirically and historically.

Summarizing, we argue that a feminist theory of social protest will encompass women-centered interpretations of who, when, how, and why women engage in social protest. A feminist methodology will attempt to record both the observer's and the subject's views, for both have to be integral parts of the process. Finally, a feminist theory of social protest will include the analysis of the roles of *all* actors in diverse spheres of life, as well as their resources and ideologies throughout the course of the struggle. A feminist analysis will also investigate empirically and historically, rather than assume as given, who are "friends" or "foes." Thus a feminist analysis of social protest includes a dynamic, historical, inclusive view of people as political beings acting collectively and individually with different resources to stake their claims and survive within systems of power and dominance. Clearly, we feel it is important not to make a clean break with existing theories of social protest. Rather, we are attempting to examine some of their shortcomings when applied to women's lives and experiences. By reexamining traditional assumptions, concepts, and definitions we hope to enhance the usefulness of these notions in political theory and analysis.

One final observation. Our work is not "value-free." We reject the idea that any political observer is value-free, regardless of her or his purported objectivity. Some may object that a book focused primarily on women and social protest is flawed to the same extent that past histories based only on men are distorted. As Dale Spender (1983c) and others point out, however, the feminist researcher's goal is not to exclude but to include. Ultimately, as a new theory emerges to explain women's participation in social protest, it will be one that reflects the reality of *all* people, not just that of women, or of men, but of all inhabitants on this earth of ours. Political thought and analysis must incorporate not only gender, but also race and class, as well as other categories that continue to divide and separate human beings (sexual preference, age, physical ability). Until it does, it must be seen as incomplete and biased. We believe that when the literature truly reflects the reality of women's lives, history will reveal the astoundingly creative "political" lives many women have led in order to survive in a male-constructed and male-dominated world.

The books and articles we identify in this chapter, and the works included in this book, are, we feel, only the beginning of an effort to reconstruct the story of women in protest. Some of women's past efforts will remain undocumented. But some existing data are being reexamined and reconstructed from a woman-centered perspective. Current research on social protest reflects greater attention to gender and the diversity within gender. No collection can be comprehensive; we offer this one as a varied, but interlinked, cross-national sampling of the type of research that is now in progress.

As research on women in social protest continues to expand—as is happening today across the globe—it is important to begin to identify and systematize some of the ideas embedded in this work. This is the aim of our next section.

PROPOSITIONS ABOUT WOMEN AND SOCIAL PROTEST

Certain recurrent uniformities emerge from our own work, that of our authors, and the new sociological literature on women and social protest. We
present these as theoretical generalizations about the sources, nature, and
consequences of women's participation in protest and illustrate them with
examples from the literature and the articles in this book. Our primary focus is
on four types of issues that draw women into social protest. These provide the
framework of the book. In addition, we examine three other areas: the relationship of participation in protest to the rise of women's political consciousness,
women's strategies for mobilizing their resources and confronting the authorities, and some of the political consequences for women in social protest.

The Types of Issues that Draw Women into Social Protest

The first proposition delineates and classifies the types of issues that draws
women into social protest. Accepting the fact that human beings have joined
together to fight collectively around a wide spectrum of issues and goals, we
need to know more about the distribution of women and men (by race and by
class) in various types of causes, and the nature of their participation.

Little classification of protest movements exists beyond such very general
and often unsatisfactory terms as liberal (reform), radical (revolutionary), and
reactionary. More recently Hess and Ferree (1985:41–42) have classified modern feminist movements into four types (using means and the ends of social
change advocated by feminists: career feminism, liberal feminism, radical
feminism, and socialist feminism). Chafetz and Dworkin (1986) differentiate
women's participation into ameliorative and revolutionary movements.

We suggest that most of the social protest in which women have been
collectively and importantly involved can be subsumed under four ideal
types. In proposing our typology, we want to emphasize its dynamic and
historical aspects. What begins as a social protest for food and shelter at the
grass-roots level may turn out to be the spark of a nationalist revolution.
Similarly, what starts as a reform movement for education and health often
turns into a women's rights revolution. Thus our typology should be viewed
as a continuum of causes for participation that may vary as internal and
external political conditions (actors and their resources) change. We also know
that ideal types, a classificatory schema of "pure" types, distort reality because of their "conscious selection." Their value is based not on their supposed approximation to reality, but on their identification of common dimensions within the type that have explanatory value. Some overlapping in real
cases is inevitable (Wilson 1973:15). Thus the types we propose are different
conceptually but nevertheless closely linked in the empirical world. They
permit classification of scattered data to help explain why and how women
have participated historically in social movements.[5] Finally, the four-part
typology developed within our first proposition will be used as the organizational framework for the articles in this book. Each of the corresponding four
sections is introduced by a brief overview of the major questions raised in

each article and how these are related to the type under discussion. An integrated bibliography containing references of all authors is found at the end.

The four types of issues that have drawn women into the protest arena historically and throughout the world are (1) those directly linked to economic survival; (2) those related to nationalist and racial/ethnic struggles; (3) those addressing broad humanistic/nurturing problems; and (4) those identified in different eras as "women's rights" issues.

Type 1. First and foremost, women have participated as leaders and as participants in organized struggles to attack problems that directly threaten their *economic survival* and that of their families and children. Most often, cross-nationally, they have been involved at the local and community levels around daily issues such as obtaining food, welfare, jobs, housing, and other needs—taking part in food riots, welfare protests, labor struggles, tenants rights, and similar collective actions.

Type 2. Women have also initiated or joined social protests focused on *nationalist* or *racial/ethnic* issues, participating either in groups demanding liberation or equality, or in countermovements demanding protection against erosion of the status quo and the threatened loss of rights. Historical examples include women in revolutionary movements in Latin American, Asian, African, and European countries, as well as women in right-wing movements to perpetuate apartheid and Pinochet- and Marcos-like regimes. Similarly, we find women in abolition and civil movements as well as right-wing women in the Ku Klux Klan and anti-busing movements in the United States.

Type 3. Women have been leaders and mass participants in movements that address broad *humanistic/nurturing* issues such as peace, environmentalism, public education, prison reform, mental health care, and hospices. Women have historically justified their collective actions in the public "male" sphere as an extension of their nurturing responsibilities within the domestic sphere to encompass national and global "families."

Type 4. Probably most visibly, women have been activists on behalf of their own *rights as women* and for various specific groups of women (battered women, older women, teenage mothers, child brides, and others) at both the national and international levels. At least one caveat is in order. Scholars are becoming increasingly aware of the fluidity of "women's issues" over time. A historical analysis of "reform" issues, "women's" issues, and "feminist" issues reveals that the boundaries shift not only over different periods of time, but also in different parts of the world.

Clearly, women have provided the bulk of participants in the struggle for women's rights (Type 4), but they have also probably been the major actors at the grass-roots level in struggles for the economic survival their families (Type 1). Similarly, the data confirm that women have also always been involved in some role in nationalistic and racial/ethnic struggles (Type 2) and in national and global humanistic/nurturing movements (Type 3).

These four types of issues that draw women into social protest are interconnected in complex ways, and we can explore only some of them here. Economic crises may lead to women to mobilize in nationalist and racial/ethnic struggles. We know, for example, that women's collective actions demanding food helped to spark the French and Russian revolutions (Dunayev-skaya 1985:80). Conversely, racial/ethnic struggles may move women to organize around economic issues, as the civil rights movement in the 1960s sparked the welfare rights protests among black women in the United States (West 1981). Collective actions around economic issues often lead to overlapping with peace movement agendas. For example, one of the prominent social protest coalitions in the 1960s was that of the welfare rights and peace movements. Symbolically, this was reflected in their call for "Welfare Not Warfare," emphasizing the meshing of economic and political goals. In New Jersey, black and white women from all walks of life led in this effort (West 1981). The interconnectedness of economics and peace is salient today as feminists throughout the world are deliberately reconstructing the term "peace" to include not only a world without war, but a world without violence of any kind, including hunger or want (Brown 1984; Kirk 1989a). Economic issues have also been an integral part of the historical struggle for women's rights. The issues of employment, housing, education, and, more recently, the feminization of poverty have been salient in the second wave of the feminist movement.

Women in peace and environmental movements, such as the Greenham Common Women and other antinuclear activists, have begun to highlight the links between the struggles against racism and the fight for a world free of nuclear weapons and pollution. For example, Kirk (1989a) reports that Asian women make a direct link between fighting for peace and against racism. They declare that the testing of nuclear bombs in so-called uninhabited areas has devastating consequences for Pacific Islanders and highlights the continuing racism of the dominant white powers in the world today.

To some degree, white women's protests in the United States and in South Africa have been linked to the struggles of people of color against white domination, increasingly so with the rise of global feminism. Similarly, peace and environmental causes have also been a part of the agenda of many women's rights movements, especially so within the recent international feminist mobilization. Speaking at a 1987 conference on ecofeminism, feminist philosopher Susan Griffin linked violence against women, people of color, and indigenous cultures to "a larger pathology that also destroys nature" (Quinn 1987). The Women's Foreign Policy Council, co-chaired by Bella Abzug and Mim Kelber, has organized a "nationwide, female coalition to help save the Family Earth from human-made global devastation" (Kelber 1989). In sum, the interconnectedness of these types of issues suggests one underlying theme that seems to unite all of them to some degree: the politics of survival. Whether we consider women fighting for food, shelter, and clothing, or for jobs, or for the right to live as a national or racial/ethnic group with the same life chances as any other, or striving to minimize the effects of "man-made" disasters, such as war and global pollution, or natural catastrophes, such as earthquakes and floods, or pursuing women's liberation struggles around the world, some common themes emerge. Women join to fight for their survival as women in many devalued roles in patriarchal society: mothers, workers, clients, students, lesbians, elderly, and second-class citizens. Clearly, the politics of survival ranges widely among various groups of women throughout history and cross-culturally and depends on resources and opportunities within their particular time and setting. Yet it is not, as Hernes (1988) points out, merely a politics of self-interest—a politics of individual rights—but, in many instances, a politics of love and caring that has propelled women to break out of their boundaries and to confront or enlist the forces of the state to change the balance of power.

The principal dimension of this typology, then, is the nature of the issues that have drawn women into protest, and not the nature of their ideological stands or tactics. Depending on the political times and opportunities, racial or nationalistic groups have at times sought limited changes and at other times the overthrow of an oppressive regime. Peace movements have engaged in petitioning, lobbying, and marching, or, alternatively, in civil disobedience—burning draft cards and physically impeding war preparation activities. The common theme in all is that at least for a critical mass within the group the situation has become intolerable and those in power have to be challenged. Among challengers, their opponents, and the witnessing public, there is generally little consensus about the degree of change being sought or about the legitimacy of the strategies being used (Wilson 1973:22). From a symbolic interaction perspective, all actors' definitions must be identified and seen as interacting and shaping protest movements and their outcomes.

We illustrate the four types briefly. In Type 1—*economic survival protests*—the focus is on women's collective actions at the grass-roots level and on economic "bread and butter" issues. Women's activism for social change at the grass-roots level throughout the world has been widely documented (Andreas 1985; Barrios 1983; Bookman and Morgen 1988; Fainstein and Fainstein 1974; Jayawardena 1986; McCourt 1977; K. Sacks 1988; Sacks and Remy 1984). Women as a group come together, spontaneously or otherwise, at a time of economic or political crisis to break down barriers that prevent them from getting the basic needs for survival. Historically, the recurring problem for women, given their traditional role within the family and society, has been to find ways to feed, shelter, and clothe their families within patriarchal, racist, and classist constraints. K. Sacks (1988:21) points out that working-class women used family and neighborhood networks as "resources of resistance" against male domination as well as class domination. Few women in any era have been in positions of power to decide on the distribution of economic resources, such as land, food, housing, jobs, and income. Consequently, we find that over the centuries and in many parts of the world, women have banded together to protest against the confiscation of land, their sources of food supplies, their homes, as well as their jobs and welfare benefits. Their activities have been well documented in accounts of food riots in Europe (e.g., Chafetz and Dworkin 1986; Cloward and Piven 1979; Kaplan 1982, 1987; Thomis and Grimmett 1982; Tilly 1981b).

Numerous writers have also noted the significant participation of women in labor uprisings throughout the world and in various periods (Bonnell 1983; Foner 1979, 1980; Jensen and Davidson 1984; Milkman 1985; Seddon 1986; Tax 1980; Thomis and Grimmett 1982; Tilly 1981a). In the Western world, women have participated as workers in separate locals (such as the sewing and women's tailor locals in the Knights of Labor in Rochester, described by Jensen and Davidson 1984:99), in separate "auxiliaries" as wives, mothers, and daughters of the men engaged in labor protests (Aulette and Mills 1988), as well as in gender-integrated workers' protests, such as strikes by white southern textile workers, young immigrant garment workers in the North, and black southern hospital workers (K. Sacks 1988:21). Increasingly, women have organized as women in caucuses within existing unions or in new female-run unions (as in the 1984–85 Yale University strike in the United States; see Ladd-Taylor 1985). In these labor struggles, women have fought primarily at the local level (generally because of family constraints and "glass ceilings" within labor unions), demanding jobs, better working conditions, and more money for themselves and their families, depending on what economic source of survival has been threatened—their own wages or those of their husbands, fathers, or brothers.

Three examples of such economic survival protests in the United States are included in Part I. Ronald Lawson and Stephen Barton's article (Chapter 2) describes the collective efforts of women as tenants in New York City fighting to safeguard their housing. Jackie Pope's article on the Brooklyn Welfare Rights movement (Chapter 3) examines a contemporary case in the United States in which poor women, most of them black, mobilized against the state to demand food, clothing, housing, and an adequate cash allowance for their children and their families. Finally, Sally Maggard (Chapter 4) documents the struggle of coal miner's wives who joined and took leadership in the labor strikes in Kentucky in the 1970s.

Turning to Type 2—*nationalist and racial/ethnic protests*—the evidence is mounting on the catalytic role of women in such struggles, despite ubiquitous cultural norms that continue even today to make their presence and contributions largely invisible and deny them formal leadership positions. For instance, Dunayevskaya (1985:80) contends that it was Russian women who initiated the revolution in February 1917, French women who led in the Paris Commune uprising in 1871, and Nigerian women who organized and revolted in the 1929 Aba "riots." In terms of leadership, she also argues that black women—Sojourner Truth, Harriet Tubman, and others—were the ones who drove white middle-class women in the 1840s to face reality. Black women, only condescendingly recognized by white women (or men), were in fact the orators, generals, and thinkers in the revolution for women's rights. Similarly, Terborg-Penn (1989) documents the historic role of black women in the United States and in South Africa in the struggles against white oppression. She emphasizes that "for Black women in both the US and South Africa, fighting oppression was an extension of their roles that predated American slavery" (Terborg-Penn 1989:2). After his release from prison in South Africa in February 1990, Nelson Mandela paid tribute to the "mothers, wives and sisters of our nation," calling them "the foundation of our struggle" ("Transcript of Mandela's Speech" 1990).

Not surprisingly, in times of national and racial/ethnic crisis, when total mobilization of the population is critical, women have often abandoned restrictive role boundaries and joined in the struggle. Men in leadership have sometimes responded by reluctantly accepting women as additional resources; at other times, by urging them to join and defining their behavior as legitimate until the crisis is passed or victory won (Bridenthal and Koonz 1977:1–10). Even then, however, their historic role is seldom acknowledged or recorded. Moreover, the collective resistance of women within rigidly authoritarian, racially repressive, and patriarchal regimes (such as German women against Hitler) is less recognized or documented than that of men (see, for example, Oldfield 1987).

In racial/ethnic and nationalist struggles, oppressed groups tend to stress "manhood" themes, rationalized on the basis of the minority male's lack of power within patriarchal societies. As we discuss later, women's attempts to participate equally in these liberation movements, and the responses of both male colleagues and male enemies to these attempts, have often sparked new political consciousness. In the struggle against one oppression, women become aware of their own oppressed condition. What they do about it is tempered at the time by their loyalty to what is usually considered the "broader" cause and the contraints they encounter within the movement, their families, and society in general. Thus feminist revolt *within* a racial or nationalistic movement may be subdued and deliberately downplayed to ensure a united front, but nonetheless be very much alive.

Within this type of protest (Type 2), we also include right-wing groups and countermovements, whose members see themselves as "auxiliaries" (e.g., in traditional supportive roles) to their men, helping to protect the dominant racist and patriarchal regimes against perceived threats. Right-wing women join protest movements to preserve the status quo or return to an earlier stage of group supremacy. They rarely challenge and, indeed, often champion women's traditional roles, recognizing men as the source of their economic survival.

Women of more privileged classes and colors have frequently joined the struggles of oppressed racial groups as allies, in causes such as abolition, civil rights, welfare rights, penal and educational reform, and the anti-apartheid movement (Blumberg 1982; J. Jones 1985; West 1981). The Black Sash, initially a white women's organization, was one of the earliest outspokenly anti-apartheid white groups in South Africa (Michelman 1975). Upon his release from prison on February 11, 1990, Nelson Mandela "salute[d] the Black Sash" for being (together with the National Union of South African Students) "the conscience of white South Africans." In the United States, some white women activists in the civil rights movement experienced a feminist awakening that later translated into active participation in the women's movement. In the past, more affluent women, such as those in the settlement house and welfare rights movements, labored long and hard on behalf of their disadvantaged sisters. Berg (1978) suggests that the reform movements organized by women in the early nineteenth century laid the foundation for the rise of the feminist movement in the 1840s.

Part II illustrates the roles of women in nationalist revolutions and racial protests and why and how they move into these arenas. Linda Lobao (Chapter 5) compares women in guerrilla movements within the revolutions in five Latin American countries (Cuba, Columbia, Uruguay, Nicaragua, and El Salvador). Tim Futing Liao (Chapter 6) explores the role of women in the Taiping Movement in China in the nineteenth century. Women in the Zionist movement that led to the establishment of Israel are the subject of Dafna Izraeli's study (Chapter 7). Marie Marmo Mullaney (Chapter 8) analyzes women in socialist revolutions in Europe in the nineteenth and twentieth centuries, focusing on leading European activists. Moving to the United States, two articles describe women in the civil rights protest in two different settings. First, Charles Payne (Chapter 9) explores African-American women's participation in the movement in Greenwood, Mississippi, in the early 1960s. Second, Rhoda Lois Blumberg (Chapter 10) highlights the 1960s activism of white northern women in the black struggle of that era.

In Type 3, we focus on *humanistic/nurturing protests*, a type in which women have been given some recognition as participants. Women are popularly believed to be "peacemakers" and the "moral guardians" of the family and the world. Relatively speaking, few would be surprised to find women protestors in these arenas, for their actions have been and are simply viewed as an extension of their primary and traditional "caretaking" role.

In fact, the data do support the common perspective that women have been the backbone of the peace movement in the United States and globally. Recently, they have also become leaders in environmental movements. In Kenya, the struggle to save and plant trees has been led by a woman—Professor Wangari Maathai—and mobilized by women, despite being attacked as subversive and the tremendous opposition of the government (Perlez 1989). At the local level, women in the United States and in other parts of the world have taken leadership in protests against hazardous-waste sites and other types of pollution. For example, Lois Gibbs uncovered the existing contamination in Niagara Falls, New York, in her home community (Love Canal), and led the collective struggle against corporate and governmental authorities to eliminate this pollution (Gibbs 1982; Levine 1982). More recently, low-income Mexican-American and black women joined together in a group called "Mothers of Los Angeles" to block construction of a toxic-waste incinerator ("Mothers' Group Fights Back in Los Angeles" 1989). Women have also participated in and led the collective protests in other such "nurturing" and "life-giving" causes, sometimes derogatorily tagged "women's issues," such as child care, health care, prostitution, alcoholism, and the abolition of lynching and the death penalty, to name a few. Because they are women, they tend to gain such dubious labels as "moral reformers" and "do-gooders" rather than recognition as actors in political struggles.

The articles in Part III of this volume help to illustrate these humanistic/ nurturing protests. Carolyn Strange (Chapter 11) examines women's participation in the current peace movement and the intersection of motherhood, feminism, and pacifism. Carolyn Schmid (Chapter 12) describes and analyzes the West German Green Movement and Party and traces the coalition process between feminists and the environmentalist, peace, and "alternative" movements. The final selection in Part III is a study by David M. Neal and Brenda

D. Phillips (Chapter 13) of women (and men) in citizen groups involved in disaster situations, such as those caused by floods, tornadoes, toxic waste, or nuclear plants, and how "domestic" and "job" concerns affect participation by women and men.

Finally, Type 4—women's rights protests—are the subject of articles in Part IV. Here we find women entering the political arena to demand rights for themselves. The unique dimension in this "ideal type" is that the women's claims are based on the rights *of* women *as* women and citizens of society. Historically, women have been in the forefront in developing autonomous feminist movements in support of all women. They have also developed support for specific groups of women uniquely disadvantaged as women. The literature is expanding on such collective efforts centered around aging women, battered women, poor women, welfare women, homeless women, pregnant women denied abortion rights, and women trapped into forced sterilization. Data also reveal new arenas of protest at the national and international levels as women mobilize collectively to stop female infanticide, rape, sexual harassment, sex tourism, and other practices that are rooted in the oppression of women in patriarchal societies. Clearly, these collective actions focus on the immediate needs of particular groups of women and are considered integral elements of the feminist movement. Nonetheless, feminists today are increasingly demanding recognition that all issues are women's issues because they affect their lives. Bella Abzug's public confrontation with President Jimmy Carter, shortly after she was appointed chair of his National Advisory Committee on Women, highlights the emerging demand by feminists that all policies be defined as affecting men *and* women. Angered by her sharp criticism of his economic policies and their impact on women, Carter dismissed her on January 12, 1979, just a few weeks after her appointment (West 1981:266–67). Today, then, women's global protests range from reproductive rights to female poverty, from violence against women to expenditures by the military, from economic legislation to sexuality and the AIDS epidemic (see also Bunch 1987:331–34).

Several authors in Part IV illustrate the struggle for women's rights in different eras, around different issues, and in different countries. In Chapter 14, Virginia Kemp Fish explores the struggles for educational rights by women and the countermovements they fostered in the United States. Verta Taylor (Chapter 15) shows how the women's rights struggle in the United States adapted and survived in the forty years between the suffrage victory and the rise of the "second wave" of the feminist movement. Janet Saltzman Chafetz, Anthony Gary Dworkin, and Stephanie Swanson (Chapter 16) compare the women's movements in the nineteenth and twentieth centuries and explore the factors—especially the socioeconomic conditions—that gave rise to different types of women's rights movements in the United States and in other parts of the world. Susan Cavin (Chapter 17) describes the sources of the gay/lesbian rights movement, with a focus on lesbian women's roles and tactics as part of this gender-integrated struggle and as independent mobilizations of lesbian women. Finally, in Chapter 18 Judith Lynne Hanna explores the innovative ways dance has been used in Nigeria and in the United States to thrust women's grievances into the political arena and help women achieve their goals.

We now turn to a brief discussion of three other propositions dealing with the relationship between participation in protest and the development of a woman-centered consciousness, gender differences within social protest movements, and some political consequences of social protest for women.

Protest and the Rise of Women-centered Consciousness

Various feminist scholars have observed that women-centered political consciousness frequently evolves through women's participation in gender-integrated struggles, whether revolutionary or reformist in nature. In fighting for any cause, women become sensitized to the multiple types of oppression experienced by members of their sex. For example, while the Women's Christian Temperance Union did not, at first, support female suffrage and feminism, its very activity challenged traditional notions of women's spheres. This protest movement "became one of the most powerful instruments of women's consciousness-raising of all time," according to Bordin (1981:159). Thus protest activity expands not only women's roles but also their consciousness.

Blumberg (Chapter 10), Evans (1980), and King (1988) recorded this phenomenon in the United States civil rights struggles of the 1960s. Freeman (1975), Thorne (1975), and others documented it in the New Left Movement. Palestinian women reported, in a 1988 news broadcast, that as they participated in the nationalist uprising against Israeli occupation, they became aware of their own subordination and lack of rights. New freedoms in a time of crisis extended their boundaries in a traditional patriarchal society and raised their consciousness about their own oppression (Amos 1988).

A number of our authors mention this pattern of increased political consciousness arising through involvement in protest activities. Women's consciousness transformation during political struggle is found throughout history and in different parts of the world. Pope (Chapter 3), in her study of Brooklyn welfare rights women, notes that poor women believed at first that they were to blame for their own poverty. Participation in group meetings and in confrontations with welfare authorities taught them that the system, rather than their own deficiencies as women and mothers, was the source of their oppression. Maggard (Chapter 4) describes changes in consciousness of the women involved in the Brookside coal miners' strike in Kentucky. Similarly, Chafetz, Dworkin, and Swanson (Chapter 16), in analyzing first-wave women's movements, find that women who participated in other movements observed a stark contrast between the movements' lofty goals and their own oppressed conditions. Struggles for educational rights also raise political consciousness: perhaps this correlation explains the widespread resistance to such movements in many parts of the world. Fish, in this volume (Chapter 14), describes the strong resistance to women's fight for educational rights in the United States in the nineteenth century. Without education, women could be denied employment, income, social recognition, and intellectual parity with men.

Thus women begin to see the contradictions in ignoring their own oppression while fighting against other injustices. They also gain leadership training in the political arena that expands their skills and confidence. Finally, attacks by men (and women) who question women's intentions or ridicule their ideas and behavior can contribute to greater consciousness and solidarity among women activists. As Professor Beth Schneider has suggested, it would be instructive to examine the case of women in right-wing movements as a possible exception. Women's traditional subordination to men may be part of the system of values they consciously espouse and fight to uphold.[6]

Diversity in race, class, age, sexual preference, and other hierarchical dimensions *within* women's movements may also lead to new consciousness of power differences among women and alter the structure of the movement. Thus in the 1970s and 1980s, women of color, poor women, older women, lesbian women, and less abled women mobilized and demanded that their particular needs be addressed not only within the society, but also within the feminist movement itself (see the agendas and reports of the 1987 and 1988 National Women's Studies Association conventions in Atlanta and Minneapolis, respectively). Inclusive movements face the problem of integrating varied groups. While diversity may broaden the movement's base, it may also exacerbate schisms and conflicts. Jonasdottir (1988:55) suggests that it is not realistic to expect "genuine sisterhood" among all women. Solidarity among many may be feasible, but to mobilize the vast majority of women over the long run, "limited alliances" may be the most viable strategy. Integrating diversity in democratically oriented movements has historically been a source of conflict within social protest groups. Established hierarchical antagonisms in society, whether by gender, race, or class, have frequently been reproduced within movements. Paradoxically, diversity often increases the resources and power of challengers (West 1979).

Racial and class oppression affect both men and women, and in a bitter struggle against common enemies, priorities may have to be chosen. Public displays of disunity are seen as harmful, and women are frequently pressured by men to lay their grievances aside "temporarily." Nationalist and racial/ethnic struggles around the globe are faced with the dilemma of maintaining an image of unity even as rising consciousness of internal hierarchies create divisions within the revolution itself. O'Barr (1984) and Urdang (1984) note this conflict in African nationalist struggles; Andreas (1985) and Barrios (1978) see it in the struggles in Peru and Bolivia; Jayawardena (1986) finds it in Third World countries. Most recently, Nora Femenia (1988) describes the proliferation of women's groups in Argentina since their 1975 protests—the Madres de Plaza de Mayo fighting for the "disappeared" loved ones—and their rising identification as feminists, or, as she puts it, moving "beyond denial and out in the open." Among the Latin American guerrilla movements studied by Lobao (Chapter 5) the issue of women's rights was recognized as significant for the movements' present and future success only in Nicaragua and El Salvador. In the U.S. civil rights and black power movements, most black women eschewed public criticism of black men, although public-opinion polls

have consistently shown black women to have a higher feminist consciousness than white women.

Gender Differentiation Within Social Protest

Three important ways that women and men differ as participants in social
protest involve the use of maternal and paternal justifications, variations in
mobilization strategies, and contrasts in confrontations with authorities.

Justifications for Protest: Maternalism and Paternalism

Maternalism is a basic theme that emerges repeatedly in explanations of the
participation of women in all kinds of social protest. In fighting to survive at the
grass-roots level, women have justified their political action as a struggle to
feed, house, and clothe their children. In joining revolutionary or racial struggles, some groups of women have also used the maternalism theme as a way of
rationalizing the expansion of their nurturing roles into the public sphere.
Women explain involvement in national liberation movements in the Third
World as being essential to ensure family survival (Andreas 1985; Barrios 1983;
Davies 1983). Perhaps most obviously, maternalism has often been integrated
into the ideologies of humanistic protests and women's rights struggles.

Women joined the WCTU (Women's Christian Termperance Union) in the
1870s as "guardians of the home" (Bordin 1981:xvi, 158). They perceived
alcoholism as a problem from which women suffered disproportionately
through battering and child abuse. In the 1980s women in the new right, the
Concerned Women of America, justified their cause as protection of the traditional home (Brozan 1987). Most recently, the protests of mothers in Argentina, Chile, Nicaragua, El Salvador, and South Africa to demand accounting
for their "disappeared" children and relatives have focused international attention on maternal participation in political struggles around the world (Agosin
1987; Femenia 1987; Kaplan 1987a).

There seems to be no direct or explicit equivalent of "paternal" sentiment
that is utilized to justify male participation in social protest. Perhaps it is
because men in patriarchal societies do not need this explanation to rationalize their participation. They define themselves—and patriarchal societies uphold their view—as legitimate actors in this arena, as defenders of national
boundaries and of religious and other ideological dogmas (as in the Cru-
sades), as conquerors and expanders of wealth and prestige for their countries, as fighters for their rights as students and workers.

Mobilization Strategies: Independent, Gender-integrated, and Gender-parallel

Historically, women and men have mobilized independently of each other, in
gender-integrated or -parallel coalitions. While we focus primarily on gender-
parallel, or "auxiliary," models in the United States, we explore the other two
types to highlight the continuum of gender integration in social protest—from
independent women's groups to those totally integrated with men. The question of how to organize politically in terms of gender is still a timely one.[7]

Women, unlike men, have often had to devise the "auxiliary"—a separate and parallel group of women linked to an all-male movement organization—if they wanted to participate in a movement. The existence of female auxiliaries in male movement organizations has been well-documented, but their flexible shifting from service to political roles has seldom been analyzed seriously. More often they are ignored or discredited as mere reflections of male-dominated organizations and agendas, with no life of their own. The idea that women's auxiliaries can be and are a political component in protest is only now being recognized by political theorists, and their significance continues to be overlooked (Aulette and Mills 1988:265). Theoretically, male auxiliaries in support of women's movements would be possible. In practice, as far as we know, this has not happened, although in the United States there is a men's movement that appears to support some feminist principles and policies.[8]

Traditionally, the auxiliary–core movement coalition has been explicitly an asymmetrical gender-power model, a patriarchal model. Female auxiliaries are linked with and subordinate to movement organizations controlled by men, reflecting the traditional gender relationship in American society. Sometimes the parallel coalitions become unstable, as women become disillusioned with their lack of power and resources as auxiliaries and spin off into independent groups. For example, in the antebellum period the Daughters of Temperance was the female auxiliary of the popular Sons of Temperance. As women became alienated because of their lack of power, they first experimented with integrated models, joining the Independent Order of Good Templars, a fraternal temperance lodge. Dissatisfied with this alliance, they organized independently after the Civil War as the Women's Christian Temperance Union (Bordin 1981:5).

A variant of the auxiliary is the "semi-independent" caucus within movements. For example, the Coalition of Labor Union Women (CLUW) emerged within the labor union movement in 1974 as the first interunion organization with an agenda for women (Balser 1987:151–210). It is still confronted with cross-cutting loyalties and conflicts between "sisterhood" as part of the women's movement and "unionhood" as part of the male-dominated labor movement.

Another example is Lasky's story (1985) of the 1934 Minneapolis Teamsters strike, during which the women's auxiliary became quasi-militant, "opening the potential of radicalizing women." Similarly, Lasky details the fascinating development of the Women's Emergency Brigade, the women's auxiliary to the workers in their strike against General Motors in 1936 to 1937. In this volume, Maggard (Chapter 4) describes the spontaneous but significant "auxiliary" role of organized coal miners' wives in the Kentucky strikes. Blee (1990) describes the prototype of this auxiliary arrangement within the Ku Klux Klan movement. In the early 1920s, KKK women used maternalism (protecting home and family) along with women's rights themes to rationalize their involvement in this white racist women's auxiliary.[9]

When women and men are integrated in a movement, women's consciousness has often been raised as contradictions between ideals of equality and the reality of traditional gender arrangements emerge. The types of protest groups in which both women and men unite around a common goal are varied. Major societal crises, such as workers' uprisings, wars, rebellions, and revolutions, tend to create new opportunities for women to expand their boundaries into previously all-male arenas. It is then that mass mobilization is needed and customary divisions between female and male roles are over-looked, ignored, or even publicly repudiated by leaders. At times, however, traditional gender roles are outwardly maintained and used to fool one's enemy. Role boundaries may dissolve at the crisis stage, but later tend to be rapidly reinstated. Renewed constraints within the movement and within women's families, as well as women's own attitudes, seem to provide the necessary pressures to bring about the return to "normalcy." For example, Likimani (1985:160–84) observes that in the Mau Mau struggle in Kenya women were highly integrated into activist roles. Their political contributions won little recognition in the days following the gaining of independence from the British, however, (O'Barr 1985:35) and their position remained largely unchanged. New rationalizations of "patriotic motherhood" called on women to serve their country by being mothers and producing the next generation. Similar findings in other parts of the world suggest this is a relatively common outcome (Davies 1983; Huston 1979).

Many, if not most, protest movements are gender-integrated to some degree, some in theory only, others in theory and in practice. For example, most of the movements discussed in this volume are gender-integrated.[10] Paradoxically, while women's participation in gender-integrated protests of-ten symbolizes a breakthrough from traditional role boundaries, their activi-ties continue to be restricted within the movement. Even when they assume leadership roles, their contributions may go unrecognized and unrecorded. Perhaps "the iron law of patriarchy" in integrated social movements is a gender-specific variation of Robert Michels's (1959) "iron law of oligarchy" (according to which a few continue to rule even within movements with democratic ideals). Feminist historians have documented cases of gender power struggles in a number of protests and revolutions. (See, for example, Engel 1977; Kaplan 1977.) When women's caucuses have emerged within integrated groups, leadership and decision making continues to be carefully guarded by men. Thus as Jayawardena (1986:258) points out, women's cau-cuses in gender-integrated but male-dominated political organizations in the Third World have little or no power in decision making.

Under another set of dynamics, women may organize a movement and exercise leadership, but later lose power as men join. As has been mentioned, Lawson and Barton (Chapter 2) found that women were leaders in initial stages of protest, mainly on the local, neighborhood level, with men taking over when tenants' organizations expanded over wider jurisdictions. Paid movement roles were usually allocated to men. We believe the findings of Lawson and Barton are widely generalizable; that is, women often initiate protest on the local level, but as protest movements expand to higher levels, men assume (or perhaps are allowed to assume) formal leadership positions. Not only have women been socialized to look to men for leadership, but men have (and are recognized as having) greater access to needed resources and legitimacy within patriarchal society.

Thus women organizers and founders of social protests have often relinquished leadership roles, assuming subordinate or merely symbolic leadership roles as men enter and shift strategies to higher jurisdictional levels. For example, West (1981) describes how in the mid-1960s poor women organized grass-roots welfare rights organizations around the country and were officially elected as leaders at the state and national levels. In practice, however, especially at the national level, men (both black and white) controlled the resources and the decision-making processes. Payne (Chapter 9) notes the paradox of the "over-participation" of women in local civil rights leadership in the early 1960s and their invisibility when people were asked to name local civil rights leaders.

Sometimes women play important roles, but without commensurate formal titles. This partially explains the historic "invisibility" of women in protest politics, a notable case being Ella Baker, who was an organizer of major civil rights groups. It is also little known that a women's political organization led by Jo Ann Robinson (Garrow 1986; Robinson 1987) provided the groundwork and much of the initial leadership that led to the historic Montgomery bus boycott. Its leadership remained behind the scenes as more traditional black leaders—male ministers—took on, or were pushed into, official roles. Recently, scholars have begun to rewrite history to incorporate the full role of women in the civil rights movement. We now know that Rosa Parks, depicted as a tired worker who spontaneously decided not to give up her seat on a bus, was a long-term activist in the NAACP and had attended a workshop at an integrated movement halfway house, the Highlander Folk School.

Most of the women activists in Montgomery were state employees, professors at a local black college, who stood to lose their jobs or endanger their colleges if their protest leadership role became known. In contrast, the black ministers were self-employed professionals, responsible to the African-American community. In other situations, especially among white middle and upper classes, women and men's traditionally unequal status in the world of paid and unpaid (household) work has made women more available as candidates for community organizing and voluntary group participation. Discretionary time is now recognized as an important resource for protestors, but it is seldom acknowledged as significant when offered by women. Consequently, their political contributions are rarely recorded under assets in the "balance sheet" of protest movements (see Nyden 1969 for an example). Exceptions to this rule appear when the risks of participation increase or fewer men are available. Then leadership becomes more open to women.

The Neal and Phillips article (Chapter 13) illustrates the above point. In contrasting gender-integrated emergent citizen groups (ECGs) in disaster situations, they find that the nature of the disaster—whether natural or human-made—appears to influence male and female participation, because the risks differ for men and women. Males tend to be leaders when the disaster is a natural one, while women predominate when the disasters are caused by industrial concerns. In the latter type, men appear to be reluctant to lead because they are afraid of being fired by the targeted firms.

Women do manage—or are allowed—to take leadership when men are unavailable for various reasons: lack of interest, repression, imprisonment, or death. A study of the Marcus Garvey movement documents how national leadership shifted to Garvey's wife, Amy Jacques Garvey, when he was incarcerated for mail fraud in the 1920s (Bair, forthcoming). The substitution of women for men in political protest is not unlike their use as a "reserve army" in the economy as marginal workers to fill gaps when men are not available.[11] Major exceptions in history are those women who are the widows or other female relatives of fallen leaders, and whose elevation to leadership symbolically extends the male's reign. Often proposed as figureheads, these women sometimes surprise the kingmakers by their strength—note, for example, Indira Gandhi and Corazon Aquino.

The articles in this book that deal with women in revolutionary or nationalistic movements (Part II) also provide additional examples of gender-integrated protest. They reveal the paradox of traditional sexual power hierarchies within "liberation" struggles. With the exception of a token few, women revolutionaries have been largely neglected in political analysis (Dunayevskaya 1985; Berkin and Lovett 1980; Rowbotham 1974). In Chapters 5 to 8, Lobao, Liao, Izraeli, and Mullaney add to the expanding literature about the significant role of women in revolutionary or nationalistic struggles around the world and in various eras.

With respect to humanistic/nurturing types of social protest, Schmid's analysis (Chapter 12) of the West German Green Movement and Party provides an open-ended case that must be watched. Here women have maintained leadership while participating in a gender-integrated movement. Their leadership has survived the transition to electoral politics thus far. For now, the successful integration of women into the Green Party looks hopeful.

We predict that as women continue to participate in different types of social protest, joining independent, gender-integrated, or gender-parallel movement organizations, their political consciousness will evolve toward greater sensitivity to their own subordination. Autonomous or female-dominated women's protest groups may expand around diverse issues. While grass-roots organizations are still the most likely model for women, national and international protests should continue to attract more women in the coming decades, especially as their political roles become more visible and opportunities for protest expand. Women are shifting boundaries in all institutions, eliminating the artificial barriers between the private and the public. The political arena, as feminists have redefined it, will become increasingly gender-integrated, despite—if not as the result of—the entrenched patriarchal power throughout the world and women's rising consciousness of sexual hierarchies.

Strategies in Confrontation with the Authorities

Women's strategies against authorities reflect creative use of resources and tactics linked to traditional gender roles. Women have used innovative mechanisms such as sexual manipulation, theatrics, and their pots and pans in efforts to effect social change. The choice of these tactics has been, of course, shaped and circumscribed by the political opportunities in any historical period. As noted, traditional women's clubs and organizations and many voluntary activities have often provided a safe harbor for potential dissidents and protestors. Such groups of women appear relatively harmless and less threatening to authorities than male counterparts. Similarly, women have used culture, art, and theatrics in creative strategies of collective protest.

Prescribed gender-role behavior in a patriarchal society has provided strategic opportunities for protest. For example, making the most of "saintly" stereotypes, women have used their long skirts to conceal weapons and their "ordinary" households to provide "safe houses" in revolutionary situations. In contrast, drawing on their "temptress" role and sexual resources, they have worked as spies. At times they have "become men" to confuse their opponents. For example, the film *The Battle of Algiers* shows how formerly secluded women cut their hair and appeared in public, unsuspected, on revolutionary missions.

Kitchen utensils in confrontational actions are common protest tools for women. Women bang their pots and pans on behalf of both right- and left-wing causes and against male violence. By creating an arena of noise, they sound the alarm to attract public support against wife beaters or against oppressive authorities. In the mid-1980s, evidence of such collective confrontations appeared in women's protests in Mexico and in the poor areas outside of London (Meeting of Women and Economic Justice, Framingham, Massachusetts, June 5, 1987, attended by Guida West; Clines 1987). Chilean women banged pots and pans to show their displeasure with the choice of President Augusto Pinochet as sole nominee in a 1988 presidential referendum ("Chilean Demonstrators Protest Presidential Pick" 1988). Similarly, a cacophony of pots and pans was used in labor struggles in seventeenth-century England (Thomis and Grimmett 1982) and in Chilean women's economic protests in the 1980s (Agosin 1987). Women in the famous Bread and Roses labor protests in the twentieth century filled their pots and pans with scalding water and used this "weapon" against strikebreakers (Cameron 1985:49). Pots and pans are so prevalent in women's protests that Kramarae and Treichler (1985:350) have defined them in their *Feminist Dictionary* as "instruments of protest." Interestingly, one finds little evidence of women as knife-wielders, but sometimes they use scissors and other sharp instruments to attack their opponents (Cameron 1985:51).

Silence was dramatically employed by the Madres de Plaza de Mayo in Argentina in the 1970s. With photographs of their disappeared loved ones, women marched silently to protest against the terrorist regime, blatantly defying martial law (Agosin 1987; Femenia 1987). Established cultural norms have also been transformed into protest resources. For example, color has been used in silent protest when more blatant tactics might incur the wrath of hostile authorities. Women in Eastern European countries and in South Africa, where protest is also banned, have silently but collectively used symbols of mourning as political protest. By dressing all in black for months on end or wearing black sashes during protests, they communicate openly but unobtrusively their forbidden political messages within traditional cultural norms. In contrast, women in "open" Western societies have opted for brilliant colors to mobilize support for their cause. Feminists in the nineteenth century chose white, purple, and gold as part of their symbolic protest, colors that continued to be used in modern American movements for equal rights and reproductive freedom.

Expressive political action is often used not only as a tactic, but also as a way of releasing emotion when more direct protest is prohibited or consequences are dangerous. In this book, Pope (Chapter 3) describes the use of guerrilla theater as a nonviolent strategy to attract the attention of authorities and gain credit for welfare mothers in New York department stores. The tactic confounded the clerks and managers and eventually won the much-needed credit. Hanna's article (Chapter 18) shows the effective use of dance by Nigerian women to harass male authorities into making proper decisions. In Africa, women have often used dance collectively to target and ridicule men who hold authority. This *anlu* tradition, according to O'Barr (1984:146), was still employed against higher level officials in Africa in the late 1950s and helped to empower women.[12]

At the other end of the political theatrical spectrum is the apparently decorous behavior of middle-class club women in most parts of the world, who, as suggested earlier, play the expected "social service" role to mask their political roles, being "careful to present themselves as apolitical" (Randall 1982:46; see also Berg 1978:145–75; Blair 1980; Bordin 1981; Giddings 1984; Gilkes 1985; Griffin 1988; J. Jones 1985 on the political dimensions of black and white women's voluntary societies in the United States). The fact that basic political science texts have generally excluded women's community, volunteer, and protest activities from political analysis, contributes to the perpetuation of women's political invisibility and powerlessness (Clark and Clark 1986:9–10).

While the voluntarism of affluent white women is known, the collective activities of black women have only recently been subjected to scrutiny. Black women's "social" and "benevolent" organizations, as well as women's groups within African-American churches, have long formed the base for their political organizing and for the creation of strong, positive self-images (Gilkes 1985; Griffin 1988; J. Jones 1985). The repression of black protest by the dominant white society provided part of the impetus for the formation of such institutions (Giddings 1984). In a climate where *any* type of political opposition might result in life-threatening retaliation by whites, black women organized and collectively promoted reforms through their voluntary organizations and clubs. According to Giddings (1984:83, 93), the National Association of Colored Women, stimulated by Ida B. Wells-Barnett's Crusade Against Lynching, united existing federations of these clubs in 1896. NACW was the first national black organization that dealt with the needs of the race as well as the special concerns of black women. Yet even as late as the 1970s, a publication of all black women's organizations in the United States categorized them as exclusively "social/service" groups, with one exception: the National Welfare Rights Organization (NWRO), which was classified as "political" (West 1981:237). Nonetheless, the evidence increasingly confirms that organized networks of black women played critical roles in political struggles in the

United States. Charles Payne (Chapter 9) finds that black women's participation in the civil rights movement in Mississippi was closely linked to their kinship and friendship networks, in which political, religious, and social agendas overlapped at the grass-roots level. Elsewhere women's local activism is tied to their participation in voluntary organizations. Such organizations exist globally.[13] For women throughout the world, service and politics have been deeply interwoven and often related pragmatically in the home, in the church, in the schools, and in places of work. For example, the Japan Housewives Association has been mobilizing women successfully over the last four decades to lobby for consumer protection, protest industrial pollution, and fight against a sales tax. In the summer of 1989, they gained national and international headlines when they led the protests that resulted in the fall of Prime Minister Sosouke Uno after he was linked to sex scandals. They succeeded in defeating many of the candidates associated with the prime minister, and journalists noted that organized women, mostly housewives, were emerging with significant political muscle (Sanger 1989). Any analysis of women's political lives must, therefore, consider both the service and political dimensions of voluntarism.

Women's voluntary organizations, usually legitimate associations in open societies, have often sustained and integrated the political resources of threatened protest movements in periods of repression until remobilization could occur. While Zald and Ash (1966) identified a stage when movements become "becalmed," they did not describe what occurs during the demobilization process. We suggest that at times (generally in more hostile periods) a movement's resources are temporarily scattered, but then channeled and temporarily integrated into other groups to reduce its salience (and its risks) within the political arena. Whether this restructuring is planned or happens spontaneously requires further investigation.

Demonstrating the continuity of the women's movement during less active periods, the article by Taylor (Chapter 15) describes an "elite sustained" stage, lasting from 1945 to the mid-1960s. Between its two peaks, when the political and social atmosphere was not conducive to mass mobilization, the American women's movement was sustained by small groups of elite women working through their voluntary organizations. These groups of middle-class and wealthy women—including many former suffragettes—kept the movement alive. There is some resemblance here to what Aldon Morris (1984) has called "movement halfway houses." Morris identified several organizations that were dedicated to civil rights goals, even in the absence of a mass base, and that could be called on when the atmosphere became more conducive to protest. For him, "a movement halfway house is an established group or organization that is only partially integrated into the larger society because its participants are actively involved in efforts to bring about a desired change in society" (139). At least in some cases, and under certain political conditions, voluntary organizations provide the seedbed and recruiting ground for later and more open protest. Blumberg (Chapter 10) found that a good portion of northern white female civil rights activists entered community life by way of such traditional organizations as parent–teacher associations, the League of

Women Voters, and YWCAs. Similarly, many of the mostly white women who organized middle-class Friends of Welfare Rights groups in support of the welfare mothers protests came from mainline liberal church women's groups and other traditional women's service associations (West 1981).

Political Consequences for Women in Social Protest

Finally, we examine some common patterns in the consequences of protest for women. One point of clarification has to be made. Consequences are time-bound. That is, in analyzing consequences, we need to specify not only for *whom* (or *what*) but also *when*. We need to state clearly the time period on which we are focusing. We need to distinguish short-term and long-term outcomes and, where data are available, discuss both types of consequences to reduce distortions in our findings.

Feminists vary in their views about the impact of protest for women. Are women punished more or less severely than men? In the case of white American society, Giddings (1984) suggests that the propensity of authorities to kill black males has often forced women of the race to initiate protest. In the women's temperance movement of nineteenth-century America, women's nonviolent tactics of praying and singing in grog shops were met first with jeers and ultimately with kicks and beatings (Bordin 1981). Charles Payne (Chapter 9) argues against the view that women were treated less harshly than men in the civil rights movement in Mississippi. In our book, Neal and Phillips (Chapter 13) point out that when women in emergent citizen groups (ECGs) expand their traditional roles of protecting the home and the family outside the domestic sphere, they are negatively sanctioned by local officials, the media, the public, and their own families.

Given the nature of patriarchal societies, women generally suffer negative consequences not only from state and corporate authorities, but also from husbands and men in their families as they break out of traditional roles. Women in Latin America and Asia are known to have endured severe reprisals from the male authorities within and outside the home. Thus participation in social protest can and often does involve a triple struggle: against the broad tyranny of state or corporate male elites, against sexism within the movement itself, and against the patriarchal machismo of men in the family (see, for example, Davies 1983). In the United States, however, Goldstein (1978) found many white couples who were partners in activism in the civil rights movement, and only a minority of women whose husbands hampered their activities. Maggard (Chapter 4) also discusses some of the tensions and renegotiations in gender relations after coal miners' wives joined the Brookside strike. The political consequences of protest again illustrate the artificiality of the boundaries that supposedly divide the political and domestic spheres.

Yet in the public arena, the negative sanctions by the authorities against challengers of the system often seem to be gender-neutral and more race-specific. For example, documentary evidence shows that black (and some white) women were on the line in protest during the modern civil rights movement, facing police dogs and fire hoses along with black (and some white) men. So many civil rights actions occurred on a mass basis—with women, children, and men taking part—that police action by white authorities tended to be indiscriminate with respect to gender. Similarly, in media reports on the student and worker protests in Tiananmen Square in Beijing, in May and June 1989, the violence appears to have been directed indiscriminately at the crowds of young and elderly women, men, and children.[14]

Violence against women and children arouses public sympathy and criticism. Fannie Lou Hamer was so severely beaten in jail during the civil rights movement that she never fully recovered. Viola Liuzzo, a white woman murdered during the Selma marches while she was transporting protestors, was viewed as a martyr by many but was criticized by nonsympathizers for playing a nontraditional role. Black children jailed by the white Afrikaner regime mobilized international sentiment against this type of repression, as women of the Black Sash movement defied the authorities and protested in the streets (Cowell 1986). As suggested earlier, women in social protest are ever subject to male violence, from verbal sexual slurs to brutal rapes. For example, Roman Catholic nuns were accused of participating in sexual orgies because they were part of civil rights marches.

Violence as a consequence of social protest is well documented throughout history. For example, the political literature on Latin American revolutions today is replete with hair-raising stories of rape and torture of women rebels by the state (Bunster-Burrotto 1986). We posit that as women become recognized as actors rather than passive victims, as portrayed by patriarchal institutions and ideologies, they will face increasingly severe political consequences for their actions. The unmasking of violence against women in all its many forms throughout the world suggests to some feminists that such challenges to male dominance may, under certain conditions, result in the tightening rather than the relaxation of controls in various institutional settings (Kirk 1989a).

Focusing now on some positive consequences of women's participation in social protest, we begin by reviewing its impact on political consciousness. Earlier, we noted widespread agreement that participation in social protest frequently raises the political consciousness of women—sometimes, but not always, contributing to a revised view of their subordinate status in society. Little data exist on the durability and direction of these changes (Agosin 1987; Femenia 1988; Jayawardena 1986). Maggard (Chapter 4) and West (forthcoming) document the impact of political protest after a few years on the lives of activist women in two different settings (Kentucky coal miners' strikes and the welfare rights protest in the United States, respectively).

Feminist scholars today vary in their views about the long-term effects of participation in social protest for women, especially in revolutionary movements. In the United States, few writers dispute that women's involvement in the abolition, suffrage, civil rights, welfare rights, and feminist movements in the nineteenth and twentieth centuries had some positive consequences for women as a group, differing significantly by race and class. Social protest was often a leadership-training ground for learning organizational and managerial skills. Combined with an added sense of empowerment and self-esteem, this movement experience was frequently translated into new careers as college or graduate students, in public- and private-sector jobs, and in electoral politics. The data, however, are still sparse.

In other parts of the world, the findings suggest that women's protest often results in limited gains. Jayawardena (1986:24) concludes that although women's movements in many Asian countries achieved official political and legal equality, they were unable to alter women's subordination within the patriarchal structures of family and society. O'Barr (1985:35) argues that revolutions are not watersheds that result in enormous gains for women. A poll of Kenyan women after the successful Mau Mau revolution supports this view (Huston 1979). Cole's (1986:308) study of women after the socialist revolution in Cuba affirms that while some changes have occurred, women remain in subordinate positions in government and in the family. While favorable changes resulted from the revolution in Mozambique, A. Rodriguez (1983:127–34) observed that customs and laws continued to inhibit women's full participation in that society. On the other hand, Urdang (1984:168–69) and Davies (1983) contend that nationalist revolutions brought about positive political and economic changes for women in some parts of Africa and Latin America.

In past U.S. labor struggles, women who supported male strikers seem to have gained little power within the family, although Maggard (Chapter 3) reports on some changes in gender-consciousness in women in the Kentucky coal miners' strike. Male control over women's auxiliary organizations sometimes resulted in conservative rather than radicalizing experiences for the women (Milkman 1985). In contrast, women involved in the 1980s "pit strike" in England reported changes in their behavior, attitudes, and consciousness in terms of their status within the family and the community (Seddon 1986).[15]

With incomplete historical data, it is difficult to weigh the long-range effects of protest participation for women as a whole. More research and analysis are needed to specify under what conditions consciousness, attitudes, and behavior are affected; how embedded the changes are; and what ideological directions they take. Most importantly, we need to recover and monitor data on how women themselves assess changes in society and under what conditions they view them as linked to their collective protests.

Although we are just beginning to understand the political, economic, and social consequences of collective protest for women in different cultures and societies, a historical, global, and women-centered perspective sheds a different light on the gender ramifications of participation. Women's engagement in social protest requires them to break out of informal customs as well as oppose the overt and formal power of patriarchal authorities in all institutions. The struggle must be waged concurrently on many levels. Women are still sanctioned within gender-integrated movements and within the family for asserting their rights, regardless of their ideology. From this perspective, the costs of participation for women are clearly higher than for men. Thus a woman-centered analysis of social protest expands our understanding of the political nature of our lives and provides new insights on the sources and consequences of such actions.

TOWARD A MORE INCLUSIVE PERSPECTIVE

Ultimately, we hope that this chapter and the articles in this book will contribute to a more inclusive perspective in political sociology and other related academic disciplines and to the ongoing reformulation of politics as inherently "human" behavior. We now know that men have no exclusive right to be defined as "political" and women as "apolitical"; that political behavior occurs within the "private" as well as the "public" sphere; that the enduring, but distorted, dualistic view of politics undermines women's power in society and inhibits them in their struggle to unite to achieve their goals. At the same time, we do not wish to get caught in the opposite trap: the romanticizing assumption that the acknowledgment of women's historical involvement in politics and social protest will somehow be the key to success in rebuilding a world with equality for women. Women need, in our opinion, not only *to understand* the past in order *to plan* for the future, but also *to act* collectively to ensure achievement of their goals. Practice must provide us with theoretical markers; and theory, in turn, must guide us in the development of our visions and strategies.

Not long ago this integrated and inclusive perspective on who is political, what it means to be political in our everyday lives, and how women must act politically to achieve our goals was brilliantly and passionately expressed by a poor woman, Domitila Barrios de Chungara (Barrios 1983:58–59), a leader in the ongoing class struggle in Bolivia:

> But *compañeras*, we are political from the day we are born. When a human being starts to cry, he or she is already making politics . . . [later on] when you complain about the lack of paraffin, you are being political. This is Left-wing politics. Our exploiters are also political, but they are Right-wing. That is why we cannot say we are apolitical. We are political, we are revolutionaries because we want to see the end of exploitation, we want better living conditions, so that we, in this country can enjoy the riches of our soil. I beg you, *compañeras*, that all we women educate ourselves and join in our people's struggle and, wherever we go, wherever we may be, that we preach what we have talked about here.

NOTES

1. The definition of "resources" is still relatively vague, and its boundaries are rather arbitrary. Lipsky (1968) includes "protest" itself as a resource. McCarthy and Zald (1977:1216, 1224) define resources simply as "money and labor" or "time and money which can be easily reallocated." Tilly (1986:52) includes "land, labor, information, arms, money and so on that can be applied to influence government." Oberschall (1973:102, 28–29) includes "anything from material resources—jobs, income, savings, and the right to material goods and services—to nonmaterial resources—authority, moral commitment, trust, friendship, skills, habits of industry, and so on." Gamson

(1987:1) calls it a "mushy concept." See also Gamson (1975:136–41), and his critique (1975:55–60) of Mancur Olson's theory of "free loaders" in collective action.

2. See Carol Mueller, "Nurturance and Mastery: Competing Qualifications for Women's Access to High Public Office?" (pp. 181–210), and Susan Welch and Timothy Bledsoe, "Differences in Campaign Support for Male and Female Candidates," in Gwen Moore and Glenna Spitze, eds., *Research in Politics and Society,* Volume 2, *Women and Politics: Activism, Attitudes and Office-holding* (Greenwich, Conn.: JAI Press, 1986).

3. In Dale Spender's (1985:201) opinion "it cannot be a matter of white women allocating space to women of colour," as sometimes "patriarchal institutions have allocated space to women," but it "must be a researching, relearning, regenerative process which reshapes the whole, and reformulates what is known."

4. See also Lein and McIntosh (1982:1–15); Andersen (1983a, 1983b).

5. George A. Theodorson and Achilles G. Theodorson, "Typology," in *A Modern Dictionary of Sociology: The Concepts and Terminology of Sociology and Related Disciplines* (New York: Crowell, 1969), p. 445. Wilson (1973:14–31) notes that typologies are used in the analysis of social movements to classify them along certain crucial variables that distinguish them from other types of social movements and to find out why these differences exist. Classification, he argues, is a prerequisite of analysis because it simplifies the overcomplex reality. He also suggests that typologies are particularly valuable "in the early stages of the growth of a study," for it is then that data tend to exist with no general theory to integrate them.

6. Comments made at session "Issues of Gender in the Analysis of Social Movements," at the annual meeting of the American Sociological Association, San Francisco, August 12, 1989.

7. In 1988, despite rising public opinion and court decisions against single-sex organizations, the thirty-first National Convention of the YWCA of the U.S.A. (June 22–26, 1988) in Chicago reaffirmed its 130-year position as an autonomous women's organization controlled by women. Its national president, Glendora Putnam, stated that "the YWCA's position is an affirmative response to inequality and disparity, which continues to be the rule rather than the exception. . . . We remain an all-women's organization to create an environment where women and girls can learn to lead effectively without the influence of a socialization process which teaches us to defer to men" (Newsletter of New Jersey State Council of YWCAs, quoted in *Here and Now,* published by the New Jersey NOW, August–September 1988, p. 8).

Another recent example of this dynamic process in changing gender relationships within social movement organizations is the case of B'nai Brith Women within B'nai Brith (Goldman 1989). B'nai Brith (Hebrew for "Sons of the Covenant") was founded by European Jewish immigrants to protect and preserve Judaism in the United States and is today widely recognized as a defender of human rights. It was established in 1843 "as a fraternal order of men only." In 1886, a women's auxiliary was organized that became B'nai B'rith Women, and that was incorporated as separate entity within the parent organization in 1962. In 1988, more than 100 years after its founding, B'nai B'rith granted women full membership in the parent organization for the first time. The women rebelled, responding by declaring their group " 'a separate, autonomous organization' that is identified with B'nai Brith but not subject to its will." In answer to B'nai B'rith International's threat to expel them, the head of B'nai B'rith Women asserted that "the intent of the expulsion threat was 'to eradicate B'nai B'rith Women as an organization . . . [but that the group] would not roll over and play dead in response to this raw grab for power and control' " (Goldman 1989:A26).

8. See James A. Doyle, *Sex and Gender: The Human Experience* (New York: William C. Brown, 1985), especially Chapters 12 and 13. See also the discussion of this coalition

model, called "twin-track" coalitions in West (1981), especially Chapter 4 on the Friends of Welfare Rights coalitions with the National Welfare Rights Organizations at the national and local levels. West discusses the sources and consequences of these parallel coalitions between unlike "power" partners: where liberal whites supported blacks, where men supported women, where middle-class Friends supported welfare rights groups. In all cases, the coalition is ideally based on a friendship or partnership model, in which both parties join to achieve a common goal, generally redistribution of power and resources within society to enhance the status of the subordinate group. Within the coalition itself, the underlying principle, however, is structural equality in decision making and control of resources, or even reversal of roles, with the subordinate group (within society) taking leadership within the "twin-track" coalition. Since they tried to test an egalitarian model of cooperation between unequals, these coalitions with reversed roles proved tenuous.

9. Interestingly, Raines (1983) noted that a few women in the KKK had become major informers in the FBI's investigation of the Birmingham church bombings of 1963. Their statements had led to the conviction and imprisonment of one KKK member in Alabama in 1977.

10. The tenant's rights movement, organized by grassroots women, became gender-integrated; the welfare rights protest was open to all poor people, regardless of gender, but in reality turned out to be made up mostly of poor women; nationalist movements and struggles of blacks and other people of color in general have been inclusive and defined as the peoples' struggle; similarly, environmental, peace, and disaster-support movements appeal to everyone to join, regardless of gender; even women's rights protests, especially in the nineteenth-century reform movements, have been gender-integrated to some degree. Today, women's rights movement organizations generally do not exclude men but set limits on their participation within the movement. Thus to understand the internal structure and processes of leadership and mobilization, it is necessary to analyze empirically the *extent* of gender-integration and its consequences.

11. Guida West thanks Barbara Bair for this insight.

12. Wipper (1984:86) believes that the decrease in use of the *anlu* tactic has diminished women's power in African societies where previously it served to protect their interests and autonomy.

13. In South Africa, Lodge (1984:141) notes that until the late 1940s African women's organized activities were focused around "church-based voluntary organizations, the exclusively female *Manyanos*," or in the Zenzele Clubs and the National Council of African Women, which were concerned with the improvement of women's social conditions.

14. See Nicholas D. Kristof, "Troops Attack and Crush Beijing Protest: Thousands Fight Back, Scores Killed," *New York Times*, June 4, 1989, p. A1. Reports in the media seem to indicate that men predominate among those condemned to death by the authorities.

15. Coal miners' strikes in England are known as "pit strikes" because coal mines are called "pits."

PART I

WOMEN IN GRASS-ROOTS PROTESTS FOR ECONOMIC SURVIVAL

Mere survival has been and continues to be a basic problem for much of the world's population—but especially for women and children. And since their children have been the primary responsibility of women around the world, the need to feed, clothe, and house them has been an impelling stimulus leading to grass-roots social protest throughout the ages. It is well documented that women have organized and been the predominant activists in local protests over survival issues—from the eighteenth- and nineteenth-century food riots in England and France (Randall 1987: 58–68) to the "march of the empty pots" organized by the middle-class Chilean women in the 1970s (Chaney 1974:271, 275).

Their names do not come down to us in history books, and the extent of women's participation in labor struggles has not yet been fully revealed. Nonetheless, there is increasing recognition that economic issues have propelled masses of women into industrial militancy as well as food riots—for example, the "matchgirls' " strike in nineteenth-century Britain, the women port worker's strike in Japan that led to the 1918 "rice riots," the women workers' strike in the Shanghai silk factories in 1922, and, in the 1970s, strikes by women textile workers in South Korea and Peru (Randall 1987:62). In 1984 women in Britain made news with their involvement in the coal pit strikes (Seddon 1985). A case study of U.S. women's involvement in the 1970s coal mining strikes is provided by Maggard (Chapter 4) for this collection. In 1989 women once again joined in the Pittston coal mining strikes in southern Virginia (Flanders 1989).

Women's economic conditions in many parts of the world continue to be harsh. The disadvantages suffered by women everywhere are made clear in a 1980 statement by the United Nations ("Women Work Twice as Hard as Men").

women are half the world's adult population; they comprise one-third of the paid labor force, and they actually perform two-thirds of the world's working hours. For this, they earn one-tenth of the world's income, but they own only one percent of the world's property.

While the status of women varies significantly from one part of the world to another, nowhere is it equal to that of men. Extreme poverty and deeply rooted discrimination in the least developed countries of Africa, the Middle East, Asia, and Latin American result in harsher conditions for the women in these areas than for those in Western industrialized countries ("Country Rankings of the Status of Women: Poor, Powerless and Pregnant" 1988:1–10).

Economic conditions for the poorest women worsened in the late 1980s because of the "debt crisis"—the $1 billion said to be owed by Third World countries to Western governments and banks and international financial institutions. The response of those affected has again been to organize and protest. In calling for such protests, women in the Dominican Republic have said that they know the intimate details of the debt crisis, because they confront it every day and it has made their oppression more severe. Citing the hunger, sickness, and lack of clothing and shelter suffered by their families, a group described as housewives, consumers, mothers, rural women, and poor women united "to raise our voices in public protest so that the hardships we suffer can be ignored no longer" ("Women Worldwide Are Confronting an Economic Crisis" 1989). In other Latin American and in Asian countries, middle-class women have joined economic protests, despite the "enormous gaps between the privileged and the poor" (Chaney 1974:275).

Examples of women's participation in grass-roots economic struggles proliferate. South African women valiantly opposed the institution of a pass system for them that would limit their migration to urban areas and hence their search for jobs. They were temporarily successful, since the state was not ready for the mass demonstrations that developed in the 1950s (Lodge 1984:140). The harsh economic conditions suffered by these women helped spark the organization of the Federation of South African Women (Lodge 1984:141). In India, millions of women struggle for their daily food, barely managing to survive, and mobilize to protect their sources of food supply. To prevent the Chipko trees—one such source—from being felled, Indian women linked their bodies to the trees in an embrace. Indian women have also organized against such male violence as rape by landlords and wife battering (Kishwar and Vanita 1984).

While economic survival needs have spurred women around the world into collective action, it has not been without cost, as we pointed out in Chapter 1. Not only do many women have to face the consequences of state control, but they may experience abuse from men within the movement as well as men within their families and communities. When protesting women take leadership and expand their boundaries for action, they often have to confront patriarchal controls, and outcomes vary. In some cases, they may simply lose their leadership roles; in others, they may experience physical violence and abuse from men (Alvarado 1987; Andreas 1985; Barrios 1983; Kishwar and Vanita 1984). While we stress the commonalities of women's grass-roots protests, we do not mean to minimize the wide variations in women's conditions around the world. (For additional information on grass-roots protests around the world, see "Women in Action" 1984.)

Part I includes three studies of women's grass-roots protests in the United States. We begin with a now-classic article by Ronald Lawson and Stephen E. Barton on gender roles in the tenant movement of New York City in the early and late twentieth century (Chapter 2). Gender roles are shown to be significantly affected by the level and scope of the protest activity. In early stages, at the local level, women frequently organize and lead. If the movement grows, gaining visibility and recognition, men tend to take over leadership, and this despite the usually larger numbers of women activists at every level. Lawson and Barton trace this subtle process of discrimination against women as the movement evolves. They note that Robert Michels (1906) suggested that this phenomenon of the rule by the few was so pervasive in social movements that he labeled it "the iron law of oligarchy." His study, however, did not include any gender analysis. Lawson and Barton document that over time, male leaders move into paid movement careers or become heads of institutionalized movement organizations. What they discuss, but do not pinpoint explicitly, is what we have labeled "the iron law of patriarchy" within protest movement organizations. Their study, along with several others, suggests that the division of roles in gender-integrated movements almost invariably results (despite temporary variations) in male superordination and domination. This occurs even when the ideology of gender equality is explicit, such as in the Russian Revolution (see Engel 1977:346–69).

Pope's article (Chapter 3) analyzes the struggle of low-income mothers who joined to demand their right to basic human needs for themselves and their children. She focuses on black women in Brooklyn (New York) who were dependent on the state for AFDC (Aid to Families with Dependent Children) during the late 1960s. These organized women became the largest local group of the national welfare rights movement in the United States. Pope shows the creativity of these women—mostly black women who fought against incredible odds for adequate governmental transfers from the welfare departments and for credit from department stores. White nuns played pivotal roles as supporters and organizers at first, but two priests (men in a patriarchal society, nonetheless) acted as brokers with the authorities and took increasing control as the movement spread. She ends on a positive note, depicting the economic (career) benefits gained by the women activists in B-WAC.

The final article in Part I describes how women struggled within the labor movement in the United States to safeguard their economic survival by supporting the strikes of their husbands, fathers, and brothers, sometimes acting behind the scenes and sometimes directly confronting the authorities. Again, we observe in this type of protest another aspect of "the iron law of patriarchy." Once the strikes were won or crushed, and women were no longer needed on the political front, most returned, either voluntarily or because of pressure, to their traditional roles. Maggard discusses the link between social protest and political consciousness, describing changes in the behavior and attitudes of the coal miners' wives after the strike. Protest for women often means breaking traditional boundaries and has many ripple effects.

Thus Part I highlights the forces that pull women into and push them out of the political protest arena. Deprivation of basic survival needs has always been a source of anguish and discontent that, at particular times in history, gives rise to collective protest and may be transformed into revolutionary consciousness.

These articles raise some important questions that deserve further investigation. Under what conditions are women with relatively limited resources and critical economic needs able to mobilize collectively? Under what conditions are they less likely to organize? What are the processes of transformation that lead women to undertake collective action? Are outsiders and their resources always present when protest erupts? Or do women mobilize family and community networks and other resources when repression by a classist, racist, or sexist regime reaches a tipping point? How does spatial organization (i.e., housing arrangements) facilitate or inhibit women's mobilization and protest? Do collective support systems in poor women's communities (in contrast to isolated, individualistic middle-class systems of caring) provide a more fertile ground for consciousness raising and revolutionary ideas and strategies? What are some of the implications for women's social protest of the widespread poverty and economic stagnation or deterioration in many parts of the world in the late twentieth century?

CHAPTER 2

Sex Roles in Social Movements:
A Case Study of the Tenant Movement
in New York City

RONALD LAWSON
AND STEPHEN E. BARTON

Many recent studies have documented the presence of sexism in American society, charted the oppressive impact of discrimination against women, and traced its sources.[1] So ubiquitous is sexism, and so pervasive the engines supporting it, that, ironically, its trace may be found even within movements for social justice. A literature is now developing that describes the part women have played in social movements and the sexism they have encountered there. This is largely descriptive, focusing on the ideological interchange between party leadership and feminists.[2] Lacking still are analyses of the means by which the sexism of the larger society reproduces itself within social movements whose aim has been to liberate people from societal oppression. This paper attempts to follow Robert Michels, whose 1915 study of the forces leading to oligarchy in the German socialist movement pioneered the sociological analysis of the internal difficulties of progressive movements (Michels 1962). The vehicle for analysis is an urban phenomenon, the tenant movement, the crusade for the recognition of tenants' rights to security within well-maintained housing at reasonable rents in New York City since 1904. Over time, the tenant movement has evolved a complex structure existing at three levels: building organizations (BOs), neighborhood organizations (NOs), and city- or statewide federations. Women pioneered as the organizers of protest in their buildings and took the lead in helping to spread it from building to building. Men, however, were at the forefront when the higher levels of the structure first emerged. They have also usually been the leaders of organizations initiating new strategies at these higher levels.[3] This pattern has occurred in spite of the presence of a clear majority of women in almost all

Reprinted with permission from *Signs* 6, no. 2 (1980): 230–47. © 1981 by The University of Chicago. All rights reserved. Some notes have been omitted in this version.

organizations at every structural level. Nevertheless, once new structures or strategies have emerged, women have assumed more leadership positions. That is, women, in the forefront of organizing a grass-roots movement that has had a rather long history have been a major force in building and then keeping the movement going. This finding runs counter to the general view of women as apolitical, following their men's wishes, relying on their men heavily, or even never involving themselves in activities that cannot be immediately connected to family life (Jaquette 1974).

We do not mean to imply that the tenant movement has been led by crass male chauvinists who "put down" women daily while working with them. Indeed, the reverse is generally the case: most of the men have a genuine concern for social justice, and the concept of sexism within the movement is quite foreign to them. When we have mentioned the sex role patterns within the movement, they have often been surprised that we could find them remarkable. Many of the women activists would agree in this response. This paper is concerned, then, with a subtle process that has had a profound impact on leadership patterns and the division of labor within the movement.

RESEARCH METHODS

The data for this paper were collected using a combination of three methods. Historical research on the period 1890 to 1972 drew on city and local press, city and state government archives, tenant organization records, and extensive oral history. Fieldwork covered the three main federations extensively from 1973 to 1978, the other four in less detail, and twenty-five neighborhood and forty building organizations during 1973 to 1975. There was considerable follow-up of these organizations and extension of fieldwork to others newly important after the initial period. Surveys in 1975 and 1976 broadened coverage to the leaders and key activists of 123 neighborhood organizations and leaders, members, and nonmembers within 108 organized buildings together with their landlords; the leaders of 120 other buildings were added later. This sample represents almost all the neighborhood groups active in 1975 and 1976 whose central purpose was to organize tenants, together with a sample of thirty-six OEO-funded housing agencies, most of which mainly serviced tenants rather than organizing them. The leaders of the buildings were interviewed twice, the second time one year after the first, in order to check the outcome of their actions and their organization survival rates. When most of the actions proved to be still in process, a new sample of buildings, each organized more than two years earlier, was drawn, twenty from the files of each of six important organizations from very different neighborhoods, and the leaders of all these were interviewed.

HISTORICAL SUMMARY

The first episode of tenant activism in New York City occurred in 1904. Sharply increasing rents provoked isolated rent strikes on the Lower East

Side, which women then spread from building to building until two thousand families were participating. Organization was initially informal, relying on networks among these Jewish people. However, when rapid mobilization revealed the issue's potential, an umbrella organization, the first NO, was formed by male members of the Socialist party. This, however, collapsed before the strike culminated with gains to tenants.

The next, larger, burst of activity in 1907 to 1908 followed a similar path: the organizers were women, the would-be NO leaders Socialist men. A third, much longer, and larger wave of activity was initiated by "tenant leagues." NOs formed by Socialist party branches after 1917. It culminated with the imposition of rent controls in 1920. Again the organizers were mainly women, but the leaders both of the leagues and of the rival "tenant associations" sponsored by the mainline parties were males. However, during the 1920s when the associations continued alone, helping tenants use the complicated new law, women became prominent as NO leaders for the first time. The associations lapsed with the rent law in 1929.

Numerous NOs reemerged in the wake of the depression, focusing on the housing decay that accompanied high vacancy rates. Most of the participants and some of the leaders were women. But when the first federation was formed in 1936, all the leaders were men. However, with time, women moved into prominent positions. In 1942, when war removed the male leaders, a women became president. Three broad federations then emerged after World War II to lobby for the retention of wartime rent controls. Men led all of them. However, when these federations were dismantled in the early 1950s following the passage of state rent controls and the onset of McCarthyite repression, movement leadership reverted to boroughwide organizations, all of which had women leaders. Women also dominated the new "Save-Our-Homes" organizations in neighborhoods threatened by urban renewal. When a federation, the Metropolitan Council on Housing (Met Council), was formed in 1959 to lobby against urban renewal, a triumvirate of two men and one woman was chosen to lead it.

Meanwhile, housing conditions had reappeared as a central issue in ghetto areas. In the winter of 1963/64 a rent strike spread outward from Harlem. Though still known as the "Jesse Gray rent strike," after the man who acted as spokesperson, it was actually run by two women. Women also predominated on the citywide Strike Coordinating Committee. During the years that followed, "housing specialists" funded under the antipoverty program appeared in ghetto areas. Whatever their sex, they administrated generally unadventurous programs. The Met Council was also broadening its interests and consolidating its position as a citywide federation of tenant organizations. Jane Benedict had been appointed chairperson, replacing the original triumvirate. She has dominated it for over eighteen years.

THE CONTEMPORARY MOVEMENT

Since 1971, tenant action in New York City has swelled considerably. Virtually every neighborhood now has at least one tenant organization, and thousands

Table 2.1 Sex of Core Activists at Different Structural Levels of the Movement, 1976–77

(%)

	Building (N = 107)	Neighborhood (N = 110)	Federation (N = 7)
Women	54.2	48.2	71.4
Sexes equal	22.4	16.4	14.3
Men	23.4	35.5	14.3

of buildings have organized and conducted rent strikes. The spectrum of socioeconomic status (SES) within the movement has also broadened considerably. The range of tenant strategies has diversified and now includes an effective lobbying presence in the state legislature, tenant-initiated court cases, the direct expenditure of rent moneys on repairs, the management and moderate rehabilitation of buildings abandoned by their landlords, the gut rehabilitation of totally abandoned buildings through "sweat equity" by would-be tenants, the fostering of cooperative ownership of their buildings by low-income tenants, and a number of different forms of rent strike. The structure of the movement has developed commensurately: there are now one statewide, four citywide, and two boroughwide federations. They represent tenants with dissimilar housing problems and of differing socioeconomic status; they also stress somewhat distinct strategies.

However, certain historical patterns have continued to hold. The movement is still largely a movement of women in the sense that they make up most of the participants. Our 1975 to 1976 survey results show that women considerably outnumber men among grass-roots members: 63.4 percent of NOs report that the majority of their members are women, only 3.2 percent that the majority are men. (The remainder indicate equal numbers.) Among core activists, women outnumber men at *all* levels. However, the situation is different when leaders are separated from other activists: the higher the structural level, the more likely are leaders to be male (Tables 2.1 and 2.2).

Significant variations occur within this pattern depending on the SES of the tenants. In general, the higher the income of tenants being organized or served, the greater the likelihood that leaders are male. We divided organizations among three categories according to the average income of their member-

Table 2.2 Sex of Leaders at Different Structural Levels of the Movement, 1976–77

(%)

	Building (N = 108)	Neighborhood (N = 123)	Federation (N = 7)
Women	50.9	40.7	28.6
Both sexes coleaders	23.1	8.9	. . .
Men	25.9	50.4	71.4

Table 2.3 Sex of Leaders of Building Organizations according to the Average Income of Membership, 1976

(%)

	Average Income		
	Low (N = 23)	Moderate (N = 22)	Middle (N = 36)
Women	65.2	54.5	52.8
Both sexes coleaders	13.0	27.3	19.4
Men	21.7	18.2	27.8

ship or clientele: less than $8,000 per family (low income), $8,000 to $12,500 (moderate income), and more than $12,500 (middle income). Among BOs, although women are in the majority among both leaders and core activists at all income levels, their predominance decreases as income rises. At the neighborhood level, where there are more male leaders, a small female plurality of leaders among low-income groups is transformed into a clear male preponderance among the heads of middle-income groups (Tables 2.3 and 2.4).

While obtaining continuous historical data concerning the leadership of NOs and federations presesnted few serious obstacles, similar data for BOs were inevitably much more patchy. We do know that the formation of BOs in large numbers among middle-income tenants is a recent phenomenon, and that these BOs are much more likely to be led by men. Since the press was consistent in reporting that women led action in buildings during the early years of the movement, we would infer from these data that the proportion of male leaders in BOs has probably increased in recent years. Similarly, the formation of NOs in middle-income communities has no doubt slowed the overall trend toward leadership by women at this level of the movement structure.

Part of the variation in participation by sex among income groups may reflect the larger political role which women play in the black community (Lamb 1976). Blacks are strongly represented among low-income organizations but far outnumbered among middle-income organizations (Table 2.5).[4] However, the historical data make it unlikely that this accounts for all the variation

Table 2.4 Sex of Leaders of Neighborhood Organizations according to the Average Income of Membership, 1976–77

(%)

	Average Income		
	Low (N = 73)	Moderate (N = 15)	Middle (N = 23)
Women	47.9	26.7	17.4
Both sexes coleaders	11.0	13.3	4.3
Men	41.1	60.0	78.3

Table 2.5 Race of Neighborhood Organizations according to the Average Income of Membership, 1976–77

| | Average Income | | |
	Low (N = 70)	Moderate (N = 15)	Middle (N = 23)
White	5.7	46.7	82.6
Black	27.1	20.0	4.3
Hispanic	31.4	6.7	0
Mixed	35.7	26.7	13.0

between income groups, since most of the groups we studied in the pre–World War II period were predominantly white. Moreover, while the proportion of women leaders among black low-income organizations is greater than for other racial groups, the leadership patterns among organizations of all races are congruent with the general SES distributions we have described. For example, sixteen out of nineteen white NOs have male leaders in the middle-income category, but only two of four in the low-income category.

Despite these general patterns, some of the most prominent leaders within the tenant movement are women. For example, Jane Benedict's long rule over the Met Council and her numerous appearances on television and radio as the outspoken champion of tenant rights have made her the best-known tenant leader in New York City today. The general patterns must also be modified by another factor that cuts across them: men tend to hold the leadership positions when new paths are being pioneered, especially when these require the development of cooperative relationships with formal organizations such as legislatures, banks, courts, and government bureaucracies. Such cooperative relationships, frequently achieved as the result of conflictual strategies, may be characterized as "conflictual cooperation." However, once the new relationships, structures, and strategies have been accepted, women have been likely to replace male leaders who drop out.

For example, in the mid-1970s a number of NOs began developing new tactics to save or reclaim buildings from abandonment: moderate rehabilitation, sweat-equity rehabilitation, the forming of low-income cooperatives. These groups deal with very poor tenants, the very range where the majority of NOs are led by women; but sixteen of the twenty organizations now using these strategies are led by men. Another example is organizations founded during the 1970s in fourteen middle-income groups based in large housing developments, that is, buildings or groups of buildings with from 3,000 to 60,000 tenants in one place with one landlord. These had never been organized until recently, but the threat of forced condominium conversion or massive rent increases mobilized them. Twelve of the fourteen are led by men.

The exceptions show that women *can* and *do* lead organizations that require skills in dealing with bureaucracies; however, they have been unlikely to do so initially. On the other hand, women are in the majority among the leaders of NOs following the more traditional strategies: those fostering rent strikes (thirteen women, eleven men), opposing demolition of buildings for redevelopment and institutional expansion—the successors to those who fought urban renewal in the 1950s and 1960s (six women, no men), and mainly or solely servicing individual tenants (twenty-one women, fourteen men).

Nevertheless, with the passage of time the new strategies have been incorporated more frequently in the repertoires of NOs led by women, as the pattern that has been detected would predict. The leaders of NOs that encourage striking tenants who are being stonewalled by landlords to spend their rent monies directly on fuel or repairs—a decision that is often tantamount to accepting de facto responsibility for managing the building—are evenly divided between men and women. Several women leaders are successfully managing city-owned buildings under community management contracts between their NOs and the city (among the twenty NOs with such contracts, five management programs are headed by women). And because most NOs have a majority of women among their activist cores, sweat-equity rehabilitation[5]—a strategy which would seem to demand traditionally male skills—often finds women working in building construction along with men on an equal basis.

This pattern, where males occupy leadership positions while new directions are evolving and females are more likely to take over once these become established, may also be illustrated structurally. The major structural innovation of the 1970s has been the emergence of multiple federations. These reflect the mobilization of new constituencies among tenants with different problems and the consequent need to introduce new strategies. The original leaders of six of the seven federations were males, or in one case a male majority with a triumvirate. The one exception, City-Wide Save-Our-Homes, a coalition of NOs fighting demolition due to institutional expansion, was really founded for mutual support rather than with specific bureaucratic targets in view. All four cases of leadership succession at this level where a change of sex was involved have been from male to female; two especially notable ones occurred early in 1979. As a result of these changes, two and one-half of the three most important federations, and three and one-half of all seven federations, are now led by women.

ANALYSIS

Most tenant leaders are so embued with goodwill and idealism, and the prejudices associated with sexism are so foreign to their consciousness, that it is tempting to explain the movement's participation patterns in terms of internal processes, where female personality variables allow males to come to dominate leadership competition. However, the actual roles of the female organizations and the strength they display in them lead up to reject this. A combination of the impact of structural variables, infringing on the movement from without, and sex-role socialization is a more parsimonious explanation, which we now wish to explore in more detail by addressing three questions.

1. *Why are women predominant among organizers, other active participants, and rank-and-file members, so that the tenant movement has been numerically largely a movement of women?*

An awareness of the division between home and community on the one hand and workplace on the other is vital to an understanding of the participation patterns we found. The home is regarded as primarily the sphere of the woman rather than of the man. Consequently, when a rent increase or a deterioration in services impinges on the home, it is usually the woman's task to deal with it since it lies within her sphere. This pattern holds true more frequently in working-class than in middle-class households because of the greater separation of the roles typically found there (Komarovsky 1964). Building organization mobilization is commonly based on a network of social ties within a building which women, whether employed outside the home or not, are much more likely to form. The homemaker activities of women in their building and neighborhood—doing the laundry, neighboring, watching over children, shopping for food—all foster the creation of common ties; men, on the other hand, often lack them (James 1974). In addition, building organizations, like PTAs, provide an acceptable avenue for social action, since activities outside the home are seen as threatening by a significant minority of working-class husbands (Rubin 1976: 176–84, 201–2). These factors surely help considerably to explain why women participate in BOs to a far greater extent than men and why their participation relative to men is more extensive among those of lower SES. They also account for the fact that employment outside the home does not affect the participation of women adversely. Indeed, while 87 percent of employed women in organized buildings report membership in the BO, this is so for only 80 percent of unemployed.

As Tables 2.1 and 2.2 demonstrate, women are also more likely to act as organizers and leaders at this local level. (These two roles frequently coincide within BOs.) Several factors are relevant here. The initiative for action often grows out of networks within buildings, where women's ties are typically much more dense than those of men. Again, because of their familiarity with their neighborhoods women are more likely to know of and to make contact with a NO when housing problems arise—and the person who makes that first contact often becomes the leader of a BO. The offices of NOs are typically crowded with women, even at night. Moreover, even though leadership roles are more demanding than the roles of the rank and file, employment status is not significant in determining who fills them: the leader/follower ratio among employed women is almost identical with that among unemployed within BOs.

Relatively few tenants active in their own BOs are drawn into efforts to help other buildings, but those doing so are much more apt to be women than men. Indeed, this is the major means of recruiting women to the ranks of NO activists, and it is the reason for their numerical predominance there: 85 percent of female activists in NOs had been recruited via BOs, compared with 56 percent of males. Men are more likely than women to choose to become active in NOs without ever having belonged to a BO (see below), but this source of male recruitment does not compensate for the predominance of women among those drawn into neighborhood activism from the grass roots.

Women begin to work with other buildings because of their involvement in neighborhood friendship networks and because they are already involved in their own BOs and have found that they are good at organizing and enjoy it; in a few instances it is also important that they are not working. Only 9 percent of NO activists do not have paid employment, but 85 percent of these are women. These make up 19 percent of women activists, compared with 2 percent of men. That is, only as activism takes them out of their own buildings does the employment status of women begin to play a determining part. The involvement of these women in a NO in turn reinforces and extends their neighborhood networks, and their experiences help to strengthen, or perhaps create, an ideological commitment.

We would also argue that female socialization for "interpersonal orientation, empathy, sensitivity, nurturance, [and] supportiveness" often develops a greater interpersonal sensitivity that is important to organizing, especially where people are fearful and distrustful, as tenants facing problems often are (Bardwick and Douvan 1971). In contrast, males receive systematic training against sensitivity and trust and for agressiveness and competition (Hartley 1974). Masculine socialization and behavior thus prove to be disabling for grass-roots organizing, particularly in domains where women are a necessary constituency. McCormack has suggested that the apparently greater conservatism of female voters may be due to the aggressive masculine style of working-class politicians (McCormack 1973). Male union organizers have failed in attempts to organize women office workers for similar reasons (Barton 1979:76). Our files contain several instances where men have fought for dominance in tenant organizations and driven out the losers. On the other hand, male socialization prepares men to handle confrontations with often hostile forces outside the organization such as landlords and courts.

Finally, in the tenant movement *both* organizers and rank and file have tended to be women. Men organizers have both neglected women and attemped to exclude them from organizations. In the tenant movement women were not ignored, for women were organizing other women. Sharing a common understanding, a language, they could appeal to a common culture (e.g., the effort of poor housing conditions on their children). Moreover, women could spend time with the women organizers without being suspected of having a sexual relationship and without husbands fearing that their wives were being seduced.[16]

2. *Why have a disproportionate number of the leadership positions been held by men?*

Men have tended to hold the positions of leadership within the tenant movement because of a societal structure in which institutions favor men and discriminate against women. Sponsoring organizations have often placed men directly in advantaged positions in the movement, and men have also gained access to relevant skills and networks as a result of external experience in organizations that have been closed to, or more restrictive toward, women. Meanwhile, women have been exposed to discriminatory policies that have imposed costs on their attempts to lead or have removed them from leadership competition altogether.

Sponsorship was especially important during the first years of the movement. The earliest NOs were sponsored by political parties which took the initiative in placing personnel directly in movement positions. Because of the sexist structures of the sponsoring organizations these personnel were almost always men, the very few exceptions being Socialists during the 1917 to 1920 period. The sponsored NO participants had several advantages: not only were the NOs actually formed around them, making them the incumbent leaders, but they also had ready access to outside resources, such as skills, networks, and money. There were also prospects of personal rewards in the sponsoring organizations.

Ties to sponsoring organizations continued to be important in later years: to the American Labor Party in the years immediately before and after World War II; to the two main parties, especially the Democrats, at various times since that war; and to various churches, particularly the Catholic church, since the mid-1960s.

Beginning in the 1930s, this force favoring males began to be intertwined with, and often replaced by, a second factor: previous access to relevant skills and networks. The early Socialist-backed NOs sought to make a political impact through the use of mass rent strikes and other confrontation strategies. Later NOs tended to become more Janus-like, separating to some extent their goals of influencing politicians and bureaucracies from those of organizing buildings, bargaining with landlords, and servicing tenants. While organizers pursued the latter goals, the leaders found that they needed bureaucratic and manipulative skills in order to deal with the former, a facet that received increasing emphasis as some NOs began to manage buildings and administer various government programs in the 1970s. For their part, federations have almost always been formed with legislative or administrative targets in view and with bureaucratic strategies in mind. For example, the New York State Tenants and Neighborhoods Coalition was formed with the express purpose of establishing an *"expert lobbying presence"* with Albany legislators.

Such organizations are very different from the home-centered BOs. Their leaders need access to influential networks and skills with which to approach experts and authorities. While social-emotional roles are important for mobilization of people, bureaucratic roles are often the key to strategic impact, and males have usually been better prepared to fill such roles. Experience in other institutions within the society has provided many men but only a few women with the relevant personal skills or access to the relevant infrastructures. Several of the early federation leaders, all of them, without exception, men, had previously held administrative posts. By the 1970s the strategies used by the movement had broadened considerably. The proportion and variety of skilled personnel among its leaders expanded rapidly. Men with formal skills still far outnumbered skilled women; among key NO activists 38 percent of the males had entered with relevant skills they had learned outside the movement compared with 16 percent of the females. Among the key activists in the multiple federations of the past decade, the comparable statistics are 77 percent of men and 54 percent of women. Perhaps the most striking example is that of Robert Schur, who in 1975 moved from a post as administrator within the City Housing and Development Administration to become director of the Association of Neighborhood Housing Developers. There he provided NOs with technical knowledge about the very programs he had previously administered, doing much of the negotiating on their behalf himself.

Professional expertise and bureaucratic manipulation are broadly transferable to other organizations and movements. On the other hand, the more movement-specific skills (familiarity with people in a neighborhood, knowledge of organizational procedures) of the secondary leaders, the majority of whom are women, are less heralded and transferable. Thus for men the motivation for pursuit of leadership positions within the tenant movement is often as a step toward future career goals, frequently in politics. Paul Ross, a federation leader from 1948 to 1952, later ran for mayor. Jesse Gray, who began organizing tenants in Harlem in the 1950s, ran for several offices before being elected to the state assembly as the "Harlem Rent Strike Leader" nine years after the event. Today one state senator and two assemblymen continue to cultivate the NOs which were their original political bases, while several other tenant leaders clearly aspire to similar advancement. All are men. By contrast, Marie Runyon, a recent single-term assemblywoman, was defeated for reelection when the predominantly male leadership of the Columbia Tenants Union turned against her because she refused to act as a figurehead.

Career goals are therefore much more potent in motivating men than women: 34 percent of men entering NOs as volunteer activists are so motivated compared with 3 percent of women. Many of these enter NOs in their communities without ever having been involved with BOs (19 percent of men, 2 percent of women); but about half of these men are active prior to becoming involved with the NO in local Democratic clubs. Of twenty-one key figures active at the outset of the present-day federations, only four, all women, seem not to have been motivated at least in part by career goals. Of the other seventeen, who included only two women, three were hoping for legislative or administrative careers which they in fact did not secure, although all three were furthered toward different administrative careers as a result of their involvement. Ten secured paid posts for themselves within the movement, and for the remaining four these positions were next steps in already existing salaried careers within the movement.

More than half of the core members of NOs (56 percent at last count and rising) are now salaried. This is a recent development, dating back a little more than ten years to the first OEO-funded "housing specialists" and mushrooming only in the last three or four years with the expansion of rehabilitation and management strategies supported by government funds. Although most of these positions pay fairly poorly, and much of the funding is in soft money, it is beginning to be possible to think in terms of a career within the tenant movement. Women have been more successful in securing these positions than might have been expected: the proportion of paid women activists matches that of men activists almost exactly. However, the women's paid positions tend not to be at the highest level. For example, only one of the four salaried federation leader positions is held by a woman, and she, a new incumbent, is the first woman to hold such a position. On the other hand, women hold four of the six voluntary federation leader positions.

Meanwhile, discrimination against women has compounded the advantages held by male leaders. It was most overt in 1904, when Bertha Liebson, the most prominent of the strike organizers, was vetoed as treasurer of the new NO on grounds that a woman was not qualified to hold such a post. Recently it has been more subtle. For example, court bureaucracies have on occasion refused to deal with organizers, who tend to be female, demanding instead lawyers, more frequently male. While the various rehabilitation and community management programs were being developed, usually as a direct result of movement pressure, members of the city housing bureaucracy were loath to deal with movement personnel, whom they considered to be "unprofessional." They stressed the need for "professional packaging." This attitude meant support for male middle-class leaders at the expense of female and less educated male leaders. Similarly, NOs have trouble gaining approval for would-be "7A" administrators of buildings when no professionals are available.[7]

The factors covered in the analysis so far also explain why men are especially likely to be at the helm when new structures or strategies are evolving. When needed skills are not part of the movement's experience, skilled personnel must be mobilized externally. Males have frequently used the advantages of broader experience to assume leadership in a changing situation by taking the initiative to found new NOs. For example, the three NOs most prominent in pioneering rehabilitation and management strategies in neighborhoods undergoing abandonment in the early 1970s were led by white, well-educated males whose bureaucratic skills and access to relevant networks enabled them to manipulate the city's housing bureaucracy to create whole new city programs. One of them, Henry Lanier, then joined the Housing and Development Administration as a commissioner, where his task was to develop and administer the new program. Women have also created new NOs in response to threats, especially the threat of demolition of their housing. But throughout most of the movement's history they have not been in a position to respond to career opportunities. While the NOs they have created have also been stategically innovative, for example, in the use of squatter takeovers to combat urban renewal and institutional expansion, they have relied more on mobilization of people than on bureaucratic skills.

It is appropriate at this point to consider the oldest existing federation, Met Council. Not only is it led by a woman, Jane Benedict, but a majority of its activists and of the leaders of its branch and affiliated NOs are women. Throughout its twenty-year history, it has refused to compromise its position on tenants' rights. Indeed, it has strengthened it by adding to its slogan of "decent, integrated housing at rents tenants can afford" a call for the replacement of private ownership with "housing in the public domain." Because of its intractability, a product of the "Old Left" ideology of its leadership, it has rarely been taken seriously as a political force. Met Council uses lobbying trips to the state capital as a tool to educate its members concerning the futility of expecting changes to be given when they must be forced by direct action. It also emphasizes that tenants must rely on the strength provided by organization and unity rather than the expertise of lawyers and other professionals. Indeed, though a federation, over the last eight years it has rejected the usual political role of federations and has instead poured most of its resources into organizing rent strikes in buildings. Thus by rejecting professionals and refusing to enter the established political arena, Met Council has avoided the main avenues of male domination within the tenant movement.

In brief, some of the factors Michels found conducive to oligarchy—the greater knowledge and skills of leadership and the vested interest of leaders in preserving and furthering their careers—also help maintain male predominance in tenant leadership. The firmly oligarchic leadership of Met Council is, however, ironic evidence that women's leadership is not inherently democratic.

3. *Under what circumstances have women replaced men in leadership positions?*

The turnover among leaders of the tenant movement has been quite substantial. For example, of eight federation leadership positions, three of which have been held occasionally by more than one person at a time, four are currently held by long-term incumbents. However, a total of fourteen leaders have come and gone during the life span of the federations, eleven in the past five years. Turnover among federation activists has been even more rapid: the average term of a member of Met Council's executive board is only two years. The NO leaders also turn over at a substantial rate, though less quickly than federation leaders. Why do movement leaders leave so frequently? Some of the leaders may be described as having vaulted up successfully from their movement bases to political or administrative careers, while others were similarly successful within the movement. These two groups together make up 15 percent of federation and NO leader turnover. For them the hope that participation in the movement would further their careers was fulfilled. Almost all of them are men. Other departing leaders are less upwardly mobile. More than a third, 38 percent, "burn out," finding their participation insufficiently rewarding. Some find the personal costs of tenant activism unmatched by the rewards and retire to private lives. Some have withdrawn because of anticipated repression: one federation leader, Alfred K. Stern, fled abroad during the McCarthy period. Organizational vicissitudes cause another 30 percent to leave: those paying their salaries run out of funds or fire them, they are voted out of office, organizations split. Smaller numbers have been removed by outside forces such as the call to military service or the 1920 split in the Socialist party. Some have been moved on by sponsoring organizations. Others, like the recent opposers of demolition, have left because the short-term goals they sought were settled or rendered moot. Some positions are vacated because of retirement, illness, or death.

The turnover has been greater among men than among women over the history of the organization: 80 percent of the male activists in presently existing federations compared with 50 percent of the females; 56 percent of the men NO leaders but only 44 percent of the women. This disparity is explained in part by the career orientation of much of the male participation; consequently, men tend to come and go while women, who are more solely committed to the movement, often serve for long periods. Jane Bendict's tenure at Met Council is only one of several examples among women. No male leader equals this record. In the past male leaders have been especially likely to drop out of the tenant movement during waning periods when rewards of the kinds that had initially attracted them seemed less likely to accrue. This finding is congruent with, though the obverse of, the experiences of other movements that have been enlarged and institutionalized to the point where they offer highly rewarding careers. There, men have often stayed in leadership for long periods in spite of predominantly female memberships. For example, all the presidents of the International Ladies Garment Workers Union and the Amalgamated Clothing Workers Union have been men.

When leadership turnover has occurred within the tenant movement, women have been more likely to succeed to the positions vacated than they were to have held the positions in the first place. Since men have been especially likely to vacate positions during periods of movement decline, when these posts appeared less likely to provide avenues to political influence or to personal career advancement, men were not knocking on the doors wanting to come in and take over. Women, in contrast, were much less likely to exit at these times: they did not have sponsoring organizations to pull them out; their skills, which they had often learned within the movement, were frequently movement-specific; and they felt a high degree of commitment to the movement itself and to their fellow workers. Moreover, they were in the majority among the activists. Because they had worked so closely with the previous leader, they often knew most about his work. Leadership, therefore, passed naturally to some of the women found so commonly among the secondary ranks where they had—on the job, so to speak—developed a fluency with the strategies in use.

This pattern parallels closely the racial transition among the leaders of the first three NOs to use tenant management and rehabilitation strategies in neighborhoods undergoing abandonment. As indicated above, these organizations were founded and led by well-educated white males from outside the neighborhoods who recruited indigenous blacks or Hispanics to subordinate positions. The latter might never have had the expectations of success to found, or the skills to run, such organizations successfully. However, by the time that the founders moved on, taking advantage of career opportunities opening to them, such subordinates had developed sufficient skills and access to networks to take over.

The result of this male-to-female succession pattern was that women gradually moved up through the ranks in the movement structure, taking over the leadership positions from men. At the outset—in 1904, 1907, and again in 1917 to 1920—they were organizers whose prominence was usurped by the men who formed the first NOs; by the 1920s they were leading NOs themselves; in 1942 a woman headed a federation for the first time; by the end of the 1970s they were as prominent at the federation level as the male volunteers, through still somewhat behind in the salaried, more technical, posts.

This whole process has accelerated since the growth of the modern women's movement, which has made it easier for women to enter male-dominated positions. Career motivation has been rising just at a time when paid positions within the movement have been opening up. Moreover, some of the women leaders are now bringing skills to the movement: of the thirteen women federation leaders and key activists, seven, including a lawyer, two social workers, a labor organizer, and two administrators with considerable political experience, have externally gained skills. Moreover, the same seven, unlike all but one of the other six, entered the movement through NOs rather than BOs. And nine of the thirteen hold salaried positions within the movement.

These are as yet a rather special group of women within the movement: such skills are rarer among activists in NOs. As noted earlier, women are more likely to lead NOs using traditional strategies. Nevertheless, these seven skilled women, the appointment of four women as leaders of the three key federations, the fact that women are competing more evenly with men in the job market within the movement, and the fact that a few of them have even gone out of the movement to promising careers outside are all evidence of considerable change.

These processes are also making their impact elsewhere, such as among community development groups at the national level. One example is National People's Action, led by Gale Cincotta from Chicago. Both the New York State Tenants' and Neighborhoods' Coalition and the Association of Neighborhood Housing Developers are in close contact with her group, taking part in its annual conference and demonstration in Washington each year.

CONCLUSION

We believe our analysis serves to show the importance of both social-emotional and functional roles for mobilization of people and strategic impact. The "social relations of reproduction," centering on the home and neighborhood and their accompanying role training, help lay the groundwork for successful mobilization at the grass roots. On the other hand, the "social relations of production," pivoting around careers and the workplace, provide the skills necessary for dealing with government and bureaucracies. We have argued that these roles have, in general, been divided according to gender, so that women have tended to be the organizers and followers and men the leaders of the tenant movement. Nevertheless, as we have demonstrated, over time, and especially recently, women have successfully learned the necessary skills and broken through the structural barriers to become leaders in their own right. One can only hope that men in turn will come to recognize the disabling features of their own socialization and the distorted values incorporated into the structures of most large, formal organizations and will come to value and, ultimately, to use the skills which women have brought to bear in organizing tenants at the grass-roots level.

NOTES

1. An excellent review of the literature is Etheridge (1974, 1978).

2. See, for example, Flexner (1971), Carden (1975), Buhle (1970), Schaffer (1979), Foner (1979), and Rowbotham (1974a, 1974b).

3. We use the term "leader(s)" to refer to the spokesperson(s) and main decision maker(s) for a social movement organization. Often this is a single person bearing a formal title; sometimes the term refers best to a group of from two to four people. Our fieldwork indicates that the numbers deserving to be so designated rarely exceed four. By the "activists" or "active core" (terms we use interchangeably) we mean the group of people in an organization who do most of the work—organizing, publicity, advising of tenants, etc. This group includes the leader(s) and extends beyond him/her (them) to include less prominent participants. However, it is often not coextensive with those holding official positions. The size of the active core is most frequently between three and six persons; in some cases it may include as many as a dozen or more persons. The term "secondary leaders" is used to refer to those members of the active core who are not spokespersons or main decision makers.

4. We identified an organization as a particular race if two-thirds or more of its members were of that race; other organizations were identified as mixed race. Almost all of the latter had strong black components.

5. Under this strategy tenants gain equity in a previously abandoned building through volunteering their labor ("sweat") in its rehabilitation. Such a building is then cooperatively owned and managed.

6. The presence of strange men, whether as organizers or as sociological researchers, is often regarded with suspicion (Lofland 1973).

7. Article 7A amending the Real Property Actions and Proceedings Law in 1965 allowed one-third or more of the tenants in a building with dangerous violations to petition the court to order that all rents be deposited in court and then spent entirely on repairs by an administrator appointed by the court. Such administrators took over the day-by-day decisions concerning the buildings they managed from the landlords. The law originally insisted that they be selected from a small list of professions, such as lawyers and architects, who were predominantly male, and excluded the most obvious candidates, the leaders of the building tenant organizations, who were frequently females, because they were not the designated professionals. However, it proved to be very difficult to find professionals who were prepared to shoulder the arduous responsibility for a deteriorated building in return for a meager portion of the rent roll. Consequently, the list of categories from which administrators could be drawn was broadened in the mid-1970s, and ultimately included the tenant leaders. The latter were being added by default around the time when this paper was originally published. Since then, tenant leaders have come to dominate the role.

CHAPTER 3

Women in the Welfare Rights Struggle: The Brooklyn Welfare Action Council

JACKIE POPE

The decade of the 1960s was one of struggle by a number of groups to obtain basic human rights. During the course of these activities, participants went through personal transformations, and sometimes the groups themselves changed. This study explores the efforts of a large number of poor urban women on welfare who organized to improve the quality of their lives, to redefine welfare as a right rather than a privilege, and to obtain what they were entitled to by law.[1] The Brooklyn Welfare Action Council (B-WAC) was created to coordinate the efforts of neighborhood groups of welfare rights advocates. At its peak in 1968, B-WAC was the largest union of welfare recipients in America, with almost 8,000 individual members and 48 welfare rights groups under its auspices. Membership was predominantly black, with smaller numbers of whites and Hispanics.

I will describe how B-WAC came to be organized, the principles and strategies it employed, its accomplishments, its effect on individual lives, and the combination of forces that eventually led to its demise. It was linked, through the involvement of a small number of priests and nuns, to a radical movement within the Catholic church, a movement growing out of the Second Vatican Council under Pope John XXIII that exhorted the clergy to focus on the needs of the poor. It was also a part of the national welfare rights movement that emerged in the mid-1960s, relatively autonomous but formally linked to the National Welfare Rights Organization (NWRO).

The welfare rights movement was unusual in that it was a movement primarily of poor women, many of them minority, who were able to overcome the obstacles of poverty, ill health, and stigma to organize and fight for their rights under the law. Some of the women participated as leaders not only in local welfare rights groups, but also in the Brooklyn coordinating group and as paid officials at the national level in NWRO.[2] The role of the Catholic clergy was that of catalyst or broker, because it sought to empower poor people. At the same time, the priests and nuns acted as supporters, initially providing valuable resources such as funds, meetings places, and information.[3]

On the national level, organized welfare recipients, also overwhelmingly women, fought and lobbied for legislation on issues of welfare reform, health care, housing, and food stamps. On the local level they developed strategies and tactics that gained increased financial benefits for their members. Personal transformations took place as the women became more politically mature and skilled. Their involvement in militant organized actions became legendary. Unlike the female leadership of many other local social movement organizations, B-WAC's leaders were tapped for paid movement positions at the national level. Ironically, the promotion of these local leaders left a resource gap in B-WAC, hastening its decline. A changing national mood and the defeat of President Nixon's Family Assistance Plan (FAP), an attempt at welfare reform, also contributed to the demise of B-WAC.

THE ECONOMIC, POLITICAL, AND WELFARE ENVIRONMENT IN THE 1960s

President John F. Kennedy signed the Public Welfare Amendments to the Social Security Act on July 25, 1962, providing for increased federal funds to enable states to expand job training, placement, and casework services to welfare recipients. The law's proponents saw it as an effort to personalize the system and put able-bodied people to work. Opponents viewed the law as a method of changing the person to fit the system, leaving the system's weaknesses intact.[4]

In 1965, under Lyndon B. Johnson's administration, the Economic Opportunity Act (EOA) was passed, and the Office of Economic Opportunity (OEO) established. The act was considered a major weapon in the war against poverty, with a number of programs developed by OEO, such as Volunteers in Service to America, Job Corps, Operation Head Start, and a Community Action Program.

This "war against poverty," as the EOA was popularly called, reached New York City neighborhoods amid considerable fanfare, providing limited numbers of first-time white-collar jobs for their residents. Hope for the future spread when low-income people saw next-door neighbors staffing community programs. Until that time, most administrators (regardless of ethnic background) lived outside the area. This change of policy was appreciated because, observed Mr. Daniels, a former department community organizer, "services improve when staff and residents are users" (personal interview, July 1983).[5] However, critics of the programs pointed out that while well-meaning, they often did not reach the people needing them most.

Welfare recipients on the economic bottom availed themselves of some of the new services but did not share the general euphoria. Their lives remained virtually unchanged. With few skills, little training, and limited formal education, women on welfare realized they were moving farther away from the mainstream of American life. They watched other classes making progress. "In our isolation, we blamed ourselves and complained about welfare-related problems," said Ms. Delta, a welfare rights and community activist (personal interview, June 1982). Society as a whole remained disdainful of people on public assistance. Sympathizing with welfare recipients would have meant acknowledging that America's cultural and economic systems had serious flaws. Still, the election of John Lindsay as mayor in 1965 brought hope to the poor of the nation's largest city, since his campaign had addressed the concerns of low- and grant-income people.

PUBLIC ASSISTANCE IN NEW YORK CITY

In 1964 the categories for public assistance, all of which required a means test to establish eligibility and benefit level, were administered by the New York State Department of Public Welfare through thirty welfare centers across the city. By 1965 aid to dependent children, by then called Aid to Families with Dependent Children (AFDC), had become the largest of the public assistance programs. A New York State Department of Social Welfare booklet (1965) stated that public assistance would be granted to any needy children under the age of eighteen to enable them to remain with their families. If the children continued in high school or in other formal training programs, then welfare assistance was available to age twenty-one. Pregnant women were entitled to prenatal care and delivery and also to special dietary needs, foods, clothing, shelter, and other supplies they might require.

Ever since colonial times, the biggest expenditure of public relief funds has been for widows, orphans, and children born out of wedlock. In modern times, however, parents or other relatives have had to provide extensive information to welfare officials about all possible sources of funds in order to establish need and eligibility.

Since benefit levels were not set by the federal government, AFDC grants varied greatly from state to state. They were lowest in southern states, with Alabama's benefits set at $2,124 per year for a family of four in 1969 (*Bedford-Stuyvesant-New York Recorder*, January 3, 1969).[6] New York City was at the other end of the spectrum, with yearly payments for a family of four, including rent, totaling $3,408 (City of New York, Department of Welfare 1963–68). The U.S. Department of Labor noted that urban renters of that family size required $5,915 a year to live above the poverty line in 1967. Consequently, New York's welfare grants were 42 percent below the poverty line, while Alabama's were 64 percent below the line. Moreover, New York State law authorized additional funds for numerous special needs (e.g., furniture, clothing, washing machines, paint, camp, and air conditioners for asthmatics).

Few New York City clients knew of such provisions and rarely did they apply for or receive additional money for any reason. As we shall see, organizers of recipients would use these "special needs" regulations as a tool for recruiting purposes. Special grants would increase for families receiving AFDC between 1963 and 1968, the crucial years of organizing welfare recipients. This strongly suggests that expanded benefits for poor families were at least partially the result of the welfare rights activism to be described.

Whether in New York or in Alabama, having one's welfare application approved by administrators involved delay and aggravation. Applicants normally made several trips to the welfare center with birth or death certificates, utility bills, school and medical records. Acceptance onto the welfare rolls did not end a life of hardship. Welfare recipients paid a high psychological price because of the degrading and patronizing process at the welfare centers. Scenes in New York City offices varied little from those in other states before 1967, with rude behavior accepted as part of the price of public assistance.

Caseworkers' attitudes mirrored the nation's prejudices against individuals they believed did not have a fully developed work ethic. In seventeenth-century tradition, services were often provided in a manner geared toward making the client's life as uncomfortable as possible. This strategy of trying to force recipients to obtain employment might have been useful had clients had alternatives, but most of them were unemployable. They either lacked work experience or were responsible for the care of children or disabled adults. The small number of employable people on welfare were unskilled; few had high-school diplomas. For example, employable persons constituted only 3.8 percent of those on welfare in 1965; of that number, 14.9 percent had never worked (U.S. Department of Labor, Employment and Training Division, Regional Manpower Administration Notice #1-72).

Despite such statistics, welfare authorities were determined to keep public assistance rolls down. Thus in June, July, and August 1963, 45 percent of the applications were rejected. Five years later, analysis of the rates in the same months revealed a 21 percent decrease in the number rejected—and this despite a 55 percent increase in applications. Total grants rose almost 500 percent between 1963 and 1968 (City of New York, Department of Welfare, June, July, August 1963–68).

The denial of aid, even temporarily, posed hardships. Loans from friends and relatives on public assistance or working in low-paying jobs were the only recourse. These loans tended to be paid back as soon as grants were received, but generally utilities and other bills had to be left unpaid, creating deepening financial difficulties.

THEORY, REALITY, AND PRACTICE OF THE WELFARE SYSTEM

A 1964 report by the New York City Department of Welfare cited its official mandate as threefold: first, to meet the common human needs of those unable to help themselves; second, to return persons to gainful employment or assist them toward self-support and a maximum of self-care; and third, to prevent dependency.[7]

Women who had survived ten to fifteen years on welfare grants maintained, however, that the system did not adhere to its mandate. They agreed with Cloward and Piven's (1971) claim that relief policies are cyclical, liberal, or restrictive depending on the problems of regulation in the larger society with which government must contend; that America's response to people in financial crisis has been to create a system of constituent dependency; and that the unspoken mandate is to maintain social and political order and reinforce the work ethic.

Women on welfare decried forced and temporary low-wage employment that provided little opportunity for advancement and no job security. In contrast to the typical American reward system, welfare mothers could not increase their income by accepting work. Instead, welfare grants were taxed at a high rate and AFDC mothers' allotments reduced if they entered the labor market. The tax rate of 67 percent of earnings was a disincentive to seeking paid work. When a job ended, readjustments by the department were slow; often the recipients had to endure hardships until their money arrived. Further, a mother's employment decreased available parental supervision, creating additional problems.

Clients who were knowledgeable could seek redress through "fair hearings," but statements of lawyers, clergy, and social workers were required to support their claims of hardship. When budget complaints subsided temporarily, department policy required staff to assume that clients had obtained funds from other sources. This was a signal to begin new investigations for possible unreported income.

These problems were common knowledge among AFDC mothers, standing as a warning against volunteering for any work program recommended by the department. Ninety percent of the women interviewed confirmed the practice of not accepting employment unless certain of leaving the welfare rolls completely. Earning subsistence-level wages guaranteed the women a double life—half in the labor force mainstream and half on public assistance through supplementary grants. One still remained a welfare recipient—poor, stigmatized, and frequently a discriminated-against woman of color.

CATALYSTS FOR ORGANIZED CHANGE

Several women from Brooklyn attended the first NWRO conference in the District of Columbia in 1966 and returned home determined to establish local welfare rights organizations. Their efforts, supported by liberal Catholic clergy, bore fruit. Within one year, storefront welfare rights centers existed in almost every low-income Brooklyn community. Nuns and priests lent personal support as well as funds to enable clients to create and run their own organizations.[8]

A Survey of Community Needs

In the course of conducting a 1966 survey of community needs and problems, a group of Roman Catholic teaching nuns became friendly with women on welfare. Despite their usual suspicion of strangers, poor black women in Brooklyn welcomed these representatives of a powerful church. It was an eye-opening experience for the nuns when they heard the women describe the horrors of a welfare existence: stolen checks that were not replaced for weeks, delayed approvals for relocation that resulted in apartments being lost or tenants evicted, and routine refusals of special allowances for shoes or winter coats.[9]

The survey revealed that insufficient funds, inadequate housing, lack of child-care centers, recurrent fires, and inadequate sanitation and police services topped the list of problems.[10] Daily reports of their parochial school students supported these findings. The nuns had tried to help these children and their families on an individual basis but soon recognized this as a short-term solution. They concluded that people on welfare had to organize for collective action (Sister Tina, personal interview, May 1983).

Such thinking was radical even in the liberalized church environment at that time. The nuns were determined to develop the principles set forth by the Second Vatican Council. They were mindful of the council's mandate that church activism should focus on the needs of the poor, and were influenced by the humanistic social dynamics of the 1960s. They came to interpret welfare organizing as an empowerment effort, respecting the desire of poor people and people of color to help themselves.

The nuns first proceeded independently of the parish priest. However, aware of the pragmatic demands of convent life and of the limitations on women in the church hierarchy, they decided to enlist the participation of a priest. A new priest had arrived at Our Lady of Sorrows in Brooklyn's Bedford-Stuyvesant section a few weeks after the completion of the survey. Father Carl Stevens had acquired a reputation as a man of action, concerned about the plight of low-income people. Strongly distrustful of officials and politicians, Father Stevens joined Sisters Mary, Joan, and Ruth in organizing the people on welfare. They compiled information from neighboring parishes where priests had achieved some successes in assisting tenants. The nuns and the priest believed that similar tactics could be effective against the Department of Public Welfare.

The Catholic Church and Social Change

Many of Brooklyn's Catholic nuns and priests interpreted the pronouncements of Vatican II literally and liberally. They believed that service to low-income people included sharing their pain and helping them to meet their needs. And so the churchwomen enthusiastically spearheaded an organizing drive that was to have national impact.

Convincing Father Stevens to join their efforts had been easy, as he was a man looking for a cause. Two years later, with another priest (Father Robert Matthews), Father Stevens submitted a proposal to broaden parish work. In it, the priests expanded their concept of theological responsibilities to include confronting directly the political and economic issues faced by community people. They had faith in and respect for people's ability, regardless of class, race, or gender. Lacking formal organizing experience, they acted on their religious beliefs and faith in organizing for community empowerment. Only later, in 1968, did they receive training at Saul Alinsky's Chicago institute, the Industrial Areas Foundation, and develop their theory.

The late Saul Alinsky was a legendary community organizer and sociologist based mainly in Chicago. In the mid-1950s, he established a privately funded institute for community organizers. Its graduates operated throughout the country, supported mainly by churches.

The Alinsky model provided poor people with a way to increase their share in the distribution of wealth and to strengthen their voice in the political process. Alinsky believed the local self-reliant and community-based organization to be the only antidote against the dangerous trend of increasing political centralization, bureaucratization, corruption, and manipulation of information.[12] Whether the clergy were advocates of everything Alinsky espoused is unknown, but in the 1960s, in Brooklyn, they applied and tested most of his tenets.

CHALLENGING THE WELFARE BUREAUCRACY

In the first week of February 1966, the nuns moved into and refurbished a decrepit storefront. They had begun by surveying the neighborhood to determine the residents' needs. They encouraged women on welfare to attend a community meeting, offering child care as an inducement. A week later, with Father Stevens as chair, twenty women and their children attended the first of many meetings at the storefront. Initially skeptical about Father Stevens's knowledge of the welfare system, they came to appreciate his information about their lawful rights and the functioning of the system. Former AFDC mothers recall that their interest was sparked because they felt that they had found a group focused specifically on their concerns. They learned that the social services department was legally bound to provide for certain basic needs and that those found eligible had the *right* to special monetary grants.

This procedure was known as *being brought up to minimum standards.* Many recipients reported at the meetings that they never owned such basic things as measuring spoons, blankets, or adequate clothing. They learned from the priests the meaning of being considered the "undeserving poor," finding out that suburban women on welfare were treated with greater respect and dignity as the "deserving poor," often receiving larger grants to cover work- or school-related expenses. Group discussions raised the political consciousness of the city women and fueled their desire to confront the department. This was a big step for people who had never before considered standing up to welfare authorities.[13]

The enthusiasm of that first meeting extended to subsequent ones. Word about the need to organize welfare recipients spread throughout the community of priests. Father Robert Matthews joined with Father Stevens to organize welfare rights organizations (WROs) throughout Brooklyn. The public legitimation of their complaints by the Catholic church proved another vital mobilizing force, as welfare mothers were coming to realize the vulnerability of the welfare system.

As their first act of client administration, the WRO women agreed to manage the storefront office when the nuns were absent. This simple act of taking control of their own organization added new feelings of self-worth.

The women felt their time and skills were needed. The women volunteers' main responsibility in political organizing was to help others compile complete and accurate standard forms, to answer phones, and to recruit interested recipients.

The First Demonstration

Bolstered by the knowledge that the power of the Catholic church was behind them, the women prepared for action. At the first meeting, Father Stevens had fueled their resolve by distributing minimum standard forms. These forms listed every item a family had a right to own. By the time the meeting ended, one respondent observed, she had begun to believe that welfare was a right rather than a privilege, and that changes in Department of Public Welfare could be made (personal interview). This view, however, was in direct conflict with that of the majority of Americans, who did not regard welfare as a right.

A week after the first session, Father Stevens and twenty-five welfare mothers, armed with their forms, confronted officials at the Livingston welfare center in downtown Brooklyn and demanded that checks be ready the next day to purchase their "special needs." Contrary to usual practice, and much to the women's surprise, checks were ready when the protesters returned the following morning. Instead of the expected long, hard fight, each woman received about $100. They had acted collectively instead of individually and had won against the powerful welfare bureaucracy. The event proved to be a major organizing lesson, showing that early success could reinforce interest and spur the recruitment of others.

More welfare recipients, almost all black women, visited the storefront office as word of the victory spread. The nuns began to transfer responsibility for daily operations to the welfare rights women. By the end of three months, the welfare mothers not only were in charge of the storefront but had become experts in helping others to complete forms, accompanying them to the welfare centers, and even making referrals to other service programs. The nuns had reached across religious, class, and racial lines and succeeded in helping a number of poor women to organize for a better life.

Two years later, the three nuns left their order and moved to another city to teach and organize. But first they witnessed an important political outcome of their efforts. In May 1966, recipients voted to establish a formal welfare rights group, naming it the Neighborhood Action Center (NAC). It was the forerunner of forty-eight centers organized under the auspices of Fathers Stevens and Matthews. NAC elected officers, including a woman president who would later become the first chair of the boroughwide welfare rights union, B-WAC.

THE EARLY DAYS OF B-WAC

The proliferation of storefront centers, expansion of membership, and increased demonstrations highlighted the need for a unifying and coordinating body—a boroughwide council or executive committee. Forty-eight storefront centers, representing almost every Brooklyn neighborhood, had been established. After a series of meetings, the women and their church supporters decided to create such a coordinating council in 1967. All welfare rights groups in Brooklyn were informed about the organization and urged to contribute their views to an ad hoc planning committee. This was the birth of B-WAC. It was funded by Catholic Charities of Brooklyn with an initial budget of $5,000 plus an additional staff salary of $5,000. By 1971, the budget had increased to $12,000.[14] Total grants disbursed by Catholic Charities for all the WROs during four years was approximately $500,000. Some federally funded community action programs joined the council, but the centers organized by Fathers Matthews and Stevens remained the strongest force.

As the movement expanded, internal problems began to surface. Some local WRO groups feared loss of autonomy and opposed the federation. Others worried about creating a bureaucracy that mirrored the institutions they were pledged to change. The Citywide Coordinating Council, headquartered in Manhattan, and B-WAC's parent group, NWRO, located in Washington, expressed qualms about the growing power of the Brooklyn group. These concerns were not grounded in reality, because B-WAC's president had strong loyalties to Manhattan's Citywide and to NWRO. While it cooperated on most issues, B-WAC did occasionally refuse to support certain actions or decisions of the larger movement, sometimes by withholding membership dues from NWRO.

The priests' role was again vital in B-WAC's formation and development. The responsibilities of Fathers Matthews and Stevens included lobbying, fund raising, and scheduling speaking engagements for the welfare rights women, with their honoraria going to the council. Arranging a meeting with the bishop was another step in gaining recognition for the recipients. The women's self-confidence and self-respect increased and, in turn, the public image of the welfare rights coalition was strengthened. The clergy negotiated across the class, race, and gender barriers that would have been insurmountable in a society that devalued women's—especially poor women's— political activism, views, and demands. Once gaining access to powerholders, the women were eloquent in presenting their own case.

Brooklyn differed from other areas where white male organizers dominated decision making and leadership, for the priests were dedicated to recipient empowerment. B-WAC members were well informed because members discussed, voted on, planned, and organized all activities. If they decided against an action, then it was abandoned, regardless of the priests' position on the issue (personal interview with Hulbert James 1982; see also Bailis 1974; West 1981). Demonstrations not approved by B-WAC received almost no support in the borough. Hundreds of loyal and disciplined members proved to be the organization's primary strength. Leadership training for and by people receiving public assistance was another important factor in its success.

A Constitution and New Headquarters

B-WAC was initially housed in the downtown Brooklyn offices of Catholic Charities' social action department. It soon moved to a large rent-free, three-story Victorian house obtained by Father Matthews in a more centrally located area. In November 1967, a constitution was drafted and approved by the membership that became a model for all Brooklyn groups.[15] The former president of NAC was elected B-WAC's first president. With Catholic Charities funding, the organization hired two staff members, a young black woman and a Jewish male VISTA worker, as coordinator and office manager, respectively. It then increased its demonstrations and confrontations with the welfare departments.

Major Demonstrations

The first action to obtain minimum standard grants, described above, was designed not only to reward those who participated, but also to enhance group solidarity.[16] In this confrontation, B-WAC members had learned the importance of unity. None had left until all had received their checks. This success attracted new members and volunteers to the movement. Minimum standard drives became routine, institutionalized organizing lessons for new members and training for client representatives. Mothers who had once feared the welfare department's response to their demands often found themselves, a few days later, representing others with similar problems. As advocates and protestors they challenged officials and demanded to be treated fairly and courteously. Their self-confidence increased as they became astute political activists. One respondent described the situation, "We were used to begging; we never demanded anything—welfare rights enabled us to walk into a welfare center unafraid, dignified, and secure in the knowledge that our needs would be met" (personal interview with Maggie Halstrum).

THE STATE'S RESPONSE TO SPECIAL NEEDS DEMONSTRATIONS

Having participated in minimum standards demonstrations, the group found other protest actions less difficult. The Brooklyn women campaigned for and obtained funds for various needs: costs of laundry; graduation; layettes; confirmation, camp, gym, and spring clothes; and washing machines. Former recipients recalled their frustrations and their children's suffering before, when they had lacked money for simple but essential items. Now their children could participate in gym classes, attend camp with the required clothing, be confirmed, and take part in graduation ceremonies.

The very success of the special needs demonstrations, however, created other problems. Awareness of the special allocations drew hundreds of members and nonmembers to the welfare centers. In an unsigned article, a caseworker depicted the rising confusion at one welfare center in April 1968, starting with the 6:00 A.M. arrival of the welfare mothers and their children. Hundreds of these recipients endured long hours of waiting for service, as they tried to take care of their crying babies (*The Tablet,* July 16, 1968).

This scene was, of course, partly the result of welfare rights organizing. Hundreds of nonmembers who heard about clothing grants went to the department independently to request them. Others continued arriving with multiple problems, such as evictions, fires, or burglaries. While WRO members' collective demands were being addressed by caseworkers and supervisors, other individuals with emergencies were forced to wait. Although WROs' disruptive strategies against the bureaucracy succeeded, the price for other clients and staff was sometimes psychologically high; resentment from nonmembers was substantial.

The state legislature eventually came to the Welfare Department's rescue by eliminating the movement's major organizing tool—the special needs grant. New York State enacted the first flat grant in 1969. Under the new law, the basic needs of recipients were now covered by only one grant, with the exception of shelter, fuel, utilities, and a few other items. This dealt a serious blow to the mobilization of welfare mothers.

As legislators attempted to change the system, criticism of welfare mounted. Two years earlier, Nicholas Kisburg of the International Brotherhood of Teamsters had begun to voice concern with the existing system. Although the welfare allowances were acknowledged as being abysmally low, the welfare family of four still had a larger take-home income than the same family whose head earned $1.50 an hour. The solution to this crisis, in Kisburg's view, was to federalize the welfare system. Many others, from liberals to conservatives, proposed welfare reform and called for a guaranteed annual income. Although Congress debated President Nixon's Family Assistance Plan (FAP) and several other national welfare reform proposals in the late 1960s and early 1970s, none became law. In the meantime, B-WAC expanded its protests into the private as well as the public sector.

THE CREDIT CAMPAIGN STRATEGY

The only financial credit generally available to those on welfare came from loan sharks or small neighborhood businesses that charged usurious interest rates. In response, and facing the loss of special needs as an organizing lever, B-WAC initiated a campaign for the extension of department store credit to people on public assistance or having fixed incomes. The B-WAC membership voted to challenge general credit policies and specifically targeted those of Korvettes, a department store that many frequented.

According to plan, B-WAC officers first attempted to negotiate for the extension of credit—and were ignored by Korvette officials. On November 21, 1968, protests began. Demonstrations were staged inside and outside Korvettes in Brooklyn's major shopping area. The outcome of this collective action was that each woman obtained between $25 and $100 of personal credit. In the aftermath of the Korvette demonstrations, a higher-priced department store, Abraham and Strauss, voluntarily opened credit negotiations with B-WAC. By December, both stores had developed and instituted procedures to review credit applications submitted by people on welfare. Shortly after that, all grant income recipients (those on pensions, Social Security, and disability) were encouraged to apply for credit.

B-WAC's victory had involved the use of diverse, unique, and theatrical strategies. For instance, the owners of Korvettes were contacted by middle-class supporters—members of Friends of Welfare Rights Organization (FWRO)—on the golf course, at their private clubs, and at their places of worship, and asked for support.[17] FWRO members also agreed to raise the credit issue at stockholders' meetings. In addition, B-WAC members received special training in sessions that were dress rehearsals for protest action. Members were assigned special roles and responsibilities: outside the store, some were picketers, others messengers, marshals, leafleteers, and spokes-persons. Inside the store, welfare rights mothers acted as "customers," some-times as "angry customers"; at other times they role-played expressing or giving sympathy to those annoyed by the disruption. Some were asked to be "real" customers or to fill in as part of crowds, as a backdrop to the militants and moderates.

Members impersonating customers selected hundreds of dollars' worth of goods and took them to cashiers, who tallied the items on the register. When requests for payment were made, the "customer" produced her welfare ID card and said, "Charge it to the Welfare Department." The cashier was impelled to call for assistance in order to clear the register of the mock charge. Such actions resulted in long lines at the cash registers throughout the store. "Irate customers" standing in line with numerous expensive items voiced their displeasure about the delay. Other "customers in the crowds" grumbled loudly about the store's incompetence to unsuspecting legitimate customers.

All this commotion at rush hour proved too much for Korvettes person-nel. The store manager, later joined by the company's regional representative, invited B-WAC's leaders to meet and negotiate. At the same time, they called in the police. The women left to avoid arrest, as previously planned. When the police arrived, everything had returned to normal except for the piles of unbought clothing surrounding most cash registers. B-WAC "customers" still browsed unnoticed alongside actual purchasers, waiting for the police to leave and the signal to begin the demonstration anew. Then the whole process recommenced. When negotiations began in earnest, "moderates" agreed to discontinue the inside demonstrations. Late in the evening, welfare members left Korvettes but vowed to return the next day if their demands were not met. These actions continued for five days.

Demonstrators met to evaluate the results of their actions following each action, discussing strengths and weaknesses late into the night. Besides devel-oping a political analysis of the process of creating change, the sessions also helped demonstrators and staff prepare for questioning by members, for ac-cording to B-WAC rules, members had to be informed promptly of the results of any major action. B-WAC members debated and voted on every decision and demonstration. The give-and-take of their often heated and acrimonious debates had some very positive effects. Members became well informed and knowledgeable about issues. In fact, Brooklyn welfare rights participants were sometimes viewed as independent, arrogant, and opinionated. This resulted from the serious consideration of each person's comments and re-marks at B-WAC meetings, a process that led to empowerment for women who had been perjoratively labeled "lumpen proletariat" by intellectuals and "brood mares" by a U.S. senator.

Regardless of the intensity of their internal conflicts, the Brooklyn women remained publicly united, acting as one on nearly every issue. Those deviating from an agreed-upon strategy had to justify their behavior at B-WAC's next meeting, a formidable and usually no-win task. B-WAC's women inspired admiration, awe, and envy within the national movement. They were "out there," somewhat "crazy," and "really together." A humorous episode that occurred during a 1968 NWRO conference will illustrate. When B-WAC's president left the conference hall, word spread among Brooklynites that B-WAC had been insulted by someone. As a result, every B-WAC member got up and left the hall, following the president. The session was halted while NWRO officials tried to determine the cause of the walkout. Meanwhile, B-WAC members discovered that their president had simply gone to the women's room. When she looked around, the room was filled with B-WACers and eventually with conference officials wanting to know why Brooklyn had "walked out."

Brooklyn's credit demonstration, watched closely by welfare clients everywhere, precipitated other protests across the nation. Actions against Sears, Roebuck and three of New York's major department stores resulted in extensions of credit to welfare recipients and national publicity. Success, however, brought forth other reactions.

GOVERNMENT REACTION TO WELFARE PROTESTS

Organizers, members, and theorists had underestimated the government bureaucracy's strength and resiliency and were surprised by its reaction to regain control. Welfare rights organizations had succeeded in transferring millions of dollars from welfare agencies to low-income people. Now an increasingly conservative government attempted to eliminate loopholes that had been used by the movement. As pointed out earlier, replacing minimum standards with one-time grants ("flat grants") removed a major organizing tool and effectively halted further mobilization. This caught advocates unprepared and without a contingency plan. They realized too late that this backlash forecast the turning of the political tide and the ultimate demise of their movement.

B-WAC was doubly devastated. Its president and staff had been invited to move to Washington to work in NWRO's national office, leaving a leadership vacuum that was hard to fill. Even had the leaders remained, it is very doubtful whether the earlier momentum could have been maintained in the absence of a supportive political climate. The environment was rapidly becoming more hostile to the demands of the poor and especially of poor women. B-WAC's resources and support rapidly shrunk, hastening its demise. In this, it followed the path of most organizations of poor people: a volatile, short-term structure organized around a single issue and dependent on outside support for funds.

THE DEBATE OVER STRATEGIES

A number of intellectuals who had been involved in the national welfare rights movement as supporters or theorists entered the debate about what "went wrong" in organizational strategies. Richard Cloward, for example, acknowledged that the organizing skills and street protests of the Brooklyn group had substantially expanded the benefits of its members. He maintained, however, that too much energy had been put into building a membership organization and institutionalizing the group. According to him, continued street demonstrations would have been more effective (personal interview, fall 1983). In retrospect, this scholar felt that the movement should have been an organization of the *poor*, a coalition of various types of groups, rather than being limited to welfare clients.

Although Cloward's evaluation of street protests has some merit, he did not consider the risk of "burnout" when people are continually in the front lines. Nor did he suggest how interest and high energy levels could be maintained over prolonged confrontation periods. Another flaw in the arguments of those who call for continued protest with minimum organization is the question of whether protesters could continue to be mobilized over extended periods of time. Finally, relying on small and vulnerable protesting cadres may invite violence by the police.

Cloward argues that large numbers of politicians elected by low-income people would provide the demonstrators protection against harm by the establishment. He opposes institutionalizing a movement yet advocates the use of traditional institutions, specifically the electoral system, to secure power and protection. Had welfare rights groups become institutionalized in the 1970s, perhaps they could have played a key role in the voter education and registration drive among the poor in the 1980s. Several participants in this debate, however, contend that relying on leaders in the establishment, elected or not, simply maintains the dependent role that protestors sought to destroy.

CONCLUSION

In the mid-1960s, women receiving public assistance from the state challenged traditional views of poverty and demanded structural changes in the provision of social welfare. During a four year period (1966–70), they mobilized thousands of recipients in the struggle. Collectively, thousands of women dependent on the state created and ran B-WAC, a unique social movement organization, bringing social change into the lives of individuals and the welfare system. It was unusual because it was managed by women on welfare and because of its large size. B-WAC's members in the early years made up almost one-third of the NWRO membership.

Brooklyn's welfare rights movement followed the pattern of most lower-economic-class protests. It lasted just a few years during a time when the political climate remained relatively tolerant of protest. The momentum was impossible to maintain, as the state reacted and clamped down. The elimination of special grants reduced the incentives for protest and organizational commitment. Membership dropped dramatically.

The reasons for the decline of this local grass-roots movement are numerous and complex. First, there was disillusionment regarding the ability to attain the long-range legislative goal of a guaranteed annual income. Second, the political tides had rapidly shifted from liberal to more conservative solutions to the problems of poverty and welfare. Third, public opinion had also become less accepting of political protest and unconventional movement organizations. Finally, the deep-rooted stigma attached to welfare recipients, especially mothers, remained entrenched, limiting support for the movement. Most of the client leaders interviewed agreed that welfare rights members were left with difficult and limited options. They could continue the demonstrations and mobilization and invite arrests; they could reconsider and change their initial objectives; or they could cease operating. Although there were varying views, there was general agreement that disruptive tactics had to be abandoned and attempts made to build an institution.

Frances Fox Piven, one of the movement's theorists, agreed that interminable mobilization was unrealistic. Yet she cautioned that imitating middle-class associations would operate against poor people's interests, for grass-roots institutions require flexibility and innovation. She believed that the infusion of new ideas and recruits often ceases when long-time members consolidate their own power. An excessive amount of organizational energy tends to be used in lobbying for support. Piven continued to have faith in the power of street demonstrations (personal interview, fall 1983).

Gains and Losses by the Movement

The Catholic church played a major role in shaping the direction of the Brooklyn welfare rights movement and its members' political views. Politically and religiously progressive, the church men and women had, nonetheless, facilitated a traditional atmosphere. They helped many people to enhance the quality of their lives within the confines of the system. Their doctrine had been one of helping others to help themselves. Nonetheless, when the political tides shifted and the movement began to decline, the Catholic diocese took over full administrative responsibilities for the centers. They became neighborhood service centers staffed by professionals. The church thus reflected the government's reversal of its original but short-lived policy of encouraging maximum feasible participation by indigenous people.

On the whole, the clergy concentrated on guiding recipients into the cultural and economic mainstream and teaching them how to negotiate rather than to change the system. The priests' idealistic but pragmatic tactics for ending poverty altered and enhanced the lives of individuals and families, while theorists such as Piven and Cloward concentrated on raising the political consciousness of clients and others regarding the inequities of the welfare system.

According to welfare rights leaders, their fundamental concern was to provide new opportunities for their children, since many believed it was too late for themselves. However, a subsequent result of their protest efforts is that most of seventeen former leaders interviewed left the welfare system. Fifteen moved off the welfare roles and no longer receive public assistance. All returned to and completed high school; four accumulated several college credits, and two received master's degrees. None of the leaders' sons and daughters, and only one grandchild, were on welfare. Their children were high-school graduates and most were in college.

Today, despite the movement's demise, many of its leaders and members remain politically active in diverse ways. Ideologically, they are still committed to confronting issues that impact negatively on poor people's lives. They have continued to be involved in various community causes, including block associations, school and planning boards, welfare recipient councils, and political clubs. All interviewed believed that B-WAC had inspired and changed many individuals. The more immediate economic results for poor people are clear. During a three-month period in 1968, New York City grant income recipients received approximately $42 million in additional payments, compared with $1.3 million in 1963. Public assistance applications were accepted 81 percent of the time in 1968, but only 65 percent in 1963 (City of New York, Department of Welfare, *Monthly Statistical Reports*). In sum, protest actions brought expanded benefits to the poor in the state.

In addition, institutional changes in the welfare system resulted in some important and enduring gains. Among them were the establishment of state procedures for fair hearings, the elimination of residency requirements, and the elimination of most home visits. Other gains were a move toward granting credit for people on fixed incomes, the seeds of a national voter education drive, and the development of community paraprofessionals. On the other hand, it seems clear that the one-dimensional nature of welfare rights impeded advances beyond these issues. The movement focused mainly on the economics of poverty and specifically on welfare reform, to the exclusion of such other factors as racism and sexism. That is, poverty was not attacked in a holistic manner.[18] To address the fundamental causes of poverty would have required far more resources than those available to B-WAC and the national welfare rights movement.

B-WAC's small core of active members joined the mainstream while the majority of recipients experienced only limited personal advancement. But despite scorn from many groups, the women activists achieved a measure of self-respect and confidence. They were minorities in the truest sense: five times, if one considers they were women, black and Hispanic, middle-aged, many fat, and economically disadvantaged recipients of public aid. Despite these obstacles of gender, class, race and age, collectively they were able to overcome their isolation and stigma and to act aggressively and politically to better their lives.

They proved that fundamental freedoms in a democratic society must not be limited to people with access to powerholders. The meaning and political impact of B-WAC was summarized succinctly and dramatically by one of its members:

I learned I am somebody. Welfare Rights meant a right to life—it freed me from emotional slavery. I am a person you can't push aside, I have the right to be. Welfare Rights showed me that my counterparts are all around; knowing this, I no longer felt alone. Welfare Rights lives, I and other people are still active, struggling for a better life. PTAs, school boards, even political clubs have former welfare rights members and we continue pushing the welfare rights agenda. B-WAC lives in the minds of everyone remotely associated with it. An organization for and by poor people, a women's movement that addressed real survival issues. Its concepts and promises live in us and our children (personal interview with Ms. Wise, summer 1983).

NOTES

1. This study is based on forty-seven in-depth interviews held from 1980 to 1984 with movement activists, mostly women who had been AFDC mothers in Brooklyn during the 1960s.

2. Lawson and Barton (1980) argue that more often than not, male leaders are elected for paid social movement positions.

3. See also the discussion of the role of the white Protestant churches in the National Welfare Rights Movement in West (1981); also the analysis of the role of "outsiders" in Marx and Useem (1971).

4. Much of the material in this section is based on Trattner (1974).

5. All identities of interviewees have been disguised to protect them.

6. In Alabama, a family of four on Aid to Families with Dependent Children received a $177 monthly check for food, shelter, and clothing. Although federal funds accounted for 83 percent of the grant, Alabama refused to contribute matching funds, forfeiting $11.6 million in federal moneys in 1967 alone.

7. The present title for the public assistance office is the Human Resources Administration, Department of Social Services.

8. The nuns were from the Sisters of St. Joseph order, which numbered 2,000 nuns nationally. Seventeen of them taught at Our Lady of Victory School in Brooklyn's Bedford-Stuyvesant neighborhood. The students at their school were primarily African-American and Caribbean.

9. Mailboxes were regularly burglarized and checks stolen in low-income neighborhoods. At times, people lost all benefits for failing to respond to a Welfare Department letter or notice that had never been received.

10. The survey conducted by the nuns was referred to in interviews but was not made public, nor is it presently available.

11. Vatican II was a council of the Catholic church's highest officials convened in Rome from 1962 to 1965 by the pope to reestablish and modernize religious guidelines for its clergy and lay people.

12. See Castells (1983) for an excellent discussion of community-based organizations.

13. See also discussion of this process of individuals and groups learning about their rights prior to moving into direct confrontation with welfare authorities in Piven and Cloward (1977), Hertz (1981), Bailis (1974), and West (1981).

14. B-WAC's expenditures increased sixfold when the organization was conducting leadership training classes, peaking at $33,000 in 1969.

15. Only welfare recipients were eligible to hold offices in the council, according to its constitution.

16. Many social movement theorists place much significance on self-serving behavior as a motivation for activism. Yet the women in the welfare rights groups quickly subordinated self-interest to the larger community's cause, a phenomenon said to be common among female activists regardless of class. Hirsch (n.d.:19) supports this observation: "Self-sacrifice in pursuit of . . . emergent group interests seems to be relatively common. . . . Self-sacrifice—to which they [female activists] are socialized— begins almost with the decision to join a group."

17. Friends of Welfare Rights Organization (FWRO) members were professional, mainly white middle-class or wealthy individuals sympathetic to the plight and goals of clients. They contributed time and money to the organization and made contacts and speeches for the organization. In almost every welfare rights group—local, state, and national—except B-WAC, FWRO members were permitted to hold office or vote.

18. For a discussion of an implied holistic approach to poverty and social planning, see Gans (1968).

CHAPTER 4

Gender Contested: Women's Participation in the Brookside Coal Strike

SALLY WARD MAGGARD

On July 28, 1973, 180 coal miners went on strike at a Harlan County coal mine at Brookside, Kentucky. For the next thirteen months they stayed off the job, holding out against officials of Duke Power Company, which owned the mine, and against managers of Eastover Mining Company, the Duke subsidiary that operated the mine. Eventually, the miners won the right to work under a United Mine Workers of American (UMWA) contract.

A multi-faceted community support base that developed around the strike was headed by a group of militant women. The miners and these supporters were backed by newly elected UMWA leaders committed to cleaning up corruption in the miners' union and to "organizing the unorganized." In the end, an unusual coalition of striking miners, reform-minded union leaders, community supporters, and women managed to bring the sixth largest utility company in the United States to its knees.

Women were at the forefront of the miners' strike at Brookside. They peopled picket lines, planned strike-support strategy, argued with union officials, devised behind-the-scenes tactics, ignored public and family criticism of their participation, dealt with the press, personally faced their opposition, got arrested, testified in court, and went to jail.

What led these women to step away from the routine of their lives and become "disorderly" public figures? What mobilized them to go up against coal company officials, union leaders, police, and even family members? What did involvement in these events mean for these women?

In the following pages I address these questions by considering the importance of gender relations to working-class women's participation in political action. First, I examine ways that gender shapes women's economic vulnerability and status within households in Harlan County, thereby structuring women's interest in political activity. Second, I consider ways that gender relations and gender ideology help to determine the form, content, and outcome of political action, as well as responses to women's participation. Finally, I look at the emergence of gender itself as contested terrain during the coal strike—that is, how gender relations were renegotiated and reshaped through women's involvement in this strike.[1]

BACKGROUND OF THE RESEARCH

This research can be situated within the context of two aspects of contemporary feminist scholarship. First, it is part of the effort to develop a full historical account of women's political action that incorporates the varied experiences of women of different racial, ethnic, and class heritages (Blee 1987; Bookman and Morgen 1988; Hall 1986; G. Jones 1985; Milkman 1985; Lebsock 1984). Second, it is part of an increasingly sophisticated attempt to identify the ways that gender and social class interact to determine women's political experience, action, and consciousness (Bookman and Morgen 1988; Benenson 1980; Crompton and Mann 1986; Hareven 1982; Kessler-Harris 1982; Petchesky 1983; Turbin 1984).

While there is general agreement now about the centrality of gender relations, as well as class relations, in any social system, the precise mechanics of their interaction remain problematic. This research suggests that gender conditions the structure of economic opportunities and household operation. In addition, it suggests that ideological dimensions of gender are felt at personal, family, and community levels. Together, these structural and ideological components of gender help to determine the onset, form, content, duration, and consequences of women's participation in working-class protest activities.

Further, this research suggests that social protest itself may significantly alter gender relations. Participation in class action in Harlan County had a dramatic impact on gender relations as they had been constituted before the mine strike. Gender relations were forced out into the open, demystified, and identified as social relations that are not immutable. Gender became the subject of conflict, debate, and change.

THE STUDY

This chapter is based on a larger comparative study of women's involvement in two union-organizing drives in eastern Kentucky in the early 1970s (Maggard 1988). Both were efforts to win union representation, and both resulted in strikes: one at the Brookside mine in Harlan County and the other at a hospital in Pike County.

The principal data for this research on the Brookside strike are drawn from twenty structured interviews with women active in the union drive. Auxiliary interviews were conducted with striking miners, relatives of the female participants, participants opposed to the union effort, and persons knowledge about the strike and eastern Kentucky. The interviews were conducted in late 1986 during five months of field research in Harlan County.

A second major and unusual source of data on the coal strike was important in the research. The Academy Award–winning documentary *Harlan County, U.S.A.* was filmed in part during the Brookside strike. Outtakes of this film housed at the University of Kentucky include footage of meetings of the women, incidents on the picket lines, meetings of the local union, informal gatherings, rallies and demonstrations, and conversations between union, company, and government officials. This archive provided a rare opportunity to compare data collected thirteen years after events occurred with actual documentation of what people said and did at the time of the strike. I analyzed the outtakes in preparing for fieldwork, for event reconstruction, and for validity checking of interview data.[2]

Women agreed to be part of my research project for a variety of reasons. Above all, they knew they had been involved in historic events in the early 1970s. Part of the story of the Brookside strike is recorded in *Harlan County, U.S.A.* Now their individual stories would be recorded as well. Repeatedly, the women described their participation in the research by saying, "We're making history."

The women trusted that I could and would accurately describe their political activities. During the early 1970s, I was employed by a coalition of grass-roots organizations and political activists whose approach to social and economic problems in Appalachia included support for union organizing. I provided direct strike support and news coverage of the Brookside strike. I was on picket lines, attended meetings, marched in demonstrations, traveled to strike-related events, worked with union organizers, wrote news stores, and spent a lot of time in people's homes. My work meant that many doors were open to me during the strike.

When I returned to Harlan County thirteen years later as a researcher from the university, I found those doors still open. I believe that the people I interviewed would not have cooperated with someone they did not know and trust. My research experience grows out of my role as a former activist and supports the position that involvement in the events and processes that one studies is an asset that sharpens rather than taints scholarship (Hess and Ferree 1987; Oakley 1981; Stacey and Thorne 1985; Thorne 1983). Far from compromising my research, familiarity with eastern Kentucky and with the people involved in the strike was essential to my ability to successfully carry it out.

THE SETTING

In the early 1970s, when miners began to organize a UMWA local at Brookside, Harlan County was a very poor county in a very poor region. There were limited opportunities for paid, full-time, stable employment. The work force was underskilled and educationally disadvantaged (Maggard 1988:48–52). For the majority of residents, making a good, honest living in Harlan County was and continues to be a tough proposition.

Harlan County is typical of counties located in Central Appalachia.[3] Its economy is dominated by one industry: coal mining. Its political structure is tightly controlled by corporate interests closely linked with coal. Although great fortunes have been made in the industry, residents of Harlan County and the coalfields suffer deep and persistent poverty.

Behind this social and economic situation, there is a long history of uneven economic development. Concentration of ownership and control of land and resources (Appalachian Land Ownership Task Force 1983; Banks 1980; Eller 1982), an uneven distribution of income, jobs, and resources (Tickamyer and Tickamyer 1987; Tickamyer and Duncan 1984; Walls 1978), sharp class distinctions (Banks 1983–84; Seltzer 1985), and antagonistic class relations (Clark 1981; Corbin 1981; Dreiser 1932; Gaventa 1980; Hevener 1978) have accompanied the exploration and development of the coalfields. Endemic poverty, restricted economic opportunity, and polarized class relations have gone hand in hand with the development and growth of the Appalachian coal economy.

These conditions set the broad terms of the class conflict that developed in Harlan County as miners tried to organize UMWA representation at the Brookside mine. But to understand women's relationship to this strike, it is necessary to look more closely at the political economy of the region and its particular consequences for women.

LABOR MARKET AND HOUSEHOLD STATUS: WOMEN'S ECONOMIC VULNERABILITY

Attention to the situational and historical contexts of events has been a methodological standard in social and labor history for several decades (Foster 1974; Thompson 1966), but attention to how different groups within a population experience this context is fairly new. Feminist scholarship has demonstrated, first, the necessity of differentiating women's experiences, activities, and interests from men's and, second, the importance of considering other axes, such as age, race, class, and ethnicity, that structure differences among women themselves (Bookman and Morgen 1988; Milkman 1985).

Applying this to women involved in the Brookside strike, it is essential to examine the differential impact of the political economy for working-class women and men in Central Appalachia. More specifically, we need to explore the different ways in which uneven economic development affects women and men and how these differences are translated into differing modes of participation in political action and class conflict.

Gender and class interact in this region to form a doubly restricted opportunity structure and create unique economic vulnerabilities for women. First, women's options for paid labor are limited to sex-segregated and low-paid sectors of an undiversified local economy dominated by an extractive industry.

In 1970 in Harlan County, the largest proportion of the working population was employed in mining, in jobs restricted to men.[4] Most employed women were working in low-paid personal service jobs, health services, or retail sales.[5] This gender-based occupational segregation was reflected in income figures for employed men and women. In 1970, median earnings in

Harlan County were $5,682 for men, but dropped sharply to $2,611 for women.[6]

Second, not only were options for economic independence very limited, but women were also in a vulnerable position as dependent members of working-class households. While mining has occasionally paid higher wages than the secondary occupations that employ women, it is a highly volatile industry subject to great swings in the demand for coal. Women in households dependent on mining wages have long been vulnerable to sudden loss of income and the recurrent unemployment of male household members.

This situation is exacerbated by the high injury and death rates in mining. Women never know whether the coal miners supporting their families are going to be disabled on the job or, for that matter, return from work at all. In 1970, 16.4 percent of the women over age fourteen in Harlan County were widows, compared with 13.1 percent in Kentucky as a whole. Widowhood figures in the large number of female-headed families in 1970 in the county: 15.2 percent, compared with 10.7 percent for the state as a whole.

Given their special position in the local labor market and the vulnerability of their households, women in Harlan County in the early 1970s faced a dismal and precarious economic situation. Their dependence and extremely low status in the labor market were key among the factors that raised their political consciousness and thrust them into collective protest at Brookside.

THE STRIKE

The coal strike at Brookside broke out soon after a new leadership had taken over the UMWA. The Miners for Democracy (MFD) candidates had won control of the union in late 1972 with a platform that included promises to rid the union of a history of corruption and to "organize the unorganized." New union leaders proclaimed the Brookside strike the "cornerstone" of a commitment to organize all of eastern Kentucky.

For the new UMWA leaders, the strike became a major test of strength. A victory at Brookside was particularly important because the UMWA was preparing to negotiate its first national wage agreement since the MFD candidates had taken office. The nation was watching the UMWA, and the Brookside strike became the new union's "flagship strike."

The opponent in the strike was Duke Power Company, an electric utility company servicing the Carolinas and a new actor on the corporate scene in the coal industry. Early in 1970, Duke Power had decided to get into the coal business and establish what is known as a captive market, mining its own coal to supply its coal-fired steam plants.

Duke set up the Eastover Mining Company to manage its coal interests. It bought the Brookside Mine in 1970 from a Harlan County family that had owned it for many years and had once broken a UMWA presence at the mine (Hevener 1978). Soon other coal properties were added. At the time of the strike, Duke was one of the largest consumers of coal in the nation.

As soon as Eastover took over, the miners were told they were working under a contract with the Southern Labor Union (SLU). Miners refer to the SLU as a "company union," signifying its lack of militancy in representing miners.

The Brookside mine was dangerous, plagued by "bad top," water accumulations, and other problems. In addition, miners believed that management was lax in its attention to safety. When the contract they had inherited with SLU was about to expire, the miners began to sign UMWA cards. They won a National Labor Relations Board–ordered election, but the company refused to sign a UMWA contract. The miners were on strike.

Household Status as a Route to Class Action

Most of the women who got involved in the Brookside strike saw themselves as housewives at the time the strike began, and they expected to continue to be housewives. They were living in a local economy where there were few other options for women, particularly with their education and skill levels. This status and expectation were major influences in their decisions to participate in the strike.

None of the Harlan County women I interviewed were working outside their homes in paid employment at the time of the strike. The few who had held paying jobs had worked in domestic or low-skilled positions—babysitting, house cleaning, washing and ironing—or in light manufacturing when they had moved out of the coalfields during coal recessions. Despite having done hard work since childhood, they had few job skills.

All but one of the women were living in traditionally structured households with their husbands and children.[7] Most had married young after completing some junior high school and had started having children at a young age. Most of their husbands had gone from grade school directly into the coal mines.

These women were keenly aware of their economic vulnerability and the need to keep mining wages coming into their households. If the strike were lost, the miners were likely to be fired at Brookside and blacklisted from other mining jobs in the county. One twenty-five-year-old mother of three said:

> The longer it [strikebreaking] went on, the less chance we had of getting a contract. They would be without a job. There were rumors that they couldn't get a job anywhere in the country. With no other type of life, or type of job that they knew, it was like we didn't have a choice in the matter. We had to make a stand.[8]

Another mother who was pregnant with her second child during the strike said:

> You knew if it went down the drain, along with it went your husband's job, your future. That's why you were there. You felt like *it was as much you as it was them*. (emphasis added)

At first glance, women's involvement in the Brookside strike might be explained as a straightforward example of gender-based collective protest: women managers of male-earned wages mobilized to protect resources essential for family survival. But women's participation was never simply a situation of participation "as wives" of striking miners. It also reflected their class interests as these interacted with their gender interests.

Women's class position in Harlan County, like men's, is determined in part by the political economy of the region. There are few opportunities for secure and well-paid employment for anyone in this single-industry, politically controlled economy. But a gendered restriction of "female" work to certain sex-segregated and poorly paid economic sectors creates a double indemnity for women. This "gender effect" overlies their working-class status and in effect sentences them to a dependent household (gender) status. In short, gendered status and interests are in fact also class status and interests for the women at Brookside.

Multilayered Political Consciousness

To further complicate matters, additional factors informed women's mobilization in collective protest at Brookside. Affective ties to a spouse on strike, links to families with UMWA histories, a shared community history, personal experiences, and a belief in the UMWA as a progressive force for Harlan County all contributed to women's involvement in the strike. These reflect a web of family, community, and economic experiences and networks that have political consequences, again suggesting that women's activism is not simply a matter of roles in the private or domestic realm.

Some women were involved in Brookside to "stand by their men" in the traditional sense of that expression:

> All I knowed, I loved [him] and I wanted to support him in what he had to do. Stick by him. That was my main goal.

Another woman said:

> I guess I done it just because I loved him so much. He was trying to do what he thought was right. I just made my mind up that they needed support. He put his life in the mines for me and my kids. If it took me to stand up to fight for the contract for the men, for my husband, I would.

Other family relationships were an important impetus for mobilization as well. One woman recalled her father's efforts to organize the UMWA in Harlan County in an earlier era:

> My father used to tell about it. He'd tell us stories at night when we would start to bed—why he fought for the UMW. Said he'd have to go

and work 16 and 17 hours a day for nothing so that we could live. I didn't want that for my family. So I fit [sic] for what I thought was right.

Memories of efforts to organize the coalfields are vivid among Harlan County residents, part of a shared, living community history passed down through generations. Union campaigns to organize the mines date back to the earliest development of the industry in the region. Operators resisted, at times with the full police and legal power of the state behind them. The result was bald-faced class warfare, waged intermittently from the late 1890s to the present (AppalShop 1986; Ardery 1983; Corbin 1981; Fetherling 1974; Gaventa 1980; G. Jones 1985). For many of the women, childhood experiences in UMWA families and memories of early organizing campaigns influenced their decisions to take an active role in the strike.

Family connections to pro-UMWA sentiments were important even for women who had not grown up around coal mining and had no personal experience with the UMWA. One women with no UMWA history in her family said that her first husband taught her to revere the UMWA:

My daddy wasn't no union man 'cause they ain't got no union in Leslie County. What caused me to be union was 'cause my husband was. He taught me about the union. He told me about having to come home and lay with his work clothes on to go back [quickly] to get his job to keep somebody else from getting it. He was strong union.

All of the women spoke often in their interviews about the importance of a UMWA presence for any hope of an improved quality of life and economic security in the coalfields. One woman said:

With the union you have a better life, that's for sure. You have more money for one thing. Some of their benefits are real good. All the benefits we have around here come through the union. They built these hospitals. The miners get their pensions.

Another woman explained why she joined the strike even though her family was not directly involved:

We had a [UMWA] medical card and we had full coverage at that time. We didn't have to worry about anything. These poor people with little kids down there and their teeth rotted out of their mouth . . . I think the kids was the main reason I got involved in it. Those poor little kids that had to live in those dumps!

One of the filmmakers of *Harlan County, U.S.A.* summed up the women's involvement this way:

Unionism was not only a way of getting better safety in the mines. Of course it was that. But it was a real force, a real force of change here. The one thing that gave them the slightest bit of power in their communities.

While women's political action at Brookside was prompted by the specific material conditions of working-class life, it was also embedded in work, family, and community needs and histories. The women made sense of their concerns and translated them into imperatives for action only in the context of these other relationships, experiences, and constraints which were prominent in their lives. Specific class/gender material conditions, such as dependent household status and economic vulnerability, cannot be abstracted from the other specific situations and personal relations that move women to political action.

"You Can't Surrender to a Coal Operator!"

Knowledge of a bitter labor history past had taught the women that "you can't surrender to a coal operator."[9] However, the Brookside strike had been under way for almost two months before women were drawn into the conflict. It was Eastover Mining Company's attempt to reopen the Brookside mine in the fall of 1973 that provoked the women to action. A court injunction had restricted the number of pickets allowed at this mine. For several days in late September, sixty strikebreakers had been crossing the picket line and working the mine.

The Brookside mine is located on the hill just above the Brookside coal camp. Many of the men who worked at the mine lived in the camp with their families. Everyone in the camp was fully aware that the company was trying to break the strike. An old Harlan County story seemed about to repeat itself: miners sign unions cards; companies lock them out; coal keeps pouring out of the hills. The women deeply resented the strikebreakers. One woman described her increasing fury:

> I'd just go out and see the men going across the line to work. I'd tell my husband, "We ought to just get us some ball bats and go out there and take care of it."

Another woman whose husband was working in a nearby UMWA mine prodded the women whose husbands were on the picket line:

> . . . if they were to do my husband that way I'd slip up behind 'em with a ball bat and knock their brains out. I really and truly felt that. I wouldn't let 'em do my husband that way.

The women knew the situation was dangerous, and they were beginning to worry about a 1930s-style coalfields war. Incensed that the court had rendered the men incapable of defending the strike, women began to talk about taking action themselves. One described a decision made by several of the women who lived in the coal camp:

A few of us got together talking about how it was going with the men under a restraining order keeping them from picketing. About twenty of us decided to go down to the mine and try to talk to the scabs. None of us had any plans about what to do.

Just at shift change, these women were met by a car caravan arriving at the mine from a "company" union rally that day in Harlan, the county seat located eight miles from the mine. One woman described what happened:

Here come these cars off the mountain. Car after car. Instead of stopping, they done their best to run over us. If I hadn't flattened against that store building, they would have killed me. I didn't even know what was going on. From that day on, I swore to God that I would do everything in my power to stop [the strikebreakers] from working.

The confrontation that resulted shut down the Brookside Mine and launched the first female picket line at a Harlan County coal mine.

Class Action, Gender Ideology, and Gender Relations

Gender relations and gender ideology were major influences in the union-organizing drive at Brookside. The following pages illustrate the ways gender shaped the content of women's strike action, the organization of the strike, the responses to the women's participation, women's relationships to the union, and the strike outcome.

Women were involved in activities usually associated with strikes: maintaining picket lines; dealing with police and the courts; keeping the mine from operating; raising strike-support money; doing community and public relations work; and keeping morale high. As activists they broke out of their traditional domestic boundaries and together were able to stop the flow of coal from the Brookside mine when the strikers could not.

Women would get together at the mine entrance, try to convince strikebreakers not to "scab," and if necessary physically stop them from going to work. One woman who jumped on the back of an armed scab said:

I asked him nicely, "How about not crossing the picket line in the morning?" He said, "If you was a man, I'd show you what I'd do to you." He tried to show me. He had a gun in his hand. But, when I was done, he ran.

Her daughter commented on her mother's success:

It really shamed them. Mom took a limb to quite a few of them. I think it upset them more having to fight a woman. They was quite a few of them left because of that.

Another woman described the women's move from persuasion to physical confrontations with strikebreakers:

> We started out . . . talking nice. They didn't heed that. So it made us mad and we got a broom stick and tobacco sticks and walking sticks. The bigger the better. Some of them called them switches, but they was the biggest switches I ever saw.[10]

The news media made much play over the fact that women "switched" scabs during the strike. One woman explained the appearance of the switches this way:

> We had sticks. Broom handles. Just whatever we could find, shaking them at the miners—the ones that was trying to cross the picket line.

A sympathetic state policeman suggested:

> Now, ladies, you get rid of the ax handles and the broom handles and the mop handles. Get you a bunch of switches. I'm telling you, there's not a man that's gonna call himself a man that's gonna get up in court and testify that a woman whipped him with a switch.

In fact, according to one woman's report, only a few miners were whipped with switches and only one testified in court that he had been switched.

The first women's picketing centered around women from the coal camp at Brookside, primarily wives of striking miners. Soon the network spread to include women known to be pro-union. These women had grown up in strong UMWA families, had husbands or relatives working in UMWA mines, and lived on UMWA pensions. Many had no direct ties to this particular strike. One woman described how she was recruited:

> [A friend] called me. Some of the Brookside [camp] women had gone to talk to the scabs and tried to talk them out of working. I said to myself, "I don't see how they can stop us. I mean, I'm not in the UMWA and neither is any of the other women." [My] first morning we shut down the mine. Closed it up completely.

The women's picket line developed into a large assortment of women as calls went out for support. The women's picketing quickly took on an organized form. Homes in the camp were identified as headquarters or gathering places. Picketing schedules were developed so that the picket line was always covered, yet women were free to come and go and attend to household and family responsibilities. A repertoire of tactics for shutting down a coal mine was discussed and tried out. Soon the women had devised an arsenal of tactics that worked.

The women soon realized that police, strikebreakers, company personnel, and union organizers often did not know how to respond to militant women turning scabs away from a coal mine. On many occasions, no one seemed to know what to do with these disorderly women. It was a situation with no rules or norms, and the women used their gender as a license to behave in extreme ways that might have gotten men beaten or arrested.

Stories of picket-line incidents are peppered with accounts of women playing on their sexuality. One woman remembered an incident when women seductively distracted the state police, keeping them off balance and preventing arrests:

> The [women] got up there and they run their fingers up the state polices' back, where their jackets is at. They would get in there next to their skin and rub . . . up against them state police. By the time that the scab cars come, them state police did not want to take us to jail.

As exciting as picket-line activity was, the women faced serious physical danger each time they went to picket. One woman remembered an early morning after the Kentucky governor had sent extra state police to escort strikebreakers across the picket line:

> Everywhere you looked there was a blue light flashing! Big, tall troopers around. It was really . . . overpowering. I just thought, "They could shoot me!"

Another woman described the shock of facing armed opponents:

> Seeing all those men . . . most of them had pistols sticking out of their pockets. It just scared me to death, afraid somebody was just absolutely going to get killed. I worried more about that than anything. It was really some dangerous times. . . . My life had always been fairly peaceful.

One of the most dramatic incidents on the picket line happened when women lay down in the road to stop strikebreakers from entering the mine. One woman recalled:

> [I was] terrified! I was scared to death. We knew that if those cars started coming through we had to stop them. The only way that we could stop them was lay down in the road. I was such a coward. I knew if I saw a car coming for me I would probably get up. So I laid down with my back to them so I couldn't see them coming!

Picketing resulted in encounters with police, arrests, and jailings. Some women were arrested several times. Many were sentenced and fined. Others served time in jail. On one occasion when there had been a large number of arrests, the women took their children to jail with them. One woman explained:

> When they arrested me . . . I took three of the kids to jail. . . . I didn't
> have nobody to stay with them. So I had to take them with me.

When photographs of women and children locked behind bars in the
Harlan County Jail hit the wire services, the Brookside strike made national
news. The nation was familiar with stories about bloodshed in Harlan County.
But women stopping strikebreakers from entering a coal mine and ending up
behind bars with their children was something new for the media.

The UMWA had not planned on a women's contingent in this strike, but
it quickly moved to exploit their participation for its symbolic value. One of
the UMWA's most successful strike strategies was a "Dump Duke" campaign
designed to hamper the company's ability to generate capital by convincing
investors to divest and to pledge not to buy Duke Power Company stock. The
women proved to be a valuable asset in this campaign.

Women attended corporate meetings, picketed at Duke headquarters,
and picketed institutions that held Duke securities or depended on Duke
philanthropy. They spoke at congressional hearings and at events around the
country describing conditions in the coal camp, violence on the picket line,
terroristic threats against union sympathizers, and their experiences in the
Harlan County jail. They talked about living with the constant fear of mine
deaths and injury, of never knowing if a husband or father or brother or son
would be coming home at the end of a shift in the Brookside mine. The stories
the women told stood as testimonials to Duke's lack of regard for the quality
of their lives or for the health and safety of Eastover employees.

Women were aware of their important role in the strike, and they built on
their unique status to develop influence in the direction of the strike. Without
formal ties to the UMWA, the women operated from an autonomous sphere of
power. They carried out their own strike strategies in collaboration with male
strikers and union officials.

At times there were fierce arguments about strike direction between the
men in the union and some women. One woman complained about the pace
the organizers set in the strike:

> I'd tell them I just figured the best way to do it, if they want to play
> rough, then you play rough. They'd tell me to shut up and go do my
> cooking.

And one of the most influential women commented:

> Sometimes we'd all get together and go up there to that motel [UMWA
> strike headquarters] . . . and talk. But really, we listened more to what
> the men said than the organizers. Because, sometimes what the organiz-
> ers said was right and made sense and other times it didn't.

Some women rejected advice from male union attorneys. One woman
beginning a jail sentence said:

He said go down there and tell them I won't go on that picket line anymore and they'd let me out. I told him to forget it.

One woman publicly attacked the president of the UMWA at a rally of 3,500 people in Harlan, disputing his suggested tactic. Her home had been shot into, and her children narrowly escaped the gunfire. After repeatedly raising her hand and asking for the floor, she walked up to the front of the room and told him, "You gotta fight fire with fire."

Late in the strike, after facing heavy machine-gun fire on the picket line, several key women threatened to pull out all women's support unless the organizers met certain demands. One woman told of the showdown between women leaders and the organizers:

> We had decided somebody was . . . going and telling [the company] everything we was doing. So we had a meeting. . . . I told them that I wasn't gonna go any more if we couldn't keep this here quiet, to ourselves. So they agreed to announce a meeting place but not say where the pickets were going to from there.

In this way they influenced the planning of picket-line locations and arranged backup support for the women picketers. The strong voice in the strike and union affairs that the women at Brookside gained is ironic. Despite their almost completely dependent status in the local economy and in their own households, these women were able to win authority and influence in a strike of male coal miners.

GENDER ROLES AS CONTESTED TERRAIN

For the miners on strike at Brookside, the role women were playing in their strike was both a good and a bad thing. They knew the women were succeeding in shutting down the mine while they had not be able to. But this did not do much to build male self-esteem. The men not only were unable to fulfill their roles as family breadwinners, but also were clearly unable to win their strike without the aid of women. This symbolic double emasculation ensured trouble.

Women, on their part, were feeling the strain of suddenly leading "double lives." They were excited and challenged by their strike work, but their primary identification during most of their lives had been as housewives. It was frightening to go on a picket line, but once there, many of the women were hooked:

> After I got involved with it, I couldn't quit. I would have liked to. It was hard . . . nerve-wracking . . . scary. I had a harder time sleeping. There was a few times that I was frightened to death. But I couldn't quit.

They set up and managed their picket line in a manner designed to resolve the ambiguity they felt about strike involvement. As one woman explained, they developed an elaborate, informal picket-duty schedule to reduce tensions between traditional household roles and their new roles in the strike:

> I walked over every morning at five a.m. Then I'd go back home about seven to get them [seven children] ready. Then I went back to the picket line and stayed. We had that planned out. The ones that didn't have children would stay over there while the ones that had children would go get them ready. That way there would always be somebody over there *all* the time.

In short, the women organized their strike duties so that they could still meet the expectations of family roles. They mounted an effective, dangerous, demanding campaign against strikebreakers. And they did the laundry, prepared the meals, cleaned houses, and picked up children at school.

All the women reported letting down on their usual standards of housekeeping. One woman commented:

> We just let everything go but what just had to be done. I done it when I come home. Sometime we'd stay down there till almost dark. I left off a lot of things that I would liked to have done. But you've got to have priorities somewhere. Something had to go.

Household duties did get tended to, however, and almost always by the women. No new household division of labor occurred because of the strike. Women continued to perform their prestrike household duties, despite the fact that they were staying on the picket line seven to twelve hours a day and despite the fact that the striking men suddenly had hours of free time every week.

By maintaining their roles as household managers and wives, the women at Brookside lessened any threat to the idea that their rightful and "proper place" was at home. Their defense of a traditional division of labor required a tremendous investment of time and energy, but it operated as a safety net reinforcing miners' self-images as breadwinners.

The women may have been "switching" scabs, taunting the company president, testifying about conditions in Harlan County, risking their lives in violent confrontations, and appearing on national television. They were also getting meals on tables, cleaning clothes, and seeing to domestic chores.

Still, there were mixed reactions among the men. One woman went to the picket line often with female members of her husband's family. Her husband did not want any of them involved. They all ignored him:

> He tried to get me and his mom and all to stay home. When I told him I was going anyway, he wouldn't say much. He just let me go on, because he knew I'd go anyway. Even if I had to sneak off.

In several instances, husband–wife teams developed as men went with their wives to the picket line. One of the most active women said:

> He always went with me. Now if I was going to leave him at the house, he probably wouldn't have let me went. He just wouldn't. He always went, too.

Some men accepted the reality that the women were needed on the picket line. One woman who was a leader in the strike described a physical confrontation with a strikebreaker who had also been on the scene in Harlan County in the 1930s:

> I whipped that gun thug. I went in with that switch and bam, bam, bam. I hit him right over the face and eyes, I don't know how many times.

In a poignant moment, a UMWA pensioner approached her and said:

> Lady, let me shake your hand. That old gun thug, he killed miners. Honey, the first of the month you're gonna get my pension check. I'm gonna give it to you because you whipped that gun thug.

One of the strikers said he and many others believed the women were the key in getting a union contract signed, adding, "If them women hadn't done what they done, I'd say we'd a lost it." Other men, however, never accepted the women's participation. One striker told one of the leading women that his wife would never behave the way she was behaving:

> He said [she] was a good Christian woman and wouldn't go on the picket line. I just let it pass. I didn't see what being a Christian had to do with being on the picket line. I was a good Christian who was standing up for what I believed in.

Relationships in some households became very strained as the strike progessed. Men were unhappy with the new behavior of their wives. The women were enjoying their expanded roles as participants in the strike and the closeness developing among them. A few women buckled to the pressure of men to drop out but others stood their ground.

After heavy machine-gun fire on the picket line, the conflict over women's participation came out openly and was captured by the film crew of *Harlan County, U.S.A.*[11] The county was fast turning into an armed camp, the homes of several pickets had been shot into, and the strikers were expecting bloodshed at any moment.

The union local called an emergency meeting and voted to ask the women to stay home the next morning. The women quickly met and voted to stay off the picket line to honor the local's request, but only after intense debate.

The women were reluctant to stay away from the picket line, despite the gunfire. The following comments reveal the determination of the women to continue their participation in the strike:

> We'll see what the men can do, and if they can't do it, we'll be right there with our sticks. If they let them go to work, then we're coming back out. That's right!

Another woman said her husband had been asking if she planned to go back out to picket:

> My husband said he feels like I want to go back on the picket line. I told him he'd know. When I got ready I'd be ready.

One woman described an ongoing argument with her husband over her participation:

> It's just about got me to where I couldn't do anything. Then I said, "Piss on it. I'm going anyway." Right? You have to after a while. You can set back so long and holler.

Other women expressed their determination to continue their strike work despite opposition at home. One woman said:

> I don't think there could be anybody else stronger in the union than he is. But he could divorce me. If I wanted to go on that picket line I would. If it come right to that!

Another woman commented:

> That's exactly where I sit. He didn't tell me not to go. He didn't tell me to go before. They tried to say in court that my husband had me go out on the picket line. I said, "He don't tell me what to do." I go when I get ready.

The women were also criticized by people other than their spouses. One women remembers a person who drove past the picket line and yelled at her:

> "If you was my wife, you'd be home where you belong." I just felt like I belonged there. It was my livelihood, really, his job. There I was.

Several women were amused by the reactions of people who took the company's side in the strike. The company attorney, for instance, made a point of refusing to call them "ladies":

> According to Eastover's lawyer we wasn't "ladies." We were "women." He kept saying any woman that would be on a picket line is not a lady. His wife was a lady. . . . He said ladies didn't go out for stuff like that.

There were also differences of opinion among other family members that caused some tension. One woman was offended because her brother criticized her:

> He went on the picket line a few times. He didn't much want me to go. He told me I ought to give it up and leave it alone. I said, "You just run your life, and I'll run mine."

This woman's mother also opposed her participation:

> She wouldn't hardly speak to me she was so mad. I just sneaked out and run on the next morning. I had to go. She worried I'd get hurt and people would talk about me. That was a big thing, too. These old timers, they're afraid somebody will say something.

The principal opposition that caused problems for the women, though, was from husbands. In the aftermath of the strike, some households broke apart. In others, relationships were renegotiated.

CONSEQUENCES OF PARTICIPATION

In spite of the pressure many women were under, most of them enjoyed being in the strike. They often talked about having fun and about the comradeship that developed:

> There were times I really had a good time. We were sitting around talking and laughing and hollering. When he [Eastover's president] was going to the office, we always hollered at him. Them bosses, we'd holler at them. Nothing vulgar. Just holler. It was always kind of fun because we felt like we was doing something.

Several women said they felt better physically during the strike. One woman said:

> I thought I was sick when the picket line started. After I went to going on the picket line, I never did take another pill. I got along real good. Since I've been off the picket line, I got sick again.

These women also said they miss the strike. One woman said:

> I miss . . . everybody getting together for those meetings. Sometimes they'd have meetings for the whole community and everybody would go.

Another woman described it this way:

There was a closeness there. I'm always tickled when I see anybody that was down there.

Still another woman said: "Just me and those girls . . . that's what I miss."

Many of the women talked of their participation as an "education." As one of the women said:

I learned more about people than I had in my whole lifetime. Things that I never even thought about before.

One consequence of this education was a change in the way women see themselves and their worlds. The oldest woman on the Brookside picket line said she was glad she had lived long enough to take a direct hand in a UMWA strike:

I'd just think, "Why shouldn't I fight?" . . . We didn't have the opportunity to be on the picket lines then [the 1930s] like we have now. I feel different in a way from the 1930s. I will say it made my mouth bigger. I've talked more and I fit [sic] more than I did then—because we didn't have the opportunity.[12]

Change also occurred as some women became role models for others. Said one Brookside woman about another:

[She] come and stayed all night this one night after they shot the house up. She influenced me a lot by standing up. Usually men wants a woman setting at home doing what they want them to do, and not really standing up for what they think is right. I believe that she really showed me that if I didn't stand up, who would? What would become of my children when they got grown? Would they back down if something like this happened to them?

Changes in consciousness and self-perception did not simply vanish when the strike ended. Some women returned to prestrike routines but in the years that followed made changes in their lives. They all continued to be homemakers, but they took on new roles and identities as well. Changes occurred in the areas of education and training, work and political action.

Five of the twenty principal women respondents took some further schooling or training after the Brookside strike. One woman went through a long depression after it ended and eventually enrolled in classes at a nearby community college. Later she went to the area vocational school, learned carpentry skills, and rebuilt her trailer. She has done custom remodeling for a few people and works when she finds a project of interest to her.

Another woman had nearly completed an undergraduate degree at the time of her interview. She was determined to finish school and had enrolled at a community college under a federal support program. She decided she was going to work and found a job a few years after the strike despite her husband's opposition:

> When I went and applied for the job I have I just said, "I'm going to find me a job." [He] said, "Naw." I said, "Yes, I am. I'm going to go to work." And, "Naw," he said, "you don't need to go to work." So I went more or less out of spite.

This woman defended her education and her work as insurance for her family. Her husband has not had a mining job since the Brookside Mine was closed in 1981. She explained what she was doing in this way:

> You can't never tell when you may need it. Even if I quit work tomorrow and [he] got a job, you can't never tell when, if it was in a coal mine, there'd be another strike. So you always need something to fall back on. If I hadn't been working we'd probably lost everything we had when he got laid off. Once all the savings and the unemployment run out, we would have probably lost it all had I not been working.

Another woman became a licensed nurse's aide after the strike. At the time of the interview she was doing private-duty work a few days a week and cleaning a grade school thirty hours a week. Another woman went to the vocational school to learn auto-body work. She has worked with her husband in rebuilding cars.

One woman finished an undergradute degree and was almost through with her master's degree at the time of her interview. She and her husband moved from Harlan County not long after the strike. She expressed her intention to continue in school while working full-time in retail sales to help with costs:

> I was the first one [in the family] to get a bachelor's. My two brothers and a sister, they had associate's or whatever. But I was the first one to get a bachelor's. I'm going to be the first to get a doctorate. Let me tell you!

Two women were self-employed and owned their own businesses at the time of their interviews. One woman was looking for work, and one woman worked full-time with a large religious mission in Harlan County. She started her first paying job to help her family get by during the strike, but she quit that job to make peace with her husband:

> He always was the breadwinner until the strike. I went to work then. But as soon as he got back to work he made me quit. I liked working. But he made me quit. He just always said, "It's a man's place," the support.

But she soon found work with the charity, and her husband began to help out after the Brookside mine was closed.

Only seven of the twenty women I interviewed were still full-time home-makers in 1986. These developments represent dramatic changes in the lives of this group of women since 1972, when the miners went on strike at Brookside.

Many of these women expected to stay active in the UMWA, which has plans to organize more mines in eastern Kentucky. One women spoke elo-quently about her intention to continue working as a union activist:

> While [my husband] is working I'll help organize Highsplint. We'll go from one mine to the next. . . . Then Arjay. Then go from Arjay some-place else. Just get the UMWA everywhere.[13]

This did not happen, however. She and her husband were divorced soon after the strike, and she moved away from the county.

Another woman (who was sixty-four years old at the time of her inter-view) dreamed of going back to school and becoming an organizer:

> If I didn't have my mommy and daddy [to care for] . . . I'd rather go back to school than anything. I'd love to. I'd just like to go back to school and make my mind up what I wanted to take. Really, I'd like to be an organizer. That's what I would like to be. I sure would. For the mine workers.

While it might be argued that some of these women would have sought employment anyway after their children were grown, the range of job options they could envision was undoubtedly enlarged after the strike. Several of them did travel to other UMWA picket lines, and some were invited to talk about their experiences at labor rallies and progressive social events in Appalachia. Some of the women were involved in strike support during the UMWA contract strike (1974–75), which broke out within a few months of the Brookside victory.

One woman was active in the Harlan County Black Lung Association for a time. The grocery store she now operated was a meeting place for UMWA miners, and she retained her strong interest in union politics. Another of the women worked with widows of a mine disaster that killed twenty-six men at the Scotia Coal Company in 1976.

Women had made difficult personal choices to participate in the Brook-side strike. They were involved in events and did things they had never dreamed about before. From having self-images only as housewives and homemakers, the women emerged after the strike with a sense of personal growth and political efficacy. There is no question that the strike changed the way they see themselves and their world.

The initial decision to join the women's picket line was a political act that required a shift in gender consciousness for these women. As their experi-ences in the strike developed, gender relationships that had structured their lives came more and more into question, in particular the right of women to take leadership in political action and, later, to hold paid jobs. Gender became just as important a terrain for conflict as the strike for many of these women, and it led them to make changes in their lives in the years following the strike.

FINDINGS

Women's involvement shaped the strike and was a key component in the successful negotiation of a union contract at Brookside. But it was also a potential threat to a preexisting division of labor between the sexes inside households and gendered beliefs about women's proper place at home and in public. The very factors that pushed women toward strike involvement—disadvantaged economic status and dependent roles as housewives—meant that their participation was likely to become problematic.

Male breadwinners accustomed to supporting dependent family members and having final authority in family matters were in a double bind in this strike. They could not provide for their families, and they could not win their strike because court injunctions rendered them powerless at the mine site. Compounding this blow to their self-image, miners' wives and female family members were increasingly taking over the strike and getting national publicity in the process. This explosive situation pushed some traditional gender relations into the realm of contested terrain. That is, gender relations that had largely gone uncontested were called into question and to some degree renegotiated.

The women devised an elaborate participation scheme to ensure that they could fulfill their traditional roles as housewives and reinforce male self-images as family breadwinners. This strategy was important for keeping peace at home; it was also intended to protect women's status inside households. These women knew there were few other options for economic survival in their area, particularly given their skill and educational levels. It was in their direct interest to maintain family and household arrangements, and they knew it.

Still, women's involvement generated many problems within households. Women were in an ambivalent position from the start of the strike. They were compelled to political action in defense of a household status that restricted women's work to domestic labor. Their action, in turn, jeopardized that status.

In some households, women were not able to resolve role conflicts and dropped out of the strike. In others, the women rode out the conflict day by day. They took their complaints to one another, and a growing sense of gender consciousness resulted as women hashed out these problems in meetings, on the picket line, and in one another's kitchens.

Conflicts first experienced in private households became public grievances discussed and debated among women. Sharing experiences of gender conflict encouraged the women to act together to shape certain directions of the strike. It also reinforced difficult decisions to continue to participate despite consequences for household arrangements. Gender relations were forced into the open and, in some cases, renegotiated.

CONCLUSIONS AND SUGGESTIONS

E. P. Thompson insisted that class is not an abstract category, but is something "which in fact happens (and can be shown to have happened) in human relationships" (1966:9). The question of when class relations become visible and class consciousness develops is problematic. Certain conditions foster this development in particular historical moments and situational contexts. Members of a class may or may not develop an awareness of shared interests and move to act on them.

This research suggests that gender also "happens" and in fact "happened" at Brookside. A certain configuration of material interests, divisions of labor, and gendered beliefs about political action; autonomous female space in the strike; and situational constraints on male participation resulted in gendered consciousness and struggle. In short, the particular interaction of class relations and gender relations in the coal strike created the conditions under which gender relations became visible and contested.

Other researchers have found that gender relations are revealed and contested when the introduction of new technology disrupts equations of work process with gender identity (Cockburn 1983; Game and Pringle 1983). Particular management styles and forms of worker control may also provoke gendered consciousness and gendered components in class conflict (Costello 1985). My research suggests that class participation in a struggle disrupts gender relations and moves them from subtext to contested terrain.

Jacquelyn Hall's (1986) work on textile workers in eastern Tennessee suggests another direction for work on the intersection of class and gender. She demonstrates the importance of an erotic undercurrent in women's collective action, and suggests that we place analytic priority on the "structure of feeling" that women bring to picket lines and union-organizing campaigns. Such analysis will be a promising next step to further exploration of the emergence of gendered consciousness and changes in self-image that accompanied class action in the mine strike.

Neither class nor gender alone is a sufficient tool for understanding political action. Gender relations in combination with class relations structure women's material interests in union organizing. This interaction is itself conditioned by the historical and situational context of the strikes. Motivation for participation in strikes and union affairs by women is complex, and contextualizing women's political activity is therefore essential. Principal motivating factors such as dependent household status and economic vulnerability are conditioned by life histories and the diverse realities of working-class life.

Finally, my research suggests that treating class and gender as independent categories of social relations creates an artificial distinction. Women's material interests in political action at Brookside are neither singularly class defined nor gender defined. Ultimately, it does not make sense to separate them. Class happens only in conjunction with gender in the Brookside strike. Gender happens here only in conjunction with class.

NOTES

Major funding for this research was provided by an American Fellowship awarded by the American Association of University Women, a Lena Lake Forrest Fellowship awarded by the Business and Professional Women's Research Foundation, a James Still Fellowship awarded by the University of Kentucky, and an Appalachian Studies Fellowship awarded by Berea College.

1. In an earlier article on the Brookside strike ("Women's Participation in the Brookside Coal Strike: Militancy, Class, and Gender in Appalachia," *Frontiers* 9, no. 3 [1987]:16–21), I argued that gender relations were strained and contested during the strike but that business as usual was restored afterward . I concluded that women "returned full-time to those prescribed roles that insured that the men of their households continued to see themselves as the coal-mining breadwinners who support and head the family" (p. 20). I based this conclusion on the facts that most households remained intact after the strike, that women reported no change in household division of labor during and after the strike, and that the women reported a return to prestrike "normalcy" in their households after the strike.

After carefully analyzing data on what women did over the years following the strike and comparing their lives with those of the women involved in the eastern Kentucky hospital strike (part of my larger research project), I have revised my initial conclusions on the return to prestrike gender relations. Although women remained housewives, they made many changes in their lives.

2. *Harlan County, U.S.A.* outtakes are housed in the Special Collection of the M. I. King Library at the University of Kentucky, Lexington, Kentucky.

3. A federally defined subregion of the larger Appalachian Region, Central Appalachia consists of sixty counties located in four states: Kentucky, Virginia, West Virginia, and Tennessee (Appalachian Regional Commission 1964).

4. There are accounts of women working in contract or family-run mines early in this century and during World War II, but coal-mining employment remained blocked to women until sex discrimination suits were filed and won under the Equal Employment Opportunity Act. As late as 1975, 99.8 percent of all U.S. coal miners were men (Hall 1977).

5. Women with education and political connections (generally middle-class women) worked in coveted and politically controlled jobs in the school system.

6. All statistics are based on state- and county-level data of the 1970 U.S. Census, which is based on 1969 income data (U.S. Bureau of the Census 1973).

7. The exception was a recently divorced young woman who had come home with her small baby to live with her parents.

8. Unless otherwise noted, all quotations are from the author's interviews with strike participants and others knowledgeable about the strike. To protect their privacy, individual participants are not identified by name.

9. Comment by Lois Scott, *Harlan County, U.S.A.* Outtakes, Box 179, CR 887. Appalachian Special Collection, M. I. King Library, University of Kentucky, Lexington.

10. June Rostan, oral-history interview with Minnie Lunsford, Harlan County, Kentucky, January–February 1977.

11. *Harlan County, U.S.A.* Outtakes, Box 142, CR 813.

12. *Harlan County, U.S.A.* Outtakes, Box 142, CR 813.

13. *Harlan County, U.S.A.* Outtakes, Box 197, CR 930.

PART II

WOMEN IN RACIAL/ETHNIC AND NATIONALIST STRUGGLES

Women have always participated in collective struggles against oppressive racial and nationalist regimes. They have also taken part in protest movements designed to protect the status quo and the threatened loss of rights and privileges. This section examines women in revolutionary struggles in Latin America, China, Israel, and Europe, as well as in the civil rights movement of the 1960s in the United States.

A number of basic themes unite these diverse studies of women's participation in social protest. First, they document gender-integrated efforts to bring about or resist change in different eras and in various part of the world. Second, it appears that women seldom consistently share leadership and decision-making positions with men even in these gender-integrated struggles that espouse class or racial equality or both. Revolutionary ideologies that call for justice and freedom from oppression seldom translate them to include gender equality. While political crises and incipient movement stages often do provide women with new role opportunities, traditional conceptions of sex roles eventually limit these. As hypothesized in the introduction to Part I, the "iron law of patriarchy"—which states that men take over rather than share leadership and power with activist women—appears to be the rule rather than the exception. The "iron law of patriarchy" posits that in gender-integrated movements—regardless of their democratic ideals and rhetoric—the leadership of the movement will remain or become dominated by men, reflecting the patriarchal nature of the society within which the movement develops. It is a process similar to that described by Lawson and Barton in Part I.

Some interesting patterns emerge from the analysis of this process. The political *level* of the collective action appears to be important. Women often predominate as leaders and organizers as long as protest remains fairly confined to the grass-roots, neighborhood level. Once the movement "takes off" and shifts to confrontations at the state, regional, or national levels, men tend to take over the leadership, especially the formal leadership positions. West (1981) and Pope (1989; Chapter 3 in this volume) document similar patterns in the U.S. welfare rights movement in the late 1960s and early 1970s. Men (especially white men) tend to have greater access to resources and opportunities at higher political and economic levels because of their structural predominance in these sectors. Men's greater command of resources in society, thus, may help to explain "the iron law of patriarchy" in social protest movements.

Kaplan (1977, 1987b) and others note that gender stratification has been common in revolutionary movements. In socialist movements in Europe, Asia, and Latin America and in the civil rights movement in the United States, this pattern is well documented. Kaplan 1987b:429–49) also discusses various examples of the vanguard role of women in the communal strikes and revolutions in Russia, Italy, and Mexico between 1917 and 1922. Although women organized these communal strikes, demanding food for their families and peace in their communities, their leadership roles were taken over by men when the strikes developed into revolutionary phases (Kaplan 1987b:436). Working-class men in these socialist and anarchist struggles often ignored or minimized the centrality of women's roles and their demands for basic survival needs (food, fuel, and mooderate rents). The issues for the men were labor conditions, political arrangments, or the conduct of war. Survival, not political or economic change, was women's goal until "periods of extreme scarcity drove women to expose their bodies to bullets in order to win resources necessary for their family's survival" (Kaplan 1987b:446). Here again we see the overlap in the types of issues that draw women into social protest—from survival to socialism—and the dynamic aspect of these struggles. Food riots have been the genesis of revolutions in many parts of the world, as Kaplan and others have documented.

A third theme deals with the political consequences of participation in revolutionary movements. The data examined thus far (see Chapter 1) suggest that women's efforts seldom result in significant change of status within the movement or within society. For example, working-class women in Veracruz, Mexico, organized and led protests for housing by calling for a rent strike. Thousands joined, and by 1923 they had won most of their goals. Yet women were excluded from positions on the tenant and landlord boards that institutionalized their victory. Kaplan argues that since the women were "inspired only by female consciousness" (not feminist consciousness), they made no attempt to take power on governing boards (1987b:445). While we agree that political consciousness is an important element in any revolutionary process, we suggest that barriers to women's political participation inherent in patriarchal society, such as men's control of the military and legal institutions, also contributed to this traditional outcome.

Finally, despite obstacles to women's participation in political protest, some of them have always found ways to resist, individually and collectively, the patriarchal authorities that rule their lives. The multiple levels of women's conflicts in social protest—against their opponents in society at large, against male oppression inside their movement, and against male oppression within their families and kinship networks—are implicitly, and at times explicitly, highlighted by our authors. The dynamics of internal conflicts within social protest have only recently been analyzed in terms of gender. Historically, scholars have focused on class and race conflicts within movements. Without gender analysis, data are lost that can help explain changes in structure, resources, strategies, and outcomes.

In this section, Lobao, Liao, Izraeli, and Mullaney add to the expanding literature about women fighting in revolutionary or nationalistic struggles. Lobao (Chapter 10) compares women's participation in various Latin American guerrilla movements, noting the factors that affect their mobilization. She finds that the issue of women's rights was recognized as significant for the overall success of the revolution in only two countries, Nicaragua and El Salvador. Lobao sees new patterns of revolutionary struggle emerging in Latin America and predicts that women will continue to play an important role. Whether they will assume leadership and make greater demands as women remains to be seen. Engel (1977:346) points out that women in the French and Russian revolutions and in the European anarchist movement in the early twentieth century "made their feminist concerns secondary and joined male-led revolutionary movements." Similar patterns still appear to be the norm in the data available from Latin America.

Liao (Chapter 6) adds to the sparse literature on Asian women in the public sphere in a research note that reexamines women's behavior in the Taiping Movement in nineteenth-century China. Again, we are shown women active in their own national liberation, but not fully supported in these efforts. Izraeli (Chapter 7) discusses the rise of women's protest within the socialist Zionist movement, a movement that called for full and equal participation of women in the building of the new Jewish nation, and the token results of this separate but not autonomous wing of the socialist movement in the early twentieth century. A rising consciousness among women stems from the contradiction between espoused equality and the practice of gender inequality within the movement. Mullaney (Chapter 5) describes the outlook and behavior of five leading socialist women in the nineteenth and twentieth centuries. She suggests that these women leaders pursued their socialism differently from men, reflecting seemingly contrasting gender-related values, social positions, and societal constraints that affected both their political views and their participation.

Racial/ethnic struggles in the United States provided another arena in which women voiced their views and engaged in political action. Payne (Chapter 8) examines the role of African-American women in the civil rights movement in Mississippi in the mid-1960s. His work contributes to the expanding, but still sparse, literature on black women in the civil rights movement. Payne's study reveals the heretofore sparingly documented but predominant role of women leaders at certain times and places within the movement and the consequences the activists endured. By drawing on African-American women's personal accounts of their recruitment, Payne uncovers the importance of religious and community ties in creating involvement in the ongoing struggle. Finally, Blumberg (Chapter 9) recounts the involvement of white middle-class women in the same movement, but in the North. She clarifies the processes through which these women creatively transformed their traditional service roles into less conventional political roles. Unpredictably, they brought in motherhood themes to link themselves to the movement for racial integration. Blumberg's work also adds to the newly accumulating record of women's presence in the racial protest movements of the United States.

Part II underscores the historical and cultural breadth of women's participation in social protest. While it provides us with new insights into women's roles in revolutionary struggles and extends our knowledge about women in racial struggles in America, it leaves some questions unanswered. For example, how and under what conditions do women's consciousness and actions become transformed in gender-integrated nationalist and racial/ethnic struggles? Under what conditions do they remain relatively unchanged? Similarly, how are men's gender consciousness and behavior transformed (or not transformed) in nationalist and racial/ethnic struggles? How might the technological revolution affect women's national and international communication networks, and how might such "new" resources transform women's protests by the end of the twentieth century? That is, what might be the effect of an expanded and "instant" network of women activists throughout the globe on national protests and revolutionary struggles?

CHAPTER 5

Women and European Socialist Protest, 1871–1921

MARIE MARMO MULLANEY

From its earliest theoretical beginnings, European socialism was particularly sympathetic to the idea of women's emancipation.[1] Socialist theorists promised women complete equality in a new revolutionary order and specifically encouraged them to embrace the new ideology. This paper discusses the careers of five women who did, women who were among the leading socialist personalities of Europe in their day. They attained prominence during a critical era in the history of European socialism, a half-century flanked by the revolutionary Paris Commune of 1871 and the consolidation of the Bolshevik Revolution. European socialism grew ideologically and matured politically during these years. Germany experienced an abortive Communist revolution, revolutionary socialism rose and fell in Italy, and England witnessed the birth of a militant labor movement impregnated with Marxist principles.

Countless women shared in these struggles, not only the five identified here but innumerable others who served obscurely as labor organizers, union members, strikers, rioters, and agitators. The hows and whys of their participation—their motivations, expectations, ideals, and hardships—seen, in microcosm, through the experiences of five of the most heralded women of the socialist pantheon, are the subject of this paper.

THE SOCIALIST POSITION ON WOMEN'S LIBERATION

Throughout the nineteenth century, a standard tenet of the developing socialist creed was that the radical restructuring of society would bring with it full personal, political, social, economic, and legal equality for women. Socialist theorists in England, France, Germany, and Russia welcomed women's participation in their movements, addressed propaganda to them, and dealt with the question of women's role in the future societies they hoped to create. Forging a powerful ideological alliance between socialism and feminism, writers like Flora Tristan, Etienne Cabet, Charles Fourier, Henri de Saint-Simon, Robert Owen, and Alexander Herzen demanded changes in social organizations and institutions that would allow women to become the full and equal partners of men in the new socialist world.

Karl Marx followed in the spirit of these early thinkers. Linking women's liberation directly with socialist revolution, he saw female oppression as a general manifestation of the evils of capitalist society. Capitalism wrecked traditional family life, drove women and children into the atrocious atmosphere of the factory, and caused both men and women to sell their souls for the tenuous security of a starvation wage. Female prostitution became for Marx the most glaring of all symbols of the "cash nexus" that bound human beings to one another in the capitalist world. Although Marx dealt with women's problems only tangentially, he enunciated what was to become the socialist movement's standard position on the woman question. Since class alliances would always separate women from one another, "bourgeois" feminist movements, with their demands for the vote, equal pay for equal work, and civil and legal rights, were meaningless without wider societal restructuring. True salvation for women lay in fighting alongside the men of their class for the achievement of socialism (Marx n.d.:405–566; 1959:22, 29; 1970:51; 1973:21–22).

Frederick Engels echoed Marx's outrage at the factory employment of women and children, providing in *The Condition of the Working Class in England* a poignant and powerful description of the disintegration of family life among the poor. Even more importantly, in *The Origin of the Family, Private Property, and the State,* he gave Marxist thought on the woman question a theoretical and quasi-historical underpinning. "The first class opposition that appeared in history," he wrote, "was the antagonism between man and woman in monogamous marriage." Tracing the roots of women's oppression to a marriage system developed to enshrine and protect private property, he tied female emancipation to the destruction of all societies based on the private ownership of the means of production (Engels 1968:161–66, 1975).

As Marxism matured into an organized political movement, the German leader August Bebel completed socialism's ideological commitment to the women question. His monumental work, *Woman Under Socialism* (1904), was destined to become the classic statement on this issue. Beginning his book with a historical survey of the position of women, Bebel connected sexual oppression with the rise of capitalism itself, explaining that the subjection of women would always remain symptomatic of the pervasive oppression of class society. Attributing female subordination to the evils of wage slavery, private property, and the marriage market, Bebel insisted that only the future socialist society could guarantee women's full equality and secure them all political, social, and economic rights. With this persuasive assurance, *Woman Under Socialism* was a sensational success. Reprinted in several million copies and translated into more than a dozen languages, it was a powerful motivating factor in attracting women to the socialist cause.[2]

LEADING WOMEN IN EUROPEAN SOCIALISM

Encouraged by this inspirational ideological heritage, many women entered socialist movements by the closing decades of the nineteenth century. Those chosen for this paper were five of the most famous. While the selection was arbitrary in some respects, certain important considerations dictated the choices made. Women selected were those who left extensive written records of their revolutionary involvement and who were recognized by their contemporaries as having taken leading roles. Although they acted within five different national contexts, they were all heirs to a common Marxist tradition, and despite national differences, similar themes emerge in the study of their lives.

Louise Michel (1830–1905), the famous "Red Virgin" of the Paris Commune, is generally regarded as the greatest female revolutionary that France ever produced. A fearless firebrand, she assumed a number of roles on the barricades in 1871—agitator, ambulance nurse, soldier, orator—and was ultimately deported to the penal colony of New Caledonia for her activities. Returning to France after a general amnesty in 1880, for the next quarter of a century the charismatic Michel was a powerful rallying symbol for the nascent French socialist movement. Active as a lecturer, propagandist, writer, and strike leader, she grew to be a legendary figure, respected even by political opponents because of her religious-like passion, acute sensitivity to human suffering, and pity for the unfortunate and exploited.

Eleanor Marx (1855–98) was the only child of Karl Marx to become an important political figure in her own right. Schooled in political consciousness from girlhood and inheriting her father's sympathy and love for the working class, Eleanor was active in the English socialist and labor movement in the years when it was first emerging into institutional maturity. Filling a variety of roles—union organizer, agitator, journalist, translator, editor, and pamphleteer—she was generally considered to be one of the most important women in the socialist world of her day.

Following in a long tradition of revolutionary Russian women, Alexandra Kollontai (1872–1952) was a Bolshevik agitator, propagandist, and theoretician who became an eloquent and outspoken pioneer in demanding sexual freedom for women. After the revolution, she was rewarded with a cabinet post and established herself as the highest-ranking woman in the new Soviet government. Working to secure equality of rights and a modicum of power for women, she achieved attention and renown for her plans to recast the social and family life of the new Russia on a truly communal basis.

Of all women revolutionaries in history, Rosa Luxemburg (1860–1919) is probably the best known. Associated with revolutionary currents in Poland, Lithuania, Russia, and Germany, she is most remembered for her starring role in the abortive German Communist revolution of 1919. Above all else, her brilliant intellectual achievements elevated her above her contemporaries. Her theoretical works, political comrades acknowledged, "were like Marx at his best," and she was considered to be "the greatest genius among the scientific heirs of Marx and Engels" (Mehring 1907).[3]

A true internationalist, Angelica Balabanoff (1878–1965) took her place among the best-known figures of European socialism in the first two decades of the twentieth century. A labor organizer, an agitator, and a propagandist in Switzerland and Italy, she was a member of the Italian Socialist Party before World War I and an associate of Benito Mussolini during his years as a socialist. During the war, she was one of the leaders of the Zimmerwald movement, the ill-fated socialist crusade for a peaceful solution to the conflict. After the Bolshevik Revolution, she returned to her Russian homeland where she became secretary of the Third International.

THE ANALYSIS OF SOCIALIST WOMEN

While the contributions made by these women deserve telling, the placing of socialist women back into history is important for more than purely compensatory reasons. Their careers present significant theoretical issues for researchers and biographers.

Although socialism may have promised women equality and opportunity, it became the task of women adherents to interpret the language of the socialist tradition and translate it into practice. Did they succeed? What most attracted women to socialist ideology? Were they accepted by their comrades? How, and on what terms? Was there a dichotomy between the kinds of roles they sought to fill in the revolutionary movement and those they were assigned by male comrades?

The most important question for researchers to consider is the extent to which women's specifically *gender-based* experiences not only propelled them to political consciousness but affected the character and content of their protest politics. Was women's understanding of the socialist movement and its creed different from that of men? What about their values, aims, priorities, and activities? Overall, how did women's experience in revolutionary socialist politics differ from that of men?[4]

The Effect of Gender on Socialist Vision

Eleanor Marx, of course, came to socialist protest politics through direct personal and family influence, and it was her political radicalism that spawned her commitment to female emancipation. A striving to be free from the oppressive restrictions imposed by their sex brought the other women of this study to radical politics. Both Balabanoff and Kollontai sought to escape from homes in which they were excessively sheltered and overprotected. Luxemburg rebelled against the oppression and discrimination that she was forced to endure as a Polish Jew in the Russian Empire. At an early age, Louise Michel rejected the traditional female role of wife and mother, convinced that she was marked for a special role in life.

Propelled by this longing for independence and bolstered by a sense of mission, these women came to see socialist politics as the vehicle that could satisfy their needs. Four were born and bred in politically conscious households, and all but Eleanor Marx learned of class differences and social injustice through their dealings with servants. All came from comfortable, if not wealthy, homes, demonstrating once again that many revolutions in history have been made by individuals from the middle and upper classes who develop, in effect, counter-class sympathies. All were well schooled in socialist thought. As a young Parisian teacher, Michel studied at a free university led by ardent republicans and opponents of Napoleon III's empire. Luxemburg, Kollontai, and Balabanoff were educated at universities known to be hotbeds of political radicalism in the late nineteenth century. In this way, all five women were taught about, or came to see, the social and political evils of the system in which they lived.

Socialism's moral, humanistic undercurrent appealed to them all in a remarkably similar way. The vision they all spoke of was the same; love not hate, brought all of them to socialism and colored their definitions, goals, and dreams. Even Eleanor Marx, who might have been expected to see socialism in a more precise economic and political way, explained her attraction in quasi-religious terms. "Socialism means happiness," she tersely proclaimed (Marx 1885). Humanism was always the essence of Balabanoff's socialist faith, while to Louise Michel, socialism meant self-sacrifice, devotion to the poor, and the end of injustice. Above all, it meant "community" to Alexandra Kollontai. The socialist society would be a "big happy family" where the needs of all would be taken care of (Kollantai 1977c:134). Even Luxemburg, who demonstrated the highest theoretical understanding of all, described the future socialist society in profoundly moral terms: "The highest idealism in the interest of the collectivity, the strictest self-discipline, the truest public spirit of the masses are the moral foundations of socialist society" (Luxemburg 1971b:369).

Interpreting their adopted ideology in this way, these women found that socialist politics as practiced by their male comrades did not always measure up to such high ideals. In their own careers, each came to show a marked hostility to the quest for personal power and aggrandizement, and each consistently condemned those socialists who sought to use the movement to enhance their own prestige.

Longing for a world "without exploiters and exploited," where all people would be happy and free, and where the needs of all would be taken care of, Louise Michel always maintained that she was ambitious "not for myself but for humanity." She consciously separated her own political motivations from those of "despotic politicians" moved only by illusions of grandeur and self-importance. A social revolutionary above all else, she was horrified by the spectacle of socialists who chose to involve themselves in the "political carnival." In her opinion, they had no other aim but personal satisfaction and ambition, a selfish desire to replace the bourgeoisie in power (Michel 1890:9, 1921:385, 1976:100, 184–86, 250, 335).[5]

The sentiments of Eleanor Marx on power, politics, and ambitious politicians were remarkably similar. In 1884 she broke away from the Social Democratic Federation, England's first modern socialist organization, because she was disgusted with the spirit of "opportunism, reformism, and electioneering" that had come to characterize it. So great was her opposition to the "dictatorial and high-handed" leader cult created by the SDF's founder, Henry Mayers Hyndman, that the new Socialist League she formed in opposition announced its hostility to leaders from the very beginning. To carry out its aims, its manifesto decreed, "no overshadowing and indispensable leader" would be required. The group adopted the principle of rotating leadership, also a consistent feature of many modern-day feminist organizations (Clayton 1926:12).[6]

Luxemburg, Kollontai, and Balabanoff all continued in the attack on the "vile disease" of careerism that had come to afflict the socialist parties of Europe by the early years of the twentieth century. Luxemburg became one of the best-known opponents of revisionism, the doctrine which proclaimed that socialist aims could be achieved by electoral and legislative reform rather than by revolution. Attacking as "parliamentary cretinism" any attempt to strip Marxism of its revolutionary core, she sharply criticized the German Socialist Party, which seemed to live not for the coming socialist revolution but for Reichstag election campaigns (Luxemburg 1961:39, 1972a:265). Her dislike of parliamentary activity for its own sake was paralleled by her contempt for "spiritually bankrupt" parliamentarians, whom she considered poseurs consumed with their own self-importance. "It is laughable," she wrote to a friend, "how being a member of the Reichstag suddenly goes to all those good people's heads" (Nettl 1966:457–58). Parliamentary posts, in her view, were only "decorative shams," egoistic preserves that insulated their holders from the real task of revolutionary creation (Luxemburg 1972e:174).

Kollontai also condemned the power-seeking socialists of the German party. According to her, fawning obedience and obsequiousness, not critical independence, had become the only way to get ahead in a movement that had lost its revolutionary spirit. Those "colorless toers-of-lines" who used the party as a springboard to personal power were rewarded with deputy's seats, while those who chose not to play the game—like Rosa Luxemburg, she noted—were kept at a distance (Kollontai 1977a:85–86). Careerism, bureaucracy, and the seductive influence of power had ruined German socialism and were on their way, she predicted, to wrecking a Russian party in which stifled criticism was the price one paid for advancement. Although Kollontai knew the consequences of oppositional activity, she chose to pursue it anyway. Willing to risk estrangement from the part hierarchy, she assumed a starring role in the Workers' Opposition, a trade union movement that sought to compel the victorious Bolsheviks to implement their popular prerevolutionary rallying cry, "Workers' control of industry!" (Kollontai 1921).

Angelica Balabanoff was also highly critical of the course Lenin's revolution had taken, excoriating the "fetishism of leadership," the leader cult, and the "hypnotic and corrupting" effect of power and success (Balabanoff 1925; 1964:20–21, 28–29, 37, 74, 102–3, 120; 1965:34; 1973:84, 165–66, 203, 222–23). She condemned the Bolshevik Revolution as an elite affair made by manipulators and profiteers who had joined the party for material reasons, power seekers who saw the world as a chessboard where they could call all the moves.

Whether socialist women saw these political differences in terms of gender remains unclear; yet various statements made by the women of this study suggest that perhaps they did. How could women, asked Louise Michel, "who had long been the victims of authority themselves, ever seek to exercise power over others?" (Girault 1906:127). "Freedom is much more precious to women than it is to men," explained Balabanoff, "because women have to go through such a tremendous struggle before they are free in their own minds" (Bryant 1918:169). Balabanoff specifically praised Luxemburg for her courage in predicting and condemning the "pernicious opportunism" that would result in the tragedies of the postwar years (1973:198). In an interesting generalization, Alexandra Kollontai attributed women's failure to obtain positions of influence in Russia to their greater political integrity. Since women had "more conscience" than men, they had no desire to obtain positions "for which they were not fitted by previous training" (Bryant 1923:114).[7]

The Effect of Gender on Socialist Activities

One key commonality emerges when one identifies the motivations that drew these five women to socialism: none equated success in the revolutionary cause with the attainment of power or with political victory, either for themselves as individuals or for the movement as a whole. "Even if we are conquered," Alexandra Kollontai told an American journalist during the height of the Russian Revolution, "we have done great things. We are breaking the way, abolishing old ideas" (Beatty 1918:380). According to Rosa Luxemburg, defeat was an integral part of the self-education of the working classes. Premature revolutions were not failures but "vital elements in the process of educating the people to revolutionary consciousness" (Luxemburg 1970b:172–73, 182–83; 1972d:117). The attitudes of the other women were similar. Because all came to socialism seeking to serve, they gauged success not by the ends attained but by the work done in the process, in the attempt itself.

Most importantly, they seemed to judge their own success in terms of their direct impact on the masses they sought to aid. Contact with the people made these women acutely aware of personal suffering on a practical, tangible level. Although the socialist creed had always insisted that the people, as an abstraction, were good, to these women the people always existed as much more than a theoretical abstraction. All showed a desire to relate to individuals on concrete terms and displayed a real interest in one-to-one personal relationships with ordinary people.

This similarity suggests that their socialism was different from men's and that men and women have brought different values and priorities to the protest process. Studies of female personality structure claim it is a "pancultural fact" that male and female personalities differ from each other in what is termed "relative concreteness vs. relative abstractness." The feminine personality tends to be involved with concrete feelings, things, and people rather than with abstract entities; it tends toward personalism and particularism (Ortner 1974:81).

This difference is explained by the quality and type of social arrangements encountered in early childhood. In modern industrial societies, the mother and her work are seen in concrete terms by both male and female children; the father and his work are seen in the abstract. What the father does when he leaves home in the early morning hours remains a mystery. The female child is taught to identify with the concrete mother figure, and the mother, in turn, enjoys a special sense of identification with her female child

(Kelly & Boutilier 1978: 209; Lynn 1969:98). The son's case is different. Not only is he treated differently by his mother, but he is also taught to identify with the abstract cluster of traits culturally associated with his father and his father's role. Cognitive psychologists have established that this process is complete by age three, and that by that age boys and girls have an irreversible conception of what their gender is (Kohlberg 1966).

Consequently, each sex acquires a different cognitive style. In solving the masculine role identification problem, the boy develops a cognitive style that involves abstracting principles. The girl, in learning the mother identification lesson, adopts a cognitive style that primarily involves both a personal relationship and imitation rather than abstraction. The girl learns from her mother's personal example what it means to be a woman, to be that person whose life revolves around active physical care and concern for other people (Chodorow 1971, 1974; Lynn 1969:23–28, 36, 42, 98; 1974:6, 103–7).

Researchers have argued that women's primary involvement with family and child care powerfully influences subconscious mental attitudes and beliefs. In her original and provocative study, *The Mermaid and the Minotaur*, Dorothy Dinnerstein suggests that a sacred sense of human value and importance is innate to all women due to their socially mandated task of "maintaining the intimate bridge between generations" (1976:153). Women, she writes,

> feel in a peculiarly primitive and intimate way what it is to be human: to be knowingly part, that is, of a process that started before we were born and continues after we die. Humanness itself, then, is in this particular sense more firmly forced on woman than on man. (1976:275)

Other studies have echoed Dinnerstein's speculations. Carol Gilligan has written extensively of women's moral development and stressed its differences from men's. In her highly celebrated *In a Different Voice* (1982), she emphasizes how important human relationships are to women, explaining that women have traditionally defined and judged themselves in terms of their ability to care.

The careers and concerns of the women of this study suggest that these gender-based characteristics did in fact have political ramifications. All specifically saw their socialism as a means of relieving individual human suffering; in some cases, they even allowed their concern for individuals, as individuals, to supersede their allegiance to socialist dogma. Although socialists had traditionally opposed charity and philanthropy as being self-defeating and harmful to the revolution in the long run, Michel, Marx, and Balabanoff came to rethink the proper socialist attitude on this issue. Well known for her wide-ranging acts of personal charity and almsgiving, Michel often took time to read to the blind, to visit the sick, and to seek aid for the poor. Contemporary accounts are replete with references to her magnanimity. Her apartments were havens for stray animals, beggars, thieves, and vagrants alike, and she routinely distributed food and money to any unfortunate who crossed her path (Bernstein 1921:246–47; Goldman 1970:167–68; Hardouin 1879:123–24; Kropotkin 1899:484; Malato 1897:24–31). In time, Michel came to be even better known for acts of this kind than for her revolutionary pronouncements. Aware of socialist views in the matter, she felt compelled to defend her individual alsmgiving, explaining that the miserable would not revolt and that she could not stand back and "let them die of hunger" (Michel 1976:260).

Like Michel, Eleanor Marx was vitally affected by the misery, poverty, and suffering of the underclass. She made frequent trips to London's East End not only to agitate and to organize among workers' groups, but also to investigate the living conditions of those who suffered there. After one visit, she wrote poignantly to her sister, "I can't tell you the horrors I have seen. Children are little skeletons . . . naked, starving, pitiable" (Florence 1975:45). Although she recognized her father's opposition to works of individual charity, she knew that he had never visited a slum house, and she found it very difficult to maintain, for herself, his veneer of theoretical hard-heartedness (Beer 1935:74).

For Marx, socialism came to have a human face. There was an almost religious essence to her view of the responsibility of humans for one another: As she wrote to Dollie Radford: "Though each one must work out his own salvation, we can make the work perhaps a little less hard for those that shall come after (Thompson 1955:433). Although she had no children of her own, she was concerned that the tenets of socialism reach and touch the younger generation. "We too want the 'little children to come unto us.' " she wrote when planning a Socialist League Christmas party in 1885. "We cannot too soon make children understand that socialism means happiness" (Marx 1885, 1886).

Both Kollontai and Balabanoff were also interested in the practical, prosaic details of social welfare work. As the minister of social welfare in the new Bolshevik government, Kollontai enacted a wide variety of reforms that touched the lives of orphans and invalids, the unemployed, the needy, and the homeless. Although she had theoretical interests herself, she criticized Lenin for being "too theoretical," too far removed from the masses he was hoping to lead (Sadoul 1920:95–96). In her work at the ministry, Kollontai was determined not to let herself lose contact with the workers whom she considered the life-blood of the revolution, giving, she always claimed, the same consideration to suggestions from scrubwomen as to those from her closest colleagues. She drew all levels of the ministry into policy making, asking the opinion even of janitors and messenger boys on a wide range of issues (Bryant 1918:130–34).

Similarly, Balabanoff's entire socialist career was marked by the urge "to touch the masses in their misery." Her earliest socialist labors occurred among Italian migrants in Switzerland, whose abysmal living conditions mandated that the socialist agitator take on the character of a social worker. This was a role Balabanoff performed well. In her speeches, she instructed audiences in the values of proper diet, clean living conditions, practical clothing, and moderation in food and drink (Eshelman 1977:100–49). Later, as minister of foreign affairs for the Ukraine during the Russian Civil War, she acquired a reputation for being "soft-hearted" because of her efforts to get the prisons opened and to distribute food to all who asked for help. Such behavior did not ingratiate her with party leaders. Lenin condemned her "inconvenient moralism," while others openly mocked her. She was no more than a "sentimental philanthropist," they said, "always wasting her time trying to procure milk for some sick baby, extra things for a pregnant woman, or old clothes for people of useless age" (Goldman 1970:763).[8]

These examples demonstrate that women like Michel, Marx, Kollontai, and Balabanoff saw their socialist involvement as a means of responding to immediate human crises rather than as the mere implementation of an abstract economic or political theory. Their interest in socialism's effect on individuals manifested itself in the importance that each assigned to the role of teacher, long identified as a female role. Each one, despite her break with traditional cultural norms of proper feminine behavior, chose this role in the socialist movement she joined. Even Rose Luxemburg, the vaunted theoretician, found solace and fulfillment in teaching. Embracing personal contact with the masses when she found herself on the outs with the German socialist hierarchy, she regarded her work as an instructor at the Central Party School in Berlin as one of the most exhilarating experiences of her revolutionary career (Balabanoff 1973:22; Kautsky 1929:36–38; Luxemburg 1975:13–14).

The interests of the other women were similar. Alexandra Kollontai believed her chief political task to be educating women to political consciousness, while Eleanor Marx emphasized the importance of children's education. Anxious to reach future workers while they were still young, she worked at a socialist Sunday school in Battersea, where she taught socialist principles in the language of traditional Christian ethics and ethical idealism. She also held language and debating classes for workers (Kapp 1976:643, 650–51).

Louise Michel, a schoolteacher before she entered revolutionary politics, was also preeminently concerned with the moral education of the socialist citizen. During the insurrection of 1871, she was centrally involved in a movement to reform popular education. She continued this work in New Caledonia among the native Kanakas and also in a school she ran for the children of the French prisoners. During the last years of her life, spent in self-imposed exile in London, she directed an international socialist school for political refugees and their children (Avrich 1980:168; Michel 1976:242).[9]

Because of her belief in the creative revolutionary potential of the masses, education also assumed a place of central importance in Angelica Balabanoff's vision of socialism. The emancipation of the workers themselves, she always insisted, had to proceed from their own initiatives and experiences alone, arising from their intimate understanding of the goal they sought to achieve. In this process of creating class consciousness, the spoken word, she felt, was immensely superior to the written one; teaching was more important than theorizing. Oral propaganda not only was the most effective, if not the only, means of socialist agitation in nations like Italy and Russia with high rates of illiteracy, but also was the best vehicle the popular agitator had to touch listeners (Balabanoff 1964:27, 1973:140, 175).

The Effect of Gender on Socialist Strategy and Tactics

Close contact with the masses strongly affected the revolutionary strategy and tactics adopted by these female socialists. Faith not in the individual leader but in the masses themselves was the linchpin of their socialist creed—a faith that always remained much more than a slogan of their adopted ideology. All shared the idea that the masses were somehow purer than their leaders and that the only chance for the success of socialism lay in following the tendencies that the people represented. Over and over again, all used different words to repeat the same idea: the socialist movement was a mass movement; the "people" must achieve their own emancipation; the masses were the "ultimate source" of the revolution, the "rock" on which the revolution would be built.

Thus the gravest error of the Bolshevik regime, according to Balabanoff, was its treacherous betrayal of the people, those whom she had always taken to be "the chief protagonists of a collective movement" (1964:119). Rosa Luxemburg also came to despise the "tartar Marxism" of the Bolsheviks, excoriating those narrow-minded disciplinarians "who sought to play schoolmaster with the proletariat." Socialism was a mass movement, she insisted, not a private club that required blind obedience and mechanical subordination (Luxemburg 1904; 1970b:198; 1972b:154; 1972c:181–85).[10] Upon joining the Workers' Opposition, Kollontai voiced similar sentiments. The group was "wonderful," she believed, precisely because it had no prominent leaders but was the product of healthy grass-roots sentiments arising from the working classes (Kollontai 1921:5).

All five women shared the belief that real political wisdom flowed from below and not from above. So sincere was their faith in the masses and so complete their condemnation of the leader principle that all were reluctant to accept positions of leadership for themselves, even if such positions might have led to greater influence and decision-making authority. Michel refused all suggestions by the French Workers Party that she stand as a candidate for elective office. Eleanor Marx, when nominated for the presidency of a union she herself had helped to organize, announced she would not serve. Kollontai was reluctant to accept a position even at the Ministry of Social Welfare, fearing that if she did, she would become "just as stupid as all other ministers" (Beatty 1918:46). For Angelica Balabanoff, personal success always seemed of "very secondary importance." She was so hostile to "personal advertising" of any kind that she often declined even to be introduced at socialist gatherings where she was to be the principal speaker. In one of the most revealing examples of this shared hostility to leadership, Rosa Luxemburg for years refused to attend conventions of the Social Democratic Party of the Kingdom of Poland and Lithuania, which she herself had helped to found. She also spurned election to its central committee, although she remained one of the party's de facto leaders and its principal policy maker and main public voice.

How does one begin to explain these women's strong resistance to organizational and hierarchical needs in the process of making a revolution? A cynical answer would be that their hostility revealed a kind of "sour grapes" mentality, a veiled recognition that they, as women, could never quite belong or even hope to belong. This explanation, while possible, skirts the fact that resistance to power and organization was consistently apparent throughout the whole course of their lives. After breaking so painfully from traditional social expectations of their roles as women, they may have been reluctant to succumb to the strictures of another, albeit revolutionary, organization and its accompanying behavioral norms.

In what appears to be a related pattern, very few women who entered the ranks of socialist movements in the nineteenth and twentieth centuries aspired to theory-making roles. Aside from the vaunted Luxemburg, the socialist movement never produced any outstanding women theorists. Certainly, there may have been many reasons for this—women's traditional socialization, personal feelings of insecurity, the hostility of male comrades. Yet gender-based reasons could have been involved as well, related again to the different cognitive styles of men and women. Angelica Balabanoff, for example, consciously and deliberately refused to involve herself in theory making because of her humanistic convictions about what was most important. She always maintained that people, not theories, dictated the course of history, that the masses, not theorists, were central to socialism. In this process of creating class consciousness, the teacher, not the theorist, was all important. It was the teacher, not the theorist, who brought the socialist creed to the working classes, those most in need of simple—not sophisticated—propaganda. And it was a teacher, not a theorist, that Balabanoff chose to be.[11]

And a final question emerges from all this. Did their gender-based sense of intergenerational connectedness and individual human importance cause women revolutionaries to differ from men in their attitude toward human expendability in the so-called consolidating stages of the revolutionary process? Significantly, it was Rosa Luxemburg, the most renowned female socialist of all, who launched a biting attack on the Machiavellian mentality of the prototypical true believer. "Each tear that flows, when it could have been spared, is an accusation," she once wrote, "and he commits a crime who with brutal inadvertency crushes a poor earthworm" (1970a:399).

Although Lenin mocked their expectations that "one can make a revolution in white gloves" (Palencia 1947:93), Luxemburg, Kollontai, and Balabanoff were all appalled by the use of terror in the process of consolidating the revolution. Victory was anathema to them if purchased at the price of human suffering and bloodshed. Their common conviction of human importance never allowed them to accept Machiavellian notions like "revolutionary necessity" or "human expendability." Luxemburg stated unequivocally that Bolshevik defeat was preferable to moral collapse.

For much the same reasons, Angelica Balabanoff, on a trip to Israel in 1962, was quite dismayed to see women bearing arms in the nation's army. While enheartened by the tenuous equality this seemed to imply, she was more disturbed by the fact that Israeli women "were destined to kill the sons of other women" (Slaughter 1981:191–92). Women, in her view, had a special capacity to work for peace—a belief that links her to thousands of other women, past and present.

The Effect of Gender on Relationships with Male Comrades

As women, the socialists of this study devoted their lifetimes to eliminating the sexual oppression they considered endemic to the old capitalist order. Yet paradoxically, except for Kollontai, who alone theorized about the moral and sexual freedom women would enjoy under socialism, the revolutionary energies of none of the others extended in a truly radical feminist direction. While all were anxious to encourage women to participate in public life, all, even Kollontai, saw feminism as a middle-class concept and staunchly believed that women's rights were only part of a larger struggle. All accepted the standard Marxist line on the woman question: that women remain eternally separated from one another by class interests, and that only socialism, which welcomed the political participation of both men and women, was the true answer to female oppression. Rosa Luxemburg was downright hostile to feminist issues, bluntly terming work among women, or "old ladies' nonsense," a waste of time. When an editor of *Pravda* once asked her to write an article about German working women, she refused, saying it was simply "not worth the trouble."[12]

Such attitudes were curious, for all come to serve a movement that while promising women equality and emancipation was in reality rather ambivalent about their presence. Significantly, a willingness to shoulder certain kinds of peripheral tasks, like translating and clerical duties, was the easiest path to acceptance in the socialist organizations these women joined. With the exception of Louise Michel, whose language talents were minimal, all were useful to their respective movement as linguists, translators, and interpreters. While language skills were necessary to the socialist movement in the best days of its internationalism, there was a plodding, behind-the-scenes, noncreative character to such tasks, a quasi-clerical, secretarial function. Friends often remarked, for example, that Eleanor Marx proved herself to be a "proletarian in the truest sense of the word," because of the "thankless and grueling work" she was usually called upon to do (Bernstein 1897–98). She was the one who balanced the Socialist League's budget, bought window cleaner for the premises, and sold tickets for various socialist events—duties more in keeping with traditional sex role division than with her illustrious heritage (Kapp 1976:72).

It is difficult to determine whether these women came to such tasks willingly, seeing them as a way to serve the movement in whatever way they could, or whether such clerical, supportive roles were automatically and perfunctorily assigned to them as women. What is clear, however, is that those who resisted such labors—Luxemburg and Kollontai, for example—were challenged. Lenin was sharply critical of Kollontai's independent theorizing. During the height of World War I, he was quick to point out those areas in which she could be most useful: translating *his* pamphlets and various Bolshevik position papers into Swedish, Norwegin. and the other languages with which she was familiar—supportive and subsidiary roles that would guarantee her allegiance to the proper Bolshevik line.[13]

Even the brilliant Luxemburg was useful to the socialist movement as a translator and interpreter, but she was confident enough of her own abilities to put up a fight when attempts were made to limit her activities to such services alone. She was "nobody's fool," she wrote to a friend, angrily refusing German leader Karl Kautsky's request to help him organize and publish Marx's unfinished fourth volume of *Capital*. Her "help," she bitterly suspected, would consist in transcribing and in taking Kautsky's dictation, and that she had no intention of doing.[14]

Revolutionary socialism, for all its emancipatory pretensions, appears to have developed its own brand of sex role stereotyping: all five women played a symbolic and inspirational role within their movements. Serving as highly touted examples of the opportunities socialist revolution held out to women as a group, they were both necessary and useful to attract more women to the side of the revolution. This "prima donna" function that she was called upon to serve was the one Angelica Balabanoff resented most of all (1973:239).

In her memoirs, Louise Michel lamented the limited and often superficial commitment to female equality voiced by male radicals of her day. While they applauded the idea of female emancipation, they were all too often, she concluded, content "with just the appearances" (1976:109). After her death, two of her closest friends revealed that Michel had suffered silently all her life because of the condescension, ridicule, and at times outright scorn displayed by male comrades (Boyer 1927:238; Girault 1906:122, 209–11). Although during her lifetime she had been flattered and feted by socialists of various factions because of her popularity, revolutionary fervor, and remarkable oratorical talents, the situation changed after her death. Then veiled criticisms and biting innuendos came to be voiced by many of her former comrades, nagging questions raised as to her real political contributions, theoretical understanding, even mental stability. There were jokes about her theoretical ability, about the fact that in one short article she had used the same phrase seventeen times to express her hope for a better future (Nomad 1959:258). Her goodness was presented as something "bizarre and abnormal," her pity and devotion to the poor as bordering on "saintly madness" (Boyer 1927:238; Vizetelly 1911:79). Political friends like Jules Guesde (1914), Paul Lafargue (1897), and George Clemenceau (1919) questioned her theoretical acumen.

Ironically, however, those socialist women who did put forth theoretical ideas of their own often found themselves ruthlessly criticized. Although Lenin had always respected Rosa Luxemburg's intellectual ability, he was quick to assail "pompous Rosa" whenever she had the temerity to challenge his ideological authority with her "childish" and "ridiculous" interpretations of Marxism (Krupskaya 1930:161–62, 226, 327; Ulam 1968:292). Upon her death, he eagerly enumerated her errors:

> Rosa Luxemburg was mistaken over the question of Polish independence. She was mistaken in 1903 in her evaluation of Menshevism. She was mistaken in her theory of the accumulation of capital. She was mistaken when . . . she stood for the unification of the Bolsheviks with the Mensheviks in July 1914. She was mistaken in her writings from prison in 1918. (1963–70:vol. 33:210)

Most of all, she was mistaken in her "not-to-be-taken-seriously nonsense of organization and tactics as a process." Through her "disastrous" and "gross" mistakes, by her own "disorganized view of organization," she had created a "utopian radical" party but it was not a Marxist party (quoted in Waters 1970:22).[15]

The drumming Balabanoff and Kollontai received was so intense that each eventually left the Soviet Union in despair and disillusionment. Balabanoff voluntarily chose exile when she realized the new regime was a "perversion" of the Marxist spirit, a vile machine that created nothing but "hatred, horror, and illusions" (1964:30–31, 34–35; 1973:184–85, 271–72). Depressed and tormented by the use of terror, she was appalled by the callousness with which human life had come to be regarded. Not only had the Bolsheviks led rather than followed the masses, but they had created a new privileged class. The slow but steady reappearance of the hallmarks of gentility—champagne and caviar at government receptions, lavish displays of silverware and wealth, special rations and modes of transport for party leaders—all convinced her that this revolution had betrayed its socialist ideals (Balabanoff 1973:200–203, 219).

Kollontai's fall from grace was even more ignominious. Estranged from the Bolshevik hierarchy because of her involvement in the Workers' Opposition, she outraged party leaders with her pioneering attempts to define the moral and psychological changes that should take place under Communism. Communism may have freed women economically and politically, but in her view there were additional aspects to female emancipation. Boldly Kollontai attacked the centuries-old double standard that allowed free sexual expression to men but denied it to women. Calling for a new morality befitting the new society, she advocated a freer form of human love as the key to women's psychological emancipation. Although her critics were quick to accuse her of celebrating "free love," Kollontai envisioned instead a new society in which larger social and economic changes would ensure that all people would be free to love: freed from economic dependency in love; from economic concerns; and from worries about child support and child care. Women would no longer need love to establish their identity, nor would they need to fear that love itself would rob them of that identity (Kollontai 1972, 1973, 1975: 1977b:255–36).

Unfortunately, Kollontai's ideas were maligned, derided, and criticized. The Bolsheviks may have made a political revolutional in Russia in 1917, but their attachment to traditional values and practices continued. The erroneous perception that Kollontai was obsessed with sex and free love alone was considered "disgusting" by party leaders. To them, her writings "reeked of pornography and the gutter" (Kollontai 1977:205).

Above all, Kollontai's concern with sexual, moral, and psychological problems was regarded as frivolous and silly, neither serious nor worthy of discussion. Lenin himself set the tone there. In a famous interview, he attacked those "who are always absorbed in sex problems, the way an Indian saint is absorbed in the contemplation of his navel." The revolution, he decreed, "called for concentration and rallying every nerve by the masses and by the individual. . . . There must be no dissipation of energy" (Lenin 1934:101, 108).

Clearly, the conflict between Lenin and Kollontai centered on their very different perception of what was truly important, of what the human side of revolutionary creation was all about. In 1922 she accepted a diplomatic post abroad—tantamount to a sentence of exile. Separation from the field of revolution was meant as punishment for her sins.

THE LEGACY OF FEMALE SOCIALIST PROTEST

Certainly these women's treatment at the hands of the socialist hierarchy presaged the real extent of women's emancipation in the modern Communist world. Although there is no disputing that more women, percentagewise, are employed in Communist countries than anywhere else in the world, their participation in public life is not coterminous with status and power. It has been over 100 years since Eleanor Marx first joined her father's cause, almost seventy-five since Communism became a fact of modern political life, but in that time women have not entered the upper echelons of Communist Party structures, and they are still virtually absent from the top policy and decision-making organs of every Communist country (Jancar 1974:217–42).

Unlike Lenin, the women of this study led no successful revolutions. Their greatest strength was their personal conception of socialist salvation, their desire to live the words of the creed they professed, to reach out and touch the masses in their misery. Each of these women knew and sensed in her own way that the crux of socialism was much more than organization—as Lenin often said (Krupskaya 1959:498; Lenin 1975:301)—or the seizure of political power, but that it was about sacrifice and spirit, caring and sensitive passion, touching people's lives as people. Years before Yugoslavian Communist Milovan Djilas (1957) reaped fame and renown for his condemnation of the new Communist class and the movement's degeneration at the hands of bureaucrats and careerists, these women sensed this in their hearts. They knew that socialism meant the creation of a truly new and truly revolutionary human society, not the mere appearance of the old under a new label.

The women of this study left a rich legacy, as they sought to impart a humane and sensitizing undercurrent to the socialist movement of their day. In view of the paths to which Lenin's revolution has led, socialist men would have done well to heed these feminine voices of protest in their midst.

NOTES

1. There is an extensive literature on this topic. See, for example, Fourier (1841–46: vol. 1: 130–144, 147, 150; vol. 2: 212–229; vol. 5: 1–7, 258–60; vol. 6: 166–70, 225–44), Cabet (1848), Marx and Aveling (1886), and Lenin (1934).

2. For Bebel's impact on women, see Popp (1912).

3. See also comments by Bruno Schönlank in Luxemburg (1971a: vol. 1: 215).

4. Elsewhere I have treated the question of how the behavior of women revolutionaries differs from social science's standard image of the "revolutionary personality" (Mullaney 1983, 1984a, 1984b).

CHAPTER 6

Women in the Taiping Movement in Nineteenth-Century China

TIM FUTING LIAO

For centuries, Chinese women were confined to the home, excluded from any outside activities, let alone the political area monopolized by men. A first challenge to this tradition was provided by the Taiping Movement in the mid-nineteenth century. Women, for the first time, not only participated but also held offices at various levels. The following pages will analyze the role of women in the Taiping Movement. Three general theories (Jennings 1983) about factors that hinder women's political participation—the situational explanation, the structural explanation, and the socialization explanation—will be considered with respect to women's position as defined by Confucianism prior to the Taiping Movement. They will also be used to analyze women's situation during the movement, when greater equality between the sexes is reported to have been achieved.

Most authors who write about sexual equality during the Taiping years maintain that it was granted *by* men *to* women. In contrast, this inquiry into women's position in the Taiping Movement will shed light on women's *active* part in the political and military revolution.

BARRIERS TO WOMEN'S POLITICAL PARTICIPATION

Chinese women, besides being pressured by unfavorable Confucian doctrines, are subject to the same hindering factors that explain why women in any society often participate politically less than men. Women may not be a major political force because of the life situation they are in, because of the niche they are assigned to in the existing social structure, or because of the way they were taught while young. (Jennings 1983). First, the situational explanation attempts to examine the characteristics of a woman's life-space in terms of her gender roles as wife, mother, divorcee, widow, and homemaker. These roles are said to be confining and isolating in the sense that they do not allow women access to such resources for political activities as "time, money,

5. See also Michel's comments in *Commonweal*, September 26, 1891, March, 26 1892; *La Bataille*, May 1, 1883; *The Torch*, March, 18 1895.

6. Wiliam Morris's letters of August 1883 to Mrs. Burne-Jones, of August 28, 1884, and December 18, 1884, to Andreas Scheu, and of January 1, 1885, to Robert Thompson, in Henderson (1950: 180–81, 212–13, 221, 228). The "Manifesto of the Socialist League" is reprinted in *Commonweal*, February 1885.

7. Interestingly enough, the Russian revolutionary terrorist Maria Spirodonova also attributed women's failure to attain positions of political power to their greater integrity and sincerity. "Politicians are usually not very fine," she told Louise Bryant. "They accept political positions when they are elected to them, not because they are especially fitted for them. I think women are more conscientious. Men are used to overlooking their consciences—women are not" (Bryant 1918: 169).

8. See also *Le Monde*, November 28–29, 1965.

9. See also *The Sheffield Anarchist*, November 1, 1891.

10. See also Luxemburg's letters to Leo Jogiches: June 24, 1898, in Ettinger (1979: 48); August, 10 1909, in Bronner (1978: 126–27).

11. Recent research on the history of the New York City tenants' rights movement (1890–1978) reveals a similar pattern. Although women formed a numerical majority in almost all organizations at every level, men dominated the planning, theorizing, and strategizing positions (Lawson and Barton, 1980).

12. Luxemburg to Leon Jogiches, February 1, 1902, and February 1913, in Luxemburg (1971a: vol. 2: 85, 290).

13. Lenin to Kollontai: December 1914; May 22, 1915; July 11, 1915; July 26, 1915; August 4, 1915; November 9, 1915; February 17, 1917; March 5, 1917; March 16, 1917; March 17, 1917, in Lenin (1963–70: vol. 35: 177–78, 189–90, 193–94, 198–99, 200–201, 210–11, 285–87, 290–93, 295–96, 297–99).

14. Luxemburg to Jogiches, May 25, 1900, in Ettinger (1979: 101–2).

15. See also Lenin (1920: 23–25; 1971: 123–27).

contacts, organizational life, channels of communication, and the general skill levels that typically accompany high rates of political action" (Jennings 1983:364). It is argued that these roles continue to inhibit women's political participation, even when women break out of them, since they cannot shake off their roles entirely and must perform the old roles along with the new ones.

The structural explanation goes beyond a woman's life-space and extends to the sphere of social structure. The educational, economic, and legal institutions, as the foundation of the society, are so constructed that they deny women the opportunities, benefits, and protection that are given to men. Women therefore occupy structural niches different from men's. For example, differences between the sexes with regard to advanced education and occupations are substantial. The social system in all countries still considers women as de facto, if not de jure, second-class citizens. These structural obstacles prevent women from becoming politically involved.

The last explanation suggested by Jennings is the socialization theory. This hypothesis explains the differential performance of men and women by going farther back into the causal chain. The argument is that males and females, before adulthood, not only are socialized into different participative roles, but also learn that adult political participation is more a male than a female activity. It is suggested that these norms, when learned early in life, cause women to resist greater political involvement, even if there is later encouragement and if the situational and structural factors favor such reform.

These hypotheses should not be taken as mutually exclusive. Each has an element of truth and can explain women's less frequent political activity: the various social and institutional forces identified here are interrelated. In fact, each of these hypotheses offers a different perspective from which factors that inhibit female political participation can be examined because very often all factors operate simultaneously. It cannot be said that one factor is the cause of another. It is true that political roles are inculcated in the young through the process of socialization. Yet on the other hand, situational and structural explanations enable us to see other ways in which society influences female political participation. Therefore, each of the three hypotheses will be used to analyze women's political participation before, as well as during, the Taiping Movement.

CONFUCIANISM AND WOMEN

The legacy of the Chinese philosopher and educator Confucius (ca. 551–479 B.C.) became a major component of Chinese culture. Confucianism served as the state ideology for the Chinese for about 2,400 years, throughout the feudal dynasties. Even in contemporary China, where the state ideology is Marxism rather than Confucianism, Confucian ideology is so deeply ingrained in people's minds and in cultural traditions and practices that to a certain extent it still governs behavior.

More important for our considerations, Confucianism is the chief source of sexual discrimination in China. It defines the inferior status of women as heaven-ordained. According to Confucius, "Women and inferior men are hard to get along with. They get out of hand when befriended and they resent it when kept at a distance" (quoted in Lin 1976:345–46). Later dynasties saw Confucianism developed into more systematic rules. For instance, Tung Chung-shu[1] explained Confucian doctrine in his Three Cardinal Guides, "the sovereign guides the minister; the father guides the son; the husband guides the wife" (quoted in Lin 1976:346). Here the superior–inferior relationship between male and female is more clearly defined. Likewise, the Chinese woman's status in successive dynasties was so depreciated that she was not only a second-class citizen, but also a lesser human being deprived of all personal freedom, including political expression.

Confucian doctrine regarding women's position is harsh, and it permeates all spheres of the society. Compared with her contemporary Chinese sisters, a woman in Confucian China did more housework, all of which was her duty. Moreover, her position in the family was qualitatively different from that of her present-day counterparts in that she was not even entitled to the de jure sexual equality that they enjoy today. In other words, taking good care of house chores was a virtue for women, as one of the Confucian Four Virtues stated. Consequently, a woman in the Confucian society not only held her life-space entirely within the home, but was revered for accepting this restriction. Stated differently, pursuing objectives, whether political or apolitical, was far from being a virtue for women. And political participation on the part of women was out of the question. Compared with contemporary women again, women in the old days differed not only quantitatively in terms of institutionalized disadvantages, but qualitatively as well because women had neither educational nor occupational opportunities.

The denial of female scholarly and vocational participation was justified by Confucianism, as seen in a maxim concocted out of this Confucian credo at the end of the Ming dynasty (1368–1644): "In woman, lack of talent is itself a virtue" (quoted in Lin 1976:346). In accord with this ideology, women were excluded from civil examinations, which were given annually only to men at the county, provincial, and national levels. These examinations, in turn, functioned as the only route to scholarly accomplishment and government offices. Although women could presumably study literature and history at home, scholarship, government, and all trades were apparently regarded as a male business. Above all, the political arena was confined to men.

Confucianism attaches great importance to moral education, and Confucian ideas were taught to children at an early age. The teaching of virtues, above all, is the essence of Confucian moral education. Yet these Confucian virtues subordinate women to men—the set of virtues for women defines female obedience and inferiority to the male. The most important virtues for women were known as the Three Obediences and the Four Virtues. The Three Obediences states that a woman must obey her father before marriage, her husband upon marriage, and her oldest son upon widowhood, and the Four Virtues required women "to know their place and act accordingly, to avoid loquaciousness or boring others, to adorn themselves for the pleasure of the opposite sex, and to perform household chores with diligence and skill" (Lin 1976:346). As a consequence, women in Confucian China were socialized into a very special set of behavioral roles defined for women only. These participative roles restricted women from taking part in any type of political activities, which were men's affairs.

Therefore, for over two millennia Chinese women were kept out of political affairs entirely, as their whole life-space was limited to the home; their chances for achievement in occupations were absolutely nonexistent; and their inculcated virtues kept telling them from deep within that both the situation that held them at home and the institutionalized biases that denied them any economic, political, and legal rights were the most necessary, most natural things. This held true for the vast majority of Chinese women for eons (the few exceptions being empresses or concubines, who on occasion obtained tremendous political power), until the Taiping women threw themselves into the thick of their movement in the mid-nineteenth century. It was through this movement that they first gained some equality on many of the issues that were impossibilities for their female predecessors.

THE TAIPING MOVEMENT

The Taiping Movement was a peasant uprising against the government of the Qing dynasty. It started in Jintian, the cradle of the Taipings, in southwestern China in 1850. There an organization called "God Worshippers' Society" was founded and grew. The members of this society accepted a new religious faith in a personal God and his guidance not only for personal salvation, but also for all other daily economic, social, and political matters—a faith quite contrary to traditional beliefs in China (Michael 1966). The society gradually attracted more and more believers who had felt suffocated by the old order in China, and they became increasingly rebellious. The society played a critical role in starting the Taiping Movement. Over time, the Taiping Movement came to control large areas in southern China, especially the Yangtse River region; it took over Nangking, a major city on that river, establishing there the capital of Taiping Tianguo, or the Heavenly Peace Kingdom. The movement was stamped out by government troops and the intervention of the British and French imperial powers in 1864.

The objective of the Taiping Movement by the Chinese peasants was to overthrow the minority rule of the Manchu tyranny and reestablish the *Chinese* government. However, the movement is also well known for its achievement in enhancing the social position of women (MacFarlane 1972).

A consideration of the causes of the movement will help us understand its political meaning. The explanations for the movement, however, are very diverse, and it is difficult to sift out which factors were more important than others. The movement can be examined as a response to five conditions (Teng, 1971): a declining empire, a defeated empire, an impoverished empire, a disintegrating society, and a new religious inspiration.

The empire had been on the decline since the turn of the nineteenth century. The widely known decline in leadership fostered stagnation of scientific and industrial development, led to corruption throughout the country, and opened the way for institutional deterioration.

The Opium War[2] with Britain resulted in defeat for the empire despite its larger army and support from the anti-British militia forces in Canton. As a consequence, the Manchu military might became a "paper tiger" in the eyes of the Chinese coastal people. The empire was also defeated psychologically. Frightened by the British steamships and weapons, the leaders were willing to sign the peace treaty without reading the articles if the British agreed to withdraw their forces. Many government leaders held an irrational xenophobia as a result of this military defeat.

China could not easily recover from the Opium War because the empire was old and poor. The rapid growth of population from 182 million in 1751 to 432 million in 1851 was much faster than the increase in arable land. The situation was worsened by administrative inefficiency in the form of inequalities and loopholes in the tax system, and by frequent floods and drought from 1826 to 1850. The economy was also depressed by the imbalance of the Chinese international trade, caused primarily by the importation of opium.

The society was disintegrating in the first half of the nineteenth century in the sense that the local level of social control and popular indoctrination of Confucianism had become nominal. The basic mechanism of social control, the *pao-chia* system, whereby ten households were grouped into a *chia* for mutual surveillance under a chief who received reports of members' misconduct, existed for the most part in name only. The mechanism of inculcating the populace with Confucian ethics such as loyalty, filial piety, and respect for the law, known as the *Hsiang-yo* system, became merely a formality.

The final causative element for the revolution, according to Teng, was religious inspiration. Rebellions in Chinese history were generally linked with religious movements, such as the rise of Taoism and Buddhism. The first half of the nineteenth century saw the rapid spread of religious societies under the influence of Western missionaries and traders. Teng (1971:32) argues that the belief system of the Taipings was "an imperfectly adopted Christianity mixed with the practices of local wizards," and that religious influence played an important role in inspiring, organizing, consolidating, and encouraging the members of the God-worshiping society.

Other authors also consider religion important. The Taiping Kingdom is seen as "a transcendental Christian monarchy which starkly challenged the Confucian conception of the state as a condominium of the emperor and the literati-bureaucracy" (Wakeman 1977). The dominant ideology of the Taipings is a mixture of some Christian concepts and some Confucian ideas, according to Nakayama (1980). Two major theories challenge Teng's notion of causation: Zagoria's monsoon Asia perspective and the Maoist historical perspective (Chung 1980). According to Chung, Zagoria argued that the wetness of the Monsoon China region, sustained by the Yangtse and the Pearl, two of the best rivers for agriculture in the world, gave birth to the Taiping Movement. The region, irrigated by the two rivers in addition to abundant rainfall, made possible the cultivation of its world-famous "rice economy," characterized by intensive utilization of farmland and a dense population. However, increasing population led to land hunger and the fragmentation of landholdings. The smallholdings were weeded out, and the peasants were proletarianized. Parasitic landlordism was responsible for the process of proletarianization, which led to destabilization, and then to revolution. Some of the proletarianized and destabilized peasants were architects of the Taiping Movement. In essence, peasant unrest is correlated with economic grievances.

Unlike Zagoria's non-Marxist approach, which focuses on peasants' organizational skills, their psychological dissatisfaction, and economic conditions, the Maoist historical perspective (Chung 1980) examines the basic contradictions in the society in terms of a Marxist framework, focusing on the mode of production. In the case of a peasant movement such as the Taiping Movement, the contradictions lay within the feudal mode of production. According to this theory, inconsistency between the relations of production and productive forces gives rise to revolution, which in turn makes society evolve (from the primitive communist to the slave, to the feudal, to the capitalist, and ultimately to the socialist society). Peasants remained the fundamental revolutionary class in feudal society, because they were the exploited and oppressed. However, since they did not represent a new mode of production, peasants could not resolve these contradictions, which could be eliminated only with the leadership of the proletariat.

The Taiping Movement did not attempt to change the whole feudal mode of production, but it at least alleviated proletarianization by a land-distribution policy that entitled every individual to a share of land through the Taiping land reform. Under the policy of equalization of land, women were made eligible for land ownership, since land was distributed according to the number of people sixteen years of age or older, irrespective of sex (Cheng 1963; Shih 1967). Those fifteen years of age and younger would receive half of the amount allotted to their seniors (Michael 1966).

The broader political goals of the Taiping Movement were, first, to overthrow the Qing (Manchu) rule and restore a Chinese nationalistic regime, and second, to attack the existing social order and eliminate corrupt and exploitative practices (Jen 1973; Michael 1966). A third goal (Jen 1973) was mainly religious. The Taiping leaders, under the Christian influence brought to China by Western missionaries, sought to establish a Christian kingdom, void of all pagan idols, under one true God. The policy toward women can be seen as part of the second and the third goals—it was not only an attack on the social order, but also an attempt to realize religious ideals. Male-oriented as it is, Christianity introduced to the Taipings a way of treating women, different from the traditional, with a little more, albeit superficial, equality. The equality between the sexes under Taiping is reported to have sprung from their Christian belief that all men were brothers and all women were sisters before God (Jen 1973; Teng 1971).

Women were given equal opportunity for education and allowed to take part in civil examinations, which had been open to men only (Lin 1976; Teng 1966, 1971). Women also were eligible to hold civil positions and military ranks equivalent to men's (Lin 1976; Teng 1966, 1971). They also participated in military affairs in their own units (Lo 1979), although Michael (1971) argues that these units were rarely used in combat and were, instead, assigned to other duties such as weaving.

The dehumanizing unhealthy practice of footbinding was banned under Taiping (Lin 1976; Lindley, 1970; Lo 1979; Teng 1966, 1971). Prostitution was totally forbidden, as was the selling of the bride (Lin 1976; Teng 1966, 1971). Marriages were generally supposed to be love matches (Teng 1966). The feudal practice of the double standard of marriage for male and female—namely monogamy as a requirement for women and polygamy as a choice for men— was abolished. Instead, monogamy for men and women was promoted (Lin 1976; Teng 1971); concubinage was banned.

In short, it is said that women in the Taiping Kingdom experienced unprecedented emancipation, owing to practices of sexual equality, which they enjoyed for the first time in Chinese history (Lin 1976; Teng 1971). This enabled women to participate in revolution and production alike (Lo 1979). There appears to be consensus among authors of the Taiping literature that women were emancipated from the previous sexual inequality.

Analysis

While it is undoubtedly true that women were treated more nearly equally than ever before, and that the sexual equality implemented under Taiping was one of the greatest achievements of the movement, there is an uncomfortable undertone to this consensus about how equality between the sexes was achieved. That is, according to most sources it was the Taiping policy, promulgated by the top leaders, who were male, that *gave* women rights not previously enjoyed. Women are depicted as receivers of equal status, with men the givers of this benefaction. A male-oriented approach can be observed in the work of most authors writing on the subject, implicitly in some and explicitly in others. For example, according to Lindley (1970:301), a participant-observer of the Taiping Movement from the West also known as Lin-Le, the Taipings abolished "the horrible custom of cramping and deforming the feel of *their* women" (emphasis added). For Teng (1971:409), "*They* encouraged monogamy among the people, prohibited footbinding, and allowed female suffrage, appointing women as commanders" (emphasis added). Thus for most authors, it is men who raised women's status to a par with their own.[3] The question for us now is to ascertain whether men, as the top leaders, *ever* practiced sexual equality and really imparted to women the right of political participation for the sake of equality.

TAIPING MEN AND SEXUAL EQUALITY

The position of Taiping women will be examined according to the three hypotheses discussed earlier to see if they were really treated with equality by men and if factors inhibiting female political activities were truly removed. The following analysis will cast doubt on the men-granted equal status of women and demonstrate that sexual equality under Taiping was not an end but a means utilized by the leaders to achieve their political goals.

First, Taiping women were able to get politically involved, because their life-space had been totally altered. The Heavenly Peace Kingdom was well-known for its separation of men and women—males and females lived in separate camps and quarters, governed by officers of their own sex, and no contact was permitted between the sexes (Jen 1973; Michael 1966). The penalty for disobeying the rule of sexual separation was once extremely rigid—capital punishment was enforced (Callery and Yvan 1969; Michael 1966). This separation of sexes is described as women's being deprived of their family, when separated from their husbands, brothers, or sons (Clarke and Gregory 1982). Apparently, the destruction of the family altered women's life-space, freed them from the former roles as wife, mother, and homemaker, and thus made possible their military and political participation.

However, sexual separation was not intended by the top Taiping leaders, who were all men, to emancipate women from their traditional roles. It was decreed that sexual relations were sinful and that chastity was God's commandment, because all men and women were brothers and sisters (Michael 1966; Teng 1971). Although based on religious doctrine, this rule was in practice an enforcement of military discipline, too (Michael 1966). The fact that the top leaders did not intend to free women from their traditional fetters is revealed by Hong's conception of women's roles. He, the Heavenly King, initiated and led the Taiping Movement. In one of his proclamations he stated:

> I hereby inform you, ministers and people, that it is proper to make a distinction between men and women. Men are to manage outside affairs; it is not proper that they hear what goes on within. Women are to manage internal concerns; it is not proper that they hear what goes on without. (Michael 1971: vol. 2: 110)

His attitude toward women is by all means surprisingly inconsistent with his posture as liberator of women. If we examine the concept of woman's roles held by Liang, Hong's major ideological source, we see that Liang believed women should be quiet, obedient, and not mettlesome. This attitude is consistent with Hong's conception of woman's roles.

Did the Taiping leaders remove the institutional obstacles to women's political participation? From the previous section, we know that women were able to hold official positions and to take the examinations that were required of candidates for government posts.

Closer examination demonstrates that the removal of structural barriers for women's political involvement was only superficial. It is true that there were women officers. These positions, however, could not be held by males, because the officers that governed the women's camps also had to live there, and the Heavenly Rules stipulated that no men could enter the women's camps. Similarly, although it has been reported that women were allowed to take the civil examinations, which were the annual tests for selection of public officials, there was reportedly only one such examination really administered for women (Michael 1966). Besides, it is doubtful if there ever were examinations for women equivalent to men's. No official Taiping literature has reported that any such examinations were held, and the examinations for women reported by non-Taiping sources might be tests at the Institute for Women to select palace attendants or to find women with special skills (Jen 1973). Therefore, there is no evidence at all that the Taiping leaders ever removed the institutional obstacles to the political involvement of women.

Taiping men also did not attempt to modify traditional socialization into gender roles. *Ode for Youth,* an official publication known to exist in three very similar editions published in the early Taiping years of 1851, 1852, and 1853, was a book written especially for children, proposed to replace Confucian classic counterparts. This work (Michael 1971: vol. 2) is composed of verses on a person's duties to God, to Jesus, and to parents, duties of various family members, and of married men and women. It also includes rules of general behavior. Amazingly, although this work was supposed to replace the Confucian classics, it defined women's roles in identical ways as Confucianism had. For instance, the wife is obliged to obey father, husband, and son, and women in general are to stay at home. Obviously, these roles for women are the very same as the Confucian virtues.

All in all, the socialization practices that inhibited female political participation remained unchanged for the Taiping girls. Under the surface, the structural barriers lingered on, for there was no intention to remove them, and any unintended removal was very limited. Similarly, the destruction of the family was not meant by the Taiping leaders to emancipate women from the traditional life-space but to keep them away from promiscuity, or even from sexual relations within marraige. Therefore, the Taiping leaders never attempted, nor did they intend, to give women equality and free them from barriers to female political participation.

Examined closely in the three aspects of situational, structural, and socialization inhibiting factors for female political involvement, sexual equality under Taiping appears inconsistent at best. That is, an inconsistency exists between the equality women actually enjoyed and the intentions of the male Taiping leaders. Stated differently, despite the unprecedented military and political involvement among Taiping women reported by various sources, there was no real attempt by men to give equality to women.

The inconsistency can be accounted for by the leaders' use of equal status as a means to achieve their political goal of overthrowing the corrupt Manchu regime rather than as a goal in itself. Two examples will further demonstrate this point. First, the Taiping leaders' lack of intention to liberate women can be inferred from their retention of the Confucian attitude toward women. Women were expected to follow the Confucian Three Obediences, as advocated in *Ode for Youth.* Other evidence is found in the poems by Hong, the Heavenly King (Michael 1971: vol. 2). Hong wrote these poems to establish authority over women in his palace. He emphasized their obedience to him and urged them to serve him with true hearts in order to fulfill their religious duties. The ban on polygamy did not apply to the kings. Most sources report that the Taiping kings were the only men under Taiping permitted to have concubines. Nakayama (1980) argues that Hong attempted to establish the Taiping Kingdom as a large family, with himself as the father and head. Equality at the individual level, achieved in part by equal distribution of land, served to achieve this political ideal of the big family of brotherhood and sisterhood (Nakayama 1980).

Second, the separation of the sexes that freed women from their traditional life-space and enabled them to hold positions was needed in order to achieve military aims. It is reported that women's camps were dissolved and the women were married off in the later years of the Taiping period (Teng 1971). The change of women's units from women's camps to women's quarters to sisters' quarters[4] over time shows that the project to separate sexes and to dissolve the family evolved according to changing military aims (Nakayama 1981). Both of the above aspects help demonstrate that the Taiping men as the top leaders did not attempt to give women equal status, but used some measures of equality between the sexes to achieve their political as well as military goals.[5]

TAIPING WOMEN AND SEXUAL EQUALITY

More importantly, the inconsistency between the male Taiping leaders' intention and sexual equality in reality, found when the three sources of inhibition of female political participation are examined, can be corroborated by women's performance in the Taiping Movement. Given the notion that political expression and revolution were considered to be within a male's sphere, women's political participation could easily have been underrepresented in documents, Western and Manchu reports, and the literature of the Taiping Movement. However, if we string together the facts found in the literature, an argument can be made that women's part in the movement was more assertive and active than usually portrayed. The image of women's role in the movement becomes drastically different. This can be demonstrated in three ways.

First, men did not initiate the abolition of the practice of footbinding. Some women unbound their feet prior to the movement. The presence of women with "large" (i.e., normal) feet in the Taiping army is referred to in various sources (e.g., Lo 1979; Shih 1967). These women with normal feet participated in the revolution and became an indispensable part of the Taiping forces. Of course, only *some* women had unbound feet before the movement started. But it is important to recognize that not every woman entered the 1850s with bound feet. In fact, there were regional, class, and age differences in regard to footbinding.

There was a north–south difference. Explicit examples, both in words and in illustrations, of normal-footed women in areas of Fujian, Guangdong, and Hong Kong abound in personal accounts of the Taiping Movement by Lindley (1970) and Scarth (1972). Also, women from Guangxi, especially those living in mountain regions, had feet of natural size (Lo 1979; Shih 1967). Obviously, many women in southern China, even though not involved in the movement, already had normal feet. This first group of women in the Taiping forces came from this part of China, mainly Guangxi. The Taiping army marched north, controlled large areas along the Yangtse River, and told adults and children alike to unbind their feet. However, this does not mean that all women of the Yangtse area had small, bound feet at that time. Some of them might already have had feet of natural size. Callery (1969) reported that one of the two Nangking girls he saw in Canton had her feet compressed, while the other had hers in the natural state. On the whole, women in southern China, such as in the areas of Guangxi, Guangdong, and Fujian, were more likely to have natural-size feet prior to the movement, whether having ever been bound or not, than females from areas farther north.

Moreover, there was a class difference in the practice of footbinding. Women of lower social class, such as peasants, were more likely to have feet of natural size. For instance, both boat girls in one of Lindley's (1970) illustrations have normal feet, and the five country women from Fujian in one of Scarth's (1972) illustrations have normal, unbound feet; one of these women, obviously a female laborer, carried two baskets with a shoulder-pole. In Lo's (1979) account, the Taiping women in the forces were chiefly from Guangxi, where they had worked in the fields and were able to climb mountains. Laboring women from the lower social class were likely to have normal feet, since footbinding would make their work almost impossible.

In addition, there is a generational difference in the practice of footbinding. It seems that the practice of footbinding had lost some popularity by the 1850s, independently of the effect of the Taiping policy. In Scarth's (1972) description, it appears that around 1850 the older women might have bound, deformed feet, while the younger ones might have natural-size feet. So it is clear that not all women were fettered by the feudal practice of footbinding before the movement. Younger women as well as laboring women in the south, some of whom joined the movement, were likely to have normal feet.

Second, the Taiping women's political participation is demonstrated by their role in military affairs. Large numbers of women were involved in the forces. Michael (1971) reports that the women's army consisted of five groups: forward, rear, left, right, and central—each with eight units. In total, there were forty units in the women's army. According to another source (Shih 1967), women officers in their army occupied 5 ranks: 40 women corps commandants, 40 women corps superintendents, 40 women corps generals (each army included 2,500 women soldiers), 1,000 women lieutenants (each in charge of 100 soldiers), and 4,000 women sergeants (each in charge of 25 women soldiers). There appear to have been 100,000 women in their army. Despite the real possibility of underenrollment, the number is amazing. Some of the women's forces actually took part in battles, although there has been controversy about the extent to which they were used. Meadows (1972) reports that two detachments (about 2,000 soldiers in each) led by two female chiefs joined Hong and served as outposts. In an 1852 proclamation, Hong beseeched both male officers and female officers to exterminate the demons with joy, firmness, majesty, and courage (Michael 1971). It is beyond question that Hong understood the importance of the female forces, although his attitude toward women was still Confucian.

The degree of activism in women's political participation becomes more obvious if we take into account the courage and valor with which women fought. It is reported that women fought on horseback, some clad beautifully, helping men defeat the Qing forces (Shih 1967). And during all the Taiping progress from Guangxi to Nanking, "the women fought by the side of the men, and conducted themselves as bravely" (Clarke and Gregory 1982:88). It has been reported also that a woman commander "led several hundred women soldiers and climbed the city wall, braver and fiercer than the men," when the Taiping army captured Chen-chiang (Shih 1967:62). In short, that the Taiping women in great numbers fought the corrupt Manchu government with courage shows they were not forced or required to fight but were assertive in action. In other words, their equality in terms of political participation was not given by men, but was of their own determination.

Third, the Taiping women did not hesitate to express their criticism of Confucianism, especially Confucian doctrine about women's roles. At the Taiping metropolitan examination for women, Fu Shan-Hsiang, noted for her beauty and literary talent, won first place (Michael 1971). The subject of the examination, different from the religious topics for men, was Confucian doctrine about the inferiority of women, a chapter from the Confucian classics (Chen 1944). More than 200 women took the civil examination that was open only to men before. Fu refuted the Confucian idea that women and mean men are difficult to get along with by demonstrating the contributions of many women, throughout history, to their husbands' career success (Shih 1967). While I have not located descriptions of other women's reactions, it is quite likely that some offered similar, albeit perhaps less eloquent, criticism of the Confucian doctrine.

In sum, women criticized the Confucian attitudes toward them, either by words, as Fu did at the examination, or by action, as many women did in the forces; participated in political as well as military affairs courageously; and often freed their feet themselves. However, the Taiping women's initiative was utilized and further channeled by male leaders to achieve their political goals, precisely because women were a sizable force to be reckoned with for military and productive purposes alike. They were especially needed in the early years of the movement. The examples used in this analysis of women's active participation in the movement are, of course, far from exhaustive, because of the paucity of data about the Taiping women. We can hypothesize that the types of activity described do not constitute all the ways in which women expressed themselves politically. There must be more than meets the eye—or than has been recorded by male-oriented historians.

CONCLUSION

The Taiping Movement as a political movement raised some important issues: it proposed a version of Christianity as an alternative to Confucianism as the state ideology; it pursued a grass-roots approach to economic policy, as in the equalization of landholdings; it reputedly employed a policy toward women that awarded them unprecedented equal status. However, that policy never removed the many situational, structural, and socialization obstacles to the political participation of women. Thus it cannot be said that women actually gained equality. The Taiping policy of equal rights for women was nominal because the Taiping leaders used it as a means to achieve their political and military goals, rather than as an end in itself. And their slogan "all men are brothers and all women are sisters" on the surface granted equal status to every person, but in essence differentiated "sisters" from "brothers"—or subordinated women to men, to be exact.

This study does not condemn the Taiping policy toward women for failing to give women full equality. The policy still surpassed that of any previous government with respect to sexual equality. Rather, this paper demonstrates that the Taiping women, although not given full access to political participation by men, actively and enthusiastically participated in the movement. Most significantly, the Taiping women's active political participation broke the still water of sexual inequality in China; their activities gave great momentum to later movements. The Red Lantern girls and the Blue Lantern widows in the Boxer uprising around 1900, who also had unbound feet but were more autonomous than their Taiping sisters, can be considered the first truly liberated women in China (Liao 1981). And the Taiping women can be referred to as the first liberating Chinese women. Even though, unlike their sisters about 140 years later, they were not really aware that sexual equality was a political issue and a basic human right, they did attack the inequality with action. Another movement, the May Fourth Movement in 1919, had more sophisticated anti-imperialist goals. Yet some of its goals, such as the equality of men and women in admission to universities and employment (Teng 1980), had already been attempted and, to a greater extent, achieved by the Taiping women in terms of the scale of the movement and the range of various civil and military offices that women held. This occurred even though the earlier group of women lacked a theoretical ideology that the May Fourth women possessed.

The Taiping women's activities will become more significant if we take another issue into consideration. The norms of political expression and behavior available are not generic, but male specific (Githens 1983). Gender-related research will be limited in its conceptual framework until we abandon Georg Simmel's equation "objective = masculine" (quoted in Githens 1983:474). In other words, our vision will be obscured if traditional male definitions of the political sphere are used to measure female political behavior. In effect, the Taiping women's unbinding of their feet was a political expression in itself. The behavior was a revolutionary manifesto against the feudal tradition. More importantly, a similar expression of behavior cannot be found among men because of their already advantageous status. Examining the situation of the Taiping women, it becomes clear that if male political behavior falls mainly into the public sphere, female political participation covers more. Women have a long way to go to catch up from their inferior status with men. At least until then, the criteria used to judge men's political behavior may not be used for women and cannot be employed for the Taiping women.

NOTES

1. The proper name for a person is spelled either as it appears in the source or as is widely accepted, either in the Wade-Giles system or in the *pinyin*, the Chinese phonetic symbols. The names of cities are presented in the Wade-Giles system, the form in which they are better known, while the names of provinces and regions are in the *pinyin*.

2. The Opium War (1839–1842), which marked the first Chinese campaign against drugs, was waged by the Chinese officially in an effort to stop large-scale opium trafficking and selling by the British. Tension became acute, and the British and Chinese fleets exchanged fire when Lin Tse-hsu, a well-known patriotic official, confiscated and destroyed the opium held by foreign firms. The British military superiority and the inability of the Chinese government to negotiate ended the Opium War in unequal treaties. The Opium War was the first clash between the Chinese and the West, a foreshadowing of what was to come as the Taiping Movement.

3. It has been argued that the Taiping Movement never raised the concept of sexual equality in the sense we share today (Rong 1983).

4. Women's camps, which existed in the Taiping progress from Guangxi to Nanking when the Taiping forces conquered the city, were units with a mainly military function; women's quarters were less military in nature, since they sheltered both fighting units and the women the forces protected after conquering a city; sisters' quarters differ from the other two in that they housed women no longer under the rules of sexual separation (Nakayama 1981).

5. It is true that unfavorable intentions may have favorable effects. Doubtless, the Taiping women had more equality than before. However, most writers of the Taiping literature fail to differentiate male leaders' roles and intentions from actions of ordinary women in the Taiping Movement or to recognize women's initiative in it.

CHAPTER 7

The Women Workers' Movement: First-Wave Feminism in Pre-State Israel

DAFNA N. IZRAELI

The Zionist women's movement in Palestine developed within the socialist Zionist movement as a reaction to the disappointment of a small group of women with the limited role they were assigned in the emerging society. From its beginnings in 1911, the movement aimed to expand the boundaries of the Jewish woman's role in Palestine and to secure her full and equal participation in the process of Jewish national reconstruction. Members of the movement were nationalists and idealists who had come as pioneers from eastern Europe during the years 1904 to 1914, and they were joined by women who arrived in Palestine after World War I, from 1919 through 1923. These periods, known in the history of Zionism as the second and third waves of immigration (*aliya*), are considered the formative periods of Israeli society. During the second wave, the dominant values of the society were formulated and the rudiments of new organizational forms appeared. During the third wave, goals were implemented and major institutional structures took shape (Bein 1954; Eisenstadt 1967; Shapira 1976).

Because they were marked by social creativity, readiness for experimentation, and remodeling of institutional forms, these periods were also crucial for the status of women in the new society. Many of the obstacles to a restructuring of sex roles were reduced, and conditions were favorable for redefining traditional role relations between men and women. That equality of the sexes was achieved during the second wave and that women played a role of importance are two of the founding myths of Israeli society. Although the career of Golda Meir and the conscription of women into the army are often invoked to lend credence to these ideas, and to link the idealized past with the present, the "facts" of the case have never been subject to systematic investigation.

While this account is a study of a specific place, time, and circumstance, it highlights dilemmas that commonly confront women in socialist movements

Reprinted with permission from a slightly longer version that appeared in *Signs* 7, no. 1 (1981):87–114. © 1981 by The University of Chicago. All rights reserved. Some notes have been omitted in this version.

generally, especially during periods of economic and political upheaval. At such time, the commitment of a movement's participants tends to be heavily taxed, and the demand for undivided loyalties is great. Identification with a larger movement creates a set of constraints on the development of feminist ideology and on the genesis of a separate feminist organization, particularly when feminist dissatisfaction is directed toward the position of women within the movement itself (Slaughter 1977). These constraints, and their consequences for the career of the feminist movement in Palestine, are the major themes of this paper.

BACKGROUND

Modern political Zionism developed in Europe and America in the last decades of the nineteenth century. The World Zionist Movement and its organizational arm, the World Zionist Organization, established in 1897, served as umbrella structures incorporating a variety of social and political ideologies for which the rebuilding of Zion was the binding element. The Palestinian women's movement developed within Labor Zionism, which was inspired by radical socialist ideas then gaining momentum in Russia. The Labor Zionist groups, based in the cities and towns of what was formerly the Russian empire, professed an egalitarian ideology.

Although Labor Zionism was ideologically committed to social equality it did not concern itself with the issues of women's emancipation. One explanation may lie in socialist theory: if the elimination of exploitive relationships automatically results in women's emancipation, then within the new society in Palestine women's emancipation must be assured. A more persuasive explanation, however, is that the Zionist movement defined the problem of Jewish existence as the fundamental and overriding social issue to which all efforts had to be directed. As Eisenstadt (1967:3) suggests: "The Zionist ideology assumed that the Jews would not be able to participate fully in the new modern societies and would become, despite their assimilation, an alien element. . . ." Jewish feminists were told that the Jewish women "must bear in mind that even those [non-Jewish] women fighting for [feminist] emancipation view her first not as a woman, but as a Jewess."[1] But, for whatever reason, within the Labor Zionist movement sexual equality was taken for granted, and the value of equality between men and women in early political Zionist ideology was institutionalized in the socialist movement through the integration of the sexes in the various groups and activities prior to immigration to Palestine. Since the subordination of women in society was not defined as a condition requiring special action, no legitimation existed for specialized institutional arrangements for its change. Women's experience in Labor Zionist groups prior to immigration created a set of expectations that later conditioned their reaction to what they encountered in Palestine.

The pioneers of the second wave emigrated from Russia following the pogroms that took place in 1903 and after the October revolution in 1905. The immigrants consisted primarily of middle-class young, single people or young couples without children or parents. In a new country, the usual restraints and obligations that bind women to domestic roles and traditional definitions of their domain were reduced, so that women were free to experiment with alternative roles. Furthermore, there are indications that these women composed a self-selected group that had "liberated" itself from the effects of traditional socialization. The move to Palestine required determination and idealism from all the immigrants, but even more so from the women. They had to combat the stronger social control traditionally exerted by parents over daughters, the stigma attached to a single woman leaving home (especially in the company of a group of men), as well as the physical hardship of the passage itself. It is not surprising that women constituted only about 30 percent of the total immigrants to Palestine, many of whom joined the religious communities in the holy cities. Among the minority who came to live productive lives as laborers—those whose initiative, energy, and ideological fervor were the dominant force for change in the structure of the Jewish community—the proportion of women was even smaller (Gorni 1975).[2]

Women came to Palestine ready to participate more fully in social life than they had been permitted to do in Jewish bourgeois circles in Russia. In the words of Sara Malchin (1912:14), a founder of the women's movement: "These young women Zionists dreamed of engaging in battle and sacrifice for the ideal of redemption, even while still in the diaspora."[3] They did not expect to struggle for women's place; they thought equality would be an accompanying feature of their move to the new homeland.

YEARS OF INCUBATION, 1904–1911

Among the two most important cultural creations of the second wave were the image of the ideal pioneer—the *halutz*—and the ideal form of social organization—the *kvutza* (forerunner of the kibbutz (Eisenstadt 1967:17). *Halutz* literally means "member of the vanguard," one who goes before the camp and fulfills its highest purposes. These include a readiness for personal sacrifice made necessary by the persistent dangers of working in the malaria-infested swamplands and of defending the young collectives from attack by Arab marauders, belief in a return to the biblical state of farming the land, and dedication to manual work. During the second wave, physical work was idealized and elevated to a religious value. These key elements of the *halutz* ideal had an essentially masculine character, which heightened the relevance of biological differences between the sexes.

The most urgent problem facing the new immigrants upon their arrival in Palestine was employment. In vain they knocked at the doors of the established farmers of the first wave (1881–91), who were unwilling to substitute Jewish labor for the cheaper, more experienced, and amenable Arab labor. Women faced greater obstacles than men. The first-wave farmers considered their insistence on having "men's jobs" "unnatural." They stigmatized and ostracized the women and forbade their own daughters any contact with them. Those who were less antagonistic feared for the women's safety. Any girl doing man's work in the vineyards might be considered easy prey by the Arab laborers, unaccustomed to such license from "respectable" women. Faced with unemployment and filled with a desire to establish a new type of Jewish society, the second wave rejected as unsuited to their purpose the existing socioeconomic structures developed by their forerunners. They moved north to the barren lands of the lower Galilee, drained the swamps, and established a new type of communal life—the *kvutza*, a small collective settlement in which everyone labored.

Two of the guiding principles of the new settlement were "conquering the land," that is, making it arable for Jewish farmers, and economic self-sufficiency (Bein 1954:53). The *kvutza* was a pragmatic solution for the pioneers who faced the problem of "how to organize some form of settlement for young people with strong socialist and nationalist aspirations, without capital and with little experience and know-how . . ." (Eisenstadt 1967:20). This form of living very quickly became a normative ideal.

In the *kvutza'* the women were automatically assigned to the kitchen and the laundry. It seems that among the men and many of the women the conscious rebellion against the traditional occupational structure of Jewish society did not extend to women's work. It remained part of the "world taken for granted" that domestic work was the woman's responsibility (Even Shoshan 1963: vol. 2: 196–97). The attitude of the men is described by one of the women pioneers in an article that appeared in the Socialist Party newspaper at the time:

> Many [of the workers] believed that the role of the young female idealist coming to Palestine was to serve them. The young women, who were still inexperienced, submitted to this view and believed that in cooking and serving they were solving most of our questions [concerning our role] in Palestine. The young woman who dared to doubt this assumption was considered strange. (Liberson 1913:11–12)

It is ironic that the women should have been expected to perform domestic tasks, which in their former homes usually had been the responsibility of domestics. They were poorly equipped for the jobs they were expected to fill so "naturally" and doubly frustrated because the roles for which they had hoped were denied them. Although the men had been neither farmers nor watchmen prior to immigration, it was assumed natural for them to undertake these "manly" roles. Plowing and loading crops were considered too strenuous and even harmful for women, a situation reflected in the following statement:

> My first six weeks in Palestine I worked in Degania [a *kvutza* established in 1909]. I listened with such admiration as the men spoke of their work tools and sounded the names of corn yields. My soul yearned to be in contact with the soil, to work the land, but that was not granted me, nor to any other women. (Shidlovsky 1964)

Since the training men received from professional agronomists in Palestine was usually not extended to women, the "ability gap" between the sexes widened. Economic considerations also encouraged the perpetuation of a traditional division of labor between the sexes. The newly formed communes were dependent on the World Zionist Organization, which had yet to be convinced that agricultural collectivism was preferable to the previous system of farms under the direction of a professional agronomist in which the pioneers were paid a wage, women paid less than men. The *halutzim* (plural form of *halutz*) had to prove that the *kvutza* was economically viable. Viewing women as less productive, they feared that their participation in agriculture would result in a deficit, and so women were confined to more "suitable" jobs. The same men who had demanded that the farmers of the first wave overlook economic considerations on ideological grounds and prefer them to Arab laborers accepted only one to three women into a *kvutza* with between ten and thirty male members on the grounds that women were economically less productive. The fact that women were so few bound them even more strictly to domestic chores because it was impossible for them to rotate between kitchen and field work. In 1909 there were 165 Jewish workers organized in *kvutzot* or workers' collectives in the Galilee, only 11 of whom were women. In 1912 there were 522 Jewish workers in *kvutzot* in Judea, 30 of whom were women. During the war years, the number of workers rose to 1,500 while the proportion of women increased to over 13 percent (200 women) (Even Shoshan 1963:213–14; Maimon 1929:27; Shapira 1961:1:226).

Domestic chores, although physical work, had low status among the pioneers who established a hierarchy of values according to both the conditions under which work was performed and the type of work engaged in. A member of a collective had higher status than someone who was an employee; "productive work," work that produced marketable goods, was deemed more valuable than "nonproductive work," such as services provided for the members of the collective. Thus cooking, laundering, and mending were not considered productive work, and they ranked low among pioneering values. Cooking for a collective held greater prestige than cooking in a private household, but it was less "worthy" than tilling the soil. Within productive work, agriculture, specifically field crops (*falcha*), became the embodiment of the *halutz* endeavor, symbolizing economic self-sufficiency as well as rejection of the pattern set by the farmers of the first wave with their dependence on Arab labor and foreign markets.

One of the unintended consequences of this pioneering ideology as well as of the new forms of social organization was that they relegated women to secondary roles in the new society. The *halutza* (female form of *halutz*) had virtually no opportunity to become a bearer of the effective symbols of the *halutz* ideology. Thus the women's dissatisfaction and growing sense of deprivation came to focus on three issues: formal status participation, and attitudes in the *kvutza*.

In these early years, women were not accorded full membership; it was taken for granted that the *kvutza* was made up of male members and the few women were helpers doing domestic work. They were not included as members in the annual contracts with the Zionist Organization, even though "they had shared the burden and dangers equally with the men" (Becker 1947:517; Bein). As Maimon (1929:91) explains, "It was argued that in point of fact the women were working for them [members of the *kvutza*], not for the Palestine Office [of the Zionist Organization] which was concerned with the farm, not with the kitchen."

In addition, the women felt deprived of the opportunity to "conquer new fields of work" through agriculture and to guard the *kvutza* as the men were doing, and they resented the restrictions placed on their participation in group decision making about the affairs of the *kvutza*. In an article, "On the Question of the Women Workers," which appeared in the workers' newspaper in 1913, Tchiya Liberson bemoaned the fact that "the men could not get used to thinking of them [the women] as real members. They did not want to come to terms with the fact that the women express their ideas freely about how matters should be handled and that they stand firm in their opinions" (Liberson 1913:27; Yanait Ben Zvi 1959:394). The problem of women's participation in group meetings was exacerbated by the fact that relatively few knew Hebrew, the language of religious instruction in the diaspora and of the pioneers in Palestine. A study of second-wave pioneers still living in Palestine in 1940 found that 60 percent of men, but only 30 percent of the women, knew Hebrew upon arrival (Gorni 1975).[4]

But the issue that most aroused the women's indignation is expressed in the Hebrew term *yachas*, which literally means "attitude" or "relation." In the context of the second wave, it referred to what women deemed degrading treatment. It combined, women argued, expressions of disregard and even derision for their yearning to work equally in the building of the country. In the words of another female pioneer:

> We young women did not encounter hardship in our work but rather in the humiliating treatment and apathetic attitude toward our aspirations. Even in the eyes of the [pioneer] laborers we were ludicrous; not only those of us who wished to destroy the natural barriers and take hold of the difficult occupations of agricultural work but even those who undertook work in which a woman is able to compete with men—even there we were ludicrous [in their eyes]. (Malchin 1912:11)

The issue of *yachas* came up most frequently in the kitchens of the communes as well as of other workers' groups. Unaccustomed to cooking, particularly with primitive utensils and unfamiliar ingredients which were, in addition, in very meager supply, the women very often produced unappetizing food. At times, when the workers preferred to be hungry rather than consume burned food, they would arrange their bowls like wagons in a train and push them along the table toward the kitchen chanting "train, train"—an act of protest on the part of the hungry pioneers but also a "degradation ceremony" for the cook (Liberson 1947:272–73).

In spite of their disappointments, however, the women pioneers in the communes of the Galilee found new hope in occasional incidents. For example, in 1908 at Sejera, a small group of farm laborers decided to form an independent agricultural collective. Among the members was Manya Scho-chat, a radical labor leader and known activist prior to her immigration as well as the first to promote the idea of collective settlement in Palestine. She succeeded in persuading the agronomist who managed the farm to train women to plow with a pair of oxen. Though a successful experiment, this did not seem a workable solution to the women. An alternative was found in vegetable gardening. In 1909, under the initiative and guidance of one of the members, Hanna Meizel, a trained agronomist, the women secretly planted the first garden, hidden behind a distant hill (Krigser 1947:506; Mamashi 1913; Yanait Ben Zvi 1976). The experience at Sejera, in which women proved them-selves capable of plowing, provided a sense of efficacy and justified the claim for participation in physical work, while the gardening experiment supplied a suitable model. Women could become farmers by creating new agricultural branches compatible with their physical abilities.

A women's training farm at Kineret (on the Sea of Galilee) was founded in 1910 after Hanna Meizel had obtained funds from a women's Zionist group in Germany. The timing was propitious because a group of men at the Kineret farm had established an independent *falcha* collective. Five women under the leadership of Hanna Meizel were apportioned a courtyard, a plot of land, and minimum facilities for establishing their own collective. One of them de-scribes the excitement:

> And for us too the young women, this was the beginning of a new period. Our male comrades would be only our neighbours. Their life and ours would flow along separate paths. We are receiving a separate plot of land which will be solely for our use, worked according to our own wishes and abilities. A period of splendor, what emancipation! (Blumstein 1937:816–17)

For the time being, at least, these women gave up the idea that their equality could be achieved in the mixed group.

BEGINNINGS OF THE MOVEMENT

The transformation of dissatisfied people into a social movement requires their awareness that they share a situation that is in some important respects unjust (Smelser 1963). This process of change first manifested itself in 1911 in Kineret at a meeting initiated by Hanna Meizel for the purpose of explaining her plans for the women's training farm. Although only seventeen women attended, this meeting—providing as it did the first opportunity for the *halutzot* (female plural of *halutz*) to exchange experiences, share their individ-ual grievances, and give one another moral support—laid the foundation for the emergence of a women's movement within the Labor Zionist camp in Palestine (Even Shoshan 1963: vol. 1:215). First, "the problem of the woman worker" emerged as a social reality and legitimized the establishment of a segregated organization. Once socially identified and labeled, the issue could become the basis for social action. Second, the meeting defined the goals of the movement's future, outlined the strategy for change, and identified a group of leaders among the second wave of pioneers. The ideological orientation first formulated at Kineret, and reiterated at every subsequent conference of women workers, emphasized the need for self-transformation. To achieve their goal—equal participation—women had to change themselves. As they proclaimed:

> We, the women laborers, like the men, aspire first and foremost to rehabilitate our spirit and bodies through work . . . in the field and in nature, and in this way we can rid ourselves of the habits, the way of life and even the way of thinking that we brought with us from the diaspora. (Group of Women Workers 1913).

Turner and Killian (1972:275) list three conditions as essential for a movement to follow the route of self-transformation rather than that of institutional change: a belief that widespread improvement is possible, a belief that "the state of the social order will reflect the integrity and character of individual man," and an acceptance by the people of responsibility "for their present unsatisfactory conditions." Belief in the possibility for transforming the Jewish *Luftmensch* of the diaspora into a manual worker and tiller of the soil, as we have seen, was fundamental to Labor Zionism. In defining self-alteration as their major goal, the *halutzot* adopted a stance that fit well with the dominant ideology and was, therefore, attractive. The women believed that they had the same potential as men, although for historical reasons it had remained dormant. Through training as manual workers they would overcome their passive, dependent character. Once the *halutza* proved her skill, not only would she be accepted as a full member in the *kvutza*, but men would seek her out. "At the dawn of the movement we thought that we had only to overcome the barrier of occupational training, and as for equality, it would all follow automatically," wrote Ada Maimon (1972:121), one of the leading figures in the struggle for women's equal participation.

Men were not to be blamed for women's unhappy predicament since they, too, were conditioned by habitual ways of thinking and behaving. However, since they seemed unable to understand the problem of women workers, they could not be relied on to bring about the necessary changes. Women would have to transform themselves ("The First Women Workers' Conference" 1923). An ideology oriented toward self-transformation rather than toward changing men and social institutions helped to legitimate the creation of a separate women's movement within Labor Zionism in that it avoided direct conflict with the male-dominated ideology and with the male pioneers. The network of social ties that linked the feminists of the second wave with the male leadership of the labor movement discouraged the development of a "we–they" dichotomy. A number of highly influential male comrades had encouraged the *halutzot*, and some of the women's leaders were members of the same political party and the same *kvutza*, or they shared backgrounds, friends, and relatives. These relationships put pressure on the women, who feared that their desire for separate institutional arrangements would lead to accusations of lack of trust and even of the betrayal of their male comrades. The ideology of self-transformation mitigated this danger by emphasizing the common goals of male and female pioneers: women must be helped to change so that they could contribute more effectively toward the realization of shared values.

The Kineret meeting defined the operational goals of the women's movement. The strategy was to push for the development of new agricultural branches, such as vegetable gardening, poultry, and dairy farming, that were considered "suitable for women." The women also demanded a monopoly over these areas of work, since they argued, men had many other jobs to do. Two main tactics were adopted. First, the farm at Kineret was to serve as a training center where women could learn technical skills and begin personal transformation within a supportive environment, unhampered by the presence of men. Second, in the future women would join only those *kvutzot* willing to accept at least ten of them, so that rotation between household and agriculture would be feasible (Maimon 1929:23). The former tactic aimed at achieving the goal of self-transformation; the latter, that of participation.

The women's desire for a separate organization resulted from their growing awareness that their goals could not be realized through the existing structures of Palestine's Labor Zionist movement. Because very few women were influential or active in the labor parties, they hesitated to raise their particular problems. In addition, there were always "more important" problems of survival that took priority. Nevertheless, the disregard for women's problems struck even a male observer, who found it necessary to comment on the point in a labor newspaper: "I have been in the country five years and have taken part in many workers' meetings where every conceivable subject was discussed. To my complete surprise there was one subject that was never discussed, not even in passing; the situation of our women workers" (Mamashi 1910:5). The failure to permit women to participate in the various decision-making forums of the labor movement organizations had a cumulative effect. When the agricultural union of the Galilee neglected to invite a woman representative to its fifth conference in 1914, the *halutzot* barged into their meeting and vociferously protested (Maimon 1929:52; Shapira 1961:140), but a more important result was the women's decision to convene their own conference of women agricultural workers only three months later. Thirty delegates met, representing 209 women workers ("First Women Workers' Conference" 1923). Thus the organizational arm of the women's movement was established. In the war years, the women's movement created two organizational structures: an annual conference, five of which were held between 1914 and 1918, and the women workers' committee to organize and coordinate the activities of the movement between the conferences. The leaders were not anonymous women but women linked to the inner circles of Palestine's emerging elites. Some had political experience, and according to the evidence none received monetary remuneration for her work in the women's movement.

The issues on the agenda of the various conferences were similar to those that had been raised at Kineret in 1911, although there were additions. When the *halutzot* gave birth the their first children, the problem of how to combine child care with public activities became urgent. If each woman had to care for her own children, she would have to give up many work tasks outside the home, and the gains made would be lost. Since women accepted child raising as their primary responsibility, the demand that men share in the responsibilities, while occasionally voiced, was never seriously considered. The arrival of children threatened the women's status. Mariam Baratz (1964), the first mother in the *kvutza*, describes her struggle against social pressure: "The general opinion was that I should devote all my time to my child. I objected to this with all my might. I knew that that way I would no longer be a part of the community and of everything that was happening in the group." The solution adopted was collective child care with women in the collective rotating the responsibility (Porat 1977). Women's participation in the labor movement was another issue at consecutive conferences, as women came increasingly to realize that doing agricultural work did not automatically lead to participation in the decision-making bodies either of the labor movement as a whole or even of the commune (Harari 1959:492).

The most pressing general issue for all the pioneers of the time related to employment. During the war years, the movement achieved some important successes in providing work. Women were trained on the Kineret farm and then integrated into the *kvutzot*. The shift in economic policy within the agricultural communes between 1914 and 1918 from total reliance on grain crops toward greater diversification opened new branches and thus new opportunities for women. In 1919 a drop in the price of grain and a drought accelerated the process toward diversification and self-reliance (Bein 1954:55, 164). Women joined grain-growing collectives and established a number of independent vegetable-growing collectives that successfully sold their produce in the markets (Etinger 1919:5–6). The vegetable gardens were usually situated next to the workers' public kitchens, where the women were employed as cooks. Most of the projects received modest financial assistance from the agricultural union and, through the intervention of the women workers' committee, from Zionist women's groups abroad.

The change in women's self-image and in their status within the labor movement is reflected in the differences noticeable between the first meeting at Kineret in 1911 and later conferences. At Kineret, the doors were closed to men. Those who showed up were accused of having come to ridicule or out of curiosity, and they were thought to be indifferent to the problems of the *halutzot*. At the opening session of the fifth conference held in Tel Aviv, apart from the seventy women delegates, there were a large number of invited guests, including several official male representatives of the parties and the agricultural union (Harari 1959:492; Maimon 1929). This change of policy manifests the increased self-confidence of the movement and its recognition by the pioneering community.

Although the women's movement brought about important cultural change in the norms regarding woman's role, it did not institutionalize a social structure to serve as a power center in relation to other organizations in the *Yishuv* or the World Zionist Organization (the major source of funds for the pioneers in Palestine). The women gave relatively little attention to organizational activity, partly because they were so few and partly because they accepted as their major structural referrent the agricultural unions, where they had gained official recognition. An important additional factor was that the women preferred "doing" to "organizing others." A characteristic of the second wave as a whole was that it was oriented more toward the implementation of ideals through direct participation in grass-roots activities associated with Zionist fulfillment than toward political activity. No organizational bodies were developed between the years 1914 and 1918 apart from the conferences and the elected committee. Whatever funds were obtained, whether from the agricultural union or from women's organizations abroad, were earmarked for specific employment and agricultural training projects. But these financial contributions were not institutionalized in a structural commitment of continuous support.

THE CAREER OF THE WOMEN'S MOVEMENT, 1918–1927

The end of World War I ushered in a period of developments in the *Yishuv*, where new dilemmas for the women's movement emerged. Comparing the *Yishuv* before and after World War I, Eisenstadt (1967:24) observes that "if the period of the second wave was the period of ideological emphasis, the [British] Mandate ushered in a period of stress on the formulation and practical implementation of the major goals of the *Yishuv*. . . ." The ability of the women workers' movement to implement its goals was affected by two major developments: first, the arrival of the third wave of immigrants (1919–23); second, the establishment of the Histadrut—the Jewish Federation of Labor. From the perspective of the women's movement, however, the third wave differed from the second in three respects. First, the proportion of women among all immigrants during the third wave was larger, 36.8 percent. Among the single immigrants, the proportion was 17 percent in 1920, increasing to 30 percent in 1922. Among the pioneers affiliated with the socialist movement, women made up some 17 to 18 percent, compared with approximately 10 percent during the second wave (Erez 1948:43; Even Shoshan 1963: vol. 1:400). Second, the pioneers arrived as members of different pioneering groups and social movements, most notably Gdud Avoda (Work Battalion) and Hashomer Hatzair (The Young Watchman). These were created in the diaspora and organized in communes committed to the principle of equality in production and consumption. Third, larger numbers of pioneers gravitated to the towns, where they formed part of the new urban proletariat. There, unemployment was particularly acute for women.

The period began ominously for the women's movement. The women's vegetable-growing collectives collapsed due to competition from British imports. The farm at Kineret was closed for lack of financial means. The settlement department of the Zionist Organization discontinued its support of women's farming collectives, believing that women would find their place in kibbutzim (Bein 1954:157–58; *Histadrut Hahalait* 1951:549).[5] The women's committee had failed to gain the recognition granted to other institutions of the labor movement, particularly the political parties, by the World Zionist Organization. In other words, in 1918, on the eve of the arrival of the third wave, the women workers' movement lacked its own mechanisms for coping with the new problems of unemployment and for pursuing its goals.

The new sources of employment that developed after the establishment of the mandate—rail and road construction and then building in the towns—did not welcome women. Nevertheless, women pressed for entry, and in 1922 they composed 16 percent of the total membership in construction collectives, although half of them supplied the domestic services such as cooking. The Construction Workers' Union in 1924 resolved to increase the number of women accepted into the work groups; train women in building crafts; establish work groups in the crafts suitable for women, such as floor tiling, plastering, and painting; and put women in line for suitable jobs ("Second Conference of the Construction Workers' Union" 1924:27). These resolutions, however, were never translated into a program of action.

Working in construction became the epic expression of the *halutz* ideal and a challenge to the women's movement seeking to conquer new fields, as agriculture had been for the *halutzot* of the second wave. Again, however, women faced strong opposition. Jobs were scarce. They were mainly allocated through the labor bureau of the political parties and, after 1920, through the Histadrut. Since work contracts were assigned to groups, getting a job depended on being accepted to a work group, which was difficult for women. As Tchiya Liberson (1975:176), a member of the Construction Workers' Union reported: "The men had quite a number of reasons for keeping us out. Some said the work was too strenuous for women. Others argued that if women were admitted to the building trade communes, which contracted for work as a group, the output would decrease and the pay with it."

Faced with resistance to their acceptance by male groups, and indignant at being accused of causing financial deficits, women formed their own work communes and even competed with men for job contracts (Erez 1948). In the mid-1920s, there were two women's construction groups and several floor-tiling communes, as well as tobacco and laundry collectives. The women's organization estabished a half-dozen training farms modeled on the Kineret experiment. Women also formed *havurot*—small collectives based on a combination of vegetable gardening and outside employment. Organizing, encouraging, and financing these projects were the major activities of the executive committee of the Women Workers' Council, the organizational arm of the Women Workers' Movement within the newly established Histadrut.

After World War I, there had been a trend toward unification among the labor groups in the *Yishuv* which in 1920 led to the establishment of the Histadrut umbrella organization. The trade unions, the sick fund, the consumers' union, the labor exchanges, the immigration office, the public works and building office, the schools, and the workers' public kitchens, which had been created by the political parties, were transferred to the Histadrut. The consolidation of these structures within a single organization, which controlled virtually all the resource-generating institutions of the labor movement, meant that the women's movement became dependent on the Histadrut.

Election of delegates to the founding convention of the Histadrut, held in December 1920, was by proportional representation of political parties. As the women's movement did not consider itself a political faction but viewed its goals as cutting across the ideological differences that segmented the labor movement, it did not submit a separate list of candidates and was not officially represented. Among eighty-seven delegates to the founding convention of the Histadrut, only four were women, all sent by the Achdut Haavoda Party (an extension of the Poalei Zion Party). The more committed feminists, such as Ada Fishman-Maimon and Yael Gordon, leading members of the Hapoel Hatzair Party, were among the thirty or so women who had been invited to attend the proceedings as guests. Restricted to passive participation, these guests objected strongly to the poor representation of women by the political factions and to the failure of the convention to deal with the special problems of the woman worker. In the last hours of the closing session, Ada Maimon, leader in the struggle for women's electoral rights in all institutions of Jewish self-government, declared that the female delegates, having been chosen by the parties and not by the women workers, did not and could not represent them. She announced that the women planned to form their own association within the Histadrut, and if refused representation on the Histadrut Council they "would feel forced to submit a separate electoral list to compete for representation on the Histadrut Council in the next election" ("Protocol of the First Convention of the Histadrut" 1970). Maimon's proposal won the support of leading figures in the major parties and was accepted by the convention. Two places were reserved for representatives to be elected directly by the women workers.

The admission of the women's movement into the Histadrut stimulated a new wave of organizational activity among the women. The leadership set out to mobilize support among the new immigrants, particularly those pioneers who had arrived as part of organized ideological movements. They were potentially most co-optable. First, they were physically concentrated and thus more accessible than the mass of individual women employed primarily as seamstresses and domestics in private homes. Second, more than other women, their immigration had been motivated by aspirations similar to those of the feminists of the second *aliya*—realization of the pioneering goals of Socialist Zionism. Third, they were the most predisposed to egalitarian ideals.

The meeting between the second- and third-wave pioneers may be analyzed in terms of an encounter between "sociological generations." The *halutzot* of the second wave had been excluded from full participation in the *kvutzot*, and their aspirations had been ridiculed. After a decade of struggle, they found that women were still discriminated against in all areas of public life. The *halutzot* of the third wave belonged to sexually mixed and strongly ideological socialist groups that provided work for their women members. They did not feel as deprived as did their forerunners. Although dissatisfaction with the sex division of labor and status existed even within such aggres-

sively egalitarian groups as the Gdud Avoda, it was expressed, if at all, within
the organization through its internal media (Erez 1922:252) and did not spark
collective action across factional boundaries. Loyalty to the group and its goals
took priority over the issues that had united the women a decade earlier.
Nonetheless, out of reverence for the women of the second wave, they attended the founding conference of the Women Workers' Council (WWC) held
in 1921 (Drori 1975:14–17).[6] The 1921 conference, with 43 delegates representing 485 workers, officially established WWC as the organizational arm of the
women workers' movement within the Histadrut. The council elected an
executive committee and representatives to each of the major departments
within the Histadrut ("The First Conference of the Women Workers' Council"
1921).

By the time of the second conference in 1922, at which 37 delegates
represented 600 women members, the underlying tensions within the
women's movement had surfaced. Two major opposing factions emerged. I
refer to them as the "radicals" and the "loyalists." The difference between
them may be analyzed in terms of degrees of commitment to feminism and
of trust in the male leadership. The old leaders, joined by the disenchanted
among the third *aliya*, were the more radical. They put little trust in a male-
dominated Histadrut to look after women's interests and advocated a strong,
separate organization—free of party control and in contact with grass-roots
members—that would initiate and monitor women's training and employment opportunities. The newly arrived third-wave pioneers held the loyalist
position, which recognized that women had special problems but believed
there was no need for a separate women's organization to solve them. They
argued that the newly constituted Histadrut should look after all workers
alike. The WWC should concentrate on reeducating and activating women
for participation in public life. In relation to the Histadrut, it should limit
itself to an advisory role and certainly not duplicate the services of the labor
exchange and other bodies that generated and allocated resources. Organizational segregation was objectionable also because it implied lack of faith in
the men, which, the loyalists felt, was not deserved (Maimon 1929; Minutes
1926).

The dispute over the WWC's role was not merely an internal matter. The
positions defended and the relative influence of the respective protagonists
were determined by the interests of the male leaders of the Histadrut, whose
response to the WWC was a reflection of its general policy toward particular
interest groups. Analysis of the events in the 1920s therefore requires some
understanding of the wider sociopolitical context.

At that time the leadership of the Histadrut faced two major organizational problems. The first was how to safeguard the stability of the new,
unifying institution, which had been forged from a variety of divergent ideological streams within Labor Zionism and incorporated a number of conflicting power groups. The second problem concerned the relationship of the
political parties to the Histadrut. Although elements within Achdut Haavoda
argued that after the establishment of the Histadrut political parties were no
longer necessary and should be dissolved, those in their favor prevailed. The

latter faction, furthermore, opposed a pluralistic structure and pressed for centralization of the party organization and for party control over the Histadrut (Shapira 1976). Clearly, a women's organization independent of party control conflicted with the interests of Achdut Haavoda, which argued that separatist tendencies among particular interest groups would waste resources and weaken the Histadrut. At the same time, the leadership was generally sympathetic toward the special problems and goals of the women pioneers.

As noted, in 1920 the Histadrut's control over the worker community was still precarious. The leaders of the Achdut Haavoda Party feared the separate organization of various factions among both the second and third waves. For Histadrut leaders at the 1920 convention, Maimon's threat that the women workers would submit an independent electoral list made it expedient to absorb the leadership into the council, especially since events outside the labor movement gave the threat greater credibility. The conflict over women's voting rights in the newly forming National Assembly, the Jewish parliament of the *Yishuv,* had made feminism a salient issue and a legitimate basis for organizational differentiation. By 1920, the Association of Hebrew Women for Equal Rights in Eretz Yisrael (Palestine) had been established and was mobilizing support outside the labor sector. In the elections to the National Assembly, some eight months before the founding convention of the Histadrut, the association submitted a separate women's list that won seven mandates (Azaryahu 1977)—the same number as there were women elected by the two labor parties to the assembly. These developments influenced the response to the demand of the women workers for representatives and their incorporation in the Histadrut Council.

THE TRANSFORMATION OF THE FEMINIST MOVEMENT, 1921–1927

From the perspective of the Histadrut and particularly that of the Achdut Haavoda party, which was struggling for dominance within the newly established political structure, the women's movement posed a problem of social control. Its accusations of discrimination undermined the legitimacy of the Histadrut's claim to represent all workers. To offset the potential costs of such allegations, the WWC was defined as an embarrassment to the labor movement. This perspective emerges in the report presented by David Ben Gurion, then leader of the Achdut Haavoda, to the second convention of the Histadrut in 1923, in which he explained that the "very existence and need for the existence of a special institution in the form of the WWC to protect the interests of the women workers does not add to our honor" ("The Second Histadrut Convention" 1923:26). This stance most affected those women in the WWC who were closely identified with the male leaders of Achdut Haavoda and committed to them; one such woman was Golda Meir, who at the same convention declared: "It is a sad and shameful fact that we are forced to create a special organization to deal with matters of the woman worker" (49).

The tactical aspect of this admission about the WWC is twofold. First, when viewed as a concession to an unfortunate and embarrassing reality, the organization became a vestige of some unresolved past rather than a positive creative force projected into the future and devoted to the creation of a better society. Second, presented as a kind of "bastard" child of the labor movement (unwanted and unplanned for by the father), the women's movement was discredited for exposing the labor movement's failure to live up to its own ideals. Another tactic employed to confine the amount of resources the Histadrut would be required to divert to satisfy the demands of the WWC was to understate the magnitude of the desired change. The women's goals were translated into specific objectives and defined in negative rather than positive terms. For example, describing women's aspirations for equality as the need to eliminate discrimination at work made fewer demands on the system than a definition that called for affirmative action in all walks of life. In the same address in 1923, Ben Guiron went on to explain that

> there is no special Histadrut for women workers nor is there a need for such a Histadrut, but we cannot ignore the bitter truth that the matter of equality for women, which we accept as a first principle, is only formal . . . there is *still* a need for a special institution for the women workers which will stand guard and concern itself with the social and economic position of the female worker so that she not be discriminated against within the community of workers. ("Second Histadrut Convention" 1923:22)

Ben Gurion's interpretation of the role of the WWC discounted the importance of the movement in the ideology and activity of national rebirth. Instead of being depicted as a creator of a new cultural image for women in the emerging socialist society, it was ascribed the role of watchdog guarding the interests of a "minority" group. Its members were thus denied the right to pride in a mission whose importance for the labor movement was discounted. According to Ben Gurion, implementation of the women's movement goals, such as creating employment opportunities, was to be left to the Histadrut. His statement that no special union for women existed, as one did, for example, for agricultural workers, was not merely a description of the facts. It was intended as a warning that separation would not be tolerated and that women would have to solve their problems through the existing structures of the Histadrut.

The need for women workers to prove that they were indeed not "creating a separate platform" for women (the phrase used to accuse the WWC of separatism) put the movement on the defensive. On all public occasions, such as the Histadrut and WWC conventions, WWC leaders repeatedly declared their loyalty to the Histadrut and denied that, in demanding greater opportunities, women were seeking a "separate platform" for themselves (Katznelson 1927; "Second Histadrut Convention" 1923:17, 99).

The election system, based on proportional representation, gave the political parties and particularly the dominant Achdut Haavoda considerable control over the Histadrut in general and over the WWC in particular. Each political faction constructed its lists of candidates so that the voter elected a party rather than an individual. Representation was indirect, since the party members elected delegates to the national convention, the convention to the council, and the council to the central committee of the Histadrut. The party bosses constructed the lists of candidates to the convention, which meant that they virtually controlled the access to all important and paid positions within the Histadrut and secured control of the top leadership over the organization. Women candidates usually made up no more than 20 percent of the list.

What weakened women's bargaining position was, first, that so few were politically active and, second, that many, particularly the "loyalists," experienced ambivalence about the definition of women as a special interest group. Sex as a basis for interest aggregation was unacceptable to those who wished to participate as individuals and not as members of a category, that, by implication, was in some way inferior. Willingly or not, however, women on a party list were almost inevitably perceived as representing women.

In the Histadrut, the political "logic" of party list construction was aimed at selecting people who could claim to represent the respective interest groups but whose loyalty to the party was not in question. Selective sponsorship of leaders by the dominant coalition, according to Gamson (1968:135), is a strategy of social control similar to co-optation. Because only the loyal are sponsored, the strategy reduces the need for direct intervention and continuous monitoring by the establishment. The sponsorship strategy is evident in the Histadrut's intervention through the selection of the leadership of the WWC and in its control over the organization's election system.

The Histadrut leadership strengthened the position of some women and weakened that of others through its appointments to policy-making and resource-allocating committees of its various agencies. Although formally the executive committee of the WWC had the right to recommend representatives to these bodies, they required the approval of the Central Committee, which used its prerogative to appoint and depose committee members in accord with its political interests. For example, in 1925 Maimon, member of the Hapoel Hatzair, was removed from the important immigration committee because she fought for 50 percent representation for women among those allocated immigration permits to Palestine. While the male leadership opposed her on this issue, they objected even more strongly to her independent behavior (Maimon 1972:252). She was replaced by a male member of Achdut Haavoda.

There is also evidence that the Histadrut intervened and affected leadership recruitment *within* the WWC. Golda Meir (1975:85) records that in 1927 David Remez, influential member of the Achdut Haavoda faction in the Central Committee of the Histadrut, invited her to become general-secretary (equivalent to chairperson) of the WWC. In 1921, Meir had immigrated from the United States, where she had been an active member of the Poalei Zion party, forerunner of the Achdut Haavoda Party. The following year, she was elected to the executive committee of the WWC, and in 1923 she and Maimon were elected to the Histadrut council ("The Activities of the Women Workers'

Council, 1922–23" 1923:81). Meir's qualifications for the post are not at issue, but it should be recognized that her election was initiated and engineered by the male leadership.

The process of centralization within the Histadrut was combined with the creation of a network of labor councils to implement Histadrut policy at the local level. Under the initiative of the WWC, committees of women workers were established within the councils in the cities and agricultural villages. The WWC defined their role as "activating" women workers and representing them in the various departments of the local labor council, such as the Offices of Public Works and Immigration, as well as in trade unions. Antagonism developed between the party functionaries of the local labor councils who controlled employment opportunities and other resources and the members of the women's committees whose direct election by the local female constituency weakened the former's control over them. Work was scarce, and the functionaries rejected the women's claim to special consideration, refusing to grant them "privileges" ("Report of the Second Conference of the Women Workers' Council" 1922:12).

The issue came to a head in a debate concerning the system to be employed for electing members of the women's committee. There were two camps in the WWC: the radical feminists, who favored direct elections by a general meeting of women workers at the local level without regard to women's party affiliation and free from party intervention, and the loyalists, who advocated that candidates be appointed by the party functionaries of the local council in cooperation with the WWC. The two views came to be known as "elected committees" and "appointed committees." The radical feminists, headed by Ada Maimon, Tova Yaffe, and other members of Hapoel Hatzair, argued that direct elections were essential to arouse women to active involvement in public life. The major concern of the radicals was that with appointed committees there would be no meaningful ties between the delegates and the women workers. Members would be selected on the basis of criteria such as compliance and party allegiance, and not on the basis of their ability and readiness to represent women's issues. Direct election of candidates, therefore, was essential to promote women's confidence in their representatives and to assure that the latter would be loyal first and foremost to the female constituency.

The loyalists argued that such low trust of the local labor council functionaries would result in conflicts, which would make the women's committee ineffective. It was, therefore, in the women's interest that the committees be appointed, with the advice of the WWC, by the local functionaries who would consequently feel more responsible for them (Cheikin 1927; Histadrut Labor Archives:225; Minutes 1926).

The issue was hotly debated during the meeting of the WWC in June 1926, at which Ben Gurion, representing the Central Committee of the Histadrut, commented: "There is no need to create a negative attitude toward the women's committees among the local labor councils from the start. A committee elected from among the community of women workers will create a negative attitude on the part of the local labor councils" (Minutes 1926). The implication that withdrawal of Histadrut support would be the price the WWC would have to pay for its independence and that by raising such demands they were intensifying interparty conflict within the Histadrut was intended to intimidate those who opposed appointed committees. These statements, however, do not reveal what appears to have been the deeper concern of the male leadership.

Achdut Haavoda feared that separate elections for women would set a dangerous precedent for other interest groups, such as the Orthodox and Yemenite communities, which could result in a weakening of the control of the center over the periphery (Sharet 1927:216). Despire pressure from the male leadership, however, the executive council of the WWC decided twelve to eight in favor of elected committees at its November 1926 meeting. Women members of Hapoel Hatzair and other parties voted for them and those of Achdut Haavoda against them, and it is apparent that the division between the radicals and the loyalists more and more paralleled that between the two labor parties ("The Women Workers' Council" 1926:13). Because the struggle among political factions for control within the Histadrut had intensified the demand for party loyalty, party rivalries were penetrating the WWC. The Histadrut leadership, which by the mid-1920s was mainly in the hands of the centralist Achdut Haavoda, encouraged the loyalists. The leaders of the ideologically pluralist Hapoel Hatzair Party, fearful of the growing control of its rival party, favored independently elected committees. At the third Histadrut convention in 1927, the majority of whose delegates came from the Achdut Haavoda Party, the vote was ninety-seven to seventy-nine in favor of appointed women's committees. In 1926, election by proportional representation of political factions was introduced into the conference of the WWC as well. At the following conference, held in 1932, all candidates were sponsored by the respective political factions, and proportional representation was officially implemented. (Even Shoshan 1963: vol. 3:165). Thus by the end of the 1920s, the struggle between the "radicals" and the "loyalists" had been determined in favor of the latter.

The Histadrut, while extending its control over the women's movement through selective sponsorship of leaders, was also under pressure to make concessions to the WWC. But in terms of its original goals, the WWC was able to exact a small price from the Histadrut for its active support. It developed six agricultural training farms as well as a number of vocational training courses for women; however, these were financed almost entirely by Zionist women's organizations abroad. By 1926 the Histadrut had not yet assigned a budget to the WWC or determined salaries for its representatives on the major Histadrut committees (Minutes 1926). The WWC conference of that year reports a list of abortive attempts to gain concessions from the local labor councils in the field of employment (Sharet 1927). The economic crisis that hit Palestine, and especially the cities, in the years 1926 to 1929 resulted in large-scale unemployment for both women and men and intensified the competition between the sexes for scarce jobs. By 1930 the proportion of women in nontraditional jobs had dropped considerably. Only 0.4 percent of the urban female labor force was then employed in construction and public works, while 46.1 percent were employed in private homes (Even Shoshan 1963: vol. 3:165). In addition, the Histadrut made only insignificant concessions to the WWC's demands for power. A few token women were assigned to various Histadrut committees in the early 1920s, but their numbers dwindled as the decade progressed. Apart from Maimon, who was a member of the economic council of Hevrat Haovdim (economic enterprises of the Histadrut), women were not found in any of the policy-making bodies of the economic organizations created by the Histadrut in the 1920s. No woman was represented on the fifteen-member committee which in 1925 negotiated the first collective agreement between the Histadrut and employers in the *Yishuv*. In this agreement, unskilled women workers employed in factories were officially discriminated against in wages—a situation that continued until the 1970s. A review of the minutes of the Histadrut Executive Council meetings held between 1921 and 1927 reveals that the problem of women was raised only four times, invariably by a woman and without response from other members.

The problem of the woman worker, which was an item on the agenda of the second Histadrut conference in 1923, was dropped from that of the third in 1927. It was argued that with the creation of the WWC the problem had been solved. Although the subject was returned to the agenda in later conferences and even became a permanent item, it was an issue to which only women gave their attention. The position of women within the new worker community was and remained the responsibility and concern of the WWC. Once the organization ceased to make unacceptable demands and its energies were harnessed to advance the interests of the Histadrut establishment, the sex division of labor and a large women's organization proved highly convenient. Looking after women's issues functioned as an outlet for the political energies of women, while it freed the men for dealing with the "more important" issues of the day. Every women who joined the Histadrut was automatically registered as a member of the WWC—a bureaucratic procedure that enabled the WWC in later years to boast of being the largest women's organization in the country.

The year 1927 marks the eclipse of radical feminism within the women workers' movement. Two events that year reflect the transformation that took place in the WWC and that led to the displacement of its original goals. The first was the decision in favor of appointed committees, which has already been discussed in some detail. The grass-roots organization was co-opted by the local councils. This discouraged sustained feminist pressure to give priority to women's emancipation, since there were always "more pressing" problems that required attention. "Pressing problems" were usually those for which pressure could not be eliminated, and the silencing of the radical elements was as much a consequence of the WWC's weakness as a cause of it.

The second event was the replacement of Ada Maimon as general-secretary of the WWC by Golda Meir. In view of their very different conceptions of the role of the WWC, this change represents the culmination of the struggle for power between the old guard and the new generation and marks the beginning of the transformation of the WWC into a social service organization for women. Although Maimon was reelected to the WWC executive committee after 1927, she and the old guard had lost ground. Power had shifted to the loyalist faction.

Meir's entrance into office symbolizes the succession of generations. The generation that had put women's self-transformation above party politics gave way to a cadre whose priorities were determined by the interests of the overall party organization. Meir, who was selected by the male leadership of Achdut Haavoda, was, according to her own report (1975:88), attracted to the WWC not so much because it was concerned with the issue of women as such, but because she was "very interested in the work it was doing, particularly in the agricultural training farms they set up for immigrant girls." For her, the WWC was a brief interlude in a long career within the male establishment of the labor party. With the election of Beba Idelson as general-secretary of the WWC in 1930, a position she held for forty years, the WWC changed its name to the Organization of Working Mothers and was finally transformed into a social service organization meeting the needs of women in their traditional roles of wives and mothers, albeit working mothers. It sponsored child day-care centers to free women to enter the labor market. Its occupational training prepared girls primarily for traditionally feminine roles as hairdressers, dressmakers, nursemaids, and the like. It turned its attention more and more to looking after welfare needs of mothers and children in the urban centers, leaving the political decisions, the trade union activities, and economic policy in the hands of the male establishment. In addition, it served ancillary political functions, the most important of which was mobilizing female support for the party at elections.

CONCLUSION

From its inception, the Zionist women workers' movement avoided defining itself as engaged in a struggle against male oppression. Nonetheless, in the period between 1911 and 1927 the commitment of the women's movement to self-transformation and equal participation in the building of the new society united its members across the competing political factions within the labor movement. As a united front it pressed for greater equality in the allocation of scarce resources such as immigration certificates, job opportunities, and participation in decision-making bodies of the various organizations of the labor movement.

The structural integration of the WWC within the Histadrut as a separate, but not autonomous part of the socialist movement, brought it under the control of the emerging power centers. From the late 1920s, two forces diverted the women's movement from a sustained struggle for sexual equality: first, the demands of the political parties within the Histadrut and particularly of the dominant Achdut Haavoda for the women's undivided commitment to the wider interests of the labor movement as these were defined by the party; and second, the party's failure to develop a real commitment to women's emancipation in the construction of the new economic, political, and social institutions of the *Yishuv*. These forces also shaped the course of the WWC for decades to come. The feminist movement, which had emerged in response to the wish of women pioneers to be equal partners in conquering new fields of work and building the nation, became the largest voluntary social service and, later, welfare organization in the *Yishuv*. In addition, the movement institutionalized and thus reinforced the categorical treatment of women at the same time it monitored their public careers. Women in the labor party (which dominated the country until 1977) were "expected" to rise through the ranks of the WWC, while its leaderhip acted as gatekeepers between the female enclave and the male establishment, allowing only a selected few, sponsored by them, to pass. Those who succeeded were rewarded with a seat in the Knesset (Israeli parliament) and other central bodies, and they provided the few tokens that bolstered public belief in the notion that "capable" women *do* "make it." The lack of institutionalized rotation in the leadership, however, set stringent limits on the number who ever did.

Despite the WWC's shift in activities, the organization remained officially committed to the full participation of women in public life. Consequently, the existence of this powerful women's organization, which claimed to be the vanguard of women's interests, helped to perpetuate the myth of equality and to discourage the emergence of alternative definitions around which women could organize.

NOTES

1. From a manifesto prepared in 1897 by the Committee of Women Zionists in Stanislaw, Galicia (Poland), quoted in Gelber (1958:2:806).

2. Throughout this paper, we are dealing with small numbers of people. According to Gorni, some 35,000 to 40,000 persons came on the second *aliya*, but most left the country or were deported by 1914. Only a fraction of those who remained formed the socialist pioneering element that gave the tone to the developments in the *Yishuv* (the Jewish community in Palestine) and influenced the course of its history. Eisenstadt, in describing the second *aliya*, points out that "although workers were in the minority . . . it is nonetheless considered as a labor immigration, since the workers' initiative and energy changed the whole structure of the Jewish community" (1967:11).

3. For an expression of similar aspirations, see the memoirs of women pioneers in Chabas (1947) Katznelson Shazar (1975), Harari (1959).

4. Gorni found that the women tended to have somewhat more formal education than the men but less Jewish instruction.

5. Kibbutzim developed during the third wave. They differed from the *kvutzot*, which were restricted to twenty to thirty members and where social relations were modeled on the intimacy characteristic of family ties, primarily in that they were larger social units with 100 and more members and consequently less selective and more open to individuals ready to share their way of life.

6. Drori recounts the report of the delegate to the 1922 WWC conference from Ein Harod—a kibbutz belonging to Gdud Avoda—that she represented those who supported the WWC, while the second delegate represented those who opposed a separate Women's Movement. See also Even Shoshan (1963:vol. 2:199).

CHAPTER 8

"Men Led, But Women Organized": Movement Participation of Women in the Mississippi Delta

CHARLES PAYNE

Ah wanted to preach a great sermon about colored women sittin' on high,
but they wasn't no pulpit for me.

ZORA NEALE HURSTON

This paper is part of a larger research project, a history of the early civil rights movement in and around Greenwood, Mississippi. The intention of the larger work is to determine how it was possible, under seemingly quite adverse circumstances, to create a vigorous and sustained movement in that town, concentrating particularly on the role played by local residents in that process. I have conducted over seventy interviews, most of them with local residents, and some with organizers from the Student Nonviolent Coordinating Committee (SNCC), the civil rights organization most active in the area. Most of the interviews were conducted in 1980 and 1981. Some respondents were then reinterviewed in 1988. I identified the original sample of local residents by asking SNCC workers for the names of people who had been central to their organizing effort in 1962 to 1963. With few exceptions, the oldest of the women I interviewed would have been in their forties during the movement days. Thus I have little first-hand information on older women.

I am most concerned with the period prior to the summer of 1964. During that period, the movement had achieved few victories in the rural South; the federal government, its rhetoric notwithstanding, was still vacillating in its support for civil rights workers; the repressive power of white supremacists was still very extensive; and most blacks in the Mississippi Delta were still afraid of any form of political involvement. The decision to join the movement in that early period, then, was very different from that decision to join later. It was a much chancier, much more dangerous proposition, so that the overwhelming response of local blacks in the Delta when organizers from SNCC or other groups first entered a town was to avoid them. The men and women who signed on in the early years were very much in the minority within their own communities.

One of the important questions emerging from my study is the question of the "overparticipation" of women. My respondents, male and female, unanimously agree with the comment of Lawrence Guyot, a member of the Student Nonviolent Coordinating Committee, "It's no secret," Guyot says, "that young people and women led organizationally" (Raines 1977:241). Women took civil rights workers into their homes, of course, giving them a place to eat and sleep, but women also canvassed more than men, showed up more frequently at mass meetings and demonstrations, and more frequently attempted to register to vote. This paper is a very preliminary attempt to suggest explanations for the greater willingness of women to join the movement in the early 1960s, a pattern all the more interesting because of its departure from the pattern of the 1950s. In that even more dangerous decade, black political activism in rural Mississippi seems to have been dominated by men, most of them associated with the NAACP, the Regional Council of Negro Leadership, or both—Amzie Moore, Aaron Henry, Medgar Evers, Clyde Kennard, E. W. Steptoe, C. J. Stringer, Vernon Dahmier, T. R. W. Howard, to name some of the most visible. It is true that, historically, black women have always had to fulfill social roles not commonly played by more privileged women in this society, but that has not always led to the kind of dominance of political activity that seems to have occurred in rural Mississippi in the 1960s. The higher degree of participation by women in the early 1960s is interesting too because the standard position among political scientists has been that "women all over the world are less active in politics than men" (Matthews and Prothro 1966:65).

The pattern of participation seems to have been age-specific. That is, among older folks, there was no clear imbalance. Indeed, a number of men in their fifties and sixties played important roles in getting the movement in Greenwood off the ground (Sinsheimer 1987). Similarly, there does not seem to have been any clear difference in the participation rate of teenage boys and teenage girls. The gender difference appears to have been strongest in the years in between, the "settle-aged" years from roughly thirty to fifty. Some of my respondents estimated that women in that age range were three or four times more likely to participate than men.

While the people to whom I have spoken generally agreed about the nature of the pattern, there was no consensus at all on the reasons. They offered a variety of conflicting, sometimes contradictory explanations, and many said simply that they had no idea what accounted for the difference. Even those who did offer explanations were not very confident about them or anxious to defend them. It was also my impression that these gender differences were not something to which my respondents had given a lot of thought. This is not surprising, since gender was not as politicized a social category in 1963 as it is now.

One background factor that should be considered is SNCC's operating style. SNCC was the most active of the organizations in the Delta, and its operating style made it relatively open to the participation of women. If anyone can be called the founder of SNCC, it is a woman, Ella Baker; and in its early years, women, many of them college students, were always involved in the development of policy. The group was antibureaucratic and antihierarchical, willing to work with anyone who was willing to have them, traditional considerations of status notwithstanding. This included sharecroppers as well as doctors, the pool-room crowd as well as the church crowd. SNCC organizers placed great emphasis on finding and helping to develop nontraditional sources of leadership. Women obviously represented an enormous pool of untapped potential. Much of SNCC's organizing activity in the Delta involved door-to-door canvassing, which meant that women were as likely as men to encounter organizers. SNCC, despite the traditional definitions of sex roles held by many of its members (Evans 1980), was structurally open to female participation in a way that many older organizations would not have been. Had SNCC employed a more traditional style of organizing—for example, working primarily through previously established leadership—it might not have achieved a high degree of female participation. Still, saying that SNCC was open to the participation of women does not explain why women were responsive.

One explanation that might seem plausible initially can be rejected. This is the demographic explanation. The argument goes that the massive migration out of the South in the 1940s and 1950s drew away more men than women in the twenty-to-forty age range. Thus there were simply more women around when the movement of the 1960s began. It is true that the migrations, especially in the early stages, took a large number of men out of the Delta, but even when one looks just at Greenwood families in which both husband and wife are present in the early 1960s, the wives were far more likely to have participated.

Some of the other suggested explanations are not so easily disposed of. One idea, mentioned by several of my respondents, is that women were less exposed to reprisals than men. The argument goes that southern whites were less afraid of black women and thus less likely to initiate either physical violence or economic reprisals against movement women. Even when economic reprisals were used, the wife's salary was likely to be perceived as less important to the family than the husband's. If anyone was going to be fired, better it be the woman. In short, it was simply safer, more cost-effective, for women to participate.

We know that, in general, how free people were from economic reprisal seems to have had a great deal to do with who joined the movement in its early days. Nonetheless, it is not clear that differences between men and women can be explained in the same way. If, under normal circumstances, whites were more indulgent of transgressions of the racial norms when they came from black women, it does not follow that the same indulgence would extend to the highly charged, quite abnormal situation of 1962 and 1963. By that time, whites in the Delta clearly felt theatened, and it seems likely that they would have struck back at whom they associated with the threat, old indulgences notwithstanding.

Moreover, if a pattern of indulgence existed in fact, it may not have been apparent from the viewpoint of women who were thinking about becoming a part of the movement. Reprisals against women in the rural South were constant and highly visible. Examination of SNCC's newsletters issued in 1962 and 1963 suggests that some of the most violent incidents of reprisal were directed against women. Women who were even rumored to be a part of the movement lost their jobs. Every adult woman I interviewed got fired, except for those who quit because they expected to get fired. Women were regularly clubbed at demonstrations or brutally beaten in jail. The homes of women activists were regularly shot into. Any woman in the Delta who contemplated joining the early movement had to be aware of all this. In such a situation, even if in fact there were some gender-related differences in the likelihood of reprisal, the women involved may not have seen it as significant.

Moreover, it is misleading to think of reprisals as being directed against merely the individual who was involved. Anyone who joined the movement placed his or her whole family at risk. When someone got evicted, the whole family was evicted. True, the man pressured by his boss to get his wife out of the movement could say, "Gee, boss, I can't do anything with that woman. You know how women are" and hope for a sympathetic response. It was only a hope, though. The White Citizen's Council, in particular, made it a point to put pressure on entire families. If anyone in a family was known to be a part of the movement, every adult in that family was likely to have trouble finding work or getting credit. Similarly, the most popular forms of violence in that period—arson, drive-by shootings into homes, and bombings—were reprisals against entire families, not just individuals.

As the severity of reprisals eventually lessened, there was not necessarily a corresponding increase in male participation. SNCC's Lawrence Guyot, drawing on his experience organizing the Mississippi Freedom Democratic Party, noted that "as the violence petered down, I did not see a correlative surging forward by black males into leadership positions" (personal interview). He recalls telling a group of women that included Fannie Lou Hamer, Victoria Gray, and Unita Blackwell, " 'Y'all step back a little bit and let the men move in now.' Fortunately, they didn't kill me." He made a similar comment at a meeting, probably around 1965, at which Ella Baker was present. He relates her response:

> Ella Baker told me, "You have proven that there are some men who can do a very good job but you have to learn never, never make the mistake of substituting men in quantity for women of quality." I haven't done that shit anymore. In fact, I've gone the other way around.

Finally, the differential-reprisal interpretation strikes me as suspicious because no woman to whom I spoke ever suggested, even indirectly, that *her own* involvement could be explained in such terms. Nor did anyone to whom I spoke ever identify any specific woman whose participation was affected by the reprisal issue. In fact, I cannot find in my interviews any form of thinking that I would consider calculation, whether calculation of probable harm to oneself or of the movement's chances of success. In contrast, both Amzie

Moore and Medgar Evers, two of the most important figures in the 1950s, referred frequently to the way in which the postwar political situation offered possibilities for making change in Mississippi which had not existed previously (Evers 1967; Garvey 1981).

When explaining their own decision to join the movement, my respondents constructed answers primarily in terms of either religious belief or preexisting social networks of kinship and friendship. For many women, both factors seem to have been operative. Thus Lou Emma Allen was drawn into the movement by her son, a junior college student. Although she was often afraid, she was sure the Lord would see her through. She frequently led the singing at mass meetings in Greenwood. Appropriately, the first song she ever sang at a mass meeting was "Take Your Burdens to the Lord and Leave Them There." Belle Johnson got involved after June, her fourteen-year-old daughter, was arrested along with Fannie Lou Hamer, Euvester Simpson, and Annelle Ponder and beaten brutally. Laura McGhee explained that she was initially interested in the movement because of her brother, a courageous NAACP officer who had been shot a few years earlier. He survived the shooting and fled the state. Susie Morgan was drawn in partly by the activity of her daughters. She prayed and prayed over the decision to join, and finally she could see that it was what the Lord wanted her to do. "It hit me like a new religion," she said. Ethel Gray was drawn into the movement by an old friend. After she had joined, people would drive by and throw rattlesnakes on her porch, but "we stood up. Me and God stood up." The pattern in their histories is one of being drawn in initially by relatives or friends and then feeling a sense of support from the Lord. (There was a third theme, which I am not going to discuss here—the growing admiration some of the women felt for the young SNCC organizers.)

The religious issue raises a series of important questions. One line of explanation for the overparticipation of women might go as follows: the movement grew out of the church. Women participate in the church more than men do. (One estimate is that across all varieties of black religious activities, women represent 75 to 90 percent of the participation [Gilkes 1985:679].) Therefore, women were naturally more drawn to the movement.

This argument confuses the church in the urban South with that in the rural South. In urban areas, the churches certainly were an early focal point of organizing activity (Morris 1984). It is not surprising that there was a high level of participation by women in the activities of the Southern Christian Leadership Converence (SCLC) because many of that organization's affiliates were large urban churches populated largely by women. Rural churches, however, were initially far less supportive of the movement. In Greenwood, as in much of the Delta, the movement grew in spite of the church. In the first six months after SNCC workers came to Greenwood, only two churches were open to them, and one of these was only halfheartedly supportive. A common theme in speeches at the mass meetings of that period was the hypocrisy and cowardice of ministers. Nine months after the first organizers came, Greenwood was fairly well mobilized—hundreds of people were trying to register, and there were almost daily marches and mass meetings. *After* the general population was aroused, twenty black ministers signed a statement of support for the movement. Even then, their support for movement activity fell short of what SNCC workers would have liked. Shortly after the ministers signed the statement of support, their lack of real cooperation was cited in a memo written by SNCC's Bob Moses as the biggest single problem still facing the local movement. (Ironically, sanctified churches, which historically have allowed women wider scope than other denominations, were probably the slowest to join the movement; Methodist churches were probably the fastest to do so.)

Those in the Delta who joined the movement in the early days, then, ordinarily did so in defiance of their church leadership. Nonetheless, even if the church as an organization did not lead people into the movement, the religiosity of the population may have been very important. I noted earlier that a distinction has to be drawn between the pre- and post-1964 periods. The victories that affected the daily life of the average person began in the summer of 1964 with the public accommodations bill. After that, we got the Voting Rights Act, bringing federal registrars to the South. The same period saw a decline in the frequency of both economic and physical reprisals and increasingly vigorous federal prosecution of those who persisted in violence.

Those who joined the movement in its early days could not have known that things would work out as they did. What they knew for certain was that those who did join were going to suffer for it. From the viewpoint of most rural black Southerners in 1962 or 1963, the overwhelming preponderance of evidence must have suggested that the movement was going to fail. Joining a movement under such circumstances may literally require an act of faith. Durkheim (1965:494) noted the empowering function of religion: "The believer who has communicated with his god is not merely a man who sees new truths of which the unbeliever is ignorant; he is a man who is stronger. He feels within him more force either to endure the trials of existence or to conquer them." Durkheim may have gotten the gender wrong, but the analysis is right. Faith in the Lord made it easier to have faith in the possibility of social change. As the slaves of a century ago, according to Du Bois, saw the fulfillment of biblical prophecy in the coming of the Civil War, residents of the Delta may have seen the civil rights movement as a sign that God was stirring. Civil rights workers had long made a practice of using religion to challenge people. Ruby Hurley, who started working in the South in the early 1950s for the NAACP noted:

> I found this [using the Bible] to be effective in saying to our people, "You go the church on Sunday or you go every time the church doors are open. You say 'amen' before the minister even has the word out of his mouth. . . . Yet you tell me you're afraid. Now how can you be afraid and be honest when you say "My faith looks up to Thee" or when you sing that God's going to take care of you? If you don't believe it, then you're not really the Christian you say you are.

Most of the organizers in the Delta in the early 1960s were native Mississippians, fully aware of the motivating power of religion. A constant element in their rhetoric was that God was with the movement, and, as Fannie Lou Hamer put it in one speech, people who could not *do* something about their Christianity needed to stop shouting so much about being a Christian. Such appeals would have the most impact on the most religious—women rather than men, older rather than younger men.

The argument that women ordinarily participate less than men in political activity may not be so inaccurate in this case as it first appears. When we call the movement "political," we are imposing our own label on it. From the viewpoint of the women involved, the movement may have seemed less "political" than an extension of their faith.

It might be helpful to know more about why women, regardless of race, age, or education, are more religious than men in the first place. Despite considerable research, there is no clear answer. The pattern seems to hold, by any measure of religiosity, for all major Western religions other than Judaism. The difference does not appear to be related to gender differences in labor force participation (Ulbrich and Wallace 1984) or to the greater role that women play in the socialization of children (Hoge and Roozen 1979). Another popular notion, in the tradition of some Marxist thought, is that the church serves to compensate those most deprived of "real" rewards—women, the poor, the elderly. Attempts to support that interpretation have generally failed (Hoge and Roozen 1979). In fact, in many populations, the most economically privileged appear more religious than the least privileged, although among blacks there seems to be no relationship between religiosity and social status (Beeghley, Van Velsor, and Block 1981).

If previous research does not provide us with any explanation of the generally greater religiosity of women, the literature has frequently been interpreted to mean that strong religious feelings militate against participation in a change-oriented movement. One review of the literature (Hoge and Roozen 1979:60) concludes that the values reinforced by traditional churches

> include a world view focused on the private sector of life and with such immediate social orientations as the family, ethnic group or local community. They are associated with conformity and conservatism in all attitude realms and with personal and privatistic commitments not oriented to social change. They value conformity and tradition more than individual freedom and tolerance of diversity, social conservatism more than social change, and definite moral codes more than individualized moral orientations.

This interpretation, consistent with the idea of religion as opiate, obviously does not cover the situation of southern blacks. If the pre-1950 history of the rural black church conforms to this model (Arbor 1935; Cohn 1948:173–84; Richardson 1947), its history since then suggests that there is nothing inherently conservative about the church, that its message can as easily be packaged in order-threatening as in order-serving ways. Similarly, it is ironic that investment in "personal and privatistic commitments" should be thought to be conservatizing. Among the women I have studied, it is just such commitments that seem to have played a large role in drawing them into the movement. A more flexible model might hold that involvement in such commitments ordinarily militates against taking part in social movements, but once any one person in the network becomes politically involved, the strength of her or his social ties is likely to draw other members in. In the Delta, two populations were predisposed from the beginning to respond to the message that SNCC conveyed. One consisted of those, mostly older men associated with the NAACP, who had been active around issues of voter registation since the 1950s. Thus when Sam Block, SNCC's first organizer in Greenwood, initially arrived, an older man named Cleve Jordan, who had a local reputation as a hell-raiser on the registration issue, introduced him to people around town who would be responsive. The other group that responded quickly was young people. Better educated than their parents, more knowledgeable about the broader society, many of them were easily attracted to the movement, frequently against their parents' wishes. Thus the situation that SNCC usually encountered in the Delta was that while most people were initially afraid, some were interested right away; and, given the tightly knit social bonds of rural communities, they were able to pull others in. Since women tend to be more deeply invested than men in networks of kin and community, it is not surprising that more women were drawn in during the early stages. When teenage children joined, for example, that seems to have had a greater effect on their mothers and aunts than on their male relatives.

It seems likely that the greater investment of women in kin and communal networks would also affect the nature of their work inside the movement, an idea consistent with Karen Sacks's (n.d.) analysis of a contemporary union-organizing drive among black women in a southern hospital. Sacks was particularly concerned with the differing styles of leadership exhibited by men and women. As one of the women participants put it, "Women are organizers, men are leaders." That is, "women created the organization, made people feel a part of it, as well as doing the everyday work upon which most things depended, while men made public pronouncements, confronted and negotiated with management" (Sacks n.d.:5). Certain women operated as network centers, to use Sacks's term, mobilizing already existing social networks around the organizing goals, mediating conflicts, conveying information, coordinating activity, and "creating and sustaining good relations and solidarity among co-workers" (16). Many of these skills seemed to be rooted in the way in which these women operated in their families.

Sacks's description of the leadership style of the women she studied fits very well the role played by rural women in the civil rights movement. Andrew Young of the SCLC (King 1987:469–70) claims, "It was women going door to door, speaking with their neighbors, meeting in voter-registration classes together, organizing through their churches that gave the vital momentum and energy to the movement, that made it a mass movement." Daily maintenance of the movement at the local level was largely in the hands of women. It seems almost certain that this would have affected the tone of the movement. Drake and Cayton (1970:393–94) claimed in their study of Chicago that black women community leaders were more trusted than men, at least in part because of the perception that women could not as easily capitalize on their activism. Similarly, the preponderance of female participation in the movement may have had the effect of helping to create an atmosphere in which it was relatively easy to establish and maintain trust. As a guess, one would think that the participation of so many women meant that relationships inside the movement would have been less competitive, more nurturing, than would have been the case otherwise. These women very clearly came to see SNCC organizers and some of the other out-of-town volunteers as their children. A movement with these familistic overtones, overtones reinforced in early SNCC by its ideal of the "beloved community," must have been a relatively supportive and empowering political environment. At a point in the movement's history when the prospects for success seemed poor, when the stresses and tensions involved in organizing were great, such a climate may have done much to sustain the activists.

While religiosity is among the issues most stressed by the people I spoke to, it may be an error to take it too literally. Alberta Barnet, a Greenwood resident who joined the movement while still in high school, said: "Round here women just go out for meetings and things more than men. Men just don't do it. They don't participate in a lot of things. The most they participate in is a trade." She suggests that much of the organizational life of black Greenwood, not just the church and the movement, was dependent upon women. Ella Baker, who had decades of experience as an organizer in the South, felt much the same way and as early as the late 1950s had tried to talk SCLC into developing programs that put more emphasis on women (Walker 1974:21). Gilkes (1988) has found that in the contemporary urban North, black women community workers are more common than men, a finding consistent with my own experience with community organizations. Lawrence Guyot, who now works with a variety of community organizations in Washington, D.C., continues to find that most of them are predominantly female. Similar patterns may sometimes exist in white communities. McCourt's (1977:42–43) study of community organizations in a working-class white ethnic Chicago community found them to be dominated by women.

Thus the pattern of relatively high levels of female participation among either black or working-class women seems to exist in several types of nontraditional political activities in widely differing circumstances. It seems unlikely that religion would have the centrality in all these circumstances that it had in the Delta.

The important element, then, may not be so much religion itself as the sense of efficacy that it engenders under certain circumstances. One way to get at this would be to look at situations in which men did participate in large numbers. In the Delta, one such place was Holmes County, just south of Greenwood. According to my interviews, Holmes County was one place where the movement was dominated by men from the very beginning. Indeed, the men of Holmes County did not wait for organizers to get around to them. They went to Greenwood and invited organizers to Holmes. Holmes has a distinctive history. It has traditionally been a black-majority county, which is not unusual for the Delta, but since before World War II it has also been a county in which most of the land has been owned by blacks. It is almost certain that landownership gave residents of this county a greater degree of freedom from economic reprisals at least, but one student of the county's history feels that the tradition of landownership and cooperative work contributed to a distinctive world-view among the men. Salamon (1979) found that compared with local sharecroppers, the landowners were more optimistic about the future, had a higher sense of personal efficacy, and were more likely to feel that they had been of help to others. He also found that landowners were far more likely to participate in the early civil rights movement. Thus it may be that landowning for men, perhaps especially when blacks own whole communities, has some of the same psychological effects as religion for women, particularly with respect to an enhanced sense of personal efficacy.

The invisibility of women in the movement is an important issue in itself. Asked to name all the women they can think of who were important to the movement, most audiences are hard-pressed to get beyond Rosa Parks and Coretta Scott King. There is a parallel with the way in which we typically fail to see women's work in other spheres. Arlene Daniels, among others, has noted that what we socially define as "work" are those activities that are public rather than private and those activities for which we get paid. Under this taken-for-granted understanding, much of the activity in which women are expected to specialize—caring for children and the home, seeing to the fabric of day-to-day relationships—does not qualify as "work" and is thus effectively devalued. In the same way, I think there is a tendency in the popular imagination to reduce the civil rights movement to stirring speeches and dramatic demonstrations. The everyday maintenance of the movement is effectively devalued, sinking beneath the level of our sight.

This paper has suggested explanations for the "overparticipation" of women in the early years of the civil rights movement in the Mississippi Delta. The differential reprisal explanation, while it certainly cannot be discounted without further evidence, is not fully convincing. If one follows the line of reasoning suggested by my respondents, an explanation would be constructed around the different sense of personal investment that women had in kin and communal networks and in their different sense of personal efficacy, the latter undergirded by the depth of their religious beliefs. Both of these issues are worth further investigation, as is the issue of how the high proportion of women in the early movement changed the movement's interpersonal tone.

CHAPTER 9

White Mothers as Civil Rights Activists: The Interweave of Family and Movement Roles

RHODA LOIS BLUMBERG

This paper examines the lives of a little-studied cohort of activists—white mothers who became highly involved participants in the American civil rights movement of the 1950s and 1960s.[1] During these years most white mothers of young children were not engaged in full-time paid work. They were relatively free to participate in appropriate community activity, provided they could arrange for child care or baby-sitting and gain the cooperation of their husbands (Goldstein 1978). Indeed, "good" mothering required that these women engage in child-related public activities, such as participation at school functions and assistance with youth groups or parent-cooperative nursery schools. However, all the subjects in this study went beyond the bounds of expected family- or church-related voluntarism to become social activists in a minority group movement. My discussion will center on the interweaving of the mother and social activist roles. The aim is to understand the processes involved in the developing life-careers of women who are committed to societal as well as familial roles and who see the two as interlinked.

The crucial role of women in the modern civil rights movement is only now being explored, with many gaps still to be filled. Only the most dramatic events that involved women gained historical attention. For example, it is generally known that the resurgent civil rights movement was signaled by the refusal of a black woman, Rosa Parks, to surrender her seat to a white man on a Montgomery, Alabama, bus on December 1, 1955 (Abernathy, 1971; King 1958; Robinson 1987). Viola Liuzzo, a white woman, gained a place in history by being assassinated while serving as a driver during the Selma to Montgomery march of 1965. At the time of Mrs. Parks's action, southern cities mandated segregation of blacks and whites in all public facilities. Talk of boycotts elsewhere followed a successful ten-day boycott of buses in 1953 in Baton Rouge, Louisiana. The situation in Montgomery was tense before Mrs. Parks took her action. Blacks were treated discourteously as well as segregated;

Reprinted with permission of the publisher from a slightly different version that appeared in Helena Z. Lopata, ed., *Research in the Interweave of Social Roles: Women and Men,* vol. 1, pp. 33–50. Copyright © 1980 by JAI Press.

there were no black bus drivers. Black riders were expected to move to the back, vacating their seats as the vehicle filled. In Montgomery and elsewhere, individuals had sometimes acted on their own to protest bus segregation by refusing to move. The Women's Political Council, a Montgomery organization led by Jo Ann Robinson, had presented a set of grievances to city officials, asking for changes in bus practices (Garrow 1985; Robinson 1987). When Rosa Parks was arrested for resisting the order of the bus driver, Jo Ann Robinson went into action, mimeographing thousands of leaflets that called for a one-day boycott. The success of that day and the massive support of Montgomery's African-American community led to the boycott's continuance. There was clearly mass sentiment that it was time to struggle for change; the conditions were right for a social movement.

Social movements arise out of mass discontent and malaise with the existing order of life and a belief that it can be changed (Blumer 1969). Such discontent must become conscious and be recognized and tapped by leadership at the appropriate time. The successful Montgomery bus boycott brought a leader to prominence—Martin Luther King, Jr.—and was the beginning of a decade and a half of civil rights activism against racial segregation and for black rights.

Social movement theory concentrates on the sense of grievance of a disadvantaged group but generally fails to explain the paths to involvement of outsiders, persons from the dominant group whose sense of justice is outraged by perceived inequalities. By assuming that people join movements only because of a narrowly conceived self-interest, such theory overlooks white people in the civil rights movement, men in the women's movement, and Christians who saved Jewish lives during the Holocaust, to cite three examples.

As a matter of fact, the civil rights movement drew support from many individuals and groups. Older civil rights and human rights organizations became more active. Numerous new organizations—many interracial—were formed, on both the national and the local level. While the main drama of the civil rights movement took place in the southern states, a parallel, less discussed, northern phase also erupted. Through branches of national organizations such as the NAACP and CORE (the Congress of Racial Equality), and through local groups such as fair housing and human relations councils, antiracist northern whites found roles to play. They supported the southern movement in several ways. But they also began to examine the patterns of unofficial, de facto segregation in their own communities. National attention was focused on civil rights issues; churches and other traditional organizations, such as YWCAs, became involved in varying degrees.

The role of white women, as a category, in the movement has generally received only negative recognition. Much of the research literature consists of limited studies of white female college students recruited for the 1964 and 1965 Freedom Summer projects in the South (see, for example, Demarath, Marwell, and Aiken 1971; Fendrich 1977; Rothschild 1979). These women have been blamed for engaging in the taboo interracial sex, thereby causing tensions between black men and black women and increasing the resentment of southern whites. Inexperienced with the South, some did not know how to handle the overtures of black males. Overgeneralization based on the behavior of these raw recruits overlooks the key group of young southern women who joined the movement at an earlier stage or the mature southern women who supported it.

My own attention to the topic of women in the civil rights movement came out of my experience as a white activist in interracial, mixed-gender groups in the Midwest and the North. Because the involvement of northern white women in the movement had received so little attention, I decided to study a sample of white activists in the state in which I resided.

Many of the women in my study first joined the voluntary associations in their communities that were considered appropriate for housewives. But, unlike some of their peers, they rarely felt satisfied and comfortable with the moderate programs of these groups, and moved on to social movement activities. As civil rights activists, they participated in demonstrations, marches, picketing, national mobilizations, and public meetings. They worked for desegregation in education, housing, employment, and recreation; raised money, wrote, and spoke publicly; and were part of leadership groups in interracial organizations. Their movement was one that, on the surface, did not appear to be related to their own interests (unlike the case of black mothers, whose children's futures were tied to movement goals). On the contrary, these white women did perceive their struggle against racial injustice as being connected to their roles as mothers. They did not see civil rights as someone else's cause.

Motherhood, women's most positively sanctioned role, has usually been characterized as a domestic one. But just as maternal concerns have brought women into other humanistic causes, so did it impel many civil rights activists to seek interracial contacts for their children and a less racist society. These women saw the family as linked to community and society. Most of them considered their ideological commitments to motherhood and to the cause of racial justice complementary and reinforcing rather than conflicting. They created a meaningful interpretation of the links between these major involvements as they solved the day-to-day and year-to-year problems of allocating time to their varied roles.

The intermeshing of demanding private and public roles over time can be examined as an interweaving of multiple personal careers. In what follows, I shall first consider the dichotomization of public and private spheres with respect to women's roles, and explain how the concept of career is used. The ways in which the dual career of mother and that of civil rights activist were interwoven, both in practice and ideology, will then be considered.[2]

METHODS

Between 1973 and 1976, in-depth interviews were conducted with a snowball sample of forty-one white women recognized for their civil rights activism, mainly within their own communities, in the state of New Jersey. Initially, fifteen women known to the author personally or by reputation were asked to suggest others. Of the total, thirty-eight were mothers, a group constituting the sample for this paper. In addition to community reputation, a criterion for inclusion was the individual's confirmation that the cause of racial justice was an important guiding value in her life. Interviews focused on the dynamics and development of each woman's activism, as related to stages in her own life course. A brief follow-up contact by mail and telephone in December 1976 brought information about work and voluntary activities up to date.[3]

Participant-observation in the processes to be described also contributed needed insights and made the gaining of rapport easy. During the 1960s, I was the mother of three young children and a known activist leader in my community.

Some relevant background characteristics of the women studied are as follows: their median year of birth is 1925, with a range from 1898 to 1944. (The woman born in 1898 was among the most active community workers at the time of the study!) Their average number of children is 2.7. At present, almost 50 percent are married to their first husband; almost 16 percent, to a second husband; a little over 25 percent are divorced; and a little over 10 percent, widowed. Current educational status does not represent education attained at the time of marriage and motherhood, since approximately 45 percent returned to college or graduate school after a period of interruption. At present, over 65 percent possess a bachelor's or higher degree.

More than 70 percent of sample members report having been socialized to a humanistic, religious, or political ethic stressing justice and equality. Most remember having had an early reaction to injustice. While it frequently became focused on racial issues during childhood or young adulthood, there was a gap between felt concern and overt behavior. More than one-third recall taking some stance against racial injustice, either independently or as part of a group, before marriage. The period between marriage and motherhood did not raise this percentage significantly. Hence, almost two-thirds entered civil rights activity after the birth of their first child. The sensitivity to racial issues, however, was a factor predisposing them to seek and utilize opportunities for movement participation. (For further discussion, see Goldstein 1977a.)

THE DICHOTOMIZATION OF PUBLIC AND PRIVATE SPHERES OF LIFE

Modern American society is said to be characterized by segmentation of activities, resulting in a pluralization of life-worlds. Many theorists consider a fundamental aspect of this segmentation to be the dichotomy between private and public spheres (Berger et al. 1974). Others dispute this separation as artificial or socially constructed.

When male and female roles have been defined in terms of this split, women have often been denied the right to education or to meaningful paid jobs. Poor and racial minority women have always had to work outside the home in larger numbers, most often in marginal, discredited jobs. The idealized division of labor by sex, relegating women to the domestic sphere, is alleged to derive, at least in part, from the "nurturant capacities" of women, a characteristic considered lacking in men (Rosaldo 1974:17–42). Maternal, humanistic, and nurturant qualities are represented as either instinctive or the product of socialization (Chodorow 1974:43–66; Riegel 1970:201). The tendency of women to be concerned with others has been used to justify "social uplift" activities. Early feminists utilized this previously restrictive concept of female nature to justify the inclusion of women in the public sphere, noting that women would have "a very uplifting influence on society if they were not forced to devote most of their energies to pleasing and placating men" (Riegel 1970:251).

Arguments about women's nature can be used for or against their participation in the public sphere. But communal and societal emergencies, which demand an all-out mobilization of human resources, provide a more obvious and immediate rationale for disregarding norms that confine women to domestic roles. The Indian revolt against the British was one such historic occasion: women were urged to leave the seclusion of their homes to aid in the national liberation struggle. Said one historian, "Women, encouraged by their men, came out in their thousands from cities, towns and villages of India to fight for the freedom of their country" (Thomas 1964:329).

Besides the acknowledged value of and need for women in time of national emergency, many mundane voluntary activities that keep society going rely on their services.[4] In a large sample of midwestern middle-class women, Lopata (1971:54–55) found that the majority of them were, had been, or would be actively concerned in out-of-home activities—such as voluntary associations, political activities, and work—that they listed as ideologically unimportant.

The contradiction suggested by Lopata is that motherhood and household roles link women to their communities, but patriarchal ideology simultaneously proclaims that they belong in the home. The way her respondents make sense out of their world is by ignoring or considering insignificant their nonfamilial roles. They are, in a sense, in collusion with those who would limit the value of women's participation in voluntary associations and in other political and societal roles.[5] Although a much higher percentage of American mothers of young children joined the paid labor force in the 1980s, their struggle to be taken seriously as workers continues, as symbolized by the absence of institutional support for day care.

The vast majority of those I studied were similar to their peers in giving the motherhood role highest priority. Here is how one of them frames it: "It never occurred to me that I would not marry and not have a family and devote my time to my family. And eventually I might go back to work. But initially, I wanted to be, I guess, as my mother . . . I wanted a big family."

The crucial difference is that these women did not devalue their community roles and in fact saw home and community as interconnected. They felt that it was their right and duty to be involved in the world. The same respondent quoted above describes her civil rights work in this way:

> This has been one of the mainsprings of my life; one of the things that has given it some reason and purpose. And I think that goes back to my early learning: you're here to do something and by golly, do it! And I guess that's what I've chosen to do.

Most members of my sample did not desire full-time employment while their children were young. Yet they did indeed combine at least two major involvements, asserting their right to active social movement participation while identifying strongly with their role as mothers. And their mothering values were, as shall be seen, reflected in their civil rights work. In later years, most of them entered or returned to the world of work, almost always choosing careers related to their humanistic concerns (Blumberg 1980).

THE SOCIAL MOVEMENT CAREER AND THE DOMESTIC CAREER

The notion of career links personal biography with social history. It can include many different types of major involvements over time that have significance for individual identity (Becker and Strauss, 1970:245–59; Hughes, 1958).

Careers, then, are not only work careers. Women until the most recent past, and some still, are more likely to endure "contingent lives . . . dependent on marriage and the husband's career"—as shown in research on women born in the 1920s (Elder 1974:202). The pioneering study of midwestern housewives referred to earlier reached a similar conclusion: regardless of their taking part in other activities, the large majority of women considered their role as homemaker as the only one crucial to their identity (Lopata 1971). Domestic careers have sometimes been recognized as a type (Becker and Strauss 1970:259), but more often women's progression through family life has been described in such terms as "life cycle" or "life course"—terms more passive and less directed than "career."

While the activists I studied were, for the most part, working only out of necessity, part-time, or sporadically in the 1960s (a familiar pattern for middle-class women of that time), their movement activity provided independent, vital, and meaningful unpaid work. This involvement was sustained over a period of time, became an important element in personal identity, and thereby constituted what I term "a civil rights career."[6]

These particular social movement careers were tied both to the stages of the women's lives and to stages in the civil rights movement. Such careers, possible in the integrationist 1960s, are unlikely to be repeated in the present stage of the movement for racial justice. The resurgence of the women's movement and the increasing flow of mothers into the paid labor force (Adams and Winston 1980:1; Kreps and Clark 1975) have spawned a new awareness of available options. The type of American woman who transcended sex roles through her social action orientation is more likely, in the present generation, to pursue an occupational career.

THE ORIGINS OF CIVIL RIGHTS ACTIVISM

Without probing the psychological roots of involvement, it is possible to note various social paths to civil rights activism. There appeared to be three major ones. First, some women were prepared from early childhood to be a part of social change movements. Second, some entered by way of traditional women's voluntary associations. Finally, a third group first came into contact with the movement in the process of seeking specific kinds of socializing experiences for their children.

In addition to the vast majority of sample members who report socialization to an ethic stressing racial equality, others became sensitized to injustice through unique experiences with personal problems, marginality, or conflict with parents. About one-quarter of the sample came from homes with radical or labor backgrounds, or joined left-oriented groups while single. These organizations were among the earliest to become involved in exposing racial inequality in the legal system and in waging campaigns against such terrors as lynching. Women with radical political beliefs never questioned their right to become involved in public issues and tended to find husbands of similar mind. Once married and settled in new communities, they were prepared to enter organizational life. A woman with socialist-labor roots talks of her early training in this way:

> I've always had to utilize my intellect and have been encouraged to do that from childhood on. It wasn't that I came from a family where girls are supposed to stay home and take care of babies after they are married. That was wanted, but it was also very clear that I was going to be educated, and that this was a big piece of what I was. . . . So that, in a way, I've always been somewhat different. . . . I was not a dependent kind of person.

Such women entered or formed civil rights groups as soon as opportunities presented themselves. This was often after they had settled in new communities with their husbands and had given birth to their first child. However, a small number of respondents first became active organizationally while attending college, and one became active as a college teacher. The women were joiners, and many became members of the community voluntary associations considered appropriate for middle-class women: church groups, parent–teacher associations, the Young Womens' Christian Association, and the League of Women Voters.

Voluntarism in traditional organizations appears to have affected them in three ways. First, they developed an awareness of and knowledge about racial inequality in the local community (of which there was much evidence) even when the particular organization, such as PTA, was relatively unconcerned. Second, when some of their church groups and other organizations took on civil rights projects, the women grasped at the chance to put long-felt commitment into practice. Such traditional organizations were frequently left behind when human relations and more specifically focused integrationist groups appeared. A third recurring element was the facility with which the women developed initial contacts with black people and acquired black friends. These networks often provided links to organizations such as the NAACP, which had many local branches. Integrationists, the women were eager for interracial contacts for themselves and their children.

ACTIVISM AND MOTHERHOOD: THE SOCIALIZING OF CHILDREN

Given their backgrounds and concerns, the women tended to view the socialization of their children to humanistic values as a major task. One means was to seek or create situations that afforded natural interracial contacts. Asked when she entered civil rights, one woman replied:

> I guess maybe the first kind of action at all was when my son, who is now twenty-five—twenty-two years ago—went to a cooperative nursery school. We put into the bylaws that it was to be interracial, nonsectarian, and we went out of our way to try to attract blacks.

Years later, a woman whose activism preceded marriage explained that concern with racism, sexism, and competition in the public schools prompted her to join in the creation of an alternative elementary school for her children.

Other women sought more informal ways of finding interracial contacts for their children, forming play groups or developing other relationships with black families. Many women became drawn into arrangements in which they shared in teaching or caring for other children. It appears that the most traditional occupational role of women, that of teacher, was highly valued by these women (note that the same was true of the socialist women leaders discussed by Mullaney in Chapter 5). In the case described below, the respondent's quest for religious training for her children led her first into teaching other children and then into her long-term civil rights work:

> I joined the Ethical Culture group in North City, just to have a place for our children to go on Sunday mornings. . . . Well, what happened was the minute I brought them there to enroll them I was pounced upon and asked to teach a class. . . . Then I became a Sunday school director, and developed a whole Sunday school from preschool up until the eighth grade. . . . I was asked to take on this huge task, which I did very willingly, because this seemed to be the beginning of what I had been looking for. . . . I began to realize what a huge world this is and how much had to be done, and I really hadn't done my share. And so, with a vengeance, it began. . . .

She joined a local human relations group as soon as it was formed, becoming very involved in a project to aid a southern black community. She says, "It was an open door. I had wanted to do something. This was the very first step." Her children's needs has pushed this woman out into society, made her aware of her own skills, and moved her on to her civil rights career.

An unanticipated but not surprising finding was that the majority of respondents had been teachers, in varied settings, in volunteer and paid capacities, part-time and full-time, at various stages of their life cycles. Teaching situations varied tremendously, from preschool through college, including religious and secular schools and public and private institutions. The activists were teachers by inclination, not training, some acquiring certification long after they had considerable teaching experience. One went back to college and became qualified to teach in high school after the main period of her civil rights work. She is now using her experiences in group relations in a newly integrated school system. Another received certification in preschool education after directing a predominantly black day-care center. In addition to the Ethical Culture school, respondents teach or have taught in Hebrew, Unitarian, and Protestant Sunday schools. Attachment to children found expression in work at interracial summer camps, with YWCA youth groups, in tutoring programs, cooperative nurseries, and day-care centers. The teaching many times sounded like mothering and tended to include minority and disadvantaged school populations. Here one of the younger mothers, a leader in the welfare rights movement who returned to school by way of a community college, expresses the nurturant quality found in so many of the women:

> I teach neurologically impaired kids. . . . I love it! It's what sustains me. . . . I have six- to eight-year-olds, working on skills . . . just beginning to read. It's very important for the rest of their lives if they're failures in my class—which they won't be! It's completely individualized. I love it.

Another woman replied affirmatively when asked whether she thought her years of part-time teaching in a religious school were important. Teaching history and social studies, she used the opportunity to inculcate human values and self-respect.

IDENTIFICATION WITH BLACK MOTHERS

Several respondents mentioned incidents that clearly showed identification with black mothers. One tells how she tried to help a black woman standing trial for charges stemming from an urban riot: "Ruth Taylor was in jail, and I was involved with several other people in getting her kids down to see her. . . ." Asked whether she had known her, she replied, "No, she was a mother in jail, and I had two little children."

A mother of four took direct action as an individual because of her concern for the safety of black children. She transported her own children to school by car and each day passed a dangerous intersection that black children had to cross. She took it upon herself to complain repeatedly to the local police chief about the situation. Every time, the chief jokingly offered her a job as a crossing guard, and finally she accepted his challenge. As a crossing guard, she made contact with the adult black community.

At the time this happened, the woman involved had an infant as well as the school-going children and was not anxious to take on another responsibility. This example leads to consideration of the main issue faced by the activists: how to manage time.

TIME MANAGEMENT OVER THE CAREER

In the early years, the domestic career tends to revolve around the birth of children, their needs at various ages, and their entrance into school. Nap time for babies and bedtime for children become important breathing spaces for the mother who is doing her own child care and also mark the time that can be devoted to other interests. This early stage can be a lonely one for the housebound mother who feels restricted in her contacts. For many, this is the stage of the "overworked mother," whose tasks are never done. But not for my respondents. It was during this early stage of motherhood that many became active either in traditional community organizations or in civil rights work. They were enthusiastic mothers who carried the main burden of housework and child care. Significantly, when husbands took over responsibility for the children it was usually referred to as "baby-sitting" rather than "fathering," although there were some highly nurturant fathers. Three women who were divorced early in their mothering careers reluctantly curtailed their movement activity, having neither a husband nor money for sitters.

The mothers found various ways to be available during most of the children's waking hours: some engaged in out-of-home pursuits while the children slept, exchanged baby-sitting with other mothers, held meetings at their own homes, or took children along to meetings and demonstrations. The last two solutions were viewed as contributing positively to the children's socialization. Statements such as the following were common:

> The meeting things were important to me and I felt that type of exposure for them was extremely important. So wherever possible and whenever they would go—I didn't force them to go—I would try to take them to meetings with me. I thought that was a part of their development.

One woman who plunged directly into civil rights while her two children were infants describes doing most of her work at night or on the phone, considering the entrance of her four-year-olds into nursery school as affording her free mornings for movement work. Another who began her community involvement in an activist YWCA explains her reaction when first asked to take a position on the Y board:

> My question about "when does it meet" had to do with "could I get a free baby-sitter in my husband," you see, because things that met in the daytime were less than no use to me at that time. I had a four-year-old and a two-year-old, and one on the way, and so I went on to the YWCA Board.

Another commented that "the League of Women Voters came to me out of the blue. I was lonely and felt pretty useless, and I think I started in the league even before my kids got into school."

Family-related community activities or children's pursuits often require the presence or active participation of a parent. Chauffering children is one of them. Numerous occasions require the ceremonial appearance of a parent, signifying that the career of the child has support—whether it is some sort of "award" night, a school concert, or a parent–teacher conference. More than ceremonial support is required for such positions as "den mother" in the Cub Scouts, "class mother" for school outings, and "participating parent" in parent-cooperative nursery schools. The interrelated lives of family members have to be coordinated, and not only is the mother chief administrator, but her day is punctuated by comings and goings on. Of course, critics of these old divisions between father and mother roles have seen disadvantages in them for both parents. Be that as it may, the divisions were real for most of those studied. One woman contrasted the various stages of motherhood in this way:

> I think it's much easier when the kids are small. . . . It was more of a problem when they were bigger and couldn't drive; they had to go to all kinds of activities. . . . You couldn't have a baby-sitter any more, but you didn't feel that you wanted to leave them for certain lengths of time.

And, in a particularly forthright statement, a woman with decades of recognized leadership in both civil rights and peace work talked about the time dilemma:

> Being a mother was always first. Everything else had to be fitted in. This doesn't mean there was no conflict, even with placing them first. There were always decisions that had to be made—always a pull both ways. There were their activities and the ones I was doing.

For many of the women, another stage was reached when they needed to supplement the financing of their children's college education. Many returned to school to prepare for careers; others looked for jobs. At this stage of the domestic career, those who were not working and were in good health had a good deal of time on their hands. The integrationist civil rights movement had changed to a separatist phase in the late 1960s and early 1970s, affording fewer interracial-group contexts for action. But a subject of concern to those who remained active was the murder trials of blacks accused of having taken part in urban riots or rebellions. A number of women became involved in defense committees for these prisoners, in attending trials, and in prison visits. One who managed to play a limited role while working explains:

> Eventually, because they weren't working and because their children were grown, Diane and Audrey attended a trial which ran for three months, and they transported the defendants back and forth; and I worked part-time by then, so I sort of kept track through them of what was going on. And whenever it seemed that some interesting part had been reached in the trial I managed to get there that day. I began to transport some of the defendants.

Nonworking older activists also tended to be freer of concern for personal safety. One joined a somewhat dangerous civil rights campaign in the South after being widowed and when her children were grown. She could not remember their being worried about her, adding, "They were not about to be concerned because they had been into it themselves."

Many respondents had attended such national mobilizations as the 1963 March on Washington. But others were deterred by relatives. Talking about the death of Viola Liuzzo in Alabama, where she was transporting black civil rights workers, one woman commented, "I can remember my brother saying, 'She really should have stayed in Detroit. She had a family to look after.' And I'm sure his opinion as well as my husband's had some effect." This was the same respondent who was transporting black prisoners to a trial in her later years.

THE ACTIVISTS' CHILDREN

The women hoped their children would grow up with humanistic attitudes. They tried to serve as models, to expose them to meetings and demonstrations, and to provide them with interracial contacts. They felt their children had gained by having had early experiences with black people. One woman claimed that her activities "had a marvelous side effect . . . this was a way of getting to know black families and being friendly with black kids, and they had associations with black kids from the earliest ages."

Another woman was more specific. Here she discusses her daughter's ability to handle herself in a high school that was experiencing racial conflict:

> There was a day when I thought it would be better for Marcy not to go to school, because it seemed that things were really going to blow up that day. But she went, and it was all right. The kids were accustomed to living in a home where they saw not only white people but black people, not just for meetings, but socially. . . . Both of them were pretty knowledgeable. Our daughter never had some of the attitudes that come largely from ignorance that some other white liberal kids have. . . . She was well aware of the depth of the anger and resentment and so she didn't do dumb things or take dumb chances. She was prepared for what could happen; she didn't feel that her white liberalism shone out of her face.

Some of the women regretted that not all of their children seemed concerned with social issues. One was exuberant when her young son, previously uninvolved, finally showed anger at antiblack remarks. One mother differentiated between her children's views on the basis of their differing experiences. The older child grew up at the height of her mother's activism, a time when the FBI had come knocking at their door. She shared her mother's sentiments more than did a younger sibling.

The children were frequently described as being proud of their mothers' activities. Some of the women had entered into publicly controversial issues and were well known for their positions. Asked if her children has suffered, one stated, "The kids had gotten in it. They agreed and took their positions to school. . . . My youngest daughter wrote an article about it for the high-school paper." Another, when asked if there were any problems, said that one of her children resented her going out to meetings. But she considered it unrealistic for him to expect her to remain at home all the time and felt that it was a good thing for the family that she was not feeling confined at home.

Almost all said that their involvement had been positive for their children. Two exceptions were women whose husbands had been even more active than they. The women felt, in retrospect, that the high degree of involvement of both parents had deprived their children of needed attention. These were the only two who showed ambivalence about their social movement roles.

CONCLUSIONS

This article has examined the interweaving of the role of civil rights activist and mother of a segment of the American women's population at a particular stage in their personal biography and in social history. The women selected for their community reputations as activists proved to be highly committed mothers as well. They found their two roles ideologically compatible and had a need to participate in the public as well as the private sphere. It was partly their concern with their own young that led them to care for and teach other children, seek interracial contacts, and help create what they considered a better, more humanistic society. Some movements have consciously used the mother role as explanation for women's rights or even duty to be involved in humanistic causes, such as peace and environmental safety. This was not the theme of the civil rights movement but a rationale developed individually by these informants. They thought it healthy for their children to observe them as models and to understand their need to express a strongly held belief. The pragmatic problem of time management was the most difficult one they faced in intermeshing their roles, and this problem changed as the children grew older. The women are viewed as sex-role transcenders who participated in at least two meaningful and linked careers—mother and civil rights activist.

NOTES

This is a revised version of an article that appeared in Helena Z. Lopata, ed., *Research in the Interweave of Social Roles: Women and Men* (Greenwich, Conn.: JAI Press, 1980), vol. 1, pp. 33–50. I would like to thank the Rutgers University Research Council for aiding this research financially over a period of years. I am grateful to Lynda M. Glennon, Laurie D. Cummings, Peter J. Stein, Cheryl Townsend Gilkes, Helena Z. Lopata, Guida West, and Meyer Goldstein for their ideas and support.

1. Some of them also took part in other movements—notably the peace movement. The modern women's movement was a later development, affecting many but drawing the sustained participation of only a few.

2. Most of those studied did not engage in full-time paid work during early motherhood; later most did.

3. For further discussion of methodology, see Goldstein (1977b). This paper and others presented or reproduced have slightly different data bases.

4. The National Organization for Women has distinguished between "political or change-oriented" and "service-oriented" volunteers, criticizing women who would devote their efforts (unpaid) toward activities that appear to support existing institutions. See McCormick (1975) for a discussion of the NOW position at that time. However, not only does voluntarism develop skills, but preexisting organizational networks provide an important resource for those moving toward more politically oriented activities.

5. In Chapter 1, West and I (following Jaquette 1974:xii) question the common assumption that American women are less involved in politics than men. Local voluntary associations are an important vehicle for women's entrance into politics (Flora and Lynn 1974:50). Literature on women in voluntary associations and in politics provides important insights relevant to their social movement participation. (See West and Blumberg, Chapter 1, for more extended discussion).

6. McCarthy and Zald (1973) use the term "social movement organization careers" to refer to the growing number of paid career positions in organizations relating to social movements.

CHAPTER 10

Women in Revolutionary Movements: Changing Patterns of Latin American Guerrilla Struggle

LINDA LOBAO

This study examines the patterns of women's participation in the guerrilla struggle of Latin American revolutionary movements. Analyses of Latin American women's political behavior tend to be directed to conventional political processes, such as voting and officeholding, reflecting gender bias as well as the ethnocentricity of North American researchers.[1] Armed struggle is generally regarded as an exclusively male political behavior;[2] in actuality, Latin American women have participated in guerrilla movements, although not in extensive numbers until recently (Jaquette 1973; Rowbotham 1972; Vitale 1981). With the influx of women into the Nicaraguan, Salvadoran, and Guatemalan movements, analysts have been forced to acknowledge and reconsider women's contributions to armed struggles.

Guerrillas are members of political organizations operating in both rural and urban areas that use armed warfare for the purpose of changing societal structure (Gilio 1970; Guevara 1969; Jaquette 1973; Kohl and Litt, 1974). According to Che Guevara (1969:4), the distinguishing feature of guerrilla warfare, as opposed to the regular warfare waged by large armies, is that guerrillas possess "a much smaller number of arms for use in defense against oppression." Rather than outfighting government forces, guerrillas concentrate more on breaking down the legitimacy of the regime and morally isolating it from popular support (Chaliand 1982:240). Latin American nations have occupied historically dependent positions in the world capitalist system. As a result, past revolutionary struggles have been directed at colonial regimes as well as at those of internal political elites that have arisen from each nation's specific pattern of dependence (Cardoso and Faletto 1979).

Several questions about the nature of women's participation in guerrilla struggles are addressed.[3] First, what factors differentially affect Latin American women's participation as compared with men's? Second, how does class affect women's ability to participate? Finally, what roles in the division of labor are *guerrilleras* most likely to perform? Patterns of women's participation are delineated in light of these questions. Movements in five nations are then examined to show variations in these patterns.

FACTORS AFFECTING WOMEN'S PARTICIPATION

Barriers to Women's Involvement

The Structurally Subordinate Position of Latin American Women and the Ideology of Patriarchy

Latin American women participate in nearly all nondomestic spheres of national life to a lesser extent than men (Chaney 1979; Flora 1973; S. Schmidt 1976; Vitale 1981). This widely documented generalization stems from their structurally subordinate position and suggests why women should be expected to participate less frequently than men in guerrilla movements. Recent Marxian and feminist theory has compellingly argued that the sphere of reproduction must be taken into account in order to describe women's roles, women's relegation to domestic activities, and the historical subordination of women (Brenner and Ramas 1984; Chodorow 1979; Deere and Leon de Leal 1982; V. Randall 1982).[4] Women, primarily, direct the reproductive activities of the household, which are necessary for the reproduction of labor power. Such activities include childbearing, socialization of children, and the care of family members. Women are thus first located in the private sphere of the home by the sexual division of labor, while men are first located in the public sphere outside the home (Chodorow 1979; Stacey and Price 1981).

The sexual division of labor in production builds on women's subordination in the sphere of reproduction (Deere and Leon de Leal, 1982:66). Women are socialized not to perform or to become expert at tasks that are incompatible with their reproductive roles. This facilitates the channeling of women into lower-status "feminine" jobs where they do not compete with men. Further, in the ocupational sphere, as well as in all areas of social organization, the energy, time, and freedom of movement available to most women are greatly limited by their role in reproductive activities (Chaney 1979:17–18; Schlegel 1977:36). This role constitutes a major barrier to their involvement in nondomestic political action such as guerrilla struggle.

In Latin America, patriarchal attitudes both reflect and reinforce the subordination of women and their relegation to the domestic sphere. These attitudes, which represent "ideal" configurations held by both men and women, are summarized by Schmidt (1976:244):

1. The sexual division of labor reflects natural differences between men and women.
2. Women's identity comes through their relationship with men.
3. Women achieve their highest fulfillment as wives and mothers.
4. Women are childlike.
5. Women are apolitical.

Patriarchal attitudes operate most profoundly at the familial level and are relatively consistent across class lines (Safa 1976:80).

The patriarchal model of Latin American family structure is characterized by the male's control over most activities related to the outside world (*calle*) (Fox 1973; 281; Nash and Safa 1976a:25; Studart 1974:47). Within the domestic sphere (*casa*), however, women maintain considerable control through their acknowledged expertise in child rearing and discipline and other household activities (Chaney 1979: Stevens 1973b).

Traditional patriarchal models of family structure and of feminine behavior are undermined by cases of women who head households or are professionals in charge of men. At the national level, however, the formal pattern of male dominance still prevails. The legal status of women in most Latin American civil codes is based upon *patria potestas*, the patriarchal right of the father to control his family. Women are legally "equated with idiots and children" (Kinzer 1973:304).

Occupational and educational statistics reveal men's predominance in public activities. In twelve Latin American nations for which data are available, an average of only 18.7 percent of women were reported as active in the labor force, as compared with 51.8 percent of men (International Labor Organization 1984). ILO employs censuses and surveys from government and other sources in compiling these data. Criteria used to define economic activity may differ from country to country. In particular, low status, informal sector employment (such as household service and agricultural work, part-time and seasonal employment, unpaid family labor, and petty commerce and home production) tends to be underestimated or unreported by government sources (Central American Information Office 1982:50; Lopez de Piza 1977:25; Molyneux 1985:246; Tinker 1981:53). Statistics on Latin American women's employment must therefore be treated cautiously, recognizing that women's labor force participation is generally higher than is cited in official counts.

Educational attainment is also much lower for women than men. Female illiteracy surpasses male rates in all Latin American nations (Nash 1976:13). Educational differences become narrower, however, as higher levels, and hence higher socioeconomic status, are attained. Women represent from 24 to 47 percent of students enrolled in higher education and from 23 to 50 percent of university graduates in Latin American nations for which such data were recorded (Wilkie and Haber 1981:143–44).

As in education and the work force, women participate less in conventional political activities (Jaquette 1976). Stacey and Price (1981:142) report that in 1975 the percentage of women in Latin American legislatures ranged from 0 in Panama to 8 in Mexico. Even women holding public office have limited commitment to political involvement. Only 20 percent of 167 female politicians interviewed in Chile and Peru had ambitions for a political or bureaucratic career, and the majority expressed no desire to remain in public office beyond their current term or appointment (Chaney 1979:137). Women generally vote less frequently than men (Camp 1979; Harkess and Pinzon de Lewin 1975; Jaquette 1976; S. Schmidt 1975).

Conventional politics, however, is limited as an indicator of feminine political participation in Latin America. First, the majority of women did not gain suffrage until after World War II (Jaquette 1976:222). Legal entry of a new group into an electorate has historically been associated with abnormally low voter turnout of group members (Schmidt 1975:480). Secondly, abstention from conventional politics may be regarded as a political act in Latin America, a refusal to participate in a system that represents only privileged minorities (Jaquette 1976:233). Finally, much political behavior in Latin American occurs outside the formal political process. While women have only recently participated in large numbers in the "public sphere" of revolution and protest, they have constantly influenced politics through their position in kinship networks and their political socialization of children (Randall 1982:44–45).

The assumption that Latin American women are more politically conservative than men has been challenged by a number of researchers (Chaney 1979; Jaquette 1976; McGee 1981; Randall 1982). An Argentine study, for example, found males more likely to support parties of the far right (Randall 1982:52). Women, however, may be "less radical than more conservative" than males on certain issues, particularly those involving the family (Jaquette 1976:229–30). As Jaquette (1976) notes, because the Latin American family is an effective institution of social control, it has been attacked by radical movements supporting social change. Women may oppose such movements because they have a stake in maintaining the family as a strong institution.

Conservative groups have also tried to gain women's support by portraying the left as antithetical to the family (Crummett 1977; Jaquette 1976). Middle- and upper-class women in Chile, for example, attempted to tie support for the family to opposition to the Allende government. The right-wing Chilean women who composed El Poder Feminino staged massive propaganda campaigns to convince other women of the "dangers" of Marxism. Right-wing Brazilian women similarly aided in the overthrow of João Goulart by raising a fictitious threat to the family (Schmidt 1976:254). That these deliberately misinformative campaigns successfully contributed to the downfall of Allende and Goulart indicates that revolutionary movements remain vulnerable to feminine attack, unless they deal skillfully with the potential ideological contradiction of support for the family coupled with a social change agenda.

In sum, the structural constraints of women's role in reproductive activities and the traditional ideological constraints (partriarchal attitudes) that define women's roles are major barriers to their participation in guerrilla struggle. Relatedly, women may oppose movements when they perceive these as incompatible with their concerns or as offering no guarantee that their personal power base, the family, will remain intact.

Factors that Facilitate Women's Involvement

While women confront greater barriers than men in participating in armed struggle, several factors can be delineated as specifically contributing to women's involvement.

The Historical Location of the Movement: Changing Patterns of Struggle and Ideological Influence

The nature of revolutionary struggle in Latin America has undergone changes, particularly since the early 1970s, that have encouraged women's involvement (Chinchilla 1980:20). Previously, revolutionary struggle tended to follow the *foquista* model.[5] A small group of revolutionaries relying on military action, in contrast to the gradual establishment of mass-based political organization, formed the center of struggle (Chinchilla 1982:20). The failure of Che Guevara in Bolivia and of *foquismo* throughout Latin America and the decimation of movements in Brazil (1969–71) and other nations pointed to the increased necessity for popular support in the face of greater repression from the right. While subjective and objective conditions must be ripe for revolution, the guerrilla organization itself must be linked to the population. To the extent these links have been absent in Latin American movements, there has been an increased likelihood of failure (Chaliand 1977:42–47; Chinchilla 1982:20–27). The mobilization of women serves to ground movements in more extensive popular support. As Chinchilla (1982:20) notes, women's participation is in line with the conception of "prolonged peoples' war" (gradual organization of all mass sectors under a variety of organizational forms and tactics, such as those inspired by the Vietnamese), which has been adopted as current revolutionary strategy in Central America. There is also the related danger that if guerrilla movements fail to politicize women, progovernment parties may attempt to co-opt feminine support. Chaney (1973b:115) has noted that Latin American politicians have historically viewed woman as "electoral capital," to be mobilized "in the case of emergencies." The mobilization of women against Allende and Goulart may be reminders to more recent guerrilla groups that conservative forces will likewise recruit women, given the opportunity.

Another factor that has facilitated women's participation is the increasing awareness of feminist issues and their implications for class struggle in Latin America (Chinchilla 1982). While the relationship between class and gender has been explored from the time of Marx, the women's liberation movements beginning in the late 1960s, primarily in advanced capitalist nations, sensitized activists to feminist issues (Chinchilla 1982:4–9; Flynn 1980:22). Submission to patriarchal attitudes reinforces acceptance of the capitalist division of labor and the class structure on which it rests. The subjugation of women has historically been responsible for their low levels of class consciousness and resistance to political development (Chinchilla 1977:95). As Molyneux (1985:37) notes, the Latin American left might have unequivocally denounced "feminism" as "counterrevolutionary diversion." Instead, from the 1970s onward, the "problems of gender oppression" were increasingly integrated with those of class oppression in leftist ideology (Flora 1984:71). Women were to be mobilized on two fronts: as members of the working class and on behalf of their own cross-class liberation (Chinchilla 1977:84; Flora 1984:71). The influence of women's liberation movements in the developed nations was felt not only on the socialist left, but also in emergent feminist movements in nations such as Mexico, Peru, and Brazil (Flora 1984:72; Molyneux 1985:236) and in the mass media (Chinchilla 1982:7–8). Thus while male dominance still "limits women in all situations, in

all social classes," there has been an increasing popular sensitivity to women's issues in Latin America (Flora 1984:91).

In sum, changes in the political nature of guerrilla struggle and the diffusion of feminist thought have encouraged more recent guerrilla movements to recruit women at a time when Latin American women are becoming increasingly more receptive to need for their own liberation. Later guerrilla movements have also been able to profit from the examples of women's involvement in earlier ones in Latin America as well as in Vietnam, Angola, and Mozambique (Chinchilla 1982). These examples, and particularly the postrevolutionary incorporation of Cuban women into production and politics vis-à-vis the attack on the "second shift" (the division of labor in household work), could guide later movements in their policies toward women (Chinchilla 1982).

Social Structural Characteristics Related to Women's Roles

Women's responsibility for the reproductive activities of the household limits the time and scope of their involvement outside the home. However, the centrality of these roles to women's lives can also provide a basis for political action. Changing socioeconomic and political conditions related to family survival have impinged on women's roles and served to mobilize women, according to a number of researchers. For example, women's beliefs in early-nineteenth-century Barcelona that government policies hampered family sustenance fostered their militancy and progressive political consciousness (Kaplan 1982). Flora (1984:78) reports that neighborhood associations established by Brazilian working-class women "stemmed from the immediate needs of *reproduction of the labor force*—their day to day needs as housewives and mothers." These associations, initially focused on day care, helped women gain organizational and tactical experience that later facilitated their involvement in broader political issues. Chinchilla (1982) describes how the politically repressive Somoza regime impelled Nicaraguan women's mobilization because it undermined their roles as nurturers and family protectors.

As industrialization increases, greater numbers of women move into the paid labor force. This increases their contact with people and issues outside the family, which, in turn, increases their potential for mobilization. Chafetz and Dworkin (1985:102–3) note that when large numbers of married women enter the labor force, they begin to see employment as an important, permanent role and to compare their labor force experiences with those of men. It is at this point that large-scale women's movements with feminist ideology are most likely to develop. A large number of households in Central American nations are dependent on female bread winners, because of high male unemployment and underemployment and males' involvement in migrant agricultural work (Chinchilla 1982:9–11). When women have major responsibility for both domestic and nondomestic aspects of family survival, and they perceive government as threatening, they may participate in revolutionary movements, especially if such movements are seen as facilitating these joint roles of mother and wage earner (Molyneux 1985; Nash 1977).

Organizational Characteristics

The historical location of the revolutionary struggle and social structural factors related to women's roles present opportunities and rationales for guerrilla movements to recruit women. Internal organizational characteristics, such as the way in which revolutionary goals are formulated and male–female relationships within guerilla groups, can also foster women's participation (Chinchilla 1982:15–20). The issues involved in revolutionary struggle—such as economic policy, political representation, and foreign hegemony—are clearly of major importance in motivating both men and women. Goals specifically directed to women's concerns, however, should increase their motivation to participate beyond these initial levels. Molyneux (1985) defines two major ways—strategic and practical—in which women's interests may be articulated by organizations seeking feminine support. Strategic gender interests are derived "from the analysis of women's subordination and from the formulation of an alternative, more satisfactory set of arrangements to those which exist" (Molyneux 1985:232). These involve essentially feminist long-term objectives directed toward ending women's subordination, such as abolishing the sexual division of labor, institutionalized forms of gender discrimination, and male control over women. Practical gender interests "arise from the concrete conditions of women's positioning within the gender division of labor" (Molyneux 1985:233). These interests usually arise in response to an immediate need, such as domestic provision and public welfare, and "do not generally entail a strategic goal such as women's emancipation or gender equality" (Molyneux 1985:233). Practical gender interests and closely intertwined with class, as economic necessity particularly affects poorer women. Molyneux (1985) notes that before most women will support movements advocating strategic gender interests, they must perceive such movements as dealing with their basic, short-term practical interests. Revolutionary groups that seek the mass support of women thus need to develop platforms with such issues in mind. To the extent that the Latin American Left has not developed a social change–family agenda compatible with women's interests, it has lost their support.

Male–female relations within the guerrilla movements can also encourage women's participation, when egalitarian relationships in the division of labor and in the opportunity for leadership are promoted. While armed struggle has traditionally been a male domain of political behavior, groups that are able to supersede some of the sexism of the larger society stand a better chance of recruiting women (Chinchilla 1982).

On balance, while women's roles in reproductive activities and the tradition of Latin American patriarchalism inhibit women's participation in guerrilla movements, certain conditions can promote feminine support. Changes in the nature of Latin American revolutionary struggle and the diffusion of feminist ideology make recent movements more likely to recruit women and make women more receptive to recruitment. Social structural characteristics related to women's roles can also be a springboard for their activism. Women's participation depends both on the nature of these external sociohistorical conditions and on the organizational response of guerrillas to these conditions through recruitment efforts, policy development, and internal relations.

Class Differences in Women's Ability to Participate

The classes that support revolutionary movements as well as their specific grievances depend on historical conditions experienced by each nation. Since Latin American nations have occupied dependent positions in the world economy, movements advocating fundamental social change have attacked the internal and external social relations that sustain such dependence: the class and political structures and foreign hegemony. Class is an important base of support for revolutionary struggle, and male and female supporters should be expected to share class locations. Most guerrilla movements have been supported by segments of the middle class and the proletariat. Traditional elites, excluding students and intellectuals, clearly tend to support the entrenched order (Halperin 1976; Horowitz 1970). The middle class, composed of heterogeneous rural and urban groups, has varied historically in its commitment to the status quo (Ratinoff 1967; Soares 1980; Weffort 1970). The urban and rural proletariat, potentially the most radical classes, face the greatest barriers to political involvement. They are generally marginalized from formal political participation. Their low level of subsistence decreases their capacity to react to exploitation, even for those conscious of class interest. They are vulnerable to employer threats, and political participation may take away from paid labor time, increasing the costs of such activism (Nash 1976).[6]

Working-class women in the labor force, because of their added role in the reproductive activities of the household, face even greater obstacles to political involvement than working-class men (Sefchovich 1980:6). Their work (two out of five Latin American women in the labor force are domestic servants) is exhausting and low-paying and tends to restrict them to domestic areas, where class consciousness is not as likely to arise (Chaney 1973b:108; Safa 1977:135). In rural areas, campesino women are similarly burdened by their contribution to both household reproductive activities and agricultural production (Deere and Leon de Leal 1982). Working-class women who do not work outside the home still share the disadvantages of their class and gender—low education, low income, few marketable skills, major responsibility for the home, and so on. The added burden of gender stratification to class is reflected in studies of conventional politics that show that in Latin America low socioeconomic status decreases women's activism more profoundly than it does men's (Chaney 1979:87; 1973b:111–12).

Despite barriers to political involvement, working-class women have at times managed to act in support of class interests. They have frequently been members of revolutionary organizations in the Nicaraguan, Salvadoran, and Guatemalan struggles (Chinchilla 1982); and Chilean working-class women were decisive in the 1970 election of Allende (Chaney 1979:97). Indeed, their experiences in the day-to-day struggle to survive may make these women tenacious political fighters.[7] Female heads of working-class households have particularly strong potential to develop class consciousness. As primary wage

earners, they are more committed to their jobs and have organizational potential around both class/work and household based issues (Safa 1976:75–76).
However, these women are also the most vulnerable to the costs of political
action, in terms of job loss or imprisonment, which may inhibit activism (Safa
1976:75–76).

Should the middle class (or as happens in some cases, segments of the
elite) also support a revolutionary movement, such women would have
greater ability to participate than working-class women. Middle-class women
have not been marginalized from formal political processes and important
areas of national life. They make up the majority of all female university
students and professional workers. Their higher education contributes to
their political awareness and to their greater participation in conventional
political activities (Chaney 1973b:108; 111–12).

These involvements of middle-class women, however, do not negate patriarchal tradition. Indeed, Jaquette (1976:230) argues that many patriarchal attitudes operate more strongly for the middle class, and Cohen (1973:328) finds
women entering Colombian universities expecting education to complement
future familial roles. Even when women enter politics, they perform in familial-
type roles that have been extended to the public arena. The "super-*madre*," or
conventional female political officeholder, treats employees like children. Moreover, the "super-*madre*" operates in areas equivalent to a macro extension of her
household expertise, such as social welfare—health care, child care, and literacy programs. Women have been virtually absent from high-level policy-
making positions throughout Latin America (Chaney 1973b:109).

If patriarchal attitudes operate equally or more effectively on middle-class
women, they cannot explain middle-class women's greater involvement in
conventional politics, education, and other areas of national life. Middle-class
women participate more because it is feasible for them to do so and because
their class has had more access to these areas. Nor do they have the basic
problems of survival faced by working-class women. Should callings to take
up a career, join a political movement, or even join a guerrilla band occur,
there are no financial considerations (such as support or family members) to
stop them. Furthermore, problems of child care and housekeeping are simpli-
fied for middle-class women. While they still face major responsibility for
rearing children and supervising the domestic sphere, middle-class women
are able to escape much of the drudgery of housework through their exploitation of lower-class women as domestic servants. The middle-class *doña de casa*
thus has more time and greater financial resources to pursue any type of
activity. Further, she possesses the ascriptive background—higher status—to
exercise institutionalized authority and to command respect from a large segment of the population (Schmidt 1975:468–69). Social status and education
may allow middle-class women easier access to, and permit vanguard positions in, political groups that also include working-class persons.

In sum, while middle-class women face gender barriers to participation,
working-class women are doubly burdened by class and gender. Women
share common motivating interests with the men of their class and may be
motivated by gender-specific interests as well. In order for the working-class

women to participate, the consciousness of these interests, which may arise from perceptions of objective socioeconomic conditions or from revolutionary ideology, must be extremely high. Grievances involving household sustenance and practical gender issues, such as child care or social welfare, are important to all women, but most crucial to the working-class. The saliency of these issues are a key factor in explaining why working-class women mobilize despite the costs.

THE DIVISION OF LABOR BY GENDER IN GUERRILLA MOVEMENTS

Guerrilla movements challenge fundamental aspects of the social order, creating new statuses and roles for members in the process. That these movements have included even small numbers of women distinguishes them from the traditional militaries of the state. Abilities, such as skill in combat or leadership, are necessarily more important than social status in the allocation of positions in guerrilla movements. Shortages in personnel may also open opportunities to play roles formerly assigned to others. As a result, gender should not be as important for determining guerrilla roles as it is for roles in the large society.

However, even guerrilla movements that challenge the division of labor by gender are located in fundamentally sexist societies. The division of labor by gender, which affects occupational, educational, and conventional political life, can be expected to filter down even into guerrilla operations. When conventional state militaries do utilize women, they place them in positions that are most compatible with the existing gender order (Enloe 1980). Enloe notes that actual practices concerning women's roles in liberation armies "frequently look strikingly similar," even though ideological reasons for recruiting women differ greatly in the two situations (1980:49). Thus women may be more likely to occupy support rather than combat positions in guerrilla struggle.

An indication that guerrillas themselves hold patriarchal attitudes, in spite of their otherwise radical orientation, is found in Che Guevara's handbook on guerrilla warfare (1969:87):

> But also in this stage [the guerrilla struggle] a woman can perform her habitual tasks of peacetime; it is very pleasing to a soldier subjected to the extremely hard conditions of life to be able to look forward to a seasoned meal which tastes like something. . . . The woman as cook can greatly improve the diet and, furthermore, it is easier to keep her in these domestic tasks; . . . [such duties] are scorned by those [males] who perform them; they are constantly trying to get out of those tasks in order to enter into forces that are actively in combat.

Halperin (1976:45) cites a similar bent toward sexism even in *Actas Tupamaras*, the manifesto of the Uruguayan Tupamara movement. Feminine contributions to guerrilla warfare include "a carefully and competently prepared meal."

While sexism within movements can operate to relegate women to support operations, strategic motives may also lead to the same result. Women can play important revolutionary roles in support positions because of sex stereotyping by the opposition. Using data compiled from news sources on 350 terrorists from around the world, Russel and Miller (1977) argue that women attract less suspicion than men. Women as a group can operate safe houses or store weapons without attracting as much suspicion as a gathering of males. Women are able to pose as wives or mothers in order to gain entrance to restricted areas. They can also act as decoys and distract males' attention in hit-run assaults, as was frequent in the Tupamaro movement. Guerrillas may thus place women in support roles more out of strategic utility than sexism, because they can manipulate patriarchal images to the movement's advantage. Logically, women would be able to do more to aid guerrilla movements by utilizing these patriarchal "images" through covert operations than by standing behind a stove in order to feed a male body and ego.

While women should be more likely to occupy support positions, actual roles may vary because of dynamics similar to those that affect the degree of their participation. The diffusion of feminist ideology may sensitize later groups to the inequities of the division of labor and alter traditional patterns of role assignment. Later movements may also profit from earlier examples of women's success in combat. Finally, when women have been heavily recruited, necessary support positions may be filled, allowing women to progress to other areas.

Patterns of Women's Participation in Guerrilla Movements: Case Studies

Key factors circumscribing the patterns of women's participation in guerrilla struggle have been suggested. Women may be expected to participate less extensively than men, since they face greater barriers to such participation. This general pattern may fluctuate, however, depending on the historical location of the guerrilla movement, social structural conditions affecting women's roles, and internal guerrilla organization. Women's class location should differentially affect their ability to participate. Middle-class women, due to time and financial resources, should have less difficulty participating. The sexual division of labor, for both strategic and ideological reasons, should result in the assignment of more to support than to combat roles. Case studies of five guerrilla movements are presented to show variations in actual patterns of participation and the factors that influenced them.

Women in the guerrilla movements of Cuba, Colombia, Uruguay, Nicaragua, and El Salvador are compared in terms of the three specified issues: the extent of their participation, class background, and roles performed. These five nations were selected because they offer a chronology of women's participation (from the late 1950s to the present) and because historical conditions affecting women's participation in each nation were sufficiently varied that important comparisons could be drawn.

Data about women in guerrilla movements are limited by the nature of the subject. We are examining an area outside of conventional politics, where data are more difficult to gather; highly gender-stratified societies with a paucity of literature on women; and nations under repressive political conditions, where censorship and political reprisals may silence reports. Information about the guerrilla tends to be impressionistic and fragmentary. Case studies examine the contribution of individual women (Franqui 1980), and a few biographies exist.[8] While female participation is mentioned in some literature, details such as number of females involved or the duties they perform are missing (Laqueur 1977; Vega 1969). Only one study has been found that presents a systematic comparative investigation of women's participation in the movements of several Latin American nations (Jaquette 1973).

Cuba

Armed struggle in Cuba was first aimed at overthrowing the Batista regime, which had seized power in a 1952 coup (Blasier 1967; Draper 1965; Laqueur 1977). Cubans were outraged at the illegal manner in which Batista took control of the government and at the dictatorship's corruption, censorship, terror, and torture. Inequalities of wealth and living conditions, failure to achieve agrarian reforms, high levels of seasonal and structural employment, and Batista's policies toward U.S. investment in Cuba were among the contributing factors in the dictator's downfall (Blasier 1967; Laqueur 1977). The Cuban Revolution succeeded through the efforts of a core group of revolutionaries. For nearly two decades, it served as the *foquista* model on which following guerrilla struggles in Latin America were based.

The Cuban government under Fidel Castro has been lauded for the mobilization it achieved among women (Jaquette 1973:347). However, they were generally mobilized after the insurgent period. They do not seem to have participated substantially in the armed struggle itself.

Jaquette (1973:346–47) mentions only three females (all linked to male leaders) who participated in the guerrilla struggle in the Sierra Maestra: Celia Sánchez (Fidel's secretary), Vilma Espín (wife of Raúl Castro), and Haydée Santamaria (wife of the party leader Amando Hart Daválos). Haydée and another woman, Melba Hernández, were members of the initial group that created the Twenty-sixth of July Movement and were participants in the attack on the Moncada (Franqui 1980:527; Lopez 1976:111). Rowbotham (1972:223) provides other evidence of female participation. She states that although a women's Red Army battalion was formed, "the conditions of guerrilla fighting did not encourage the emergence of women." Men took control of the revolution. They "were not accustomed to taking orders from a woman" (Che Guevara, quoted in Rowbotham 1972:224). Chapelle (1962:327) estimates that by December 1958, one in twenty Fidelista troops was a woman.

While there is disagreement about the social origins of those who participated in the insurgency, most analysts acknowledge the important contributions made by the middle class and the peasantry (Blasier 1967:45–46; Torres and Aronde 1968:56). Fidel's core group who survived the 1956 landing were middle class, as were the majority of the leadership (Blasier 1967; Draper 1965). Evidence that middle-class women participated is suggested from the backgrounds of the women previously discussed and the existence of student guerrilla organizations that sometimes included women (Franqui 1980:186, 526–27, 532; Lopez 1976:111). Peasant women probably participated less frequently. Vilma Espín, president of the Federation of Cuban Women, noted that campesino women were generally not organizationally active until mobilized by the federation after the insurgency period (Purcell 1973:263).

Women performed basically support and relief roles. Franqui (1980) has examined the revolution through letters and interviews with Cuban revolutionaries. He provides evidence of support rather than combat performance. Women were "mobilized" to obtain a guerrilla corpse from the police; a Santiago woman delivered secret correspondence; women participated in street demonstrations (1980:215, 219, 229). According to Lopez (1976:112), women were combatants, nurses, messengers, scouts, and teachers, and withstood battle conditions "to perform domestic tasks on guerrilla fronts." Che Guevara (1969) noted, however, that women were not routinely combatants, but were sometimes placed in such positions when needed for relief purposes. Thus as substitutes for males, women could gain initial combat opportunities. Chapelle (1962: 327) observed that with the exception of one sniper platoon, women in the guerrilla army did housekeeping and supply assignments. Celia, Haydée, and Vilma are exceptional in that they held actual combat positions. Fidel's letters to Celia illustrate her combat experience. He states, "Even when a woman goes around the mountains with a rifle in hand, she always makes our men tidier, more decent, more gentlemanly . . ." (Franqui 1980:192). In a later letter, Fidel orders Celia to arrest a guerrilla charged with malperformance of duties (1980:352).

Apparently, Cuban women were not actively recruited during the insurgency. For example, excerpts from broadcasts of Radio Rebelde, the major revolutionary station, reveal no attempt to mobilize them (Franqui 1980: 297–99, 391–94). Certainly, inequality between the sexes was incompatible with the classless, egalitarian society the Cuban Revolution was committed to create, as the Castro government early recognized (Purcell 1973: 261–62), but widespread mobilization of women did not occur until the establishment of the Federation of Cuban Women in 1960. When asked by Fidel Castro to organize the federation, Espín responded: "I asked precisely why do we have to have a women's organization? I had never been discriminated against. I had my career as a chemical engineer. I never suffered, I never had any difficulty" (Azicri 1979:29). Thus women did not participate extensively in the Cuban struggle. While Guevara's comments indicate that Celia, Haydée, and Vilma took part in actual combat, they seem to have been exceptions. The Cuban *guerrilleras* performed mainly support roles. Their combat opportunities came generally in relief capacities, as substitutes for males.

Colombia

Revolutionary struggle in Colombia during the mid-1960s was affected by the aftermath of La Violencia, a violent civil war between the Liberal and Conservative parties from 1946 to 1953. La Violencia left oligarchic rule intact. In 1966, President Carlos Lleras Restrepo was elected with only 20 percent of the votes cast. Sixty-five percent of eligible voters abstained, indicating their frustration with an electoral agreement that allowed competition between only two indistinguishable parties serving elite interests (Gott 1971:242). The Colombian Communist Party, as early as 1950, had organized peasants fleeing from La Violencia to occupy areas from which they could defend themselves. Independent Communist republics were established in peasant areas, which survived until the last major army offensive against them in 1965 (Gomez 1967). Peasants formed a decentralized guerrilla organization with the major aims of ending oligarchic rule and instituting land reforms (Gilly 1965). Gomez (1967:61) reports that women were organized in committees but provides no detail as to their activities. He does note, however, that during an invasion of one peasant republic, women and children were not permitted to accompany the guerrilla detachments. After 1965, peasants were still well organized and continued the struggle, although the army occupied many of their former strongholds.

Women do not seem to have participated in any great numbers in two important guerrilla organizations of the mid-1960s: the Army of National Liberation (ELN) of Camilo Torres, a Fidelista movement; and the People's Liberation Army (EPL), a Maoist group (Gomez, 1967; Gott 1971; Jaquette 1973). Goals of both groups included an end to oligarchic rule and imperialism and the institution of agrarian reform (Gott 1971:525–34). Jaquette (1973:348) notes that "progressively educated" women in Torres's movement researched conditions of women in various areas of Colombia so that policies could be developed toward these groups. When Torres was killed by the army at Pato de Cemento in 1966, a female who escaped into the forest was said to be seen firing at troops (Jaquette 1973:348). The EPL, which was formed after Torres's death, allowed women to join an auxiliary. The EPL's declaration of 1968 stated: "Countless women from the people could only rely on poverty, slavery, and prostitution. Now their path is clear and bright; they can join the ranks of one of the auxiliary units of the EPL, helping with their own hands to build a true fatherland." (Gott 1971:533) However, there is no evidence that women performed extensively in these units.

The women who participated in Torres's group were most likely middle-class, based on the support Torres received from students in general and the reference to "progressively educated" women (Broderick 1975). Peasants also composed part of Torres's organization, but in somewhat lesser numbers than students (Gott 1971:227). According to U.S. major "Pappy" Shelton, the EPL has "real peasant support," though its organizers seem to have been educated and middle-class (Gott 1971:303–4). Based on the previous organizational experience of Colombian peasants, it would be expected that some peasant women participated in both movements. The role women may have performed in both movements is unclear. Participation in combat activities is alluded to only in the the "presumed" account of an armed *guerrillera* at Torres's death.

Both Torres and the EPL seemed to have made no real attempt to recruit women (Broderick 1975; Gott 1971; Jaquette 1973). Torres's platform (Gott 1970:528) stated that "protection for women and children [would] be provided by the law by means of effective sanction" and that both men and women would be drafted into civic, rather than military, service. The EPL offered women branches to join but presented little rationale for why they should join them (Gott 1971:533). Thus women seem not to have participated extensively in the Colombian movements.

Uruguay

The Tupamaros arose as a response to the economic crisis faced by Uruguay from the mid-1950s onward. Production had stagnated, and unemployment and inflation were rising. The nation was dependent on a monoculture, export economy (animal products) that experienced price fluctuations and market decline. Uruguayans protested with strikes and riots during the late 1960s. The government responded by enacting states of siege and engaging in repression (Kohl and Litt 1974; Porzecanski 1973). The Tupamaros, founded in 1962, attributed Uruguay's economic stagnation to the contradictions and malfunctions inherent in capitalism (Porzecanski 1973:3). Among their major goals were the establishment of socialism, and hence an end to foreign hegemony, oligarchic rule, and government repression (Movimiento de Liberación Nacional 1974:293–96).

In contrast to the previous movements, women participated in substantial numbers in the Tupamaros. Porzecanski's study (1973:31) of Tupamaro arrest records indicates that in a relatively early year of the movement, 1966, females composed approximately 10 percent of the group. By 1972, they represented over 25 percent of all Tupamaro members. Female participation rates, as estimated from arrest records, partially reflect the willingness of the police to apprehend women. However, a variety of analysts have noted the importance of women to the movement (Halperin 1976:45; Jaquette 1973:351; Madruga 1974:290; Wilson 1974:85).

The Tupamaros recruited members from all classes of society, but primarily from the middle class. As Kohl and Litt (1974:191) note, since Uruguay is a middle-class and highly urbanized nation, the movement tends to reflect this composition. Porzecanski's data also reveal a middle-class base of support. In 1966, 61 percent of the guerrillas were students or middle-class professionals, while 32 percent were workers. These figures remained approximately the same in 1972. The data have not been broken down by sex and class simultaneously, so it is unclear what proportion of females were middle- or working-class. However, since middle-class participation in general was nearly double that of the working class, it is likely the movement was composed of women largely from the middle class.

Women seem to have filled both support and combat roles. All active Tupamaro squads had one or two female members, but more emphasis was placed on support activities such as liaison, logistics, and operation of safe houses (Halperin 1973:45). Tupamaro reports, according to Jaquette (1973:351), indicated large numbers of women involved in robberies and kidnappings, often acting as decoys. Gilio's (1970) descriptions of the movement portray women guarding prisoners, robbing banks, and passing out leaflets. In order to distract government forces, women would strike provocative poses, feign accidents, and so forth, playing an important tactical role in guerrilla action.

According to Jaquette (1973:351), the Tupamaros were the only group (as of 1973) to have developed a detailed position on "revolutionary women." This position stressed an end to cultural and educational discrimination against women and advocated complementary sharing of tasks rather than a rigid division of labor. The Tupamaros also developed a program for revolutionary government that would seem to appeal to women. The program called for, in part, free education, equitable distribution of income, state control of the health industry, state aid to the elderly, and nationalization of food wholesaling enterprises (Movimiento de Liberación Nacional 1974:293–96). Since the proportion of women in the Tupamaro movement was substantial and, according to Porzecanski's data, more than doubled in six years, an argument can be made that the Tupamaros adopted effective strategies to recruit women. Although this movement was largely *foquista* in character and never achieved a mass base of support, it occurred at a period when educated, middle-class Uruguayans were increasingly exposed to gender issues.

In sum, middle-class women (as well as men) seemed to be most responsive toward the movement. Women soon filled both combat and support positions. This contrasts with the movements in Cuba and Colombia, where low rates of participation were associated with basically noncombatant performance.

Nicaragua

In contrast to the previous guerrilla movements, revolution in Nicaragua followed the pattern of protracted people's war, with mass-based participation (Chinchilla 1982). According to the Sandinista National Liberation Front (FSLN), the objectives of the Nicaraguan Revolution were "to take political power by destroying . . . the dictatorship and to establish a revolutionary government based on the worker–peasant alliance and the convergence of all the patriotic anti-imperialist and anti-oligarchic forces in the country" (FSLN 1983:139). The immediate aim of the revolution was thus to overthrow Somoza and his National Guard, who brutally repressed the population in the attempt to maintain privilege for a small elite. Nicaragua was tied to the world economy through cotton, sugar, and coffee exports. Dependent "development" meant the dispossession of small farmers, the creation of a landless proletariat, high urban and rural and unemployment, a low standard of living, and short life expectancy (Ramirez-Horton 1982). It also meant the destabilization of family life, as men abandoned families and migrated in search of seasonal or other employment and higher wages (Chinchilla 1982; Ramirez-Horton 1982). The number of female-headed households has thus been high, an estimated one-third of all families in 1978 (Chinchilla 1982:11). Nicaragua's history of dependent capitalism also produced high participation of women in the labor force (as compared with other Latin American nations), since they have had to work to support their families. Data from 1977 indicate that 86 percent of women who were family heads worked outside the home, and 45 percent of married women did so (AMNLAE 1982:24). Thus according to Chinchilla, "capitalist development in Nicaragua made impossible the realization of bourgeois ideals of the nuclear family and economically dependent women" (1982:14).

Female membership in the Sandinista movement during the final offensive in mid-1979 has been estimated at 30 percent (Flynn 1980:29). A central factor in the large proportion of women in the Sandinista movement was active recruitment by the Association of Women Confronting the National Problem (AMPRONAC), founded in 1977 by an FSLN cadre (Chinchilla 1982:24). AMPRONAC served as a forum for women whose families or relatives had been victimized by the Somoza regime. Demonstrations and petitions were principal activities, although it clandestinely encouraged women to join the FSLN (Schultz 1980:37). In March 1978, AMPRONAC openly announced its support for the Sandinistas (Flynn 1980:29).

The earliest organizers of AMPRONAC had been mainly middle- and upper-class women, such as lawyers, journalists, and bureaucrats (Flynn 1980:29; Ramirez-Horton 1982:151). Ramirez-Horton (1982:147) interviewed one woman, for example, who "decided to use her university education and leave her daughter with the maid, over the strong protests of her husband, to begin organizing women in the urban areas in defense of human rights." By 1978, the organization had achieved mass support, incorporating women from all social classes opposed to the dictatorship: peasants, workers, students, as well as the middle class and segments of the upper class (AMPRONAC 1982:3–4; Booth 1982:97–126).

Women initially participated in the Sandinista struggle in support operations but later took combat roles. They secured positions of leadership in combat operations, commanding "everything from small units to full battalions" (Flynn 1980:29). At the final battle of León, four of the seven Sandinista commanders were women (Schultz 1980:38).

The organizational conditions created by the Sandinistas are an important reason why so many women participated in the movement. As Chinchilla (1982:14) notes, women's commitment to their families, which had been a traditional barrier to their participation in revolutionary movements, actually facilitated participation under the Sandinistas. The FSLN responded to the immediate problems faced by women under Somoza. First, it attempted to counter the repression felt keenly and uniquely by women: women were expected to protect their children, but their children had increasingly become targets of repression due to their real or fabricated opposition to the dictatorship; and many women needed to work outside the home, but they, too, were subjected to harassment from Somocista troops (Chinchilla 1982:11).

Second, the FSLN incorporated longer-term objectives important to women into its formal platform. It called for the "struggle to end discrimination against women, particularly in the forms of prostitution and domestic servitude," and encouraged women to organize "in defense of their rights" under the dictatorship (FSLN 1979:112). AMPRONAC's (1982:4–5) 1978 platform included among its major demands: "Better living conditions, improved housing, education. Equal salary for equal work . . . An end to prostitution and the usage of women as economic commodities . . . Abolishment of all laws that discriminate against women." Major goals of the Luisa Amanda Espinoza Association of Nicaraguan Women (AMNLAE), the organization created from AMPRONAC after the 1979 victory, indicate the continuation of such objectives. These include establishing child-care, health-care, and educational programs; organizing workers (particularly domestics, with the long-term goal of completely eliminating domestic service); eliminating female unemployment; establishing forums to encourage female political participation; and creating laws to end legal discrimination against women (Flynn 1980:31). The FSLN goals were thus oriented around more immediate social-welfare issues as well as the long-term end to discrimination. Such goals bolstered rather than undercut the familial roles of many women and tended to promote family survival, especially for lower-class and female-headed households. The repression of the Somoza regime coupled with poor socioeconomic conditions undoubtedly impinged on many women's ability to sustain their families. While women from the lower classes face greater barriers to participation, the extensive involvement of such women in the FSLN indicates the great appeal of its objectives.

The FSLN also created internal organizational conditions conducive to female participation. According to Chinchilla (1982:17), it stressed "correct relationships" among members, based advancement on merit and skill, and cultivated respect and support for women. Relations between men and women in the organization contrasted sharply with the sexism outside the movement (Chinchilla 1982:15–20). This organizational climate was not easily achieved. The first women recruited into the FSLN during the 1960s experienced isolation and an undervaluing of their achievements. As more women entered the movement, sexism began to break down (Chinchilla 1982:15–20). Chinchilla (1982:18) notes that the opportunity for respect based on merit provided important motivation for women to join the movement.

Nicaragua clearly demonstrates the possibility of the mass mobilization of women, in spite of class and gender barriers to participation. The FSLN gained extensive support by focusing on issues relevant to the whole society and the overthrow of a repressive regime, as well as gender-specific issues related to the role of women in Nicaraguan society. It created AMPRONAC specifically to mobilize women and fostered internal organizational conditions conducive to feminine participation.

El Salvador

In October 1979, young Salvadoran officers seized power in a coup against General Oscar Humberto Romero. The coup was undertaken to combat the structural inequalities that placed most Salvadorans in poverty, to protest increasing human rights violations, and because of the unpopularity of the military, which was tarnished by its involvement with a regime considered corrupt and repressive (NACLA 1984:14). The coup was supported by many factions of the Left. However, the first junta established by the coup lasted only three months before its reforms were blocked by the oligarchy, big business, and right-wing military officials. In the following years, government by the moderate Christian Democrats did little to combat the power of the oligarchy and big business, while repression by the Right continued to increase (Forche 1982; NACLA 1984). The major opposition to right-wing forces now consists of the joint opposition fronts of the Farabundo Martí Front for National Liberation/Democratic Revolutionary Front (FMLM/FDR). Their present platform includes demands for direct power sharing, extensive agrarian reform, reform of the financial system and foreign trade, a mixed economy, a pluralistic polity, and restructuring of the army and security forces (NACLA 1984:16). At this time, women are not specifically mentioned in principal objectives of the struggle (Baloyra 1982:165; NACLA 1984;16).

Women make up a great part of the popular organizations that compose the FMLM/FDR (AMES 1982; Armstrong 1982; Armstrong and Shenk 1980; Castillo 1982; Central American Information Office 1982; Herrera 1983; Montgomery 1982; WIRE 1982a). The FMLN is a coalition of four political–military organizations and the Communist Party of El Salvador. The Popular Forces of Liberation (FPL) and the National Resistance (RN), two of the organizations within the FMLN, have high-ranking female *commandantes* (Armstrong 1982:28). Female participation in the FPL has been estimated at 40 percent (Armstrong and Shenk 1980:20). The FDR is an umbrella organization for socialist, social-democratic, student, and worker parties. It is directed by considerable female leadership, with women constituting 40 percent of the Revolutionary Council (Central America Information Office 1982:57).

The FMLM/FDR has a broad base of support and includes people from the middle and working classes: students, union workers, and professionals (Armstrong and Shenk 1980:32; WIRE 1982a:34). In rural areas, local peasants play a key part in guerrilla operations (NACLA 1981:12). Middle-class women, in particular teachers and students, were the first to be drawn into political–military organizations in the late 1960s. Rural working women soon followed. In the late 1970s, urban workers entered the struggle (Castillo 1982:8).

Women are involved in both support and combat operations (AMES 1982; Castillo 1982; WIRE 1982b, 1982c). Relations between men and women seem egalitarian. One guerrilla comments on women's roles:

> We are trying to teach the women that they do not have to accept only the traditional roles for women, that they should try to examine their potentialities. We have some peasant women who join us as cooks but they soon realize that they have opportunities to do other things. They become combatants, medics, or leaders. (NACLA 1981:13)

Montgomery (1982:151) presents another example:

> One guerrilla said in an interview that the "process of coming to see women as *compañeras* and not as sex objects" was one he and his fellow guerrillas had had to go through in the mountains. In his particular unit, two-thirds of the combatants were women. "There is a great concern," he said, "to destroy *machismo*."

The FMLN/FDR has no unified mass organization for women on the scale of the Sandinista AMPRONAC. Rather, there are various smaller organizations affiliated with the FMLN/FDR that deal with gender-related issues, such as the Association of Salvadoran Women (AMES), incorporating housewives,

professionals, teachers, students, and previously unorganized groups; organizations of peasant women in the zones of FMLN Central, such as the Association of Women of Guazapa "Lil Milagro Ramirez"; the Committee of Mothers and Relatives of the Disappeared, Assassinated, and Political Prisoners; the National Association of Salvadoran Teachers (ANDES); and the Association of Market Vendors and Workers (AUTRAMES) (Castillo 1982; Latin American Working Group 1983; WIRE 1982a).

The FMLM/FDR tacitly supports women's issues and encourages women to share tasks and leadership with men. But it has not developed a formal platform on women's issues comparable to that of the FSLN. Principal objectives of the struggle do not mention women (Baloyra 1982:165; NACLA 1984:16). The platform of the FDR advocates issues important to women (the development of social services, literacy programs, and low-cost housing programs), without referring to women (Armstrong and Shenk 1980:31–33). According to FMLN/FDR official Norma Guevara, "the resources for which we are struggling belong to all so that the possibility of resolving the problems of women and children exists only in the context of a project that takes account of all the social, political, and economic problems of our country" (Montgomery 1982: 154–55). National liberation is thus to include the liberation of both men and women (Montgomery 1982: 154).

The Association of Salvadoran Women (AMES 1982:19) has noted that movements of the Left have "not dealt with the problems of women with the same consistency with which they confront other social problems. Their pronouncements in this regard are limited to the realm of class struggle . . . they do not make reference to the specific condition of women. . . ." (AMES 1982:23) further states that while "the struggle for women's liberation must be immersed in the struggle for the liberation of our peoples," women's "specific demands" must be recognized. The various women's organizations affiliated with the FMLM/FDR therefore have the major task of organizing women around gender- as well as class-based issues (WIRE 1982c:3). AMES itself was created to mobilize women on the basis of such demands. Its platform includes an end to forced sterilization, safe family planning, free child care, and the right to education and training (WIRE 1982c:3). As in Nicaragua, the number of households headed by women is high (due to migration during coffee, cotton, and cane harvests and high unemployment), so that problems of family support also become exacerbated (Criollo 1982:4; Dunkerley 1982:67).

In sum, the FMLM/FDR has formally tended to focus on class-based issues that would appeal to women as well as men, and has created internal organizational conditions conducive to equal participation by women. Women's organizations in the FMLN/FDR have the major task of addressing gender-based issues.

DISCUSSION AND CONCLUSIONS

Three questions were addressed regarding the nature of women's participation in guerrilla movements. First, what factors differentially affect Latin

American women's participation as compared with that of men? Second, how does class affect the ability to participate? Finally, what roles in the division of labor do women tend to perform? The movements in five Latin American nations were examined in light of these questions. Our conclusions are necessarily limited by the paucity of information about the *guerrillera*.

In all the movements, women participated less extensively than men. The structural constraints of women's roles in reproductive activities and the patriarchal nature of Latin American society, which reflects and reinforces this role, were major reasons suggested for this limited participation. While it is impossible to ascertain directly the extent to which women failed to participate because of these reasons, a statement by AMES (1982:18–19) acknowledges women's structural role in reproductive activities and the attitudes associated with this role as major limiting factors. The following passage is taken from the section entitled "The Difficult Task of Being Members of an Organized Movement."

> If men have, for centuries, devoted themselves to political work and have fulfilled themselves in it, it is because they have always had the support of one or several women who have provided them with children, with domestic services; to these women are diverted all psychological tensions, thereby freeing men from the small and large problems of domestic life.
>
> We women, on the other hand, do not have such support systems available to us, and in order to utilize our intellectual potential we must organize ourselves in such a way that the private sphere does not interfere with our specific political work. It is indeed dramatic to organize ourselves physically and psychologically to exercise this role without experiencing guilt vis-à-vis the "neglected" roles of mother and wife, which relegate us to the domestic sphere.
>
> For a woman to be active in sociopolitical organizations implies the assumption of a definitive commitment, a commitment which, she feels, will have repercussions on her activities as woman, wife, mother, and in some cases, as paid worker. This situation is aggravated by the fact that until now it has not appeared that men have the intention of truly assuming some of the responsibility which for centuries has been delegated to women. It is not easy for men, even with good intentions, to raise their consciousness concerning the privileges conveyed by masculinity and to relinquish their role as the star members of the cast, becoming instead comrades who share daily life and struggle.

While women were expected to participate less than men, certain factors might foster greater female involvement. The historical location of the movement, social structural conditions, and internal organizational characteristics of the movement were expected to influence the extent of actual participation. The Colombian and Cuban struggles, occurring prior to the 1970s, tended to follow the *foquista* pattern of struggle in contrast to the prolonged "people's wars" of Nicaragua and El Salvador. Mass mobilization of those

groups opposed to the government in conjunction with guerrilla action was not general revolutionary strategy. These movements also occurred before feminist thought had begun to diffuse throughout Latin America. The two earlier groups thus neither developed special platforms for women nor tried to recruit them. Likewise, gender egalitarianism was overlooked as an essential component of internal organizational relations. There was, correspondingly, only a small degree of female involvement in the Cuban and Colombian movements.

In contrast, the three later movements with substantial female participation (the Tupamaro, Sandinista, and Salvadoran) varied on the previous characteristics. The Tupamaro movement of the late 1960s and early 1970s tended to be *foquista* in character. Mass mobilization of Uruguayans was never achieved. The Sandinista and Salvadoran movements were based on current revolutionary strategy of protracted, mass-based struggle, which increased the possibility that women (as well as men) from all segments of society would participate. The three later movements occurred during a period of increasing awareness of feminist issues and of women's involvement in previous struggles that encouraged women's recruitment.

Social structural characteristics present in the three nations seem to have fostered women's participation. Although statistics on women's economic activity must be approached cautiously, data for the 1970s indicate higher economic participation of women in Uruguay, Nicaragua, and El Salvador, as compared with other Latin American nations, including Colombia and Cuba (Wilkie and Haber 1982:174).[9] Economic participation is said to sensitize women to class work-based issues more readily than domestic work inside the household (Chafetz and Dworkin 1985:102–3). Nicaragua and El Salvador also had more female-headed households than other Latin American nations. In these two nations, issues of family sustenance and political repression by the government seemed particularly threatening to women's roles as family nurturers and protectors. The case studies thus suggest that women's roles in both domestic and nondomestic aspects of family survival may serve as a base of participation.

Internal organizational characteristics may also influence the extent of women's participation. The Tupamaros, Sandinistas, and Salvadorans promoted routine policies of egalitarian relations between men and women. Women were to share in leadership, decision making, and task performance. These movements also employed platforms attractive to women, which seemed to be of two types. First, in opposition to patriarchalism, women were offered some feminist objectives, in line with long-term, strategic gender interests—an end to discrimination in such areas as the work force, the polity, and education. Second, programs stressing shorter-term, practical gender interests, such as child care, health care, and literacy, which maximized social welfare and facilitated women's roles in the workplace and household, were advocated. The Tupamaros and Sandinistas formally offered women both types of platforms. In the Salvadoran case, the FMLN/FDR offers social welfare policies in conjunction with the feminist planks offered by its affiliated women's organizations.

All three movements advocated gender interests that were compatible with the wider goals of the revolution, such as social welfare, the reduction of social inequality, and the need for mass political mobilization. Molyneux (1985:245) notes that in much current socialist policy, "women's emancipation is not just dependent on the realization of the wider goals, but is pursued insofar as it contributes to the realization of those goals." According to Molyneux (1985), the latitude that revolutionary movements possess in addressing gender issues depends, in part, on the severity of the struggle and the need for popular support. Advocating feminist or strategic gender interests in patriarchal societies becomes more problematic when the need for mass support is great. This may help explain why the Salvadorans have formally made little reference to women, except through their affiliate women's organizations. According to Molyneux (1985:244), the current invasion of Nicaragua by the contras has likewise pressured AMNLAE to table highly feminst issues for fear of alienating popular support.

In sum, while women face greater barriers to participating in guerrilla movements than do men, a number of factors may foster women's participation. The later three movements illustrate how these factors can alter traditional patterns of participation.

The guerrilla movements in all five nations attempted to alter internal and external relations that characterized each nation's pattern of dependent development. While specific objectives varied as a result of each nation's unique historical conditions, the movements emphasized such changes as more egalitarian relations within the economic or political structure and between the nation and the hegemonic core. The successful revolutions in Cuba and Nicaragua indicate additional possibilities for mobilization due to the unpopularity of a repressive regime. Class has been an important factor in revolutionary struggle and seems to be an overriding basis of participation for both men and women. Indeed, there is no evidence to suggest that female supporters belong to classes different from their male comrades.

The analysis of the five movements indicates that middle-class women probably faced fewer barriers to participation than did other women. Where both the middle classes and the working class/campesinos participated, middle-class women were somewhat more likely to be at the forefront of guerrilla activity. In Cuba, as Jaquette (1973) notes, "exceptional" middle-class women formed the core of the Twenty-sixth of July Movement. In Colombia, Torres's group had early student organizers. Initial organizers of the Sandinista AMPRONAC and the Salvadoran female recruits of political–military organizations tended to be middle-class. Working-class and campesino women seemed to enter the movements somewhat later. The Tupamaros' middle-class base remained relatively consistent throughout the life of the movement, reflecting a demographic pattern specific to Uruguay and the absence of mass-based support.

The early participation of middle-class women may be linked to their higher education and perhaps greater awareness of political issues. However, even campesino and working-class women who recognized the benefits of involvement faced the burdens of class as well as gender. Since these women pay the highest costs for political participation, it is not surprising that they would enter movements later—when they become conscious of fundamental interests, such as those related to household survival, and when revolutionary groups provide the means of addressing these interests. In Nicaragua and El Salvador, working-class women's roles in sustaining the family were continually eroded by government oppression and poor economic conditions. The mass-based strategy of the Sandinista and Salvadoran groups called for addressing the needs for all potentially mobilizable groups. Hence these groups begin to recruit large numbers of working-class and campesino women through attention to their specific class and gender interests. For example, practical gender interests, such as social welfare and child care, are critical because of the many female-headed households in both nations.

Women were more likely to occupy support than combat positions, although actual roles varied by movement. Women played important revolutionary roles in support positions in which, given the patriarchal nature of Latin American society, their male comrades would stand limited chance of success. Strategic utility may therefore have overridden sexism as the major reason for placing women in such positions, although sexism was indeed apparent in accounts of the earlier movements. Women performed mainly in support capacities in the Cuban and Colombian struggles, which had limited female participation. In the later three movements, women participated extensively in combat as well. Several factors may have contributed to the broadening of women's roles, such as the diffusion of feminist thought and examples of women's previous successes in combat. The influx of women in the Tupamaro, Sandinista, and Salvadoran movements also meant that necessary support positions could be covered, while additional women would be available for combat. Finally, under conditions of mass mobilization, as in Nicaragua and El Salvador, the need for combatants is especially great. Previously excluded groups, such as women and youth, may be given the opportunities formerly reserved for adult males.

The extensive participation of women in guerrilla movements, their mobilization from varied social classes, and their greater participation in combat indicate new patterns in Latin American revolutionary struggle. Women's participation in the Cuban Revolution conformed little to these patterns. The Cubans were successful in spite of their limited mobilization of women. Only two decades later, however, such participation was a critical component of the Sandinista victory and was being reproduced in other Latin American nations as well. Guerrilla movements of the future will be hard pressed to ignore the significant role that women can and must play in their struggles.

NOTES

The author gratefully acknowledges the comments of Maxine Atkinson, Norma Chinchilla, Barbara Risman, Michael Schulman, Richard Slatta, and editors Guida West and Rhoda Lois Blumberg. This study draws from a previous article: "Women in Latin American Guerrilla Movements: A Comparative Perspective," *Comparative Politics* 18 (January 1986): 147–69.

1. A number of political scientists argue that much of the political behavior in Latin America occurs outside "conventional" processes through guerrilla movements, military coups, strikes, and demonstrations (Jaquette 1976:235; Schmidt 1976:252; Wiarda and Kline 1979:42). The paucity of studies on women's participation in such activities is frequently noted (Jaquette 1976; Knaster 1976; Schmidt 1976).

2. For example, the major studies on guerrilla warfare by Richard Gott (1971) and Walter Laqueur (1977) do not even reference "women."

3. While this paper generically refers to "Latin American women," it should be kept in mind that Latin women differ on a number of important characteristics—for example, nationality, class, race, and rural or urban background. Valid generalizations about Latin American politics and gender stratification, however, incorporate "Latin American women" as a useful category (Jaquette 1976).

4. See Schlegel (1977) for a concise discussion of theories of sexual stratification.

5. The *foco* theory was first formulated by Che Guevara. He argued that guerrilla fighters could defeat the regular army; that guerrilla warfare should take place in the countryside; and that "objective conditions" need not be ripe for revolution to occur, "since the *foco*, the mobile focal point of insurrection, [could] by its very existence . . . create them" (Chaliand 1977:43). For a Marxist critique of the *foco* theory, see Silva (1968).

6. A variety of sociological theories have attempted to deal with the mobilization of deprived groups. Chafetz and Dworkin (1985) argue for use of an eclectic model in which the intensification of a social structural change results in a movement mounted by direct beneficiaries as well as by external organizations and leadership. In Latin America, economic and political crises impinging on the urban and rural proletariat have historically resulted in activism when these classes could be linked to labor movements and popular or political organizations (Chaliand 1977; Chinchilla 1980; Horowitz, 1970).

7. Louise Tilly (1981a) outlines specific conditions under which working-class women have tended to act collectively. When women are involved in wage labor, characteristics related to the organization of production—such as women's contact with other workers of similar interests, engagement in structured associations, ability to withdraw labor without incurring great cost, and household division of labor that allows them to act autonomously—promote collective activity. Working-class women also tend to act collectively when the household unit itself is mobilized on the basis of shared interests. According to Tilly (1981a:417), these factors differ little from those leading to working-class male mobilization, with the exception that women are much more likely to act when household sustenance or consumption is threatened. Research on Latin American working-class women similarly argues that the structural position of women in production and household is an important mobilizing factor (Chinchilla 1982; Flora, 1984; Safa 1976).

8. See Marta Rojas and Mirta Rodriguez Calderon, eds., *Tania* (New York: Random House 1971); and Margaret Randall, *Doris Tijerino: Inside the Nicaraguan Revolution* (Vancouver: New Star Books, 1978).

9. The percentage of the total female population that is economically active, by nation and year of data, are as follows: Colombia, 15.4 (1973); Cuba, 11.5 (estimated in 1970); El Salvador, 20.5 (1978); Nicaragua 18 (1977); and Uruguay 22 (1975) (Wilkie and Habor 1982:174). It should be noted that Cuban statistics reflect the period prior to the drafting off the Family Code and women's increased economic participation during the 1970s.

PART III

WOMEN IN SOCIAL-NURTURING/ HUMANISTIC PROTESTS

Peace and environmental concerns are issues that have historically attracted women into protest. A common theme in all these movements is protection of life within potentially life-threatening contexts, such as war, environmental pollution, or natural disasters. In such situations, women have organized and joined social-nurturing/humanistic protests to protect themselves, their families, and their communities. In the process, they have expanded role boundaries and defined their public behavior as an extension of their traditional caretaking roles. Thus another theme that emerges within this section is that of maternalism and peace politics. Sara Ruddick (1989:34), in examining the role of women in Argentina and Chile, suggests that the myth of maternal peace politics—which portrays women as "peacemakers without power" engaged in the "business of life," in contrast to men's involvement in the "business of war"—has been "shattered by history." Women throughout history have mobilized collectively to exert power to stop violence against their children, their families, and their communities. Their power and their resources have emerged from the contradictions between their prescribed roles as nurturers and as passive actors within patriarchal regimes that destroy what they are bound to protect.

In this section, Strange (Chapter 11) explores the ideologies that inform women's participation in the current Canadian peace movement, considering the intersection of motherhood, feminism, and pacificism. She weighs the potential of these ideologies to mobilize women to the cause and considers some of the conflicts between traditional and nontraditional women activists. Strange explores the problems for feminists as they assess the strategic value of maternalistic arguments. Historically, the banner of "maternalism" has mobilized women activists into both left- and right-wing protests, and it continues to fuel the debate among feminists as well.

Another theme explored in Chapter 1 emerges in this section (as it did in Parts I and II)—that of women's tenuous leadership positions in protest movements that are or become gender-integrated. In an unusual case, Schmid (Chapter 12) finds that as women worked as organizers of the Green Movement in West Germany and developed coalitions between feminists, environmentalists, and peace activists, they were able to maintain leadership. From this united struggle to transform the world into a safer place for all people, women gradually moved into electoral politics, campaigning for elections and retaining significant leadership positions. This example of a gender-integrated movement in which women have held control over an extended period seems to be a unique phenomenon in the history of women and social protest. Perhaps it reflects both the nature of the protest—its humanistic thrust—and its convergence with two other factors: first, the increasing visibility of women's mobilization for global survival as women and as part of the human race, and, second, the rising international concern about repeated Bhopals and Chernobyls. By the end of the 1980s and beginning of the 1990s, the Green Movement had gained widespread significance in world politics and in the press; seven leaders at the 1989 economic summit proclaimed the environment as an important item on their agenda. As the movement becomes legitimized at the international level, it will be interesting to observe the emerging gender patterns of leadership within the movement and party in different countries (Simons 1989). To what extent, if any, will the movement and the party's leadership structure and agenda change?

Finally, Neal and Phillips (Chapter 13) examine the roles and responses of women and men in natural and industrial disasters. They investigate emergent citizen groups (ECGs) that organize before or after disasters, such as those caused by floods, tornadoes, toxic waste, or nuclear plants, and why women tend to be the leaders in certain of these local groups. Neal and Phillips argue that participation in such movements is viewed as an extension of women's (especially white and middle-class women's) domestic concerns and their different patterns of labor market participation. For men, involvement in natural disasters is relatively risk-free economically and politically and offers social recognition. Thus males tend to be leaders when the disaster is a natural one. However, women leaders predominate in disasters caused by industry. In these cases, men's employment by the very firms the movement has targeted inhibits their participation. This study raises the question of how women's participation in industrial protests may be affected as their employment in, and ties to, industry continue to increase. Will the economic risks—the threat of losing their jobs—inhibit women's leadership in protests against industry as their situations change? Or will women continue to be in the forefront of such movements? What other factors converge to affect their participation in such protests?

Thus women and men's involvement in nurturing/humanistic protests are closely correlated with their expected and traditional roles in society. The economic and political consequences of participation in protest affect not only protest goals and targets, but also leadership and membership of both women and men. That is, some of the most critical resources of a social movement—its leaders and its members—are dependent on gender (as well as class and race) ideologies and gender structure in society. As gender differences in labor force participation are reduced (as current trends indicate), we predict that, even in nurturing/humanistic movements, the perceived and real costs of protest participation may rise for women and perhaps decrease their involvement. At the same time, if men (and women) conclude that the benefits of safer and less violent environments outweigh the economic risks of job loss, they may join such movements in greater numbers.

There are a number of related questions that bear investigation. Under what conditions do men emerge as leaders and members of protest movements that address nurturing and humanistic issues, which are from a traditional perspective more feminine than masculine concerns? Under what conditions to women tend to join and leave such movements? How do leadership styles, goals, and strategies differ by gender? How are these related to the resources available to women as a group? to men as a group? How do outcomes in male-led versus female-led humanistic movements vary, if at all? How can any observed differences be explained? If we take a global perspective, what are the commonalities and variations that emerge in the data on women in such nurturing/humanistic mobilizations over time?

CHAPTER 11

Mothers on the March: Maternalism in Women's Protest for Peace in North America and Western Europe, 1900–1985

CAROLYN STRANGE

THE POWERS AND PITFALLS OF MATERNALISTIC PROTEST

One of the themes of this volume has been that women traditionally find their political voice in social protest rather than in formal politics. In supporting a variety of causes, they have approached political issues primarily from a familial perspective, particularly as mothers. As protectors of life, providers of nurturance, and the bearers of the next generation, women have historically used their "female consciousness" on the political stage (Kaplan 1982:551).[1] Some marched for "bread and the Constitution," as did Parisian women in 1795, while others, such as female Nazi leaders, drew women into Hitler's Third Reich under the slogan "Kinder, Kirche, Kuche." The basis of their activism—the conviction that women's maternal role extends beyond the family to society—was similar, but their goals differed radically. When women mobilize as mothers on behalf of their families, they become a potent political force, but one as adapatable to repressive as to liberating causes.

The women's peace movement in North America and Western Europe has emerged in this tradition of maternally oriented protest. Women have banded together in the 1980s in the face of the growing likelihood of nuclear war and once again assumed prominent roles as spokespersons in the larger peace movement. Many of them, previously apolitical, have come to sense their power to resist a threatening social order and contribute to a more humane world. While women join for a variety of reasons, perhaps the most common one is familiar: women, and mothers in particular, share a set of values distinct from men's;[2] as natural guardians of future generations, moreover, they have a particular responsibility to create a world free of nuclear threats. You can't hug kids, they declare, with nuclear arms.

There is no denying that the call to mother society through its nuclear crisis has evoked a tremendous response. The peace movement could have gained no greater weapon than the participation of hundreds of thousands of mothers. Besides contributing to the strength and breadth of a popular protest movement, these "ordinary" women have lent respectability to the antinuclear cause. A British mother pushing a pram through a park on a peace march or a Japanese mother singing a protest song with a toddler strapped to her back signals to observers that one need not be a flower child to promote peace. The significance of these practical gains cannot be overestimated: the peace movement needs mothers in a world that needs peace to survive.

Yet feminists caution against equating what is good for the peace movement with what is progressive for women. They are especially critical of women who justify their protest on the basis of their maternal feelings. Maternalist pacifists apparently garner social approval because they operate within the prescribed boundaries of femininity. Thus many feminists fear that while campaigning for a nuclear-free world, the mothers for peace perpetuate their own and all women's enslavement under patriarchy ("Politics Without the Punch" 1983:42). In fact, maternally inspired protestors may march for peace one day and speak out against feminist demands such as abortion, day care, or the availability of safe and effective birth control the next (Carroll 1984). Radical-lesbian and socialist feminists in particular worry that these protestors, by basing their pacifism on "womanly" or "maternal" concerns, will abet the growing antifeminist, heterosexist backlash that idealizes women solely as mothers and keepers of the hearth. The opponents of feminism are only too ready to enlist the support of conservative maternalists and to exploit these divisions between women to further their aims. Feminists warn that maternalism is too shaky a platform to support women's protest.

This phenomenon of motherly pacifism is not, however, a creature of the 1980s. For over a century, women in Western Europe and North America have spoken out against war from a motherly perspective. The history of their protest indicates that a maternalistic approach does not necessarily prevent women from adopting a political and economic analysis of war and peace. Collective action in the peace movement has also been an effective means of political education for women who otherwise might not have considered joining a formal political party. The experience of several women's peace groups in the early twentieth century, the 1950s, and, more recently, the 1980s has shown that this education can also spur the development of feminist consciousness. It would be dangerous to applaud the tradition of maternal pacifism, however, without looking at two recurring problems: the conservatism and antifeminism often hidden beneath maternal rhetoric; and the capacity of patriotic maternalists to rally for war. The challenge for women in the peace movement of the 1980s seems to be to tap the mobilizing powers of maternalism while avoiding its ideological pitfalls. The historical record of women's peace activism suggests that maternal concern has a viable place in pacifist protest, but only when incorporated into a broader analysis of imperialism, sexism, racism, and militarism.

NINETEENTH-CENTURY ROOTS OF PACIFISM AND MATERNALISM

Just as the road leading to World War I was a long one, so was the path of women's efforts to quell international conflict. Female pacifists worked throughout the nineteenth century to avert war, contrary to their conventional portrayal as enthusiastic war supporters. As early as 1844, feminist Eugenie Niboyet founded *La Paix des deux mondes,* a weekly devoted to the promotion of international peace based on domestic justice. Ten years later, during the Crimean War, European women formed the Women's Peace League. In Britain, almost fifty years before British women gained the vote, Mrs. Henry Richard became the first president of the Women's Association of the British Peace Society. While the peace movement lacked support after the Franco-Prussian War of 1870 to 1871, it regained momentum in the 1880s as increasing friction between imperialistic powers prompted an upsurge of women's peace activism. One of the leaders was Bertha Von Suttner, the founder of the Austrian Peace Party. Her antiwar novel, *Lay Down Your Arms* (1889), rapidly became an international bestseller, rivaled only by *Uncle Tom's Cabin* (Cooper 1984). The time had come for women to assume leadership in the campaign against war.

When women denounced the rising spirit of militarism at the end of the nineteenth century, they spoke in the idiom of maternalism. Whether biological or "social" mothers, maternalists believed that their familial role as nurturers and caretakers prepared them for similar social responsibilities; moreover, they sensed an obligation to ameliorate society through their distinctive, motherly abilities. Indeed, most turn-of-the-century women's groups accepted the notion that they were society's mothers and shrewdly used that role to gain a political voice on the public stage where they demanded everything from the vote to the suppression of alcohol. Even feminists used maternalistic arguments to challenge the notion that women's role in the state was solely to prepare their sons for responsible citizenship and to instill the virtues of domesticity in their daughters. They sought a more active, direct role in the public sphere, one that would draw their domestic talents from their parlors into politics. Not surprisingly, when female pacifists voiced their concern, they spoke through the maternalistic rhetoric that characterized the discourse of the nineteenth-century women's movement.

PATRIOTIC AND PACIFIST CURRENTS OF MATERNALISM IN WORLD WAR I

What did surprise maternalist pactifists was the willingness of many society's mothers to support militarism once war was declared. In 1914, the millions of women across North America, Europe, Scandinavia, and Australia already organized into myriad social and political groups, split into two opposing camps: those who supported the war effort, and those who opposed their country's involvement. The most familiar women are the former, the hearthkeepers, nurses, ammunitions workers, and auxilliary military personnel depicted in popular films, posters, and novels. Women from the belligerent nations did, in fact, take up the gauntlet of war and fought with the resources at their disposal. They quickly transformed existing charity, reform, and suffrage associations into war support agencies. In Canada, for instance, leaders of the largest women's federation—the National Council of Women in Canada (NCWC)—turned their organization into a "ready-made forum for patriotic and enfranchised feminity" (Strong-Boag 1976:290). Maternalist suffragists in the NCWC and the wider suffrage movement saw the war as a splendid opportunity to assume the spotlight in a country where only months earlier demands for the vote had been denied. They persuaded Canadians that "a nation engaged in the masculine business of war needed the mothering skills of its women all the more" (Strong-Boag 1976:293). A successful war effort required mother-headed, domestic support, for without a "strong home life," a "strong national life" was impossible. Women of the NCWC and other liberal organizations believed that maternalism and patriotism were linked in much the same way as mothers and fathers provided mutual support within the ideal family. "The victory won on the battlefield," argued NCWC president Rosalie Torrington, "must be followed by a realization of the power of consecrated motherhood. To us, it is a testing time." The official position of her organization was unequivocal: "Canadian women and Canadian societies of women are not in sympathy with the pacifist movement of today" (Strong-Boag 1976:296, 329).

Women's paramilitary training advocates were even more clearly aligned with the forces of militarism than the women who rolled bandages and knitted socks. Organizers of the largest women's national defense group in the United States—the Women's Section of the Navy League—stated that their main purpose was to "arouse patriotism among American women." As mothers, they felt they had the right to a public voice on matters that might endanger the lives of their children, but their maternal mission prompted them to bolster America's defenses against external enemies. These patriotic maternalists considered themselves hard-headed realists, as opposed to the old-fashioned sentimentalists who wept upon the mere mention of a cannon" (Steinson 1980:265, 266).

Despite overwhelming pressure from both the government and patriotic organizations to support the war effort, there were pockets of women in each country who worked for peace. With the same sense of responsibility expressed by patriotic social mothers, maternalist pacifists risked opprobrium and, in some cases, sedition or treason charges to speak out against war. Whereas patriotic maternalists interpreted their social role as including the duty to support their sons against all foes, pacifists urged women to exert their motherly power by preserving life and diminishing conflict. These pacifists felt that motherly power had to be enlisted in the battle against such militaristic influences as war toys, parades, and films. They tried to develop what they considered to be innate female characteristics for pacific ends, for they believed that, according to Alice Chown, "women as a class are naturally opposed to war" (Strong-Boag 1976:328). According to their interpetation, women's instinctual ability to nurture and to conciliate made them the logical choice for peace makers.

The most famous product of women's resistance to World War I was a liberal coalition of pacifists who met at The Hague in 1915. There they attempted to convince world leaders to abandon the folly of destruction and to pursue avenues toward a peaceful solution of conflict. Although theirs was not specifically a mothers' organization, members borrowed their reasoning from the ideology of social motherhood to justify their involvement. Jane Addams, president of the conference, cast her statements in a particularly maternal light, even though she herself never had children. Just as an artist could not fire on a beautiful building, she argued, "so women, who have brought men into the world and nurtured them until they reach the age for fighting, must experience a peculiar revulsion when they see them destroyed" (Addams 1975:128). What was wrong with the world was that these nurturing sentiments had been forgotten in the face of dominant, militaristic reasoning. In calling on the most conventional aspects of womanhood—the biological capacity to bear children and the social prescriptions to raise them—delegates differed from their jingoistic counterparts. Where these antiwar lobbyists distinguished themselves, though, was through their interpretation of maternalism for pacific ends.

Maternalists who lobbied for peace did not tackle the prevailing gender system, but many did adopt a feminist consciousness in the course of their campaigns. In The Hague Conference Resolutions, for instance, delegates refuted "the assumption that women can be protected under the condtions of modern warfare." Under "Principles of Peace," they included a demand for the political enfranchisement of women, adding that "women can only have full responsibility and effective influence when they have equal political rights with men" (Addams 1975:150, 154). As maternalist feminists, these women did not repudiate all forms of oppression, yet they did manipulate the ideology of motherhood to pursue a "muted form of autonomy" (Roberts 1978:18). Thus they demonstrated the capacity of maternalistic protestors to support both pacifism and feminism.

Maternalists were more likely to maintain an anti war stance if they linked motherly concern to a leftist political agenda. The most stalwart opponents of militarism came from the ranks of women who had campaigned for suffrage, birth control, workers' rights, socialism, or anarchy before the war broke out. Through their involvement in these struggles for social justice, many came to see the fatal connections between patriarchy, militarism, and imperialism (Vellacott 1985:6).[3] In Britain, pacifist suffragist leaders Kathleen D. Courtney, Helena Swanwich, and Catherine E. Marshall developed an antimilitaristic stance that encompassed a "much more radical view of the changes necessary in society than could be accommodated simply by their own admission to existing political structures" (Vellacott 1985:6). Their pacifist work enriched their feminist agenda, as their criticism of the war included a general indictment of militarism's connections with class, race, and sex oppression.

Socialist pacifists also linked their antimilitarism to a maternalistic ethos of peace. Gertrude Richardson, a Canadian socialist feminist, wrote in the leftist press, directing her antiwar columns to the "mother heart" in her readers. Like Violet McNaughton, another Canadian feminist, she criticized the brand of mothering that produced jingoistic patriotism and called instead for the power of mothers to be turned toward peace. A socialist analysis of the costs of war, in both human and economic terms, led these women to extend their maternal sympathy toward all mothers and children who suffered as a result of military aggression. Marion Frances Beynon, another socialist maternalist, urged that a "new spirit of national motherhood" be roused on behalf of children from every warring nation, and not exclusively those from the mother's own country. Her understanding of war and peace was far from sentimental, however. She perceived that "imperialism motivated by greed, and the jingo nationalism so carefully propagandized at every level of society by the militarists" were the roots of war. The only road to a lasting peace, Beynon concluded, was to reconstruct and regenerate the economy and the social order. Thus maternalistic thinking, located in the leftist–feminist theoretical context, led a small group of women toward a radical vision of peace (Roberts 1985b:7, 12).

MATERNALISTIC PROTEST IN THE INTERWAR PEACE MOVEMENT

Despite the decline of the feminist movement and the Left in general in the postwar period, women continued to work for the preservation of peace. The devastation of the war pulled most nations into isolationism, but it also drew a minority of citizens into a movement for peaceful cooperation and internationalism. The most prominent of these groups was the Women's International League for Peace and Freedom (WILPF), the permanent peace lobby that Hague delegates formed after the 1915 conference. In WILPF, women worked closely with the League of Nations. They added their explicitly maternal stance against war to the league's guiding principle of collective security (Strong-Boag 1984). Elsewhere, the British Women's Co-operative Guild formed a "Mother's International" in 1921 to promote similar aims. Like WILPF members, they spoke against war from a maternalistic perspective, as General Secretary Margaret Llewelyn Davies's statement indicates:

> There is no class to whom the cause of Peace can make a stronger appeal than to International Co-operative Guildswomen, for war casts its dread shadow in a special way on the lives of wives and mothers. Nor is there any class whose ideals can more effectively undermine the causes of war. (Black 1984:471)

Both WILPF and the guild worked toward the establishment of a genuine peace based on a "new national order" instead of the nineteenth-century "balance of powers." The sense of starting afresh, however, faded by the late 1920s as it became clear that the old spirit of militarism had reawakened in the rise of fascist regimes. WILPF's disarmament conferences, economic commissions, and peace pilgrimages seemed futile when the same nations that had fought the "war to end all wars" veered once again toward the path of destruction. The open aggression and totalitarianism of the fascist states tested the fundamental principles of women's peace groups: could "positive peace-making" become the "appeasement of brute force" (Bussey and Tims 1965:130)?

MATERNALISM IN THE NUCLEAR AGE

The faltering peace movement was swept aside in the 1940s by a torrent of outrage at fascist aggression and a general sense that World War II was a "moral war." The U.S. bombing of Nagasake and Hiroshima revealed the destructive capabilities of these nuclear weapons, yet few Westerners expressed their fears until the Russians challenged U.S. monopoly over the new weaponry. Not even the U.S.–backed intervention in Korea in 1950 inspired the rebirth of the peace movement. The only women's group to maintain a consistent critique of both nuclear weapons and militarism was WILPF, whose members blasted the Korean War as a "flagrant extension of the East–West conflict to a new, and hotter, theatre of war" (Bussey and Tims 1965:205). For the most part, North American and Western European maternalists remained silent in the face of conventional warfare waged in this Asian nation across the globe. Only in the late 1950s, when the threat of nuclear war *at home* seemed likely, did maternalists rally their resources for survival.[4] Without a strong base for women-only organizing, women in the 1950s tended to join mixed peace groups to voice their protest against nuclear weapons. Yet even in an era so hostile to women's independent political action, a few exclusively women's peace groups did emerge in reaction to the tensions of the Cold War. Women who mobilized outside of male-dominated, mainstream coalitions like the Campaign for Nuclear Disarmament (CND) offered what they felt to be their unique perspective on peace—a maternal one. While WILPF continued to pursue its prewar policies, its prominence declined in the face of two new women's peace groups. The Voice of Women (VOW), in Canada, and Women Strike for Peace (WSP) in the United States offered their motherly advice as a lucid alternative to the Cold War mentality of "brinksmanship." VOW grew out of the failure of the Paris Summit Conference over the U-2 incident in 1960, while members of WSP became active during the Cuban missile crisis of 1962.[5] In a period of escalating tension, these women organized to transform fear into strength.

VOW stood for the survival of "civilization as we know it," but it directed its campaigns at Canadian women and their maternal responsibilities to "turn men's minds from war." VOW members opposed war and nuclear weapons because they believed that "the power of a spiritual or moral force latent in women [had] been stirred to assert itself as the conscience of mankind." Their activities included letter-writing campaigns, petitions, and the submission of antinuclear briefs to the Canadian government and international bodies. Women active in VOW considered theirs an advisory role in an international political system where men made the decisions. In the context of the Cold War, male decision makers seemed to need all the maternal advice they could get. Thus VOW's statement of beliefs declared: "By working through women's common interests and their *instinctive* concern for their children and the human family, VOW can assist in the creation of a climate of understanding and trust which will enable world powers to resolve their differences without war or threat of war" (emphasis added) (Tucker 1962:27). Like most pacifists before them, VOW members constructed their vision of peace on a maternalistic platform that also supported conservative notions of women's familial role.

The experience of the WSP demonstrated that concern for the welfare of others does not necessarily stunt the growth of a broader political analysis. Their anti–Cold War activities resembled VOW's, and their slogan—End the Arms Race, Not the Human Race—became a popular call for life over death.

As maternalists, they articulated their stance through the language of mother-hood, but in the course of their protest, they "used the feminine mystique to justify their radical dissent from Cold War politics (Swerdlow 1982). When brought before the House Un-American Activities Committee in 1962 for al-leged ties to the Communist Party, the women drew on their "women's cul-ture" and responded to committee interrogators with "female common sense, openness, humor, hope, and naivete" (Swerdlow 1982). Once they expressed their personal fears on a political level, many resolved never to retreat into the domestic sphere, where they had comparatively little power to shape their own lives or those of their children. Working in this exclusively female, mater-nally oriented group also encouraged members to develop a more overtly feminist consciousness than they had previously possessed. Their emergence into the political sphere was not a finite event, but a process that led some members to adopt feminist politics.

Maternalism in the Current Women's Peace Movement

Not until the 1980s, however, did women's activism for peace match the level of organization established in the early twentieth century. Separate women's peace groups arose within the context of a reawakened women's movement, just as the World War I–era peace movement was an offshoot of the "second wave" of feminism. But the differences between the first and second phases of the women's movement in the twentieth century are significant. While most turn-of-the-century feminists had turned outward to infuse the public sphere with a maternal spirit, feminists in the 1970s tended to turn inward toward "the personal." Consciousness-raising taught women to incorporate their per-sonal experience of oppression into a social analysis of women's subordinate position under patriarchy. Above all, biology was *not* destiny; feminists coun-tered that women were merely conditioned to be men's servants, their wives, and, most significantly, their mothers. According to the theoretical bases of feminism now being laid out by writers like Shulamith Firestone, motherhood and the very capacity to bear children was a patriarchal trap to be avoided. Feminist leaders urged women to reject their "feminity," especially the pre-scription to nurture and protect, and to keep the peace. Sisterhood, not moth-erhood, was the rallying cry for feminist unity.

The women's "conditioning" described by feminists did not stop hun-dreds of thousands of women from swelling the ranks of the peace movement in the 1980s. Most joined out of the fear inspired by a new age of nuclear terror, where hydrogen bombs have been eclipsed by cruise and MX missiles, Trident submarines and "Star Wars." An exclusively women's peace move-ment did not emerge as much from a feminist base as it grew from a revival of maternally inspired protest. When feminists did participate in the peace move-ment, they found themselves holding hands outside military bases with women who seemed to accept their conditioning as self-sacrificing mothers concerned solely with the safety of their children.[6] The result has been an ironic twist on the situation seventy years earlier: the greatest critics of mater-nalist pacifists in the 1980s have been not patriotic mothers, but feminists.

What do these latest maternalist pacifists stand for? They speak out for peace in the same voice traditionally invoked by mothers engaged in social protest. They go no further than their innate, maternal feelings to explain their actions, as one member of Babies Against the Bomb responded to feminist criticism:

> Should we all feel ashamed of this deep gut feeling [to ensure the survival of our children]? For me, feminism is about choice, about every woman's freedom to feel and act and be valued. Does it make me any less of a person if my immediate, *instinctive* reaction to nuclear war is in my capacity as a mother? (emphasis added) (Jones 1983:67)

She, like most female pacifists, argues that the priority is peace: "What does it matter," she asks, "how we come to want it?" Members of Babies Against the Bomb work squarely within the maternalist tradition of protest; their title underlines that they protest on behalf of others more vulnerable or innocent than themselves. The weakness in these maternalists' single-issue politics lies in their refusal to analyze any form of oppression other than the threat of nuclear war in their children's lives.

Oxford Mothers for Nuclear Disarmament is another group explicitly concerned with its maternal responsibilities to ensure peace. One middle-class, white spokesperson revealed that she had joined the group because there was no other place for her in a movement dominated by "radicals." She found the common bond of motherhood a powerful unifying force, whereas dealing with issues like "class, religion, and politics" proved too divisive. What could a mother find more compelling than a "deep fear for [her] children's futures hanging in a mushroom cloud above [her] head" (Jones 1983:70)? For the purposes of organizing, the Oxford members define "mothers" as white, middle-class, Protestant, and liberal women. "Deviants" only cause disunity.

While these maternalists' stance is narrow and conservative, their motherly motivations do offer important political advantages to the peace movement. Like the delegates at The Hague peace conference and members of Women Strike for Peace, the Oxford Mothers and leaders of Babies Against the Bomb fully realize the persuasiveness of their actions among conservatives. One Oxford mother explained her strategy in planning a demonstration march: "We all felt that the idea of mothers and children . . . had by far the greatest impact, both emotionally and visually . . . and that as mothers we could appeal to many women who like ourselves were politically unsophisticated and who perhaps had never taken part in a demonstration before" (Jones 1983:71). The tactical advantages of this approach are considerable: on the one hand, the moderate image of the peace mothers makes their message acceptable to a broad spectrum of observers; on the other, their emphasis on motherhood has proved the most potent device to mobilize previously apolitical women. Where the call for sisterhood in the 1970s apparently fell on deaf ears for many women, the appeal to motherhood rings clearly in the 1980s.

Feminist Criticism of Maternal Pacifism

Feminists remain understandably wary about this latest form of maternal protest. Those within the peace movement argue that a reliance on maternalistic rationales hurts the cause as well as women. Their greatest objection relates to maternalists' acceptance of traditional motherhood under patriarchy. In stressing their nurturing qualities, the mothers for peace absolve men of their equal responsibility to value and protect life ("Politics Without the Punch" 1983:44). A concern for peace, argue feminist pacifists, should not demand that women express their "true natures" as mothers of others, but that they become angry on their *own* behalf. Members of Babies Against the Bomb and similar organizations pander to popular, sentimental notions of helpless infants protected by doting mothers; never do they question the position of women within the patriarchal family. Protest based on "instinctive reactions" instead of incisive political analysis will end neither the threat of nuclear war nor the oppression of women ("Politics Without the Punch" 1983:44).

Feminists *outside* the peace movement are even warier. To them, pacifism is a dangerous red herring in women's more immediate struggle for liberation.[7] The London Revolutionary Feminists spoke for skeptical outsiders when they launched a stinging attack on the women's peace movement. They claimed that the popularity of female pacifism in the early 1980s paralleled declining support for the women's liberation movement. One of their most contentious issues was the media respect accorded to women for peace, particularly when participants were white, middle-class, "respectable" mothers who pinned baby clothes to air-base fences. Feminist critics point out that at women's peace camps, the protestors' image is that of "peace-loving, idealistic givers of life," hardly a challenge to prescriptive, patriarchal notions of womanhood:

> This [image] reinforces the assumption that women should and mostly do conform to those stereotypes. It also implies that those who conform are not oppressed other than by the possibility of nuclear war. Being woman-only doesn't make this [peace] campaign a feminist one, on the contrary, the ideas behind this kind of organizing are actually in opposition to feminist aims. (Alderson 1983:12)

The media loses interest, however, if women protest on behalf of their own needs rather than the welfare of their and others' children. When radical feminists—whether young or old, lesbian or heterosexual, women of color or whites—demand the right to reproductive freedom, for instance, they are not the darlings of the media, but pariahs. For these feminists, "the peace movement is a means of diverting us from the real struggle—our struggle" (Alderson 1983:15, 16).

Critics caution that saving the world for humanity, rather than changing the world for women and all exploited people, feeds a growing stream of neoconservatism. Andrea Dworkin observes that an alarming number of women are joining the ranks of the Right out of the same concerns that inspire maternalist–pacifists. Arguments for women's political participation that hinge on "different" female nature ultimately work against all women. For Dworkin (1983:14) maternalists "follow a biological imperative derived directly from their reproductive capacities that translates necessarily into narrow lives, small minds, and a rather mean-spirited puritanism." Mothers cannot be real moral agents, for they are nothing more than symbols of goodness in patriarchy. Their subservient position in the family is the prototype of their subordinate role in society. Thus, she concludes, "mothers are the immediate enforcers of male will, the guards at the cell door, the flunkies who administer the electric shocks to punish rebellion" (Dworkin 1983:15).

MATERNALISM IN A FEMINIST–PACIFIST CONTEXT

The women's peace movement needs a watchful, feminist eye. As one theorist cautioned, "We cannot allow a feminist agenda to be reduced to a concern for children." Yet that eye need not be blind to the positive potential of maternalism. The "moral mother" approach to peace may not challenge protestors to "think in complex ways about the sources of military threat," but neither does it prevent women from reaching an analysis of the political and economic roots of violence and oppression (Leonardo 1985:613). The most sophisticated analyses of women and peace in the past, however, have come from feminists and socialists, many of whom were maternalists as well. The fact that socialist feminists in the 1980s have again found ways of tapping maternalistic sentiment in their work against war and injustice suggests that it is possible to adopt a progressive, internationalist perspective on peace that leaves room for motherly concerns.

Several women's peace groups have begun to develop a feminist stance on peace that accommodates maternal sentiment without succumbing to sentimentalism. These feminist pacifists have constructed an alternative vision of a peaceful world by borrowing from, but not relying on, maternalistic reasoning and organizational tactics. In Britain, Women Opposed to Nuclear Technology (WONT), and in the United States the Women's Pentagon Action (WPA) criticize not only the arms race but also the inequities and injustice of capitalist patriarchy. Nuclear weapons to these women are the most dramatic products of societies already fraught with violence; preventing nuclear war requires an attack on the roots of violence—sexism, racism, and imperialism. To hide "women's" issues such as rape, abortion, battering, and poverty behind the cloak of antinuclear protest is to miss the connections between the everyday violence in women's lives and the nuclear threat. Feminist pacifists are quick to underline that their participation in the peace movement stems from a rejection of the prevailing gender structure. As Lynne Jones (1983:23) reports, one WONT member declared:

> We don't think women have a special role in the peace movement because we are "naturally" more peaceful, more protective, or more vul-

nerable than men. Nor do we look to women as the "Earth Mothers" who will save the planet from male aggression. Rather, we believe that it is this very role division that makes the horrors of war possible.

Male domination, they assert, links women's oppression with war because sex role stereotypes devalue the life-affirming qualities women are socialized to cultivate. In short, the peace movement will gain strength once pacifists, both male and female, denounce the matrix of injustice, not simply the threat of nuclear war.

Feminist pacifists who espouse a set of values that emerges from women's social position promote peace without enslaving women in the "instincts" of motherhood. Many have also adopted an internationalist perspective on peace and justice in their protests. In a unity statement drafted in 1980, for instance, the WPA presented a comprehensive condemnation of oppression and not merely an indictment of atomic bombs. A protest against nuclear weapons heads their long list of objections against cuts in day dare, restricted abortion rights, unemployment, the exploitation of Native Americans, and apartheid in South Africa. From global tensions to domestic violence, the connections are clear: the same "dominance which is exploitive and murderous in international relations [is] also dangerous to women and children at home" (Jones 1983:42). Although they are as anxious about the fate of future generations as the most ardent maternalists, members of the WPA do not resort to apolitical, motherly sentiment to express their political concerns; rather, their statement concludes with a call to eradicate all manifestations of sexism, racism, capitalism, and imperialism. The women who drafted these principles had the courage to confront the inequalities that Babies Against the Bomb protestors preferred to ignore. Instead, WPA protestors developed a broader vision of peace in the tradition of the feminists who opposed World War I and the WILPF members in the 1950s who refused to regard the possibility of nuclear war as the only real threat to life.

Must peace protestors therefore deny maternal sentiment a place in their programs? Both WONT and WPA members assert that they do not "wish to capitulate to the traditional role of women forced to clean up after everyone else and to nurture men while denying [themselves]" (Jones 1983:59). At the same time, however, they do not repudiate concerns voiced by peace mothers. The WPA unity statement put motherhood issues into the context of reproductive freedom: "We want the right to have or not to have children— we do not want gangs of politicians and medical men to say we must be sterilized for the country's good" (Jones 1983:59). Similarly, they support life-affirming values from a less divisive, daughterly perspective: "We understand all is connectedness. The earth nourishes us as we with our bodies will eventually feed it. Through us our mothers connected the human past to the human future" (Jones 1983:59). Through their integration of maternal values into a complex, political analysis of the social and economic bases of peace, WPA members have helped open a dialogue between maternalists and feminists.

This dialogue began at the grass-roots level of pacifist protest. The Greenham Common encampment is only the most famous example of women's collective protest against nuclear weapons. Peace camps across Europe and North America in the 1980s have become political melting pots, where women from diverse political backgrounds debate a range of issues connected to pacifism (*Tribune* 1985).[8] Even single peace actions have opened women's eyes to a range of issues connected with peace, feminism, and social justice. In Canada, for instance, the proposed testing of the cruise missile drew women out of their homes and into the public eye. The Primrose Lake Weapons Testing Range became the site of a women's peace camp in 1983 as eighty women from across western Canada "refused the cruise." The camp's success prompted protestors to set up a permanent camp at Cole Bay, Saskatchewan, where "women could put into practice their vision of a society based on the principles of collectivism and non-violence." Their actions included the re-working of traditional symbols of womanhood in an effort to "celebrate community and re-affirm the dignity of human life (Bennet and Gibson 1983:20, 23). For many of the women, participating in the peace camp introduced them to far more than nuclear weapons issues:

> Through the sharing of personal and political knowledge, women saw that militarism's greatest stronghold exists in the internalized value system which accepts violence, exploitation and dominance as fundamental precepts of human society. They understood that the structuring of social relationships along these lines is necessary to the maintenance of both capitalism and patriarchy and that militarism must therefore be confronted on both the material and psychological levels. (Bennet and Gibson 1983:23)

Thus women who entered the camp to stop the cruise left with a broadened political awareness and a radical revisioning of their world.

MATERNALISM AND THE FUTURE OF PACIFIST PROTEST

Will maternally inspired pacifists "necessarily" capitulate to reactionary forces intent on restricting women's political, economic, and social rights? Should women protesters abandon images of motherhood for fear that they will be used against them? Feminist social analyst Sara Ruddick and writer Adrienne Rich say no. They have contributed to a resurrected theory of maternalism that once again urges women to expand the values of mothering through social action. Rich begins with the experience of giving birth and explores the potential for bonding between mother and daughter that is seldom realized under patriarchy. The "victimization of the mother" within male-dominated societies, she observes, "mutilates the daughter who watches her for clues as to what it means to be a woman" (Rich 1976:247). Thus Rich remarks that "motherhood as experience and institution" are two very different phenomena; the institution of patriarchal mothering demands that one female teach another to "conform to a degrading and dispiriting role." One can only imagine the positive potential of mothering in a society of women equally valued as citizens. In the present, male-dominated world, however, Rich (1976:246) urges that "the power of our mothers, whatever their love for us and their struggles on our behalf, is too restricted."

If this "power" is to be more than an idealistic notion, it must be resurrected within a feminist framework, according to Sara Ruddick. Like Rich, she rejects the "mothering typical of patriarchies," for it "perpetuates hierarchical societal arrangements" (Treblicot 1983:1). In its place, she turns to the material sources of "maternal thinking." In the "practice of mothering," and not merely the biological capacity to bear children, women develop a unique way of thinking. Ruddick celebrates a set of values traditionally associated with women, but by no means biologically ordained to be women's alone. For Ruddick and Rich, it is not so much a question of men or women being more closely connected to war or peace through their biological makeup, but the fact that those human qualities praised as masculine virtues—aggressiveness, strength, and competitiveness—are no longer expedient, whereas stereotypically feminine qualities of nurturance, empathy, and cooperation are essential to world survival.

Ruddick shares the traditional maternalistic faith in women's greater commitment to survival. She believes women's mothering work has led them to develop a sense of "preservative love," their "distinctive contribution to . . . the cause of peace" (Ruddick 1983:233). Maternalist theorists find themselves tempted to envision the creative potential of mothering "as it might exist in woman-centred communities" (Treblicot 1983:vii). As Sara Ruddick (1980:344) muses: "That maternal love, pleasure in reproductive powers, and a sense of maternal competence survive in a patriarchal society where women are routinely derogated, makes one wonder at the further possibilities for maternal happiness in decent societies." Charlotte Perkins Gilman imagined such a decent social system during the heyday of maternalism, and described it in her 1915 utopian novel, *Herland*. In the peaceful all-woman paradise of Herland, the benign powers of mothering are permitted full expression; mothers foster creativity and harmony rather than act as the undercover agents of women's exploitation. Rich (1976:290) has kept Gilman's utopian vision alive, hoping that in the *real* future, feminists will embrace the unique experience of motherhood, and

> will come to view our physicality as a resource, rather than a destiny. In order to live a fully human life we require not only *control* of our bodies . . . we must touch the unity and resonance of our physicality, our bond with the natural order, the corporeal ground of our intelligence.

Until that time, women will continue to struggle within the real limitations of "motherhood as institution." Even Ruddick (1983:232) concedes that feminists must question "the effectiveness of a virtue acquired in conditions of powerlessness." After all, women have demonstrated their ability to use their maternal position both to oppose feminist goals and to fuel the fires of war. Maternalism remains a volatile force, capable of stirring women to support repressive campaigns under some circumstances as well as progressive causes under others. The history of women's protest in peace movements over the past century is encouraging, though, for it indicates that women can transcend the limitations of maternal logic if they adopt a feminist viewpoint. Female pacifists from the World War I era, the 1920s, and the 1950s demonstrated that it is possible to join peace groups out of a motherly concern for others, but in the context of peace activism develop a feminist awareness of their own interests as women. This transition is an evolutionary process, accelerated through the education of political activism. Maternalism can be liberating, concludes Ruddick (1980:356–57), only when "transformed by a feminist consciousness."

But feminism itself may not push maternalists to develop a complex analysis of war and oppression. Even a feminist-inspired desire for peace offers poor guidance for those women who must confront the reality of war. If antinuclear activists mobilize against the *possibility* of nuclear war in North America and Europe, yet ignore the fact of ongoing conventional wars in Central America, Africa, and Asia, for instance, they cannot hope to usher in a just world order, even if they express concern about the equality of women. Until maternal feminists come to identify the roots of war, not only in sexism, but also in imperialism, economic exploitation, and racism, they will do little to disarm the forces of militarism. Protestors must, like socialist feminists in the early twentieth century and participants in more recent peace actions such as the WPA, look beyond their own fears for survival to search out the political and economic causes of war if they seek a just peace. Unless they do, the women's peace movement will continue to be dominated by those who march against bombs because they pose a threat to their children's future. Women who refuse to nurture life only to see it destroyed undoubtedly threaten the political order; the most profound challenge, however, will come in the form of protest that weds that love for life to a passion for social justice.

NOTES

Many people assisted in the production of this paper. In particular, I would like to thank Phyllis Mack and E. Ann Kaplan for their initial comments, and Marianna Valverde for her helpful criticism in the final stage of revision. I am also grateful to Guida West for encouraging me to write an article after hearing an earlier version of the paper in 1984.

1. A more recent example of this phenomenon is discussed in Zabaleta (1983: 152–55).

2. Not all arguments concerning an exclusively female set of values center on motherhood. Because the motherhood rationale looms so large in the women's peace movement, however, it will be the focus of this paper.

3. Vellacott (1985) argues that constitutional suffragists, but not the militant suffragettes, were unwilling to trade their support for the war in exchange for the vote. In Canada, most conservative leaders of the suffrage movement, including Nellie McClung, offered to support their government's war effort once the vote was offered.

4. Opposition to the development of atomic weapons began on a large scale in

the mid-1950s, primarily in response to the testing of the new hydrogen bomb. In the United States, the Committee for a Sane Nuclear Policy, established in 1957, pressured governments to halt the development of nuclear bombs. One year later, the Campaign for Nuclear Disarmament (CND) arose in reaction to the British testing of H-bombs at Christmas Island; soon there were CND branches in West Germany, the Scandinavian countries, Canada, New Zealand, and Australia (Duff 1979: 17).

5. The U-2 incident arose when an American U-2 spy plane was shot down over the Soviet Union just before the Paris Peace Summit was scheduled to begin. The Cuban missile crisis refers to the U.S. reaction to evidence that Cuba was constructing sites for Soviet missiles. President Kennedy threatened to set a naval blockade around Cuba, pushing Soviet leader Krushchev to the "brink" of declaring nuclear war.

6. One cartoon by Cath Jackson illustrates this tension. It depicts a white mother pushing a pram addressing another, younger black woman. "I want my child to have a future," declares the mother. "I wouldn't mind a future myself," the other retorts (*Breaching the Peace* 1983:33).

7. On the cover of *Breaching the Peace* is another Cath Jackson cartoon. This one features two women looking at a missile-laden truck. "It's the new cruise missile," one woman states. "It's called the red herring."

8. The editors of the *Tribune* estimate that since 1980, women have established at least twenty-six peace camps, from Puget Sound to Mount Fugi, and organized thirty-two demonstrations and peace marches on every continent.

CHAPTER 12

Women in the West German Green Party: The Uneasy Alliance of Ecology and Feminism

CAROL SCHMID

West Germany today offers the latest setting for feminism's historical confrontation with the important questions concerning the causes of war, the exploitation of nature, and the conditions for establishing equality in postindustrial society. The formation and evolution of West Germany's Green Party provides an important case study of the role of women and a feminist agenda in the Federal Republic's newest party. In March 1983, the Green Party became the first new party for thirty years to enter the federal parliament, the Bundestag (Hutchings 1985). According to Langguth (1986:87), the women's movement provides the fourth most important source of Green support, ranking after the ecological, alternative, and peace movements.

After the dissolution of Students for a Democratic Society (SDS) in the early 1970s, many protest groups competed with one another in an attempt to establish a broad-based movement to change the structure of German society. The search for an alternative society led in the second half of the 1970s to the so-called new social movements that attempted to construct a new model of a harmonious, ecologically balanced society that provided more input from the "basis," or masses, of the society. Langguth (1986:5) observes that "the adherents of these movements considered themselves politically part of the Left, but they did not wish to identify with any existing socialist structure." Rather, "the primary emphasis was to change the everyday life of the individual and to develop a life-style critical of consumerism."[1] The new movements blended anarchistic ideas, Marxism, German romanticism, and existentialism, as well as philosophies advocating alternative lifestyles.

The evolution from social movement to formation of the Green Party took place in number of distinct stages, encompassing approximately a decade. The first stage included local citizen initiatives on the environment, primarily in opposition to nuclear power, beginning in 1973. According to the Federal Office of Environmental Protection, in 1980 approximately 5 million citizens were active in the citizen initiative movement. In the second phase, starting around 1977, there was a consolidation of various groups (including women's groups) on the state (*Land*) level that formed ecological and alternative lists.[2] The third phase saw the first nationwide consolidation of local Green lists into a Green association, which was formed prior to the election of the European Parliament in 1979. Among the top candidates was Petra Kelly, who has been a consistent advocate of feminist issues. The fourth phase witnessed the founding of a federal Green Party in January 1980, which participated in the federal German elections in 1980. In the final phase, the Greens became a party in parliament beginning on March 6, 1983 (Langguth 1986:6–21). A crucial test for the evolution from movement to party was the ability of the Green Party to again surpass the 5 percent hurdle in January 1987, when it received 8.3 percent of the popular vote. (Five percent must be obtained for parties to be represented in the federal Parliament.) Joschka Fischer, a Green from the realist wing, confirmed this fact when he remarked, "Political success is now the measure. The founding stage of the party is closed" ("Knacken im Gebaelk" 1989).

Since 1980, the Greens have worked continually on the elaboration of a program guided by "fundamental principles" that all its actions be "ecological, social, democratic, and nonviolent." Ecological politics is based on an "active partnership between nature and human beings," and therefore on cooperation rather than on exploitation and destruction of the environment (Programme of the German Green Party 1985).

In this paper, I shall first briefly trace the background and origins of the Green Party and its connection with the women's, ecological, alternative, and peace movements. The second section will address the participation of women in the Green Party at the federal and local levels. The third section will examine the program of the Green Party and its congruence with feminist issues. Finally, the paper will conclude with an assessment of the present and future role of women and feminist issues within the Green Movement.

ORIGINS OF THE GREEN PARTY

An assessment of the Green Party and the feminist movement must begin with their origins in recent German politics. The most significant of these is the rise of massive, fundamental political alienation, especially among Germany's educated youth. The development of the Green Movement and Green local and federal parties is unimaginable without the student protest movement of the late 1960s through the mid-1970s. Individuals who identify with the Greens are largely composed of this younger generation in West Germany. Many leaders of the Greens came out of the student protest groups and are supporters of leftist causes (Deutscher Bundestag 1983; Langguth 1983). The continuity of activism from the campus to the community seems to support Mannheim's (1973) and Heberle's (1951) notion of a political generation that continues rather than abandons previous political involvement (see also Luebke 1981:261).

The massive influx of students into the universities, the weakening of traditional values, and the increasing alienation of youth provided fertile soil for the student protest movement known as the APO, or Extra-Parliamentary Opposition. In the Federal Republic of Germany, the existence of a coalition that governed from 1966 to 1969 without any major opposition served to radicalize left-leaning students. The student movement dominated German university life and alternative politics from the violent protests of 1968 (when there was an assassination attempt on Rudi Dutschke, an outspoken protest leader, and a hostile campaign was waged against the state of emergency that was imposed) until around the mid-1970s. Anti-Americanism was also an important theme in the student protest movement. The Vietnam War resulted in deep disillusionment with the United States, a remarkable change from the positive, idealized American image fostered during the Adenauer era. This anti-Americanism was easily mobilized by the peace movement,[3] which is one important strand of the Green Movement and a movement in which women have been particularly active.[4]

The APO reached its peak in 1967 to 1969 and then dissolved into numerous splinter groups. A few activists went into radical political K-Gruppen (Communist groups) (Szabo 1983). Two more significant realignments, however, were the entry of many APO activists into the Young Socialists (Jusos), the youth organization of the Social Democratic Party (SPD), and the creation of the autonomous women's movement.

The Jusos increased in membership by 222,048 between 1969 and 1972, workers increasingly being displaced by white-collar employees, students, and civil servants (Szabo 1983). The installation of the Social Democratic–Liberal coalition government of Willy Brandt and Walter Scheel in 1969 produced great expectations among the student Left of a more open society and a shift away from the anti-Communism of Adenauer toward the direction of *Ostpolitik* or détente. In the early 1970s, the main concern of the Jusos was a domestic policy that would renew the socialist orientation of the SPD and overcome capitalism. They increasingly equated the two superpowers, considering both imperialistic, and urged a policy of détente, which they hoped would relax tensions with the East. After 1974, however, when Brandt was replaced by Helmut Schmidt in the chancellery, the Jusos influence in the SPD waned. Many Young Socialists became critical of the Schmidt government policies, holding the SPD responsible for defense, energy, environment, and transport policies that they viewed as either wrong or watered down to obtain the support of the Free Democratic Party (FDP). By 1977 the Jusos active membership was only about half what it had been in 1972. The SPD had little appeal for a younger generation of Germans who were less interested in the large ideological movements of the 1960s and were increasingly disenchanted with the major political parties. This disillusionment led many students to search for new channels for their efforts and protests. The ecology and antinuclear, peace, alternative, and autonomous women's movements provided important outlets for them to express their dissatisfaction (Braunthal 1985; Papadakis 1984).

Other attempts to elaborate a theoretical structure for conceptualizing the

Green's electoral success have concentrated on the demographic changes in the voting population (Bürklin 1984; Dalton 1981) and the increasing process of party dealignment, which is taking place in many European countries and helping smaller parties to develop (Dalton et al 1984). Two of the more developed explanations of the emergence of the Greens point to the consequence of the fundamental value change in West Germany (Inglehart 1979, 1984) and the significance of new social movements as a basis of support for the Green Party. In Germany, fundamental changes in values and attitudes were influenced by increased access to education, detachment from traditional partisan politics, and an economic climate of rapid expansion followed by a contraction, with relatively high levels of unemployment for university-educated individuals, who provide the core support for the Greens (Bürklin 1985a, 1985b; Schmid and Luebke 1986).[5]

The second explanation for the emergence of the Green Party emphasizes the significance of the new social movements as a social base for the new party and is most compatible with the resource mobilization approach. In terms of this theory (McCarthy and Zald 1973, 1977), the ability of the Green Party to appeal to a wide spectrum of new social movement organizations is one of its strengths. As Zald and Ash (1966) have pointed out, the most viable movement is one with several organizations that can play different roles and pursue different strategic possibilities.

THE NEW SOCIAL MOVEMENTS AND THE GREEN PARTY

The breakdown of the student movement led to new forms of political protest, including the new women's movement and the ecological, alternative (of which the women's movement may be considered a part), and peace movements (Holmes 1983). The story of exactly how segments of these movements came together remains to be told. Mewes (1983:56) indicates that

> in retrospect, the steps toward founding an environmental protest party could easily be construed as obeying the developmental sequence of the movement itself. According to this view, a permanent party organization was necessary first to express the unity of ecological politics, and secondly, to provide the continuity and coherence to dispersed citizen groups who might in the absence of a party lose their dynamics and direction.

Another, probably more significant reason, and one that is less apparent to most Americans, is the prominence of political parties in the German political system. In the United States, there is a relative openess to interest groups (such as NOW and the Sierra Club) outside the major political parties, but this is not the case in the German Republic, where access to politics and the public realm are dominated by the traditional political parties. Thus there was a much greater incentive (seeing that political parties must only obtain 5 percent of the voting citizenry) to challenge the traditional political parties on their own grounds.

The Autonomous Women's Movement

In West Germany, as in the United States, feminism grew out of and in reaction to the claims of the student movement (Brand, Büsser, and Rucht 1983; Kitschelt, 1985). According to Altbach (1984:461–64), the alienation of feminists from the Left seems more complete in the Federal Republic than in the United States. German feminists are more likely to refer to the "autonomous women's movement" and less likely to use designations such as "socialist-feminist" or "Marxist-feminist." From the beginning, the new feminist movement[6] was dominated by the radical feminist tendency, which sought separation from, instead of integration and moderate reform within, the existing male-oriented society (Randall 1982).

The conflict between the New Left and feminism surfaced most dramatically in Frankfurt in 1968 when groups of women broke away from male members at the delegate conference of the Students for a Democratic Society (SDS). Women protested against their second-class status in the political struggle of the Extra-Parliamentary Opposition (APO), where they were called on to do traditional tasks such as making coffee, typing pamphlets, and duplicating and distributing information, as well as serving as sexual objects (Altbach 1984; Haug 1986; Schlaeger 1978). At this meeting, Helke Sanders addressed the delegates in a now-famous speech exposing males inside and outside the movement as being the practical beneficiaries and agents of the day-to-day oppression of women. She further observed that women live not only under capitalism, but also under patriarchy, and that in order to overcome this condition it would be necessary for them to unite into an autonomous movement to resist the customary supremacy of men (Haug 1986:52–53).

Various segments of the women's movement in West Germany developed their own unique infrastructure of movement groups, organizations, and particular strategies, such as consciousness-raising groups. The women's movement experienced its greatest mobilization successes in the campaign for abortion rights in the early 1970s. Like their American counterparts, German feminist groups founded and supported a network of alternative self-help organizations, such as clinics for women and shelters for battered wives (Altbach 1984; Schlaeger 1978). However, unlike the radical feminist movement in America, which has declined in recent years, the movement is still growing in West Germany and is actively involved in a far broader sector revolving around compatible grievances including the environment, peace, and an alternative economy (Kitschelt 1985).[7]

The Ecology Movement

Ecological politics, conceived in the 1960s and born in the 1970s, has been the most significant strand contributing to the Green Party's coming of age during the 1980s. Emerging from the youth movements of the 1960s and early 1970s, the ideology and issues of the ecological movement in the Federal Republic are affected by their legacy.

An ecological consciousness was molded during the early 1970s by the widely read *Limits to Growth* (Meadows et al. 1974), published by the Club of Rome, and later by *Ein Planet wird geplündert* (1975) by Herbert Gruhl, a conservative politician who subsequently became one of the founders of the Greens. Fears about the deterioration of the environment were shared by the population at large, focusing not only on the potentially destructive effects of nuclear power stations and chemical factories, but also on the gradual increase in the pollution of air, water, and land (Capra and Spretnak 1984; Müller-Rommel 1985; Papadakis 1984).

The politicization of the environmental issue was first actively pursued by the Social Democrat–Liberal coalition's so-called reform policy. However, on the whole, the government remained unresponsive to public opinion concerning the environment and nuclear energy. In order to change this situation, independent citizen initiatives (*Bürgerinitiativen*) emerged on the local level, most of them spontaneously, to protest for single issues such as the provision of parks and against urban renewal, new highways, and the construction of nuclear plants. The success of the civic-initiative groups led to the establishment of the Federal Association of Citizen Initiatives for the Protection of the Environment (BBU) in 1972 (Müller-Rommel 1985).

The BBU was founded as a national umbrella organization to promote the professionalization of the environmental movement all over West Germany. By using the tactics of the student movement, including sit-ins, demonstrations, and occupations of sites, and by mobilizing older networks of left-leaning individuals, many of whom had experience in the student movement, the BBU quickly grew in membership to over 1,000 affiliated groups and around 2 million members. The environmental movement and the BBU were undoubtably important factors in the later emergence and electoral success of the Greens on a local and later national level.

By the mid-1970s, nuclear energy came to dominate the BBU and the citizen initiatives. One of the first major confrontations was fought out at a proposed nuclear-energy site in 1975 in Wyhl, a small German village in the state of Baden-Württemberg. A peaceful demonstration of about 150 people, mostly area residents, took place. The police eviction of this group of people led thousands of demonstrators to become involved in the campaign in Wyhl, which eventually encompassed the entire region (Sternstein 1978:19–50).

Between 1977 and 1981, a series of demonstrations took place, some ending in violent confrontations—for example, in Grohnde, Lower Saxony, and in the later stages of the occupation around Frankfurt Airport. In Grohnde, 1,000 to 2,000 people, helmeted and heavily armed, destroyed sections of fence surrounding the nuclear site and attemped to occupy it. Nearly 5,000 police were dispatched, and in the encounter approximately 240 police and 80 demonstrators were injured (Pilat 1980:48). These demonstrations both polarized the population and allowed for maximum publicity for the new environmental movement. The activities of the citizens' initiatives and the mass mobilization against nuclear-power stations and government policies made it apparent that certain interests were not adequately represented by the main political parties.

The Alternative Movement

The environmental protests in Gorleben, site of a proposed nuclear-waste reprocessing plant, and around Frankfurt Airport revealed another element within the Green Movement—groups committed to alternative lifestyles. Alternative groups, supported primarily by young, well-educated people, made one of their most dramatic appearances in the protest at Gorleben. These activists went further than the citizens' initiatives in their opposition to technology and the evolution of industrial society. The Green Movement, according to Papadakis (1984:77), "could not have grown at such speed without this committed activity which strove to unify the spheres of personal existence and objective social reality."

When the federal government decided to build the plant in Gorleben, which was partially a nature reserve, local citizens were joined by many youthful protestors from large cities, including West Berlin, Hannover, and Hamburg. These protests culminated in a mass demonstration by 40,000 people in Hannover, the capital of the state of Lower Saxony, in March 1979 (Pilat 1980:84).

Although the protestors were able to get the Christian Democratic government of Lower Saxony to exclude Gorleben as a site for the plant, the authorities still hoped to store radioactive waste in the underground salt deposits in the area. This precipitated a new occupation on a drilling site that was being used by the nuclear-energy industry to investigate the salt deposits. Activists, primarily from outside the area, sought to practice grass-roots democracy and nonviolence.

The eviction of the occupants prompted solidarity marches in some of Germany's largest cities (Papadakis 1984:77–82). The events in Gorleben showed the close links between the ecology and alternative movements. These links have remained important, even though alternative groups do not constitute a majority within the Green Movement.

The alternative movement also covers a broad spectrum of political, social, and economic activity that reflects the themes and concepts that arise in the Green Movement. All the groups within the alternative movement have attempted to find new ways of dealing with or organizing society. The women's movement has had an important influence in creating new lifestyles and demanding more active roles for women in society. Another strand of the alternative movement became involved in various projects concerned with providing services for a particular subculture. These include alternative stores, publications, schools, health centers and therapy groups, and alternative technologies.

The squatters' movement is identified with alternative groups that have a close association with the Greens—86 percent of the supporters of the Greens in a national survey of young people also supported the squatters (Fischer 1982:686). According to Papadakis (1984:128), "the squatters' movement offered to many people who had little idea of what they wanted to do a perspective and a shelter from the outside world, which they experienced as hostile and alien." This was probably as important a reason for occupying vacant apartment buildings as the lack of housing.

The conflict around the Frankfurt Airport reflected a number of key themes within the Green Movement—opposition from ecological and alternative groups, growing disappointment with the policies of the Social Democrat–FDP alliance, and increasing tension between pragmatic radical reformists and utopian fundmentalist tendencies within the Green Movement. On November 3, 1980, about 15,000 people took part in a protest over plans to construct a new runway at Frankfurt Airport and to destroy a large section of woodland. A year later, on November 14, 1981, more than 100,000 people participated in a rally in Wiesbaden against the extension of the airport. In the autumn of 1982, the Green list gained enough votes in Hesse to enter the state parliament in Frankfurt and to hold the balance of power between the SPD and the Christian Democratic Union (CDU). Their support was particularly strong around Frankfurt Airport, even though many politicians from the major parties also opposed the runway (Papadakis 1984). The experiences of the environmental, alternative, and women's groups with the bureaucratic organizational structure of the established parties and interest groups became a major reason for the growth of the Greens in West Germany.

The Peace Movement

Between 1979 and 1983, a peace movement grew in West Germany that brought together church, left-wing, and pacifist groups as well as groups and individuals from established political parties and organizations, offering another important outlet for extending the basis of Green support. The major role played by the Greens in the larger West German peace movement was to serve as a catalyst, especially in their policies and demonstration aimed at halting the deployment of Pershing II and cruise missiles.

Initially, the Women's Initiative for Peace (Anstiftung der Frau zum Frieden [AFF]), a group inspired by Scandinavian women who collected signatures on a petition for peace, was supported by women from the Green Movement. This group, although it numbered only about 40 women, collected 80,000 signatures for a peace initiative by May 1980 (Papadakis 1984:134).

The emergence of the peace movement offered an opportunity for the Green Party to present itself as the representative of more than just ecological issues and to relate the question of nuclear energy to nuclear weapons. Around 1980, there was a shift of emphasis from opposition to nuclear energy toward antimilitarism and peace.

The peace movement escalated around 1980 in response to the NATO dual-track decision, which attempted to increase the number of Pershing missiles while offering to negotiate a reduction of armaments. Inspired by church groups such as the Service for Peace (Aktion Sühnezeichen/Friedensdienste [ASF]), the Green Party in cooperation with the Jusos, environmentalists, and other groups sponsored a peace rally in October 1981 that was attended by

300,000 people (Mushaben 1984:178; Papadakis 1984:135–37). As December 1983 approached, when deployment was to start if negotiations failed, opposition to the decision gained further momentum. To weaken their potential impact, opponents predicted a violent "hot autumn," but this turned out to be far milder than expected (Braunthal 1985).

Thus we have seen that the evolution of the federal Green Party has been a complex one, including many strands. At first, independent candidates agreed to set up lists of environmentalists and antinuclear groups, together with various independent leftists and alternative groups, including women's groups, for local and state elections. After a number of victories at the polls, a decision was made to establish a national Green Party. The Greens emerged as a federal party from a series of meetings at Offenbach (November 1979), Karlsruhe (January 1980), Saarbrücken (March 1980), and Dortmund (June 1980). Approximately 1,000 delegates from local and regional Green groups and 250 alternative groups were represented and agreed after considerable debate to create a federal Green Party by January 1980, with a party platform being passed in March 1980.

WOMEN IN THE GREEN MOVEMENT AND PARTY

Women have played an active part in all phases of the evolution of the Green Movement, from citizen initiatives to the entrance of the Green Party into the federal parliament in 1983. Nevertheless, feminists have argued that women were underrepresented in the leadership of the ecology and peace movements (Brockman 1981) in the first phase of the evolution from Green Movement to Party.

The second phase saw the Green Movement evolve from locally based groups to *Land*, or state, organizations. What had begun as a grass-roots movement dedicated largely to environmental issues had by 1977 become the major political vehicle for the antinuclear movement. The first Green electoral list, the Green List for Environmental Protection (Grüne Liste Umweltschutz [GLU]), was established in Lower Saxony by activists involved in demonstrations and citizens initiatives against the nuclear reactors at Gorleben and Kalkar (Mombauer 1982:135–39). The GLU also experienced a number of electoral successes at the local level in 1977. Support of women was critical in these victories and in the second phase of the movement. A 1978 Emnid poll found that 47.1 percent of women either sympathized with or supported the Greens, as compared with 43.6 percent of men, even though the Greens generally received less than 10 percent of the vote from both sexes (Scharping and Hofmann-Göttig 1982:402).

The decision to create a national organization to run candidates for election to the European Parliament marked the third stage in the creation of a national Green Party. According to the election rules of the European Community, candidates must be members of a designated party. Part of the incentive for forming a coalition of ecologists was to acquire sufficient finances to build a national Green Party. (Article 21 of the Basic Law of West Germany awards political parties 3.50 DM [about $2.00] from the state for each vote received [Smith 1983:360]). In March 1979 near Frankfurt, a loose coalition of environmental groups (with approximately 500 delegates) came together to form a unified Green list for the European Parliament elections, calling themselves "An Alternative Political Union: the Greens" (Sonstige Politische Vereinigung: Die Grünen [SPV]). Members of the women's movement were well represented among this group and were a major reason for the inclusion of a policy statement on women. The convention approved a platform consisting of two major issues: a nuclear-free Europe, mainly centered on opposition to the European Economic Community's investment in nuclear power plants, and a decentralized "Europe of regions." In addition, it contained a women's platform, noting the "wide-spread use of force against women" in German society and criticizing the underrepresentation of women in all areas of public life, discrimination against women and their treatment as objects of male needs, and the reduction of women to the role of mothers. In their program, the Greens demanded the complete removal of all legal sanctions against women who have abortions and the doctors who assist them (the repeal of Paragraph 218 of the German Judicial Code) (Langguth 1986). The Greens won 900,000 votes in the 1979 European election, although their 3.2 percent of the total vote fell short of the 5 percent necessary for representation.

The linking of the peace and ecology movements within the Green Party was largely the work of Roland Vogt and Petra Kelly, who met at the 1975 Easter rally at Wyhl, site of one of the first large-scale demonstrations against a proposed nuclear-energy plant (Capra and Spretnak 1984:68). Petra Kelly was one of the best-known leaders of the Greens and a central figure in the discussions leading to the founding of a national Green Party (Mewes 1983). In 1972, she joined the staff of the European Community in Brussels and became involved with the Social Democrats and the BBU. Like many young, left-wing Social Democrats, she became disenchanted with the centralist policies of the SPD, especially its acceptance of nuclear power and nuclear weapons (Markham 1983:71). There can be little doubt that Kelly and other women who played important leadership roles in the evolution of the federal Green Party have deeply influenced its direction and social policies. As we shall see in a later section, however, women have not always presented a unified voice in the Green Movement.

In the fourth phase, the various Green factions were combined into a loose coalition to run as national and local parties in the 1980 elections. Shortly after the European Parliament elections, a consolidating trend began. Between October 1979 and January 1980, when the next SPV convention was held in January in Karlsruhe, the Greens membership rose from 3,000 to 10,000 (Langguth 1983; Papadakis 1984). They saw their most important task as the maintenance of a viable organization. After a poor showing in the 1980 federal election (1.5 percent of the national vote), the Greens (with the help of the other allied protest groups) rebounded and entered the legislatures in Berlin (1981), Lower Saxony (1982), Hamburg (1982), Hesse (1982), and

Bavaria (1986). They had previously surmounted the 5 percent hurdle in Bremen (1979) and Baden-Württemburg (1980).

It is significant that the platform of the federal Green Party was more reticent than the platform of Greens for the European Parliament in calling for the repeal of Paragraph 218, the anti-abortion paragraph. Langguth (1986:87–88) traces this development to the more influential role played by the feminist component in the European Parliament elections than in the writing of the platform of the federal Green Party.

The final phase in the evolution from movement to formal party was started when the Greens scored a significant victory on March 6, 1983, winning 5.6 percent of the popular vote, enough to give them representation in the Bundestag (the West German Parliament). The Green Party also made spectacular advances in the European Parliament, jumping from 3.2 percent of the West German vote in 1979 to 8.2 percent in 1984. In the period after the 1980 federal elections, the Green Party was able to utilize two important factors to broaden its basis of support. The first factor was connected with the politicization of the issue of peace and nuclear weapons on German soil. As an active participant in the peace and antinuclear movements, the newly formed Green Party attracted a great deal of media attention and the sympathy of young people alienated from existing institutions (Laquer 1985:51). Müller-Rommel (1985:59) nevertheless maintains that there are more active supporters of the ecology movement (which also is supported by the SPD and church groups) than of the peace movement among the voters of the Greens. He concludes that the Green Party is mainly the parliamentary arm of the members and followers of the local and district environmental, women's, and antinuclear-power movements as well as of the citizen-participation groups.

Women played an important role in the successes at the polls. Among young women under the age of twenty, 6 percent said they were members of the Green Party, and 53 percent identified politically with the party. Kolinsky (1984a:436) notes that prior to the 1970s female voters had been reluctant to support new political parties. With the founding of the Green Party, this situation changed considerably, with young women and men being equally supportive of the new party. In addition, the position of women is evident in the parliamentary representation of the party. Of the 520 members of the Bundestag in 1983 who belong to the four parties represented, 51 were women, and 10 of these were members of the Green Party. In contrast with the CDU/CSU (Christian Socialist Union), FDP, and SPD, women are relatively well represented in the Green faction (or Party). Almost 38 percent of the Green delegation were women, compared with 10.4 percent in the SPD, 6.6 percent in the CDU/CSU, and 8.5 percent women in the FDP (the coalition partner of the CDU/CSU) (Kolinsky 1984a: Schrüfer 1985).

By 1987, the percentage of women in the Bundestag had increased for all parties. The largest increase, however, was registered by the Green Party, where women made up 56.8 percent of the forty-four-member delegation. In contrast, women made up 16.1 percent of the SPD, 12.5 percent of the FDP, and 8.1 percent of the CDU/CSU ("Mehr Frauen in die Politik" 1988). It has been estimated that one-third of Green deputies in *Land* parliaments and the Bundestag together were women, compared with 10 percent of the other three parties put together.

Estimates of the share of women in the Green Party membership range from a low of one-fourth (Hoecker 1986:66) to a high of one-half (Kolinsky 1984a:436); Lovenduski 1986:151), with figures probably closer to the latter. Despite the relatively high proportion of women in comparison with those in the three established parties, the goal of "parity on all party committees, leadership positions, commissions, and particularly on the party lists" has not been realized (Schrüfer 1985:34).

An analysis of how women in the Green Party were able to obtain leadership positions in the state and federal Green parties remains a largely untold story. Some indication of the inside dynamics of the struggle between males and females was illustrated in a *Spiegel* article ("Frausein allein adelt noch nicht" 1986) about the Hamburg Green Alternative List (GAL). An exclusively female list of candidates ran for election to the Hamburg parliament, although 65.6 percent of the Hamburg Green Party is male.

One of the most important ingredients in the female victory was a small circle of outspoken, radical women in the Hamburg Green Party who referred to themselves as the Freche Frauen (fresh women). They argued that a completely female slate was necessary for two reasons. First, they maintained that what was good for women was good for all humankind (including men). Second, they insisted that constitutional equality of rights was not enough to equalize the age-old inequality of the sexes, since men held the vast amount of power in the society. The exact policies that the women's list intended to pursue in the parliament were left open. At first it seemed unlikely that they would be able to push through their demand for an all-women's slate of candidates. Arguments against the women's list were made by more socialist women and some men who said that running for office based exclusively on biology was unacceptable. Gay men in the party argued that they were also the victims of a patriarchal society and therefore should be considered separately from heterosexual men. In spite of these counterarguments, the feminists were able to get their slate through by strong-arm tactics. They vowed to step down en bloc (so that there would be insufficient women on the Green list and the unity of GAL would be threatened) if they were not voted in as a unified slate. By continually applying pressure within the party and forcing the more socialist female candidates to withdraw their names from candidacy, the Freche Frauen were able to prevail. Other factors within the Hamburg Green Party also worked to their advantage. Although forty delegates consistently voted against them, many men did not want to be labeled as chauvinists or bourgeois. When in doubt, there is a tendency for the Greens to take a more radical stance so as not to appear as part of the establishment and to differentiate themselves from the Social Democratic Party ("Frausein allein" 1986).

THE TREATMENT OF WOMEN'S ISSUES IN THE 1983 PLATFORM
OF THE GREEN PARTY

The Green's were the first political organization to achieve a victory at the national level that expressly gave prominence to the goals of women's liberation in their program (Haug 1986). In the preamble to its 1983 program, the Green Party explicitly notes its link "to all those working together in the new democratic movement: groups for the protection of life, nature and environment, citizen's initiatives, the workers' movement, Christian initiatives, peace, human rights, women's, and Third World movements" (Programme of the German Green Party 1985:6).

While there is no plank dealing exclusively with feminist issues, there are important statements on sex roles and the status of women in the sections "Education and Work," "Pensions," "Violence Against Women," "Children," "Pregnancy," and "Abortion." In these sections, there are demands for equal job training and educational opportunities for men and women, including courses in domestic science and child care for both sexes at the compulsory school level. The desire for complete equality between the sexes and the recognition of the special position of women is also echoed in demands for equal pay for equal as well as equivalent work, special job security and protection from dismissal for single parents, subsidized child care, recognition of housework and child care as full-time work meriting suitable compensation and pension benefits, and an eighteen-month parental leave for either parent of a new baby. Furthermore, there are demands for autonomous women's centers for abused females, enforceable legal sanctions against discrimination in the workplace, assault, and rape and violence within marriage (Programme of the German Green Party 1985:39–43). The strong women's platform on the federal level is related to the fact that women in the party have veto power on women's issues.

Perhaps the women's issue that has generated the most controversy within the Green Party is the policy on abortion. There is a lack of consensus on this issue, which brings into conflict two of the basic ideals of the Green Party, "on the one hand, to support wholeheartedly the right of women and men to self-determination; on the other, to protect human life in all areas . . . including care for the further development of humanity" (Programme of the Green Party 1985:43). The party was severely divided on this issue at the national convention in Saarbrücken in 1980. The feminists, including Petra Kelly, argued that a woman must have control over her own body, while the conservative Green women (two out of the ten federal Green representatives, including a Catholic nurse) and a majority of the men agreed that much of Paragraph 218 (which declares abortion illegal in the first three months unless the pregnant women can get permission from three doctors on the basis of her or the fetus's health) should be retained (Capra and Spretnak 1984:108–9). Delegates finally reached a compromise, rejecting Paragraph 218 and calling for ecological and safe forms of birth control (what these are exactly was never spelled out), greater male responsibility for contraception, and funding of abortions by the state health insurance.[8] Some feminists outside the Green

Movement criticized the Green stance for raising ecological issues concerning abortion rather than proposing an unqualified rejection of Paragraph 218.

The political attitudes of the general public and of the Green voters generally reflected the opinions of the policy makers. In post election studies in 1980 and 1983, supporters of the Greens were the most positive of the four parties toward a liberal reform of the abortion law. On a 7-point scale (with 7 the most favorable), the Green supporters averaged 5.3 in both 1980 and 1983, in comparison with 3.8 for the SPD in the same years, 3.9 (1980) and 3.5 (1983) for the FDP, and 2.8 (1980) and 2.5 (1983) for the CDU/CSU (Pappi 1984:22).

PROBLEMS OF INSTITUTIONALIZATION

Despite the avowed feminist orientation of the Greens, in practice, they have experienced many of the problems of the traditional parties. In the summer of 1983, former Green Bundestag parliamentarian Klaus Hecker, the chairman of the Committee for Research and Technology, had to give up his seat in Parliament after female colleagues complained publicly about his roving hands. In a party that champions women's rights, the incident was acutely embarrasing. The Greens realized that actions they vehemently rejected in their own program could happen among their own members (Langguth 1986).

The organizational structure of the Green Party is intended to institutionalize participatory democracy. At the federal level, the party is characterized by efforts to discourage any tendency toward formation of a permanent leadership structure, development of oligarchy, bureaucratization, and professionalization by means of frequent rotation of offices. Despite these attempts to limit power, the parliamentary party faction, with its daily involvement in national politics, tends to be the most active and politically visible group (Mewes 1984). The faction elects its own leadership.

From April 3, 1984, to March 30, 1985, the leadership of the Green Bundestag faction was totally in the hands of six women.[9] This was symbolic of the importance of the women's movement in the party. The move to name these six women was also a tactical maneuver to remove the previous leadership, including Petra Kelly, who was accused of becoming a media star. Kelly criticized this move. "They acted just like men. They tricked me. I was not informed. The strategy was, unfortunately, very male" (Langguth 1986:89). This event illustrates the difficulty of both providing strong female leadership and avoiding the concentration of power in a few hands. While a significant number of voters (47 percent) who had heard of it disagreed with this change, among Green voters 82 percent of the women and 57 percent of the men approved (Langguth 1986:89). Events such as these point to many unresolved problems in the Green Party.

THE PRESENT AND FUTURE ROLE OF WOMEN AND FEMINIST ISSUES WITHIN THE GREEN PARTY

It would be premature at this point to offer a final assessment of the Green Party's integration of women and feminist issues into its party organization.

There can be little doubt that the Greens have realized a degree of participatory democracy and grass-roots control that has been to the advantage of women, even if the first signs of strain are now emerging.

The party has clearly remained more responsive to a feminist platform and the participation of women than the three traditional West German parties. In 1983, women represented 23 percent of the membership of the Christian Democrats, 14 percent of the Christian Socialists, 25 percent of the Social Democrats, 24 percent of the Liberals, and 50 percent of the Greens (Lovendusky 1986). Men, however, in the most recent national election in 1987 were still slightly more likely to vote for the Green Party than were women. Of the entire voting population, 8.3 percent of the male voters and 7.7 percent of the female voters cast their second ballot for the Green Party (*Statistisches Jahrbuch* 1987:90).[10]

Since their appearance on the political scene, the Greens have demanded quotas. From the beginning, even though they have not always been successful, they have taken pains to promote parity between men and women. As we have seen, the federal party leadership was made up of only women for an entire year. On the local level in Hamburg, the Greens put forward a women's list ("Frausein allein adelt noch nicht" 1986; "Quoten verschaffen uns einem Fuss in der Tür" 1986:37).

Even more noteworthy on the local level is the result of the recent West Berlin election, which took place on January 29, 1989. The ruling CDU was voted out of office when its coalition partner, the FDP, failed to surpass the 5 percent hurdle. This left the SPD to form a government with the Alternatives, the Berlin equivalent of the Greens. For the first time in German history, the ruling cabinet (Senat) has a majority of women. ("Revolutionaere Geduld" 1989).

The three Alternative members of the Red–Green coalition cabinet are all women who have been active in feminist organizations. The occupy the cabinet positions for education, environment, and women. Anne Klein, who is the head of the women's cabinet, is an avowed lesbian. They mayor, Walter Momper, selected five men and five women from his ruling Social Democratic Party to complete the cabinet. The women in the Berlin City Council (Abgeordnetenhaus) are also well represented outside Momper's cabinet. Of the 138 representatives, 37 (or almost 27 percent) are women. Over one-third of the 55 representatives from the SPD are female. Almost half of the Alternative delegation is female (8 out of 17). The percentage for the CDU is 14 (8 of the 55 representatives), while there are no women among the 11 members of the Republican delegation. (The Republican Party is a right-wing, anti-foreigner party that received 7.5 percent of the vote in the January 1989 Berlin election.)

In general, in West Germany today the most left-leaning the party, the higher is the proportion of women. This finding also seems to be true for other European democracies. More research needs to be conducted in this area, particularly on the role of the socialist parties and the new environmental parties in promoting the status of women. The comparative study of women politicians, feminist policies, and the party structure in Western European democracies continues to be an under-researched area of social science.

Opinion polls in West Berlin show that women are more supportive of the female-dominated cabinet than men. Fifty-three percent of women, as compared with 47 percent of the men, are in favor of this arrangement. Among party voters, the majority female cabinet is most highly endorsed by Green voters: 67 percent, compared with 56 percent of SPD voters, 58 percent of FDP voters, 43 percent of CDU voters, and 38 percent of Republican Party voters. In reply to the question "Which party is the most supportive of equal rights for men and women?" 39 percent of those responding said the SPD, compared with 36 percent for the Greens, 11 percent for the CDU, and 4 percent for the FDP ("Urknall mit Joghurt" 1989).

The Greens have adopted the most radical position of the West German political parties in promoting a feminist agenda. In addition to requiring parity in all party positions since 1986, the Greens have also proposed a far-reaching antidiscrimination law in the parliament. They demand that 50 percent of all paid jobs, training slots, and official positions be filled by women.

The SPD has responded to the Greens by placing more emphasis on the role of women in party politics. In the 1984 European Parliament elections, the SPD was forced to place a woman at the head of its party list in order to compete successfully with the Greens. SPD posters and campaign fliers placed all women in the front row, creating the false impression that the party was running numerous women candidates (Lovenduski 1986:152). The party convention, in August 1988, voted that women should hold at least 30 percent of all party functions. Beginning in 1994, this will be increased to 40 percent ("Emanzen-Sieg" 1989:56).

The Green Party has not always been very receptive to women. In their conversations with Green women, Capra and Spretnak (1984) observe that they complain of the patriarchal and competitive style of politics of many of the men in the federal Green Party. Many women in the grass-roots citizen-initiative movements refuse to join the Green Party, where they feel they are not taken seriously, but treated as tokens.

Despite pledges to the contrary, the Greens appear to be moving toward a more formalized established party structure. The passivity of some members and their limited involvement in political undertakings have forced the Greens toward the very professionalization of politics they proclaimed to have overcome through the principle of Basisdemokratie ("Die Gruenaen: Eine Anti-Volkspartei" 1989; Kolinsky 1984b:311).

CONCLUSION

Many questions remain with respect to the position of women in the Green Party and German politics on the eve of the German national election that will take place in late 1990. At this writing in November 1989, Chancellor Helmut Kohl's center-right coalition is at a low in public-opinion polls. The Christian Democratic Union is in serious trouble according to most polls. Of concern also to the CDU is the FDP, its coalition partner, which has failed to surpass the 5 percent hurdle in several recent elections.

The national Social Democratic leadership, meanwhile, is looking at West Berlin as a field test of a coalition the part had previously ruled out on the national level. If the Berlin experiment should fail, this situation will only aid the CDU. The only other time the Greens shared power in a *Land* election, in Hesse in 1986 with the Socialists, the coalition collapsed within fourteen months in a dispute over atomic power ("For West Berlin, Is Socialist–Green Rule Coming?" 1989).

Meanwhile, in the national Green leadership, pragmatic "realos" made major gains over the uncompromising "fundis" at a congress in Duisberg. This raises the question of whether the Greens would be willing to cooperate with the Social Democrats on a national level. In order to share power at the federal level, the Greens would probably have to compromise some of their more radical policies. In Berlin, Walter Momper won major concessions on three basic issues: the presence of allies, legal ties to West Germany, and the government's monopoly on the legal use of force ("For West Berlin, Is Socialist–Green Rule Coming?" 1989).

The extent to which the Greens would be willing to compromise on the 50 percent quota for women remains an unanswered question. Nevertheless, in West Germany where women's organizations like those in the United States exist but are less influential, the Green Party has given parliamentary expression to feminist demands and varied antiestablishment attitudes (Edinger 1986). As an alternative party still in its infancy, the Greens are undergoing a transformation in the midst of a larger sociopolitical transformation they have helped to precipitate. Although it has had only rather modest success in getting its platforms on women accepted above the local level of government, especially in the Bundestag, the Green Party has forced previously ignored or neglected issues onto the policy agenda of the ruling establishment.

NOTES

1. The citizen initiatives, especially organizations such as the BBU and the Federal Association of Citizen Initiatives for the Protection of the Environment, viewed "destruction of the environment, economic inequality, social injustice, and increased dependence of the individual on the authorities" as "essential characteristics of the system" and therefore the proper object of criticism (Langguth 1986:8).

2. The electoral system in the Federal Republic of Germany is based on a complex proportional system. Each voter has two votes, one to choose the individuals in local districts by plurality vote and the second vote for lists presented by the parties in each *Land*. The second vote is decisive for determining a party's total number of seats in the Landtag (state parliament) or Bundestag (federal parliament). The first vote partly influences which members of the party will have seats (Smith 1983). Small parties such as the Greens and Free Democrats (FDP) may not win any district outright. However, if they surpass the 5 percent barrier required by the constitution representatives in proportion to the popular vote will be drawn from the party list.

3. As Markovits (1985:22–23) observes, the anti-Americanism of the peace movement and the Greens is very misunderstood in the United States. As the Greens themselves note, "Green peace politics is not anti-American in the sense of an attitude against

the American people. It is directed exclusively against the warmongering politics of those who, as politically and militarily responsible, have the say in the U.S." (quoted in Markovits, 1985:23). The Greens (except for some of the most Marxist-oriented) also condemn the Soviet Union. This has been underscored by direct action, such as Petra Kelly's 1983 antinuclear demonstration in East Berlin, which resulted in the brief detainment of Kelly and the other protestors by the German Democratic Republic.

4. It is significant that two of the Greens most widely known in America are both women who have lived in the United States. Marieluise Beck-Oberdorf attended high school in Quincy, Michigan, as an exchange student, and Petra Kelly graduated from American University in Washington, D.C. The social unrest of the Vietnam War era affected both women deeply. The methods of the American antiwar protest have influenced the Greens and the peace movement.

5. As long as the economy and private consumption rose, job prospects for university graduates remained bright. But with the onset of stagflation, job prospects have declined drastically, especially in the public sector, where 80 percent of all university graduates in West Germany were employed in the late 1970s. According to Bürklin (1985a:476–77), "the future expectations of the new potential elites have been seriously frustrated, and their protest against the established elites has found substantial electoral support."

6. The second wave of feminism in Germany can be dated from the mid- to late 1960s. A relatively strong German feminist tradition, going back to the nineteenth century, was obliterated by Nazism. To a great extent, the postwar generation of women in the Federal Republic was very apolitical until the campus unrest of the 1960s (Randall 1982:155).

7. It is too early to tell if the Green Party, which is the smallest and least stable of the German parties, will continue to attract and represent feminist programs and policies. There are considerable differences between the organization of traditional German and American parties. Although women in both countries were organizing into distinctive interest groups during the 1970s, American party and campaign organizations, according to Christy (1985:97), appear to have been more easily penetrated by these newly organizing interests. One contribution of the Green Party may be to make the traditional German parties more receptive to women and women's issues.

8. In her speech on abortion on May 5, 1983, Green parliamentarian Waltraud Schoppe, a high-school teacher and single parent, broke the usually staid atmosphere of the Bundestag. She criticized Paragraph 218 for humiliating women, especially women from lower economic strata, facing a crisis and abandoning them to the arbitrary mercy of male experts. She continued: "We are living in a society where uniformity is the norm—uniform dress, living quarters, opinions, and also uniform morality. This uniformity is carried even into bed, where, just before falling asleep, people conduct a uniform exercise, with the man most commonly executing a careless penetration . . . careless, for the majority of men do not use any contraceptive devices. Men are as responsible for pregnancy as women, but they evade their responsibility. The law punishes only women for abortion. It is only after the fact that men intervene again as the defenders of our morals, drafting legislation. . . . A majority of the Greens, including myself, demand the elimination of Paragraph 218 and thus place ourselves behind the demands of the women's movement" (Capra and Spretnak 1984:110–11).

9. The six women were Heidemarie Dann, Annemarie Borgmann, Antje Vollmer, Erika Hickel, Waltraud Schoppe, and Christa Nickels.

10. The first vote is cast for a candidate, who must secure a plurality of the votes to be elected. No Green Party candidate received a plurality of votes.

CHAPTER 13

Female-Dominated Local Social Movement Organizations in Disaster-Threat Situations

DAVID M. NEAL AND BRENDA D. PHILLIPS

Research on women's participation in social movements and related group activities has tended to focus on marginal leadership and membership roles (Evans 1979). Thomis and Grimmett (1982: 9) note that "it is possible that most prominent writers on the question of social protest have not said as much about women as their role warrants." For example, research on social movements, social movement organizations, and other forms of collective protest of the 1960s virtually ignores women's involvement in such activities (e.g., Keniston 1971; Lipset 1971; Masotti and Bowen 1968). Yet a massive survey by Baird (1970: 126–27) shows that the percentage of male and female college students who considered themselves "activists" was essentially the same (about 12 percent). Although some accounts suggest that males dominated much of the civil rights, antiwar, and other related movements during the 1960s and early 1970s (Braungart and Braungart 1980), other accounts indicate that women were highly involved (Blumberg 1984; Evans 1979; Morris 1984). When women have been a focus of social movement and social movement organization research, feminist and related movements are studied (e.g., Cassell 1977; Freeman 1979; Glennon 1979).

One exception is Lawson and Barton's 1980 study of female predominance in tenants' organizations in New York City (Chapter 2 in this volume). Their research suggests that the higher the hierarchical position in the social movement organization, the more likely the position was male-dominated. National leaders seem to be predominantly male, while less so locally. Other types of social movement organizations that have a large proportion of female involvement (although often dominated by male leadership, such as some New Right organizations (Taylor 1983), are neglected.

In this study, we hope to expand the knowledge of membership and leadership composition, especially the role of women, in one type of local movement organization, the emergent citizen group (ECG) in disaster. During a nationwide study of over forty such grass-roots groups, we found that women predominated in the leadership and membership structure. As we will explain, ECGs fall under the rubric of social movement organizations (McCarthy and Zald 1977) and movement organization locals (Lofland and Jamison 1984).

We contend that factors such as task structure, preexisting social networks, type of issue, and other conditions facilitate women's increased membership and leadership in ECGs. Drawing on varied studies of women's involvement in social movements and their related organizations, we demonstrate how historical and situational factors influence the composition of certain types of movement organizations, including ECGs.

LITERATURE REVIEW

The social organizational or structuralist perspective is currently more prominent in the study of social movements and collective behavior than the earlier psychological or social psychological perspectives. We adopt the current approach. A number of works over the past twenty-five years promoting the social organizational view (e.g., Dynes and Quarantelli 1968; Lofland 1981; Lofland and Jamison 1984; McCarthy and Zald 1973, 1977; Smelser 1963; Turner 1964; Weller and Quarantelli 1973) and questioning social psychological approaches (Marx and Wood 1975; McPhail 1971) are partially responsible for this current theoretical trend.

Authors of the social movement organization (SMO) and resource mobilization (RM) literature also specifically argue for a social organizational approach in studying social movements and their related organizations. The first important statement from this perspective originates in the work of Zald and Ash (1966: 320), who delineate the concepts of social movement and social movement organization. McCarthy and Zald (1977:1217–18) later specify this differentiation, defining a social movement as "a set of opinions and beliefs in a population which represents preferences for changing some elements of the social structure and/or reward distribution of a society." An SMO is defined as a "complex or formal organization which identifies its goals with preferences of a social movement or countermovement and attempts to implement those goals."

Lofland and Jamison (1984) specify criteria for defining movement organization locals. Advocating a structuralist approach toward studying such entities, they contend that local movement organizations must have three or more people who have (1) a specific boundary for the group, (2) regularly planned meetings, (3) long-term goals with no planned date of extinction; (4) coordinated goals, (5) a formal name, (6) a place to gather and meet, (7) boundary personnel and means for communicating internally and externally. Using criteria similar to those of McCarthy and Zald (1977), Lofland and Jamison (1984:4) consider the characteristics of movement organization locals listed above as "features of formal organization." We use the term "SMO" as defined by these two sets of authors, with the difference that whereas McCarthy and Zald assume that the SMO is attached to a national social movement, the ECGs in our study are not necessarily so attached.

To date, the impact of leadership and membership composition in local, regional, and national SMOs is difficult to determine. Boyte (1980: Chap. 6) notes that women's participation may be increasing in social movements (e.g., especially those concerned with land use, the environment, and health) but offers no explanation for this trend.

We find most SMO research, except on the women's movement, has focused on male leadership and membership. Explanations provided by these studies fail to give us an adequate data base or theory to interpret our findings. We will suggest a historical typology to aid in the interpretation of our data.

METHODOLOGY

The data for this paper are drawn from a nationwide study of ECGs in disaster. We conceptualize ECGs as groups formed by private citizens before or after a disaster. ECGs consist of private citizens who formally organize at the neighborhood or community level to pursue general or specific nonemergency goals with respect to actual or potential disasters. For example, we include here local ECGs that have worked to mitigate hazards from floods, tornados, toxic waste, landslides, nuclear plants, and the like.

As in many studies of complex organizations, it is difficult, if not impossible, to define the actual population of ECGs in disaster in the United States. To locate ECGs, the following categories of people and groups were contacted: disaster officials (both locally and nationally), environmental groups, relevant government agencies (such as civil defense and mayoral offices), media, and volunteer organizations (the Red Cross, the Salvation Army). As figures later in the chapter show, we achieved our goal of finding a mix of disaster agents (technological and natural) in varied geographical settings. To minimize geographical bias, our sample included at most two ECGs per city, five ECGs per state, and no more than eight agent-specific ECGs. Here "agent" is used to refer to particular types of disasters, such as those caused by earthquakes or toxic-waste sites.

Once in the field, we conducted interviews with ECG members (including core, active, and peripheral members), public officials, the media, and other private citizens and organizations involved with the ECG. Additionally, we collected documents (e.g., newspaper accounts, private memos, letters) and field observations (e.g., photographs of disaster sites, notes from ECG or other related public meetings, videotapes). Over 500 individuals were interviewed concerning the 44 ECGs in this study. Both the qualitative and the quantitative data obtained are used in the analysis.

Our impressions from the field indicate that women were key participants or leaders in ECGs. To specify the degree to which this was the case and ascertain the conditions of female participation, we followed Glaser and Strauss's (1967: 185–220) suggestion of creating general duty indices. Both female participation and female leadership patterns were determined by consulting membership rosters, newsletters, and taped interviews with informants. We used ECG composition found at the time of the study, while carefully noting changes that occurred over time. This enabled us to study both structural and processual change over time. Other general indices included type of disaster (natural, technological, mixed), time of impact (pre-impact, post-impact, mixed; that is, some groups tried to mitigate a disaster, some to recover from a disaster, and others both to recover from and to prevent a future disaster), location of ECG in terms of area (urban, suburban, rural), and neighborhood social class (upper, middle, lower).

Due to the nature of our sampling, nonparametric statistics are used in our cross-tabular analysis. Although we recognize that problems exist with such statistics, we believe that these problems are outweighed by their advantages, and that our technique is the appropriate one for such research (see Spiegel 1956: 32–33). We believe this approach is at least a useful heuristic device for interpreting the data and is better (and more correct) than using parametric statistics or no statistics at all. Since our data are nominal, the test of significance is determined through chi square, and the contingency coefficient is used as our measure of association (Spiegel 1956: 196–202: Welkowitz et al. 1976: 255–56).

WOMEN'S PARTICIPATION IN SMOs: A TYPOLOGY

As we noted earlier, SMO composition is rarely discussed in sociological studies. We analyze both leadership and membership of disaster-related ECGs by sex. Three categories are used for our analysis: female-dominated ECGs (100 percent to 61 percent female), mixed (60 percent to 40 percent female), and male-dominated (39 to 0 percent female). The distribution of membership and leadership patterns of ECGs is shown in Figure 13.1. These data clearly indicate that females predominate as members and leaders in approximately 50 percent of the cases. When these totals are added to groups with mixed membership and leadership traits, we find that only 20 percent of the ECGs are male-dominated. An important question to ask, then, is why do women predominate in ECGs?

Figure 13.1.

Gender Distribution

		Female-dominated	Mixed	Male-dominated	
ECG Characteristic	Leadership	50.0% 22	27.3% 12	22.7% 10	100% (n = 44)
	Membership	47.7% 21	34.1% 15	18.2% 8	100% (n = 44)

The predominance of women in ECGs can be explained through a historical sociological perspective. Women's associations and reform societies developed in the years between 1800 and 1860 (Berg 1978; Ryan 1979). These
associations were concerned with issues threatening the perceived well-being
of the home and local community. Women were the predominant participants
in these types of organizations, which over time began to take on the characteristics of SMOs. Women came to be seen as the moral guardians of their
communities as they organized around such social problems as prostitution,
social purity, and moral education (Gordon, 1976; Sklar 1973; Welter 1966).
These associations represented several local urban social problems.

Some associations seem to be the forerunners of a social movement and
certain SMOs that appeared in the latter part of the nineteenth century. Blair
(1980) describes the women's clubs that first appeared as literary organizations around 1870. These clubs not only engaged in self-improvement types of
activities, but eventually extended to such community projects as reforming
mental asylums and jails and building public libraries. According to Blair,
these local clubs were concerned with issues that were an extension of
women's traditional sphere in the community. This female influence, known
as "domestic feminism," later became known as "municipal housekeeping."
Civic reform was an example of extending women's sex roles beyond their
homes. In a similar theme, Gonzales (1973) contends that even though the
state has taken over many of the domestic matters traditionally dealt with by
women, it is women who are politically active in dealing with these matters
(see also Lawson and Barton 1980).

For example, in the 1870s the local clubs described by Blair (1980) were
more traditional than the feminist movement. The General Federation of
Women's Clubs (GFWC) was national and is traditional. The GFWC did not
support women's suffrage until 1914, and then only as a way to further apply
its principles of municipal housekeeping.

ECGs fit into a pattern that is traditional and local. Women in ECGs view
their activity as an extension of their traditional gender role. These ECGs are
concerned with issues that are perceived to pose a threat to the well-being of
the home and community. Essentially, the women in these groups are furthering their families' interests in the face of actual or potential disaster. Based on
the history of women's participation in SMOs that form around traditional
roles at the local level, we expect that ECGS will have high female leadership
and membership. ECGs form to protect the family and community and as
such are capable of drawing women's participation.

We present a typology to further clarify these points. Our typology is
intended to remedy the inadequate treatment of women in historical and
sociological studies and to provide a systematic approach for the explanation
of female participation in SMOs (Figure 13.2). Our analysis proceeds along
two axes. The first, geographical focus, indicates whether the specific issue
around which the SMO is organized is a local or national concern. Some local
SMOs may be considered part of a national umbrella group; here, we treat
local and umbrella (national) groups separately. Also, a local group may even-

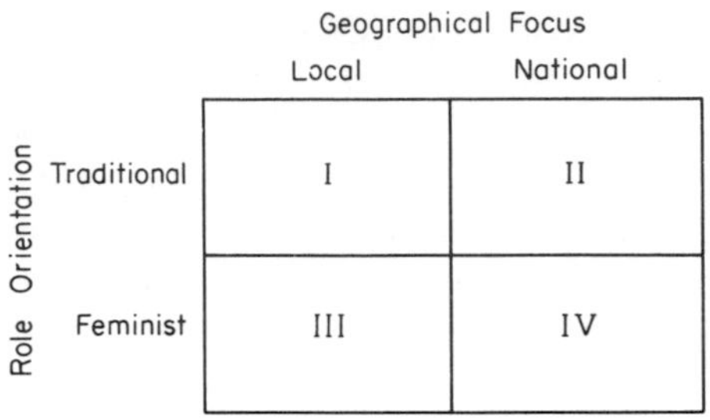

Geographical Focus

	Local	National
Traditional	I	II
Feminist	III	IV

Role Orientation

Figure 13.2. Women's participation in SMOs: a typology.

tually develop into a national movement. The length of a group's existence may also determine whether it has a local or national focus. ECGs and their members most often have a local focus. Even if they become somewhat coupled with national movements or members, their focal point is still the local issue.

The other axis is role orientation, having the categories of traditional or feminist. Traditional role orientations hold in SMOs in which home and community actions are considered important by the participants and are reflected as such by the group's actions. Consumer groups may fit into this category, as do ECGs. Feminist role orientations are reflected in those SMOs in which feminist political concerns take precedence. Suffrage associations are an example.

Type I SMOs are characterized by a traditional role orientation and a local focus. ECGs fit such a category, as do the initial stages of such groups as Mothers Against Drunk Drivers. Earlier efforts to improve jails and mental asylums, as well as local attempts to improve the moral standards of a community (described by Berg 1978; Blair 1980; Ryan 1979), are other illustrations.

Type II SMOs are characterized by a traditional role orientation with a national focus. Groups associated with temperance movement laws such as the Women's Christian Temperance Union, the national Mothers Against Drunk Drivers, and today's peace or anti–nuclear war movement organizations are examples.

Type III SMOs, which are feminist and local, include the early 1970s consciousness raising (C-R) groups (Cassell 1977; Freeman 1979) and probably the early-twentieth-century birth control movement (Gordon 1976). Finally, Type IV groups, which have a feminist and national focus, would include groups associated with women's suffrage and the Equal Rights Amendment. Our paper focuses on Type I SMOs, but can be totally understood only within the context of the whole typology.

To summarize, our contention here is that ECGs fall under the rubric and tradition of Type I SMOs. Like other examples within this category, those involved in forming and maintaining ECGs are concerned with protecting the family and home environment. That is, women participate in ECGs not because of some inherent political ideology, but as an extension of traditional gender ideology.

WOMEN'S INVOLVEMENT IN ECGs

Although ECGs fit the Type I category, some characteristics of ECGs reflect ongoing changes in the American social structure. One key change is the type of strategy required. Women in ECGs are much more inclined today to lobby city, state, or even federal officials or use the courts to achieve their goals. A key structural characteristic of American society related to these tactics is what is known as the supradomestic realm. This concept refers to an area of agencies and related social agencies that connect domestic-household issues to the public-jural domain. Gonzales (1973) defined this as the supradomestic realm, or the place where domestic matters are at least partially controlled by the state apparatus. Gonzales argues that concern with public health, like the fight against pollution, is an extension of private, domestic, and family health concerns. She further suggests that domestic issues of consumerism, health, and education have been usurped or impinged upon by jural institutions, with the result that the family, small groups, and individuals acting as private citizens have little control over this domain. Women in ECGs who enter this supradomestic realm are often concerned with issues that are extensions of the domestic or private domain. Quality of life, health, and investment in the home community which disaster threatens or has already struck are central to the goals and issue-defining process of ECGs. These concerns have been traditionally expressed and acted on by women rather than by men in SMOs.

Other factors also seem to be related to women's involvement with ECGs in disaster. For one, the type of disaster impact is important (Figure 13.3). ECGs dominated by female leadership seem to occur in technological-disaster situations, whereas male leadership patterns tend to occur more in natural-disaster situations. Mixed leadership patterns occur mostly when the disaster agent is mixed. The location where the ECG originated (i.e., urban, suburban, rural) is related to the ECGs gender leadership characteristic (Figure 13.4). Female leaders predominate in rural areas, male leaders are most often found

Figure 13.3.

Type of Disaster

Gender Leadership Characteristic		Natural	Technological	Mixed	
	Female-dominated	8 (36.4%)	13 (59.1%)	1 (4.5%)	22 (100%)
	Mixed	5 (41.7%)	4 (33.3%)	3 (25.0%)	12 (100%)
	Male-dominated	8 (80.0%)	2 (20.0%)	0 (0.0%)	10 (100%)

$\chi^2 = 10.42 \quad a = .03 \quad c = .438$

Location of ECG

Gender Leadership Characteristic		Urban	Suburban	Rural	
	Female-dominated	4 (18.2%)	7 (31.8%)	11 (50.0%)	22 (100%)
	Mixed	5 (41.7%)	6 (50.0%)	1 (8.3%)	12 (100%)
	Male-dominated	1 (10.0%)	8 (80.0%)	1 (10.0%)	10 (100%)
		10	21	13	

$\chi^2 = 12.40 \quad o = .01 \quad c = .469$

Figure 13.4.

in the suburbs, and mixed leadership has a slight edge over female leadership in urban areas. Other characteristics, such as geographical location and time of ECG impact (pre- or post-disaster), were not statistically significant. We add that the leadership patterns of ECGs resulted in significant relationships in our cross-tabulations, whereas membership patterns did not result in any significant relationships. With all the relationships tested, elaboration techniques were used and none of the relationships varied significantly. The consequence of the importance of the leadership patterns is discussed later in this paper.

EMERGENCE AND GROWTH: THE ROLE OF FRIENDSHIP NETWORKS

Not only do the issues themselves affect membership and leadership composition in ECGs, but so does the mobilization and recruitment process during emergence. Aveni (1977) and Snow et al. (1980), among others, have documented the role of friendship networks in the mobilization and recruitment patterns in crowd and SMO activities. A focus of friendship networks suggests that recruitment may be viewed as a function of such structural conditions as proximity, availability, and recruitment into ECGs.

Our data clearly show that the core leadership develops before the total membership exists. Not surprisingly, predominantly female leadership patterns lead to predominantly female membership patterns, or more generally the composition (i.e., male or female) of leadership patterns influences the composition of membership patterns. A pattern of recruitment based on sex is seen in Figure 13.5. The implication from these data is that the networking and recruitment process for ECGs is strongly based on same-sex relationships. This pattern holds even when other characteristics mentioned above are used in our elaboration techniques. Hence, not only are friendship pat-

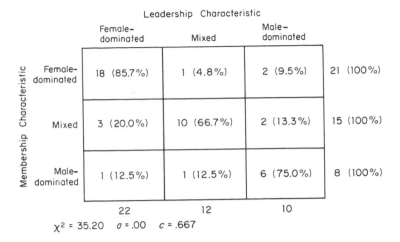

Figure 13.5.

terns important, as the literature suggests, but friendship patterns within the same sex are of at least equal importance.

Our cross-tabulations show the relationships between the various characteristics and conditions of ECGs; our qualitative data show the process from which these relationships emerge. Our study shows, as a prevalent pattern, that a problem is gradually identified and the need to take some action is recognized through extensive contacts between same-sex friends. This occurs over coffee, cards, car-pooling, and day-to-day informal interaction. These friends, often women who live in the same neighborhood, if not on the same street, then form a group with themselves as the core (if not sole members) to attempt to prevent, remove, minimize, or recover from the disaster agent. This process is very similar to Lawson and Barton's (1980) description of how various tenant unions began to emerge in informal settings (such as laundry rooms) where women discussed problems within their building. The probability of male activity under this pattern is low, because women tend to network with other women.

The second pattern involves a widespread local recognition of the actual or potential disaster agent. In these cases, although small acquaintance networks may exist, people have not frequently interacted prior to the precipitating incident. These people eventually mobilize. Frequently, the disaster agent has been identified as such by the media, by the announcement of a permit application for potential pollution (in the air, water, or soil), or by an actual disaster impact on the area. Acquaintances and friendships develop throughout the mobilization period, as demonstrated by the number of non-disaster-related interactions these people have after mobilization. These patterns of interaction can be attributed to the initial meeting and group assignment to various tasks. One feature of these newly formed friendships or relationships between the members is the formation of female dyads and triads, which occur much more frequently than with males in ECGs. These groupings then proceed to recruit nonmembers (females) into the ranks of ECGs. Neighborhoods where this pattern occurs are frequently heterogeneous, especially with respect to socioeconomic status. This pattern also occurs, however, in larger areas such as residential suburbs and the cities. In these areas, blanket recruitment through the media is tempered by class and perhaps occupationally related channels of participation. Organizational meetings, although open to all interested, may be held at private clubs or homes. Also, before the formal meetings, a number of individuals may formulate an agenda of organization. As a result, these individuals (generally female) usually assume leadership positions within the ECG.

PERCEIVED LEGITIMACY AND FEMALE MEMBERSHIP

ECGs' core members note that their groups' major problem is being acknowledged as legitimate by various public and private persons and organizations. They state that having a majority of female members or participants, or a lack of male participants, decreases their degree of perceived legitimacy with the ECGs' contacts. Members of predominantly female ECGs feel that the groups' perceived legitimacy would increase if they had a male to represent the ECG, even though other tasks would be accomplished by female members. The ECGs' members reason that males' occupationally related contacts, organizational knowledge, and easier entrée to powerful groups could have increased both their success in various tasks and goals, and the degree of perceived legitimacy for the group.

These observations by female ECG members reflect their understanding of the limits of female power, authority, and perceived legitimacy within the larger society. Yet despite such experiences and perceptions, these women do not change their orientation from traditional to feminist. (Further longitudinal analysis would reveal whether such experiences change traditional role orientations toward a feminist perspective, such as Ferree [1980] has found when working-class women join the labor force.)

ECG members are correct in believing that gender roles act as structural constraints on perceived legitimacy and group success. Officials from industry, the media, and public organizations as well as elected representatives frequently use such phrases as "a bunch of hysterical housewives," "concerned mothers," "neighborhood women," and the like to summarize their impressions of group characteristics. Female ECG members also label themselves as "housewives," "concerned mothers," and "neighborhood women," but in a different and more positive fashion.

A structural contradiction exists in this situation. All groups involved seem to assume that the only legitimate role of female-dominated ECGs and female ECG members is traditional. Yet different perceptions exist regarding what that role entails. Females in ECGs are active because of their concern for the household and family in the role of mother and homemaker. As long as the women stay in the home, their claims are perceived, to a small extent, as legitimate. If these women collectively leave the home or the neighborhood to organize as a group to protect their homes, their concerns lose their perceived legitimacy in the eyes of many public and private organizations and officials. In other words, women's traditional roles do not tend to legitimate action outside the domestic realm, especially if taken in a collective manner. Even though women perceive such behavior as part of their role, they are negatively sanctioned by local officials and others.

This treatment by officials should not be surprising. Type I SMOs have historically experienced a lack of legitimacy in the public realm. In the case of female-dominated ECGs, the absence of legitimacy is very evident. In the cases we studied, many public and private officials saw these disaster issues as trivial.

In further explaining the lack of male ECG members, women (who are homemakers) perceive themselves as having more discretionary time than male ECG members and leaders. Further, ECG members have indicated that using one's discretionary time for ECG-type protest is a source of internal family conflict. For example, some female ECG participants point to the disruption of the "normal household routine," and some have even explained that this has led to an extreme strain on their marriages. Male members have also experienced conflict, although externally, in using their discretionary time for such protest. We will expand on this shortly.

This fact leads us to add that McCarthy and Zald's (1973: 11) concept of discretionary time, especially among professionals, needs to be modified. We contend that *perceived* discretionary time within households and friendship networks is as important as "objective" discretionary time. On the other hand, the role of housewife certainly fits McCarthy and Zald's (1973: 11) contention that "any occupation whose members are not tied to specific and sharply delineated time and work spaces may arrange their work loads to increase participation in social movements." This is precisely what female ECG members did: they shifted their time schedule.

We suggest that one reason why women take such an active role in ECGs, even if family conflict increases as a result, is that the majority of women involved consider themselves responsible for the family, household, and community. A great deal of their activity in the ECG is an actual extension of their perceived traditional role as being primarily domestic and community-oriented. When a disaster or potential disaster threatens, the female ECG member becomes active through an extension of her traditional role orientation. Blair's (1980) example of "municipal housekeeping" clearly fits within our logic.

Given the historical and social background of women in Type I SMOs, we find the major characteristic of traditional role orientation significant. A majority of female ECG members are not otherwise politically active, especially in ways that could be considered to the left of the political spectrum. During interviews, female ECG members often disclaimed association with the women's movement or feminist politics.

THE LACK OF MALE PARTICIPATION

The decision-making procedures in ECGs also affect participation. Many of the maintenance activities and much of the decision making are carried out informally rather than at formal meetings. The ability of a small number of members to meet or talk frequently (often three to four times a day, over the phone, or over coffee) is an important prerequisite to active, constructive participation. Members point to this as one reason for low male participation. This prerequisite also increases the general difficulty that ECGs encounter in recruiting members outside their own friendship and networking patterns.

In conjunction with the lack of formal, regularly scheduled meetings (except during the initial two- to six-month period following emergence), the male-recruitment dilemma hinders individuals from "coming up through the ranks," a pattern that perhaps could later alter the sex-ratio composition. If the group is to maintain its existence, recruitment is important because the core of the ECG members generally do most of the tasks and many suffer a form of burnout after a year or two of extensive activity.

Actual or perceived occupational sanctions may also prevent male participation in larger numbers. Males of the mobilized population are often employed by an organization that may be responsible for creating, monitoring, mitigating, or defining the disaster agent. Therefore, these males are constrained by the perceived possibility of job loss or other economic or social sanctions. For example, in a number of cases, blue-collar families were concerned about toxic-waste sites or water and air pollution. The husbands' jobs and the local economy were directly linked to the technological agent. The worker-husbands were not inclined to become involved for fear of losing their jobs. Another example involves middle- and upper-middle socioeconomic-status groups. The wives were quite active in clean-air or environmental activities aimed at corporations that, ironically, employ their husbands in white-collar and higher managerial positions.

Conflicts between the husband's job and the wife's participation are not limited to technological-disaster situations. Small businessmen and politically active, upwardly mobile men are not inclined to participate in helping to define a disaster because doing so might entail, for example, rezoning a flood area or redeveloping a business district after a tornado. If, in the process, men challenge the business norms of the community, they may not have business licenses renewed or may be deprived of normally obtained political favors. With technological disasters, however, wives in ECGs continue to battle the proper authorities to mitigate or aid recovery from a natural hazard. Only in extreme cases have women commented that they have had to temporarily "drop to the background" during some debates because of their husbands' employment.

CONCLUSION

In this paper, we have taken mainly a structuralist perspective. The emergent group is the focus, or level, of analysis, using the SMO approach initially advocated by Zald and Ash (1966) and further developed by Mc-Carthy and Zald (1973, 1977). Lofland and Jamison's (1984) work has also aided our analysis of local SMOs, a topic neglected by collective behavior and SMO researchers.

We focus on one type of local SMO, emergent citizen groups (ECGs), developed to mitigate or recover from disaster, which are part of the current efforts of neighborhood groups to solve community problems. Our research found that women often predominate in leadership and membership composition within ECGs.

Male or female composition is a topic that is neglected in much research on social movements and SMOs. In this study, we describe the distribution of female membership and leadership patterns of ECGs in disaster to explain why women are a majority of those involved in ECGs. First and most important, we demonstrate that the type of localized issues involved follows a pattern of domestic feminism and municipal housekeeping that can be traced in American culture back to the early nineteenth century. Activity in this type of SMO, which includes ECGs, is related to social perceptions that women's main role is protecting and tending to the family and the home. Obviously, a potential or an actual disaster threatens the domain of the family and home.

The nature of preexisting networks among female friends enhances the predominance of women in ECGs. Also, perceived notions of discretionary time and perceived potential job sanctions impede male membership and leadership. ECG members feel that the lack of male members or leaders initially inhibits group legitimacy due to perceptions by outsiders who view these female ECG members as illegitimately exercising power.

NOTE

A much earlier version of this paper, by Susan McCabe and David M. Neal, was presented in 1983 at the annual meeting of the North Central Sociological Association. The data in this paper were obtained through National Science Foundation Grant Number CEE-8113191 to the Disaster Research Center; however, any opinions, findings, or conclusions are solely those of the authors and do not reflect the views of the National Science Foundation. The authors' names appear in alphabetical order and designate equal authorship. The authors would like to thank E. L. Quarantelli and Susan McCabe for their comments on earlier drafts of this paper.

PART IV

WOMEN IN WOMEN'S RIGHTS PROTESTS

Women have been present most visibly in the historic struggles for their own rights. Part IV brings together six articles about women's collective efforts to expand their boundaries and to make known their political, economic, and social grievances. Various themes emerged from these studies of women's rights protests. First, women's mobilizations throughout history have included a wide variety of demands. That is, women have organized to demand their rights not only to food and shelter, but also to education, jobs, and suffrage in order to survive economically as individuals and as caretakers of children and families. Second, women are not a monolithic group. Indeed, women have often mobilized into opposing camps—on issues involving peace and war, abortion rights, affirmative action, and education, to mention only a few. For example, Fish (Chapter 14) analyzes women's struggle for education as a primary and recurrent goal in every country where women have been subordinated. In describing the active countermovement to women's education, Fish reveals how serious a threat to male supremacy it appeared to pose in the United States. Interesting parallels are demonstrated between the arguments against female suffrage and female education. As pointed out in Chapter 1, Jayawardena (1986) has highlighted a similar pattern of demands by women for education and resistance by men in other parts of the world into the late twentieth century. Thus educational rights still provide the stimulus for women's mobilization and men's (and some women's) countermobilizations around the world.

A third theme highlighted in this section is the continuity between the women's rights struggles and the survival forms that enable such movements to persist over extended periods of time. Although the traditional literature often describes social movements in terms of their rise and fall—implying a beginning and an end—feminists and others

have begun to question this perspective. They suggest that some movements do not "wither away," but merely adapt to changing political
(usually more hostile) conditions in order to survive. They reemerge
when these conditions become more favorable. For example, Taylor
(Chapter 15) links more traditional clubs and organizations with the
feminist movement. She argues that they have been unrecognized as
possible seedbeds, or "halfway houses"—using Aldon Morris's (1984)
concept—for resurgent feminism. Taylor claims continuity between
elite organizations, such as the National Women's Party, and protest
organizations, with the former helping to sustain the women's movement between its peak periods. The extensive history of women's
rights struggles worldwide are documented by Chafetz, Dworkin, and
Swanson (Chapter 16). They maintain that role expansion combined
with changed consciousness, within a climate of rapid urbanization
and industrialization, provided the necessary conditions for the emergence of the first wave of women's movements around the world.
They also indicate how socioeconomic conditions produced ameliorative rather than radical feminist ideologies at that time.

A fourth theme—the prevalence and importance of diversity *within*
the women's rights movement—is underscored by Cavin's (Chapter
17) article on the struggles of lesbians to organize and effect policy in
the United States. Cavin examines the origins of the lesbian movement
and its roots in the gay liberation and feminist movements. Setting it
within a historical and international framework, Cavin describes and
analyzes the forces that led to the birth of the gay/lesbian movement in
Europe and the United States. Her data provide another glimpse into a
semi-gender-integrated protest and the consequences of this mobilization strategy for women. The lesbian rights struggle has been an integral part both of the feminist movement and of the gay movement. She
compares gender-independent and gender-integrated confrontational
strategies within this linked but separate gender-based social protest in
the United States in the last three decades.

The creativity of women's modes of protests is a fifth theme that
provides a link among women's rights protests, political actions, and
their other types of protests. Ruddick (1989:38) differentiates these
types as "feminist politics" and "women's politics of resistance," respectively. As an example of the latter, the silent and dramatic actions
of the Madres of the "disappeared" in Argentina and Chile in the 1970s
demonstrated the creative and sustained struggles of mothers, grandmothers, and others to subvert militarism and totalitarian power
(Ruddick 1989; see also Agosin 1987; Femenia 1987). In addition to
marching defiantly and silently with the photographs of their disappeared loved ones, they talked and made tapestries (*arpilleras*) to dis-

seminate the truth about what had happened to their relatives. They used drama, speech, and other art forms to publicize their political message to the ruling authorities and to the world. Some evidence exists of similar use of drama and art in the suffragist movement. McAllister (1988) notes the use of songs and singing in her study of women's nonviolent ways of bringing about social change. Thus despite their variability, it is clear that women's rights protests and other types we have examined often overlap in terms of structure, issues, and innovative strategies of confrontation.

In confronting their opposition—whether at the local grass-roots level or at the state level—women have creatively transformed some of their traditional behavior into political protest. At times, they explicitly draw on their "culture's symbols of femininity" to resist oppressive conditions (Ruddick 1989:38–39). In Part I, Pope (Chapter 4) described the use of guerrilla theater by welfare rights women who demanded that authorities transform the public-assistance program. Women acting collectively in protest do not necessarily subscribe to feminist goals (such as the repudiation of women's traditional place in society). In fact, resistance by traditionalist women often develops when ruling authorities interfere with expected female roles.

Regardless of their location on the left–right continuum of political ideology, women who protest commonly view the struggle as necessary for family and group survival and betterment against perceived enemies. But only rarely are men or male power–based structures, as such, identified as the enemies. More often, race, class, or religious differences distinguish friends from foes. The state, the job, the church, or the local governing bodies are reified and ungendered, despite the ubiquitous male hegemony throughout history.

Some women on the right have organized to safeguard their perceived security under existing patriarchal relationships and regimes. For feminists, the struggle has been fueled by the desire to eradicate what they see as multiple-gendered sources of oppression. As discussed in Part I, protests have frequently emerged at the grass-roots level, when a threat is perceived. Yet despite the basic and recurring common thread of "survival" (however that is defined by the group), differing experiences, resources, and opportunities contribute to the diversity of women's protest. While all social life is gendered, women's modes of resistance, Ruddick (1989:42) notes, "are as various as the cultures from which they arise."

Hanna's article (Chapter 18) provides another example of women's creative use of "feminine" traditions—dance—as social protest. She first analyzes dance as a form of *protest* (in Nigeria) and then examines dance as a mode of *rebellion* within the dance institution (in the United

States). Art, in a form such as literary work, is widely recognized as a form of protest. Music, songs, paintings, and posters have similarly been acknowledged to serve this purpose. These types of art have generally been treated as being produced by males, or at least as being gender-neutral.

In contrast, more "feminine" art forms have eluded political analysis until recently. In the last few years, feminist researchers have begun to analyze dance for its potential political implications. This form of protest was vividly demonstrated at the Greenham Women's Peace Camp in January 1983, as women joined hands and danced on top of the silos that housed nuclear missiles. Only recently has the political significance of "feminine" art forms—such as sewing, embroidery, and quilting—begun to capture the attention of analysts. Although historical data on this topic are sparse, except for such highlights as Mme. Defarge's knitting during the French Revolution, we know that today women often use these art forms to communicate political messages, especially under totalitarian regimes (for example, the Chilean women's *arpilleras* mentioned earlier).

When we examine dance as a form of protest, however, the relationship generally is subtle and consequently easily ignored. Or, perhaps, protest masked in the form of dance has in fact been recognized but largely unacknowledged by traditional scholars. It may be that the soldiers who fired on unarmed Native Americans during the Ghost Dance (the massacre at Wounded Knee) understood the political nature of these expressive activities. With few exceptions, however (for example, the study of "cargo" cults in Melanesia), a masculine perspective in the sociopolitical literature has generally biased our thinking by focusing primarily on the more aggressive and "action-oriented" aspects of protest: war, revolution, riots, marches, and demonstrations. Hanna's work contributes to the new feminist literature that shows how various types of art have been and are still being used as protest.

Hanna focuses on the use of dance in two different settings: in Africa in the early twentieth century, and in the United States today. She describes the many ways in which dance is used by Nigerian women, showing how it was employed as a major tactic in the Nigerian Women's War of 1929. Rebelling against oppressive British rule, the women mobilized at the grass-roots level, transforming their traditional dances into political activities. Hanna then provides a contrast and a parallel, exploring rebellion within the institution of dance and the way in which women changed the nature of this art form in the United States. Modern dance emerged as women's rebellion against ballet, the most male-dominated institution of dance. Breaking established boundaries, women moved into the public arena through theater dance, drastically altering the rules of the game and the assumptions about women's physical capabilities. Thus Hanna shows how creative artistic protest has at times transformed patriarchal institutions. Social innovations—such as modern dance—reflect the new freedoms sought by women in society and a new and liberating aggressiveness. Analyzed from a woman-centered perspective, modern dance becomes both the means and the outcome of protest against patriarchal control over women's way of artistic expression and submissive scripts.

The literature on women's struggles for their own rights has expanded rapidly since the rise of the second wave of feminist protest. We know a great deal about the involvement of white women, especially middle-class and affluent women's roles in the first and second wave of feminism. Knowledge is accumulating on the various sources and consequences of feminist revolts, rebellions, and revolutions in the Western world. Cross-cultural data on feminist struggles have only recently become more available, as feminist scholars, internationally, try to integrate and analyze the commonalities and differences of women's experiences. In particular, African-American women have been developing a body of theory that explains the uniqueness and complexity of the black woman's historical position and, consequently, the complexity of her feminism (Collins 1989; Dill 1979; King 1988). The small but growing body of writings by other racial/ethnic minority women are also providing insights into situations of extreme double or triple jeopardy, based on race/ethnicity, gender, and class.[1]

We conclude by raising some questions: What do varied protests for women's rights encompass? How is "feminist politics" understood and linked to other types of women's rights protests and "women's politics of resistance" in various parts of the globe? What are the core issues that have united women historically? Which ones have divided them? What strategies and tactics have been used across the ages to confront patriarchal systems in different areas? How do women activists who demand rights *as women* fare today in Latin America, Africa, Australia, and Asia? How do women combine the fight for their rights as women with the other major struggles against sources of inequality that draw them into protest? How does one affect the other? What new insights can we gain from the political lives of women by using a global perspective? What new insights can we gain by emphasizing the diversity among women, as well as their commonalities as women in a patriarchal world? What are some of the potential consequences for women's rights and women's rights protests in Western and Eastern

European, African, and Latin American countries that have undergone revolutionary political upheavals?

NOTE

1. See, for example, "Common Grounds and Crossroads: Race, Ethnicity, and Class in Women's Lives" [special issue], *Signs* 14 (Summer 1989).

CHAPTER 14

The Struggle over Women's Education in the Nineteenth Century: A Social Movement and Countermovement

VIRGINIA KEMP FISH

This article focuses on one facet of the feminist social movement of the nine-teenth century in the United States: women's attempts to gain bona fide access to universities and colleges that had previously enrolled only men, and thereby to expand their social space. Not surprisingly, most of the activists in this movement were white, native-born, upper-middle-class women (with some men as well). A social movement can be simply defined as a large number of people who have joined together to bring about or to resist social change (Robertson 1981:651). A countermovement may be termed reactionary or regressive if its goal is to restore prior agreements that have been over-turned (a "turn back the clock" effort) or conservative if its goal is to resist prospective social change (Babbie 1980:526–27). The feminist movement, which was intertwined with the abolition movement, took shape at the Sen-eca Falls Convention of 1848, at which time a Declaration of Sentiments and Resolutions, modeled after the Declaration of Independence, was drawn up. The following excerpt from the "Declaration of Sentiments" details in a suc-cinct fashion the social position of women in the society at that time, citing in particular the denial of college education:

> The history of mankind is a history of repeated injuries and usurpations on the part of man toward woman, having in direct object the establish-ment of an absolute tyranny over her. To prove this, let facts be submit-ted to a candid world.
>
> He has never permitted her to exercise her inalienable right to the elective franchise.
>
> . . . compelled her to submit to laws, in the formation of which she had no voice.
>
> . . . made her, if married, in the eye of the law, civilly dead.
>
> . . . taken from her all right in property, even to the wages she earns.

. . . denied her the facilities for obtaining a thorough education, all colleges being closed against her.

. . . usurped the prerogative of Jehovah himself, claiming it as his right to assign for her a sphere of action, when that belongs to her conscience and to her God. (reprinted in Gurko 1974: 308–9)

The movement that came out of the Seneca Falls Convention of 1848 was a women's rights movement that posed a "relatively radical and fundamental challenge to patriarchal power," including a critique of the sexual division of labor. As the century neared an end, the movement increasingly made concessions to the existing power structure and reduced its program for social change to a much more limited and restricted set of goals. In time, the movement embraced the notion of separate spheres and a romanticized conception of sexual differences that located women in home-centered and family-based roles (Buechler 1986:37).

Many of the educational pioneers who are the focus of this article accepted the domestic and child-rearing role as paramount for their sex. Nonetheless, their efforts to enter universities involved a form of social protest in which they sought to redefine and expand their roles. Not only did these pioneers attempt to enter the public sphere, but they attempted to legitimate the place of women within that sphere.[1] The very act of matriculating as students challenged the notion of women's confinement to a separate sphere. The nineteenth-century movement (as well as this century's second wave), however, "articulated grievances" about private as well as public-sphere concerns, and "hence about the dual sided nature of women's subordination" (Buechler 1986:47–48).

COUNTERMOVEMENT

A countermovement can be described as a particular kind of protest movement that arises as a response to the social change advocated by the initial movement. The process by which changes (or threatened changes) in the position of groups generate protest, followed by counterprotest, can be seen as part of a dialectical process (Mottl 1980:620). This conflict of opposites ultimately creates a new reality, which in turn creates contradictions and new challenges in a never-ending process. Therefore, social movement and countermovement are intertwined in a dynamic relationship that creates a changed environment (Hess, Markson, and Stein 1982:549).

Whether one emphasizes the reactionary or the conservative aspect of the countermovement that emerged in response to the feminist movement, out of it came elaborate arguments and attempts by males (for the most part) at universities—students, faculty, administrators, members of governing boards—to maintain the traditional boundaries between the sexes and thus to continue to constrict and to limit the social space of females. Even though a great deal of the opposition came from individuals, there was organized opposition by faculty bodies and by boards of regents. Their efforts did not involve the formation of new countermovement organizations (as occurred in the suffrage movement), but were expressed within the authority context of their formal roles. For example, at the University of Michigan from 1858 until 1870, the board periodically discussed and then went on record opposing coeducation; in some cases, the board equivocated by tabling a motion or referring the matter to a committee. Likewise, during this same period, faculty bodies at Michigan went on record opposing coeducation several times. Even in 1870, after women had been admitted to Michigan, the medical school faculty on two occasions recorded its opposition to the admission of women to the medical school (McGuigan 1970: 17–29, 36–37).

Tentative evidence suggests that sustained organizational mobilization may not be as necessary or important a resource for reactionary countermovements resisting change as it is for progressive social movements promoting change (Buechler 1986:49). Thus the opponents of coeducation often operated on an ad hoc basis in response to a crisis. For example, at its March 1858 meeting the board of regents of the University of Michigan was informed by letter that twelve young women intended to present themselves for admission as students the following June. It might seem that some kind of response had to be made, but the regents quickly tabled the letter. (Proceedings of the University of Michigan Board of Regents, 1837–1864, cited in McGuigan 1970:17). Thus the activities of the opponents were sporadic, but it was their ideology that was significant. Opponents defined the context within which the ideas favoring coeducation were articulated, posed the problems the proponents had to solve, and asked the questions the proponents had to answer (e.g., will women's health withstand the rigors of seeking higher education?) (Kraditor 1971:12).

The fierce opposition of countermovements becomes understandable when one remembers that their constituents are often prone to make symbolic readings of the formalistic goals of the movement. For example, any social change proposed by movement members that involves legislation (such as that enabling women to enter universities as students or to vote) is read as linking the formalistic goals of the movement to an agenda involving significant social changes that the countermovement regards as threatening to the social order. Social changes of this sort have consistently been interpreted by countermovements as "relatively innocuous tips of potentially threatening icebergs" (Buechler 1986:50). The countermovement's perception has often been that the fight is not really over women's entrance to universities, voting rights, or whatever, but over "the family, the decline of womanhood, the elimination of sexual differences, and the like" (Buechler 1986:50). Discussion later in the article shows the parallels between the arguments used against suffrage and coeducation, lending support to the tip of the iceberg thesis.

WOMEN'S ENTRANCE INTO PREVIOUSLY ALL-MALE INSTITUTIONS OF HIGHER LEARNING

The influx of women into previously all-male institutions did not swell until around 1870, although Oberlin admitted women as early as 1833. The University of Iowa, which began instruction in 1855 with eighty-nine students, four of whom were women, "appears to be the only state university with a continuous record of coeducation for over 100 years."[2] By 1870, eight state universities were accepting women, but in most cases with reservations. For example, a female department had been provided for in the original University of Michigan charter in 1837, but the regents failed to appropriate money for it. Continuing demands for the admission of women were successful only in 1870, after administrators who opposed coeducation were gone and the composition of the board of regents had changed (McGuigan 1970:29).

The words "coeducation" and "coed" entered the English vocabulary sometime during the 1850s; both words, which had disparaging meanings, quite possibly originated in Ann Arbor. The Michigan student *Chronicle* in 1881 called the word "coed" a "synonym for ignominy." If any single person was responsible for removing the stigma from these words, it was James Burrill Angell, third president of the university, who arrived on campus in June 1871, just a year after women had been admitted. During his thirty-eight-year tenure, President Angell, who was a forthright and staunch defender of coeducation, was called on repeatedly, not only in the United States but also in Europe, to explain and defend his liberal views on women's education (McGuigan 1970: 39–40).

Another of the early university presidents who played a positive role in bringing about social change in this realm was William Watts Folwell, who in 1869 became the first president of the University of Minnesota, the first state university to offer its classes on an equal basis to both women and men. Many years before (1852), Folwell had written a letter to his sister Jennie encouraging her to consider educating herself as a physician. "I cannot bear this idea," he concluded, "of having you wear out your life in the family of some man, going down to the grave 'unwept, unhonored, unsung.' " (Roberts 1981:10).

The stance taken by both these university presidents illustrates the positive role those in positions of power in a society can play in legitimizing social changes and thus in smoothing the passage of participants in those social changes. Those in positions of power who choose, for example, not to enforce legislation reflecting social changes severely undermine the gains of the social movement itself. Both ridicule and nonenforcement of legal changes are powerful tools in the hands of officials in positions of authority, such as university presidents.

Oberlin College (first Oberlin Collegiate Institute) was seen as a herald of a new order, not only because of its early admission of female students, but also because students were admitted irrespective of color. While women students could enter the program leading to a B.A., the new college also offered a diluted and abridged ladies' course as an alternative. Many women students seemed to prefer this less-demanding curriculum. Out of nearly 250 women enrolled at Oberlin by 1856–57, only 20 had enrolled in the degree courses (Goodsell 1924: 24–25). Out of the black women students enrolled in the period from 1833 to 1865, many were also in the ladies' (or literary—no higher mathematics and no ancient languages were required) program, but three had received the B.A. in what was occasionally referred to as the gentleman's course (Henle and Merrill 1979:8).

The background of these early black women students appears to have been quite different from that of their white sisters. While most of the latter were from rural New York and New England, black females were more likely to come from urban areas (e.g., Cincinnati, Pittsburgh, Washington, D.C.). Most of the white women were far from wealthy and found the work–study program at Oberlin a welcome way of meeting college costs. The black students, on the other hand, were diverse in origin, in status at birth (free or slave), and in degree of color (light mulatto to African). Most were light-skinned, however, which may have facilitated their reception at a predominantly white school (Henle and Merrill 1979:8, 11). In addition, some of them were from a nuclear family with sufficient status and income to afford a college education for its daughters.

RECEPTION ON UNIVERSITY CAMPUSES OF WOMEN STUDENTS

The appearance of the first women students on university campuses was, not surprisingly, met with hostility, derision, and scorn. Attempts were made to cast them into the role of deviants and to put them on the defensive, a very effective tactic, as feminists a century later learned. In 1870, for example, when the first woman, Madelon Stockwell, appeared on the Michigan campus, a male student wrote in his diary about the "she-sophomore." She was at once the "target of curious stares . . . pointed fingers, and whispered remarks—not only from her thousand or so fellow students, but of the men on the faculty and the people in Ann Arbor." Stockwell later wrote to a friend that her admission exams had been "longer and more severe than those given the young men" (quoted in McGuigan 1970:1). The local newspapers in both Ann Arbor and nearby Ypsilanti ran editorials excoriating the regents for permitting an experiment "detrimental . . . to the best interests of the University" and accusing the regents of "floating on the tide of the radical party" (*Ypsilanti Sentinel*, January 1870, quoted in McGuigan 1970:2).

In the September following Stockwell's admission as a student at the University of Michigan, thirty-three more women enrolled: thirteen joined her in the Literary Department; eighteen were admitted to study medicine, and two into law. They made up just 3 percent of the enrollment. The scorn heaped upon women who entered the medical school seemed especially vitriolic. During commencement exercises in 1871, Amanda Sanford, the first woman to be made a Doctor of Medicine at Michigan, was "hooted and showered with abusive notes from the [crowd of] young men students sitting in the balcony." Additionally, the early women medical students were disparagingly called "hen medics" on the campus and in town as well (McGuigan 1970:38).

Certainly, these pioneers possessed exceptional ability and motivation with which to withstand the discriminatory behavior and prejudicial attitudes of those first years. Even to reach college, most had to overcome far greater obstacles than their brothers. Generally, the sons in a family had first claim to any available money for education. In order to persuade her parents to allow her to go to the university, Alice Freeman Palmer, an early Michigan student who later became president of Wellesley College, had to promise not to marry until she had paid her younger brother's way through medical school; she kept her promise. Also, daughters were viewed as having heavier obligations to their families than sons. In the large extended families of that era, an older daughter often had to care for younger children, and perhaps an aged relative or two. Finally, parents of daughters viewed with apprehension all the dangers thought to be "lying in wait for young ladies in the jungle of a coeducational college" (McGuigan 1970: 31–32).

POINTS OF ATTACK BY THE COUNTERMOVEMENT

The question of higher education for women had been controversial for centuries, but whether that education might be pursued side-by-side with men was not argued until the nineteenth century. Attempts by males on university campuses to maintain their hegemony for social control and to oppose coeducation centered around three issues. First, the question was raised as to whether women were intellectually capable of advanced learning. Some college presidents, university faculty, and male students contended that women were mentally inferior to men and would be quite unable to meet the standards set for men's higher education. It was claimed that to admit women to classes with men would only pull down the standards and impair the quality of men's education. A second issue revolved around the notion that women's physical constitution could not stand the rigors of higher education. Women were thought to be frail, and often were in the days of wasp waists and no exercise. Over-study would surely give them brain fever. Further, if women should manage to survive college, their children would be sickly, if they were able to have children at all (Newcomer 1959:25–28). Finally, the question was put "whether in any case, it was both a mistake and a waste to educate women for anything except their proper sphere—and everyone knew what that sphere was" (McGuigan 1970:3).

The little band of women students at Ann Arbor in the early 1870s were somewhat amused by these allegations. Among this group of pioneers was a bright, lively young woman named Olive San Louie Anderson, who immortalized her adventures in a little autobiographical novel (McGuigan 1970:47). Through the words of her heroine, Wilhelmine Elliott (Will for short), Anderson (1878) recounted, largely in a light, humorous manner, what were undoubtedly her own experiences as well as those of her network of friends.[3] In detailing her first semester at college, Will commented that when the professors were asked how the young ladies stood in their classes, they were compelled to say that the female students had done "as well as the best in the class," but the professor always added, "their health will break down either during the course or after!" She continues:

"They have changed base somewhat," said Nell merrily; "at first the cry was that we were mentally incapable, now we are only 'physically incapacitated.' Strange, isn't it, that we will either die during our college course or after, and we will not have a head or finger ache for the next decade that can't be directly traced to the higher education?" (Anderson 1878: 65–66)

As time went on, the evidence that women were intellectually capable of advanced study began to mount, however. President Angell of Michigan, for one, emphasized that the women students were performing as ably academically as the men. In fact, he declared that "there is no branch taught in college which women have not shown themselves entirely competent to master" (Report to the Board of Regents, June 1872, quoted in McGuigan 1970:53). Writing over thirty years later, Helen Olin (1909: 119–20) noted that when the Phi Beta Kappa chapter at the University of Chicago was established in 1899 forty-three women and twenty-nine men were elected to membership. Further, for four consecutive quarters in 1899 and 1900, among the senior and the junior colleges, thirty-five of the honor students were women, while seventeen were men. Whatever influence these facts may have had in the eventual decision to segregate the sexes at Chicago (1902), Olin (1909:120) pointed out that "the fear of lowering the intellectual standard by admitting women to competition with men is certainly effectively dispelled."[4] More than fifty years later, Newcomer (1959:29) indicated that some Phi Beta Kappa chapters were known to *ration* the number of women elected in order to make the honor acceptable to men. Additionally, she cited the president's report of the University of Michigan to note that for 1956/57 (a presumably typical year), women constituted only 32 percent of the enrollment but earned 45 percent of the academic honors.

Although many skeptics said that women would not be able to do college work, those who had "experience with coeducation reported almost without exception to the contrary," according to Thomas Woody (1929: 272–73) in a thorough history of women's education in the United States. "In fact," he added, "in due time, the superior scholarship of women and girls, in some subjects, became a new objection to coeducation." The men, in other words, did not do so well competing with women. This argument, though obviously an embarrassing one, was very frequently used. It became the target of ridicule in Alice D. Miller's (1915: 34–35) lines on "the protected sex":

> There, little girl, don't read,
> You're fond of your books, I know
> But Brother might mope
> If he had no hope
> Of getting ahead of you
> It's dull for a boy who cannot lead
> There, little girl, don't read.

As evidence kept mounting that women were fully capable of performing well academically as university students, the opponents then rallied their forces to focus on the second argument—that women's health would invariably suffer from the strain of competitive study with men; this argument, however, proved harder to refute. In fact, in 1873 the argument exploded into national prominence in a little book, *Sex in Education, or A Fair Chance for the Girls,* written by Dr. Edward H. Clarke, formerly on the medical staff of Harvard College and a well-known Boston physician. The title and the contents of the book were highly provocative for that time; the book was a bestseller overnight. Within a few years, seventeen editions were printed, and the book was widely quoted even in the early years of the twentieth century (McGuigan 1970: 53–54).

Friends of coeducation suspected that Clarke's book represented a gatekeeping attempt by Harvard College, which had been reluctant to admit women students. According to McGuigan (1970:55), Clarke was a "pamphleteer and an ardent and persuasive one." His a priori arguments were sufficient to prove to thousands of doubtful parents and educators that "identical education of the two sexes is a crime before God and humanity, that physiology protests against, and that experience weeps over" (Clarke 1873:127). Clarke's arguments pointed to the necessity for separate women's colleges as well as lower academic requirements for them. Although his statistical evidence was limited to the cases of only seven women, not a single one of whom had attended a coeducational school, the book confirmed prejudices, giving credence to the opponents' attempts to repress educational gains by women and to reestablish the old boundaries (McGuigan 1970:55).

The heads of women's colleges and of coeducational universities alike would protest Clarke's conclusions and insist that the health of their women students was excellent, but Clarke had forestalled them. Educators, he contended, could not possibly judge the "heinous effects" of coeducation by the *apparent* good health of women students while still in college, as it might be years before the "catastrophic" results could be discerned in "grave and even fatal disease of the brain and nervous system . . . in torturing . . . imperfections of the reproductive apparatus that imbitter [*sic*] a lifetime" (Clarke 1873:116).

Clarke's book was doing a brisk business in Ann Arbor in 1873. The local bookseller, who had sold more than 200 copies in a single day, opined that "the book bids fair to nip coeducation in the bud" (Anderson 1878:96). In the academic community the girls as well as the boys read it and delivered their opinions at length among themselves. The pastor of the local Presbyterian church, taking Clarke's book as a basis, "inveighed against the whole women's movement" (Anderson 1878:102). Olive San Louie Anderson (1878:97) commented on Clarke's book through her heroine, Will:

> What does the precious doctor propose to do with us after he has cajoled us into believing that we are born and predestined to be invalids from the foundation of the world? Send us home to embroider chair-covers and toilet sets, I suppose; . . . just as soon as women are beginning to have a

cals. Many of the ACA branches were delighted to have the findings available to them for ammunition; for example, the Milwaukee, Wisconsin, branch was organized specifically to fight the allegation that finishing schools were adequate for the education of those young women who intended to marry, while a college education was necessary only for those who wished to become teachers, or for pedants, or for the socially unattractive (Talbot and Rosenberry 1931:119, 124). Further research substantiated Wright's findings. In fact, later research concluded that women college graduates were healthier than other women. An additional effort disclosed that proportionately more students at Amherst (an all-male college) dropped out for reasons of health than did college women.[6]

Remnants of all three of the contentions launched by those who opposed women's entrance into previously all-male colleges and universities remain within our cultural framework. However, it is probably the third argument— why educate women if they are only to fulfill their natural function as wives and as mothers—that has been the most tenacious in resisting social change. Arguments in this vein in the nineteenth century were, to say the least, contradictory. On the one hand, some opponents worried that educated women would somehow be either unfit or unable to bear children. Conversely, some feared that coeducation would be "conducive to mating" (Woody 1929:301). The latter charge was acknowledged openly and gladly by some proponents. President Angell of the University of Michigan indicated that many of the happiest marriages he had known resulted from coeducation. Further, he asked, was not an acqaintance of four years in the classroom a better basis for choosing a mate than someone who was a chance acquaintance in a ballroom (Woody, 1929:301–2)?

ANALOGY WITH THE SUFFRAGE MOVEMENT

An analogy can be drawn between the rationale and arguments used against women's right to vote and those used against women's access to higher education. The arguments, which were an arsenal of pseudo-science and theology, are explainable only by realizing again how very threatening to opponents was the notion of women's meaningful participation in the public sphere. The argument was ostensibly about the right of women to vote or to enter universities as students, but deeper fears lurked beneath the surface. If women did enter the public sphere as active and rational participants, they might go on to experience a thoroughgoing intellectual reorientation, with a new assessment of self and an expanding of boundaries.

The ideology that underlay opponents' arguments rationalized a particular set of arrangements in the society—that is, women as inferior, dependent beings appropriately confined to the private sphere—and was based on the link of women to the home and to the notion that each woman's vocation was determined not by her individual capacities or wishes, but by her sex. While men were expected to have a variety of ambitions and capabilities, all women were destined from birth to be full-time wives and mothers. Close to the heart show in education, up starts your erudite doctor with his learned non-sense, embellished with scarecrow stories, trying to prove that women's complicated physical mechanism can't stand any mental strain.

The obvious fact that the great majority of women students enjoyed good health had to be documented with scientific studies. It was at this point that the newly formed (1882) Association of Collegiate Alumnae (ACA), a network of college-educated women, took action.[5] While the manifest function of the ACA was to "unite alumnae of different institutions for practical educational work" (Talbot and Rosenberry 1931:12), a latent function was to provide a support structure for the small body of women college graduates of that time. The ACA provided its early members with a sense of community and helped them to overcome the isolation—actual as well as symbolic—that many of them felt.

The obstacles met by the young women who were the first members of the ACA in their insistence on a college education had been many, but none was more serious than the almost universally held opinion that young women could not, except at a high price physically, undergo the intellectual strain that their brothers seemed to find no strain at all. In spite of the dire prophecies that they heard on every side, these first ACA members persisted in their contention that the regular life and engrossing interests of college work tended to give women greater, rather than less, physical vigor. Therefore, they wished to use all means at their disposal to extend the scope of collegiate education for women (Talbot and Rosenberry 1931:116).

Thus the ACA, as one of its first research endeavors, undertook a series of investigations into the health of women college graduates, pledging that the work would be conducted fairly. A committee of the association prepared a series of questions that were heartily endorsed by physicians, teachers, and others and then distributed to the 1,290 graduates belonging to the ACA. Colonel Carroll D. Wright, then chief of the Massachusetts Bureau of Statistics of Labor, characterized the inquiry as one of great value to the commonwealth and offered to tabulate and publish the results (Talbot and Rosenberry 1931:118–19). When the results were published in 1885, Wright—after a careful assessment—concluded that

> the facts which we have presented would seem to warrant the assertion . . . that the seeking of a college education on the part of a woman does not in itself necessarily entail a loss of health or serious impairment of the vital forces. Indeed, the tables show this so conclusively that there is little need, were it within our province, for extended discussion of the subject. (quoted in Newcomer 1959:29)

The findings were widely distributed, not only among ACA members, but also among college women in general. They were sent to the leading medical and educational journals of the day. Members living in the major cities of the country played an active role in presenting the subject to the public through editorials and articles in influential newspapers and period of many opponents was a "sentimental vision of Home and Mother, equal in Sanctity to God and the Constitution" (Kraditor 1971:12). This ideology was reinforced by the "cult of the true lady," which had been present as a concept in American society since colonial days and had become the accepted ideal of femininity toward which *all* women should strive (Lerner 1979:25–26). This ideal was epitomized by such characteristics as purity, piety, domesticity, and submissiveness. As Welter (1966) has pointed out, submissiveness, which colleges subverted by encouraging independence in their women students, was always the weakest link of the cult. Opponents feared that allowing women to vote and go to college would destroy the whole image and what it stood for.

Opponents of suffrage and of higher education for women set forth theological, biological, and sociological arguments. The commonest theological contention was really no argument at all, but the mere announcement that God had ordained men and women to perform different functions in the state as well as in the home (Kraditor 1971:12–13). This clearly spelled out that the public sphere was for males; the private, for females. Thus casting a vote and matriculating at a university were clearly inappropriate behavior for females.

The biological argument was designed to appeal to people who needed a scientific sanction for their beliefs. This argument rested on two assumptions. The first, that souls as well as bodies had sexual attributes, underlay arguments that identified femininity with inherent emotionalism and illogicality, traits inconsistent with the proper exercise of suffrage (or with entering universities, for that matter). The second assumption was that women's physical constitution was too delicate and thus incapable of undertaking the various duties involved with voting (Kraditor 1971:14–15). This contention is reminiscent of Dr. Clarke's declaration that women could not endure the rigors of higher education without possible neuralgia, hysteria, and uterine disorder (Clarke 1873:47).

The sociological argument against both women's suffrage and higher education hinged on the "separate but equal" doctrine of the respective spheres of man and woman. This point of view declared that social peace and the welfare of the human race depended on woman's staying home, having children, and refraining from active participation in the public sphere (Kraditor 1971:16). Dr. Clarke, in fact, concluded that the coeducational experiment would spell the doom of the human race (1873:63).

THE BACKLASH: REACTION AGAINST COEDUCATION

In retrospect, the first generations of college-educated women were no doubt naive in the optimism with which they faced their expanding horizons and in the confidence they felt in their new liberty. After the great progress toward coeducation made in the 1870s and 1880s in the Midwest and Far West, a lull occurred. Men's colleges in the East failed to follow the lead of midwestern universities, adopting instead the principle of annexes or coordinate women's colleges. Not until the 1950s would any more all-male universities open their doors to women (McGuigan 1970:95–96).

Beginning in the early 1900s, a reaction set in. A number of previously coeducational colleges (e.g., the University of Chicago) began a policy of segregating women from men (at least in certain areas or departments) and applying quotas to limit the number of women who might enter (McGuigan 1970:97). The overall numbers of both sexes seeking higher education in the closing years of the nineteenth century had climbed astronomically. The chief reason for the reactionary countermovement was that the proportion of women to men choosing higher education had increased sharply. Male administrators began to express openly the fear that some departments were in great danger of being feminized. Biological arguments resurfaced. It was claimed that higher education damaged the breeding function of women, that college women were marrying later and producing fewer children.

Underlying this reaction, which represented the tip of the iceberg, was the new fear, "rooted in a reactionary political climate and openly expressed," that higher education of women was "endangering the supremacy of the Anglo-Saxon, native born, ruling class in America" (McGuigan 1970:101). What alarmed conservative social scientists in the early twentieth century was that the great many immigrants to the United States were producing nearly twice as many children as native-born, middle-class women.[7] Some of these social scientists, as well as certain physicians and biologists, blamed the falling birthrate of middle-class America on the emancipated woman, especially the college educated woman (McGuigan 1970:101–2).

CONCLUSION

This article has described the efforts of women in the late nineteenth century to gain access to higher educational opportunities as part of a larger social movement to expand the social space of women and to legitimize their place as active participants in the public sphere. The countermovement engendered by this social movement had both conservative features—*resisting* prospective social change, as in the proposed shift from segregated to coeducational universities—and reactionary features—attempting to *restore* a pattern of segregation after the system of coeducation had been implemented. As with other social movements, those who felt threatened and who perceived an invasion of their social space responded with scorn, derision, and attempts to trivialize the movement. As in all social movements, symbols of various sorts helped to give the movement credibility or helped to denigrate it.[8] Verbal symbols such as "hen medics" and "coed," with their derogatory meanings, played a role in discrediting the movement, as did the use of what is termed glittering generalities, a propaganda technique that uses vague, abstract words to bring forth a response. Use of the words "God," "Home," "Constitution," and "Mother(hood)" exemplify these.[9]

Additionally, the "separate but equal" theme was used both by the conservative branch of the countermovement to resist coeducation and by the reactionary branch to restore a segregated system after a coeducation pattern had begun in many schools. The "separate but equal" thread has been used repeatedly in American society as a way of dealing with what have been perceived as threatening demands by disadvantaged groups, and as a way of protecting the supremacy of white, middle-class, native-born males.

Certainly, the view that woman's rightful place is in the home was not eradicated by these nineteenth-century movements. Today, manifestations of it are numerous. The assumption is still made that women are the natural and best caretakers of children based on their ability to bear and nurse infants. A closely allied assumption is that the broader domestic role is and should be the primary concern of all women, not of men. Although many two-parent families now have two wage-earners, division of labor *within* the household has changed little. Women perform essentially two full-time jobs. The plethora of popular books and manuals concerned with "How to Juggle Home and Job" are written largely for women rather than men. The main responsibility for the care of the household and of the children is seen as the woman's problem, not the man's, regardless of the former's level of education or occupational attainment. The presence of female students on college campuses today is no longer controversial, but resistance is still encountered by women who wish to train in nontraditional fields (e.g., as engineers or as forest rangers). Female and male college students still appear to have differing role expectations for the future, both for themselves and, should they marry, for the other spouse.[10]

Although they have abated to some extent, "old prejudices, old prerogatives, linger on: Those habits of thought Virginia Woolf labelled 'tough as roots, but intangible as sea mist' " (McGuigan 1970:106).

NOTES

1. Elshtain (1974) traces the roots of the public–private dichotomy back to Aristotle's work. The public (political) realm is seen as appropriately occupied by free males who make decisions and wield power in the life of the polis; however, males are also allowed to occupy the private (nonpolitical) realm of nonfree females. Here males receive support and sustenance to enable them to carry on their onerous duties in the outside (political) world. Females, however, are not allowed to enter the public sphere, but are relegated entirely to the life of the lesser association (i.e., the household), which is seen as inferior in nature, in intent, and in purpose to the more inclusive association of the polis.

2. For this information, Newcomer cites J. L. Pickard, "Historical Sketch of the University of Iowa," in *Annals of Iowa* (Iowa City, 1899), 31.

3. In the caption under a picture of Anderson, McGuigan (1970:n.p.) notes that Anderson's heroine, Will, "burned her corsets as a gesture of emancipation."

4. Marion Talbot (1858–1948), who served as the first dean of women at the University of Chicago from 1892 until her retirement in 1925, was a staunch supporter of women in higher education, both as students and as faculty. She noted in *More Than*

Lore (1936:175), a book of reminiscences about her years at Chicago, that the proportion of women students at Chicago was 24 percent in 1892/93, but had risen to 43 percent in 1898/99 and to 52 percent in 1901/2.

5. The Association of Collegiate Alumnae, which Marion Talbot helped to found, ultimately became the American Association of University Women.

6. This research is discussed in more detail in Newcomer (1959:29–30), who points out that since only comparatively well-to-do and well-educated parents were sending their daughters to college during this period, college women were undoubtedly not a representative sample of all women in the society. Further, the courses in hygiene and physiology taken by college women as well as the "regimen of exercise and other health measures enforced by the women physicians of the colleges . . . may well have made some contribution to the outcome."

7. This period witnessed the influx of the second wave of immigrants, who were mainly from Eastern and southern Europe, poor, of the working and lower classes, and visibly different (in dress, names, and customs) from earlier immigrants. See Weinberg's (1972: chap. 7) biography of E. A. Ross, for a discussion of the sociologist as nativist. Ross (1866–1951), a progressive sociologist at the University of Wisconsin, whose thought represented a fusion of liberalism and nativism, subscribed to a melioristic version of nativism that was Midwestern and rural in origin (Weinberg 1972:172).

8. Jokes as well as verbal symbols play a role in this denigration. McGuigan (1970:32–33) recounts that some professors at Michigan had their little jokes, such as the following, which was printed in the student *Chronicle* soon after Madelon Stockwell arrived: "A dog had wandered into the classroom, and a couple of students rose to remove it. The professor stopped them. 'That dog . . . is a resident of Michigan. Don't you know we now recognize the right of every resident of the state to enjoy the privileges afforded by the University?' " (*Chronicle*, February 12, 1870, quoted in McGuigan 1970:33).

Nearly fifty years after Stockwell was referred to as the "she-sophomore," a woman practicing law in New York City (Siegel 1982:360), was asked by a judge, who first mistook her for an office stenographer, "My God! What do I call you? . . . 'she' lawyer, 'woman' lawyer or 'female lawyer' "? Siegel suggested that "counselor" would be appropriate.

9. These glittering generalities are again common currency in the twentieth-century countermovement's attempts to discredit the feminist movement.

10. Data from colleagues suggest that within the past six or seven years, plans and expectations of male and female students enrolled in introductory sociology classes show some revealing differences. While many males envision having a satisfying full-time career and a traditional wife who is a full-time housewife and mother ten years after graduation, a great many females do not envision themselves playing that role. Instead, they see themselves as involved in a full-time occupation outside the home, even if they indicate a desire to marry eventually (Skelton n.d.).

CHAPTER 15

The Continuity of the American Women's Movement: An Elite-Sustained Stage

VERTA TAYLOR

In 1957, Rose Arnold Powell wrote to director Cecil B. DeMille suggesting that he make a film on the "Woman Movement" along the lines of *The Ten Commandments*.[1] Powell, who devoted her life to winning recognition for the nineteenth-century suffrage pioneers, had ruminated in her diary in 1955 that injustices toward women had resulted "in an ORGANIZED effort known as the Woman Movement, which has continued to this day to secure a status of equality for women established in the 'law of the land.' "[2] Powell was not alone in seeing her efforts as part of a larger women's movement. Many women involved in promoting women's rights in the 1940s and 1950s as a continuation of their participation in the early-twentieth-century suffrage movement used the term "women's movement" or its nineteenth-century equivalent, "woman movement" to refer to their activities. These women did not see themselves as creating a movement but as maintaining one. Yet despite the significance these women attached to their own political work, scholars of the American women's movement have characterized the 1940s and 1950s as devoid of an organized women's movement. In a discussion of group mobilization, Charles Tilly (1978: 61) warns that it "takes confidence, even arrogance, to override a group's own vision of its interests in life." What, then, might it mean to take seriously the perspective of these women and to consider their efforts as part of a social movement? This is the question that this paper addresses.

The traditional view of the American women's movement is that it peaked in two periods. The first wave of feminism grew out of the abolitionist struggle of the 1830s, reached a stage of mass mobilization in the years between 1900 and 1920, and culminated in the passage of the Nineteenth Amendment, guaranteeing women the right to vote. The second wave emerged out of the civil rights and New Left movements of the 1960s, reached a stage of mass mobilization around 1970, carried on with vigor through the 1970s, and is still in progress in the 1980s (Chafe 1972; Conover and Gray 1983; Evans 1979; Ferree and Hess 1985; Freeman 1975, 1979; Klein

1984; Rupp and Taylor 1986; Taylor 1983). During the forty years between the ratification of the Nineteenth Amendment and the resurgence of feminism, there was no widespread, highly visible feminist activism, at least compared with these other periods in American history. Scholars have, therefore, assumed that the women's movement died in the 1920s and was not resurrected again until the mid-1960s.

Recent work by scholars of both the British and the American women's movements, however, provides strong evidence of the continuation of feminist activity in both countries between the two world wars, even though no highly visible mass women's movement existed (Banks 1981; Becker 1981; Cott 1984; Harrison 1982; Hartman 1982; Klein 1984; Lemons 1973; Scharf 1980; Scharf and Jensen 1983; Spendor 1983). British sociologist Olive Banks (1981) argues that one reason that scholars have overlooked the continuity of the women's movement in both countries is that, organizationally, feminism has taken various forms throughout its history, including that of a mass movement, a pressure group, and a radical sect. It is not surprising, then, that when asked by Dale Spender what she had done during the time when there was no women's movement, feminist Mary Stott proclaimed, "What do you mean, when there was NO women's movement? There has always been a women's movement this century!"[3]

This chapter examines feminist activity from 1945 to the mid-1960s from a social movement perspective. Its goal is to contribute to an understanding of the historical continuity of the American women's movement by documenting the existence of a self-defined movement that continued to work for equal rights for women in the years after 1945. Viewing the women's movement as a continuous phenomenon from the nineteenth century to the present requires that we pay attention to significant variations in the movement's legitimacy, organizational form, patterns and base of mobilization, and strategies at different periods in its history. By no stretch of the imagination can the women's rights movement that functioned in the 1940s and 1950s be seen as broad-based and having wide influence. This analysis focuses, therefore, on the organizational and strategic patterns the movement used to ensure its continuation and survival in hostile circumstances and introduces the concept of an "elite-sustained movement" to describe the kind of movement that existed in the period in question. It then explores the consequences that this round of feminist activity had for the later cycle of the women's movement that unfolded with the founding of NOW and the movement's more radical branch in the mid-1960s.

There are two reasons for singling out the post-1945 years for closer scrutiny. First, historians have generally recognized that the National Woman's Party (NWP), which originated as the militant branch of the suffrage movement, continued to devote itself to women's rights throughout the interwar years (Rupp 1985). By the end of World War II, its membership was aging and had dwindled from approximately 60,000 in the last years of the suffrage movement to about 4,000, only 600 of whom paid dues. Yet under the leadership of Alice Paul, the NWP pursued doggedly and single-mindedly the passage of the Equal Rights Amendment (ERA), a campaign it first launched on the heels of

the suffrage success in 1923 as the principal strategy for attaining equality for women. Although most groups involved in the suffrage struggle kept their distance from the NWP and its work on behalf of the ERA in the 1930s and early 1940s, support for the ERA bloomed during World War II as large national women's organizations joined the previously short list of endorsers and the amendment made headway in Congress. However limited the National Woman's Party's impact, members who were active in the post-1945 period saw their efforts on behalf of the ERA as continuing the movement for women's rights. Since the surviving feminist activity of the 1940s and 1950s came on the eve of the growth of a more massive women's movement in the late 1960s, any connections that might have existed between the two phases are significant for our understanding of the women's movement's historical continuity.

The second reason for focusing on the post-1945 years is the traditional image of the period as particularly hostile to feminism and women's rights. The end of World War II ushered in an antifeminist backlash that preached domesticity, motherhood, and suburbia, or conformity to what Betty Friedan (1963) labeled "the feminine mystique." Women who did not conform to the image of the "happy housewife" that permeated the mass media were denounced as "neurotic" and held responsible for the ill fate of their children (Rupp 1982). Feminist protest, associated with the nineteenth-century suffragists, had become "as quaint as linen dusters and highbutton shoes" (Coughlan 1956). It is not surprising that most scholars have assumed that in the face of the strong antifeminism, the baby boom, the flight to the suburbs, the Cold War, and the silencing of dissident voices by the McCarthy witch-hunts, the women's movement died.

DATA SOURCES

The data for this study come from two sources: documentary material in public and private archival collections, and tape-recorded interviews with women involved in activities geared toward obtaining equal rights for women in the period from 1945 to the 1960s.[4] A fuller description of the movement and complete documentation are available in Rupp and Taylor (1987).

The first sources of archival data were the papers of the National Woman's Party and the League of Women Voters, the two major factions of the suffrage movement, and the papers of the President's Commission on the Status of Women (1961–63), a group whose activities facilitated the resurgent women's movement of the mid-1960s (Freeman 1975). Other documentary material examined included unofficial and official organizational documents, publications, personal letters, and memos available in public and private archival collections, most of which were housed at the Schlesinger Library at Radcliffe College or at the Library of Congress. The papers of individual women were another important source of information, not only about feminists' organizational careers, but also about the activities of women's organizations in this period, which included the National Federation of Business and Professional Women, the Connecticut Committee for the Equal Rights Amendment,

the National Association of Women Lawyers, the Lucy Stone League, the National Association of Colored Women, and other voluntary service and professional organizations.

The second source of data was open-ended, semi-structured, tape-recorded interviews with leaders and key members of the most central groups involved in feminist activity in the period. Twelve women active at the national level were interviewed, and thirty-three women were interviewed who were involved at the local level in organizations such as the League of Women Voters, the Young Women's Christian Association, the American Association of University Women, Zonta International, Planned Parenthood, Jewish women's organizations, Church Women United, and other groups that coalesced around feminist issues such as the Equal Rights Amendment. A final source of interview data was twelve transcribed interviews conducted by other researchers, most of which came from the Twentieth Century Trade Union Women Project and the Suffragist Oral History Project at the University of California.

AN ELITE-SUSTAINED MOVEMENT

Scholars of social movements have, in recent years, shifted from an emphasis on studying discontents, grievances, and psychological dispositions as explanations for the rise and decline of social movements to studying the structure of social movement organizations, their position in the political system, and the factors that influence their success or failure (Gamson 1975; Gerlach and Hine 1970; Jenkins 1983; McAdam 1982; McCarthy and Zald 1973; Oberschall 1973; Perrow 1979; Tilly 1978; Tilly, Tilly, and Tilly 1975). This newer work has been loosely grouped together under the term "resource mobilization theory" because of the emphasis it places on the role of resources—money, expertise, access to publicity, and the support of influential groups and individuals outside the movement—in determining the nature, course, and outcome of a movement.

Among the major contributions of the resource mobilization approach is its emphasis on the dynamic nature of social movements. Earlier work had assumed that social movements inevitably pass through a standard "life cycle" from their emergence to their decline as a result of either institutionalization and bureaucratization or failure and collapse (Blumer 1951; Edwards 1927; Hopper 1950; Lang and Lang 1961; Perry and Pugh 1978). Recent approaches see social movements as taking diverse paths that lead to different outcomes (Gusfield 1981; Jenkins 1983; Miller 1983; Oberschall 1978; Perrow 1979; Snyder and Kelly 1979; Zald and Ash 1966; Zald and McCarthy 1979). Put simply, the history of any social movement is determined by an interplay between factors internal to it and factors in the outside world that influence its ability to mobilize resources in pursuit of its aims. By conducting research on movements at different developmental stages, it can be shown that the same social movement is likely to adopt different structural forms and mobilization strategies at various periods in its history depending on whether it is in a

stage of formation, success, continuance and survival, or decline (Bromley and Shupe 1979, 1983).[4]

Scholars have, in fact, found this to be the case by applying the concepts of resource mobilization theory to understand the development of the American civil rights movement. For example, Aldon Morris (1984) characterizes the civil rights movement in its formative stages, from 1953 to 1963, as an indigenous movement. An indigenous movement owes its existence to preexisting institutions—in the case of the civil rights movement, the black church, black colleges, and other black organizations—that provide the leadership, ideas, communication network, money, membership, and specialized expertise necessary to mobilize. Having strong ties to its mass base through indigenous institutions, this kind of movement primarily draws on resources *within* the previously organized dominant group. By the early 1970s, a period marked by the decline of widespread black protest, the civil rights movement could no longer be characterized as an indigenous movement, but functioned as a professional social movement (Jenkins 1986; McAdam 1982; McCarthy and Zald 1973). Lacking strong ties to its mass bass, the movement depended for its existence on a core of trained movement entrepreneurs capable of securing financial resources and other kinds of support for civil rights from government agencies, foundations, political elites, the mass media, and other influential groups. This meant that the nature and direction of the movement was shaped increasingly by resources obtained *outside* the dominated group.

This paper follows in the tradition begun by scholars of the civil rights movement and introduces the concept of an elite-sustained movement to characterize the cycle of the women's rights movement that existed from 1945 to the mid-1960s. These years mark a period of decline in the history of the American women's movement. The movement that survived was largely, although not exclusively, a remnant of the twentieth-century suffrage movement and provided an environment in which already committed feminists could pursue their goals. To indicate why the term "elite-sustained" has been chosen for describing the women's movement of the 1940s and 1950s, it is necessary to describe the organizations and networks of women that participated in the struggle for women's rights in this period.

John D. McCarthy and Mayer N. Zald (1977:1218) define a social movement as a "set of opinions and beliefs in a population which represents preferences for changing some elements of the social structure and/or reward distribution of a society." Social movements are generally composed of a number of social movement organizations that compete and cooperate in pursuit of specific goals (Freeman 1983; Gerlach and Hine 1970; McCarthy and Zald 1977).

In the decade following World War II, a number of women's groups favored a change in status for women. But by the post-1945 period, only a small group of organizations and individuals who saw themselves as the heirs of the suffrage movement claimed to be part of an organized women's rights movement. Drawing the boundaries of any social movement is difficult. Three criteria set apart those groups and networks of women who identified as part of the women's rights movement from those who did not:

feminist ideology, commitment to equal rights, and interaction with the National Woman's Party. In a period when feminism had come to be seen as anachronistic and abrasive and feminists as "more hysterical than historical," groups and individuals who remained committed to women's rights were regarded as peculiar, if not deviant.[5] In "What Has Happened to the Feminist Movement?"—published in an anthology on leadership in 1950—the authors explicitly contrasted these women who were a part of the "old-fashioned, separatist, militant feminist" movement with the modern "shoulder-to-shoulder stand with American men" characteristic of other 1950s women leaders (Green and Melnick 1950: 283).

The clearest case of a self-proclaimed feminist organization in this period is the National Woman's Party. Best known for its use of disruptive tactics such as picketing the White House during the suffrage campaign, the National Woman's Party committed itself exclusively to passage of the ERA. Never popular with mainstream suffragists because of its militant feminism, the Woman's Party broke away from other groups in the women's movement in the years following the suffrage victory when it launched its relentless and unswerving campaign for the ERA. The story of the National Woman's Party in the post-1945 decades is a story of decline and survival, since the group failed to achieve its single goal, passage of the ERA; lost membership and failed to attract new and young members; suffered serious internal conflicts that hampered its effectiveness; and developed a reputation as a group of amusingly eccentric and anachronistic old feminists. But because the Woman's Party sustained a feminist community that made continuing activity possible in a hostile social context, the distinctive character of the women's rights movement in the two decades after the end of World War II owed a great deal to it (Rupp 1985).

The movement consisted of a number of autonomous organizations and networks of women grouped in a core and periphery pattern around the NWP (Table 15.1). As the only self-proclaimed organization devoted exclusively to women's rights, the Woman's Party had influence out of all proportion to its numbers. This was not because it was well liked. To the contrary, most other women's organizations detested the party, especially if they opposed the ERA, or at best distrusted it because of its proprietary attitude toward the amendment. It seemed sometimes as though the NWP would rather see the Equal Rights Amendment go down to defeat than relinquish leadership of the struggle. Even a woman with ambivalent reactions to the Woman's Party admitted that it "is of course the spearhead of the movement. . . ."[6]

The core movement organizations clustered around the National Woman's Party supported the Equal Rights Amendment, the issue that had divided women activists in the aftermath of the suffrage victory and had come to symbolize the definition of "women's rights" that characterized the women's movement. Most of these groups existed prior to the 1940s and 1950s and had purposes broader than passage of the ERA. Still, their activities on behalf of the amendment were central to the functioning of the movement. Preexisting organizations that formed the core of the movement included groups of professional women, such as the National Federation of Business and Professional

Table 15.1   Women's Movement Organizations, 1945–1960s

	Core	Periphery
Preexisting	National Woman's Party Business and Professional Women's Clubs National Association of Women Lawyers American Medical Woman's Association pioneers of the women's movement network	General Federation of Women's Clubs National Council of Women American Association of University Women National Association of Colored Women Federation of Women Shareholders women in politics network Zonta Soroptimist Altrusa
Emergent	Connecticut Committee Massachusetts Committee Lucy Stone League Women's Joint Legislative Committee Industrial Women's League for Equality St. Joan Society	Women in World Affairs Multi-Party Committee of Women Assembly of Women's Organizations for National Security

Women's Clubs (BPW), the National Association of Women Lawyers, and the American Medical Women's Association. In addition, a loose network of women dedicated to winning recognition for the pioneers of the suffrage movement can be considered part of the core.[7]

Not all those interested in women's rights could be traced directly to the suffrage movement. Several new groups emerged in the 1940s and 1950s and enlarged the core of the movement. The Connecticut Committee for the Equal Rights Amendment, founded in 1943, was a state group active on the ERA and other feminist issues. It spawned other state groups, the most successful of which was the Massachusetts Committee, established in 1955. The Lucy Stone League, a women's rights group established in New York in 1950, was a revived and broadened organization based on the Lucy Stone League of the 1920s, which had fought for the right of a married woman to retain her own name. The National Woman's Party also organized a number of new groups that included the Women's Joint Legislative Committee, set up by Alice Paul in 1943 as a coalition lobbying group; the Industrial Women's League for Equality, established in 1944 by Alice Paul and another Woman's Party member to counter arguments that women workers did not support the ERA; and the St. Joan Society, a group of pro-ERA Catholics founded in 1963 to defuse Catholic opposition to the amendment.

On the periphery of the movement were a variety of preexisting and emergent groups that supported women's rights and cooperated periodically with core movement organizations to pursue common aims, but not with the same level of interest and consistency as core groups. Included among these were the General Federation of Women's Clubs, the National Council of Women, the American Association of University Women (AAUW), the National Association of Colored Women, the Federation of Women Shareholders, a network of women in politics, and service organizations such as Zonta International, Soroptimist International, and Altrusa International. Women in World Affairs and the Multi-Party Committee of Women formed in 1946 to support the appointment of women in policy-making positions.

All these diverse organizations and networks of women, some of which owed their existence to the suffrage struggle and others newly formed in the period, made up a loosely connected women's rights movement. As one woman in the National Woman's Party described it, "The movement is a huge mosiac [sic]" in which "every little fragment of work contributed by some one" was important.[8]

There were other women's organizations devoted to improving women's lives but generally hostile to those who identified as part of the women's rights movement. The Women's Bureau of the Department of Labor is a good example. Although it worked hard to improve the conditions of working women, the assistant director in 1954, in planning a conference on woman-power, sought a title that would "avoid the old battle of the sexes idea and pitch a conference around the idea of men and women working together and maintaining the Nation's economy."[9] Organizations such as the Women's Bureau and the National Council of Negro Women often perceived their interests as antagonistic to those of the self-identified women's movement, largely because of the long tradition in the movement of defining "women's rights" as property rights, the right to vote, and other legal and political rights relevant mostly to white, middle-class women.

A clear-cut case of an organization that was born out of the women's movement but chose to dissociate itself from the movement in this period is the League of Women Voters. Successor to the mainstream suffrage organization, the league shifted its focus after the passage of the suffrage amendment to educating voters about political issues and candidates. Of course, some individual women in the league continued to identify themselves as feminists in the 1940s and 1950s. But the distance that the league maintained from women's rights work is evident in the comments of one leading member who contrasted "those primarily interested in women (the old line 'feminists') and those primarily interested in seeing women play their part in world affairs."[10]

From this description of the movement's organizational composition, it is clear that the women's movement in the post-1945 period was not in a stage of mass mobilization. Feminist organizations and networks of women directed little effort toward expanding the base of support for women's rights, as the women's movement of the late 1960s and early 1970s did (Cassell 1977; Freeman 1975; Klein 1984). Rather, the movement functioned primarily by channeling preexisting group and individual feminist commitment and the other resources necessary to survive when, for the most part, the odds were against its success. The term "elite-sustained" seems appropriate for describing the stage of the movement in this period.

ORGANIZATIONAL DILEMMAS AND TACTICAL CHOICES

To illustrate what is meant by an elite-sustained movement, the discussion of the post-1945 women's rights movement will be organized around four analytical themes that parallel major organizational dilemmas and tactical choices any movement confronts in attempting to mobilize. First, the analysis will examine the ways in which the movement sought, in a social climate inhospitable to its aims, to attain legitimacy. Second, the consequences of adopting a decentralized structure rather than a centralized one will be discussed in light of the movement's objectives. Third, the nature of the infrastructural supports available to the movement and the ways they shaped its mobilization strategies will be examined. Finally, the discussion focuses on major constraints on the tactical choices that could be made by the movement.

Movement Legitimacy

There are two principal kinds of legitimacy that a movement strives to achieve: legitimacy of numbers and legitimacy of means (Useem and Zald 1982). Legitimacy of numbers is achieved by mobilizing a large number of people committed to challenging the existing distribution of power. The rationale behind this strategy is that the polity accepts only those challenging groups that are able to mobilize a sizable number of supporters (Oliver and Marwell 1988; Tilly 1979). Legitimacy of means is achieved by convincing the public, through particular aims and strategies, that the movement is the most appropriate vehicle for achieving the goals of its constituency (Gamson 1975; Turner 1969). This kind of legitimacy is necessary for recruiting new members and for obtaining access to the mass media and other elites (Zald and Ash 1966). To achieve legitimacy of means, a movement must make certain that its grievances are seen as credible and serious enough to warrant its existence as a social movement (McCarthy and Zald 1977; Turner 1969).

By the post-1945 period, the women's movement had dwindled in size so that it no longer could claim a large and active base of supporters. From the perspective of the mass media, the public, and others that the movement hoped to influence, the small size and the selective composition of the movement made it easy to question whether those active on behalf of women's rights legitimately represented the interests of American women. An analysis of 108 women whose national participation was substantial enough to give them visibility found that the majority of the women active in the period were white, middle- or upper-class, well-educated, employed in professional or semiprofessional occupations, and were in their fifties, sixties, or seventies by 1950.[11] Leaders of national organizations made up an important component of the membership. Because these kinds of women might be seen as having access to other more institutionalized means of influence, the movement for women's rights had difficulty convincing the public that it truly represented a disadvantaged group for whom a social movement was the appropriate vehicle for expressing grievances. An example of the way in which the motives of women who advocated changes in women's status was questioned is found in a letter to the *Washington Star,* complaining about a feature on a major woman leader of the period:

> Whenever I see these smug pictures of women who have abdicated their normal functions and entered the field of politics and the like I instinctively say failure and slacker. Such women have flunked at their own jobs and yet pretend to tell men what they should do in their normal field.[12]

Recognizing that it was important that the movement appear to represent a larger sector of women than it actually was able to mobilize, feminists used strategies available to them because of their elite social status to give the appearance of having a mass constituency. Among the small core of intensely committed members of the movement were a number of well-known and admired women who headed national women's organizations. These women typically were able to command a following when support for a particular goal became essential. Thus when a national organization supported an issue such as the ERA, movement leaders claimed the entire membership of that organization in listing numbers of women who supported the movement's position. The BPW's "Buttonhole Campaign," in which state and local members were urged to "buttonhole" their senators and representatives to ask for passage of the ERA, is an example of the ways in which the national leadership of women's organizations mobilized their membership. Another tactic used to inflate the movement's numbers was seeking paper membership by, for example, copying the National Woman's Party's practices of listing as members those who paid one-time nominal dues or seeking the establishment of state branches by a single member.

To try to counter the image that the movement was a small, exclusive, and eccentric group whose claims of injustice and discrimination might not be warranted, movement leaders sought to establish organizations that would give the impression of a large and broad-based membership, such as the Women's Joint Legislative Committee for the ERA, the Women's Industrial League for Equality, and the Massachusetts Committee for the Equal Rights Amendment. The most important strategies devised to establish legitimacy of means were those that attempted to give the appearance that the movement had wide grass-roots appeal among less privileged women, such as working-class, union, and black women.

The support of women from labor was extremely important because a primary source of opposition to the ERA in this period was organized labor, which justified its opposition to the amendment on the grounds that the ERA was a threat to protective legislation. In an effort to persuade the public and elite groups that women in labor supported the women's movement, the few working-class and union activists were used as spokespersons whenever possible. The National Woman's Party also financed the Women's Industrial League for Equality to give the appearance of a coalition between labor and the women's movement. The same kind of tokenism was evident in the way in which black women were dealt with by the movement in order to advance the cause of the ERA. Although women's movement organizations made no large-scale efforts to open their membership to black women, they did encourage the participation of particular women like Mary Church Terrell, founder of the National Association of Colored Women, in order to obtain her group's endorsement of the ERA. The kinds of actions taken by women's movement organizations with regard to union women and black women suggest that feminists were not committed to creating truly meaningful political alliances with other contituencies. Rather, they tended to use individuals and groups for their own ends, to give the impression that the movement represented a truly aggrieved group whose demands for change were legitimate.

Movement Decentralization

Considerable debate exists in the social movement literature over the relative effectiveness of centralized bureaucratic movement structures as compared with decentralized structures for achieving a movement's goals (Gamson 1975; Gerlach and Hine 1970; Piven and Cloward 1971). Scholars generally agree that each type of movement structure has its advantages. Centralized bureaucratic structures tend to produce the organizational stability, technical expertise, and coordination necessary for accomplishing movement goals of institutional change. Decentralized structures, on the contrary, maximize participation benefits, such as commitment and community, and encourage the development of multidirected strategies for change. But they can also contribute to factionalism and intense conflict between movement organizations, which can impede a social movement's overall strategic effectiveness (Zald and Ash 1966).

The structure of the women's movement in this period was decentralized. Although the National Woman's Party formed the center of the movement and attempted, whenever possible, to direct all efforts on behalf of women's rights in the period, other movement organizations and groups took leadership on various issues and actions, and leadership by individual women able to command a following also changed depending on the issue or action.

Three major goals received the most attention in the movement: the ERA, the appointment of women to policy-making positions, and advocacy of women's history. Alice Paul, the founder of the Woman's Party, who by 1945 had already established an almost legendary reputation as a dedicated, iron-willed "superfeminist," fanatic, and martyr to the cause, directed ERA lobbying activities. But when the BPW made the ERA a priority, it often worked independently—much to the dismay of the Woman's Party, for which the ERA had become the raison d'être.

Support of the appointment of women to policy-making positions through the compiling of rosters of women qualified for posts in government and industry and the backing of women candidates was coordinated by the heads of organizations such as the BPW, American Association of University Women, and the National Council of Women. Such efforts often relied on the participation of women in politics, such as India Edwards, the highest-ranking woman in the Truman administration. Individuals such as Rose Arnold Powell rebelled against the "utter man-mindedness" she saw around her by devoting her life to winning recognition for the pioneers of the suffrage movement.[13] From the 1920s until her death in 1961, Powell sought to honor the memory of suffrage pioneer Susan B. Anthony by working to have her face carved on Mount Rushmore, have schools named after her, make her birthday a national holiday, and have calendar companies mark Anthony's birthday. Other women worked with the support of Emma Guffey Miller, Democratic national committeewoman, to have the Postal Service develop a stamp to raise the awareness of women throughout the country concerning the history of the women's movement.

The decentralized structure benefited the movement in two ways. First, it encouraged the development of varied goals and strategies in the pursuit of women's rights. State and local groups engaged in independent activities that could not have been undertaken by the national leadership. For example, the leader of the Connecticut Committee, because of close personal ties to members of the American Civil Liberties Union, worked to influence the organization to change its position opposing the ERA. The Little Below the Knee Club, in Dallas, Texas, protested the exploitation of women by the fashion industry by refusing to change the hemlines on their skirts. In addition, strategies were used by movement organizations that would not have been encouraged under the tightly directed leadership of Alice Paul and the National Woman's Party, because of the party's view that the ERA was the only strategy for winning equality for women. For instance, Rose Arnold Powell drafted a declaratory act that would guarantee that the generic "man" in the Constitution included women. Neither did the Woman's Party trust or expend much energy on tactics like those employed by the Women's Division of the Republican National Committee, which fought for a series of breakfasts with Eisenhower—dubbed "hen breakfasts" to match the "stag breakfasts" that already existed.[14]

Second, decentralization functioned to sustain individual commitment by creating a strong sense of community among those involved in working toward common goals and, thus, helped ensure the survival of feminist activity in the face of strong opposition to the movement from the larger society (Gerlach and Hine 1970). Many of the women literally devoted their lives to feminist activity. One woman described the intense commitment and close personal bonds among National Woman's Party members as "ingrown to the point of fanaticism," while another woman apologized for her lack of activity, explaining, "I am interested but not with that dedicated drive I so admired."[15] Clearly, the separate organizations and networks of women that made up the movement were held together by rather loose ties, and most were hierarchical organizations in which leaders enjoyed tremendous respect and influence. It is not surprising that the movement as a whole was ridden with intense conflict and competition (Ross 1983).

To a large extent, this conflict centered around the fact that the National Woman's Party, throughout its history, believed that no other organization could be trusted to devote itself wholeheartedly to the ERA. Criticizing the

Woman's Party for thwarting other efforts on behalf of the amendment, the president of the BPW commented in 1953 that "a great many people are saying that they have come to the conclusion that certain leaders in that organization do not actually want the Equal Rights Amendment passed because they would no longer have a 'cause' for which to work."[16] In effect, the continuing competition and conflict between different movement organizations, together with the emphasis placed on moral commitment to the cause and on maintaining close personal ties among core members of the movement, contributed at times to a lack of emphasis on the movement's larger goals for institutional change.

Even though the movement's decentralized structure promoted conflict and continuing factionalism among movement organizations, this type of configuration had one important advantage in the struggle for the ERA. Each of the separate organizations, groups, and networks of women that composed the movement had a different base of support and sphere of influence and was able to make use of its ties to and status in established institutions to promote the amendment in ways that might not have been possible had the Women's Party remained the only organizational voice for the movement.

Movement Infrastructure

Social movement scholars generally agree that the mobilization potential of a movement is affected by the degree of preexisting organization among dominated groups (Freeman 1983; Jenkins 1983; McAdam 1982; Morris 1984; Oberschall 1973; Tilly 1978). If the social base of a movement is already linked together in some sort of primary network so that people have common values and moral commitments, interpersonal ties, and communication on a regular basis, then this prior group solidarity can serve as a basis for mobilization (Aveni 1978).

The infrastructure or organizational base of the post-1945 women's movement can be traced to three main sources: a shared bond of participation in the suffrage struggle, business and professional ties, and friendship and other close personal relationships. It should not be surprising that participation in the suffrage struggle would hold together a community of women across the years; women who had demonstrated in front of the White House during World War I and suffered imprisonment and forced feeding were not likely to forget the sacrifices they had made "for the cause." Lamenting the passage of that period in her life, Florence Kitchalt, the force behind the Connecticut Committee for the ERA, asked a fellow suffragist in 1950 whether she ever felt "as I do, that the 'modern' woman is missing something very thrilling, uplifting as well as unifying in not being able to take part in a suffrage campaign? Those were the days!"[17] Not only were women who had themselves participated in the suffrage struggle likely to remain committed to women's rights in this period, but women with illustrious suffrage mothers, grandmothers, and other relatives were often recruited to do feminist work in various organizations. Such women sometimes even used their ancestry as a credential when vying for leadership positions in the movement. By connecting the fight for the ERA to the struggle for the vote, the Woman's Party sought to make women who were not involved in the suffrage movement feel as though they were a part of an historical movement for women's rights. One member described the sense of community she felt through participation as "the warm glow that always comes when old Suffrage ties are renewed."[18] Katharine Hepburn, mother of the actress, in a speech to the Connecticut Committee, described her experiences in the suffrage struggle. "That whole period of my life I remember with the greatest delight," she said. "We had no doubts. Life was a great thrill from morning until night."[19]

Professional ties also played a part in recruiting women to feminist activity and sustaining their commitment. Since many of the women held professional positions, it was not uncommon for them to have become involved in women's rights work through professional associations, such as the BPW, the AAUW, or the National Association of Women's Lawyers. A number of women in Democratic Party politics who held posts in government became fast friends and worked together to improve political opportunities for women. Margaret Hickey, a president of the BPW, an editor of the *Ladies' Home Journal*, and later a member of the President's Commission on the Status of Women, attributed her interest in the women's movement to her contact with a network of powerful women lawyers involved in women's rights work.

Friendship and primary group networks, then, were at the root of most women's involvement in the movement. Whether these grew out of a common suffrage heritage, professional ties, or other strong emotional and social bonds, the community of women that formed the core of the movement was held together by close and loving friendships. Correspondence among women rang with expressions of intimacy and friendship, indicating the intensely personal nature of the political work, and close friendships frequently were what led those women who did join the movement in this period to participation in feminist activity.

Intense devotion to a woman leader and to the tight friendship circle that formed around her was another reason given by women for joining the struggle for women's rights, and these leader–follower relationships also played a major role in tying together the feminist community. Alice Paul, often described as a charismatic leader, was the object of intense love and admiration, although she was not the only woman leader to inspire the loyalty and devotion of other women. Indicative of the superhuman characteristics attributed to Paul is the fact that she was addressed in one letter as "My Beloved Deity."[20] Not surprisingly, both adoration and denunciation of Alice Paul tended to focus on the same qualities: her complete absorption with but one thing and her perennial lack of gratitude for the effort others spent on behalf of women's rights.

A fair number of core activists were involved in longtime committed couple relationships with other women (Rupp 1980). As far as can be determined from the data, these women would not have identified their partnerships as lesbian, although charges of lesbianism, especially in conjunction with "red-baiting," were occasionally whispered. Being involved with another woman seemed to facilitate feminist work because these women's personal lives meshed well with their political commitments, thus removing one of the obstacles to participation that women with families or nonsupportive husbands sometimes experienced (Cook 1977). Women involved in the movement in this period created a homosocial world through which they carried out their political work and maintained the kind of female public sphere that historian Freedman (1979) argues is so essential to the survival of feminism.

Myra Marx Ferree and Frederick Miller (1980) discuss three general strategies a movement can use to mobilize participants: conversion that creates new ideological commitments among individuals; coalition-formation that mobilizes ideological commitments already held by individuals and groups; and direct mobilization that relies on network ties and situational factors to bring about participation without ideological commitment. Because the women's movement in this period was rooted in strong primary relationships and intense personal ties, the movement principally relied on coalition-formation among previously connected networks and groups and, to a lesser extent, direct mobilization of the membership of large organizations by the leadership. Movement organizations published newsletters as a way of keeping members and others informed of their programs and actions. Multiple organizational memberships were common: many National Woman's Party members belonged to the BPW and the AAUW, and some even to the anti-ERA League of Women Voters, and they used these multiple memberships in order to try to win or maintain endorsements for the ERA. For example, a number of NWP members who belonged to the BPW attended a BPW convention and, concealing their Woman's Party membership, mingled with the delegates and gathered at intervals in a central room to map out strategy for winning wider support in the organization for the ERA.

Preexisting organizations and networks of women, although they were unable to effect widespread change or disseminate their views to large audiences, had access to important resources that made it possible to maintain a commitment to women's rights in a climate of antifeminism. Belmont House, the National Woman's Party headquarters, was used by members of the NWP and nonmembers as a feminist hotel, meeting place, and center of organizational activities. Leaders of women's organizations had access to politicians and other decision makers and to existing networks of women who could be mobilized for direct action, such as letter-writing campaigns, on a particular issue. And because feminists were largely middle- and upper-class women with the financial means and time to devote themselves to the cause, many of them were able to make the movement their life work. Yet the very factors that served to integrate feminists into this close-knit community of women and made it possible for them to sustain their commitment also isolated movement organizations and made it difficult to recruit younger and less privileged women.

Preexisting structures, then, played a larger part in developing and maintaining the movement in this period than did spontaneous individual and group actions aroused by a sense of injustice. At a time when large numbers of American women were not drawn to feminism, the women's movement had to rely on available resources from preexisting organizations and networks. It is important, however, in examining the historical development of a movement, to distinguish between different types of resources necessary for movements mobilizing for survival and continuance compared with movements undergoing mass, or "white-hot," mobilization (Lofland 1979). The women's movement, from the end of World War II until the resurgence of more widespread feminist activism in the 1960s, was in a continuance stage that required a highly dedicated core of activists held together by a willingness to devote themselves almost single-mindedly to the cause, close interpersonal ties, a shared moral commitment, and strong leadership capable of coordinating and devising multiple strategies and actions (Taylor 1989).

Constraints and Strategic Choices

The actions and strategies of social movements are, by definition, noninstitutionalized (Killian 1964; Turner and Killian 1972; Wilkinson 1971; Wilson 1973). There is a tendency, however, to think of only those actions that are dramatic and discontinuous from everyday acts of social institutions as constituting social movement activity. But social movements can and do employ a range of tactics, respectable and nonrespectable, disruptive and nondisruptive, threatening and nonthreatening, violent and nonviolent, covert and overt, depending on whether their aim is to bargain, to persuade, or to coerce (Turner 1970). Jo Freeman (1983) identifies four factors that affect the strategies adopted by social movements: available resources, constraints on the use of those resources, a movement's own organization, and its expectations about the groups it hopes to influence.

As mentioned earlier, the core activists of the women's movement in the post-1945 period were white, middle- or upper-class, well-educated, and employed in professional or semiprofessional occupations, many of whom were lawyers. Given this composition and the kinds of support and other resources feminists could realistically expect to mobilize in a period in which the political establishment was not particularly receptive to pressure from feminist groups, the movement had available to it only certain kinds of strategies. On the whole, groups adopted persuasive strategies aimed at affecting national issues and actions and pursued tactics that could be accomplished with the support of elites in government and politics, while avoiding actions like public demonstrations and protests that required the involvement of large numbers of participants. For example, the National Woman's Party instigated the inclusion of a prohibition on sex discrimination in Title VII of the 1964 Civil Rights Act through its contacts with conservative representative Howard Smith (Brauer 1983). Women's organizations worked for the ERA by lobbying Congress, seeking endorsements from candidates for political office and other organizations, establishing coalitions to support the amendment, and educating the public through newspaper and magazine articles, letters to the editor, and radio and television appearances. Commenting on the persistence of feminists' lobbying efforts, one representative from Connecticut wondered in 1945 "whether or not the Congress meets for any other purpose but to consider the Equal Rights Amendment."[21]

Women organized letter-writing campaigns on every issue the movement supported: not only the ERA, but also the election of pioneer feminists like Susan B. Anthony to the national Hall of Fame and the support of women candidates for elected offices and government appointments. Sometimes these campaigns were undertaken by a single individual, but attempts were almost always made to make the efforts of individuals appear to represent a wider constituency by, for example, printing up organizational letterhead even if only one individual wrote all the letters and constituted the entire membership. For example, one woman did almost all the work of the Connecticut Committee for the ERA, as did another for the Spokane branch of the National Woman's Party.

The core activists in the movement, although relatively homogeneous in terms of social characteristics, were diverse politically. They were Democrats and Republicans, liberals and conservatives, integrationists and segregationists, and McCarthyites and anti-McCarthyites who agreed on little else politically except their feminist goals. Despite the fact that these women's efforts on behalf of feminism went against the broad social trends of the times, the movement as a whole sought respectability in its relationship to almost all social and political issues other than women's rights as narrowly defined by the movement. Because the ERA was in this period opposed by labor, liberals, left-wing organizations, and most women's groups, feminists did not generally align their efforts with other progressive interests. When they did, it was out of self-interest, as was the case with the attempt to include sex discrimination in civil rights legislation, an effort that was viewed with suspicion by many civil rights groups. Similarly, the National Woman's Party tried to give the appearance that women in labor were involved in women's movement activities by spotlighting token union women who supported the ERA. But the movement never seriously addressed the concerns of women in labor about the issue of protective legislation and how it would be affected by the ERA.

At the same time, feminists were willing to use almost any strategy, no matter how contradictory to the basic principles of social equality, to further their goals as long as it did not involve engaging in mass protest and other disruptive tactics. For example, the National Woman's Party attempted to win support for the ERA by using the fact that the Communist Party opposed the amendment to threaten vulnerable groups and individuals; the NWP pointed out that organized labor, by being against the ERA, was on the side of the Communists. In effect, the relationships that feminists established with other major social movements of the period—McCarthyism, the labor movement, and the civil rights movement—were limited and undertaken only to further the women's movement's own relatively narrow feminist goals.

Consistent with what other scholars have found, the strategies and tactics of the women's movement in this period were influenced not only by its limited opportunities for collective action, but also by its base of mobilization and its position in the power structure (Useem and Zald 1982). The movement operated from a small social base of well-educated and economically privileged women with ties to established institutions who, for the most part, had

developed their commitment to feminism during an earlier stage of the movement. Recognizing the unlikelihood of generating wide support for its aims,
the movement had little choice but to adopt legal change and institutional
reform as its ultimate goals and to use strategies that were respectable and
nondisruptive in trying to persuade political elites and other established
groups of the righteousness of its cause.

CONSEQUENCES FOR THE RESURGENT MOVEMENT

Although the women's movement that survived in the period from 1945 to the
mid-1960s made some limited progress toward its goals, clearly it did not
achieve them. But a more important question for understanding the historical
continuity of the American women's movement is what consequences, if any,
the actions of the elite-sustained women's movement of this period had for
the revitalized movement that took up the fight for gender equality by the end
of the 1960s. The founding of the National Organization for Women (NOW) in
1966 serves as a useful signpost in mapping the course of the transition from
the women's movement of the 1940s and 1950s to the resurgence of the
contemporary women's movement. At about the same time, women involved
in the civil rights and New Left movements began forming the more locally
organized radical branch of the women's movement. Analyses of the origins
of both branches of the movement of the 1960s and 1970s have seldom recognized the connections the existing women's movement made with the resurgent movement.

To understand the ways in which the elite-sustained movement was connected to the feminist challenge that followed, it is useful to think of this
phase of the movement as providing crucial resources that molded the strategies and possibilities for action in subsequent years. Following Freeman
(1979), movement resources can be distinguished as tangible or intangible.
Tangible resources include such things as money, space, and publicity a movement needs to maintain an existence and to make its program known, while
intangible resources refer to such things as specialized expertise, access to
networks, access to decision makers, status in the larger society, status within
the movement, and the time and commitment of supporters.

The women's movement of the 1940s and 1950s provided the resurgent
movement with time, money, and physical facilities, tangible resources that
stemmed largely from the fact that most women active in the movement in
this period were relatively affluent, capable of paying membership dues and
leaving bequests that supported the activities of their organizations and networks. For example, once NOW endorsed the ERA in 1967, the Belmont
House, the Woman's Party headquarters, was used as a central location for
lobbying for groups other than the Woman's Party, for celebrations of the
women's movement's history, and as a temporary residence for scholars and
students engaged in feminist research in Washington. Other organizations,
too, such as the BPW and AAUW, had headquarters in Washington that were
focal points of activity, information, and support as the movement coalesced

around the ERA and other activities in the 1970s. The newsletters of groups such as the BPW, the Woman's Party, professional women's organizations, and women's service organizations continued into the 1980s to reach a sector of women that otherwise would never have been influenced by the publications of NOW, much less by the newsletters and writings of the more radical groups of younger women. In addition, the elite-sustained movement had access to established media that helped to publicize feminist activity when new groups such as NOW had yet to establish such connections. For example, the *Christian Science Monitor* and the New York *Herald Tribune* supported the ERA from the 1940s on, and journalists looked to groups like the National Woman's Party and the BPW for information about the ERA before NOW gained visibility and wider support.

Far more important than the tangible resources, however, were the intangible ones that preexisting feminist groups provided new organizations and groups concerned with equality for women that emerged in the late 1960s. Since the elite-sustained movement had been active for many years on behalf of the ERA, participants had developed regular procedures for lobbying senators and representatives, maintained records of supporters and opponents, and had some access to key decision makers in government and politics. The struggle to include sex discrimination in Title VII of the Civil Rights Act of 1964 illustrates how the National Woman's Party used its connections and expertise on behalf of a legal change that eventually would become a major issue propelling the resurgent movement. National Woman's Party members wrote to Representative Howard Smith suggesting that he introduce an amendment forbidding sex discrimination, which he did. They then used their traditional lobbying techniques to support passage of the amendment. Although in actuality a number of women in government assisted the Woman's Party in the fight for the amendment, Alice Paul insisted, characteristically, that the NWP "bore the entire burden of this battle with absolutely no help of any kind from other women's organizations."[22] Another member of the Woman's Party involved in the struggle said, "I seriously doubt that women could have gotten Title VII without just a very small number of us." Eventually, Title VII and the issue of its enforcement by the Equal Employment Opportunity Commission helped spark the founding of NOW, shaped its earliest actions, and rendered the political system vulnerable to the feminist challenge by facilitating collective action around sex discrimination in the workplace (Freeman 1975).

The movement in the post-1945 period also had access to existing networks of women within a variety of established organizations, such as the AAUW, BPW, and National Association of Women Deans, that might otherwise have remained isolated from feminism as it increasingly became identified in the 1970s as an opposition movement. By 1970, most women's organizations supported the ERA and frequently took up support of some of the newer goals of the movement. But some feminists who had been active in the 1940s and 1950s, especially some of the most ardent supporters of the ERA, dissociated themselves from the actions of the later movement, sometimes out of opposition to newer feminist issues and sometimes out of reluctance to have their life's work taken on by a new and younger constituency. For example, a past president of the National Woman's Party used her influence in the Democratic Party to attempt to keep Betty Friedan from speaking in favor of the ERA and abortion rights at the 1968 convention. She feared that Friedan's support, since it would be viewed as coming from a militant and radical feminist, would harm the cause of the ERA.

Although the women's movement in the post-1945 period did not always reach the wider public with its program, probably the best evidence that the women's movement did have some impact on the larger society, even if limited, was that John F. Kennedy in 1961 appointed the President's Commission on the Status of Women. Part of the reason for establishing the commission was to devise an alternative to the ERA and thus placate the amendment's opponents, including Kennedy and the Democratic Party. That the position of feminists on the ERA entered into the deliberations of the commission is clear from the attitude expressed by one member, who hoped that "we could steer a complete path between not opposing the equal rights amendment and not bringing down the wr[a]th of the very influential Woman's Party . . . upon our fresh green heads."[23] It was to no one's surprise that the commission's final report did not favor the ERA and that its deliberations did forestall, temporarily, further action on the amendment. However, as scholars have pointed out, the real significance of the President's Commission on the Status of Women was that, through recommending the establishment of state commissions, it ultimately served as a stimulus for the growth of a new and more broad-based cycle of the women's movement (Freeman 1975).

Perhaps the most important resource that the elite-sustained movement brought to the movement in subsequent years was status within the feminist world. With the founding of NOW in 1966, a new group of women who had not identified with the women's movement in the 1940s and 1950s took up the feminist cause. Not surprisingly, some members of the Woman's Party were among the early members of NOW, and, most important, NOW's endorsement of the ERA in 1967 resulted largely from Woman's Party prompting. Alice Paul reported that a great many Woman's Party members joined NOW and voted for endorsement of the ERA at the convention; in her mind, "we captured the NOW people."[24] Although the two organizations did cooperate for a time, as NOW grew into a vigorous organization with a multi-issue platform and took leadership of the ERA struggle, the Woman's Party's attitude toward it hardened. One longtime activist disapproved of NOW's attention to "problems of sexual or psychological supremacy," which she felt debased the struggle for equal rights to the "battle of the sexes."[25]

Whatever else can be said about the impact of the elite-sustained stage of the movement on the women's movement that was to follow, one thing is clear: the Equal Rights Amendment, written in 1923 by the Woman's Party, was handed to a new generation of women and became, for almost a decade, one of the major issues around which the women's movement mobilized. In 1978, fifty-five years after the National Woman's Party arranged for the introduction of the ERA in Congress for the first time, a small contingent from the party joined the massive march of 100,000 people for the Equal Rights Amendment sponsored by NOW in Washington, D.C. At no time in its history could the Woman's Party have mobilized as many people to march for the ERA as NOW did on that day. But that does not belie the significance of the Woman's Party in the history of the American women's movement.

In many ways, the National Woman's Party functioned for the resurgent women's movement as what has been termed a "movement halfway house" (Morris 1984). A movement halfway house is an organization whose members are working to promote change that lacks broad-based support but provides important resources, such as skilled activists, media contacts, specialized knowledge, experience with past movements, and a vision of the future. As a movement halfway house, the National Woman's Party had resources of value to the newly developing women's movement; at the same time, the growth of a women's movement that drew from a much wider base of support by the end of the 1960s provided preexisting feminist groups like the National Woman's Party the opportunity to pursue their goals on a broader scale. Although some of the organizations that had been part of the movement in the 1940s and 1950s faded away in the 1970s, the Woman's Party remains symbolically important even today for its ties to the suffrage movement and its ownership of Belmont House. In fact, in 1981 a group of young feminists called the Congressional Union tried to take control of the Woman's Party during the final struggle to win ratification of the ERA.

In summary, the post-1945 elite-sustained women's movement, although its roots were firmly planted in the suffrage struggle, had connections also to the resurgent women's movement through individuals, organizations, specific interactions, and goals. While new organizations emerged in the late 1960s and 1970s and took up a broader range of feminist issues, mobilized a larger and more diverse constituency, and developed new and varied strategies, the women's movement of the 1940s and 1950s was clearly a source of mobilizable resources for the round of feminist activism that was to follow.

CONCLUSION

For many scholars, the most interesting and debated research question has been why the women's movement emerged. When new groups come into being that challenge the status quo by attempting to alter accepted relations of power and their ideological underpinnings, the suddenness and seeming unexpectedness of their claims almost compels us to take note of them. It is this general preoccupation with movement beginnings, however, that has led scholars to recognize only two waves of the American women's movement: the suffrage movement of the early 1900s, and the resurgent movement of the late 1960s and 1970s. By ignoring movement activity in stages of decline and continuance, when feminists have been unable to mobilize large numbers of supporters, scholars have overlooked the continuity of the American women's movement and its full significance in bringing about changes in the status of women. Arguing a similar point, Joe Gusfield (1981) states that "it is a matter crying for study that movements remain dormant and reemerge with their rhetoric shining and seemingly unused."

Olive Banks (1981) argues that the American women's movement is best understood as "one single historical process." This case study provides evidence for the historical continuity of the American women's movement by describing the structure and functioning of what has been characterized as an "elite-sustained" stage of the women's movement in a period in which it was assumed that no organized feminist activity existed. The term "elite-sustained" was chosen because the women's movement throughout the 1940s and 1950s was made up of a small, relatively affluent, well-educated, and highly dedicated core of women who, despite little support and strong opposition from the wider public, carried on the struggle for women's rights begun with the suffrage movement. Lacking any real mass base, the women's rights movement relied on moderate tactics and sought limited goals. Yet as encapsulated as the movement might have been in its own time and as little progress as it made toward its major goal, the ERA, the activities of feminists in the post-1945 period had an impact on the goals and strategies, ideology, and composition of the resurgent women's movement that grew in the late 1960s.

The question of when and why a movement takes this shape is critical to understanding different cycles of movement activity. Proponents of the resource mobilization perspective suggest three factors that affect the nature and development of a movement: (1) the structure of political opportunities, especially events external to the movement that influence the availability of resources and the success of tactics; (2) the organizational strength of movement forces that influence its base and breadth of mobilization and tactics; and (3) the nature of the group's own resources, including its ideology, which influence its tactical and structural choices (Gamson 1975; Jenkins 1983; McAdam 1982; McCarthy and Zald 1977; Zald and Ash 1966).

Applying these factors to this case, it is evident, first, that groups and individuals that attempted to sustain the struggle for women's rights from 1945 to the 1960s recognized that they were working in a social climate that was generally hostile to feminism. They expected and found little external support—publicity, financial assistance, and favorable sentiment—for the cause of women's rights. Second, the movement that managed to survive the antifeminist backlash suffered organizational problems that prevented it from broadening its base of support. Its core group, the National Woman's Party, was, in essence, a remnant of a previous stage of more successful mobilization. Born out of factionalism that split the suffrage movement, conflict over goals, strategies, and movement leadership continued to plague the Woman's Party and the women's rights movement as a whole throughout the post-1945 years. Failure to resolve the continuing problem of internal conflict between movement organizations, together with the fact that women's rights advocates lacked sufficient ties to other organized constituencies, such as women in labor, socialist women, and black women, prevented the movement from launching a unified and broad-based challenge on behalf of women's rights. The third factor that contributed to the movement's structural and tactical choices was the nature of the resources that its constituent groups had available to them. Most of the organizations and networks of women who composed the movement were privileged groups that, because of the sponsorship of a loyal supporter or group of supporters, pursued limited goals consistent with the kinds of resources they were able to obtain from the high status of movement participants, such as financial resources, informal connections to decision makers in politics and government, legal expertise, and communication networks with mainly middle-class professional and semiprofessional women. Given these factors, the movement form that has been described as elite-sustained appears to have been one of the few options open to the women's rights movement in this period.

This case study of the post-1945 movement has important implications for our understanding of the contemporary women's movement. Much was written in the 1980s about the decline of the women's movement and the "postfeminist generation." While few would claim that the feminist movement of today has suffered the same devastating loss of participants and influence that characterized the movement of the 1940s and 1950s, most observers found the 1980s less supportive of feminist activism than the previous two decades (Taylor 1983). By illustrating one way in which an unfavorable political climate can affect the structural and strategic options of the movement, this case study provides some insight into the factors that contribute to the increasingly elite social status of participants in the contemporary women's movement and the growing isolation of the movement from other constituencies.

It will not be surprising if feminist activists and scholars are uncomfortable with the term "elite-sustained," for it admits outright what scholars of social movements have long known, that many movements start as small minorities and often continue as minorities, even though they can act as harbingers of significant social and political change (Wilkinson 1971). In a 1982 interview, Caruthers Berger, an activist from the 1940s and 1950s, looked back at the impact that such a minority can have:

> We were, in a way, a little bit like the story about Sergent York, the famous hero of World War I. He hid behind a log, and he was such a crack shot that he annihilated a whole regiment. As they came by the log he got one, and pow! another. In other words, he was such a dead aim shot that they thought he was a regiment because he was hitting everything that he shot at. I think for the short period of time that it took for us to get protection for women in Title VII, we were able to get the Congress to take women seriously enough to do it.[26]

Thus even if some parts of the story of the women's movement of the 1940s and 1950s disappoint contemporary feminists, one fact cannot be denied. These groups and networks of women managed to sustain a commitment to women's rights until the equation of forces changed, making it possible for a later generation of women to resume more overt, mass-based protest.

NOTES

This chapter is part of a larger collaborative study of the American women's movement from 1945 to the 1960s conducted with Leila Rupp (Rupp and Taylor 1987). The research was supported by a Basic Research Grant (RO-*0703-81) from the National Endowment for the Humanities and by grants from Ohio State University. In addition, a fellowship from the Radcliffe Research Scholars Program for 1979–80, awarded to Leila Rupp, supported a great deal of the documentary research. SL in the notes stands for the Schlesinger Library at Radcliffe College, Cambridge, Massachusetts. LC stands for the Library of Congress.

1. Rose Arnold Powell to Cecile B. DeMille, August 27, 1957, Powell Papers, box 2 (21), SL.

2. Rose Arnold Powell, diary entry, July 19, 1935, Powell Papers, box 1, vol. 7, SL.

3. Quoted in Spender (1983b).

4. Blumer (1951: 199–200) defines a "general social movement" as a movement such as the women's movement or the labor movement whose background is "constituted by gradual and pervasive changes in the values of poeple. . . . As movements they are unorganized, with neither established leadership nor recognized membership, and little guidance and control."

5. Remarks of Margaret Hickey, Chair, Women's Responsibility in Public Affairs, n.d., Hickey Papers, Archive and Manuscript Division, University of Missouri, St. Louis.

6. Florence Kitchelt to Evelyn Samras, November 23, 1945, Kitchelt Papers, box 8 (224), SL.

7. This network consisted of Rose Arnold Powell, a Minnesota woman who belonged to both the National Woman's Party and the General Federation of Women's Clubs; the Susan B. Anthony Memorial in Rochester, New York; the Susan B. Anthony Memorial Library in California; and the Committee on Pioneers of the Woman Movement of the National Woman's Party, chaired by Ethel Adamson.

8. Anna Kelton Wiley to Anita Politzer, November 7, 1945, Babcock-Hurlburt Papers, box 7 (96), SL.

9. Winifred G. Helmes to Helen Loy, October 15, 1954, Alice Leopold Papers, box 2 (8), SL.

10. Dorothy Kenyon to Anna Lord Strauss, October 5, 1946, League of Women Voters (LWV) Papers, box 696, LC.

11. This profile of the membership is based on a careful reading of archival material, particularly correspondence, as well as research in biographical sources. For 108 women identified as core members, information was recorded about race, class, education, occupation, age, place of residence, political affiliation, political views, marital status, number of children (if any), living situation, and time of first involvement in the women's movement. In addition, any comments made by participants about the social characteristics of the membership were noted.

12. Letter to the editor of the *Washington Star*, November 3, 1946; carbon in LWV Papers, box 700, LC.

13. Rose Arnold Powell to Mary Beard, June 23, 1948, Powell Papers, box 2 (27), SL.

14. " 'Miss Republican' Goes 'Politikin' ' Eastern Shore Style," *Salisbury Advertiser* and *Wicomico Countian*, March 20, 1952; " 'Breakfast with Ike'—Here's What It's Like," *Washington Sunday Star*, May 29, 1955.

15. Florence Kitchelt to Margaret Bruton, July 11, 1947, Kitchelt Papers, box 4 (93), SL; Julia Pemberton to Alice Paul [November 1955], NWP Papers, reel 101.

16. Helen G. Irwin to Nina Horton Avery, June 21, 1954, NWP Papers, reel 100.

17. Florence Kitchelt to Katharine Ludington, August 14, 1950, Kitchelt Papers, box 6 (175), SL.

18. Caroline Babcock to Grace Cook Kurz, July 8, 1946, NWP Papers, reel 89.

19. Katherine Hepburn, speech to the Connecticut Committee, n.d. [1946?], Kitchelt Papers, box 6 (153), SL.

20. Lavinia Dock to Alice Paul, May 9, 1945, NWP Papers, reel 86.

21. Joseph E. Talbot to Florence Kitchelt, February 12, 1945, Kitchelt Papers, box 8 (234), SL.

22. Memo from Alice Paul, July 10, 1964, NWP Papers, reel 109.

23. Transcript of Proceedings, Committee on Political and Civil Status of Women, August 24, 1962, President's Commission on the Status of Women's Papers, box 14, John F. Kennedy Library, Boston, Massachusetts.

24. Alice Paul, "Conversations with Alice Paul: Woman Suffrage and the Equal Rights Amendment," interview in 1972 and 1973 with Amelia R. Fry, Regional Oral History Office, University of California, 1976.

25. Miriam Holden to (Mary Glenn) Newell, February 11, 1967, NWP Papers, reel 110.

26. Interview no. 8, May 15, 1982.

CHAPTER 16

Social Change and Social Activism: First-Wave Women's Movements Around the World

JANET SALTZMAN CHAFETZ, ANTHONY GARY DWORKIN, AND STEPHANIE SWANSON

For millennia, at least since the emergence of advanced horticultural societies, women have been substantially disadvantaged relative to their male compatriots (Blumberg 1978; Chafetz 1984; O'Kelly 1980). Rarely, however, have women collectively revolted against their common plight, and movements oriented *explicitly* to changing women's status date only to the mid-nineteenth century. During the 100 years from the mid-nineteenth to the mid-twentieth centuries, societies around the world experienced social movements on behalf of women's rights. These are often termed "first-wave" women's movements, as compared with "second-wave" movements, or those that emerged after the mid-1960s. In this paper, we will discuss first-wave movements in twenty-nine societies for which we have sufficiently complete information. These data come from a larger project that describes and explains the relative size and ideological scope of women's movements across time and space (Chafetz and Dworkin 1986). We will argue theoretically, and demonstrate empirically, that first-wave women's movements arose as a response to the interrelated processes of industrialization and urbanization. Where these processes were most highly developed, but not elsewhere, such movements generally achieved substantial size. In addition, we will argue that first-wave women's movements nearly always adopted an ameliorative, reformist ideology that supported rather than challenged traditional gender roles because the socioeconomic conditions that might have spawned a more radical feminist ideology were absent during the early stages of industrialization.

THEORETICAL APPROACH

The unit of analysis in this paper is the independent·women's social movement. Social movements are a form of collective behavior involving grass-roots group mobilization. They arise as a response to social strains (Turner and Killian 1972) and are typically composed of several groups or organizations connected by a communications network; some sort of leadership, however informal; at least some adherents who belong to no movement organizations but agree with some, many, or all movement goals (i.e., "fellow travelers"); and at least some shared definitions among movement adherents concerning the nature of the strains or problems confronting them and the changes desired to rectify these (i.e., "conciousness"). By "women's movement" we mean a social movement mounted primarily by females, whose members explicitly and consciously focus on actions intended to alleviate strains experienced by women on the basis of their sex (regardless of any other social attributes, such as religion, class, race, nationality). That is, the *first priority* for a women's movement is to bring about change in some aspects of the status or roles of women in society in order to rectify disadvantages faced by women as women.

Women have often participated extensively in social movements on behalf of a disadvantaged category based on a status other than sex, especially socialist movements and movements for national liberation. Often such movements—at least the leaders and the formal ideology—have manifested sympathy with the women's cause. Socialist and Communist parties in particular have frequently voiced strong official support for women's rights and sexual equality. In virtually all such cases, however, women's issues have received low priority. Women have been routinely told to wait until the "larger" cause was accomplished, that to pursue their own issues would divide the "broader" movement. As Lipman-Blumen (1984: 40; also 181–82) noted:

> . . . when women in the forefront of major social movements did try to address women's equality, they were forcefully reminded that the "women's issue" must wait until the "larger" social question was resolved. Abolitionists, socialists, Zionists, nationalists, civil rights workers all admonished women that they were selfish, elitist, or politically inept to press the women's question of social justice and power relationships.

When victorious, many such movements have metamorphosed into totalitarian states governed by one party. In these instances (e.g., the Soviet Union, China), party-sponsored women's organizations oriented to substantially altering the status, rights, and roles of women have indeed been established, and have often been at least minimally successful in their efforts. However, as Lapidus (1977:137) argued with respect to the *zhenotdel* in postrevolutionary Russia, the primary purpose of such organizations has been to mobilize women to support the regime (see also Andors's [1983:30] discussion of postrevolutionary China). By definition, social movements are grass-roots phenomena, organized by interested citizens. Organizations sponsored by governments on behalf of women therefore do not constitute women's movements, regardless of how successful their endeavors on behalf of women. In this chapter we address only *independent* women's movements, by which we mean those that are organizationally free from control by male-dominated organizations, political parties, and governments.

The broader project from which this chapter derives seeks to explain variation in both ideological scope and size of women's movements. First-wave movements were overwhelmingly ameliorative in ideology—that is, focused rather narrowly on women's rights without seriously questioning traditional gender roles or the sharp division between men's and women's "spheres." In the absence of variation on the ideological dimension, we will concentrate in this chapter on the size dimension. The information available cross-culturally is very uneven in the extent of movement description, and allows for only gross estimates of size. We have developed a three-point scale, ranging from incipient through intermediate to mass. At the incipient level, only a few groups or organizations exist, involving a few thousand adherents at most (depending on the size of the total population), confined to one or a few locales, and receiving little, if any, support from the rest of the society. At the mass level, a plethora of groups and organizations are involved in movement activity. The movement is spread over communities throughout the society, receives substantial support for at least some demands from the broader society, and involves at least 1 million (or in small societies a significant percentage of all) women. Of course, intermediate-size movements fall somewhere between these two extremes. In all cases, when we speak of movement size, we refer to the largest size to which it grew.

Societies not included in our study are of two types. It is likely that in some societies movements existed concerning which no English-language sources were available to us. Most such cases would probably have been incipient, as historians publishing in the sources available to us appear to have done a rather substantial amount of research on first-wave women's movements in recent years and are unlikely to have missed larger movements. Other societies probably did not experience any organized *movement* activity during this period, which is not to say that they had no women's rights or feminist advocates. Such advocates would have been relatively isolated individuals or cadres too small to even be considered an incipient movement.

The Causes of Women's Movements

Before we address the issue of the determinants of movement size, we will review briefly the theory that we have developed to account for why women's movements (regardless of ideological scope or size) emerge in the first place (for a complete explication, see Chafetz and Dworkin 1986: chap. 3; see also Chafetz and Dworkin 1983). All movements are contingent on the existence of social-structural strain—that is, ambiguities, tensions, conflicts, discriminations, deprivations, and discrepancies within a social order characterized by inequality (Smelser 1963). While the amount of strain to which women are subject has varied historically and cross-culturally (Chafetz 1984), in virtually every society (except for some technologically simple tribal ones) females have been subject to substantial strain for several millennia. In short, there has long been ample reason for a women's movement almost everywhere. Yet such movements did not occur before the mid-nineteenth century, and then not everywhere.

The nineteenth and early twentieth centuries witnessed the beginnings of massive social changes in many societies, brought about by the intertwined processes of industrialization and urbanization. Two results of these processes are an increase in the skill level (and therefore the education) required for many jobs and an increase in the size of the middle class and in the leisure time of members of that class. In turn, these changes resulted in altered and expanded roles for females. Women in urban industrial societies began to become better educated, in line with the general societal increase in educational attainment. At least before marriage, some of these better-educated middle-class women worked outside the home, albeit typically in poorly paid (and even unpaid) occupations such as schoolteacher, writer, social worker, or nurse. Large numbers of middle-class women, including married women, used their increased leisure to join clubs, organizations, and social movements (e.g., temperance, antislavery, national liberation), moving out of the home and often into the public arena.

Role expansion, in turn, tended to produce "status/role dilemmas" for women. By this term we mean contradictions resulting from discrepancies between the socially defined appropriate roles and the reality of emerging new roles. Women were socially defined as domestic and dependent. Yet in their new roles, many women functioned outside the home in a relatively or completely independent fashion. In interactions with males (and many other females), they would have been treated according to traditional definitions of femininity. But increasingly their own accomplishments—educational, organizational, even occupational—would have led such women to expect to be treated with more respect and credibility.

Role expansion, especially within the context of the high population density characteristic of urban life, also served to bring women experiencing such dilemmas into increased contact with other women undergoing the same process. Increased communication among such women likely resulted in an increasing consciousness that, relative to males, they faced unjust disadvantages. That is, as they met at work, in school, in clubs, in social movement organizations, women began to communicate their shared frustrations and develop an awareness that "something is wrong with the system"—not with themselves as individuals. Moreover, the skills and resources they had developed in their new roles helped give them not only the confidence that they could change the social order, but also the resources to mount a movement of their own (e.g., the ability to organize and to communicate publicly, money for travel and publications, fund-raising skills, and the like).

We need to note what might appear to be a contradiction at this point. On the one hand, we are arguing that role expansion constitutes a critical variable in explaining the emergence of first-wave women's movements. On the other hand, we have stated that such movements were overwhelmingly ameliorative and stressed women's traditional domestic roles as wives and mothers. Role expansion for middle-class women in the era under discussion was primarily into public but not employment roles. Many women were indeed employed, but few of them were married. During the early stages of industrialization there was not a great demand for female labor, especially the kind of labor that middle-class women would be willing to provide. The result was that their demands were for tools that would allow them to function better in traditional roles and in their new public roles, which were often extensions of their domestic concerns. For instance, they wanted suffrage in many societies chiefly in order to be more effective in their other social movement activities, especially social and moral reform movements (e.g., for temperance, against prostitution, for protective legislation for child and female industrial workers). Their consciousness of the extent and nature of women's deprivations was limited by the fact that their roles expanded only partially. Thus the demands they made were limited, as we shall see more clearly in the next section. In recent decades in some highly industrialized societies, economic changes have occurred that have radically increased the demand for female labor and hence the proportion of women in the labor force. In such societies, large numbers of married middle-class women (the bulk of potential adherents to independent women's movements) have experienced further role expansion. As this occurred, consciousness of continued sex-based inequities grew by the same general process as an ameliorative consciousness developed earlier. However, much greater role expansion has resulted in a more radical, fully feminist ideology in second-wave women's movements (for more detail on this wave, see Chafetz and Dworkin 1986: chaps. 3, 5–6).

A women's movement was likely to emerge when the kind of consciousness described above spread substantially among women and combined with the development of potential leaders with adequate resources. However, independent of this process, the political conditions extant in a given society could impede movement development (Dahrendorf 1959). On the one hand, politically repressive regimes may effectively prevent any social movement activity, including, of course, the emergence of a women's movement. On the other hand, sympathetic governing elites may co-opt emergent social movements by quickly acquiescing to some initial demands, thereby seeming to render further activism and movement development moot. Therefore, women's movements were most likely to emerge and grow where free political association was permitted but the government was essentially unresponsive to women's demands.

Determinants of Movement Size

The logic of the theoretical synopsis just presented may be summarized as follows. Industrialization and urbanization combined to expand the roles of women, especially middle-class women. In turn, such women experienced increased status/role dilemmas. Role expansion also produced increased opportunity for communication about those dilemmas, encouraging the development of gender consciousness. Furthermore, role expansion provided a skilled leadership cadre with resources to mount a movement. In the absence of political obstacles or co-optation, a women's movement was likely to emerge.

It would seem reasonable, then, that the more widespread each of the processes was, the larger the pool of potential recruits to a women's movement, and therefore the larger the resultant movement would tend to be. In short, we hypothesize that for first-wave women's movements, there was a direct relationship between movement size and level of urbanization, level of industrialization, average educational level of women, relative size of the middle class, and proportion of women participating in roles previously monopolized by men.

The logic of our theoretical argument suggests the need to compare not only movements of various sizes, but also cases where no women's movement emerged at all. Unfortunately, neither historians nor social scientists tend to examine the absence of a phenomenon. We cannot know if there was no movement in a society, or simply no study of a movement available to us. Therefore, our study must be confined to documented movements, which nonetheless varied substantially in size.

DESCRIPTION OF MOVEMENTS

In this section, we report a summary based on more or less detailed descriptions of the twenty-nine cases examined. About eighty-five references were used in the process of developing the descriptions, and it is clearly beyond the scope of this chapter to report either the details of each case or the bibliography. (Readers who wish more information on the cases, or who wish to examine the way in which we reached the conclusions reported here, should see Chafetz and Dworkin 1986: chap. 4.)

In Table 16.1 we present our conclusions concerning the relative size and ideological scope of each movement examined. In cases where the movement spanned a relatively long time and experienced a substantial shift in ideology or size at some point during its history, we separate out the two movement stages (United States, Great Britain, France, Germany, and Japan).

Several things are immediately apparent when this table is examined. First, women's movements of this era were overwhelmingly ameliorative in ideology, irrespective of where or exactly when they occurred, as stated earlier. Moreover, in the few cases where they existed, ideologically broader feminist movements never grew beyond the incipient stage. If a society experienced a feminist movement and subsequently the movement developed beyond the incipient stage, the ideology narrowed to the ameliorative level (e.g., United States and France). In other cases, the larger ameliorative movement coexisted with a much smaller feminist branch (e.g., Great Britain and Mexico). Of the twenty-nine societies examined, only two (United States and Great Britain) achieved unambiguous mass women's movements at some point in their history. Six more may have reached mass proportions (Germany, Sweden, Denmark, Iceland, Holland, and Japan), while four were intermediate in size (Canada, France, Cuba, and Mexico), and two others may also have reached a level between incipient and mass (Australia and New Zealand). In all, at least fifteen societies, or over half the cases for which data are available, never grew beyond the incipient stage.

Two kinds of cases that remained small or experienced retarded growth are

Table 16.1   Estimates of Relative Size,* Scope of Ideology, and Approximate Dates of Independent First-Wave Women's Movements

Nation	Dates	Size	Ideology
United States	1848–1870	Incipient	Feminist
	1870–1920	Mass	Ameliorative
Great Britain	1860–1900	Incipient	Ameliorative
	1900–1918	Mass and incipient	Ameliorative and feminist
Canada	1880–1918	Intermediate	Ameliorative
Australia	1880–1901	Incipient or intermediate	Ameliorative
New Zealand	1885–1893	Incipient or intermediate	Ameliorative
Finland	1880–1906	Incipient	Ameliorative
Norway	1885–1913	Incipient	Ameliorative
Sweden	1870–1910	Intermediate or mass	Ameliorative
Denmark	1870–1910	Intermediate or mass	Ameliorative
Iceland	1894–1910	Intermediate or mass	Ameliorative
Holland	1894–1913	Intermediate or mass	Ameliorative
France	1870–1900	Incipient	Feminist
	1900–1914	Intermediate	Ameliorative
Russia	1905–1918	Incipient	Amelioriative
Germany	1865–1914	Incipient	Ameliorative
	1914–1920	Intermediate or mass	Ameliorative
Italy	1867–1914	Incipient	At least partially feminist
Austro-Hungarian Empire	1893–1920	Incipient	Ameliorative
China	1911–1927	Incipient	Ameliorative
Japan	1880–1923	Incipient	Ameliorative
	1923–1930	Intermediate or mass	Ameliorative
India	1917–1950	Incipient	Ameliorative
Persia/Iran	1906–1950s	Incipient	Ameliorative
Egypt	1919–1935	Incipient	Ameliorative
Dominican Republic	1931–1942	Incipient	Ameliorative
Cuba	1914–1927	Incipient or intermediate	Ameliorative
Mexico	1904–1940	Intermediate and incipient	Ameliorative and feminist
Argentina	1900–1930s	Incipient	Ameliorative
Brazil	1920–1937	Incipient	Ameliorative
Chile	1915–1949	Incipient	Ameliorative
Peru	1915–1925	Minimally incipient	Ameliorative
Uruguay	1916–1932	Incipient	Ameliorative

*Relative size refers to the largest size achieved by a movement during the period in question.

especially interesting in light of political considerations raised in the last section. In the cases of New Zealand, Australia, Norway, and Finland, suffrage and some other reforms were granted to women before World War I by sympathetic and powerful male leaders. In those nations, movement activism was rendered largely moot relatively soon after it began, preventing the development of larger movements. In a number of other cases, government repression retarded movement development. In Germany, Russia, China, and Japan, laws existed at the time their movements began which specifically restricted the right of women to join political organizations, attend political meetings, or publicly discuss political issues. In these cases, a few women (along with male allies) braved arrest and demanded the repeal of such laws, which eventually occurred. After repeal, these movements grew rather rapidly, and in two cases may have eventually approached mass size. In addition, at some point in their history, women's movements in France, Russia, China, Japan, Persia/Iran, Brazil, and Peru were directly although temporarily repressed by their governments, sometimes quite brutally (e.g., China).

Regardless of size or ideological scope, independent women's movements were overwhelmingly middle-class, urban phenomena. Especially the leaders, but apparently most of the followers as well, were considerably better educated than the average women of their society. Many were employed, at least at some point in their lives (usually before marriage), as educators, as journalists or writers, or in the medical profession. In addition, in most societies, women's rights activists were typically involved in social welfare and philanthropic activities as well. In all but six cases we documented growing middle-class female involvement in public-sphere, nonemployment roles before or during the time of the women's movement. These include philanthropic societies, moral reform organizations, and nationalistic and other types of political movements and parties. Information on those six cases was scarce, so we simply do not know if such role expansion was occurring. These attributes of movement adherents are precisely those predicted by our theory.

In a number of societies, socialist or nationalist movements ostensibly supported women's rights; these movements often attracted sizable numbers of women from the lower socioeconomic strata, as well as some middle- and upper-class women. As we argued earlier, however, in almost all such cases women's issues not only were low priority, but were routinely sacrificed to the "larger cause." Since our focus is on *independent* women's movements, it is safe to charcterize them all as overwhelmingly middle-class phenomena.

There was considerable similarity in the issues addressed by the various movements and in the process of movement development. In Table 16.2, the major issue areas stressed by a substantial number of movements are enumerated. Two countries, Chile and Peru, have been deleted from this table because of insufficient information, leaving a sample of twenty-seven societies. A "yes" in Table 16.2 means that there is clear evidence that the issue was of concern in a given case. A blank space means that we lack data to determine whether or not that issue was raised; it does not mean that the issue was definitely absent from the movement's priorities.

Educational Opportunity

In twenty of the cases, educational opportunity was definitely an issue. In nations where literacy rates were high—North American and European societies—the educational opportunity issue focused on access to higher education. While movement activists everywhere were well-educated relative to other women in their societies, their education usually occurred in female seminaries, by private tutoring, or in normal schools. In some of the later-developing movements, activists were often educated abroad. In the rest of the cases (i.e., Asian, Middle Eastern, and most Latin American and Caribbean societies), the issue focused on basic literacy for women, often beginning

Table 16.2 Issues Addressed by First-Wave Women's Movements

Nation*	Educational Opportunity	Legal Reform	Economic Opportunity	Protective Legislation	Temperance	Sexual Double Standard	Suffrage	Other	Traditional Justification
United States (pre–Civil War)	Yes	Yes	Yes			Yes	No	Sex stereotypes; dress reform; physical fitness	No; equal rights
United States (post–Civil War)				Yes	Yes (WCTU)	Yes	Yes		Yes
Great Britain	Yes	Yes	Yes	Yes	Yes (WCTU)	Yes	Yes	Socialist feminists critique entire system	Yes except Socialist feminists
Canada	Yes		Yes	Yes	Yes (WCTU)		Yes		Yes
Australia		Yes			Yes (WCTU)	Yes	Yes		Yes
New Zealand		Yes			Yes (WCTU)		Yes		Yes
Finland	Yes	Yes				Yes	Yes		
Norway	Yes	Yes	Yes		Yes (WCTU)		Yes		
Sweden	Yes	Yes	Yes		Yes	Yes	Yes		
Denmark			Yes		Yes		Yes		
Iceland	Yes		Yes				Yes		
Holland							Yes		
France	Yes	Yes	Yes	Yes		Yes	Yes	Religion; voluntary motherhood; some advocate free love	Yes partly; part equal rights

Country							Socialist feminists critique entire system	Yes except Socialist feminists
Russia	Yes	Yes	Yes		Yes	Yes	Yes†		Yes
Germany	Yes	Yes	Yes	Yes	Yes	Yes	Yes†		Yes
Italy	Yes		Yes	Yes		Yes	Yes		Yes
Austro-Hungarian Empire				Yes		Yes	Yes†		Yes
China	Yes	Yes	Yes	Yes (WCTU)	Yes	Yes	Yes	Foot-binding; child and arranged marriage	Yes
Japan	Yes	Yes	Yes	Yes (WCTU)	Yes	Yes	Yes		
India	Yes	Yes	Yes			Yes	Yes†	Seclusion; child marriage	Yes
Persia/Iran	Yes	Yes	Yes		Yes	Yes	Yes†	Seclusion and veil	Yes
Egypt	Yes		Yes	Yes (WCTU)	Yes	Yes	Yes†	Child and arranged marriage	Yes
Dominican Republic	Yes	Yes	Yes	Yes	Yes	Yes	Yes		Yes
Cuba	Yes	Yes	Yes		Yes	Yes	Yes		
Mexico	Yes	Yes	Yes	Yes	Yes	Yes	Yes	Land to women; free love by some	
Argentina	Yes	Yes	Yes	Yes	Yes	Yes	Yes†	Day care; physical fitness	Yes
Brazil	Yes	Yes	Yes	Yes	Yes	Yes	Yes		
Uruguay	Yes	Yes			Yes	Yes	Yes		Yes

*Chile and Peru were omitted due to insufficient information.

†Suffrage issue was of minor importance or emerged relatively late in movement history.

with women of the middle and wealthy classes. In several cases, Westernized or politically liberal males raised the issue of basic education for females late in the nineteenth century (e.g., Japan, India, Persia/Iran, Egypt, and Argentina). These men would typically educate their daughters and other female relatives, who then became the nucleus of a women's movement in the next generation, one of whose chief demands was educational opportunity for women. In both types of cases, educational opportunity was usually one of the earliest demands made, sometimes preceding all other demands by a generation.

Legal Reform

The precise nature of the legal reforms demanded varied from nation to nation, in accordance with the precise legal disabilities women faced. However, there were some relatively prevalent issues. In eighteen cases, there was definitely demand for legal reforms. Virtually everywhere married women faced a variety of inequities, and it was on these that the movements concentrated. Equal authority over children (especially in the event of divorce), property rights for married women, control over inheritance and earnings, and divorce-law reform were frequent reforms demanded. In general, legal reforms also constituted early reform demands, surfacing either at the same time or as the very next issue after educational opportunity.

Economic Opportunity and Protective Legislation

In eighteen cases, economic opportunity for women constituted an issue. This issue was focused largely on access to high-prestige positions requiring at least college credentials, and especially the medical profession, which was barred to women in most places in the nineteenth century. As overwhelmingly middle-class phenomena, independent women's movements were composed of relatively well-educated women whose credentials could not be translated into many jobs. By and large, however, the demand for access to high-level jobs was a demand on behalf of unmarried women. Rarely did any of the movements argue that women should have the right to pursue both careers and family roles. Rather, the justification for expanded economic opportunity built upon the recognition of the need of single women and widows for economic self-sufficiency. This issue tended to surface somewhat later than those of educational opportunity and legal reform, inasmuch as it was prompted primarily by a growing pool of well-educated, unemployable women.

In eight countries we are sure that the issue of protective legislation arose, and most of these were relatively industrialized when the issue surfaced. Unlike their middle-class sisters, working-class women in such societies were often employed as industrial workers. They were cruelly exploited, financially and otherwise, and faced horrid working conditions. Moreover, they were usually shunned by the members of male-dominated unions who defined them as a threat, arguing that women were willing to accept lower wages, which therefore helped to keep male wages depressed. In fact, in most nations unions fought for a "family wage" for men that would "allow" their wives to absent themselves altogether from the labor force (Foreman 1977; Kessler-Harris 1975; Thomis and Grimmett 1982). Where working-class women organized separately, often under the leadership of socialist feminists, protective legislation for female workers was sought. Sometimes this issue placed them in direct, bitter conflict with middle-class women's movements. The latter saw protective legislation as defining women as in need of special consideration, and therefore as antithetical to their call for increased employment opportunity and equality. The result was that in several cases where female working-class activism arose, no cooperation between it and the middle-class women's movement came to pass. This was especially notable in France and Germany.

Temperance and the Sexual Double Standard

Independent women's movements of this era overwhelmingly accepted a notion of fundamental differences between the sexes. They accepted traditional notions of "separate spheres" for the two sexes, women's "sphere" clearly being that of the home and family. They tended to justify movement demands in large measure in terms of strengthening the family, raising "better" children, hence benefiting the total society. Toward this end, two moral reforms appeared in a large proportion of the cases: temperance and an end to the sexual double standard.

Alcoholism was extremely destructive to nineteenth-century families, especially given married women's lack of legal control over children and money (including their own). Since men drank but women did not during this era, temperance was seen primarily as a "women's issue"; they and their children were the major victims of alcohol abuse. The Women's Christian Temperance Union (WCTU) grew up in the 1870s in the United States and rapidly spread to many other nations, including some non-Christian ones (see Table 16.2). Quite early in the United States, the WCTU began to realize that its members needed the vote to gain needed legislation. It became an active supporter of suffrage and other reforms concerning the rights of women (Bordin 1981; Epstein 1981). In some cases, it was the major or at least the original organization fighting for women's suffrage (e.g., Canada and Australia). Even in the WCTU's absence, the temperance issue was often raised by women's movements. In all, sixteen of our cases definitely included temperance in their demands, and in nine of those cases we can document WCTU activism.

In seventeen cases, there was definitely a call for the end of the sexual double standard. Where legalized or state-controlled prostitution existed, the call was to abolish it. Where concubinage was practiced, the demand was for its end. Polygyny was attacked in societies where it was permitted. White slavery was likewise attacked. In the absence of these, the informal sexual double standard was decried. In all such cases, women demanded that men be required to act as they do: monogamously or chastely. A few female proponents of "free love" spoke out in several Western nations, but they were quickly ostracized by the overwhelming bulk of movement activists.

Suffrage

In every society examined, women's suffrage eventually emerged as an issue. In many cases, however, this issue emerged relatively late in a movement's history, usually for one of two reasons. First, in many cases no member of the society was enfranchised for much of the movement's history, as the government was a traditional monarchy (e.g., Russia) or a colonial power (e.g., India). Where males were not enfranchised, females were not likely to demand the vote, unless they were also involved in a political movement to democratize or free the society—as was often the case. In this instance, however, the principle of universal suffrage was usually sacrificed in order to attain male suffrage or in response to male antipathy to women's rights. Second, in many societies, such as the United States and Germany, women's suffrage was initially considered a very radical demand, and one less likely to succeed than other demands. Repeated frustration in achieving various other goals eventually resulted in a redefinition of suffrage as a necessary tool to achieve other demands. Ironically, despite the widespread initial definition of suffrage as a means to other reform ends, in many cases it ultimately became the de facto chief priority. This tended to happen most notably in societies that experienced movements beyond the incipient level, including Great Britain and the United States. Women with widely diverse goals came to agree on one: suffrage. In such cases, the means became the end, and after it was achieved, these movements rapidly died because few, if any, other interests were widely shared by participants in the suffrage campaign.

When we discussed employment opportunity and protective legislation, we noted a conflict, sometimes bitter, between middle- and working-class women. Sometimes suffrage was also a divisive issue. In some instances, such as in the United States, many suffrage advocates called for enfranchisement of literate women only, reflecting a general middle-class fear of lower-class radicalism. On the other hand, in some nations, such as France, left-wing and radical women opposed female enfranchisement because they feared the religious, conservative, and monarchist commitments of the mass of women in their societies.

Other Issues

In some cases (e.g., pre–Civil War United States, Great Britain, Mexico, France, and Germany), a small but ideologically feminist movement existed, usually alongside a larger ameliorative one. In a few instances, it was composed almost entirely of socialist females. Where a cadre of feminists existed, it raised issues pertaining to a wide range of social institutions, in much the same manner as do most contemporary women's movements.

The primary miscellaneous issues of central importance to various movements arose in Asia and the Middle East. An end to child and arranged marriages and to female seclusion (purdah) constituted major demands in societies where such practices existed (along with footbinding in China). The end of such practices was deemed necessary if females were even to be able to acquire an education. They thus appeared among the very first demands made by newly forming women's movements. Indeed, such demands were often first voiced by Westernized males, as much as a generation before women organized themselves (e.g., China, India, Persia/Iran, and Egypt).

Movement Justification

In thirteen cases, virtually the entire justification of movement demands (excepting only the socialists) was stated in terms of women's traditional roles. In only two cases is there an indication that movement demands were justified on the basis of the simple assertion that women as human beings deserve equality with men. This is not to say that no one asserted this position, only that the organized groups constituting the core of movement activism did not. The usual justification assumed that women's primary roles were those of wife and mother. Further, women were assumed to be innately more moral, compassionate, and peaceable than men. The various reforms demanded were thus predicated on one or both of two goals:

1. Women would be better wives and mothers and the family would be strengthened.
2. National policy would be enriched by the inclusion of women's "special" virtues and concerns.

It is, of course, this type of justification that contributed to our assessment of most first-wave women's movements as ameliorative.

One final aspect of first-wave women's movements is worthy of note. Of fourteen nations that may have experienced movements larger than incipient, ten were predominantly Protestant (United States, Great Britain, Canada, Australia, New Zealand, Sweden, Denmark, Iceland, Holland, and Germany). Moreover, the only two Protestant societies that failed to develop movements larger than incipient in size were Finland and Norway, where women were enfranchised very early. Many scholars have argued that there is a direct connection between theology and women's rights activism, and it would certainly appear so from this data. However, we believe that this is a spurious relationship. It is our contention that educational level, not religion per se, accounts for this phenomenon. Because of their theologies, the various Protestant faiths were the first historically to stress literacy for all people, to enable the direct reading of the Scriptures. Therefore, Protestant nations had much higher proportions of educated women earlier than other societies. These women provided the pool available for mobilization into a women's movement. Where the pool was smaller, the movement was smaller. But in all cases, movement activists were relatively well educated, regardless of religion.

MOVEMENT SIZE AND SOCIOECONOMIC INDICATORS: A PARTIAL TEST OF THE THEORY

We have hypothesized that the size of first-wave women's movements varied directly with the level of urbanization and industrialization, the size of the

middle class, and expansion of women's roles and education. We have already presented some evidence that women's non-labor-force, public roles
were expanding by the time women's movements were emerging, and that
intermediate and mass movements were primarily confined to Protestant nations whose female populations were probably better educated than elsewhere. What follows is an attempt to test the other hypotheses. Unfortunately, the available data do not permit a further test of the role expansion or
female-education hypotheses at this time.

When one works with census data from the nineteenth and early twentieth centuries from a diversity of nations, one rapidly discovers how little
uniformity there is across time and space, and how many counting and other
methodological errors pervade censuses. Thus we have had to operationalize
our variables in terms of data collectible from most, if not all, of the national
censuses, with the result that our measures are quite simple. Nonetheless, the
findings are highly suggestive of the utility of our approach.

The data utilized to test our model are from the census nearest to the end
point of the women's movement for each nation, except in those few cases
where such an end point was also the beginning of a more massive movement
or a major ideological shift. In the cases of the United States, Great Britain,
France, Germany, and Japan, we selected a point in time approximately mid-
way between the emergence and the end of the movement to demarcate the
first phase of each movement, while retaining the end point for the later
phase.

The dependent variable, movement size, was presented in Table 16.1 and
its measurement described in the theoretical section. Following is a description of our measurements of the independent variables.

Industrialization

The form of industrialization has varied across time and space, with few
nations exactly duplicating the conditions present in Great Britain or the
United States. However, one obvious and readily accessible common denomi-
nator has been a diminished percentage of the population engaged in the
primary economic sector (agriculture, forestry, mining, and related extracting
industries). We therefore expect that movement size varied directly with the
percentage of the employed population in nonprimary labor.

Urbanization

Nations have rarely been consistent in their measures of urban areas. Some
define as urban any location with a population of 2,500 or more, others set
limits closer to 25,000, and still others did not develop such indices. We
elected to count the population of the largest cities (those in excess of 100,000)
and divide that figure by the total national population. The resulting figure
represents the proportion of the population in the largest cities. We hypothesize that the larger the percentage of the population living in the largest cities,
the larger the size of the women's movement.

Size of the Middle Class

Statistics on the distribution of wealth are often unavailable, especially for nineteenth-century censuses. However, it has long been argued that in the absence of traditional claims to authority, the middle class tends to rely on meritocratic criteria, of which educational attainment is the most universal (e.g., Durkheim 1953; Williams 1960). Thus we assess the size of the middle class by the proportion of the school-aged population (i.e., children ages 5 to 19) who actually enrolled in school. Since social movements are not mounted by children, we have used the percentages two decades prior (or the closest date available) to the end point of the movement. We hypothesize that the greater the proportion of children enrolled in school twenty years before the end point of the movement, the larger the size of the women's movement.

The sources used to collect the data to be presented are too numerous to document within the space confines of this paper. Readers who wish more information should refer to Chafetz and Dworkin (1986: chap. 6).

Findings

In Table 16.3, we present the demographic data on industrialization, urbanization, and the size of the middle class for twenty-two of the nations for which data were available, resulting in twenty-seven cases (given that five nations experienced two movement phases). For ease of analysis, the table also indicates the approximate size of the women's movements for the nations, distinguishing between those that were incipient and those that were intermediate or mass. On inspection, it is apparent that there are generally clear cutting points associated with the size of the movements. When less than 50 percent of the labor force was in nonprimary occupations, movements never were more than incipient. When less than 10 percent of the population lived in the largest cities, again movements were never more than incipient. With only the exception of Cuba, the same is true when less than 40 percent of the school-age population was enrolled in school twenty years prior to the end point of the movement. Cuba is only a partial exception, because the census of 1899 (two decades before the end point of the movement) reported that nearly 80 percent of the school-age population of Havana (where most movement activity was located) attended schools.

Given these clear cutting points, we shall directly test our hypotheses using dichotomous measures of each variable. Presented in Table 16.4 are a series of tests of significance of difference between each independent variable and the dependent variable, movement size. Also included for each test is the appropriate measure of association (Yule's Q). Each part of the contingency table displays the majority of the cases along the diagonal, and thus is supportive of our hypotheses. The subtables are also what Francis (1961) has referred to as "less restrictive models." When the levels of industrialization and urbanization were low, movement size was always restricted to incipient. With the already noted exception of Cuba, a small middle class also always resulted in an incipient movement. However, when the levels of the independent vari-

Table 16.3 Assessment of Industrialization, Urbanization, and Size of the Middle Class Across Societies

Country	Movement Date	Movement Size	Percent in Non-Primary Occupations	Percent in Large Cities	5–19 in School 20 Years Earlier
United States 1	1860	Incipient	45.8	5.5	47.2
United States 2	1920	Mass	71.1	24.4	61.8
Great Britain 1	1880	Incipient	82.0	27.3	12.5
Great Britain 2	1918	Mass	85.6	28.6	48.6
Canada	1918	Intermediate	85.6	20.0	65.4
Finland	1906	Incipient	30.8	5.5	6.0
Norway	1913	Incipient	58.9	9.6	47.0
Sweden	1910	Intermediate/mass	60.0	11.3	48.8
Denmark	1910	Intermediate/mass	58.3	20.0	50.7
Holland	1913	Intermediate/mass	69.6	14.4	45.9
France 1	1890	Incipient	44.9	8.4	48.6
France 2	1914	Intermediate	58.5	11.0	56.7
Russia	1918	Incipient	40.8	7.2	N/A
Germany 1	1890	Incipient	42.5	7.3	45.1
Germany 2	1920	Intermediate/mass	65.6	16.3	56.7
Italy	1914	Incipient	43.9	7.0	26.5
Austro-Hungarian Empire	1920	Incipient	40.5	4.7	41.2
China	1927	Incipient	N/A	2.2	N.A.
Japan 1	1900	Incipient	35.7	11.3	33.6
Japan 2	1930	Intermediate/mass	50.1	19.0	51.1
India	1950	Incipient	25.9	4.9	10.3
Iran	1950	Incipient	43.3	6.8	-13.0
Egypt	1935	Incipient	39.3	12.7	12.3
Dominican Republic	1942	Incipient	39.7	4.7	31.5
Cuba	1920	Intermediate	50.0	12.5	17.4
Mexico	1940	Incipient/intermediate	67.6	10.7	N/A
Chile	1949	Incipient	63.6	28.5	36.7

Table 16.4 Cross-Classification of Movement Size by Industrialization, Urbanization and the Size of the Middle Class

Industrialization				
Low Industrialization, Incipient Movement	Low Industrialization, Intermediate/ Mass Movement	High Industrialization, Incipient Movement	High Industrialization, Intermediate/ Mass Movement	Statistical Analysis*
12	0	3	11	$\chi^2 = 13.28$ p. = .001 Q = 1.00
Urbanization				
Low Urbanization, Incipient Movement	Low Urbanization, Intermediate/ Mass Movement	High Urbanization, Incipient Movement	High Urbanization, Intermediate/ Mass Movement	Statistical Analysis*
12	0	4	11	$\chi^2 = 11.62$ p. = .001 Q = 1.00
Size of Middle Class				
Small Middle Class, Incipient Movement	Small Middle Class, Intermediate/ Mass Movement	Large Middle Class, Incipient Movement	Large Middle Class, Intermediate/ Mass Movement	Statistical Analysis*
9	1	5	9	$\chi^2 = 5.50$ p. = .02 Q = .87

*Yates's corrections applied to χ^2 statistics.

ables were high, intermediate or mass movements predominate, but some incipient movements also existed.

Examining those nonfitting cases where on at least one variable a larger movement would have been predicted, the total number is ten. However, in seven instances (Mexico, Japan 1, Egypt, United States 1, France 1, Germany 1, and Austro-Hungarian Empire) two of the three variables predicted the incipient movement found. In the remaining three cases, two of the three variables predicted a larger movement than was found. In the case of Norway, political co-optation was noted and may account for the discrepancy. Both Great Britain 1 and Chile, while sufficiently urbanized and industrialized for a larger movement, lacked an appropriate-size middle class. In the absence of a sufficiently large middle class, the pool of the type of women who mount women's movements, was simply too small.

The statistically significant chi-square values and the magnitude of their accompanying measures of association provide substantial support for our thesis. In addition, in only one case did we find a movement beyond the incipient level when the level of any one independent variable predicted otherwise. Moreover, in every case with full data, when all three independent variables predicted a movement of a given size, such a movement was found.

CONCLUSION

In the 100 years between the mid-nineteenth and the mid-twentieth centuries, women in nations across the globe organized to seek amelioration of some of the social, legal, and political disadvantages under which they lived. The strains to which they were responding were for the most part ancient. The absence of such movements before the mid-nineteenth century was the result of the absence of conducive social-structural conditions. With the beginning of industrialization and urbanization came a set of processes that encouraged a proportion of the growing number of middle-class women to develop a collective consciousness, albeit limited, of their sex-based deprivations and the wherewithal to organize to seek change. The revolt of these women was partial because socioeconomic conditions restricted the degree to which their roles could expand. A more radical feminist challenge was socially premature, and where it emerged it failed to attract any sizable following. The more heavily industrialized and urbanized the society, the larger the pool of women who experienced role expansion and developed gender consciousness, and thus the larger the resultant movement whose members were drawn from that pool. The "unfinished revolution" had to await a further set of socioeconomic changes, those sometimes called the "postindustrial revolution," to continue. In such societies, a new role expansion—the movement of middle-class, and especially married, women into full-time labor force roles—served to set the process of movement development in motion once again nearly twenty-five years ago. This time, conditions were right for a more radical, feminist ideology to attract substantial numbers of adherents.

NOTE

We thank the Center for Public Policy, College of Social Sciences, University of Houston for partial funding of the research project from which this paper derives.

CHAPTER 17

The Invisible Army of Women: Lesbian Social Protests, 1969–1988

SUSAN CAVIN

This chapter explores the political invisibility of lesbian protests within social movements generally and the feminist and gay liberation movements in particular. It describes the diverse strategies used by organized lesbians to gain visibility and legitimacy in the process of achieving their goals. Finally, the chapter examines the changing nature of gender politics *within* the gay liberation movement in the United States in the late 1980s, focusing on the impact of the AIDS crisis.

LESBIAN INVISIBILITY AND THE ORIGINS OF LESBIAN PROTEST

Lesbian protests have remained largely invisible, even as the women's and gay liberation movements have gained recognition within the political arena. Although this study focuses on lesbian social protests between 1969 and 1988 in the United States, lesbian collective actions date back to the nineteenth century with the rise of the homosexual emancipation movement in Germany in 1864 and lasting until the Hitler regime exterminated over 200,000 alleged homosexuals in the 1930s (Lauritsen and Thorstad 1974; Steakley 1975). The German movement is generally recognized as the first wave of gay/lesbian protests (1864–1935). The tendency of researchers of this period was generally to see homosexual movements in terms of gay men. Women activists, who were assumed to be heterosexual, were viewed as part of the feminist movement. Within such limited frameworks, lesbian women disappeared through analytical cracks despite their participation in collective actions from the earliest time to the present. Even today, social scientists and journalists tend to ignore lesbians when writing about the gay movement, gay life, homosexuality, or AIDS. The issues and struggles of lesbians within the gay world are still usually ignored by all—academics, the media, and politicians. The last often choose, however inaccurately, to clarify lesbian activism under the rubric of feminist protests. For instance, Reagan administration officials labeled Title IX (a federal law guaranteeing women equal educational opportunity) as "the Lesbian's Bill of Rights" (Connell 1987).

While lesbian social protests may be more prominent in the feminist movement today, they continue to be relatively invisible as part of other progressive movements, such as the black, pacifist, environmental/ecology, antinuke, and socialist movements (Deming 1974; McCallister 1982; Meyerding 1984). One reason for this is that lesbians involved in many of these struggles choose to remain "in the closet," as they take a stand for a certain cause.[1] For example, Karen Silkwood remained a closeted lesbian even as she became a political activist against the government (Cavin 1981; Kohn 1981).

Although lesbian feminist protest is rooted in the intersection of the women's and gay movements in the nineteenth and twentieth centuries, both movements have tended to ignore "the lesbian question" (Cavin 1985; Rich 1980). Within the women's movement, homophobia and fear of being labeled lesbian by the patriarchal establishment led many feminists to minimize lesbian contributions (Cook 1979). Lesbians were, and still are, largely invisible in the gay movement because of the sexism and misogyny of gay men.

While remaining hidden may help individual lesbians avoid discrimination, it is the major source of lesbian oppression in patriarchy (Cruickshank 1982). Thus "coming out of the closet" is a significant political act, an intrinsic act of social protest within homophobic environments (Vida 1978). Coming out of the closet has several dimensions beyond the conventional parameters of social protest. It counters social and sexual taboos; it breaks the conspiracy of silence on "the love that dares not speak its name" in an erotophobic society (Jackson-Brewer et al. 1988); it forces public discourse about sensuality and sexual desire—the power of the erotic (Snitow et al. 1983). Coming out psychologically reverses the stigma of a "spoiled identity" (Goffman 1963), turning social shame into political pride. With new consciousness, the once-reviled untouchable becomes the proud and political pariah. Therefore, all lesbian and gay social protests, almost by definition, involve the political act of coming out into a new arena. In feminist language, this means "the person is political," or breaking through the old private–public dichotomy. It means bringing private sexual matters into the public domain. Lesbian social protest cannot be understood outside of this context (Hoaglund and Stanley 1988; Kitzinger 1987; Radicalesbians 1973).

THEORIES OF LESBIAN/GAY PROTESTS

Political theorists, including gay and feminist scholars, suggest that macro factors—social, political, and economic—contributed to the rise of lesbian/gay protests. Laud Humphreys (1972) argues that the gay and lesbian movement became conceivable only after the publication of the Kinsey reports. These reports documented the prevalence of homosexuality and appear to have reduced individual isolation. D'Emilio (1983) contends that World War II played an important role in the development of the urban gay subculture and in the increase in lesbian/gay bars. Out of this, the Stonewall "riot" later erupted, unleashing the second wave of the gay/liberation movement in 1969. While it is often noted that wars alter sexual relations between men and women, scant attention has been paid to their effects on female homosexual and homosocial relations.

Several gay male scholars have written about the importance of urbanization in the formation of a visible gay male subculture and its links to gay political resistance (Boswell 1980; D'Emilio 1983). Feminist scholars also argue that industrialization and urbanization altered women's roles and laid the foundation for their protests in the nineteenth and twentieth centuries.[2] No theorist, however, has yet analyzed the relationships between lesbian feminist protest, patriarchal wars, industrialization and urbanization, and socio-sexual transformations in society. I suggest that the increased rate of lesbian feminist protests in the nineteenth and twentieth centuries is closely tied to the rise of industrialization, urbanization, and patriarchal wars, reflecting lesbian feminism's position at the intersection of the gay and women's movements.

Theories about the development of lesbian politicization[3] help explain changes in the visibility of lesbian feminist protest. According to Weitz (1984), U.S. lesbians went through three stages in moving from accommodation to political mobilization to challenging the dominant system. In the 1950s, their strategy was one of accommodation and self-censorship of outward differences between themselves and heterosexuals. By the 1960s, they had shifted to what Weitz calls "tertiary deviance," defining lesbians as a group entitled to civil rights and discarding past strategies of adjustment. By the 1970s, they had moved to a "radical deviant stance," celebrating deviance as "honorable resistance" and deliberately shifting their focus from changing individuals to changing society. Thus toward the close of the turbulent 1960s, the politicized groups of lesbians and gays were ready to challenge publicly their historical oppression.

THE ORIGINS AND TACTICS OF THE SECOND WAVE OF LESBIAN PROTEST

While the first wave of lesbian/gay protests dates back to the nineteenth century, the second wave is generally defined as beginning in the late 1960s.[4] The event that sparked this new wave of mobilization and protest is known as the "Stonewall incident." The records focus on the role of drag queens and gay men more than lesbians at Stonewall, probably because most of the historians have been gay male writers. Yet the account by Lucien Truscott IV, a *Village Voice* reporter who witnessed the event, places an unnamed lesbian in a central role in this protest.

On June 27, 1969, the conflict erupted when the New York City police attempted to close down a gay bar called the Stonewall Inn (Marotta 1981; Truscott 1969). At first, the gay men laughed as the police separated those with IDs (who they would not arrest) and those without IDs and drag queens (who they did arrest). All of a sudden the mood of the crowd changed, as a paddy wagon arrived and some of "the more blatant queens—in full drag"— along with others were loaded inside. Lucian Trescott wrote that the scene became "explosive" when police tried to arrest a "dyke" who put up a tremendous struggle. At that point, people began pelting the police with cans and bottles (Truscott 1969). A full-scale lesbian/gay riot erupted and lasted for three days. The 1969 Stonewall incident is celebrated annually throughout the world on the last Sunday in June as Lesbian/Gay Pride Day. In the next decade, the movement gradually changed from essentially scattered local struggles to national mobilization. The first national march for lesbian/gay rights in Washington, D.C., in 1979 reflected the expansion of the movement.

In addition to marches, lesbian/gay protests have employed unusual and varied tactics in their confrontations with the authorities. Challengers have used not only direct actions, but also legal strategies. Lesbians and gay men have resisted arrest by throwing beer bottles at police. They threw chicken blood at psychiatrists at the American Psychological Association (APA) convention to signify that they had blood on their hands as gays demanded declassification of homosexuality as a mental illness. This goal was achieved in 1973. Between 1975 and 1980, their repertoire expanded to include a national lesbian/gay boycott of Tropicana orange juice, targeting its antigay spokesperson, Anita Bryant. Although Bryant was dethroned from this position, the campaign marks the beginning of an anti–lesbian/gay backlash movement in the United States.

Collective effort has taken place in the courts and legislatures, directed at the passage and implementation of civil rights ordinances. As a result of these efforts, lesbian/gay civil rights ordinances were passed in various cities around the country (ten cities in the early period, 1969–74; twenty-six cities in the later period, 1975–80). In addition, many types of antidiscrimination lawsuits were filed by openly lesbian/gay lawyers: on behalf of lesbian mothers for custody of their children, for lesbian reproductive rights, for lesbian/gay employment and housing rights, as well as lawsuits against the military and the immigration service. Over time, lesbian/gay tactics have shifted from spontaneous direct action to include more planned strategies using judicial and legislative channels, but some notable exceptions need to be highlighted.

After the 1978 assassinations of gay San Francisco supervisor Harvey Milk and Mayor George Moscone by Dan White, lesbians, gays, and their supporters united in a massive nonviolent candlelight march. However, when Dan White was given only a light sentence, lesbians and gays in San Francisco rioted, set fire to police cars, broke windows at City Hall, and engaged in hand-to-hand combat with police on the streets. This became known as the "White Night Riot" (Shilts 1987).

Similarly, direct action reemerged in New York City when lesbian feminists poured cement down toilets of movie theaters showing "SNUFF" films (in which unsuspecting porno actresses were actually murdered on film). In Philadelphia, lesbian feminists executed a commando raid of a "SNUFF" theater, stormed the projection room, and seized the film.

In San Francisco lesbians protested police brutality by buying a block of 200 seats at a televised women's pro basketball game and unfurling a protest banner in front of television cameras. The media, however, blacked out the protest by cutting this segment of the ball game (Martin and Lyon 1988).

In addition, the women and men in the movement have used various means to publicize their political and collective "coming out" as lesbians and gays. In the early movement days (1969–1974), some of the lesbian tactics included guerrilla theater, mass street demonstrations, taking over radio and television shows, picketing homophobic establishments, writing lesbian graffiti, and pasting lesbian stickers on sexist-homophobic ads in subways and on billboards.

To mobilize others, strengthen solidarity, and heighten their political visibility, lesbians created militant separatist organizations where no men were allowed; wore lesbian buttons and jewelry (labyris, double women's symbols) and lavender T-shirts with lesbian slogans ("A Woman Without a Man Is Like a Fish Without a Bicycle," "Dyke"); published lesbian protest poetry (e.g., Judy Grahn's *Edward the Dyke*, a biting critique of psychiatry's treatment of lesbians); and in general created a lesbian feminist counterculture with books, films, plays, satire, comedy, art, and periodicals as well as unique dressing in "gender fuck" drag (lesbians in dresses with unshaven legs, male haircuts, and combat boots).

Finally, choosing another strategy, numerous openly lesbian and gay candidates have run for public office—for example, Harvey Milk in California, Elaine Noble in Massachusetts, and Ginny Apuzzo in New York.

In sum, lesbian and gay protests emerged in Europe in the nineteenth century and in the United States during the turbulent 1960s, reflecting in part the changing political and social sexual climate. Using both spontaneous and planned strategies, the movement in the United States attempted to change public policies at all levels.

SOME CONSEQUENCES OF PROTEST IN THE REAGAN YEARS

While the Anita Bryant attack against lesbians and gays symbolized the beginning of a backlash, the conservative political climate of the AIDS–Reagan era—1981 to 1988—exacerbated and fueled the antilesbian furies. Protests by lesbians and gays were met by increasing police repression and attacks from other sectors of society. Led by Jerry Falwell's Moral Majority, virtually every fundamentalist, conservative religious group scapegoated lesbians and gay men. Some called for outright "extermination of homosexuals," others for "quarantine" in concentration camps. As reported by Michael Musto (1990), conservative columnist William F. Buckley called for "tattooing the buttocks" of gays. Violence against lesbians and gays increased in every U.S. city that kept records on homophobic assault.[5]

Despite the pain caused by the homophobic hysteria of the AIDS–Reagan era, the attacks have had a positive effect on politicizing and mobilizing members and supporters. Large numbers of closet-apolitical lesbians and gays, who heretofore felt no need to join, have now become active participants. A historical overview of the numbers participating in marches supports this generalization, for the annual lesbian/gay marches to commemorate Stonewall grew larger every year of the 1980s, and this despite large numbers of gay men dead from AIDS. For example, the first national march on October 14, 1979, drew a disappointing turnout of only 100,000, in contrast to the New York City and San Francisco lesbian/gay marches, which routinely bring out from 150,000 to 300,000, respectively. The second national lesbian/gay march on October 11, 1987—eight years later—exceeded all expectations. The estimates of the number of marchers on that day ranged from 500,000 to 800,000.

Additional evidence suggests that the ferocious antigay backlash has helped unite and expand the movement. Lesbian separatists, who refused to work with men in the 1970s, returned to the gay fold in the 1980s in order to show solidarity. Protest organizations, such as the Anti-Gay Violence Projects and the Gay and Lesbian Anti-Defamation Leagues, have emerged to counter the effects of the backlash. In addition, lesbians and gays have joined together to boycott industries and media that discriminate against them. Boycotts were organized against the *New York Post* for gaybaiting, *Time* and *Newsweek* for their complete blackout of the 1987 March on Washington for Lesbian/Gay Rights, as well as Coors beer for homophobic ads.

Expanding unity and solidarity are also reflected in the thousands of lesbians who have joined the movement in the 1980s, risking arrest in various direct actions at the Seneca Falls Peace Camp, the Women's Pentagon Action, the U.S. Supreme Court, and St. Patrick's Cathedral; on Wall Street; and even at the White House. Mobilization, mass radical/gay street actions, and nonviolent civil disobedience have increased since the U.S. Supreme Court's *Hardwick* decision (July 1986), which upheld the criminalization of private consensual oral and anal sex between adults. Thus the protest of the late 1960s and 1970s by lesbians and gays gave rise to a widespread backlash that, in turn, helped to mobilize supporters and strengthen the lesbian/gay movement in the 1980s.

The expanded movement continues to struggle for visibility and a voice in the political arena through diverse and creative tactics. Recent strategies include a mass wedding of several thousand lesbian and gay couples at the Internal Revenue Service in October 1987 to protest the IRS's refusal to recognize lesbian and gay marriages or domestic partnerships, lesbian/gay bloc voting campaigns, mobilization of lesbians and gays for Jesse Jackson for president in 1988 as a protest vote, flooding the White House and Congress with telegrams to pass the federal gay civil rights bill, blocking traffic with sit-downs to protest the *Hardwick* Supreme Court decision, making computer calls every few seconds to the Moral Majority's toll-free number to tie up the lines, and a "National Coming Out Day."

The Sharon Kowalski–Karen Thompson case became a major lesbian cause célèbre in the 1980s. Kowalski, brain-injured in an accident, was not allowed by the hospital or her parents to see her lover, Thompson. This case brings together two important movement issues: the struggle for legal-medical recognition of lesbian/gay relationships, and the fight against the patriarchal family's legal control over adult lesbian/gay children who are disabled. It is not surprising that mobilization and protests around this case swept the lesbian/feminist community.

THE POLITICS OF GENDER AND RACE WITHIN THE LESBIAN/GAY MOVEMENT

The lesbian/gay movement, like other gender-integrated movements, originally reflected patriarchal gender patterns, with men leading and controlling decision-making positions. In recent years, as the separate movement of lesbians became stronger, this appears to have changed. Modifications in the gender distribution of decision-making positions and power are reflected in certain actions of the lesbian/gay movement in 1987.

Unlike previous mobilizations, lesbians played a prominent part in the national leadership of the second march on Washington in 1987. A year before, a policy of gender and racial parity within the movement had been adopted by the leaders of the movement. As a result, two of the three cochairs for the march were lesbians (one of whom was black). Four of the seven-member executive board were lesbians. The march's fifty-member steering committee consisted of nearly two-thirds lesbians (64 percent) and about one-third (36 per cent) gay men. Regionally, also, lesbians predominated. Only the South Central region (Texas, Oklahoma, Arkansas, and Louisiana) had less than half lesbian organizers (40 percent). The leadership also adopted the policy that at least one-fourth of the organizers for the march had to be people of color.

In this researcher's opinion, one of the major reasons why the second national lesbian/gay march was successful (as reflected in the high number of participants noted earlier) was because of its inclusiveness and wide representation of lesbians and gays of all colors. This event seems to have marked a reversal of the business-as-usual sex and color distributions in most gay organizations, particularly national ones. Previously, the pattern had been one of a white-male and middle-class gay movement, with only about one-third (36 percent) of the national steering committee members being lesbians. It is interesting to note, however, that despite this change in structure, only one public demonstration surrounding the march was actually led by women. This was the civil disobedience action at the U.S. Supreme Court on October 13, 1987, coordinated by Michele Crone and organized primarily by lesbians.

Lesbians predominated in a number of cities. Civil disobedience coordinators in New York City, San Francisco, Boston, St. Louis, Seattle, and Washington, D.C., were all lesbians. Most were white, although some were people of color; most notably, Hispanic organizers played key roles in the preparation and execution of the civil disobedience tactic.

A question may be raised: How did lesbians gain such strong national leadership in the march and civil disobedience actions of October 1987? Historically, in the United States, gay men have tended to relegate lesbians to subordinate and invisible positions within the movement, a fate not uncommon to many gender-integrated movements. Several explanations emerge. First, the gender-parity policy really worked in practice. Second, the AIDS epidemic in the gay male community may have allowed or forced women to take the lead, as the death and disabling of men usually does in times of national crisis (e.g. war, revolution). Third, a very seasoned group of lesbian feminist local activists linked up for the first time to pool all the political skills they had learned from working in every civil rights and social justice movement of the 1960s, 1970s, and 1980s. This created the first national lesbian leadership pool working solely on lesbian protest issues. Finally, when given an opportunity, lesbians tend to be disproportionately represented among women leaders. That is, estimates place the gay population (men and women combined) at about 10 percent of the total population. Yet, in my twenty years of participant observation, the number of lesbian leaders in gender-integrated movements where women are allowed to lead appears to be much higher than 10 percent.[6] Clearly, further research is needed to illumine this rarely discussed topic.

THE POLITICS OF AIDS AND GENDER

In some ways, the AIDS epidemic has left the old political agenda of "gay" civil rights up to lesbian leadership. For example, the 1987 lesbian/gay civil rights ordinance that passed in Boulder, Colorado, was led to victory by lesbian organizers.

Both the mass media and the medical establishment have exacerbated distortions about AIDS, especially in the early AIDS period (1981–87). Both spread the misconception that AIDS was a "homosexual disease" or a "disease caused by homosexuality," even as the U.S. Centers for Disease Control announced that lesbians are at zero risk of AIDS (Gross 1987). New York City health statistics supported this generalization. In 1987, the Greater New York Blood Program secretly conducted a blood drive among lesbians in the city; the results revealed that lesbians who were non-IV drug users had the lowest statistical probability of being contaminated with the HIV virus of all sexually active adults. It did not, however, make these results public.

The important question within the framework of the politics of AIDS and gender is: Why was the public never told this? The suppression of information about lesbians and AIDS, and the historic sexism and homophobic controls that have kept lesbians invisible, have skewed information available about the very low probability of their being contaminated. All homosexuals have been scapegoated by the right wing. As I have noted elsewhere (Cavin 1987:30),

> this phenomenon is part of a much broader sexist tendency to either: 1) lump lesbians and gay men together as a homogeneous, undifferentiated mass called "homosexuals" in the same way that uninformed writers lump women and men together, study the men, assume that women are the same and call it a study of "human nature"; or 2) unconsciously use the term "homosexual" or "gay" to really mean male—ignoring the existence of lesbians altogether.

In fact, one political side effect of AIDS has been to increase lesbian invisibility within the gay movement.

Interestingly, lesbians did not choose to make a public issue of the fact that they were different sexually from gay men for fear of being divisive within the lesbian/gay community while it was under ferocious attack from outside. In addition, most lesbians wanted to display public solidarity with their besieged brothers by standing by them in their hour of need. But privately, lesbians expressed outrage at the careless sexism of the press.

Although the AIDS epidemic has been and continues to be a very difficult and painful period for gays and lesbians and the movement as a whole, it has had some positive effects from a social change perspective. Most importantly, the epidemic has altered social norms and traditions of public discourse about sexual preferences and forced recognition of the oppression of homosexuals in our society. First, it has achieved what the lesbian/gay movement never did: the almost daily mention of the taboo words ("gay," "homosexual") in the national news, albeit a negative mention. (To the invisible, a negative mention is better than no mention at all.) The fact is that the AIDS epidemic has compelled a homophobic society to modify its rules about language. Second, because of the AIDS crisis, explicit descriptions of gay male sex acts have been taught to nongay audiences. Regardless of the established taboos, the overriding fear of the consequences of AIDS has impelled some in authority to expand the boundaries of what is acceptable information in daily discourse. Third, AIDS has revealed to the public that the gay community in major metropolitan areas has organized institutions to take care of its own. Fourth, AIDS has broken asunder the liberal argument that liberals and gays are not really oppressed and therefore do not need legal protection. Fifth, the violence and bigotry against gays and lesbians engendered by AIDS in the 1980s (e.g., the burning down of homes of children with AIDS in Florida) has turned the more moderate sector of society from indifference to sympathy and sometimes to outright support. Thus as noted in other movements, extremism and heightened outside pressures sometimes paradoxically serve to mobilize new resources. The politics of AIDS within the society (the right-wing repression and open scapegoating of lesbians and gay men) has actually increased the ranks of protest and brought more people out of the closet than ever before. AIDS has been a defeat so negative that something positive emerged out of it.

In sum, AIDS has already altered and will continue to alter the lesbian/gay protest movement in profound ways. First, growing numbers of gay men are joining AIDS protests and leaving the traditional civil rights agenda of the movement more up to lesbian leadership than ever before. Second, the sex ratios of the leadership and the rank and file of the protest movement may be greatly altered in the coming years. Third, the invisibility of lesbians within the movement appears to be on the rise, particularly as reported by mainstream journalists and scholars, in spite of their increased prominence as leaders. Fourth, AIDS has changed the priorities within the gay movement, creating internal tensions. It has polarized the priorities of gay men and lesbians. For example, the issue of sexism is not a priority for most gay men but is a top priority for lesbian feminists working in mixed-gender groups. Finally, given all these complex gender divisions within the gay movement, several prominent gay activists with AIDS have publicly recognized the important role of lesbians and other women in support services for people with AIDS (PWAs). They have even gone so far as to suggest that lesbians and other women have been less likely to abandon men with AIDS than have men, gay or straight. This is one more fascinating, yet painful, complexity in the relationships between gender, sexuality, and AIDS. An interesting question to be explored is why women have been so supportive despite rising tensions. Some of this female support is obviously attributable to the traditional gender socialization of women to nurture and care for the sick. Another possible explanation is that lesbians face the contradiction that they are scapegoated as people with AIDS and yet are physically well. This paradox seems to draw lesbians into AIDS protest and support groups.

SUMMARY AND CONCLUSIONS

This paper has examined the origins, theories, and strategies of lesbian protests in the United States and described the impact of the AIDS epidemic on the gender politics within the movement. The lesbian and gay protest, emerging in the late 1960s, gained momentum, visibility, and power within the political arena as it organized collectively to confront authorities on various fronts. Using a range of strategies—from direct action, electoral politics, and legal redress in the courts—lesbians were in the vanguard of the collective struggle to demand their civil rights and to establish themselves as a political force to be reckoned with by those in power. At the same time, lesbians had to organize and protest against the continuing oppression by gay men within the movement. The schisms and traditional sexist hierarchies contributed to the invisibility of lesbians in these protests and distorted the reality of their contributions and goals.

In conclusion, the increasing trend toward unity between lesbians and gay men, reflected in the cooperative efforts during the mobilization for the national march on Washington in 1987, can be explained in part as the result of rising attacks by the right-wingers who used AIDS hysteria to exacerbate homophobia in the Reagan years. As the entire political spectrum shifted to the right in this decade, the lines between radicals and liberals blurred. Radicals within the gay and feminist movements began to support liberal issues as liberals shifted to support the previous positions of moderates. In other words, everyone seems to have moved one step to the right. Radical lesbian separatists, who previously refused to work with liberal gay men in the 1970s (Marotta 1981), came back to the gay fold to band together against the right-wing threat of annihilation. Thus the increasingly hostile political climate within society toward homosexuals in the 1980s seems to have resulted in greater cooperation and unity within the movement.

The alliance between lesbians and gay men forged as a result of these outside attacks, however, appears to be internally fragile because it is essentially "a one-way-street" phenomenon; that is, lesbians feel that they support gay men's issues around AIDS, but most gay men do not support feminist health issues, such as abortion. Lesbians essentially face the same sexist problems with gay men that other women face in all gender-integrated movements. A public curtain has been drawn over these issues for the sake of unity, given the increasing attacks, in much the same way that women of color have often had to repress their internal problems with men of color for the sake of movement unity. How long lesbians and other women will continue to keep gender issues on the back burner, ironically in order to preserve gender-integrated movements, may depend on how long the external right-wing attack continues and how long the AIDS epidemic is viewed as the highest priority by those in decision-making positions within the movement.

Finally, it must be noted that the study of lesbian protest teaches us that the definition of feminist protest must be expanded to include coming out publicly as one's private self. This is a political act. Celebrating a woman-identified-woman identity in a male-identified society is a legitimate form of social protest that requires further research. This much is clear: breaking lesbian invisibility is always the central ingredient of lesbian feminist protest.

NOTES

1. Several other U.S. movements that lesbians tend to join are the animal rights, labor, New Left, Native American, Puerto Rican independence, Chicano, farm workers, prisoners' rights, anti–U.S. intervention, anti-apartheid, and differently abled movements, where a disproportionately high number of lesbian organizers work behind the scenes. For homophobic reasons, most of these movements tend to keep their lesbian membership a secret.

2. Although Bunch and Myron (1975) connected sexism, homophobia, and classism, lesbians of color gave the movement insight about racism, homophobia, and "passing." See Bethel and Smith (1979); Clarke (1983); Cliff (1980); Lorde in Cavin (1983); Moraga and Anzaldua (1981); Roberts (1981).

3. I theorize that lesbians and gays are a sexuality caste because heterosexist society views them as ritually unclean, impure, and thus excluded from the religious performance of purifying rituals (e.g., the Catholic Church's expulsion of Dignity, a gay Catholic group). Judy Grahn (1984) views lesbian/gay culture as tribal, with an oral tradition and rites of passage; she also refers to the gay tribe as "an underground."

4. However, Martin and Lyon (1988) believe that the gay/lesbian liberation movement "started before Stonewall . . . in 1950 in Los Angeles with the Mattachine Foundation, *One* magazine in 1953, then Daughters of Bilitis (DOB) in 1955," which was founded by Martin and Lyon.

5. A record high of 7,008 antigay violence incidents were reported to the National Gay and Lesbian Task Force in 1987, compared with 4,946 incidents in 1986 across the United States (NGLTF 1987). According to the 1987 report of the National Institute of Justice (Finn and McNeil 1987), "The most frequent victims of hate violence today are Lesbians, Gay Men, Blacks, Hispanics, Southeast Asians, and Jews. Lesbians and gay men are probably the most frequent victims."

6. Astute political observers have noted a disproportionately high number of lesbians among political radicals in general. The question why needs further research. The most common analysis suggests that lesbians suffer from at least two oppressions:

sexism and homophobia. Some say that "lesbianphobia" is a third kind of oppression in its own right. "Lesbianphobia" defines lesbians as "angry and sick . . . cantankerous . . . just refusing to cooperate." People who are lesbianphobic, when they see something lesbian (e.g., a book, film, or person), feel "an absolute horror . . . the outrage that is suddenly there, that you dare to bring this material to them. But it's not always anger. Sometimes they laugh at you . . . like geeks on display" (Kron, a lesbian comic, interviewed by Stone 1988).

CHAPTER 18

Dance, Protest, and Women's "Wars": Cases from Nigeria and the United States

JUDITH LYNNE HANNA

Can the arts be a vehicle of social protest? What is their potential? their potency? Western theater theory and history are replete with recognition of the power of the arts to move and persuade (Carlson 1984).

Aristotle, whose *Poetics* is a central reference point, wrote about the dangerous potential of the arts (which included dance in Greek theater) to arouse people and thereby subvert the state and religion. The Christian church, also fearing the passion of dance, nevertheless used the arts to instruct and delight in the Middle Ages. Many governments have harnessed the arts in service of the state. George Bernard Shaw believed the aim of the arts should be didactic: telling truths society would rather not hear. Conceiving the goal of theater to be educative, Bertolt Brecht argued that it could intervene in history by explaining that the world can be other than it is and altering spectators' consciousness. Somewhat in agreement, Antonin Artaud viewed theater as an instrument of revolution to reorder human existence. In a similar vein, Jean-Paul Sartre considered dramatic creation a process of commitment dealing with rights. Herbert Blau stated that theater should be a forum pitted against the outrages humanity commits upon itself. Another theorist, Wolfgang Wildescheimer, suggested dramatic creations may be indirectly moving as symbolic ceremonials in which the spectator assumes the role of questioner to a performance that gives no reasonable response but leaves the spectator to decide.

Herein theater is broadly conceived as performance that includes all kinds of "stages"—from proscenium to village compound.

What about the specific potential and potency of dance as a medium of protest? First, what kind of art is dance? On the basis of a worldwide survey of behavior generally called dance, we can say dance has these elements: purpose, from the dancer's perspective, which is usually shared by the audience members of the dancer's culture; intentional rhythm; culturally patterned sequences; use of extraordinary nonverbal movement with inherent and aesthetic value; manifestation through the body instrument in time, in space,

and with effort; an interactive dynamic process; and transformational potential (this conceptualization is elaborated in Hanna 1979a, 1979b, 1983a, 1983b,
1987a).

Dance is communicative behavior, a "text in motion" or "body language."
A physical instrument or symbol for feeling and thought, dance is sometimes
a more effective medium than verbal language in revealing needs and desires.
Humans are multisensory. Occasionally they verbalize and listen; more often,
they act and watch or feel. Movements in dance become standardized, patterned symbols understood by members of a society to express and communicate experiences in the external and psychic world.

Dance is also one of the means by which human groups identify themselves. It is often part of a culture's inventory of signs to promote self-identity,
prescribe and assert social values and roles, mediate between persons and
their situations, evoke emotion, and rally people to action. Since early humankind, we have evidence of the use of dance to help individuals and groups
explore the spectrum of possibilities for coping with life (Hanna 1988b).

Both reflecting and influencing society, dance is a "safe" arena to play with
the dangerous and to explore the unknown without the consequences of real-
life risks and failures. For example, Western ballet conveys fairy tales and
contemporary narratives from *Cinderella* (treating problems of equity and growing up) to *A Soldier's Tale* or *Green Table* (both dealing with horrors of war and
hypocrisy). Dance portrays the range of emotions and human relationships
such as "prince and princess" coming together, parent and child parrying, or
males touching and lifting each other. As people confront changing sex roles,
they can see issues of the gender gap played out when men dance the step-
sisters in Mikhail Baryshnikov and Peter Anastos's production of *Cinderella* and
the queen in Paul Taylor's *Snow White,* women catch men who leap through the
air, and male and female performers dress alike and dance the same movements in the same style in other dances (Hanna 1987a, 1987b, 1988a).

Whether ritual, social, or theater art, dance has important yet little recognized potential for influencing attitudes and behavior. The Puritan and Industrial Revolution heritage diverted attention from the study of dance because
its instrument, the body, had to be harnessed or denied in service of economic
morality and productivity. However, we now know that dance, part of the
cultural communication system that is one means of adaptation to an environment, may convey information purposefully or serve as an open channel.
Shared knowledge about the form, experience in its use, and notions about
when, where, how, and why messages are sent, as well as information sufficiently lucid to be perceived through surrounding distractions or impedi-
ments, are conditions for effectiveness (Hanna 1983b).

The power of dance lies in its cognitive-sensorimotor and aesthetic capabil-
ity to create moods, motivations, and guideposts for performer and spectator
alike. Motion, research indicates (Arnheim 1954:361; 1969), has the strongest
visual appeal to attention, for it implies a change in the conditions of the
environment which may require reaction. In contrast with the ritualized displays of other animals, humans not only express immediate emotion, drive,
and autonomic rhythms, but also communicate abstract concepts, removed

from an immediate stimulus, distanced in time and space and in deliberately chosen rhythms, as well as transform experience symbolically using various devices of encoding meaning. Note that dance is more like poetry (with its multiple, symbolic, and elusive meanings) than prose.

Moreover, the body, instrument of dance, is the first means of human power, with which everyone can identify. For women, the body also has the power of creativity and change. They bear human life and direct it.

From Africa to America, one can find illustrations of women's use of dance as social protest. (It should be noted that through history men, too, have used the dance as a medium of social protest [Hanna 1987c, 1988a, 1988b]). I will present a case of dramatic social dance from Nigeria and a case of theater dance from the United States. Conducting field research in another society can lead one to a different perception of processes in one's own. In a culture relatively new to literacy, where the arts and society intermesh, it is not surprising to find informal media of communication and protest through dance, with influence similar to the institutions of school, press, and television. However, in Western society, where dance is relegated to the separate realms of art, entertainment, and recreation, finding dance as a medium of social protest and a mechanism to empower women or engender a sense of empowerment is unexpected.

Yet in disparate continents, societies, and cultures, women's issues, goals, targets, and strategies were similar. African and American women told their stories and expressed their feelings and visions through dance. Although they experienced male control of knowledge, they independently conveyed knowledge visually, and sometimes also verbally, through the performances they put on. The women danced to articulate problems about the general condition of women and to protest against matters that directly threatened them. Through means at their disposal, they combated the tendency to be overlooked and ignored by male-dominated structures. The dance groups became conscious collective efforts to bring about change. Dance performance took place through the initiative of women's voluntary associations.

Of course, there were differences in the use of dance as social protest. Nigerian women responded to a specific perceived lack of control over their economic situation, whereas American women reacted to a general lack of economic power as well as dominance over their own bodies. In addition, they also focused on broader issues of war and poverty that affected both men and women. In Nigeria, women's voluntary associations have a long-standing kin-based tradition dating to precolonial times, whereas in the United States, the dance associations were newly constituted small groups of nonrelated elite women. In contrast with Nigerian women's nearly captive audiences, American women had to build audiences.

THE NIGERIAN "WOMEN'S WAR"

What level of power do Ubakala Igbo women of eastern Nigeria (now Imo State) have when their society traditionally requires them to leave their birthplace to live among strangers in a situation that excludes them from formal political and religious decision making? The answer is dance! And when the messages of the dance go unheeded, the women have been known to resort to less peaceful persuasion. The Nigerian Women's War of 1929, which I describe later, is the most notable case.

The Ubakala people trace family descent on the father's side. Women leave their natal home upon marriage to live among their husband's kin, many of whom may be strangers. Another indicator of apparent male domination is the exclusion of women from the formal, traditional political and ritual decision-making bodies. Most women's activities center on the domestic scene, agricultural fields, and market network.

However, Ubakala women are not merely subordinate domestic creatures of exchange and family alliances. They also provide men with mates, privileges in a new group (husbands gain special support from a wife's family), and labor. The Ubakala recognize that female fertility and energies complement male virility and strength in human and economic production. Furthermore, women have prestige and power apart from that of their husbands: achieving wealth, developing persuasive verbal eloquence, and bearing many offspring are indicators of a woman's success. With these assets, women past menopause may even attend men's political meetings if they choose. Women have their own groups and leaders who are considered powerful among both themselves and the men. Moreover, women may assert themselves and become especially visible in dance-play performance.

With its requisite components of music, song or theme, and dance, the dance-play is similar to Western opera in having several channels of communication. There are various genres of dance-plays with specific participants, occasions, purposes, functions, movements, accompaniment, and costume. For example, there are dance-plays for young single-sex groups, coeds, families of a deceased, and elite male societies (Hanna 1976, 1987a). The occasions for these dance-plays—birth, death, harvest, markets, visits by dignitaries, and religious celebrations—provide a virtually captive audience. Ubakala women knowingly use the dance-play to assert and laud their creative power as mothers, lineage maintainers, and family integrators. They also self-consciously use the dance-play for political power.

Three kinds of dance-plays focus on women's special creative powers. One kind is the dance-play for the birth of a child. The performance takes place immediately after a normal healthy child is born, and again when the child has survived for one year. The performers are married women from the compound of the new infant's father who are at least fifteen years old and have themselves given birth and achieved the status of womanhood. Using movements and song text that clarify the meaning of the movement, these women glorify fertility and generously praise childbearing women and midwives. After performing for about three hours at the father's home, they move on—dancing, singing, and playing along the way—to the compound of the mother's parents where they perform again, informing all of the blessed event.

Thus the women contribute to enhancing group and society-wide emotional bonds. Families unite to celebrate the birth of a new member. Women contribute by introducing the young and reminding adults of Ubakala values. Song lyrics suggest these—for example, "Praise to the expert in bearing children." Husbands are advised in song: "Whether or not I know how to behave, exercise patience and live with me"; and "An old woman whose beauty is fading away is not seen" (suggesting that husbands should behave properly even after the beauty of youth has passed). "My grandmother, the birth has cleaned my perspiration," refers to women caring well for their children so that they may participate in the parent's second burial. This final mortuary rite, sometime after interment, assists the deceased on his or her journey to the land of the ancestors.

A second kind of dance-play focusing on women's creative power is performed after the death of an important aged woman. The deceased would have lived at least to the age of seventy, borne many children, and become independently wealthy through trade in agricultural products or some craft items. This dance-play eulogizes, propitiates, and shows respect for the deceased on behalf of her kin. The spirit of the deceased is believed to exist in limbo between living and ancestral states—perhaps wreaking havoc upon living kin instead of joining other ancestors—until the performance of the second burial. Ancestors are believed to be reincarnated later. The ancestors may interfere in politics, punish persons who misbehave on earth, and intercede on their living kin's behalf before the supreme deity. The relatives of the deceased are invited to the second burial, and anyone may join the dancing, although the primary performers are the close female relatives, some of whom may travel long distances for the occasion. Once again, lineages unite.

A third kind of dance-play that stresses women's power is the "outsider" relations' society dance-play. This society originated as an expression of unity by related women who marry into the same village. Their goals are to rejoice in the fact that they have children, to confront the problems of family life jointly, to share economic resources, and to affirm friendships among married women originally from the same village. Living as they do among "strangers," and having little part in formal political and religious activities, women who hail from the same village seek one another out. This can be seen as their attempt as "outsiders" to counter the bonds of blood and kin that bind their husbands. These women especially use the dance-play to adjust wrongdoings and work through the contradictions of social life. This dance-play centers on women's creative and political powers.

Fundamental and sometimes conflicting, Ubakala values move people to social actions (Turner 1974). An emphasis on individualistic competition and achievement is juxtaposed with the need for cooperation and interdependence (community spirit, group solidarity, and sharing the wealth; personal aggrandizement is not emphasized). The desire for and expectation of change often run counter to the principle of respect for authority, which is largely based on seniority. Innovation generally involves criticism or rejection of what those older than oneself have established. The principle of respect and obedience to leaders is opposed both to the egalitarian distaste for assertive authority and to the norm of bringing things into the open.

The pursuit of one part of a pair of opposites to the exclusion of the other creates an imbalance, a dilemma, and a social drama. When one value is expressed such that it violates another equally valid value and an individual or a group feels threatened and desires to contain, modify, or reverse it, the dance-play mediates between persons and their situations (in much the same way as speech mediates between persons and their situations or a shaman mediates unbalanced forces in a healing ritual).

Mediation refers to reconciling action. The dance-play mediates social relations and political situations by encapsulating the issues and phases of social dramas. The four phases of social drama are (1) a breach of the norms of a social group, (2) a mounting crisis, (3) a legal or ritual redressive process, and (4) public and symbolic expression of an irreparable schism or conciliation (Turner 1974). Accordingly, the dance-play may communicate the breach, foment the crisis, ameliorate the conflict (or at least hold it in suspension so that it is present, viewable, and ponderable), and proclaim the schism or celebrate the reintegration.

The Ubakala allow a special kind of license in the dance-play that protects the individual and the group from libel. But the dance-play has the potential for more than letting off steam or catharsis; it can guard against the misuse of power and produce social change without violence. However, dance-play messages are often implicit, and a symbolic system is a weak vehicle of control unless enforcement is implied. The dance-play is a political form of coercion in a shame-oriented society. Energy (force), the ultimate means of social control, is symbolically related.

The famous 1929 "Women's War," in which the dance-play communication went unheeded, illustrates the potential of this women's medium. Repercussions of this spectacular protest movement of women's resistance to male dominance and the imposition of colonial practices were widespread on both local and intercontinental levels. Contemporary politicians and leaders refer to this notorious episode of feminine protest (Gailey [1970] provides one of the fullest accounts) as reason for considering women's views. They remember how the women moved the mighty British to alter their colonial administration of eastern Nigeria. (O'Barr [1984] and Wipper [1984] report other patterns of African women's protest using the dance strategy. See Hanna [1988c] on African Americans' protest against white dominance.)

Njaka (1974:22) argues that women's intrusion in the affairs of state and their imposition of sanctions makes them the custodians of the "constitution." Because women marry outside the village group into which they were born, their kin organization cuts across and goes beyond any one level of political structure. The organization is thus potentially powerful in rallying numerous groupings behind any single member.

The women's dance-play as a boycott is sometimes called "sitting on a man" (Van Allen 1972). The aggrieved gather at the compound of an offender and dance and sing to detail the problem. Movement presents a dynamic image emphasizing the argument as well as releasing and generating physical and psychological energy and tension. The accompanying song, with its potent ridicule and satire, serves as a vehicle for specific social criticism.

The British colonial government of Nigeria was generally aware of the potential for public disturbance in this cultural expression. Thus its native council was empowered by the 1901 Proclamation, Section 36(3) to regulate "native plays . . . [gatherings] of natives in any public street or market, or in any house, building, or in any compound adjoining a public street or market for the purpose of dancing or playing native music" (City Ordinance 591/2, in Nwabara 1965:188–89). In some areas, licenses and permission from the British district commissioner were necessary to hold plays.

A breach of understanding between women and the colonial government began the first phase of the Women's War social drama. In 1928, the British government introduced taxation applicable to men. Late in 1929, women incorrectly believed that this tax was to be extended to them. This misunderstanding signaled the beginning of an example of "sex solidarity and political power which women can exercise when they choose to do so" (Meek 1937:201). The women viewed taxation as an infringement on their economic competitive patterns. In the latter part of the nineteenth century, women started to amass considerable wealth from the growing trade in palm kernels, a woman's crop. Not appreciating the economic and political position of women, the British attempted to focus hitherto diffuse power on colonial government–appointed Nigerian male warrant chiefs. Since women had not become representatives of the colonial government, as Nigerian men had, they did not see the benefits from the imposition of taxes. The women's economic and political grievances coalesced. Women were aggrieved by the European control of market prices and what the women considered abusive and extortionist practices of many warrant chiefs (for example, some obtained wives without paying full bride wealth; others took property improperly).

In the midst of a depression era, the effects of which hurt women, the spark igniting the conflagration was supplied by a young British assistant district officer in Bende Division. (This was the same division where the district officer A. L. Weir, deceived the people in 1927 about the purpose of the initial tax census.) Because census registers were incomplete and inaccurate, the administrative officers were supposed to revise the initial counts in their spare time. In October, Captain John Cook (who had taken over from Weir) decided on his own authority to obtain information on the number of men, women, children, and livestock.

The massive protest was incited when Warrant Chief Okugo, of Oloko Village near the town of Aba, employed a schoolteacher, Mark Emeruwa, to take charge of the census. Inquiring about the possessions of a local woman, Nwanyeruwa, the messenger engaged in argument and physical scuffle with her. She then reported the incident to her village women's meeting.

A mounting crisis as women gathered to discuss what had occurred marked the second phase of the social drama. The alarmed women sent palm leaves, symbols of warning and distress, to women of neighboring and distant villages summoning them to Okoko to join the protest. Women from far and near, even pregnant women, met in the Okoko square on November 24.

The third stage was the potentially redressive process of "sitting on a man," which usually works to resolve conflicts. (The audience-captivating dance-play medium serves as a socially acceptable vehicle to express displeasure about something and has the effect of catalyzing people to act to ameliorate the cause of dissatisfaction.) The irate women trooped to the mission that employed Emeruwa, the chief's messenger, to demonstrate against him. They camped in front of his compound at the Niger Delta Mission and "sat on him"—the man was kept from sleeping and carrying out his usual tasks. They danced and sang outside the mission compound all night, eating, drinking palm wine, and singing that Nwanyeruwa had been told to count her goats, sheep, and people (Nwabara 1965:231). A song was quickly improvised to meet the situation. The women sent their message. Yet no satisfactory response was forthcoming.

The next day, with the problem still unresolved, the social drama reached the schism phase. The women became more excited and went to the chief's compound. They besieged Chief Okugo at his house and demanded his cap of office, symbol of authority. He escaped to seek refuge on the Native Court compound. Captain Cook met over 25,000 women in the market to assure them they were not to be taxed; however, the women insisted that Chief Okugo and Emeruwa be arrested and tried.

The women were skeptical of government assurances that they were not to be taxed, and their rampages began to spread. Late in December, the women forced the Umuahia warrant chiefs to surrender their caps. In Aba, women sang and danced to no avail about their antipathy toward the chiefs and the court messengers. Then they proceeded to attack and loot the European trading stores and Barclays Bank and to break into the prison and release the prisoners (Perham 1937: 208).

The riots spread, involving about 10,000 women in 2 provinces. Destruction was directed primarily toward the warrant chiefs and buildings representing this detested authority. Finally, in panic the British authorities called troops and police into the area. The most extreme violence was triggered by a car accident and heated passions. In the town of Opobo in Calabar Province, the police opened fire in one of the worst episodes; thirty-two women were killed and thirty-one wounded (Nigerian Government Reports 1930a, 1930b; Perham 1937:206–20; Onwuteaka 1965). News of the slaughter spread, and local disturbances persisted well into 1930.

The women's rapid mobilization was possible because of their strong societal organizations and effective communication networks based on concentration in the markets and dispersal along the trade routes. Colonial government reorganizations in 1930 and 1931 followed reports of two commissions of inquiry and anthropological study. The women succeeded in their destruction of the warrant chief system. The cost would have been less had the audience been more attentive initially. Thus the contemporary women's dance-play performance serves as a metaphor for their power (Hanna 1979b).

Related to the memories or stories of dramatic instances of unheeded dance-plays is a dynamic concept of play that may help to explain the role of the dance-play in conflict management. Schechner (1973:28–36) builds on the concepts of Huizinga (1955) and Loizos (1969) concerning play. However, he rejects Huizinga's exclusion of function in the concept of play and accepts the possibilities of play as a school or practice, a safe arena for exploring beyond the known or working through problems, an exercise of mental or physical faculties. He suggests that play has survival value in that it is derived from life situations of flight, fight, sexual, and eating behavior. Schechner points out that play maintains a "regular, crisis-oriented expenditure of kinetic energy" that can be "switched from play energy into crisis or flight energy."

In presenting this case of women's social protest, I have tried to suggest that although Ubakala men dominate the traditional political organization and ritual of the egalitarian society, the women also have power. They perpetuate the husband's lineage, integrate villages through marriage ties, and mediate imbalances in social life as viewed from the perspective of Ubakala values. The women express their wishes and power in dance-plays. They can transform these performances into usually persuasive boycotts called "sitting on a man" and dance and sing their grievances. However, when their dance-play communication goes unheeded in both a usual performance and a boycott, the woman can switch from playfully dancing to violently waging war—their ultimate means of enforcing their will. The 1929 Women's War was a dramatic extension of the traditional method women used to settle grievances with men who acted badly toward them.

AN AMERICAN REVOLUTION

In the United States, women as a group have been subject to prejudice and discrimination. Some have sought escape from social and economic constraints through theatrical "high art" dance. Note that dance can be a metaphor of existence, for life is movement.

A sketch of some key facts in the history of ballet and the situation of women is relevant to an understanding of women's social protest through dance. Men have dominated classical ballet since its origin in France during the time of Louis XIV. They controlled the technical relations of production (how work is organized by the sexual division of labor) and social relations of production (allocation of resources) as well as artistic decisions. At first, men danced both male and female roles. Then women began to appear onstage, and by the mid-eighteenth century Romantic period—when Marie Taglioni established a foothold for women by elevating herself *en pointe*, a special nonmale prowess—women were in the spotlight. Nonetheless, they continued to be directed from backstage by male producers, choreographers, and ballet masters.

The French Revolution and the Industrial Revolution dealt serious blows to the esteem of physical activity and male dancing. As the importance of dance declined, men abnegated the dance profession. Although women gained more opportunities, their public dancing marked them as part of the demimonde or echelons of prostitution. Until the mid-twentieth century, female performers generally came from the lower classes. For an attractive girl, dancing could be an avenue of social mobility, an alternative to sweatshops, agriculture, or domestic work. The ballet "leg show" enticed wealthy men who relished the sight and fell in love with the beautiful dancers, enduring their punishing rejection and begging their rewards of intimacy. Becoming mistress to a wealthy man usually meant success and the option of leaving the stage. Some less fortunate dancers in the "parade" left the theater to become teachers or common prostitutes.

Gordon (1983:13 passim) notes that contemporary ballet choreographers and directors—"almost always male—mold ballet's young women to the idea of feminine that equates beauty and grace with excessive thinness," an aesthetic that is punitive and misogynist. The men treat dancers like children, calling them "girls" or "kids," school them in obedience and deference, and ignore the fact that relentless pursuit of the unnatural "ideal" female body arrests puberty, imbalances hormones, contributes to hypothermia and low blood pressure, and often leads to psychosomatic disorders of starvation, vomiting, and the use of laxatives. Anorexia and injury are interconnected.

Modern dance, a new form of theater art in rebellion against male-dominated ballet, was birthed and nurtured by women. The advent of pioneers from the educated middle class, such as Ruth St. Denis and Martha Graham, both of whose parents were trained in medicine, and, later, women's introduction of dance to universities helped to make dance respectable.

The turn-of-the-century modern dance was in part a rebellion against male domination in both dance and society. Role strain characterized the Victorian era, a period of rapid change. While men were expected to be sexually aggressive, the middle class was at the same time expected to be self-denying in order to serve the need of the bureaucratized industrial society of managers, professionals, and entrepreneurs. Charles Rosenberg (1973:243) speaks of the expository metaphor of the mercantilist body, an image of "a closed energy system, which could be either weakened through the discharge of energy or strengthened through its prudent husbanding." The work imperative demanded that men bottle up emotion, repress sex, and regulate population. Women's bodies were viewed as being thoroughly saturated with sexuality and governed by sex-linked irrationality (Foucault 1978:6).

Slotted in this way, daring women in the nineteenth and twentieth centuries, who were cut off from male prerogatives in society, economy, and polity, took advantage of the emotional behavior attributed to their gender: they acted emotionally through the physical medium of dance. Note that the cognitive aspects of dance went unrecognized until recently (Hanna 1983a). Men generally manifested emotion indirectly through other more "intellectual" arts that use the body indirectly, through, for example, a pen or paintbrush.

One thrust of women's critique of the nineteenth-century system that excluded them from key economic and political roles and relegated them to the home and the realm of morals was modern dance. Women looked to themselves for inspiration as they chose to be agents rather than objects and formed female-dominated dance companies similar to the small businesses that ethnic groups owned, governed, and found to be vital instruments of upward mobility. Women had to be as econmically astute, competitive, and strong as a man would be.

From a cross-cultural perspective, Rosaldo (1974:71) notes that women appear oppressed or lacking in value and status to the extent that they are relegated to the domestic world: "Women gain power and a sense of value when they are able to transcend domestic limits, either by entering the men's world or by creating a society." Emphatically beyond traditional domestic life, theater dance epitomizes a public role.

Women had also been constrained physically by the male-imposed style of dress that distorted the body and hampered natural movement. Moreover, women received restricted education and were taught health practices that prevented getting fresh air and a sensible diet. Innovative female choreographers with strong personal character displayed their displeasure with traditional roles when they broke the rules of the rigidly codified traditional ballet to extend the boundaries of dance with the creation of revolutionary movement vocabularies, grammars, composition techniques, and themes as well as new costumes. Women offered new dance systems and images alongside the *danse d'école* developed by men. The dance medium also permitted women to control and sublimate their sexuality, which had been dominated by men. To get ahead in an uncharted avant-garde, some women had a nun-like dedication; other respectable middle-class women had love affairs in and out of marriage in a manifestation of their new sense of social and sexual equality; and some had lesbian relations.

Asserting themselves as individuals against traditional female destiny, ground-breaking modern dancers through onstage models helped decorset sensually alluring wasp-waisted females. Tight lacing oppressed the body and enforced sexual taboos, whereas unlacing meant sexual release. While the corset worn in ballet helped pull up the body and gave the woman's male partner a good grip when lifting her, it also prevented him from feeling her flesh (Kunzle 1982:84).

What women wore closely mirrored their changing role in American society. The women's rigid silhouette of earlier years collapsed with the quest for changes in feminine education, health, and professional opportunity. Intrigued with the interplay of body, intellect, and spirit, female dancers investigated and experimented. Braless, corsetless, and barefoot, the modern dancer's free style of dress symbolized a host of freedoms and a renewed, diversified self-image. As the twentieth century progressed, taboos on what parts of the body could be seen slowly disappeared.

Modern dancers' aggressiveness paralleled other developments of the late nineteenth and twentieth centuries: women's challenge to patriarchy, the growth of free choice of a spouse, the rise of marital equality and mutual decision making, campaigns for female voting and higher education, and the entry of women into the labor market during and after World War II. Modern dancers extended women's fight to gain control over their own bodies.

Initially women's achievement, modern dance bore their style-setting stamps. Females were choreographers, dancers, company founders, and managers—that is, creators, performers, entrepreneurs, and administrators. They established schools. Harbingers of innovation include Isadora Duncan, Loie Fuller, and Ruth St. Denis; later, Martha Graham, Doris Humphrey, Agnes de Mille (who combines modern and Broadway styles in the ballet idiom); and more recently, Yvonne Rainer, Trisha Brown, Twyla Tharp, Laura Dean, and Lucinda Childs.

Duncan believed ballet projected a socially pernicious image of women: virginal, disembodied sylphide, frail, sexually passive. She denounced the recruitment of dancers from the slums as exploitation of the poor by the rich and a perversion of artistic values in favor of the prurient (1938:49, 56, 69, passim). Considering movement activity in human life to be an antidote to the rigidities of modern life. Duncan, with messianic zeal, founded schools for children.

St. Denis, mother of the most flourishing lineage of modern dance, began her career in the flurry of vaudeville, where she had been performing a number with rapid-fire stunts about eleven times a day on a stage adjacent to the presentation of midgets and two-headed calves in jars. She turned to exotica, for non-Western cultures offered visual beauty and spiritual messages in contrast to Western industrial life. The critique of traditional women's options through new forms of dance was thus in some ways indirect and symbolic; ballet choreographers had also drawn on exotic cultures, but to make their art innovative.

Graham, who began teaching in 1925, redefined the art of dance with innovative movement: stunning, sharp, and percussive patterns of torso contraction (with sucked in pelvic organs) and release (the combination of movements corresponding to life's breathing and sexual tension); twisting and spiraling spinal movements (ballet focused on limbs); parallel and inward-rotated positions of the legs (ballet uses a turn-out); flexed foot (ballet feet are pointed); pelvic isolation; and falls to the floor. Thematically, Graham presented earthy and socially relevant *Sturm und Drang* dynamics dealing with dominance, unbridled passion versus duty, attraction and repulsion, and submerged guilt and open eroticism to counter ballet's ethereal fantasies.

A younger writer and dancer puts into words what has been a resounding feminine theme: "What I have been interested in from a woman's point of view, what I have experienced in my own dancing, is trying to tie up movement with one's own image as a woman" (Luger and Laine 1978:66).

Movements carry the inner feelings and cultural overlays of sexuality and sex role identities. Much of the female choreography centered on heroic women who took fate into their own hands, if only, says Jochen Schmidt (1983:64), "with an axe, like Lizzie Borden in Agnes de Mille's 'Fall River Legend,' who murdered her parents in order to free herself from their rules and strictures." Graham portrayed settler women of America's pioneer history in *Frontier* and *Appalachian Spring*. She also dealt with the great lovers and haters of Greek tragedy.

Contributing to the foundation for the popular androgyny of the 1980s exemplified by singer Michael Jackson, some women such as Ann Halprin and Meredith Monk have fulfilled their gender movement impulses and gone on to express the male and female possibilities within us all in a performance context. That is, either or both sexes do the same movements in abnegation of stereotyped sex-role actions. Monk has also experimented with makeup and costuming to obscure sex identity; for example, she sometimes wears a mustache. Postmodern dance, a rebellion against modern dance developing since the 1960s, has tended to deemphasize sexuality and gender-specific movement. It has grown in tandem with an increasing acceptance of recreational sex and unisex dress and behavior.

Senta Driver's choreography continues with women's early use of weight and power. She extends the latter by reversing dancers' traditional gender roles: her women lift and carry men.

Laine (1983:64) noted a female gender bias in the Brooklyn Academy of Music "New Wave" series (1981–83) of interdisciplinary, collaborative presentations, an avant-garde sequel to postmodern minimalism: "Of eleven programs of produced choreography . . . only one featured male choreographers (Bill T. Jones and Arnie Zane). . . . Can we conclude that modern dance is still dominated by female creativity?"

Female dancers, by no means passive bystanders, have moved to draw on the repertoire of strategies available to them to protest about women's oppression. They have thus challenged the typical male supremacist and female submissive scripts. Women, and some men, now call for men to pay attention to their own bodies and sensuality so that they may discover physical desires apart from a socialized desire to dominate. Moreover, women have also focused on broader issues of war and poverty through dance (Hanna 1988b).

CONCLUSION

I have tried to suggest that the arts, specifically dance, can be a vehicle of social protest. Both theory and empirical evidence call attention to the power of dance in dramatic communication. The Nigerian Women's War in the early twentieth century is a case in point. Dance encapsulated economic and political issues deemed critical to women's condition, and dance marked phases of a social drama that led the British to reevaluate their colonial policy of indirect rule.

Lest one think that dance as protest is only part of the Third World, the case of American modern dance in this century should dispel such thought. Women "lobbied" for their economic, physical, and social well-being through public kinetic, visual images and asserted creative and production control backstage. The dance has served as an arena for exploring alternative processes and roles, critiquing the status quo, and suggesting change.

Although both the Igbo Nigerian and American societies were called "egalitarian," men in each have had more options than women. In Nigeria, the women's call for change through the dance medium had implied enforcement—that is, the evidence of the 1929 episode in which the play of dance became nonplay. Sanctions for women's unheeded dance messages in the United States are hard to document. Yet a key indicator of the potential of dance, with its attention-attracting, language-like, and emotion-evoking qualities to bring about change, is the extent to which totalitarian governments go to control the arts.

NOTE

Parts of this paper are taken from Hanna 1976, 1979a, 1983a, 1987a, 1987b, 1988a.

Bibliography

Abbott, Sidney, and Barbara Love. 1972. *Sappho Was a Right-On Woman*. New York: Stein and Day.

Abernathy, Ralph D. 1971. "The Nonviolent Movement: The Past, the Present and the Future." In Rhoda L. Goldstein, ed., *Black Life and Culture in the United States*. New York: Crowell.

Ackelsberg, Martha. 1985. "Separate and Equal? *Mujeres Libres* and Anarchist Strategy for Women's Emancipation." *Feminist Studies* 11 (Spring): 63–83.

"The Activities of the Women Workers' Council, 1922–23." 1923. *Pinkas Hahistadrut* 5. [In Hebrew]

Adams, Carolyn Teich, and Kathryn Teich Winston. 1980. *Mothers at Work: Public Policies in the United States, Sweden, and China*. New York: Longman.

Addams, Jane. [1917] 1975. *Women at The Hague*. New York: Macmillan.

Adelson, A. 1972. *SDS*. New York: Scribner.

Agosin, Marjorie. 1987. *Scraps of Life: Chilean Arpilleras—Chilean Women and the Pinochet Regime*. Tarfon. N.J.: Red Sea Press.

Alderson, L. 1983. "Greenham Common and All That . . . A Radical Feminist View." In *Breaching the Peace: A Collection of Radical Feminist Papers*. London: Onlywomen Press.

Alpert, Jane. 1973. "Mother Right: A New Feminist Theory." *Ms.* 8 (August).

Altback, Edith Hoshino. 1984. "The New German Women's Movement." *Signs* 9: 454–69.

Altman, Dennis. 1971. *Homosexual Oppression and Liberation*. New York: Outerbridge and Dienstfrey.

Alvarado, Elvia. 1987. *Don't Be Afraid, Gringo: A Honduran Woman Speaks from the Heart*. Translated and edited by Medea Benjamin. San Francisco: Institute for Food and Development Policy.

AMES (The Association of Salvadoran Women). 1982. "Participation of Latin American Women in Social and Political Organizations: Reflections of Salvadoran Women." *Monthly Review* 34 (June): 11–23.

AMNLAE (Luisa Amanda Espinoza Association of Nicaraguan Women). 1982. "Our Participation in the Economy." In Women's International Resource Exchange, *Nicaraguan Women and the Revolution*. New York: Women's International Resource Exchange.

Amos, Debra. 1988. "Palestinian Women in the West Bank Struggle" [Radio news report]. "Morning Edition" [National Public Radio]. May 16.

AMPRONAC (The Association of Women Confronting the National Problem). 1982. "Nicaraguan Women: Struggle for a Free Homeland." In Women's International Resource Exchange. *Nicaraguan Women and the Revolution*. New York: Women's International Resource Exchange.

Anderson, Olive San Louie (Sola). 1878. *An American Girl. and Her Four Years in a Boys' College*. New York: Appleton.

Andors, Phyllis. 1983. *The Unfinished Liberation of Chinese Women, 1949–1980*. Bloomington: Indiana University Press.

Andreas, Carol. 1985. *When Women Rebel: The Rise of Popular Feminism in Peru.* New York: Macmillan.

Appalachian Land Ownership Task Force. 1983. *Who Owns Appalachia: Landownership and Its Impact.* Lexington: University Press of Kentucky.

Appalachian Regional Commission. 1964. *Appalachia.* Washington, D.C.: Government Printing Office.

AppalShop. 1986. "Mine War on Blackberry Creek" [AppalShop Headwaters television series]. (Videotape, VHS, 28 min., 30 sec.). Whitesburg, Ky.: AppalShop.

Arbor, J. Edward. 1935. "Upon This Rock." *Crisis* (April): 110–11.

Ardery, Julia S., ed. 1983. *Welcome the Traveler Home: Jim Garland's Story of the Kentucky Mountains.* Lexington: University Press of Kentucky.

Armstrong, Robert. 1982. "The Revolution Stumbles." *NACLA Report on the Americas* 16 (March–April): 23–30.

Armstrong, Robert, and Janet Shenk. 1980. "There's a War Going On." *NACLA Report on the Americas* 14 (July–August): 20–36.

Arnheim, Rudolf. 1954. *Art and Visual Perception.* Berkeley: University of California Press.

———. 1969. *Visual Thinking.* Berkeley: University of California Press.

Ash, Roberta Garner. 1977. *Social Movements in America.* Chicago: Rand McNally.

Astin, A., et al. 1975. *The Power of Protest.* San Francisco: Jossey-Bass.

Atkinson, Ti-Grace. 1974. *Amazon Odyssey.* New York: Links.

Aulette, Judy, and Trudy Mills. 1988. "Something Old, Something New: Auxiliary Work in the 1983–86 Copper Strike." *Feminist Studies* 14, (Summer): 251–68.

Aveni, Adrian F. 1977. "The Not-so-lonely Crowd: Friendship Groups in Collective Behavior." *Sociometry* 40: 96–99.

———. 1978. "Organization Linkages and Resource Mobilization: The Significance of Linkage Strength and Breadth." *Sociological Quarterly* 19: 185–202.

Avrich, Paul. 1980. *The Modern School Movement.* Princeton, N.J.: Princeton University Press.

Azaryahu, S. 1977. *The Association of Hebrew Women for Equal Rights in Eretz Yisrael.* 2d ed. Haifa: Foundation for Women's Aid. [In Hebrew]

Azicri, Max. 1979. "Women's Development Through Revolutionary Mobilization: A Study of the Federation of Cuban Women." *International Journal of Women's Studies* 2 (January–February): 27–30.

Babbie, Earl 1973. *Survey Research Methods.* Belmont. Calif.: Wadsworth.

———. 1980. *Sociology: An Introduction.* 2d ed. Belmont, Calif.: Wadsworth.

Baccioccio, E. 1974. *The New Left in America.* Stanford, Calif.: Hoover Institution Press.

Bailis, Lawrence N. 1974. *Bread or Justice: Grass Roots Organizing in the Welfare Rights Movement.* New York: Heath.

Bair, Barbara. (Forthcoming). *Our Women and What They Think: Gender and Power in the Garvey Movement.*

Baird, Leonard. 1970. *Activists in Protest! Student Activism in America.* Clinton, Mass.: Colonial Press.

Balabanoff, Angelica. 1925. In *New York Times.* December 27.

———. 1964. *Impressions of Lenin.* Ann Arbor: University of Michigan Press.

———. 1965. "Lénine et la création du Comintern." In Jacques Freymond, ed., *Contributions a l'histoire du Comintern.* Geneva: Droz.

———. 1973. *My Life as a Rebel.* Bloomington: Indiana University Press.

Baloyra, Enrique. 1982. *El Salvador in Transition.* Chapel Hill: University of North Carolina Press.

Balser, Diane. 1987. *Sisterhood and Solidarity: Feminism and Labor in Modern Times.* Boston: South End Press.

Banks, Alan. 1980. "Land and Capital in Eastern Kentucky, 1890–1915." *Appalachian Journal* 8:8–18.

———. 1983–84. "Coal Miners and Firebrick Workers: The Structure of Work Relations in Two Eastern Kentucky Communities." *Appalachian Journal* 2:85–102.

Banks, Olive. 1981. *Faces of Feminism: A Study of Feminism as a Social Movement.* Oxford: Martin Robertson.

Baratz. M. 1964. "How I Conquered Work." In R. Katznelson Shazar, ed., *With the Steps of the Generation.* Tel Aviv: Histadrut HaKlalit—Moetzet Hapoalot. [In Hebrew]

Bardwick, J. 1971. *Psychology of Women.* New York: Harper & Row.

Bardwick, Judith, and Elizabeth Douvan. 1971. "Ambivalence: The Socialization of Women." In Vivian Gornick and Barbara K. Moran, eds., *Women in Sexist Society.* New York: Basic Books.

Barrett, Nancy B. 1983. "The Welfare System as State Paternalism." Paper presented at the Conference on Women and Structural Transformation, Institute for Research on Women, Rutgers University. November.

Barrios de la Chungara, Domitila. 1978. *Let Me Speak: Testimony of Domitila, a Woman of the Bolivian Mines.* Translated by Victoria Ortiz. New York: Monthly Review Press.

———. 1983. "Women and Organization." In Miranda Davies, ed., *Third World/Second Sex: Women's Struggles and National Liberation.* London: Zed Books.

Barton, Stephen. 1976. "Understanding San Francisco: Social Movements in Headquarters City." Unpublished manuscript.

Basu, Amrita. 1987. "Alternative Forms of Organizing Women in India: The Challenge of Difference in the Indian Women's Movement." *Barnard Occasional Papers on Women's Issues* 2 (Fall): 39–61.

Baver, A. 1972. "Institutional Correlates of Faculty Support of Campus Unrest." *Sociology of Education* 45: 76–94.

Beatty, Bessie. 1918. *The Red Heart of Russia.* New York: Century.

Bebel, August. 1904. *Women Under Socialism.* New York: Labor News Press.

Beck, Evelyn Torton. 1982. *Nice Jewish Girls: A Lesbian Anthology.* Watertown, Penn.: Persephone.

Becker, E. 1947. "From the Life of a Watchman's Family." In B. Chabas, ed., *The Second Aliya.* Tel Aviv: Am Oved. [In Hebrew]

Becker, Howard S. 1963. *Outsiders: Studies in the Sociology of Deviance.* New York: Free Press.

Becker, Howard S., and Anselm Strauss. 1970. "Careers, Personality and Adult Socialization." In Howard S. Becker, ed., *Sociological Work.* Chicago: Aldine.

Becker, Susan. 1981. *The Origins of the Equal Rights Amendment: American Feminism Between the Wars.* Westport, Conn.: Greenwood Press.

Beeghley, Leonard, E. Van Velsor, and E. W. Block. 1981. "Correlates of Religiosity Among Black and White Americans." *Sociological Quarterly* 22 (Summer): 403–12.

Beer, Max. 1935. *Fifty Years of International Socialism.* New York: Macmillan.

Bein, A. 1954. *The History of Jewish Agricultural Settlement in Palestine.* 3d ed. Tel Aviv: Massada Press.

Benenson, Harold. 1980. "The Theory of Class and Structural Developments in American Society: A Study of Occupational and Family Change, 1945–1970." Ph.D. diss., New York University.

Bennet, Jean, and Pat Gibson. 1983. "Women Gather to Stop the Cruise." *Canadian Dimension* 17 (December): 20, 23.

Berg, Barbara J. 1978. *The Remembered Gate: Origins of American Feminism.* New York: Oxford University Press.

Berger, Peter, Brigitte Berger, and Hansfried Kellner. 1974. *The Homeless Mind.* New York: Random House.

Berkin, Carol R., and Clara M. Lovett, eds. 1980. *Women, War and Revolution.* New York: Holmes and Meier.

Bernstein, Eduard. 1897–98. "Eleanor Marx: Erinnerungen von Eduard Bernstein." *Die Neue Zeit:* 120–21.

———. 1921. *My Years of Exile.* New York: Harcourt, Brace, and Howe.

Bethel, Lorraine, and Barbara Smith, eds. 1979. "The Black Women's Issue." *Conditions* 5 (Autumn).

Black, Naomi. 1984. "The Mothers' International: The Women's Co-operative Guild and Feminist Pacifism." *Women's Studies International Forum* 7: 467–76.

Blackwood, Caroline. 1984. *On the Perimeter.* London: Heinemann.

Blair, Karen J. 1980. *The Clubwoman as Feminist: True Womanhood Redefined, 1868–1914.* New York: Holmes and Meier.

Blasier, Cole. 1967. "Studies of Social Revolution: Origins in Mexico, Bolivia, and Cuba." *Latin American Research Review* 2: 28–62.

Blee, Kathleen M. 1987. "Gender Ideology and the Role of Women in the 1920s Klan Movement." *Sociological Spectrum* 7: 73–97.

———. 1990. "Political Mobilization of Women: Insights from the 1920s Women of the Ku Klux Klan." *Feminist Studies.*

Blumberg, Rae Lesser. 1978. *Stratification: Socioeconomic and Sexual Inequality.* Dubuque, Iowa: Brown.

Blumberg, Rhoda Lois. 1980. "Careers of Women Civil Rights Activists." *Journal of Sociology and Social Welfare* 7 (September): 708–29.

———. 1982. "Women as Allies of Other Oppressed Groups: Some Hypothesized Links between Social Activism and Female Consciousness." Paper presented at the Tenth World Congress of the International Sociological Association, Mexico City. August 16–22.

———. 1984. *Civil Rights: The 1960s Freedom Struggle.* Boston: Twayne.

———. 1988. "Progress in the Historical Reconstruction of the Civil Rights Movement: Women Leaders Rediscovered." Paper presented at the Dream and Reality conference, Hofstra University. February 19.

Blumer, Herbert. 1951. "Social Movements." In Alfred McLung Lee, ed., *Principles of Sociology.* New York: Barnes & Noble.

———. 1969. "Social Movements." In Barry McLaughlin, ed. *Studies in Social Movements.* New York: Free Press.

Blumstein, S. 1937. "Life in the Kineret Commune." In A. Ya'ari, ed., *Memoirs of Eretz Yisrael.* Vol. 2 Jerusalem: Zionist Organization Youth Department. [In Hebrew]

Boles, Kay. 1975. "Political Science" [Review essay]. *Signs* 1 (Autumn): 161–74.

Bonnell, Victoria E. 1983. *Roots of Rebellion: Workers' Politics and Organization in St. Petersburg and Moscow. 1900–1914.* Berkeley: University of California Press.

Bookman, Ann, and Sandra Morgen, eds. 1988. *Women and the Politics of Empowerment.* Philadelphia: Temple University Press.

Booth, John A. 1982. *The End and the Beginning: The Nicaraguan Revolution.* Boulder, Colo.: Westview Press.

Bordin, Ruth. 1981. *Women and Temperance: The Quest for Power and Liberty, 1873–1900.* Philadelphia: Temple University Press.

Boswell, John. 1980. *Christianity, Social Tolerance and Homosexuality: Gay People in Western Europe from the Beginning of the Christian Era to the Fourteenth Century.* Chicago: University of Chicago Press.

Bourque, Susan, and Jean Grossholtz. 1974. "Politics an Unnatural Practice: Political Science Looks at Female Participation." *Politics and Society* 4:114–66

Boyer, Irma. 1927. *Louise Michel: La Vierge rouge*. Paris: André Delpeuch.

Boyte, Harry C. 1980. *The Backyard Revolution*. Philadelphia: Temple University Press.

Braga, J., and R. Doyle. 1971. "Student Activism and Social Intelligence." *Youth and Society* 2: 387–424.

Brand, Karl-Werner, Detlef Büsser, and Dieter Rucht. 1983. *Aufbruch in eine andere Gesellschaft*. Frankfurt: Campus Verlag.

Brauer, Carl M. 1983. "Women Activists, Southern Conservatives, and the Prohibition of Sex Discrimination in Title VII of the 1964 Civil Rights Act." *Journal of Southern History* 49: 37–56.

Braungart, Richard G., and Margaret M. Braungart. 1980. "Political Career Patterns of Radical Activists in the 1960s and 1970s. Some Historical Comparisons." *Sociological Focus* 13: 237–54.

Braunthal, Gerald. 1985. "Economic Perspectives, Ideology, and Coalition-Building: Prospects for an SPD–Green Coalition." Paper presented at the Fifth International Conference of Europeanists, Washington, D.C. October 18–20.

Breaching the Peace: A Collection of Radical Feminist Papers. 1983. London: Onlywomen Press.

Brenner, Johanna, and Maria Ramas. 1984. "Rethinking Women's Oppression." *New Left Review* 144 (March–April): 33–71.

Bridenthal, Renate, Atina Grossman, and Marion Kaplan. 1984. *When Biology Became Destiny: Women in Weimar and Nazi Germany*. New York: Monthly Review Press.

Bridenthal, Renate, and Claudia Koonz, eds. 1977. *Becoming Visible: Women in European History*. Boston: Houghton Mifflin.

Bridenthal, Renate, Claudia Koonz, and Susan Stuard. 1987. *Becoming Visible: Women in European History*. 2d ed. Boston: Houghton Mifflin.

Brockmann, Anna Dorothea. 1981. "Wider die Friedfertigkeit: Gedanken über den kriegerischen Alltag." *Courage* 6 (March): 20–22.

Broderick, Walter J. 1975. *Camilo Torros: A Biography of the First Priest-Guerrillero*. New York: Doubleday.

Bromley, David G., and Anson D. Shupe, Jr. 1979. *"Moonies" in America: Cult, Church, and Crusade*. Beverly Hills, Calif.: Sage.

———. 1983. "Repression and the Decline of Social Movements: The Case of the New Religions." In Jo Freeman, ed., *Social Movements of the Sixties and Seventies*. New York: Longman.

Bronner, Stephen Eric, ed. 1978. *The Letters of Rosa Luxemburg*. Boulder, Colo.: Westview Press.

Brown, Rita Mae. 1972. "The Woman-Identified Woman." *Ladder*. 16 (April–May): 21.

Brown, Wilmette. 1984. *Black Women and the Peace Movement*. Bristol, Eng.: Falling Wall Press.

Brozan, Nadine. 1987. "Politics and Prayer: Women on a Crusade." *New York Times*. June 15: C18.

Bryant, Louise. 1918. *Six Red Months in Russia*. New York: Doran.

———. 1923. *Mirrors of Moscow*. New York: Seltzer.

Buechler, Steven M. 1986 "Social Change, Movement Transformation, and Continuities in the Illinois Woman Suffrage Movement." In Gwen Moore and Glenna Spitze, eds., *Research in Politics and Society*. Vol. 2, *Women and Politics: Activism, Attitudes, and Office Holding*. Greenwich, Conn.: JAI Press.

Buhle, Mari Jo. 1970. "Women and the Socialist Party. 1901–1914." *Radical America* 4 (February): 36–55.

Bunch, Charlotte. 1987. *Passionate Politics*. New York: St. Martin's Press.

Bunch, Charlotte, and Nancy Myron. 1975. *Lesbianism and the Women's Movement*. Oakland, Calif.: Diana.

Bunster-Burrotto, Ximena. 1986. "Surviving Beyond Fear: Women and Torture in Latin America." In June Nash and Helen Safa, eds., *Women and Change in Latin America*. South Hadley, Mass.: Bergin and Garvey.

Bürklin, Wilhelm P. 1984. "The *Grünen*: Ecology and the New Left." In S. Wallachand and G. Rosmoser, eds., *West German Politics*. New York: Praeger.

———. 1985a. "The German Greens: The Post-Industrial Non-Established and the Party System." *International Political Science Review* 6: 463–81.

———. 1985b. "The Split Between the Established and the Non-Established Left in Germany." *European Journal of Political Research* 13: 283–93.

Bussey, Gertrude, and Margaret Tims. 1965. *Women's International League for Peace and Freedom*. London: George Allen & Unwin.

Bustos, Jorge. 1976. "Mythology About Women, with Special Reference to Chile." In June Nash and Helen Safa, eds., *Sex and Class in Latin America*. New York: Praeger.

Cabet, Etienne. 1848. *La Femme*. Paris: Le Populaire.

Caldecott, Leonie, and Stephanie Leland, eds. 1983. *Reclaim the Earth: Women Speak Out for Life on Earth*. London: Women's Press.

Callery, J.-M., and M. Yvan. 1969. *History of the Insurrection in China*. Translated by J. Oxenford. New York: Paragon Books Reprint Corp.

Cambridge Women's Peace Collective. 1984. My Country Is the Whole World: An Anthology of Women's Work on Peace and War. London: Pandora Press.

Cameron, Ardis. 1985. "Bread and Roses Revisited: Women's Culture and Working Class Activism in the Lawrence Strike of 1912." In Ruth Milkman, ed., *Women, Work and Protest: A Century of Women's Labor History*. Boston: Routledge and Kegan Paul.

Camp, Roderic A. 1979. "Women and Political Leadership in Mexico: A Comparative Study of Female and Male Political Elites." *Journal of Politics* 41: 417–41.

Capra, Fritjof, and Charlene Spretnak. 1984. *Green Politics*. New York: Dutton.

Carden, Maren Lockwood. 1975. "The New Feminist Movement in the U.S." Paper presented at the Eighth World Congress of Sociology.

Cardoso, Fernando Henrique, and Enzo Faletto. 1979. *Dependency and Development in Latin America*. Berkeley: University of California Press.

Carlson, Marvin. 1984. *Theories of the Theatre: A Historical and Critical Survey from the Greeks to the Present*. Ithaca, N.Y.: Cornell University Press.

Carroll, Berenice. 1984. "Feminism and Pacifism: Historical and Theoretical Connections." Paper presented at the Conference for Women and Education for Peace and Non-Violence, Ontario Institute for Studies in Education. September.

Cassell, Joan. 1977. *A Group Called Women: Sisterhood and Symbolism in the Feminist Movement*. New York: McKay.

Castells, Manuel. 1983. *The City and the Grass Roots*. Berkeley: University of California Press.

Castillo, Caroline. 1982. "The Situation of Women in El Salvador." In Women's International Resource Exchange, *Women and War: El Salvador*. New York: Women's International Resource Exchange.

Cavin, Susan. 1981. "Was Karen Silkwood a Lesbian?" *Big Apple Dyke News (B.A.D. News)* 1 (December).

———. 1983. "Interview with Audre Lorde on the Intersection of the Black, Feminist, and Lesbian/Gay Movements." *Big Apple Dyke News (B.A.D. News)* 3 (October–November).

——. 1985. *Lesbian Origins*. San Francisco: ISM.

——. 1987. "Lesbian Feminist Non-Violence." *Big Apple Dyke News* (*B.A.D. News*) 7 (Summer).

——. 1987. "Rutgers Sexual Orientation Survey." Unpublished manuscript.

——. 1988. "To Be Young or Old. Gifted or Ungifted and Gay." *A Critique of America* (June–July).

Central American Information Office. 1982. *El Salvador: Background to the Crisis*. Cambridge, Mass.: Central American Information Office.

Chabas, B., ed. 1947. *The Second Aliya*. Tel Aviv: Am Oved. [In Hebrew]

Chafe, William H. 1972. *The American Woman: Her Changing Social, Economic, and Political Roles, 1920–1970*. New York: Oxford University Press.

Chafetz, Janet Saltzman. 1984. *Sex and Advantage: A Comparative, Macro-Structural Theory of Sex Stratification*. Totowa, N.J.: Rowman and Allenheld.

Chafetz, Janet Salzman, and Anthony Gary Dworkin. 1983. "Macro and Micro Processes in the Emergence of Feminist Movements: Toward a Unified Theory." *Western Sociological Review* 14: 27–45.

——. 1986. *Female Revolt: Women's Movements in World and Historical Perspective*. Totowa, N.J.: Rowman and Allanheld.

Chaliand, Gerard. 1977. *Revolution in the Third World*. Baltimore: Penguin.

——. 1982. *Guerrilla Strategies*. Berkeley: University of California Press.

Chaney, Elsa. 1973a. "Old and New Feminists in Latin America." *Journal of Marriage and the Family* 35 (May): 331–43.

——. 1973b. "Women in Latin American Politics." In Ann Pescatello, ed., *Female and Male in Latin America*. Pittsburgh: University of Pittsburgh Press.

——. 1974. "The Mobilization of Women in Allende's Chile." In June S. Jaquette, ed., *Women in Politics*. New York: Wiley.

——. 1979. *Supermadre: Women in Politics in Latin America*. Austin: University of Texas Press.

Chapelle, Dickey. 1962. "How Castro Won." In Franklin Mark Osank, ed., *Modern Guerrilla Warfare*. New York: Free Press.

Cheikin, Bat-Sheva. 1927. "Protocol of the Third Histadrut Convention." *Pinkas Hahistadrut*. July 22–25. [In Hebrew]

Chen, P. T. 1944. *Taiping Tianguo* (The Taiping kingdom). Peking: Xinping Yinshuguan.

Cheng, J. C. 1963. *Chinese Sources for the Taiping Rebellion: 1850–1864*. Hong Kong: Hong Kong University Press.

"Chilean Demonstrators Protest Presidential Pick." 1988. *Newark Star Ledger*. August 31: 5.

Chinchilla, Norma Stoltz. 1977. "Mobilizing Women: Revolution in the Revolution." *Latin American Perspectives* 4 (Fall): 83–102.

——. 1980. "Class Struggle in Central America: Background and Overview." *Latin American Perspectives* 7 (Spring–Summer): 2–23, 44.

——. 1982. "Women in Revolutionary Movements: The Case of Nicaragua." Paper presented at the annual meeting of the American Sociological Society, San Francisco.

Chodorow, Nancy. 1971. "Being and Doing: A Cross Cultural Examination of the Socialization of Males and Females." In Vivian Gornick and Barbara K. Moran, eds., *Woman in Sexist Society*. New York: Basic Books.

——. 1974. "Family Structure and Feminine Personality." In Michelle Rosaldo and Louise Lamphere, eds., *Women, Culture and Society*. Stanford, Calif.: Stanford University Press.

——. 1979. "Mothering, Male Dominance, and Capitalism." In Zillah R. Eisenstein, ed., *Capitalist Patriarchy and the Case for Socialist Feminism*. New York: Monthly Review Press.

Christy, Carol A. 1985. "American and German Trends in Sex Differences in Political Participation." *Comparative Political Studies* 18 (April): 81–103.

Chung, T. 1980. "A New Look at Peasant Rebellions in China." *China Report* (India) 16: 33–35.

Clark, Cal, and Janet Clark. 1986. "Models of Gender and Political Participation in the United States." *Women and Politics* 6 (Spring): 5–25.

Clark, Paul F. 1981. *The Miners' Fight for Democracy: Arnold Miller and the Reform of the United Mine Workers*. Ithaca, N.Y.: Cornell University Press.

Clarke, Cheryl. 1983. "The Failure to Transform: Homophobia in the Black Community." In Barbara Smith, ed., *Homegirls: A Black Feminist Anthology*. New York: Kitchen Table/Women of Color Press.

Clarke, Edward H. 1873. *Sex in Education: A Fair Chance for the Girls*. Boston: James R. Osgood.

Clarke, P., and J. S. Gregory. 1982. *Western Reports on the Taiping: A Selection of Documents*. Honolulu: University Press of Hawaii.

Clayton, Joseph. 1926. *The Rise and Decline of Socialism in Great Britain*. London: Faber and Gwyer.

Clemenceau, Georges. 1919. *La Mêlée sociale*. Paris: Charpentier.

Cliff, Michelle. 1980. *Claiming an Identity They Taught Me to Despise*. Watertown, Mass.: Persephone.

Clines, Francis X. 1987. "Doing the 'Lambeth Walk': A Vote for Britain's Poor." *New York Times*. June 5:A6.

Cloward, Richard A., and Frances Fox Piven. 1971. *Regulating the Poor: The Functions of Public Welfare*. New York: Vintage Books.

———. 1979. "Hidden Protest: The Channeling of Female Innovation and Resistance." *Signs* 4 (Summer): 651–69.

Cockburn, Cynthia. 1983. *Brothers: Male Dominance and Technological Change*. London: Pluto Press.

Cohen, Lucy. 1973. "Female Entry to the Professions in Colombia." *Journal of Marriage and the Family* 35 (May): 322–30.

Cohn, David. 1948. *Where I Was Born and Raised*. Boston: Houghton Mifflin.

Cole, Johnetta B. 1986. "Women in Cuba: The Revolution Within the Revolution." In Jack A. Goldstone, ed., *Revolutions: Theoretical, Comparative, and Historical Studies*. New York: Harcourt Brace Jovanovich.

Collins, Patricia Hill. 1989. "The Social Construction of Black Feminist Thought." *Signs* 14 (Summer): 745–73.

Colwill, N., and H. Lips. 1978. *The Psychology of Sex Differences*. Englewood Cliffs, N.J.: Prentice-Hall.

"Combahee River Collective Statement." 1984. In Alison Jaggar and Paula Rothenberg, eds., *Feminist Frameworks*. New York: McGraw-Hill.

Connell, Christopher. 1987. "Ron's Ex-Aide Recalls Slurs: Bell Blames Some Reaganites." *Daily News* (New York). October 20.

Conover, Pamela, and Virginia Gray. 1983. *Feminism and the New Right*. New York: Praeger.

Cook, Blanche Wiesen. 1977. "Female Support Networks and Political Activism: Lillian Wald, Crystal Eastman, Emma Goldman." *Chrysalis* 3: 43–51.

———. 1979. "The Historical Denial of Lesbianism." *Radical History Review* 20: 60–65.

Cooper, Sandi. 1984. "Women's Participation in European Peace Movements: The Struggle to Prevent World War I." Paper presented at the Conference for

Women and Education for Peace and Non-Violence, Ontario Institute for Studies in Education, Ontario. September.

Corbin, David Alan. 1981. *Life, Work, and Rebellion in the Coal Fields: The Southern West Virginia Miners, 1880–1922*. Champaign: University of Illinois Press.

Costello, Cynthia B. 1985. " 'WEA're Worth It!': Work Culture and Conflict at the Wisconsin Educational Insurance Trust." *Feminist Studies* 11: 497–515.

Costin, Lela B. 1982. "Feminism, Pacifism, Internationalism, and the 1915 International Congress of Women." *Women's Studies International Forum* 5: 301–15.

Cott, Nancy F. 1977. *The Bonds of Womanhood*. New Haven, Conn.: Yale University Press.

———. 1984. "Feminist Politics in the 1920's: The National Woman's Party." *Journal of American History* 71: 43–68.

Coughlan, Robert. 1956. "Changing Roles in Modern Marriage." *Life*. December 24.

"Country Rankings of the Status of Women: Poor, Powerless, and Pregnant." 1988. *Population Briefing Paper*, no. 20. Washington, D.C.: Population Crisis Committee.

Cowell, Alan. 1986. "South Africa Rights Group Accuses the Security Forces of Brutality." *New York Times*. October 16:B1.

Crain, W. 1972. "Young Activists' Conceptions of an Ideal Society." *Youth and Society* 4: 203–36.

Crain, W., and E. Crain. 1974. "Growth of Political Ideas and Their Expressions Among Young Activists." *Journal of Youth and Adolescence* 3: 105–33.

Criollo, Cecelia. 1982. "Is Revolution Men's Work?" In Women's International Resource Exchange, *Women and War: El Salvador*. New York: Women's International Resource Exchange.

Crompton, Rosemary, and Michael Mann, eds. 1986. *Gender and Stratification*. Cambridge: Polity Press.

Cruikshank, Margaret, ed. 1982. *Lesbian Studies: Present and Future*. New York: Feminist Press.

Crummett, Maria. 1977. "*El Poder Feminino:* The Mobilization of Women Against Socialism in Chile." *Latin American Perspectives* 4 (Fall): 103–13.

Dahrendorf, Ralf. 1959. *Class and Class Conflict in Industrial Society*. Palo Alto, Calif.: Stanford University Press.

Dalton, R. 1981. "The Persistence of Values and Life Cycle Changes." In H. D. Klingemann and Max Kaase, eds., *Politische Psychologie*. Opladen: Westdeutscher Verlag.

Dalton, R., S. Flanagan, and P. Beck, eds. 1984. *Changing Electoral Forces in Western Democracies*. Princeton, N.J.: Princeton University Press.

Daniels, Arlene Kaplan. 1987. "Invisible Work." *Social Problems* 34 (December): 402–15.

Davies, Miranda. 1983. *Third World/Second Sex: Women's Struggles and National Liberation*. London: Zed Books.

Deere, Carmen Dianna, and Magdalena Leon de Leal. 1982. "Peasant Production, Proletarianization, and the Sexual Division of Labor in the Andes." In Lourdes Beneria, ed., *Women and Development*. New York: Praeger.

Demarath, N. J. III, Gerald Marwell, and Michael T. Aiken. 1971. *Dynamics of Idealism*. San Francisco: Jossey-Bass.

D'Emilio, John. 1983. *Sexual Politics, Sexual Communities: The Making of a Homosexual Minority in the United States, 1940–1970*. Chicago: University of Chicago Press.

Deming, Barbara. 1974. *We Cannot Live Without Our Lives*. New York: Viking Press.

Deutscher Bundestag. 1983. *Kürschners Volkshandbuch*. Tenth Election Period. Rheinbreitbach: Neue Darmstadter Verlagsanstalt.

Diamond, I. 1977. *Sex Roles in the State House*. New Haven, Conn.: Yale University Press.

"Die Gruenen: Eine Anti Volkspartei". 1989. *Das Parliament*. August 4–11: 11.

Dill, Bonnie Thornton. 1979. "The Dialectics of Black Womanhood." *Signs* 4 (Spring): 543–55.

Dinnerstein, Dorothy. [1963] 1976. *The Mermaid and the Minotaur: Sexual Arrangements and Human Malaise*. New York: Harper Colophon Books.

Djilas, Milovan. 1957. *The New Class: An Analysis of the Communist System*. New York: Praeger.

Donovan, J., and M. Shaevitz. 1973. "Student Political Activities." *Youth and Society* 4: 379–412.

Drake, St. Clair, and Horace Cayton. 1970. *Black Metropolis*. Chicago: University of Chicago Press.

Draper, Theodore. 1965. *Castroism: Theory and Practice*. New York: Praeger.

Dreiser, Theodore. 1932. *Harlan Miners Speak: Report on Terrorism in the Kentucky Coal Fields*. New York: Harcourt, Brace.

Drori, C. 1975. "From Soviet Russia to the Conference in Haifa." In R. Katznelson Shazar, ed., *The Plough Woman*. New York: Herzl Press.

Duff, Patricia. 1979. "What You Don't Know About the Arms Race." *Our Generation* 13 (Winter): 17–23.

Dunayevskaya, Raya. 1985. *Women's Liberation and the Dialectics of Revolution: Reaching for the Future*. Atlantic Highlands, N.J.: Humanities Press International.

Duncan, Isadora. 1938. *The Art of Dance*. New York: Theatre Arts.

Dunkerley, James. 1982. *The Long War: Dictatorship and Revolution in El Salvador*. London: Junction Books.

Dunlap, R. 1970. "Radical and Conservative Student Activists." *Pacific Sociological Review* 13: 171–81.

Durkheim, Emile. 1953. *Sociology and Philosophy*. Translated by D. F. Pocock. Glencoe, Ill.: Free Press.

———. [1915] 1965. *Elementary Forms of the Religious Life*. New York: Free Press.

Dworkin, Andrea. 1983. *Right Wing Women*. New York: Perigee Books.

Dynes, Russell R., and E. L. Quarantelli. 1968. "Group Behavior Under Stress: A Required Convergence of Organizational and Collective Behavior Perspectives." *Sociology and Social Research* 52: 416–29.

Edinger, Lewis J. 1986. *West German Politics*. New York: Praeger.

Edwards, Lyford P. 1927. *The Natural History of Revolution*. Chicago: University of Chicago Press.

Eisenstadt, S. N. 1967. *Israeli Society*. London: Weidenfeld and Nicolson.

Eisenstein, Zillah. 1981. *The Radical Future of Liberal Feminism*. New York: Longman.

———. 1983. "The State, the Patriarchal Family, and Working Mothers." In Irene Diamond, ed., *Families, Politics, and Public Policy*. New York: Longman, Green.

Elder, Glen. 1974. *Children of the Great Depression*. Chicago: University of Chicago Press.

Eller, Ronald D. 1982. *Miners, Millhands, and Mountaineers: Industrialization of the Appalachian South, 1880–1930*. Knoxville: University of Tennessee Press.

Elshtain, Jean Bethke. 1974. "Moral Woman and Immoral Man: A Consideration of the Public–Private Split and Its Political Ramifications." *Politics and Society* 4: 453–73.

———. 1982. "Feminism, Family and Community." *Dissent* (Fall):442–50.

———. 1983. "Antigone's Daughters: Reflections on Female Identity and the State." In Irene Diamond, ed., *Families, Politics, and Public Policy*. New York: Longman, Green.

"Emanzen-Sieg." 1989. *Spiegel.* April 17: 56–59.

Engel, Barbara. 1977. "Women as Revolutionaries: The Case of Russian Populists." In Renate Bridenthal and Claudia Koonz, eds., *Becoming Visible: Women in European History.* Boston: Houghton Mifflin.

Engels, Frederick. 1968. *The Condition of the Working Class in England in 1844.* Stanford, Calif.: Stanford University Press.

———. 1975. *The Origin of the Family, Private Property, and the State.* New York: International.

Enloe, Cynthia. 1980. "Women—The Reserve Army of Army Labor." *Review of Radical Political Economics* 12 (Summer): 42–52.

———. 1983. *Does Khaki Become You? The Militarisation of Women's Lives.* London: Pluto Press.

Epstein, Barbara Leslie. 1981. *The Politics of Domesticity.* Middletown, Conn.: Wesleyan University Press.

Erez, Y. 1922. In *Mc'Chayinu* [newspaper of the Gdud Aavoda], no. 25. [In Hebrew]

———. 1948. *The Third Aliya.* Jerusalem: Zionist Organization Youth Department.

Eshelman, Nancy Gorman. 1977. "Angelica Balabanoff and the Italian Socialist Movement: From the Second International to Zimmerwald." Ph.D. diss., University of Rochester.

Etheridge, Carolyn. 1974. "The Dynamics of Changing Sex-Roles: An Integrated Theoretical Analysis." Paper presented at the Annual Meeting of the American Sociological Association.

———. 1978. "Equality in the Family: Comparative Analysis and Theoretical Model." *International Journal of Women's Studies* 1: 50–63.

Etinger, Y. 1919. "Cooperative Groups in the Year 1919." *Kontres* 12.

Ettinger, Elzbieta, ed. and trans. 1979. *Comrade and Lover: Rosa Luxemburg's Letters to Leo Jogiches.* Cambridge, Mass.: MIT Press.

Evans, Sara. 1979. *Personal Politics: The Roots of Women's Liberation in the Civil Rights Movement and the New Left.* New York: Vintage Books.

Even Shoshan, Z. 1963. *The History of the Workers' Movement in Eretz Israel.* Tel Aviv: Am Oved. [In Hebrew]

Everett, Jana. 1985. "Class, Gender and Political Participation." Paper presented at the Annual Meeting of the American Political Science Association, New Orleans. August 29–September 1.

Evers, Myrlie. 1967. *For Us the Living.* New York: Doubleday.

Fainstein, Norman I., and Susan S. Fainstein. 1974. *Urban Political Movements: The Search for Power by Minority Groups in American Cities.* Englewood Cliffs, N.J.: Prentice-Hall.

Farah, B., and M. Jennings. 1978. "Ideology, Gender, and Political Action: A Cross-national Survey." Paper presented at the Annual Meeting of the American Political Science Association, New York. September.

Femenia, Nora. 1987. "Argentina's Mothers of Plaza de Mayo: The Mourning Process from Junta to Democracy." *Feminist Studies* 13 (Spring): 9–18.

———. 1988. "Beyond Denial and Out in the Open: From Women's Groups to Feminism in Argentina 1988." Paper presented at the Annual Conference of the National Women's Studies Association, Minneapolis. June 22–26.

Fendrich, James M. 1977. "Keeping the Faith or Pursuing the Good Life: A Study of Participation in the Civil Rights Movement." *American Sociological Review* 42 (February): 144–57.

Fendrich, James M., and Ellis S. Krauss. 1978. "Student Activism and Adult Left-Wing Politics: A Causal Model of Political Socialization for Black, White and Japanese

Students of 1960s Generation." In Louis Kriesberg, ed., *Research in Social Movements: Conflicts and Change*. Vol. 1. Greenwich, Conn.: JAI Press.

Ferree, Myra Marx. 1980. "Working-class Feminism: A Consideration of the Consequences of Employment." *Sociological Quarterly* 21: 173–84.

Ferree, Myra Marx, and Beth Hess. 1985. *Controversy and Coalition: The New Feminist Movement*. Boston: Twayne.

Ferree, Myra Marx, and Frederick Miller. 1980. "Mobilization and Meaning: Toward an Integration of Social Psychological and Resource Mobilization Perspectives on Social Movements." Unpublished paper.

Fetherling, Dale. 1974. *Mother Jones: The Miners' Angel*. Carbonadale: Southern Illinois University Press.

Finn, Peter, and Taylor McNeil. 1987. "The Response of the Criminal Justice System to Bias Crime: An Exploratory Review" a [Report commissioned by the United States Department of Justice, the National Institute of Justice]. Cambridge, Mass.: ABT Associates.

"The First Conference of the Woman Workers' Council." 1921. *Pinkas Hahistadrut*. [In Hebrew]

"The First Women Workers' Conference." 1923. Hapoel Hatzair 37: 12–13. [In Hebrew]

Fischer, Arthur, ed. 1982. *Jugend '81: Lebenswürde, Alltagskulturen, Zukunftsbilder*. Jugendwerk der Deutschen Shell. Opladen: Leske.

Flanders, Laura. 1989. "Pittston Women Fight On." *New Directions for Women* 18 (November–December): 1, 9.

Flexner, Eleanor. 1971. *Century of Struggle: The Women's Rights Movement in the United States*. New York: Atheneum.

Flora, Cornelia Butler. 1973. "The Passive Female and Social Change." In Ann Pescatello, ed., *Female and Male in Latin America*. Pittsburgh: University of Pittsburgh Press.

———. 1984. "Socialist Feminism in Latin America." *Women and Politics* 4 (Spring): 69–93.

Flora, Cornelia Butler, and Naomi B. Lynn. 1974. "Women and Political Socialization: Considerations of the Impact of Motherhood." In Jane S. Jaquette, ed., *Women in Politics*. New York: Wiley.

Florence, Ronald. 1975. *Marx's Daughters*. New York: Dial Press.

Flynn, Patricia. 1980. "Women Challenge the Myth." *NACLA Report on the Americas* 14 (September–October): 20–32.

Foner, Philip S. 1979. *Women and the American Labor Movement: From Colonial Times to the Eve of World War I*. New York: Free Press.

———. 1980. *Women and the American Labor Movement: From World War I to the Present*. New York: Free Press.

Forche, Carolyn. 1982. "El Salvador: The Next Vietnam?" In Women's International Resource Exchange, *Women and War: El Salvador*. New York: Women's International Resource Exchange.

Foreman, Ann. 1977. *Femininity as Alienation: Women and the Family in Marriage and Psychoanalysis*. London: Pluto Press.

"For West Berlin, Is Socialist Rule Coming?" 1989. *New York Times*. March 8: A8.

Foster, John. 1974. *Class Struggle and the Industrial Revolution: Early Industrial Capitalism in Three English Towns*. New York: St. Martin's Press.

Foucault, Michel. 1978. *The History of Sexuality*. Vol. 1, *An Introduction*. Translated by Robert Hurley. New York: Pantheon Books.

Fourier, Charles. 1841–46. *Oeuvres complètes*. Paris: Librarie Sociétaire.

Fox, Geoffrey E. 1973. "Honor, Shame, and Women's Liberation in Cuba." In Ann

Pescatello, ed., *Female and Male in Latin America*. Pittsburgh: University of Pittsburgh Press.

Francis, Roy G. 1961. *The Rhetoric of Science*. Minneapolis: University of Minnesota Press.

Frank, Carrolyle M. 1974. "Politics in Middletown: A Reconsideration of Municipal Government and Community Power in Muncie, Indiana, 1925–1935." Ph.D. diss., Ball State University.

Franqui, Carlos. 1980. *Diary of the Cuban Revolution*. New York: Viking Press.

"Frausein allein adelt noch nicht." 1986. *Spiegel*. November 3: 74–92.

Freedman, Estelle. 1979. "Separatism as Strategy: Female Institution Building and American Feminism 1870–1930." *Feminist Studies* 5 (Fall): 512–29.

Freeman, Jo. 1975. *The Politics of Women's Liberation*. New York: McKay.

———. 1979. "Resource Mobilization and Strategy: A Model for Analyzing Social Movement Organization Actions." In Mayer N. Zald and John D. McCarthy, eds., *Dynamics of Social Movements*. Cambridge, Mass.: Winthrop.

———. 1983. *Social Movements of the Sixties and Seventies*. New York: Longman.

Friedan, Betty. 1963. *The Feminine Mystique*. New York: Dell.

FSLN (Frente Sandinista de Liberacion Nacional). 1979. "Why the FSLN Struggles in Unity with the People." *Latin American Perspectives* 6 (Winter): 108–13.

———. 1983. "The Historic Program of the FSLN." In Peter Rossett and John Vandermeer, eds., *The Nicaragua Reader*. New York: Grove Press.

Gailey, Harry A. 1970. *The Road to Abe: A Study of British Administrative Policy in Eastern Nigeria*. New York: New York University Press.

Game, Ann, and Rosemary Pringle. 1983. *Gender at Work*. London: George Allen & Unwin.

Gamson, William A. 1968. *Power and Discontent*. Homewood, Ill.: Dorsey Press.

———. 1975. *The Strategies of Social Protest*. Homewood, Ill.: Dorsey Press.

———. 1987. "Introduction." In Mayer N. Zald and John D. McCarthy, eds., *Social Movements in an Organizational Society: Collected Essays*. New Brunswick, N.J.: Transaction Press.

Gans, Herbert. 1968. *People and Plans: Essays on Urban Problems and Solutions*. New York: Basic Books.

Garrow, David J. 1985. "The Origins of the Montgomery Bus Boycott." *Southern Changes* (October): 21–27.

———. 1986. *Bearing the Cross: Martin Luther King, Jr., and the Southern Christian Leadership Conference*. New York: Morrow.

Garvey, Michael. 1981. "An Oral History with Amzie Moore." Mississippi Oral History Program, University of Southern Mississippi.

Gaventa, John. 1980. *Power and Powerlessness: Quiescence and Rebellion in an Appalachian Valley*. Champaign: University of Illinois Press.

Gelber, N. 1958. *The History of the Zionist Movement in Galicia, 1875–1918*. Jerusalem: Histadrut Hazionit.

Gerlach, Luther P., and Virginia H. Hine. 1970. *People, Power, and Change: Movements of Social Transformation*. Indianapolis: Bobbs-Merrill.

Germani, Gino. 1970. "Mass Society, Social Class, and the Emergence of Fascism." In Irwin Louis Horowitz, ed., *Masses in Latin America*. New York: Oxford University Press.

Gibbs, Lois. 1982. *Love Canal: My Story*, as told to Murray Levine. New York: Grove Press.

Giddings, Paula. 1984. *When and Where I Enter: The Impact of Black Women on Race and Sex in America*. New York: Morrow.

Giel, Lawrence A. 1967. "George R. Dale—Crusader for Free Speech and a Free Press."
    Ph.D. diss., Ball State University.
Gilio, Maria Esther. 1970. *La Guerrilla Tupamara*. Havana: Casas de las Americas.
Gilkes, Cheryl Townsend. 1983. "From Slavery to Social Welfare: Racism and the
    Control of Black Women." In Amy Swerdlow and Hanna Lessinger, eds., *Class,
    Race and Sex: The Dynamics of Control*. Boston: Hall.
————. 1985. " 'Together and in Harness': Women's Traditions in the Sanctified
    Church." *Signs* 10 (Summer): 678–99.
————. (1988). "Building in Many Places: Multiple Commitments and Ideologies in
    Black Women's Community Work." In A. Bookman and S. Morgan, eds.,
    Women and the Politics of Empowerment. Philadelphia: Temple University Press.
Gilligan, Carol, 1982. *In a Different Voice*. Cambridge, Mass.: Harvard University Press.
Gilly, Aldolfo. 1965. "Guerrillas and 'Peasant Republics' in Colombia." *Monthly Review*
    17 (October): 30–40.
Gilman, Charlotte Perkins. [1915] 1975. *Herland*. Introduction by Anne J. Lane. New
    York: Pantheon Books.
Girault, Ernst. 1906. *La Bonne Louise*. Paris: Bibliothèque des Auteurs Modernes.
Githens, M. 1983. "The Elusive Paradigm: Gender, Politics and Political Behavior." In
    A. D. Finifter, ed., *Political Science: The State of the Discipline*. Washington, D.C.:
    American Political Science Association.
Gittell, M., and T. Shtob. 1980. "Changing Women's Roles in Political Volunteerism
    and Reform of the City." *Signs* 5, Supplement (Spring):S67–S78.
Glaser, Barney G., and Anselm L. Strauss. 1967. *The Discovery of Grounded Theory:
    Strategies for Qualitative Research*. Chicago: Aldine.
Glazer, M. 1966. "Field Work in a Hostile Environment." *Comparative Education Review*
    10: 367–76.
Glennon, Lynda M. 1979. *Women and Dualism: A Sociology of Knowledge Analysis*. New
    York: Longman.
Goffman, Erving. 1963. *Stigma: Notes on the Management of Spoiled Identity*. New York:
    Simon and Schuster.
Goldberg, Susan, ed. 1985. *Facing the Nuclear Age: Parents and Children Together*. Toronto:
    Annick Press.
Goldman, Ari L. 1989. "B'nai B'rith Is Threatening to Expel Its Women's Unit." *New
    York Times*. December 7: A26.
Goldman, Emma. 1970. *Living My Life*. New York: AMS Press.
Goldstein, Rhoda L. (Blumberg) 1977a. "The Committed Revisited: Civil Rights
    Careers of White Female Activists" [Revised from "Civil Rights Careers"].
    Paper presented at the Annual Meetings of the Eastern Sociological Society.
    March.
————. 1977b. *Involvement in Civil Rights: The Case of White Women*. Washington, D.C.:
    ERIC Clearinghouse on Urban Education.
————. 1978. "Wife–Husband Companionship in a Social Movement." *International
    Journal of Sociology of the Family* 8 (Spring):101–10.
Gollan, Donna. 1985. "Nurturing the Sensibilities." *Broadside* 6 (June): 10.
Gomez, Alberto. 1967. "The Revolutionary Forces of Colombia and Their Perspec-
    tives." *World Marxist Review* 10 (April): 59–67.
Gonzales, W. 1973. "Women and the Jural Domain: An Evolutionary Perspective." In
    Dorothy McGuigan, ed., *A Sampler of Women's Studies*. Ann Arbor: University of
    Michigan Press.
Goodsell, Willystine. 1924. *The Education of Women: Its Social Background and Its Problems*.
    New York: Macmillan.

Gordon, Linda. 1976. *Woman's Body, Woman's Right: A Social History of Birth Control in America*. New York: Viking/Grossman.

Gordon, Suzanne. 1983. *Off Balance: The Real World of Ballet*. New York: Pantheon Books.

Gorham, Debra. (1984). "Vera Brittain, Flora MacDonald Dennison and the First World War: The Failure of Non-Violence." Paper presented at the Conference on Women and Education for Peace and Non-Violence, Ontario Institute for Studies in Education, Toronto. September.

———. 1985. "Vera Brittain and the Great War." Paper presented at the Canadian Historical Association Conference. May.

Gorni, Y. 1975. "Changes in the Social and Political Structure of the Second Aliya between 1904–1940." In D. Carpi, ed., *Zionism: Studies in the History of the Zionist Movement and the Jewish Community in Palestine*. Tel Aviv: Massada Press.

Gott, Richard. 1971. *Guerrilla Movements in Latin America*. Garden City, N.Y.: Doubleday.

Grahn, Judy. 1984. *Another Mother Tongue: Gay Words, Gay Worlds*. Boston: Beacon Press.

Green, Arnold W., and Eleanor Melnick. 1950. "What Has Happened to the Feminist Movement?" In Alvin W. Gouldner, ed., *Studies in Leadership*. New York: Russell & Russell.

Griffin, Farah Jasmine. 1988. " 'Layin' On of Hands': Organizational Efforts Among Black American Women, 1790–1930." *Sage*, Student Supplement: 23–29.

Gross, J. 1987. "The Devastation of AIDS: Many Dead, More Dying." *New York Times*, March 16.

Group of Women Workers. 1913. "In Answer to Mrs. Tahon. *Hapoel Hatzair* 26:12–13. [In Hebrew]

Gruhl, Herbert. 1978. *Ein Planet wird geplündert*. Frankfurt: Fisher.

Guevara, Che. 1969. *Guerrilla Warfare*. New York: Vintage Books.

Gurko, Miriam. 1974. *The Ladies of Seneca Falls: The Birth of the Women's Rights Movement*. New York: Schocken Books.

Guesde, Jules. 1914. *Ça et là*. Paris: Marcle Rivière.

Gusfield, Joseph R. 1981. "Social Movements and Social Change: Perspectives of Linearity and Fluidity." In Louis Kriesberg, ed., *Research in Social Movements: Conflict and Change*. vol. 4. Greenwich, Conn.: JAI Press.

Hadden, J. 1970. "Reflections on the Social Scientist's Role in Studying Civil Violence." *Social Science Quarterly* 51: 328–38.

Hall, Betty Jean. 1977. "Background Paper on Sex Discrimination in the Coal Industry." Coal Employment Project, Jacksboro, Tenn.

Hall, Jacquelyn Dowd. 1986. "Disorderly Women: Gender and Labor Militancy in the Appalachian South." *Journal of American History* 73: 354–82.

Halperin, Ernst. 1976. *Terrorism in Latin America*. Beverly Hills, Calif.: Sage.

Hanna, Judith Lynne. 1976. "The Anthropology of Dance-Ritual: Nigeria's Ubakala Nkwa di Iche Iche." Ph.D. diss., Columbia University. Ann Arbor: University Microfilms.

———. 1979a. "Movements Toward Understanding Humans Through the Anthropological Study of Dance." *Current Anthropology* 20: 313–39.

———. 1979b. "Toward Semantic Analysis of Movement Behavior: Concepts and Problems." *Semiotics* 25: 77–110.

———. 1983a. "The Mentality and Matter of Dance." *Art Education* (Art and Mind) 36: 42–46.

———. 1983b. *The Performer–Audience Connection: Emotion to Metaphor in Dance and Society.* Austin: University of Texas Press.

———. 1987a. *To Dance Is Human: A Study of Nonverbal Communication.* Chicago: University of Chicago Press.

———. 1987b. "Gender 'Language' Onstage: Moves, New Moves, Countermoves." *Journal of the Washington Academy of Sciences* 77: 18–26.

———. 1987c. "Patterns of Dominance: Men, Women, and Homosexuality in Dance." *Drama Review* 113: 22–47.

———. 1988a. *Dance, Sex and Gender: Signs of Identity, Dominance, Defiance, and Desire.* Chicago: University of Chicago Press.

———. 1988b. *Dance and Stress: Resistance, Reduction, and Euphoria.* New York: AMS Press.

———. 1988c. *Disruptive School Behavior: Class, Race, and Culture.* New York: Holmes and Meier.

Harari, Y. 1959. *Woman and Mother in Israel.* Tel Aviv: Massada Press. [In Hebrew]

Hardouin, C. La *Detenue de Versailles en 1871.* Paris: C. Hardouin.

Hareven, Tamara K. 1982. *Family Time and Industrial Time: The Relationship Between the Family and Work in a New England Industrial Community.* New York: Cambridge University Press.

Harkness, Shirley, and Patricia Pinzon de Lewin. 1975. "Women, the Vote, and the Party in the Politics of the Colombian National Front." *Journal of Inter-American Studies and World Affairs* 17 (November): 439–64.

Harrison, Cynthia E. 1982. "Prelude to Feminism: Women's Organizations, the Federal Government, and the Rise of the Women's Movement." Ph.D. diss., Columbia University.

Hartley, Ruth. 1974. "Sex-Role Pressures and the Socialization of the Male Child." In Joseph Pleck and Jack Sawyer, eds., *Men and Masculinity.* Englewood Cliffs, N.J.: Prentice-Hall.

Hartmann, Susan M. 1982. *The Home Front and Beyond: American Women in the 1940s.* Boston: Twayne.

Haug, Frigga. 1986. "The Women's Movement in West Germany." *New Left Review,* no. 155: 50–74.

Heberle, Rudolf. 1951. *Social Movements.* New York: Appleton.

Henderson, Philip, ed. 1950. *The Letters of William Morris to His Family and Friends.* London: Longmans, Green.

Henle, Ellen, and Marlene Merrill. 1979. "Antebellum Black Coeds at Oberlin College." *Women's Studies Newsletter* 7 (Spring): 8–11.

Hermann, Ursula. 1984. "German Social Democratic Women in the Struggle for Peace Before the First World War." Paper presented at the Conference of Women and Education for Peace and Non-Violence, Ontario Institute for Studies in Education, Toronto. September.

Hernes, Helga Maria. 1988. "The Welfare State Citizenship of Scandinavian Women." In Kathleen B. Jones and Anna G. Jonasdottir, eds., *The Political Interests of Gender: Developing Theory and Research with a Feminist Face.* Sage Modern Politics Series, vol. 20. Sponsored by the European Consortium for Political Research/ECPR. London: Sage.

Herrera, Norma de. 1983. *La Mujer en la Revolución Salvadorena.* Morelos, Mexico: CCOPEC/CECOPE.

Hertz, Susan Handley. 1981. *The Welfare Mothers Movement: A Decade of Change for Poor Women?* Washington, D.C.: University Press of America.

Hess, Beth B., and Myra Marx Ferree. 1985. *Controversy and Coalition: The New Feminist Movement*. Boston: Twayne.

———, eds. 1987. *Analyzing Gender: A Handbook of Social Science Research*. Newbury Park, Calif.: Sage.

Hess, Beth B., Elizabeth W. Markson, and Peter J. Stein. 1982. *Sociology*. New York: Macmillan.

Hevener, John W. 1978. *Which Side Are You On? The Harlan County Coal Miners, 1931–39*. Champaign: University of Illinois Press.

Hewitt, Nancy A. 1984. *Women's Activism and Social Change: Rochester, New York, 1822–1872*. Ithaca, N.Y.: Cornell University Press.

Hidalgo, Hilda. 1984. "The Puerto Rican Lesbian in the United States." In Trudy Darty and Sandee Potter, eds., *Women-Identified Women*. Palo Alto, Calif.: Mayfield.

Hirsh, Eric. N.d. "The Creation of Political Solidarity in Social Movement Organizations: A Critique of the Resource Mobilization Approach." Unpublished report.

Histadrut Hahalait—The Union of Agricultural Workers in Its Thirtieth Year. 1951. Tel Aviv: Vaad Hapoel. [In Hebrew]

Histadrut Labor Archives. 206/1V.

Hoaglund, Sarah, and Julia Penelope Stanley. 1988. *For Lesbians Only: A Lesbian Separatist Anthology*. London: Onlywomen Press.

Hoecker, Beate. 1986. "Frauen in der Politik: Gängige Hypothesen zum Päsendefizt auf dem empirischen Prüfstand in Bremen." *Zeitschrift für Parliamentsfragen* 17: 65–82.

Hoge, Dean, and D. Roozen. 1979. *Understanding Church Growth and Decline*. New York: Pilgrim Press.

Hollander, Nancy. 1973. "Women: The Forgotten Half of Argentine History." In Ann Pescatello, ed., *Female and Male in Latin America*. Pittsburgh: University of Pittsburgh Press.

Holmes, Kim R. 1983. "The Origins, Development, and Composition of the Green Movement." In Robert L. Pfaltzgraff, Kim R. Holmes, Clay Clemans, and Werner Kaltefleiter, eds., *The Greens of West Germany: Origins, Strategies, and Transatlantic Implications*. Cambridge, Mass.: Institute for Foreign Policy Analysis.

Hopper, Rex D. 1950. "The Revolutionary Process." *Social Forces* 28: 270–79.

Horn, J. and P. Knott. 1977. "Activist Youth of the 1960s." *Science* 171: 977–85.

Horowitz, Irving Louis. 1970. "Masses in Latin America." In Irving Louis Horowitz, ed., *Masses in Latin America*. New York: Oxford University Press.

———. 1972. "Social Deviance and Political Marginality." In *Foundations of Political Sociology*. New York: Harper & Row.

Hubbard, Ruth, Mary Sue Henifin, and Barbara Fried, eds. 1982. *Biological Woman—The Convenient Myth: A Collection of Feminist Essays and a Comprehensive Bibliography*. Cambridge, Mass.: Schenkman.

Huber, Joan, and Glenna Spitze. 1983. *Sex Stratification: Children, Housework, and Jobs*. New York: Academic Press.

Hughes, Everett C. 1958. *Men and Their Work*. Glencoe, Ill.: Free Press.

Huizinga, Johan. 1955. *Homo Ludens: A Study of the Play Element in Culture*. Boston: Beacon Press.

Humphreys, Laud. 1972. *Out of the Closet: The Sociology of Homosexual Liberation*. Englewood Cliffs, N.J.: Prentice-Hall.

Hurley, Ruby. 1968. Interview. Moorland Spingarn Collection, Howard University. September 26.

Hurston, Zora Neale. 1938. *Their Eyes Were Watching God*. London: Dent.

Huston, Nancy. 1982. "Tales of War and Tears of Women." *Women's Studies International Forum* 5: 271–82.

Huston, Perdita. 1979. *Third World Women Speak Out: Interviews in Six Countries on Change, Development, and Basic Needs.* Foreword by Arvonne S. Fraser. New York: Praeger.

Hutchings, Ian. 1985. "The Five-Percent Hurdle and Federal Elections in West Germany." *Parliamentary Affairs* 38: 455–71.

Inglehart, Richard. 1979. "Value Priorities and Socioeconomic Change." In Samuel Barnes and Max Kaase, eds., *Political Action*. Beverly Hills, Calif.: Sage.

———. 1984. "The Changing Structure of Political Cleavages in Western Society." In R. Dalton, S. Flanagan, and P. Beck, eds., *Changing Electoral Forces in Western Democracies*. Princeton, N.J.: Princeton University Press.

International Labor Organization. 1984. *Year Book of Labour Statistics*. Geneva: ILO.

Isenberg, P., et al. 1977. "Psychological Variables in Student Activism." *Journal of Youth and Adolescence* 6:11–24.

Jacklin, C., and E. Maccoby. 1974. *The Psychology of Sex Differences*. Stanford, Calif.: Stanford University Press.

Jackson-Brewer, Karla, Liz Margolies, and Martha Becker. 1987. "Internalized Homophobia: Identifying the Oppressor Within." *Lesbian Psychologies*. Champaign: University of Illinois Press.

Jacobs, P., and S. Landau. 1966. *New Radicals: A Report with Documents*. New York: Vintage Books.

Jaquette, Jane S. 1973. "Women in Revolutionary Movements in Latin America." *Journal of Marriage and the Family* 35 (May): 344–54.

———, ed. 1974. *Women in Politics*. New York: Wiley.

———. 1976. "Female Political Participation in Latin America." In June Nash and Helen Safa, eds., *Sex and Class in Latin America*. New York: Praeger.

———. 1986. "Women, Feminism and the Transition to Democracy in Latin America." Paper presented at the Twentieth Anniversary Meeting of the Latin American Studies Association. June 23–26.

Jaquette, Jane S., and Kathleen A. Staudt. 1988. "Politics, Population, and Gender: A Feminist Analysis of US Population Policy in the Third World." In Kathleen B. Jones and Anna G. Jonasdottir, eds., *The Political Interests of Gender* London: Sage.

James, Selma. 1974. "A Woman's Place." In Mariarosa Dalls Costa and Selma James, eds., *The Power of Women and the Subversion of the Community*. Bristol, Eng.: Falling Wall Press.

Jancar, Barbara W. 1974. "Women Under Communism." In Jane S. Jacquette, ed., *Women in Politics*. New York: Wiley.

Jay, Karla, and Allen Young, eds. 1977. *Out of the Closets: The Voices of Gay Liberation*. New York: Jove.

Jayawardena, Kumari. 1986. *Feminism and Nationalism in the Third World*. London: Zed Books.

Jen, Y. W. 1973. *The Taiping Revolutionary Movement*. New Haven, Conn.: Yale University Press.

Jenkins, J. Craig. 1983. "Resource Mobilization Theory and the Study of Social Movements." *Annual Review of Sociology* 9: 527–53.

———. 1986. "Black Insurgency and the Role of Elite Patronage and Professional SMOs." Paper presented to the Department of Sociology, Ohio State University.

Jennings, M. K. 1983. "Gender Roles and Inequalities in Political Participation: Results from Eight-Nation Study." *Western Political Quarterly* 36:364–85.

Jensen, Joan M., and Sue Davidson, eds. 1984. *A Needle, a Bobbin, a Strike: Women Needleworkers in America.* Philadelphia: Temple University Press.

Johnston, Jill. 1973. *Lesbian Nation.* New York: Simon and Schuster.

Jonasdottir, Anna G. 1988. "On the Concept of Interest, Women's Interests, and the Limitations of Interest Theory." In Kathleen B. Jones and Anna G. Jonasdottir, eds., *The Political Interests of Gender.* London: Sage.

Jones, G. C. 1985. *Growing Up Hard in Harlan County.* Lexington: University Press of Kentucky.

Jones, Jacqueline. 1985. *Labor of Love, Labor of Sorrow: Black Women, Work, and the Family, From Slavery to the Present.* New York: Vintage Books.

Jones, Kathleen B. 1988. "Towards a Revision of Politics." In Kathleen B. Jones and Anna G. Jonasdottir, eds., *The Political Interests of Gender.* London: Sage.

Jones, Kathleen B., and Anna G. Jonasdottir, eds. 1988. *The Political Interests of Gender.* London: Sage.

Jones, Lynne, ed. 1983. *Keeping the Peace: A Woman's Handbook.* vol. 1. London: Pandora Press.

Kaledin, Eugenia. 1984. *Mothers and More: American Women in the 1950s.* Boston: Twayne.

Kaplan, Temma. 1977. "Other Scenarios: Women and Spanish Anarchism." In Renate Bridenthal and Claudia Koonz, eds., *Becoming Visible: Women in European History.* Boston: Houghton Mifflin.

———. 1982. "Female Consciousness and Collective Action: The Case of Barcelona, 1910–1918." *Signs* 7 (Spring): 545–66.

———. 1982. "Female Consciousness and Collective Action: The Case of Barcelona, 1910–1918." In Nannerl O. Keohane, Michelle Z. Rosaldo, and Barbara C. Gelpi, eds., *Feminist Theory: A Critique of Ideology.* Chicago: University of Chicago Press.

———. 1987a. "Community and Resistance: Women's Political Cultures in Historical Perspective." Paper presented at the University of California, San Diego. October.

———. 1987b. "Women and Communal Strikes in the Crisis of 1917–1922." In Renate Bridenthal, Claudia Koonz, and Susan Stuard, eds., *Becoming Visible: Women in European History.* 2d ed. Boston: Houghton Mifflin.

Kapp, Yvonne. 1976. *Eleanor Marx.* Vol. 2. New York: Pantheon.

Katz, Jonathan. 1976. *Gay American History: Lesbians and Gay Men in the U.S.A.* New York: Crowell.

———. 1983. *Gay, Lesbian Almanac.* New York: Harper & Row.

Katznelson, R. 1927. "The Participation of the Female Workers." *Kontres* 14: 15–20. [In Hebrew]

Katznelson Shazar, R., ed. 1975. *The Plough Woman.* New York: Herzl Press.

Kautsky, Luise. 1929. *Rosa Luxemburg: ein Gedenkbuch.* Berlin: Laubsche.

Kelber, Mim. 1989. "The Daughters of Mother Earth." *New Directions for Women* July–August): 2.

Keller, Evelyn Fox. 1985. *Reflections on Gender and Science.* New Haven, Conn.: Yale University Press.

Kelly, Rita Mae, and Mary Boutilier. 1978. *The Making of Political Women.* Chicago: Nelson-Hall.

Keniston, Kenneth. 1968. *Young Radicals.* New York: Harcourt, Brace & World.

———. 1971. *Youth and Dissent: The Rise of a New Opposition.* New York: Harcourt Brace Jovanovich.

Kerpelman, L. 1972. *Activists and Nonactivists.* New York: Behavioral Publications.

Kessler-Harris, Alice. 1975. "Where Are the Organized Women Workers?" *Feminist Studies* 3 (Fall):92–109.

———. 1982. *Out to Work: A History of Wage-Earning Women in the United States.* New York: Oxford University Press.

Killian, Lewis M. 1964. "Social Movements." In Robert E. L. Farris, ed., *Handbook of Modern Sociology.* Chicago: Rand McNally.

King, Deborah K. 1988. "Multiple Jeopardy, Multiple Consciousness: The Context of a Black Feminist Ideology." *Signs* 14 (Autumn): 42–72.

King, Martin Luther, Jr. 1958. *Stride Toward Freedom: The Montgomery Story.* New York: Harper & Row.

King, Mary. 1987. *Freedom Song: A Personal Account of the Civil Rights Movement.* New York: Morrow.

Kinzer, Nora Scott. 1973. "Priests, Machos, and Babies." *Journal of Marriage and the Family* 35 (May):300–11.

Kirk, Gwyn. 1989a. "Blood, Bones, Connective Tissue: Issues for Feminist Peace Politics." Paper presented at the Laurie New Jersey Chair Seminars, Rutgers University.

———. 1989b. "Our Greenham Common: Feminism and Non-Violence." In Adrienne Harris and Ynestra King, eds., *Rocking the Ship of State: Towards a Feminist Peace Politics.* Boulder, Colo.: Westview Press.

Kishwar, Madhu, and Ruth Vanita, eds. 1984. *In Search of Answers: Indian Womens' Voices from Manushi.* London: Zed Press.

Kitschelt, Herbert. 1985. "New Social Movements in West Germany and the United States." *Political Power and Social Theory* 5: 273–324.

Kitzinger, Celia. 1987. *The Social Construction of Lesbianism.* London: Sage.

Klein, Ethel. 1984. *Gender Politics: From Consciousness to Mass Politics.* Cambridge, Mass.: Harvard University Press.

"Knacken im Gebaelke." 1989. *Spiegel.* March 12:10.

Knaster, Meri. 1976. "Women in Latin America: The State of Research 1975." *Latin American Research Review* 11: 3–74.

Koen, Susan, and Nina Swain, eds. 1980. *Ain't No Where We Can Run: Women in the Nuclear Mentality.* Norwich, Vt.: WAND.

Kohl, James, and John Litt. 1974. "Urban Guerrilla Warfare: Uruguay." In James Kohl and John Litt, eds., *Urban Guerrilla Warfare in Latin America.* Cambridge, Mass.: MIT Press.

Kohlberg, Lawrence. 1966. "A Cognitive-Developmental Analysis of Children's Sex Role Concepts and Attitudes." In Eleanor E. Maccoby, ed., *The Development of Sex Differences.* Stanford, Calif.: Stanford University Press.

Kohn, Howard. 1981. *Who Killed Karen Silkwood?* New York: Summit Books.

Kolinsky, Eva. 1984a. "The Greens in Germany: Prospects of a Small Party." *Parliamentary Affairs* 37: 434–47.

———. 1984b. *Parties, Opposition and Society in West Germany.* New York: St. Martin's Press.

Kollontai, Alexandra. 1921. *The Workers' Opposition in Russia.* Chicago: International Workers of the World.

———. 1972. *Sexual Relations and the Class Struggle.* Translated by Alix Holt. Bristol, Eng.: Falling Wall Press.

———. 1973. "La Crise de la famille." In Judith Stora-Sandor, ed., *Alexandra Kollontai: Marxisme et révolution sexuelle.* Paris: Maspero.

———. 1975. "The New Woman." In *The Autobiography of a Sexually Emancipated Communist Woman.* New York: Schocken Books.

———. 1977a. "Excerpts from a Diary." In Alix Holt, ed. and trans., *Selected Writings of Alexandra Kollontai*. Westport, Conn.: Laurence Hill.

———. 1977b. "Theses on Communist Morality in the Sphere of Marital Relations. In Holt, *Selected Writings*.

———. 1977c. "Working Woman and Mother." In Holt, *Selected Writings*.

Komarovsky, Mirra. 1964. *Blue-Collar Marriage*. New York: Random House.

Kraditor, Aileen S. [1965] 1971. *The Ideas of the Woman Suffrage Movement: 1890–1920*. New York: Columbia University Press; Garden City, N.Y.: Anchor Books.

Kramarae, Cheris, and Paula A. Treichler. 1985. *A Feminist Dictionary*. Boston: Pandora Press.

Kreps, Juanita, and Robert Clark. 1975. *Sex, Age and Work: The Changing Composition of the Labor Force*. Baltimore: Johns Hopkins University Press.

Krigser, S. 1947. "Our First Agricultural Training." In B. Chabas, ed., *The Second Aliya*. Tel Aviv: Am Oved. [In Hebrew]

Kropotkin, Peter. 1899. *Memoirs of a Revolutionist*. Boston: Houghton Mifflin.

Krupskaya, Nadezhda. 1930. *Memoirs of Lenin*. Translated by E. Verney. Vol. 1. New York: International.

———. 1959. *Reminiscences of Lenin*. Moscow: Foreign Languages Publishing House.

Kunzle, David. 1982. *Fashion and Fetishism: A Social History of the Corset, Tight-Lacing and Other Forms of Body Sculpture in the West*. Totowa, N.J.: Rowman and Littlefield.

Ladd-Taylor, Molly. 1985. "Women Workers and the Yale Strike." *Feminist Studies* 2 (Fall):465–89.

Ladner, Joyce. (1988). "A Sociology of the Civil Rights Movement: An Insider's Perspective." Paper presented at the Annual Meeting of the American Sociological Association, August.

Lafargue, Paul. 1897. "Socialism in France from 1876 to 1896." *Fortnightly Review*, n.s., vol. 62: 452.

Laine, Barry. 1983. "Whose Wave Is It Anyway?: The New, the Next, and the Permanent . . ." *Dancemagazine* 57: 59–67.

Lamb, Curt. 1976. *Political Power in Poor Neighborhoods*. New York: Schenkman.

Lang, Kurt, and Gladys Engel Lang. 1961. *Collective Dynamics*. New York: Crowell.

Langguth, Gerd. 1983. *Die neue Linke seit 1968*. Cologne: Verlag Wissenschaft und Politik Berend von Nottbeck.

———. 1986. *The Green Factor in German Politics: From Movement to Political Party*. Boulder, Colo.: Westview Press.

Lapidus, Gail. 1977. "Sexual Equality in Soviet Policy: A Developmental Perspective." In D. Atkinson, A. Dallin, and G. W. Lapidus, eds., *Women in Russia*. Stanford, Calif.: Stanford University Press.

Laqueur, Walter. 1977. *Guerrilla: A Historical and Critical Study*. London: Weidenfeld and Nicolson.

———. 1985. *Germany Today*. Boston: Little, Brown.

Lasky, Marjorie Penn. 1985. " 'Where I Was a Person': The Ladies' Auxiliary in the 1934 Minneapolis Teamsters' Strikes." In Ruth Milkman, ed., *Women, Work and Protest: A Century of U.S. Women's Labor History*. Boston: Routledge and Kegan Paul.

Latin American Working Group. 1983. "El Salvador." In *Central American Women Speak for Themselves*. Toronto: Latin American Working Group.

Lauritsen, John, and David Thorstad. 1974. *The Early Homosexual Rights Movement (1864–1935)*. New York: Times Change.

Lawson, Ronald. 1983. "A Decentralized but Moving Pyramid: The Evolution and Consequences of the Structure of the Tenant Movement." In Jo Freeman, ed., *Social Movements of the Sixties and Seventies*. New York: Longman.

Lawson, Ronald, and Stephen Barton. 1980. "Sex Roles in Social Movements: A Case Study of the Tenant Movement in New York City." *Signs* 6:230–47.

Le Bon, Gustave. [1895] 1969. *The Crowd: A Study of the Popular Mind.* New York: Ballantine Books.

Lebsock, Suzanne. 1984. *The Free Women of Petersburg: Status and Culture in a Southern Town. 1784–1860.* New York: Norton.

Lee, P., and R. Steward. 1976. *Sex Differences.* New York: Urizen.

Lein, Laura, and Peggy McIntosh. (1982). "Putting Research to Work: Applied Research on Women." Working Paper, no. 97. Wellesley College Center for Research on Women. August 1–15.

Lemons, J. Stanley. 1973. *The Woman Citizen: Social Feminism in the 1920s.* Urbana: University of Illinois Press.

Lenin, V. I. 1920. *"Left" Communism: An Infantile Disorder.* London: The Toiler.

———. 1934. *The Emancipation of Women.* New York: International.

———. 1963–70. *Collected Works.* Moscow: Progress.

———. 1971. "Réponse à Rosa Luxemburg." In Daniel Guérin, *Rosa Luxemburg et la spontanéité révolutionnaire.* Paris: Flammarion.

———. 1975. "The Dual Power." In Robert C. Tucker, ed., *The Lenin Anthology.* New York: Norton.

Leonardo, Micaela di. 1985. "Mothers and Militarism: Antimilitarism and Feminist Theory." *Feminist Studies* 11 (Fall): 599–617.

Lerner, Gerda. 1979. "The Lady and the Mill Girl: Changes in the Status of Women in the Age of Jackson." In Gerda Lerner, ed., *The Majority Finds Its Past: Placing Women in History.* New York: Oxford University Press.

Levine, Adeline Gordon. 1982. *Love Canal: Science, Politics and People.* Lexington, Mass.: Heath.

Liao, F. 1981. "Emancipation of Women Ended Footbinding." *China Daily.* September 5.

Liberson, T. 1913. "On the Question of the Women Workers." *Hapoel Hatzair* 6. [In Hebrew]

———. 1975. "Women Build Houses." In R. Katznelson Shazar, ed., *The Plough Woman.* New York: Herzl Press.

Liberson, Z. 1947. "The Workers' Kitchen in Hadera." In B. Chabas, ed., *The Second Aliya.* Tel Aviv: Am Oved. [In Hebrew]

Likimani, Muthoni. 1985. *Passbook Number F.47927: Women and Mau Mau in Kenya.* Introductory essay by Jean O'Barr. London: Macmillan.

Lin, S. T. 1976. "Chinese Women on the Road to Complete Emancipation." In L. B. Iglitzin and R. Ross, eds., *Women in the World: A Comparative Study.* Oxford: Clio Books.

Lindley, A. F. 1970. *Ti-Ping Tein-Kwoh: The History of the Ti-Ping Revolution.* New York: Praeger.

Lipman-Blumen, Jean. 1984. *Gender Roles and Power.* Englewood Cliffs, N.J.: Prentice-Hall.

Lipset, Seymour Martin. 1971. *Rebellion in the University.* Boston: Little, Brown.

Lipsky, Michael. 1968. "Protest as a Political Resource." *American Political Science Review* 62 (1968):1144–58.

———. 1970. *Protest in City Politics: Rent Strikes, Housing and the Power of the Poor.* Chicago: Rand McNally.

Lo, E. K. 1979. *Taiping Tianguo Shishi Kao* (Studies of the Taiping Kingdom). Peking: Sanlian Shudian.

Lodge, Tom. 1984. "Women's Protest Movements in the 1950s." In *Black Politics in South Africa Since 1945.* London and New York: Longman.

Lofland, John. 1977. *Doomsday Cult*. New York: Irvington.

———. 1979. "White-Hot Mobilization: Strategies of a Millenarian Movement." In Mayer N. Zald and John D. McCarthy, eds., *Dynamics of Social Movements*. Cambridge, Mass.: Winthrop.

———. 1981. "Collective Behavior: The Elementary Forms." In M. Rosenberg and R. Turner, eds., *Social Psychology: Sociological Perspective*. New York: Basic Books.

———. 1985. *Protest: Forms of Collective Behavior and Social Movements*. New Brunswick, N.J.: Transaction Books.

Lofland, John, and Michael Jamison. 1984. "Social Movement Locals: Modal Member Structures." *Sociological Analysis* 45: 115–29.

Lofland, Lyn. H. 1973. "The 'Thereness' of Women: A Selective Review of Urban Sociology." In Marcia Millman and Rosabeth Moss Kanter, eds., *Another Voice: Feminist Perspectives on Social Life and Social Science*. New York: Anchor Books.

Loizos, Caroline. 1969. "Play Behavior in Higher Primates: A Review." In Desmond Morris, ed., *Primate Ethology*. Garden City, N.J.: Anchor Books.

Long, Priscilla. 1985. "The Women of the Colorado Fuel and Iron Strike, 1913–14." In Ruth Milkman, ed., *Women, Work and Protest: A Century of U.S. Women's Labor History*. Boston: Routledge and Kegan Paul.

Lopata, Helena Z. 1971. *Occupation Housewife*. New York: Oxford University Press.

Lopez, Olga. 1976. "Las Guerrillas Cubanas." In Michele Flouret, ed., *La Guerrilla en Hispano America*. Paris: Masson.

Lopez de Piza, Eugenia. 1977. "La labor doméstica como fuente importante de valor de plusvalía en los países dependientes." *Revista de Ciencias Sociales* 14 (October): 19–29.

Lovenduski, Joni. 1986. *Women and European Politics: Contemporary Feminism and Public Policy*. Amherst: University of Massachusetts Press.

Lowe, Marianne, and Ruth Hubbard, eds. 1987. *Woman's Nature: Rationalizations of Inequality*. New York: Pergamon Press.

Luebke, Paul. 1981. "Activists and Asphalt: A Successful Anti-Expressway Movement in a 'New South City.'" *Human Organization* 40:256–63.

Luger, Elaine, and Barry Laine. (1978). "When Choreography Becomes Female." *Christopher Street* (November): 65–8.

Luxemburg, Rosa. 1904. "Organisationfragen der russischen Sozialdemokraten." *Die Neue Zeit*. July 13, 20:484–92, 529–35.

———. 1961. *The Russian Revolution and Leninism or Marxism?* Ann Arbor: University of Michigan Press.

———. 1970a. "Against Capital Punishment." In Mary Alice Waters, ed., *Rosa Luxemburg Speaks*. New York: Pathfinder Press.

———. 1970b. "The Mass Strike, the Political Party, and the Trade Unions." In Waters, ed., *Rosa Luxemburg Speaks*.

———. 1971a. *Lettres à Léon Jogichès*. Paris: Denoël Gonthier.

———. 1971b. "What Does the Spartacus League Want?" In Dick Howard, ed., *Selected Political Writings of Rosa Luxemburg*. New York: Monthly Review Press.

———. 1972a. "The National Assembly." In Robert Looker, ed., *Selected Political Writings*. London: Jonathan Cape.

———. 1972b. "The Next Step." In Looker, ed., *Selected Political Writings*.

———. 1972c. "Political Mass Strike." In Looker, ed., *Selected Political Writings*.

———. 1972d. "The Revolution in Russia." In Looker, ed., *Selected Political Writings*.

———. 1972e. "What Now?" In Looker, ed., *Selected Political Writings*.

———. 1975. *Letters to Karl and Luise Kautsky*. Edited by Luise Kautsky. New York: Gordon Press.

Lynd, Robert, and Helen Lynd. 1929. *Middletown*. New York: Harcourt, Brace.

Lynn, David B. 1969. *Parental and Sex-Role Identification*. Berkeley, Calif.: McCutchen.

———. 1974. *The Father: His Role in Child Development*. Monterey, Calif.: Brooks/Cole.

MacFarlane, C. 1972. *The Chinese Revolution*. Wilmington: Scholarly Resources.

Madruga, Leopoldo. 1974. "Interview with Urbano." In James Kohl and John Litt, eds., *Urban Guerrilla Warfare in Latin America*. Cambridge, Mass.: MIT Press.

Maggard, Sally Ward. 1988. "Eastern Kentucky Women on Strike: A Study of Gender. Class and Political Action in the 1970s." Ph.D. diss., University of Kentucky.

Maimon (Fishman), A. *Women Workers' Movement in Eretz Israel*. Tel Aviv: Hapoel Hatzair. [In Hebrew]

———. 1972. *Along the Way*. Tel Aviv: Am Oved. [In Hebrew]

Malato, Charles. 1897. *Les Joyeusetés de l'exil*. Paris: Stock.

Malchin, S. 1912. "The Women Worker in Kineret." *Hapoel Hatzair* 11 (1912). [In Hebrew]

Mamashi. 1910. "The Question of the Woman Worker in the Galilee." *Hapoel Hatzair* 4. [In Hebrew]

———. 1913. "On the Question of the Women Workers." *Hapoel Hatzair* 27.

Mannheim, Karl. 1973. "The Problem of Generations." In Paul Kecksckmeti, ed., *The Sociology of Knowledge*. New York: Oxford University Press.

Markham, James. M. 1983. "Germany's Volatile Greens." *New York Times Magazine*. February 13: 37, 39, 41, 77–79.

Markovits, Andrei S. 1985. "On Anti-Americanism in West Germany." *New German Critique* 34 (Winter): 3–27.

Marotta, Toby. 1981. *The Politics of Homosexuality: How Lesbians and Gay Men Have Made Themselves a Political and Social Force in Modern America*. Boston: Houghton Mifflin.

Martin, Del, and Phyllis Lyon. 1972. *Lesbian/Woman*. New York: Bantam.

———. 1988. "The History of Daughters of Bilitis (DOB)." Speech sponsored by the New York City Lesbian Herstory Archives and the Office of the Mayor of New York to commemorate Lesbian/Gay Pride, New York City. June 23.

Martin, Jane Roland. 1986. "Questioning the Question." *Women's Review of Books* 4, (December):17–18.

Marx, Eleanor. 1885. In *Commonweal*. December.

———. 1886. In *Commonweal*. May 15.

Marx, Eleanor, and Edward Aveling. 1886. "The Woman Question: From a Socialist Point of View." *Westminster Review*, n.s., vol. 69: 207–22.

Marx, Gary, and Michael Useem. 1971. "Majority Involvement in Minority Movements: Civil Rights, Abolition and Untouchability." *Journal of Social Issues* 27: 81–104.

Marx, Gary, and James Wood. 1975. "Strands of Theory and Research in Collective Behavior." In Alex Inkeles, James Coleman, and Neil Smelser, eds., *Annual Review of Sociology*. Vol. 1. Palo Alto, Calif.: Annual Reviews.

Marx, Karl. n.d. *Capital*. New York: Modern Library.

———. 1959. *The Communist Manifesto*. In Lewis S. Feuer, ed., *Marx and Engels: Basic Writings on Politics and Philosophy*. Garden City, N.Y.: Anchor Books.

———. 1970. *The German Ideology*. New York: International.

———. 1973. *Critique of the Gotha Program*. Edited by C. P. Dutt. New York: International.

Masotti, Louis H., and Don R. Bowen, eds. 1968. *Riots and Rebellion: Civil Violence in the Urban Community*. Beverly Hills, Calif.: Sage.

Matthews, Donald, and James Prothro. 1966. *Negroes and the New Southern Politics*. New York: Harcourt, Brace & World.

McAdam, Doug. 1982. *Political Process and the Development of Black Insurgency, 1930–1970*. Chicago: University of Chicago Press.

Mc Allister, Pam. 1988. *You Can't Kill the Spirit*. Philadelphia: New Society.

————, ed. 1982. *Reweaving the Web of Life: Feminism and Nonviolence*. Philadelphia: New Society.

McCarthy, John D., and Mayer N. Zald. 1973. *The Trend of Social Movements in America: Professionalization and Resource Mobilization*. Morristown, N.J.: General Learning Press.

————. 1977. "Resource Mobilization and Social Movements: A Partial Theory." *American Journal of Sociology* 82 (May): 1212–41.

McClung, Nellie. [1915] 1972. *In Times Like These*. Introduction by Veronica Strong-Boag. Toronto: University of Toronto Press.

McCormack, Thelma. 1973. "Toward a Nonsexist Perspective on Social and Political Change." In Marcia Millman and Rosabeth Moss Kanter, eds., *Another Voice: Feminist Perspectives on Social Life and Social Science*. New York: Anchor Books.

McCormick, Pat. 1975. "NOW Task Force on Volunteerism." *Ms.* (February): 73.

McCourt, Kathleen. 1977. *Working Class Women and Grassroots Politics*. Bloomington: Indiana University Press.

McGee, Sandra F. 1981. "Introduction to Women and Politics in Twentieth Century Latin America." In Sandra McGee, ed., *Women and Politics in Twentieth Century Latin America*. Williamsburg, Va.: Department of Anthropology, College of William and Mary.

McGuigan, Dorothy Gies. 1970. *A Dangerous Experiment: 100 Years of Women at the University of Michigan* Ann Arbor, Mich.: Center for Continuing Education of Women.

McPhail, Clark. 1971. "Civil Disorder Participation: A Critical Examination of Recent Research." *American Sociological Review* 36: 1058–73.

Meadows, Donella H., et al. 1974. *Limits to Growth: A Report for the Club of Rome's Project on the Predicament of Mankind*. New York: Universe.

Meadows, T. T. 1972. *The Chinese and Their Rebellions*. New York: Harper & Row.

Meek, C. K., 1937. *Law and Authority in a Nigerian Tribe*. (London: Oxford University Press.

"Mehr Frauen in die Politik." 1988. *Das Parliament*. December 16: 9.

Mehring, Franz. 1907. "Historisch-materialistiche Literatur." *Die Neue Zeit*, July 17: 507.

Meir, G. 1975. *My Life*. London: Futura.

Merritt, R. 1970. *Systematic Approaches to Comparative Politics*. Chicago: Rand McNally.

Merritt, S. 1978. "Sex Differences in Role Behavior and Policy Orientations of Suburban Officeholders." Paper presented at the Annual Meeting of the American Political Science Association, New York. September.

Mewes, Horst. 1983. "The West German Green Party." *New German Critique* 28 (Winter): 51–85.

————. 1984. "The Green Party Comes of Age." *Environment* 27 (June): 13–39.

Meyerding, Jane, ed. 1984. *We Are All Part of One Another: A Barbara Deming Reader*. Philadelphia: New Society.

Michael, F. 1966. *The Taiping Rebellion: History and Documents*. Vol. 1. Seattle: University of Washington Press.

————. 1971. *The Taiping Rebellion: History and Documents*. Vols. 2, 3. Seattle: University of Washington Press.

Michel, Louise. 1890. *Prise de possession*. Paris: Saint Denis.

————. 1921. *La Commune*. Paris: Stock.

————. 1976. *Mémoires de Louise Michel*. Paris: Maspero.

Michelman, Cherry. 1975. *The Black Sash of South Africa: A Case Study in Liberalism.* London: Oxford University Press for the Institute of Race Relations.

Michels, Robert. [1906] 1959. *Political Parties: A Sociological Study of the Oligarchical Tendencies of Modern Democracy.* New York: Dover.

——. [1915] 1962. *Political Parties: A Sociological Study of the Oligarchical Tendencies of Modern Democracy.* New York: Free Press.

Milkman, Ruth, ed. 1985. *Women, Work and Protest: A Century of U.S. Women's Labor History.* Boston: Routledge & Kegan Paul.

Miller, Alice Duer. 1915. *Are Women People? A Book of Rhymes for Suffrage Times.* New York: Doran.

Miller, Frederick. 1983. "The End of SDS and the Emergence of Weathermen: Demise Through Success." In Jo Freeman, ed., *Social Movements of the Sixties and Seventies.* New York: Longman.

Minutes of the Second Meeting of the Executive Committee of the Women Workers' Council. 1926, June. Labor Archives, Tel Aviv. [In Hebrew]

Molyneux, Maxine. 1985. "Mobilization Without Emancipation? Women's Interests, the State, and Revolution in Nicaragua." *Feminist Studies* 11 (Summer): 227–54.

Mombauer, Martin. 1982. "Die Doppelstrategie der grünen Niedersachsen." In Jorg R. Mettke, ed., *Die Grünen.* Hamburg: Spiegel-Verlag.

Montgomery, Tommie Sue. 1982. *Revolution in El Salvador.* Boulder, Colo.: Westview Press.

Moraga, Cherrie, and Gloria Anzaldua, eds. 1981. *This Bridge Called My Back: Writings by Radical Women of Color.* Watertown, Mass.: Persephone.

Morris, Aldon. 1984. *The Origins of the Civil Rights Movement: Black Communities Organizing for Change.* New York: Free Press.

Morris, David, and Karl Hess. 1975. *Neighborhood Power.* Boston: Beacon Press.

"Mother's Group Fights Back in Los Angeles." 1989. *New York Times.* December 5: A32.

Mottl, Tahi L. 1980. "The Analysis of Countermovements." *Social Movements* 27 (June): 620–35.

Movimento de Liberación Nacional. 1974. "The Tupamaro's Program for Revolutionary Government." In James Kohl and John Litt, eds., *Urban Guerrilla Warfare in Latin America.* Cambridge, Mass.: MIT Press.

Mullaney, Marie Marmo. 1983. *Revolutionary Women: Gender and the Socialist Revolutionary Role.* New York: Praeger.

——. 1984a. "Gender and the Socialist Revolutionary Role, 1871–1921: A General Theory of the Female Revolutionary Personality." *Historical Reflections/Réflexions historiques* 11: 99–151.

——. 1984b. "Women and the Theory of the 'Revolutionary Personality': Comments, Criticisms, and Suggestions for Further Study." *Social Science Journal* 21: 49–70.

Müller-Rommel, Ferdinand. 1985. "Social Movements and the Greens: New Internal Politics in Germany." *European Journal of Political Research* 13: 53–67.

Mushaben, Joyce. 1984. "Anti-Politics and Successor Generations: The Role of Youth in the West and East German Peace Movements." *Journal of Political and Military Sociology* 12: 171–90.

Musto, Michael. 1990. "AIDS, Hope, and Charity; Gay Fundraisers Ask: Do We Accept Money from Our Oppressors?" *Village Voice.* February 27: 31–34.

NACLA (North American Congress on Latin America). 1981. "No Easy Victory." *NACLA Report on the Americas* 15 (May): 8–17.

——. 1984. "El Salvador 1984: Locked in Battle." *NACLA Report on the Americas* 18 (March–April): 14–17.

Nakayama, Y. 1980. "Taihei Tengoku Fujin Seisaku" (The Taiping policy of women). *Kita Kyushu Daigaku Gaikokugo Gabuku Kiyo* 42 (October): 9–37.

———. (1981). "Taihei Tengoku ni Okeru Josei no Koudou" (The activities of women in the Taiping Movement). *Kita Kyushu Daigaku Gaikokugo Gabuku Kiyo* 43 (February): 65–90.

Nash, June. 1976. "A Critique of Social Science Roles in Latin America." In June Nash and Helen Safa, eds., *Sex and Class in Latin America*. New York: Praeger.

———. 1977. "Women in Development: Dependency and Exploitation." *Development and Change* 8:161–82.

Nash, June, and Helen Safa. 1976a. "Introduction to Part I: The Family and Ideological Reinforcement of Sexual Subordination." In June Nash and Helen Safa, eds., *Sex and Class in Latin America*. New York: Praeger.

———. (1976b). "Introduction to Part II: Women in Productive Roles." In June Nash and Helen Safa, eds., *Sex and Class in Latin America*. New York: Praeger.

Nelson, Barbara J. 1989. "Women and Knowledge in Political Science: Texts, Histories and Epistemologies." *Women and Politics*. 9: 1–25.

Nestle, Joan. 1987. *A Restricted Country.* Ithaca, N.Y.: Firebrand.

Nettl, J. P. 1966. *Rosa Luxemburg.* Vol. 2. London: Oxford University Press.

Newcomer, Mabel. 1959. *A Century of Higher Education for Women.* New York: Harper & Brothers.

NGLTF (National Gay and Lesbian Task Force). 1987. *Anti-Gay Violence, Victimization and Defamation in 1987.* Washington, D.C.: NGLTF.

Nigerian Government. 1930a. Aba Commission of Enquiry: Minutes of Evidence.

———. 1930b. Report of the Commission of Inquiry Appointed to Inquire into the Disturbances in the Calabar and Owerri Provinces, December 1929. Sessional Paper of the Nigerian Legislative Council, no. 23.

Njaka, Mazi Elechukwu Nnadibuangha. 1974. *Igbo Political Culture.* Evanston, Ill.: Northwestern Univ. Press.

Nomad, Max. 1959. *Aspects of Revolt.* New York: Bookman.

Nwabara, Samuel Nkankwo. 1965. "Ibo Land: A Study in British Penetration and the Problem of Administration, 1860–1930." Ph.D. diss., Northwestern University. Ann Arbor, Mich.: University Microfilms.

Nyden, Philip. 1972. "Welfare and Welfare Rights: An Analysis of Organizations in the Newark Metropolitan Area." Paper submitted to Drew University, Madison, N.J.

Oakley, Ann. 1981. "Interviewing Women: A Contradiction in Terms." In Helen Roberts, ed., *Doing Feminist Research*. Boston: Routledge & Kegan Paul.

O'Barr, Jean. 1984. "African Women in Politics." In Margaret Jean Hay and Sharon Stichter, eds., *African Women: South of the Sahara*. London: Longman.

———. 1985. "Introductory Essay." In Muthoni Likimani, *Passbook Number F.47927: Women and Mau Mau in Kenya*. London: Macmillan.

Oberschall, Anthony. 1973. *Social Conflict and Social Movements.* Englewood Cliffs, N.J.: Prentice-Hall.

———. 1978. "The Decline of the 1960s Social Movements." In Louis Kriesberg, ed., *Research in Social Movements: Conflict and Change.* Vol. 1. Greenwich, Conn.: JAI Press.

O'Brien, M. 1981. *The Politics of Reproduction.* London: Routledge & Kegan Paul.

O'Kelly, Charlotte G. 1980. *Women and Men in Society.* New York: Van Nostrand.

Oldfield, Sybil. 1987. "German Women in the Resistance to Hitler." In Sian Reynolds, ed., *Women, State and Revolution: Essays on Power and Gender in Europe Since 1789.* Amherst: University of Massachusetts Press.

Olin, Helen R. 1909. *The Women of A State University: An Illustration of the Working of Coeducation in the Middle West*. New York: Putnam.

Oliver, Pamela E., and Gerald Marwell. 1988. "The Paradox of Group Size in Collective Action: A Theory of the Critical Mass, II." *American Sociological Review* 53: 1–8.

Onwuteaka, J. C. 1965. "The Aba Riot and Its Relation to the System of Indirect Rule." *Nigerian Journal of Economic and Social Studies* (November): .

Ortner, Sherry B. 1974. "Is Female to Male as Nature Is to Culture?" In Michelle Zimbalist Rosaldo and Louise Lamphere, eds., *Women, Culture, and Society*. Stanford, Calif.: Stanford University Press.

Palencia, Isabel de. 1947. *Alexandra Kollontay: Ambassadress from Russia*. New York: Longmans, Green.

Papadakis, Elim. 1984. *The Green Movement in West Germany*. New York: St. Martin's Press.

Pappi, Franz Urban. 1984. "The West German Party System." In Stephano Bartolini and Peter Mair, eds., *Party Politics in Contemporary Western Europe*. London: Frank Cass.

Park, Robert E., and Ernest W. Burgess. 1921. *An Introduction to the Science of Sociology*. Chicago: University of Chicago Press.

Parsons. T. 1976. "Family Structure and the Socialization of the Child." In P. Lee and R. Steward, eds., *Sex Differences*. New York: Urizen.

Participants in the Puget Sound Women's Peace Camp. 1985. *We Are Ordinary Women: A Chronicle of the Puget Sound Women's Peace Camp*. Seattle: Seal Press.

Pateman, Carol. 1987. "Introduction: The Theoretical Subversiveness of Feminism." In Carol Pateman and Elizabeth Gross, eds., *Feminist Challenges: Social and Political Theory*. The Northeastern Series in Feminist Theory. Boston: Northeastern University Press.

Pateman, Carol, and Elizabeth Gross, eds. 1987. *Feminist Challenges: Social and Political Theory*. The Northeastern Series in Feminist Theory. Boston: Northeastern University Press.

Pearce, Diana M. 1984. "Farewell to Alms: Women and Welfare Policy in the Eighties." In Jo Freeman, ed., *Women: A Feminist Perspective*. 3d ed. Palo Alto, Calif.: Mayfield.

Perham, Margery. 1937. *Native Administration in Nigeria*. London: Oxford University Press.

Perlez, Jane. 1989. "Skyscraper's Enemy Draws a Daily Dose of Scorn." *New York Times*. December 6: A4.

Perrow, Charles. 1979. "The Sixties Observed." In Mayer N. Zald and John D. McCarthy, eds., *The Dynamics of Social Movements*. Cambridge, Mass.: Winthrop.

Perry, Joseph B., and M. D. Pugh. 1978. *Collective Behavior*. St. Paul: West.

Petchesky, Rosalind Pollack. 1983. "Reproduction and Class Division Among Women." In Amy Swerdlow and Hanna Lessinger, eds., *Class, Race, and Sex: the Dynamics of Control*. Boston: Hall.

———. 1985. *Abortion and Women's Choice: The State, Sexuality and Reproductive Freedom*. Boston: Northeastern University Press.

Pilat, F. 1980. *Ecological Politics: The Rise of the Green Movement*. Vol. 8, *The Washington Papers*. The Center for Strategic and International Studies. Beverly Hills, Calif.: Sage.

Piven, Frances Fox. 1976. "The Social Structuring of Political Protest." *Politics and Society* 6:297–326.

———. 1980. "Social Problems as the Institutional Nexus of Rebellion." President's Statement of the Theme for the Annual Meeting of the Society for the Study of Social Problems. Preliminary Program Booklet.

————. 1981. "Deviant Behavior and the Remaking of the World. *Social Problems* 28 (June):489–508.

————. 1985. "Women and the State: Ideology, Power, and the Welfare State." In Alice S. Rossi, ed., *Gender and Life Course.* New York: Aldine.

Piven, Frances Fox, and R. A. Cloward. 1971. *Regulating the Poor.* New York: Pantheon Books.

————. 1977. *Poor People's Movements: Why They Succeed, How They Fail.* New York: Pantheon Books.

"Politics Without the Punch?" 1983. *Spare Rib* (July): 42–45.

Popp, Adelheid. 1912. *The Autobiography of a Working Woman.* London: Fisher Unwin.

Porat, R. 1977. *Education in the Collectives and Kibbutzim.* Tel Aviv: Hakibbutz Hameuchad. [In Hebrew]

Porzecanski, Arturo C. 1973. *Uruguay's Tupamaros: The Urban Guerrilla.* New York: Praeger.

Programme of the German Green Party. 1985. London: Heretic Books.

"Protocol of the First Convention of the Histadrut, December 1920." 1970. *Asufot* 1: 5–80.

Purcell, Susan Kaufman. 1973. "Modernizing Women for a Modern Society: The Cuban Case." In Ann Pescatello, ed., *Female and Male in Latin America.* Pittsburgh: University of Pittsburgh Press.

Quinn, Robin. 1987. "Mothering Earth." *Ms.* (September): 86.

"Quoten verschaffen uns einem Fuss in der Tür." 1986. *Spiegel.* August 25: 32–47.

"Radicalesbians." 1970. *Come Out!* (December):10.

————. 1973. "The Woman-Identified Woman." In Anne Koedt et al., eds., *Radical Feminism.* New York: Quadrangle.

Raines, Howell. 1977. *My Soul Is Rested.* New York: Putnam.

————. 1983. "The Birmingham Bombing: Twenty Years Later." *New York Times Magazine.* July 24:12–13, 21–23, 28–29.

Ramirez-Horton, Susan E. 1982. "The Role of Women in the Nicaraguan Revolution." In Thomas W. Walker, ed., *Nicaragua in Revolution.* New York: Praeger.

Ramos, Juanita. 1988. *Compañeras: Latin American Lesbian Anthology.* New York: Kitchen Table.

Randall, Margaret. 1978. *Doris Tijerino: Inside the Nicaraguan Revolution.* Vancouver: New Star.

Randall, Vicky. [1982] 1987. *Women and Politics.* New York: St. Martin's Press.

Ratinoff, Louis. 1967. "The New Urban Groups: The Middle Classes." In Seymour Martin Lipset and Aldo Solari, eds., *Elites in Latin America.* London: Oxford University Press.

"Report of the Second Conference of the Women Workers' Council." 1922. *Hapoel Hatzair* 37. [In Hebrew]

"Revolutionaere Geduld." 1989. *Spiegel.* April 14: 73.

Reynolds, Sian, ed. 1987. *Women, State and Revolution: Essays on Power and Gender in Europe Since 1789.* Amherst: University of Massachusetts Press.

Rich, Adrienne. 1976. *Of Woman Born: Motherhood as Experience and Institution.* New York: Bantam Books.

————. 1980. "Compulsory Heterosexuality and Lesbian Existence." *Signs* 5 (Summer): 631–60.

Richardson, Harry. 1947. *Dark Glory: A Picture of the Church Among Negroes in the Rural South.* New York: Friendship Press.

Rieder, Ines, and Patricia Ruppelt. 1988. *AIDS: The Women.* Pittsburgh: Cleis.

Riegel, Robert E. 1970. *American Women: A Story of Social Change.* Rutherford, N.J.: Fairleigh Dickinson University Press.

Roberts, Barbara. 1985a. " 'An International Calamity Caused by Greed': Feminist Pacifist Responses in Canada to the Great War, 1914–1918." Paper presented at the Canadian Historical Association Conference, Montreal. May.

———. 1985b. " 'Why Do Women Do Nothing to End the War?': Canadian Feminist Pacifists and the Great War." CRIAW Paper, no. 13.

Roberts, J. R. 1981. *Black Lesbians: An Annotated Bibliography.* Tallahassee, Fla.: Naiad.

Roberts, Norene. 1981. "A Woman's Place in Minnesota." *Roots* 9 (Winter): 2–31.

Roberts, Wayne. 1978. "Rocking the Cradle to Rule the World: Maternal Feminists in Toronto, 1880–1910." In Linda Kealey, ed., *A Not Unreasonable Claim: Women and Reform in Canada, 1880–1920.* Toronto: University of Toronto Press.

Robertson, Ian. 1981. *Sociology.* New York: Worth.

Robinson, Jo Ann Gibson. 1987. *The Montgomery Bus Boycott and the Women Who Started It: The Memoir of Jo Ann Gibson.* Edited, with a foreword, by David J. Garrow. Knoxville: University of Tennessee Press.

Rodriguez, Anabella. 1983. "Mozambican Women After the Revolution." In Miranda Davies, ed., *Third World/Second Sex: Women's Struggles and National Liberation.* London: Zed Books.

Rodriguez, Mario Menendez. 1983. *Voices From El Salvador.* San Francisco: Solidarity Publications.

Rong, T. 1983. "The Women's Movement in China Before and After the 1911 Revolution." *Chinese Studies in History* 16: 159–200.

Rosaldo, Michelle Zimbalist, and Louise Lamphere, eds. 1974. *Women, Culture and Society.* Stanford, Calif.: Stanford University Press.

Rosenberg, Charles E. 1973. "Sexuality, Class and Role in 19th-Century America." *American Quarterly* 35: 131–53.

Ross, Robert J. 1983. "Generational Change and Primary Groups in a Social Movement." In Jo Freeman, ed., *Social Movements of the Sixties and Seventies.* New York: Longman.

Rothschild, Mary Aickin. 1979. "White Women Volunteers in the Freedom Summers: Their Life and Work in a Movement for Social Change." *Feminist Studies* 5 (Fall): 466–95.

Rowbotham, Sheila. 1972. *Women, Resistance, and Revolution.* New York: Random House.

———. 1974a. *Hidden from History.* London: Pluto Press.

———. 1974b. *Women, Resistance, and Revolution: A History of Women and Revolution in the Modern World.* New York: Vintage Books.

Rubin, Lillian. 1976. *Worlds of Pain: Life in the Working Class Family.* New York: Basic Books.

Ruddick, Sara. (1980). "Maternal Thinking." *Feminist Studies* 6 (Summer): 342–67.

———. 1983. "Preservative Love and Military Destruction: Some Reflections on Mothering and Peace." In Joyce Treblicot, ed., *Mothering: Essays in Feminist Theory.* Totowa, N.J.: Rowman and Allanheld.

———. 1989. "Maternal Peace Politics and Women's Resistance: The Example of Argentina and Chile." *Barnard Occasional Papers on Women's Issues* 4 (Winter):34–55.

Rupp, Lelia J. 1980. " 'Imagine My Surprise': Women's Relationships in Historical Perspective." *Frontiers* 5: 61–70.

———. 1982. "The Survival of American Feminism: The Women's Movement in the Postwar Period." In Robert H. Bremner and Gary Reichard, eds., *Reshaping*

America: Society and Institutions, 1945–1960. Columbus: Ohio State University Press.

————. 1985. "The Women's Community in the National Woman's Party, 1945 to the 1960s." *Signs* 10 (Summer): 715–40.

Rupp, Leila J., and Verta Taylor. 1986. "The Women's Movement Since 1960: Structure, Strategies, and New Directions." In Robert H. Bremner, Gary Reichard, and Richard Hopkins, eds., *American Choices*. Columbus: Ohio State University Press.

————. 1987. *Survival in the Doldrums: The American Women's Rights Movement, 1945 to the 1960s*. New York: Oxford University Press.

Russell, Charles A., and Bowman H. Miller. 1977. "Profile of a Terrorist." *Terrorism* 1: 17–33.

Ryan, Mary P. 1979. "The Power of Women's Networks: A Case Study of Female Moral Reform in Antebellum America." *Feminist Studies* 5:66–85.

Sacks, Karen Brodkin. n.d. "Gender and Grassroots Leadership." Unpublished paper.

————. 1988. "Out of the Frying Pan, into the Fire: Macroeconomic Trends and Women's Life Chances." In Martha A. Ackelsberg, Randall Barlett, and Robert Buchele, eds., *Women, Welfare and Higher Education: Toward Comprehensive Policies*. Northampton, Mass.: Smith College.

Sacks, Karen, and Dorothy Remy, eds. 1984. *My Troubles Are Going to Have Trouble with Me: Everday Trials and Triumphs of Women Workers*. New Brunswick, N.J.: Rutgers University Press.

Sacks, Oliver. 1988. "The Revolution of the Deaf." *New York Review of Books*. June 2.

Sadoul, Jacques. 1920. *Notes sur la révolution bolchévique*. Paris: Editions de le Sirène.

Safa, Helen Icken. 1976. "Class Consciousness Among Working-Class Women in Latin America: Puerto Rico." In June Nash and Helen Safa, eds., *Sex and Class in Latin America*. New York: Praeger.

————. 1977. "The Changing Class Composition of the Female Labor Force in Latin America." *Latin American Perspectives* 4 (Fall): 126–36.

Saffioti, Heleith B. 1977. "Women, Mode of Production, and Social Formations." *Latin American Perspectives* 4 (Fall):27–37.

Salamon, Lester. 1979. "The Time Dimension in Policy Evaluation: The Case of the New Deal Land Reform Experiments." *Public Policy* (Spring):129–83.

Sale, K. 1974. *SDS*. New York: Random House.

Sanger, David E. 1989. "Uno Finds Himself Japan's No. 1 'Women's Issue.' " *New York Times*. July 3:A1, A4.

Sapiro, Virginia. 1984. *The Political Integration of Women: Roles, Socialization and Politics*. Urbana: University of Illinois Press.

Scarth, J. 1972. *Twelve Years in China: The People, the Rebels, and the Mandarins*. Wilmington: Scholarly Resources.

Schaffer, Robert. 1979. "Women and the Communist Party, USA." *Socialist Review* 45 (May–June): 73–118.

Scharf, Lois. 1980. *To Work and to Wed: Female Employment, Feminism, and the Great Depression*. Westport, Conn.: Greenwood Press.

Scharf, Lois, and Joan M. Jensen. 1983. *Decades of Discontent: The Women's Movement, 1920–1940.*. Westport, Conn.: Greenwood Press.

Scharping, Rudolf, and Joachim Hofmann-Göttig. 1982. " 'Alternative' Politik in den Landesparlament? Ideologiekritische Inhaltsanalyse von 300 Redebeiträge 'grüner' Parlamentarier." *Zeitschrift für Parliamentsgragen* 3:391–415.

Schechner, Richard. 1973. "Drama, Script, Theatre, and Performance," *Drama Review* 17:5–36.

Schlaeger, Hilke. 1978. "The West German Women's Movement." *New German Critique* 13 (Winter): 59–68.

Schlegel, Alice. 1977. "Toward a Theory of Sexual Stratification." In Alice Schlegel, ed., *Sexual Stratification.* New York: Columbia University Press.

Schmid, Carol, and Paul Luebke. 1986. "West Germany's Greens as a Social Movement: Institutionalization or Decline?" Paper presented at the Meeting of the American Sociological Association, New York. August 30–September 3.

Schmidt, Jochen. 1983. "The Granddaughters Dance Themselves Free: From Fanny Elssler to Pina Bausch or from Female Other-Directedness to Self-Determination in Ballet." *Ballet International Köln* 5: 12–19.

Schmidt, Steffen W. 1975. "Women in Colombia: Attitudes and Future Perspectives in the Political System." *Journal of Interamerican Studies and World Affairs* 17 (November): 469–89.

———. 1976. "Political Participation and Development: The Role of Women in Latin America." *Journal of International Affairs* 30 (Fall–Winter): 243–60.

Schrüfer, Gertrud. 1985. *Die Grünen im deutschen Bundestag: Anspruch und Wirklichkeit.* Nuremberg: Pauli-balleis Verlag.

Schultz, Victoria. 1980. "Organizer! Women in Nicaragua." *NACLA Report on the Americas* 14 (March–April): 36–39.

Schuster, Marilyn R., and Susan R. Van Dyne, eds. 1985. *Women's Place in the Academy: Transforming the Liberal Arts Curriculum.* Totowa, N.J.: Rowman and Allanheld.

———. 1988. *Selected Bibliography for Integrating Research on Women's Experience in the Liberal Arts Curriculum.* 6th ed. Northampton, Mass.: Smith College.

"Second Conference of the Construction Workers' Union." 1924. *Pinkas Hahistadrut* 21.

"The Second Histadrut Convention." 1923. *Pinkas Hahistadrut* 2.

Seddon, Vicki, ed. 1986. *The Cutting Edge: Women and the Pit Strike.* London: Lawrence and Wishart.

Sefchovich, Sara. 1980. "América Latina: La Mujer en Lucha." *Fem* (January–February): 5–12.

Seltzer, Curtis. 1985. *Fire in the Hole: Miners and Managers in the American Coal Industry.* Lexington: University Press of Kentucky.

Shapira, Y. 1961. *Work and Land—Fifty Years of the Histadrut of Agricultural Workers.* Tel Aviv: Am Oved. [In Hebrew]

———. 1976. *Achdut Haavoda Party: The Power of Political Organization.* Tel Aviv: Am Oved. [In Hebrew]

Sharet, Moshe. 1927. "Protocol of the Third Histadrut Convention." *Pinkas Hahistadrut.* [In Hebrew]

Shelley, Martha. 1969. "Stepin Fetchit Woman." *Come Out!* November 14:7.

Shidlovsky, A. 1964. "Kineret in Its Jubilee." In R. Katznelson Shazar, ed., *With the Steps of the Generation.* Israel: Histadrut HaKlalit—Moetzet Hapoalot. [In Hebrew]

Shih, V. Y. C. 1967. *The Taiping Ideology: Its Sources, Interpretations, and Influences.* Seattle: University of Washington Press.

Shilts, Randy. 1987. *And the Band Played On: Politics, People, and the AIDS Epidemic.* New York: St. Martins Press.

Siegel, Mary G. 1982. " 'Crossing the Bar': A 'She' Lawyer in 1917." *Women's Rights Law Reporter* 7 (Summer): 357–63.

Siim, Birte. 1988. "Towards a Feminist Rethinking of the Welfare State." In Kathleen B. Jones and Anna G. Jonasdottir, eds., *The Political Interests of Gender.* London: Sage.

Silva, Clea. 1968. "The Errors of the *Foco* Theory." *Monthly Review* 20 (July–August): 18–35.

Siltanen, Janet, and Michelle Stanworth, eds. 1984. *Women and the Public Sphere: A Critique of Sociology and Politics*. New York: St. Martin's Press.

Simons, Marlise. 1989. "Ecologists Rush for Seats on European Parliament." *New York Times*. May 31: A3.

Simpson, Ruth. 1976. *From the Closet to the Courts*. New York: Viking Press.

Sinsheimer, Joe. 1987. "Never Turn Back." *Southern Exposure* 15 (Summer): 37–50.

Skelton, Gail. n.d. Unpublished manuscript on future plans for students enrolled in introductory sociology classes.

Sklar, Kathryn K. 1973. *Catherine Beecher: A Study in American Domesticity*. New Haven, Conn.: Yale University Press.

Skolnick, Jerome. 1969. *The Politics of Protest*. Special foreword by William H. Grier and Price M. Cobbs. New York: Ballantine Books.

Slaughter, Jane. 1977. "Women and Socialism: The Case of Angelica Balabonoff." *Social Science Journal* 14: 57–65.

———. 1981, "Humanism versus Feminism in the Socialist Movement: The Life of Angelica Balabanoff." In Jane Slaughter and Robert Kern, eds., *European Women on the Left*. Westport, Conn.: Greenwood Press.

Smelser, Neil J. 1963. *Theory of Collective Behavior*. New York: Free Press.

Smith, Barbara, ed. 1983. *Homegirls: A Black Feminist Anthology*. New York: Kitchen Table/Women of Color Press.

Smith, Dorothy. 1978. "A Peculiar Eclipsing: Women's Exclusion from Man's Culture." *Women's Studies International Quarterly* 1:281–96.

———. 1988. *The Everyday World as Problematic: A Feminist Sociology*. Boston: Northeastern University Press.

Smith, Gordon. 1983. "Federal Republic of Germany." In George E. Delury, ed., *World Encyclopedia of Political Systems and Parties*. Vol. 1. New York: Facts On File Publications.

Smith-Rosenberg, Carroll. 1986. *Disorderly Conduct: Visions of Gender in Victorian America*. New York: Oxford University Press.

Snitow, Ann, et al. 1983. *Powers of Desire*. New York: Monthly Review Press.

Snow, David., Louis A. Zurcher, Jr., and Sheldon Ekland-Olson. 1980. "Social Networks and Social Movements." *American Sociological Review* 45:787–801.

Snyder, David, and William R. Kelly. 1979. "Strategies for Investigating Violence and Social Change." In Mayer N. Zald and John D. McCarthy, eds., *The Dynamics of Social Movements*. Cambridge, Mass.: Winthrop.

Soares, Glaucio Ari Dillon. 1980. "Mobilidade e Politica." *Revista Brasileira de Estudos Politicos* 50: 101–119.

Spender, Dale. 1983a. *Feminist Theorists: Three Centuries of Key Women Thinkers*. Introduction by Ellen Carol DuBois. New York: Pantheon Books.

———. 1983b. *There's Always Been a Women's Movement This Century*. London: Pandora Press.

———. 1983c. *Women of Ideas (and What Men Have Done to Them)*. London: ARK Paperbacks.

———. 1985. *For the Record: The Making and Meaning of Feminist Knowledge*. London: Women's Press.

Spiegel, S. 1956. *Nonparametric Statistics for the Behavioral Sciences*. New York: McGraw-Hill.

Stacey, Judith, and Barrie Thorne. 1985. "The Missing Revolution in Sociology." *Social Problems* 32 (April):301–16.

Stacey, Margaret, and Marion Price. 1981. *Women, Power, and Politics*. London: Tavistock.

Statistisches Jahrbuch fuer die Bundesrepublik Deutschland. 1987. Weisbaden: Statistiches Bundesamt.

Steakley, James. 1975. *The Homosexual Emancipation Movement in Germany.* New York: Arno.

Steinson, Barbara J. 1980. " 'The Mother Half of Humanity': American Women in the Peace and Preparedness Movements in World War One." In Carol R. Berkin and Clara Lovett, eds., *Women, War and Revolution.* New York: Holmes and Meier.

Sternstein, W. 1978. *Überall ist Wyhl.* Frankfurt: Haag und Herchen.

Stevens, Evelyn P. 1973a. *"Marianismo:* The Other Face of Machismo in Latin America." In Ann Pescatello, ed., *Male and Female in Latin America.* Pittsburgh: University of Pittsburgh Press.

———. 1973b."The Prospects for a Women's Liberation Movement in Latin America." *Journal of Marriage and the Family* 35 (May): 313–21.

Stone, Laurie. 1988. "Funny Girls." *Village Voice.* June 28: 30, 39.

Stoper, Emily. 1973. "The Student Nonviolent Coordinating Committee: Rise and Fall of a Redemptive Organization." In Jo Freeman, ed., *Social Movements of the Sixties and Seventies.* New York: Longman.

Strong-Boag, Veronica. 1976. *The Parliament of Women: The National Council of Canada, 1893–1927.* Ottawa: National Museum of Man Mercury Series.

———. 1984. "Internationalism and Peace: The Effort of Canadian Women, 1919–1939." Paper presented at the Conference for Women and Education for Peace and Non-Violence, Ontario Institute for Studies in Education. September.

Studart, Heloneida. 1974. *Mulher: Objecto de Cama e Mesa.* Petrópolis, Brazil: Editora Vozes.

Swerdlow, Amy. 1982. "Ladies' Day at the Capitol: Women Strike for Peace Versus HUAC." *Feminist Studies* 8 (Fall): 493–516.

Szabo, Stephen F. 1983. "The New Generation in Germany: Protest and Postmaterialism." In Robert Gerald Livingston, ed., *The Federal Republic of Germany in the 1980s.* New York: German Information Center.

Szyliowicz, J. 1972. *A Political Analysis of Student Activities.* Beverly Hills, Calif.: Sage.

Tabak, Fanny. 1982. "Women and Authoritarian Regimes." In Judith Hicks Stiehm, ed., *Women's Views of the Political World of Men.* New York: Transactional Publishers.

Talbot, Marion. 1936. *More than Lore: Reminiscences of Marion Talbot.* Chicago: University of Chicago Press.

Talbot, Marion, and Lois Kimball Mathews Rosenberry. 1931. *The History of the AAUW, 1881–1931.* Boston and New York: Houghton Mifflin.

Tax, Meredith. 1980. *Feminist Solidarity and Class Conflict, 1880–1917.* New York: Monthly Review Press.

Taylor, Verta. 1983. "The Future of Feminism in the 1980's: A Social Movement Analysis." In Laurel W. Richardson and Verta Taylor, eds., *Feminist Frontiers: Rethinking Sex, Gender, and Society.* Reading, Mass.: Addison-Wesley.

———. 1989. "Social Movement Continuity: The Women's Movement in Abeyance." *American Sociological Review* 54: 761–75.

Teal, Donn. 1971. *The Gay Militants.* New York: Stein and Day.

Teitelbaum, M. 1976. *Sex Differences.* Garden City, N.Y.: Anchor Books.

Teng, S. Y. 1962. *Historiography of the Taiping Rebellions.* Cambridge, Mass.: Harvard University Press.

———. 1966. *New Light on the History of the Taiping Rebellion.* New York: Russell & Russell.

———. 1971. *The Taiping Rebellion and the Western Powers: A Comprehensive Survey.* Oxford: Oxford University Press.

Teng, Y. 1980. "Remembrance of the May Fourth Movement." *Chinese Studies in History* 14:90–103.

Teodori, M. 1969. *The New Left: A Documentary History.* New York: Bobbs-Merrill.

Terborg-Penn, Rosalyn. 1989. "Black Women's Resistance and Civil Rights in South Africa and America: A Comparative Analysis." Paper presented at the Institute for Research on Women, Rutgers University, New Brunswick, N.J.: February 16.

Thomas, P. 1964. *Indian Women Through the Ages.* Bombay: Asia Publishing House.

Thomis, Malcolm I., and Jennifer Grimmett. 1982. *Women in Protest, 1800–1850.* London: Croom Helm; New York: St. Martin's Press.

Thompson, Dorothy, ed. 1983. *Over Our Dead Bodies: Women Against the Bomb.* London: Virago Press.

———. 1984. "Women, Peace and History—Notes for a Historical Overview." Paper presented at the Conference for Women and Education for Peace and Non-Violence, Ontario Institute for Studies in Education. September.

Thompson, E. P. 1955. *William Morris: Romantic Revolutionary.* London: Laurence and Wishart.

———. 1966. *The Making of the English Working Class.* New York: Vintage Books.

Thorne, Barrie. 1975. "Women in the Draft Resistance Movement: A Case Study of Sex Roles and Social Movements." *Sex Roles* 1: 179–95.

———. 1983. "Political Activist as Participant Observer: Conflicts of Commitment in a Study of the Draft Resistance Movement of the 1960s." In Robert M. Emerson, ed., *Contemporary Field Research: A Collection of Readings.* Boston: Little, Brown.

Tickamyer, Ann, and Cynthia Duncan. 1984. "Economic Activity and the Quality of Life in Eastern Kentucky." *Growth and Change* 15:43–51.

Tickamyer, Ann R., and Cecil Tickamyer. 1987. *Poverty in Appalachia.* Appalachian Data Bank Report, no. 5. Lexington: The Appalachian Center, University of Kentucky.

Tilly, Charles. 1978. *From Mobilization to Revolution.* Reading, Mass.: Addison-Wesley.

———. 1979. "Social Movements and National Politics." Working Paper, no. 197. Ann Arbor: Center for Research on Social Organization, University of Michigan.

———. 1981. "Introduction." In Louise A. Tilly and Charles Tilly, eds., *Class Conflict and Collective Action.* Beverly Hills, Calif.: Sage.

———. 1986. "Does Modernization Breed Revolution?" In Jack A. Goldstone, ed., *Revolutions: Theoretical, Comparative, and Historical Studies.* San Diego: Harcourt Brace Jovanovich.

Tilly, Charles, Louise Tilly, and Richard Tilly. 1975. *The Rebellious Century: 1830–1930.* Cambridge, Mass.: Harvard University Press.

Tilly, Louise A. 1981a. "Paths of Proletarianization: Organization of Production, Sexual Division of Labor, and Women's Collective Action." *Signs* 7 (Winter): 400–417.

———. 1981b. "Women's Collective Action and Feminism in France, 1870–1914." In Louise A. Tilly and Charles Tilly, eds., *Class Conflict and Collective Action.* Beverly Hills, Calif.: Sage.

Tilly, Louise A., and Charles Tilly, eds. 1981. *Class Conflict and Collective Action.* Beverly Hills, Calif.: Sage.

Tinker, Irene. 1981. "New Technologies for Food-Related Activities: An Equity Strategy." In Roslyn Dauber and Melinda L. Cain, eds., *Women and Technological Change in Developing Countries.* Boulder, Colo.:Westview Press.

Tolerance. (1923). Chicago: American Unity League.

Torres, Simon, and Julio Aronde. 1968. "Debray and the Cuban Experience." *Monthly Review* 20 (July–August): 48–62.

Touraine, Alain, and Daniel Pecaut. 1970. "Working-Class Consciousness and Economic Development in Latin America." In Irving Louis Horowitz, ed., *Masses in Latin America.* New York: Oxford University Press.

"Transcript of Mandela's Speech at Capetown City Hall: 'Africa It is Ours!' " 1990. *New York Times.* February 12:A15.

Trattner, Walter 1974. *From Poor Law to Welfare State: A History of Social Welfare in America*. New York: Free Press.

Treblicot, Joyce, ed. 1983. *Mothering: Essays in Feminist Theory*. Totowa, N.J.: Rowman and Allanheld.

The Tribune: A Woman's Development Quarterly. 1985. Newsletter, no. 32, 3d quarter.

Truscott, Lucian, IV. 1969. "Gay Power Comes to Sheridan Square." *Village Voice*. July 3:1, 18.

Tucker, Helen. 1962. "Voice of Women and the Conference for International Cooperation Year." *Our Generation* 1 (Summer):26–34.

Turbin, Carole. 1984. "Reconceptualizing Family, Work and Labor Organizing: Working Women in Troy, 1860–1890." *Review of Radical Political Economics* 16:1–16.

Turner, Ralph H. 1964. "Collective Behavior." In R. Faris, ed., *Handbook on Modern Sociology*. Chicago: Rand McNally.

———. 1969. "The Public Perception of Protest." *American Sociological Review* 34:815–31.

———. 1970. "Determinants of Social Movement Strategies." In Tamotsu Shibutani, ed., *Human Nature and Collective Behavior*. Englewood Cliffs, N.J.: Prentice-Hall.

Turner, Ralph, and Lewis Killian. 1972. *Collective Behavior*. 2nd ed. Englewood Cliffs, N.J.: Prentice-Hall.

Turner, Victor C. 1974. *Dramas, Fields, and Metaphor: Symbolic Action in Human Society*. Ithaca, N.Y.: Cornell University Press.

Ulam, Adam B. 1968. *The Bolsheviks*. Toronto: Collier.

Ulbrich, Holley, and Myles Wallace. 1984 "Women's Work Force Status and Church Attendance." *Journal for the Scientific Study of Religion* 23:341–50.

Urdang, Stephanie. 1984 "Women in Contemporary National Liberation Movements." In Margaret Jean Hay and Sharon Stichter, eds., *African Women: South of the Sahara*. London: Longman.

"Urknall mit Joghurt." 1989. *Spiegel*. April 24: 73.

U.S. Bureau of the Census. 1973. *Characteristics of the Population*. Vol. 1, part 19, *Kentucky*. Washington, D.C.: Government Printing Office.

Useem, Bert, and Mayer N. Zald. 1982. "From Pressure Group to Social Movement: Organizational Dilemmas of the Effort to Promote Nuclear Power." *Social Problems* 30 (December): 144–56.

Useem, Michael. 1975. *Protest Movements in America*. Indianapolis: Bobbs-Merrill.

Van Allen, Judith. 1972. " 'Sitting on a Man': Colonialism and the Political Institutions of Igbo Women." *Canadian Journal of African Studies* 6:165–81.

Vega, Mercier. 1969. *Guerrillas in Latin America*. New York: Praeger.

Vellacott, Jo. 1984. "Feminist Consciousness and the First World War." Paper presented at the Conference for Women and Education for Peace and Non-Violence, Ontario Institute for Studies in Education. September.

———. 1985. "Feminism and Anti-militarism: Some Historical and Theoretical Connections." Unpublished paper.

Vida, Ginny, ed. 1978. *Our Right to Love: A Lesbian Resource Book*. Englewood Cliffs, N.J.: Prentice-Hall.

Vitale, Luis. 1981. *Historia y sociología de la mujer latinoamericana*. Barcelona: Editorial Fontamara.

Vizetelly, Ernest Alfred. 1911. *The Anarchists*. London: Lane.

Wakeman, F., Jr. 1977. "Rebellion and Revolution: The Study of Popular Movements in Chinese History." *Journal of Asian Studies* 36:201–37.

Walker, Eugene. 1974. "Interview with Ella Baker: 9/4/1974." Southern Historical Collection, University of North Carolina at Chapel Hill.

Walls, David. 1978. "Central Appalachia in Advanced Capitalism: Its Coal Industry Structure and Coal Operator." Ph.D. diss., University of Kentucky.

Watts, William A., Steve Lynch, and David Whittaker. 1969. "Alienation and Activism in Today's College-age Youth." *Journal of Counseling Psychology* 16: 1–7.

Weffort, Francisco. 1970. "State and Mass in Brazil." In Irving Louis Horowitz, ed., *Masses in Latin America*. New York: Oxford University Press.

Weinberg, Julius. 1972. *Edward Alsworth Ross and the Sociology of Progressivism*. Madison: State Historical Society of Wisconsin.

Weitz, Rose. 1984. "From Accommodation to Rebellion: The Politicization of Lesbianism." In Trudy Darty and Sandee Potter, eds., *Women-Identified Women*. Palo Alto, Calif.: Mayfield.

Welkowitz, Joan, Robert B. Ewen, and Jacob Cohen. 1976. *Introductory Statistics for the Behavioral Sciences*. New York: Academic Press.

Weller, Jack M., and E. L. Quarantelli. 1973. "Neglected Characteristics of Collective Behavior." *American Journal of Sociology* 79:665–85.

Welter, Barbara. 1966. "The Cult of True Womanhood, 1820–1860." *American Quarterly* 18:151–74.

West, Guida. 1979. "Twin-Track Coalitions in the Black Power Movement." In Rhoda Goldstein Blumberg and Wendell James Roye, eds., *Interracial Bonds*. Bayside, N.Y.: General Hall Press.

———. (1981). *The National Welfare Rights Movement: The Social Protest of Poor Women*. New York: Praeger.

———. Forthcoming. *Protest Leadership Outcomes: Welfare Rights Leaders Two Decades Later*. New York: Praeger.

Wiarda, Howard Jr., and Harvey F. Kline. 1979. "The Latin America Tradition and Process of Development." In Howard J. Wiarda and Harvey F. Kline, eds., *Latin American Politics and Development*. Boston: Houghton Mifflin.

Wilkie, James W., and Stephen Haber, eds. 1981. *Statistical Abstract of Latin America*. Vol. 21. Los Angeles: UCLA Latin American Center for Publications.

———. 1982. *Statistical Abstract of Latin America*. Vol. 22. Los Angeles: UCLA Latin American Center for Publications.

Wilkinson, Paul. 1971. *Social Movements*. New York: Praeger.

Williams, J. 1977. *Psychology of Women*. New York: Norton.

Williams, Raymond. 1960. *Culture and Society*. Garden City, N.Y.: Anchor Books.

Wilson, Carlos. 1974. *The Tupamaros*. Boston: Branden Press.

Wilson, John. 1973. *Introduction to Social Movements*. New York: Basic Books.

Wiltsher, Anne. 1985. *Most Dangerous Women: Feminist Peace Campaigners of the Great War*. London: Pandora Press.

Wipper, Audrey. 1984. "Women's Voluntary Organizations." In Margaret Jean Hay and Sharon Stichter, eds., *African Women: South of the Sahara*. London: Longman.

WIRE (Women's International Resource Exchange). 1982a. "An Interview with Sister Margarita Navarro, Member of Human Rights Commission for El Salvador." In Women's International Resource Exchange, *Women and War: El Salvador*. New York: Women's International Resource Exchange.

———. 1982b. "Reconciliation Is No Longer Possible: An Interview with Ana Guadelupe Martinez, Member of FMLN and FDR." In Women's International Resource Exchange, *Women and War: El Salvador*. New York: Women's International Resource Exchange.

———. 1982c. "Women's Lives in El Salvador: An Interview with Miriam Galdemez, an El Salvadoran Refugee." In Women's International Resource Exchange, *Women and War: El Salvador*. New York: Women's International Resource Exchange.

Wittner, Judith G. 1984. "Steps Toward a Feminist Sociology." Working Paper, no. 147. Wellesley, Mass.: Center for Research on Women, Wellesley College.

"Women in Action." 1984. *ISIS International Women's Journal*, Special Supplement, no. 1.

"Women March on the Pentagon." 1981. *Our Generation* 14 (Summer): 23–4.

"Women Work Twice as Hard as Men." 1980. Press release for the 1980 World Conference of the United Nations Decade for Women Conference. July 14–30.

"The Women Workers' Council." 1926. *Hapoel Hatzair* 27. [In Hebrew]

"Women Worldwide Are Confronting an Economic Crisis." 1989. *Tribune* 42 (June):4.

Wood, J. 1974. *Political Consciousness and Student Activities*. Beverly Hills, Calif.: Sage.

Woody, Thomas. 1929. *A History of Women's Education in the United States*. Vol. 2. New York and Lancaster, Penn.: Science Press.

Woolf, Virginia. 1938. *Three Guineas*. London: Hogarth Press.

Yanait Ben Zvi. R. 1959. *We Ascend: Memoirs*. Tel Aviv: Am Oved. [In Hebrew]

———. 1976. *Manya Schochat*. Jerusalem: Yad Ben Zvi. [In Hebrew]

Zabaleta, Marta. 1983. "The Mothers Do Not Disappear." In Leone Caldecott and Stephanie Leland, eds., *Reclaim the Earth: Women Speak Out for Life on Earth*. London: Women's Press.

Zald, Mayer N., and Roberta Ash. 1966. "Social Movement Organizations: Growth, Decay, and Change." *Social Forces* 44:327–41.

Zald, Mayer N., and John D. McCarthy, eds. 1987. *Social Movements in Organizational Society: Collected Essays*. Introduction by William A. Gamson. New Brunswick, N.J.: Transaction Books.

Contributors

STEPHEN E. BARTON received his B.A. from Haverford College and studied social movements at the University of Paris at Vincennes. He received his Ph.D. in city and regional planning from the University of California, Berkeley, where he is a research associate with the Institute of Urban and Regional Development. He has published articles on neighborhood and tenant organizations, mandatory homeowners' associations as private governments, housing policy, and beliefs about property rights. He is currently working on a book about the politics of housing tenure.

RHODA LOIS BLUMBERG is Professor of Sociology at Rutgers University and the author of books and articles in the field of race relations, gender, and organization. Among the articles are several based on her study of women in the civil rights movement. Her most recent books are *Organizations in Contemporary Society* (Prentice-Hall, 1987) and *Civil Rights: The 1960s Freedom Struggle* (Twayne, 1984, revised edition forthcoming). Blumberg was a visiting scholar at Stanford University's Institute for Research on Women and Gender in 1986.

SUSAN CAVIN, author of *Lesbian Origins* (ISM, 1985), is currently Assistant Director of Women's Studies at Rutgers University. In 1984, she was the first woman president of the Gay & Lesbian Press Association. In 1987, she was the national spokeswoman for the October 13 Gay & Lesbian Civil Disobedience at the Supreme Court.

JANET S. CHAFETZ is Professor of Sociology at the University of Houston. Her areas of interest are sociological theory and gender inequality. She is the author of *Sex and Advantage* (Rowman and Allenheld, 1984), *Feminist Sociology* (Peacock, 1988), *Gender Equity* (Sage, 1990), and, with Anthony Dworkin, *Female Revolt* (Rowman and Allenheld, 1986). Chafetz and Dworkin recently published a paper analyzing antifeminist movements cross-culturally and historically.

ANTHONY GARY DWORKIN is Professor and Chair of Sociology at the University of Houston. He is the author of *When Teachers Give Up* (Texas Press, Hogg Foundation for Mental Health, 1985), *Teacher Burnout in the Public Schools* (State University of New York Press, 1987), and, with Margaret LeCompte, *Giving Up in School* (Sage, 1990). His areas of research include minority group relations and the sociology of education. He serves as editor of a book series entitled The New Inequalities, published by the State University of New York Press.

VIRGINIA KEMP FISH is Professor Emerita of Sociology at the University of Wisconsin, Stevens Point. Her research interests have focused largely on a group of six women—Edith and Grace Abbott, Sophonisba Breckinridge, Alice Hamilton, Florence Kelley, and Julia Lathrop—that she has called the Hull House Circle and whose contributions to the founding years of sociology at the University of Chicago and to various reform movements and organizations, such as the Woman's Peace Party and the Women's Trade Union League, have not been acknowledged until recently. Additional areas of research include emerging models of feminist scholarship as well as the roles and positions of frontier women.

JUDITH LYNNE HANNA received her Ph.D. from Columbia University and is a senior research scholar at the University of Maryland and a consultant in the arts, education, health, and public policy. She is the author of *To Dance Is Human* (University of Chicago Press, 1987), *The Performer–Audience Connection* (University of Texas Press, 1983), *Dance, Sex, and Gender: Signs of Identity, Dominance, Defiance, and Desire* (University of Chicago Press, 1988), *Disruptive School Behavior: Class, Race and Culture* (Holmes and Meier, 1988), and *Dance and Sex* (AMS, 1988) and of more than three-score articles, as well as coauthor of *Urban Dynamics in Black Africa* (Aldine, 1981). She has taught and lectured at numerous universities in the United States and abroad.

DAFNA N. IZRAELI is Professor of Sociology and current Chair of the Department of Sociology and Anthropology at Bar-Ilan University in Israel. She received her M.S.W. from McGill University and her Ph.D. from Manchester University, and she did postdoctoral work at the University of California, Berkeley. She has published numerous articles in various scholarly journals, focusing on the interface of women, work, organizations, and power. Izraeli is coauthor of *The Double Bind: Women in Israel* (Kubbutz Hameuchad, 1982 [in Hebrew]), and is co-editor of *Women in Management Worldwide* (Sharpe, 1988). She is currently researching dual-career couples and the perception of the status of women as a social problem. She serves as a member of the National Council on the Status of Women and the Advisory Committee to the Chief of the Women's Army.

RONALD LAWSON completed his Ph.D. in history and sociology at the University of Queensland in Australia and then did postdoctoral studies in the Department of Sociology and the Bureau of Applied Social Research, Columbia University. He is now Professor in the Department of Urban Studies at Queens College, the City University of New York, having taught earlier at Hunter College, CUNY. He is the author of *The Tenant Movement in New York City: 1904–1984* (Rutgers University Press, 1986) and *Brisbane Society in the 1890s: An Australian Urban Society* (University of Queensland Press, 1973). The latter book was reprinted in 1988 to mark the bicentennial of the founding of Australia. Lawson is currently writing a sociological study of the Seventh-day Adventist Church around the world.

TIM FUTING LIAO, a native of China, is Assistant Professor in the Department of Sociology at the University of Georgia. His research interests include sex and gender studies, fertility, demographic theories, and sociological methodology. Currently, he is studying the cross-cultural variation of women's fertility in terms of their rational basis for sustaining a certain level of fertility.

LINDA M. LOBAO is Assistant Professor in the Department of Agricultural Economics and Rural Sociology at Ohio State University. Her research areas are the sociology of economic change and political sociology. Her interest in Latin America centers on women's political mobilization and on women in development issues. In her domestic research, she is studying women's response to the recent farm crisis and completing a book, *Locality and Inequality*, on the impact of farm and industry structure on socioeconomic conditions in rural areas. Her articles have appeared in numerous journals.

SALLY WARD MAGGARD is Assistant Professor in the Department of Sociology and Anthropology at West Virginia University. She is writing a book about women's involvement in two labor-union-organizing drives in the early 1970s in eastern Kentucky: the Brookside Mine strike in Harlan County, Kentucky, and the Pikeville Methodist Hospital strike in Pike County, Kentucky. At the time of these strikes, she was a writer for *Mountain Life & Work*, a Central Appalachian newsmagazine, and was employed by the Council of the Southern Mountains. She has been Assistant Director of the Appalachian Center at the University of Kentucky. Her other research interests include the economic and social development of lagging regions, gender and inequality, and coalmine health and safety.

MARIE MARMO MULLANEY is Professor of History and Chair of the Department of History and Political Science at Caldwell College. A Danforth Fellow, she holds an M.A. and a Ph.D. in modern European history from Rutgers University. She is a specialist in women's history and the author of *Revolutionary Women: Gender and the Socialist Revolutionary Role* (Praeger, 1983), as well as numerous other articles and reviews in this field. Her most recent publication is "Sexual Politics in the Career of Louise Michel," which appeared in the Winter 1990 issue of *Signs*.

DAVID M. NEAL is currently Assistant Professor in the Department of Sociology and the Emergency Management and Administration Program at the University of North Texas. He received his Ph.D. in sociology from Ohio State University in 1985 and has published articles in *Mass Emergencies, Sociological Focus*, and *Disasters*. His current research focuses on collective behavior, social movements, and organizational response in disasters.

CHARLES PAYNE has taught at Southern University, Haverford College, and Williams College and is currently Associate Professor of African-American Studies, Sociology, and Urban Affairs at Northwestern University. Interested primarily in social change, social inequality, and Afro-American culture, he is the author of a book on urban schooling, *Getting What We Ask For* (Greenwood

Press, 1984), and is currently completing *This Little Light of Mine*, a study of local participation in the Mississippi civil rights movement.

BRENDA PHILLIPS is Assistant Professor of Sociology at Southern Methodist University. She received her Ph.D. in sociology from Ohio State University and has published in *Mass Emergencies* and *Sociological Focus*. She is currently studying social movements and gender, and, with the aid of National Science Foundation grants, is continuing her research on disaster. Her article in this book, co-authored with David M. Neal, grew out of shared experiences while doing research at the Disaster Research Center at Ohio State University.

JACQUELINE POPE is Associate Professor of Public Administration at Stockton State College. She received her Ph.D. in urban planning from Columbia University, and her doctoral dissertation was recently published as a book entitled *Biting the Hand that Feeds Them: Organizing Women on Welfare at the Grass Roots Level* (Praeger, 1989). Her research on welfare reform policies has been published in the *Black Scholar*. She is now studying ethics in public bureaucracies.

CAROL SCHMID teaches sociology at Guilford Technical Community College. Her scholarly work focuses on women and minorities in West Germany, Switzerland, Britain, Canada, and the United States. She is the author of *Conflict and Consensus in Switzerland* (University of California Press, 1981) and of articles on foreign workers in West Germany and Switzerland, and social movements in Canada, Britain, Germany, and the United States. Her interest in the Greens dates from 1983 when, as a visiting professor at the University of Trier, she was able to observe their role in the German federal and local elections. In 1987, as a visiting scholar at the Free University in West Berlin, she researched the position of women in the Alternative Party, which is affiliated with the Greens. She is attending law school.

CAROLYN STRANGE is a doctoral candidate in history at Rutgers University. She has written on maternalism in women's prisons and in the women's peace movement. She has taught history and women's studies at Rutgers, the University of Ottawa, and Queen's University. Currently, she is a visiting junior fellow at the Centre of Criminology at the University of Toronto. Her dissertation, "The Perils and the Pleasures of Urban Living: Single, Wage-Earning Women in Toronto, 1880–1930," is nearing completion.

STEPHANIE A. SWANSON is a research assistant in the Department of Psychology at the Baylor College of Medicine. She is a recent master's graduate in sociology from the University of Houston, where she worked as a research assistant for Dworkin and Chafetz, helping to collect and analyze data reported in the article in this book. She elaborated on these data in her master's thesis, "An Analysis of Women's Movements Through Time: A Structural Process Model for the Study of Minority Social Movements."

VERTA TAYLOR is Associate Professor of Sociology at Ohio State University. She is the co-editor, with Laurel Richardson, of a women's studies anthology, *Feminist Frontiers II: Rethinking Sex, Gender and Society* (Random House 1988), the coauthor, with Leila J. Rupp, of *Survival in the Doldrums: The American Women's Rights Movement, 1945 to the 1960s* (Oxford University Press, 1987; Ohio State University Press, 1990 [paperback]), and a member of the editorial board of *Gender and Society*. Her recent publications on the women's movement also appear in the *American Sociological Review* and *Gender and Society*. Taylor's current research focuses on the emotions of childbirth and early motherhood and on social movement culture and mobilization in the lesbian and gay movement.

GUIDA WEST was born and raised in Brazil. She received her Ph.D. from Rutgers University in political sociology. She has been a researcher and an activist in the civil rights, welfare rights, and feminist struggles during the past thirty years. Her book *The National Welfare Rights Movement: The Social Protest of Poor Women* (Praeger, 1981) examined the rise and decline of this movement. She is now completing a study of what happened to the welfare rights leaders after NWRO's collapse in the mid-1970s, which will be published as a book called *Protest Leadership Outcomes* (Praeger, forthcoming). She taught at Rutgers University for many years and was Special Projects Administrator at the Rutgers Institute for Research on Women. Currently, she is Director of Policy, Advocacy, and Research at the Federation of Protestant Welfare Agencies in New York City.

Index